What Social Workers Do

2nd Edition

What Social Workers Do

2nd Edition

By Margaret Gibelman

NASW PRESS

National Association of Social Workers
Washington, DC

Gary Bailey, MSW, *President*
Elizabeth J. Clark, PhD, ACSW, MPH *Executive Director*

CHERYL Y. BRADLEY, *Publisher*
PAULA L. DELO, *Executive Editor*
MARCIA D. ROMAN, *Managing Editor, Journals and Books*
JACKIE RODRIGUEZ, *Editor*
LOU GOINES, *Copy Editor*
LEONARD ROSENBAUM, *Proofreader*
LEONARD ROSENBAUM, *Indexer*

Cover and interior design by Metadog Design Group, Washington, DC
Printed and bound by Port City Press, Baltimore, MD

©NASW Press

Library of Congress Cataloging-in-Publication Data

Gibelman, Margaret.
    What social workers do/by Margaret Gibelman.—2nd ed.
    p. cm.
Includes bibliographic references
    ISBN 0-87101-364-9 (pbk.)
    1. Social service—United States.   2. Social service—Vocational guidance—United States.   3. Social workers—United States.   I. Title.
    HV91.G447 2004
    361.3'2'02373—dc22

Printed in the United States of America

Table of Contents

ACKNOWLEDGEMENTS

As a master of social work student at Rutgers University just over 30 years ago, I was required to take a course entitled "The Profession of Social Work." It was a one-credit course that focused on the mission, values, and history of the profession and was taught by then Dean Werner Boehm. To my chagrin, I received the grade of "C" in this course, with the admonishment from Dean Boehm that I didn't seem to "get it". Only a few years ago, I had occasion to see Dr. Boehm at a retirement dinner. Noting that I had written three books on the profession of social work and the social work labor force, I wondered out loud whether I had finally "gotten it" and, if so, whether he would change my grade. "No way," he said. And so I keep trying.

I cannot claim, however, that the grade of "C" stimulated my interest in what social workers do. A family friend not long ago commented that I had followed in my father's footsteps. I was taken aback because my father was an economist, not a social worker. But, I was reminded, he spent the bulk of his career heading up the New York State Department of Labor's Division of Research and Statistics. And didn't I remember—my parents had met when they were both on loan to set up a post-depression Department of Welfare. How easy it is to avoid making the obvious connections.

Undertaking to describe and analyze the enormous range of roles social workers carry out in our society is a daunting task. Any boundaries are artificial and the selection of what to include and what to exclude is challenging. These choices are solely those of the author. Exclusion of some areas of service does not suggest that they are unimportant. However, the focus, consistent with the first edition, is on those areas of service in which the majority of social workers actually work. Since the earliest days of social work, there have been debates about how to conceptualize the profession. The decision to follow the National Association of Social Workers' (NASW) classification system regarding areas of service is one of expediency; some framework is necessary and many have merits.

The source material used in this volume draws heavily from the publications of the NASW, thus suggesting a slant toward viewpoints and information considered to be newsworthy and of priority by this professional association. This bias is acknowledged. Also acknowledged is my personal interest in macro practice, reflected in the decision to devote a chapter to this subject even though it is not an area of service, per se. The relationship between social work and the society in which it is practiced at any time has become even more clear to me in the course of preparing this second edition. The imperative to influence the direction of that society seems equally apparent in a political environment in which rebuilding other nations, cutting taxes for the rich, and paring down the role of government appear to take priority over human well-being within our own society. The phenomenon of globalization has also taken on new meaning as events in one nation have repercussions for the economy and stability of other countries.

As with any project of this scope, many people provided invaluable assistance. During work on the first edition of this book, Laura Kuzma served as my research assistant. Her input to that volume continues to be reflected in this second edition.

Throughout this volume, definitions are drawn from the R. L. Barker's *The Social Work Dictionary*, 4th ed (NASW Press, 1999).

The vignettes that appear throughout the volume are based on countless conversations with social work colleagues about the nature of their practice and represent composites of actual or typical situations. Several of the vignettes represent real people and events and are so noted.

Material presented in many of the case studies was drawn from discussions and observations with supervisees, colleagues, students, and friends over many years and current events as reported in newspaper and professional newsletters. "Poetic license" was taken in these cases to highlight specific social problems, functions performed, types of social work interventions, levels of social work practice, and agency context. Several people loaned their substantive knowledge of areas of service to fill in the gaps. Susan Kleszewski, my sister, provided her expertise in mental health. Abbe Greenberg (working with people with disabilities), Robin Kahan (working with the aging), and Eileen Gelman (hospital social work), three friends and colleagues, shared their stories and experiences and reviewed the text to ensure accuracy. Lou Levitt and Aaron Beckerman, both professor emeritus at Wurzweiler School of Social Work (WSSW), provided their current experiences and expertise in organizing a grassroots movements for health care reform. Their efforts are also instructive for those who ponder how they will use their post-retirement time for the greater good. Jay Sweifach used his extensive background in Jewish communal service to help me construct a representative case that may confront a Jewish Community Center social worker. Jane Joseph, a college friend whose friendship has endured several decades and geographic distance, is a full-time mediator in Houston, Texas. I built upon the stories she has relayed over the years about her work in exploring the role of the social work mediator. David Dempsey of the NASW National Staff submitted to a "process analysis" of staff efforts involved in influencing welfare reform reauthorization legislation.

Appreciation is also extended to the National Association of Social Workers for its continued interest in articulating who social workers are and what they do. I also want to thank Cheryl Y. Bradley, Beth Ledford, Jackie Rodriguez, Marcia Roman, and Katrina Alaman-Murray of NASW Press for their assistance in the editorial and production process.

One of the delights in directing a doctoral program is how much I learn from the extensive research in which my students engage. Some of their work is cited in this volume, with special thanks for the new knowledge to Maina Fridman, Evelyn Laureano, Kim Lorber, Michelle Maidenberg, Jessica Rosenberg, Jay Sweifach, and Juann Watson. Sheldon Gelman, dean, Wurzweiler School of Social Work, Yeshiva University, and my colleagues at WSSW continue to provide a supportive environment within which to pursue scholarly interests.

The world keeps changing and the pace of change continues to accelerate. Each change brings new issues and problems that confront our society and its citizens and, consequently, results in new opportunities and challenges for social workers. Thus, the profession continues to evolve and no volume about what social workers do will ever be a finished tale.

Margaret Gibelman, DSW
New York, NY

Chapter One OVERVIEW

What do social workers do? Ask this question of a group of social workers and one is likely to get a broad range of responses:

- a request to reiterate the question
- a description of the place or agency in which one works
- a description of the client population—"I work with homeless people"
- a job title—"I'm a case manager" or "I'm a therapist"
- a broad brush—"I'm a social worker"
- a description of rank or title—"I'm an executive director" or "I'm a supervisor"
- a description of interventions—"I practice psychotherapy."

Why do social workers have a difficult time answering this question? One explanation is that social work, more than other professions, has expansive boundaries. Thus, the configuration of practice is affected by the setting of practice, area of practice, auspice of practice, characteristics of the presenting problems of clients, level of practice, and methodologies employed in practice. The configuration may vary from one social worker to another and change for the individual social worker over the course of his or her career. Because of the many variables that define the profession and practice of social work, it is often easier to explain where one works and with whom rather than what one does.

But the question remains: What do social workers actually do? This book examines what social workers do in their day-to-day work across the broad range of social work settings, levels of practice, and fields of practice (for example, aging, child welfare). The focus is on the roles and functions social workers assume in their work. An exploration of the activities in which social workers engage highlights the dynamism and vitality of the social work profession.

Social workers provide services in a variety of practice settings and at all levels of practice. For example, social workers deliver services in private practice, hospitals and health clinics, school systems, child welfare and mental health agencies, and correctional facilities.

Social work is a diverse profession with fluid boundaries. It is carried out, for example, in nonprofit medical, legal, and educational settings, in state and local governments, and in proprietary (for-profit) agencies. Social workers intervene with and on behalf of individuals, groups, and communities and provide preventative and ameliorative services. The clients represent all populations of our society—children, families, and adults—who have problems that run the gamut of the human condition from substance abuse to developmental disabilities.

Despite the long history of the profession in U.S. society, there is a scarcity of information devoted to the spectrum of career options within the field of social work. In part, this is because social workers do so many different things in so many places. Although attorneys may specialize in tax law or family law, they tend to work in a firm, small group practice, or independent practice. Social workers, on the other hand, may specialize in one of many practice areas and practice their specialization in an even larger array of sites under public, for-profit, or not-for-profit auspices.

Social work is becoming increasingly specialized, and those considering a career in social work or those now enrolled in social work education programs may be confused about career options. Students frequently ask for information about the range of jobs open within social work. They know they want to be social workers, but generally do not have access to information about where the social work jobs are located and what different kinds of things social workers do in a variety of settings. Both those currently practicing social work (and perhaps wondering about other social work career options) and those interested in entering the profession will profit from a book devoted to exploring the diversity and commonalities that constitute the social work profession.

What Social Workers Do seeks to fill the void about the profession of social work by providing a panoramic look at the profession in action; offering practical information about the current status of the different service areas and the types of jobs available; making extensive use of case studies; and highlighting the intersection among practice functions (for example, direct practice, supervision, management, policy analysis), practice settings (for example, schools, courts, hospitals, private practice), and practice areas (for example, child welfare, mental health, substance abuse, employment related, and so forth). This approach demonstrates the unity of the profession and shows the connections among what appear to be diverse specializations.

PURPOSES AND USES OF THIS BOOK

What Social Workers Do provides responses to a number of questions that are consistently posed by people interested in a career one of the helping professions, by students enrolled in social work programs, by practitioners in the field interested in knowing more about career paths within their profession, and by policymakers and government agencies that are responsible for establishing standards of care and requirements for professional credentialing and licensing. Questions include the following:

- Where do social workers work?
- What are the characteristics of the clients with whom social workers work?
- What kinds of problems do social workers address?
- How is the practice of social work influenced by larger sociopolitical developments?
- What impact does social work have on defining social problems and potential remedies?
- What are the different levels of social work practice?
- What technologies do social workers use?
- How fluid are social work careers both vertically and horizontally?
- In what ways do social workers interact with professionals in other disciplines?
- What career opportunities are available?
- What distinguishes social work from other helping professions?

These questions are addressed in this book through illustrative vignettes that highlight what social workers do across settings, practice areas, and levels of practice.

There are many audiences who will find the information contained in this volume to be of use. The book should provide a useful reference guide in high school and college libraries throughout the country to assist students who are exploring career options. It can serve as an introductory text in BSW and MSW programs, particularly in courses that provide an overview of the profession of social work and the characteristics of social work practice. Similarly, the volume will be of interest to social work students and practitioners as a reference manual to guide career development. Social work educators will find the case studies useful in stimulating class discussions about situations that arise in practice. Agencies, schools, and practitioners will have a comprehensive resource by which to respond to requests for information about the profession.

ORGANIZATION

The majority of social workers who are members of the National Association of Social Workers (NASW), and from whom routine data are collected, work in the following areas of service:

- mental health
- health
- family and children's services
- aging and the elderly population
- schools
- substance use and abuse.

Earlier NASW categorizations were more far reaching and included crime, delinquency, and justice; developmental disabilities and mental retardation; and occupational and industrial services. These categories have been subsumed under more global areas of service because of the relatively small number of social workers who practice them.

The book is organized to reflect the major service areas delineated by NASW. An additional chapter focuses on other service areas that constitute long-standing important areas of practice, but in which relatively small numbers of social workers work. Finally, a chapter is devoted to a crosscutting area: *macro* social work practice. Here, attention is focused on social workers with functional responsibilities related

to community organization, policy development, implementation and evaluation, politics (including holding office and advocacy), mediation, and consultation.

The National Association of Social Workers has struggled for years to classify the social work labor force in a way readily understandable to its members, government, and the public at large, and in a way that accurately reflects the totality of the profession. *Person-in-environment*, the purview of social work, encompasses most of the human condition experienced by people individually and collectively. The complexities of this classification task are accepted as a given, and it is recognized that efforts to organize and categorize what social workers do are, to some extent, arbitrary.

There are many ways in which the organization of social work can be conceptualized:

- field of practice (for example, health, mental health)
- practice setting (for example, community mental health, schools, courts)
- agency type (for example, not-for-profit, government)
- functions performed (for example, direct services, supervision)
- client population served (for example, people who are homeless, children with learning disabilities, individuals with chronic mental illness)
- methods used (for example, social group work, casework, community work)
- practice goals (for example, prevention, problem resolution, symptom alleviation)
- services provided (for example, marital therapy, case management, discharge planning)
- type of presenting problem (for example, marital discord, depression, unemployment).

The breadth of the social work profession means that any classification of the field has inherent limitations. The service areas used by NASW for classification of its membership and the literature of the profession also have limitations. Is homelessness, for example, a mental health problem, or a problem affecting families and children, or a community organization or housing problem? Are employee assistance programs components of mental health services, substance abuse services, or industrial social work?

The classifications of areas of service used by NASW highlight some of these dilemmas. For example, aging is considered a service area, but it is also a population group. Thus, in the chapter entitled "Aging", the subject area is the population. Most other areas of service, such as health and mental health, across all population groups. Another service area is schools, but this also is one of the settings in which social workers practice. Mental health, or mental illness, refers to a population (people with mental illness), a range of social problems, and settings in which social workers practice (for example, community mental health centers). The areas of service are most notable for their overlap with practice settings, populations, and social problems. Thus, there is constant fluidity in conceptualization and categorization.

Within each of the areas of service listed, social workers occupy positions in direct services, supervision, and management. Also within each of the service areas, social workers may concentrate on certain targeted population groups, such as people with chronic mental illness and people who are homeless. Thus, an individual social worker may have a service area of mental health, occupy a supervisory position, and work on problems related to the homeless. And, of course, to add to the complexity, some service areas actually are special populations, for example, elderly people, and other service areas, such as schools, are also practice settings.

Social workers working in the defined areas of service deal with social issues that crosscut the broad spectrum of problems that affect individuals, groups, and communities within this society. These include civil and legal rights, economic status and poverty, employment, rural and urban issues, and problems unique to special populations.

Each chapter includes a discussion of the range and types of practice areas within the category, nature and scope of the problems addressed in the particular area of service, enabling legislation and the programs that flow from laws. Vignettes illustrate the functions social workers carry out, as these are affected by the type and auspice of the employing agency, the position held by the social worker, and the characteristics of the clients served. The range of job opportunities in the areas of service are presented in sample classified advertisements abstracted from the *NASW News* (the newspaper of the National Association of Social Workers) between 1998 and 2002. The *NASW News* provides a national panorama of social work jobs rather than the (usually) local-based notices that appear in newspapers. These ads do not portray current listings to which readers may apply. Rather, they provide clues about the types of positions available to social workers, by area of practice, and the qualifications needed for them. The concluding chapter includes a discussion of the trends evident in social work practice and employment.

Information was derived from a number of sources. Publications of the National Association of Social Workers were relied as the "pulse" of the profession's development. The *NASW News* provided a particularly rich source of material about what social workers do and the context in which they practice. All issues of the *NASW News* published between 1995 and early 2002 were reviewed, augmented for this same time period by a review of articles in *Social Work* as well as the 19th edition of the *Encyclopedia of Social Work* (1995) and *Supplement* (1997) to gain a perspective on the growth and change experienced by the profession. Other references included textbooks and major social work journals used in graduate and undergraduate social work education programs that provided an overview of the profession and articles or chapters concerned with social work areas of practice and functions carried out by professional social workers. Definitions were, for the most part, drawn from the *Social Work Dictionary* (Barker, 1999). In some cases, older literature, as used in the first edition of this book, is maintained as it continues to highlight salient points or historical trends.

In early 1995, when the first edition of *What Social Workers Do* was completed, the search for information involved extensive time in the library culling through the professional literature. In 2001 and the first half of 2002, the time frame in which this second edition was prepared, the impact of the information revolution became clear. With the click of the mouse, information was readily available. For example, updated information about the characteristics of the elderly population with whom social workers work was available within minutes by turning to the Web sites of the American Association of Retired Persons (AARP), the National Institute on Aging, and the National Council on Aging. The use of an academic search engine—Proquest—allowed instant access to all major U.S. newspapers and revealed a plethora of stories about social workers, not only for the present time period, but also retroactively. The good news lies in the richness of the material now available to describe the functions and accomplishments of social workers. The daunting news lies in the need to sift through and cull out major themes that represent the totality of the profession.

The case studies exemplifying what social workers do are drawn from interviews, newspaper articles, and the *NASW News*. Many of the case studies are composites of real people and events. In some instances, the case studies portray actual people or events, and these are so noted. In these instances of real people and situations, there is a bias toward portraying what social workers do in the northeast corridor of the United States. Although unintentional, this bias is hopefully understandable. Because the author lives and works in the northeast, many case situations were drawn from the immediate environment.

All references were selected because of their relevance to understanding what social workers do and the types of issues they confront in their work. Therefore, however worthy, literature pertaining to diagnosis and assessment; treatment approaches and modalities; dynamics of interventions, social programs, or program development; staff development; the nature of social problems and policy or practice options; special populations; evaluation of services; or theoretical constructs per se is generally not included. The exception is literature pertaining to social work functions that may also touch some or all of the areas mentioned earlier.

The sequence of chapters reflects the primacy of the area of service within the social work profession as reflected in the NASW membership; for example, mental health is the first chapter because the largest proportion of NASW members are employed within this area. Similarly, "A Potpourri of Areas of Service" appears toward the end of the volume, as the service areas reflected in this catchall category represent only a very small proportion of the NASW membership. In the first edition, statistics regarding the proportion of NASW members in each service area were drawn from *Who We Are: The Social Work Labor Force as Reflected in the NASW Membership* (Gibelman & Schervish, 1993). For this second edition, data were drawn from *Who We Are: A Second Look* (Gibelman & Schervish, 1997). The ranking of areas of service by proportion of NASW members remains consistent.

Any effort to define what social workers do must indicate the limitations of that endeavor. The social work profession is broader than most professions in regard to types of problems social workers address, settings in which social workers work, levels of practice, interventions used, and populations served. The scope of social work practice has always been wide, and its boundaries continue to expand. *What Social Workers Do* attempts to highlight what social workers do within the context of a highly diverse and ever-evolving profession.

REFERENCES

Barker, R. (1999). *Social work dictionary* (4th ed.). Washington, DC: NASW Press.

Edwards, R. L. (Ed.-in-Chief). (1995). *Encyclopedia of social work* (19th ed.). Washington, DC: NASW Press.

Edwards, R. L. (Ed.-in-Chief). (1997). *Encyclopedia of social work* (19th ed., 1997 Suppl.). Washington, DC: NASW Press.

Gibelman, M., & Schervish, P. (1993). *Who we are: The social work labor force as reflected in the NASW membership*. Washington, DC: NASW Press.

Gibelman, M., & Schervish, P. (1997). *Who we are: A second look*. Washington, DC: NASW Press.

Chapter Two DEFINING THE PROFESSION

LANGUAGE OF THE PROFESSION

Each profession has its own vocabulary. We use certain words that have special meaning to those who practice social work, but may not mean the same thing or be readily understandable by people in different fields. A key example is the use of acronyms—the short-hand terms used to describe organizations or credentials. If we use these acronyms with our family or friends, they might look at us as if we are speaking a foreign language.

In addition, the vocabulary used by social workers to describe their profession and their practice is by no means standard (Gibelman & Schervish, 1997). The same phenomenon may be referenced using different words. For example, the voluntary sector—the sector in which the largest proportion of social workers are employed—is also called the third sector, the nonprofit sector, the nongovernment sector, and the not-for-profit sector. It is also subsumed under the rubric of the private sector, along with for-profit enterprises.

The language of social work continues to expand and become more complex and refined. *The Social Work Dictionary* has grown from a modest 205 pages in the first edition to nearly 600 pages in the fifth edition (Barker, 1991, 2003). Given the broad range of specialties within the profession, it is not surprising that clear communication within the profession and across professions remains a challenge.

The confusion is understandable. As Barker (1999) noted:

> As the profession of social work enters its second century, its language continues to grow in volume and complexity. This is a positive trend, the result of both increased social work knowledge and the profession's desire to communicate with greater precision. It is also the product of closer relationships with other professions and segments of society, each of which has its own jargon and terminology. (p. xiii)

The desire to communicate with precision has also led to a refinement in the language of the profession; the social work vocabulary has changed. In 1961 *caseworker* was the term used to describe social workers engaged in direct practice. Their practice was that of *casework*. Now, those engaged in one-to-one interventions with clients are referred to as *clinical social workers* or *clinicians*.

Attention to the profession's vocabulary is also important because there are so many components to social work. For example, clinical social workers frequently identify themselves as *psychotherapists*. It has been found that self-identification is significantly correlated with preferred client group, practice activity, and interest in private practice (Bogo, Raphael, & Roberts, 1993). But to the outside world, the use of the term psychotherapist to describe a social worker can obscure professional identification rather than clarify it.

The definitions provided in this chapter are offered to establish a common base of understanding of professional language. The beginning point is the profession itself. The task of defining the profession has encompassed its entire history.

WHAT IS SOCIAL WORK?

In 1956 the Commission on Social Work Practice of the then newly formed National Association of Social Workers prepared a "working definition" of social work practice with the intent to provide a "temporary and tentative" base for the commission's programs. A delineation of the purposes of social work was included in the statement, as follows:

- to assist individuals and groups to identify and resolve or minimize problems arising out of disequilibrium between themselves and their environment
- to identify potential areas of disequilibrium between individuals or groups and the environment in order to prevent the occurrence of disequilibrium
- in addition to these curative and preventive aims, to seek out, identify, and strengthen the maximum potential in individuals, groups, and communities. (NASW, 1956, pp. 1028–1029)

The commission's statement was presented as a "beginning formulation with the understanding that it would be revised continuously as knowledge and understanding of social work practice grew" (NASW, 1956, p. 1028). Future revisions were seen as desirable and necessary. Indeed, such revisions have been debated and adopted. For example, in 1970 the NASW Board of Directors adopted the following definition of social work:

Social work is the professional activity of helping individuals, groups, or communities

enhance or restore their capacity for social functioning and creating societal conditions favorable to this goal. (NASW, 1973, p. 4)

Other definitions, of course, have been offered over the years. In 1979, for example, Crouch identified the need for a concise definition of social work built around the profession's diverse fields and specialties. He offered the following:

Social work is the attempt to assist those who do not command the means to human subsistence in acquiring them and in attaining the highest possible degree of independence. (Crouch, 1979, p. 46)

In 1981 NASW made another attempt to develop an overarching definition of the profession. As defined by the NASW Task Force on Labor Force Classification (1981):

The profession of social work, by both traditional and practical definition, is the profession that provides the formal knowledge base, theoretical concepts, specific functional skills, and essential social values which are used to implement society's mandate to provide safe, effective, and constructive social services. (p. 5)

A recent definition of the profession comes from the NASW *Code of Ethics* (1996):

The primary mission of the social work profession is to enhance human well-being and help meet the basic human needs of all people, with particular attention to the needs and empowerment of people who are vulnerable, oppressed, and living in poverty. A historical and defining feature of social work is the profession's focus on individual well-being in a social context and the well-being of society. Fundamental to social work is attention to the environmental forces that create, contribute to, and address problems in living. (p. 1)

Barker (1999) offered a succinct definition of social work as the "applied science of helping people achieve an effective level of psychosocial functioning and effecting societal changes to enhance the well-being of all people" (p. 455). In common to all of these definitions is the focus on both the person and the environment; this duality and the interaction between them constitute the special purview of the profession and make it distinct from other helping professions.

The periodic call to re-examine the definition of social work relates, in part, to the varying degrees of influence of different segments of the professional community. From its beginning in the 19th century, social work has maintained a dual focus of concern (see, for example, Bartlett, 1970; Germaine, 1979; Hollis, 1970; Reynolds, 1942). One stream has emphasized the personal needs of individuals, families, and groups. A coexistent stream has emphasized social reform and social justice—the common collective good (Falck, 1988).

SOCIAL WORK AS A PROFESSION

Social work is a profession. Barker (1999) defined a profession as "a group of people who use in common a system of values, skills, techniques, knowledge, and beliefs to meet a specific social need" (p. 379). Professions also have been characterized as a "calling requiring specialized knowledge and often long academic preparation" (Merriam-Webster, 1999, p. 580).

In 2001 the Council on Social Work Education (CSWE) articulated the principles and purposes of the profession as follows:

The social work profession receives its sanction from public and private auspices and is the primary profession in the development, provision, and evaluation of social services. Professional social workers are leaders in a variety of organizational settings and service delivery systems within a global context.

The profession of social work is based on the values of service, social and economic justice, dignity and worth of the person, importance of human relationships, and integrity and competency in practice. Within these values as defining principles, the purposes of social work are as follows:

- to enhance human well-being and alleviate poverty, oppression, and other forms of social injustice
- to enhance the social functioning and interactions of individuals, families, groups, organizations, and communities by involving them in accomplishing goals, developing resources, and preventing and alleviating distress
- to formulate and implement social policies, services, and programs that meet basic human needs and support the development of human capacities
- to pursue policies, services, and resources through advocacy that promote social and economic justice
- to develop and use research, knowledge, and skills that advance social work practice
- to develop and apply practice in the context of diverse cultures. (p. 5)

Social work, as with most professions, is formally recognized through legal regulation in the form of licensing. A professional social worker is an individual who qualifies for membership in the profession; uses its practices, knowledge, and skills to provide services to clients; and always adheres to the profession's code of ethics (Barker, 1999). According to the U.S. Department of Labor (2002), approximately 468,000 jobs are held by professionally trained social workers.

SOCIAL WORK PRACTICE

The definition of social work adopted by NASW in 1970 included clarification about the nature of social work practice:

Social work practice consists of the professional application of social work values, principles, and techniques to one or more of the following ends: helping people obtain tangible services; counseling and psychotherapy with individuals, families, and groups; helping communities or groups provide or improve social and health services; and participating in legislative processes. The practice of social work requires knowledge of human development and behavior; of social, economic, and cultural institutions; and of the interaction of all these factors. (NASW, 1973, pp. 4–5)

Virtually all professions include specializations within their professional education and practice. The legal profession, for example, includes members who are specialists in tax, criminal, or family law. Medicine, of course, has a wide range of specialty areas; the social work profession is equally complex and broad.

As the profession has evolved, the definitions of the profession and its practice have been subject to periodic debate, re-examination, and change. Social work is a profession that interrelates with and seeks to have an impact upon the larger socioeconomic and political environment; it is not surprising that the definition of social work would be dynamic in nature rather than rigid and static.

In 1981 the NASW Board of Directors adopted the *Standards for the Classification of Social Work Practice* developed by the NASW Task Force on Labor Force Classification. The intent of the standards was "to identify the specific social work content of social service employment and to provide a basis for differentiating among levels of practice" (NASW, 1981, p. 3). As defined by the NASW task force (1981), social work practice

consists of professionally responsible intervention to (1) enhance the developmental, problem-solving, and coping capacities of people, (2) promote the effective and humane operation of systems that provide resources and services to people, (3) link people with systems that provide them with resources, services and opportunities, and (4) contribute to the development and improvement of social policy. (p. 6)

Most recently, CSWE, in its new *Educational Policy and Accreditation Standards* (2001), defined social work practice as that which

promotes human well-being by strengthening opportunities, resources, and capacities of people in their environments and by creating policies and services to correct conditions that limit human rights and the quality of life. (p. 3)

Over the years, these definitions of practice have shared in common the anchoring of professional practice in the *person-in-environment* paradigm. Furthermore, the definitions have always encompassed interventions at the individual, group, community, and societal levels.

HUMAN SERVICES: THE ARENA OF SOCIAL WORK PRACTICE

Human services are defined as those services oriented toward the prevention, amelioration, or resolution of health, mental health, social, or environmental problems that afflict individuals, families, specific groups, or communities (Gibelman, 1995). Barker (1999) further delineated the human services as "programs and activities designed to enhance people's development and well-being, including providing economic and social assistance for those unable to provide for their own needs" (p. 224). Included are the planning, developing, and administering of programs for and providing direct services to people unable to provide for their own needs. The term "human services" has been used synonymously with "social services" and "welfare services". However, the term human services is more encompassing in that it incorporates the full range of professions involved in the delivery of health, economic, and social services (Barker, 1999).

Human services organizations, the means through which most human services are provided, are viewed as organizations that assist in the growth and development of individuals and families (Wellford & Gallagher, 1988). They may be public (government) at the federal, state, or local level; proprietary (for profit); or nonprofit. No sector has a monopoly on the provision of a particular type of service. However, the largest proportion of social workers deliver services through not-for-profit organizations (Gibelman & Schervish, 1997).

Types of Agencies in Which Social Workers Practice

The auspice of practice refers to the legal authority of organizations or individuals to provide human services. Lowenstein (1964) referred to auspice as that which

> differentiates between the private provision of a service and the provision of that service by an organization set up by the community at large, either through government or voluntary association, with accountability for, and control over, the service resting with the community at large. Such control and accountability are in contrast to the private control of the contractual relationship mutually exercised by a private practitioner and his [or her] client. (p. 4)

The practice of social work has traditionally been carried out in organizational settings. Throughout the profession's history, these settings have basically been of two types: public and private. Public agencies are generally associated with bureaucracies, such as large public assistance or child welfare agencies. Distinctive characteristics of these agencies include clearly defined rules; a vertical hierarchy with power

centered at the top; formal channels of communication; and selection, promotion, compensation, and retention based on technical competence (Gibelman, 1999). Social workers who work for the government typically fall under civil service rules and regulations.

Public human services organizations, also known as government agencies, are created by legislative bodies composed of elected officials. Within the human services, some public organizations are federally operated but have decentralized structures within local communities across the country. For example, the network of hospitals under the U.S. Department of Veteran Affairs is under federal auspices even though the hospitals themselves are locally based. Public child welfare programs and programs for older adults are typically under the jurisdiction of state or local public agencies, although a sizable proportion of the budget for such services comes from the federal government. Each state has substantial leeway in how it organizes its services delivery system—thus, there is no one "structural format" that applies to all states.

The mission of public agencies, which are funded through tax dollars, is described in legal codes and government regulations (Horejsi & Garthwait, 1999). This funding base is sometimes offset, to some degree, by fees for services or copayments that clients and consumers may be required to pay to be eligible for public services. An example might be a fee for health inoculations. The fee, however, generally does not cover the full cost of the service.

The majority of public social services agencies no longer provide most social services under their jurisdiction directly, but rather contract with other agencies to deliver the services (Gibelman & Demone, 1998). Examples of public services that are "contracted out" include foster care, day care, residential treatment, family preservation services, and group home care.

The private sector includes not-for-profit and for-profit agencies. Within the not-for-profit sector (or nonprofit sector as it is also referenced) there are two types of agencies: sectarian and nonsectarian. Sectarian agencies have their origins in or have the financial support of religious organizations or are oriented toward providing services primarily to members of a specific religious group. Examples include Catholic Charities USA and its affiliates across the country, Jewish Family Services, Lutheran Social Services, and Methodist Board of Child Care (Barker, 1999). Nonsectarian agencies are not religiously affiliated. Nonprofit social welfare agencies, both sectarian and nonsectarian, may be under a national rubric, such as the affiliates of the Child Welfare League or Alliance for Children and Families, but also may be located communities and therefore may attempt to be responsive to community needs within the parameters of their national standard-setting organizations.

About half of all nonprofit organizations in the United States fall under the category of "charitable"—meaning that donations to them are permitted and are tax deductible to the donor (National Center for Charitable Statistics [NCCS], 2002). This status relates to their purpose—to serve the broad public interest. They include educational, religious, scientific, social services, and other public benefit organizations. Most social workers in the nonprofit sector work in charitable organizations that promote or provide a broad range of social or human services to individuals or families, such as family, child welfare, mental health, and personal social services; personal enrichment services; and residential or custodial care (NCCS, 1993).

Most of the traditional social services and social change organizations are not-for-profit organizations. A not-for-profit agency is accountable to its board of directors, which sets overall policy. The largest proportion of social workers deliver services through not-for-profit organizations. In 1995, the last year for which comprehensive data are available, 38.6 percent of NASW members indicated that they worked in not-for-profit organizations, both sectarian and nonsectarian (Gibelman & Schervish, 1997). The bylaws of the agency articulate which clients are to be served, what problems are the focus of the agency's attention, and what methods are to be used in providing services (Barker, 1999). Revenue to carry out their programs comes from a variety of sources—contributions, donations, grants, purchase of services, and fees for services.

In recent years, for-profit organizations, also known as proprietary organizations, have increasingly entered the human services market, particularly in settings such as nursing homes, home health care, residential treatment centers, and adult and child day care. Although these organizations employ social workers and other mental health professionals, for-profit organizations are owned and operated as any other business (Gibelman, 2000). Their purpose is to sell a set of services, and their operations reflect the goal of yielding a profit for investors and stockholders (Horejsi & Garthwait, 1999). Many such businesses are part of super corporations, such as the Psychiatric Institute, which owns and operates inpatient and outpatient psychiatric facilities across the country, and nursing home chains, such as Beverly Enterprises. The mission of the for-profit organization is quite straightforward. As with any entrepreneurial business, the purpose or reason for being is to make a profit (Weinbach, 1994).

Although there are similarities among all human services organizations (particularly in relation to their people-serving activities), auspice does have an impact on how the work of the organization is carried out. Such differences include financial and legal bases, focus of services, clients served (for example, fee-for-service versus means-tested), operating philosophies, governing structures, and technologies employed.

Practice Setting

Social workers provide services in a variety of practice settings, also referred to as *fields* of practice (Barker, 1999). For example, social workers deliver services in settings that include private practice, institutions, hospitals, school systems, clinics or centers, and correctional facilities; the range of practice settings is broad.

LEVELS OF SOCIAL WORK PRACTICE

Social workers function in direct services, supervision, management, policy development, research, planning, and education and training capacities. These levels of practice typically are distinguished by their skill and experiential requirements. For example, those holding management positions tend to have several years of direct service or supervisory experience. In an agency setting, there are typically three major levels of practice: direct services, supervision, and administration. In some agencies, however, there may be additional levels of practice or positions, such as paraprofessionals or case aides. And within administration, there may be middle managers who occupy program management positions and upper level managers who carry overall responsibility for the operations of the agency.

Another conceptualization of levels of practice is that of direct and indirect. Direct practice refers to the range of professional activities in which social workers engage on behalf of clients. The specified goals for clients are reached through personal contact with and immediate influence of the social worker. In indirect practice, the activities of the social worker are oriented toward achieving social goals or developing human opportunities (Barker, 1999).

Social workers engaged in administrative practice have responsibility for a social agency or subunit of an agency (department or division, such as the social work department of a hospital) and carry out some or all of the following functions:

- determine organizational goals
- acquire resources and allocate them to carry out the programs of the agency
- coordinate activities to achieve selected goals

- monitor, assess, and make necessary changes in processes and structures to improve effectiveness and efficiency
- engage in activities that contribute to transforming social policy into social services. (Barker, 1999, p. 8)

The term "administrator" is often used synonymously with manager. Similarly, the terms administration and management are interchangeable.

The levels of social work practice have also been distinguished as *macro*, *micro*, and *mezzo*. *Macro* refers to that level of social work practice oriented toward bringing about change and improvement in the general society (Barker, 1999). The functions performed in this regard include political action, community organizing, and agency administration. *Mezzo* is that level of social work practice primarily carried out with families and small groups. Related activities include facilitating communication, mediating, negotiating, and linking people together (Barker, 1999). *Micro practice* refers to professional activities that address the problems faced primarily by individuals, families, and small groups. The functions performed are, for the most part, in the form of direct intervention on a case-by-case basis in a clinical setting (Barker, 1999).

All social workers engage in the three levels of practice to some extent, even though the major focus of their attention may be at one or two of the levels (Barker, 1999). Social workers share in common their commitment to help people increase their capacities to problem solve and cope. They do this through by helping clients (who may be individuals, families, groups, communities, organizations, or society in general) obtain needed resources, facilitating interactions between individuals and between people and their environments, making organizations responsive to people, and influencing the development and implementation of social policies (Barker, 1999).

SOCIAL WORK FUNCTIONS

In diverse practice settings, social workers carry out a series of functions, each of which is comprised of a set of distinctive tasks. The relationships between the goals of social work practice, the objectives related to particular goals, and the functions and tasks involved are illustrated in Table 2.1. Functions are defined as major groupings of tasks and activities that, when performed by social workers, meet the four practice goals identified in Table 2.1.

The ability to carry out these functions is predicated on the use of social work knowledge and skills in ways that are consistent with social work values. In the performance of social work roles, 12 skill areas are identified as essential.

Social workers should be able to

(1) listen to others with understanding and purpose

(2) elicit information and assemble relevant facts to prepare a social history, assessment, and report

(3) create and maintain professional helping relationships

(4) observe and interpret verbal and nonverbal behavior and use knowledge of personality theory and diagnostic methods

(5) engage clients, including individuals, families, groups, and communities, in efforts to resolve their own problems and to gain trust

---

TABLE 2.1

Summary of Social Work Functions

GOAL 1	GOAL 2	GOAL 3	GOAL 4
To enhance problem-solving, coping, and development capacities of people	To link people with systems that provide resources, services, and opportunities	To promote effective and humane operations of systems	To develop and improve social policy
FUNCTIONS	**FUNCTIONS**	**FUNCTIONS**	**FUNCTIONS**
Advice and Counseling	Diagnosis	Administration and Management	Planning
Advocacy and Enabling	Exchange	Consultation	Policy Advocacy
Assessment	Mobilization	Coordination	Policy Analysis
Detection and Identification	Negotiation	Evaluation	Policy Development
Diagnosis, Support, and Assistance	Organizing	Program Development	Reviewing
	Referral	Staff Development	
		Supervision	

Source: National Association of Social Workers. (1981). *Standards for the classification of social work practice: Policy statement 4* (p. 12). Silver Spring, MD: Author.

(6) discuss sensitive emotional subjects supportively and without being threatening

(7) create innovative solutions to clients' needs

(8) determine the need to terminate the therapeutic relationship

(9) conduct research or interpret the findings of research and professional literature

(10) mediate and negotiate between conflicting parties

(11) provide interorganizational liaison services

(12) interpret and communicate social needs to funding sources, the public, or legislatures. (NASW, 1981, pp. 17–18)

NASW's *Standards for the Classification of Social Work Practice* (1981) offered a classification scheme for social work values, knowledge, and skills. These classifications were intended "to provide a basis for differentiating among levels of practice" (p. 1). The standards, though over 20 years old, have never been updated. However, their relevance to the nature of the work carried out by social workers today has withstood the test of time.

More recent works on social work job classification include Teare and Sheafor's (1995) task descriptions of social work practice and O'Hare and Collins' (1997) scale for measuring social work practice skills. These more recent tools, although not as comprehensive as the NASW standards, are consistent with the classification initially developed by NASW, as highlighted in Table 2.2. Teare and Sheafor (1995), for example, sought to categorize social work tasks into 18 clusters of work activities. NASW, on the other hand, deduced social work tasks from overarching functions that, in turn, related to four primary goals of the profession. The 18 tasks identified by Teare and Sheafor appear in Column 1. In Column 2, their relationships to social work functions, as delineated by NASW, are illustrated.

FACTORS AFFECTING WHAT SOCIAL WORKERS DO

What social workers do depends, in part, on their age, level of experience, highest degree, and gender. A study of the NASW membership (Gibelman & Schervish, 1997) revealed that the overwhelming majority of members have a primary function of direct services. Since 1988, a baseline year for later comparisons, the proportion of NASW members in direct services has increased, whereas the proportion in other functional areas, such as management, research, supervision, and policy, has decreased. However, because the membership of NASW represents slightly less than 30 percent of the total number of professional social workers identified by the U.S. Department of Labor, Bureau of Labor Statistics (2002), it is not possible to speculate whether the skewing toward direct practice occurs throughout the profession or only among NASW members.

There are some important differences in what social workers do on the basis of their highest degree. For example, 72.1 percent of BSW level NASW members indicated that their primary function was direct service; for MSWs, it was 69.7 percent; and for PhDs and DSWs, 39.1 percent. Across the three educational levels, those with a PhD or DSW were more likely to identify research as their primary function than were BSWs or MSWs (Gibelman & Schervish, 1997). More doctoral and MSW social workers than BSW social workers occupied management positions. The findings revealed that 17.3 percent of doctoral-level members had a primary function of management, compared with 16.4 percent of MSWs and 9.3 percent of BSWs.

Experience is also a significant factor affecting what social workers do. There is a decided shift in function that occurs between two and five years of practice and between six and 10 years of practice. The proportion of NASW members reporting supervision as their primary function increases sharply from two to five years of experience. Similarly, the proportion of

TABLE 2.2

Linking Classification Systems

SOCIAL WORK TASKS[a]	SOCIAL WORK GOALS[b]
Case planning and maintenance Dispute resolution Group work Individual and family treatment Interpersonal helping Protective services Risk assessment and transition Service connection Tangible service provision	To enhance problem-solving, coping, and development capacities of people
Case planning and maintenance Dispute resolution Group work Interpersonal helping Professional development Protective services Service connection Staff deployment Staff information exchange Staff supervision Tangible service provision	To link people with systems that provide resources, services, and opportunities
Case planning and maintenance Delivery system knowledge development Dispute resolution Instruction Organizational maintenance Professional development Program development Research and policy development Service connection Staff deployment Staff information exchange Staff supervision	Delivery system knowledge development
Delivery system knowledge development Dispute resolution Instruction Professional development Program development Research and policy development	To develop and improve social policy

Source: [a] Adapted from Teare, R. J., & Sheafor, B. W. (1995). *Practice-sensitive social work education* (p. 22). Alexandria, VA: Council on Social Work Education. [b] Adapted from National Association of Social Workers. (1981). *Standards for the classification of social work practice: Policy statement 4.* Silver Spring, MD: Author.

members reporting management as a primary function increases from 11 to 15 years of experience (Gibelman & Schervish, 1997).

Gender is an extremely important factor affecting the type of practice in which social workers engage. A higher proportion of women are in direct services than men. The proportion of men is higher when the primary function is supervision, management, or education (Gibelman, 2000; Gibelman & Schervish, 1997).

It is not unusual for social workers to carry out multiple functions either within the same job (such as supervising and providing direct services) or in two different settings. In 1995, approximately 28 percent of employed NASW members indicated that they had a secondary practice. Some social workers held a full-time job and an additional part-time job; some had two part-time jobs. A typical pattern is for social workers to work in an agency as their primary job and then engage in part-time private practice. There are monetary incentives involved, but another factor motivating social workers to have more than one practice area is to fulfill occupational interests. Also, the mobility that is possible within the profession may encourage social workers to develop expertise in a new area through part-time employment while remaining in their primary practice setting (Gibelman & Schervish, 1997).

PREPARING FOR SOCIAL WORK PRACTICE

Formal training and subsequent experience prepare social workers for their professional roles (Barker, 1999). The purposes of social work education are, according to CSWE (2001), to "prepare competent and effective professionals, to develop social work knowledge, and to provide leadership in the development of service delivery systems" (p. 5).

There are two points of entry into the profession based on education: the baccalaureate in social work and the master of social work. The BSW is a degree awarded to qualified students who major in social work in a CSWE-accredited college or university (Barker, 1999). The NASW established the Academy of Certified Baccalaureate Social Workers (ACBSW) in 1991 to evaluate and certify the practice competence of baccalaureate social workers. Those who have obtained a BSW from an accredited school of social work are eligible for ACBSW after they complete two years of full-time or 3,000 hours of part-time postgraduate employment, commit to adhere to the NASW *Code of Ethics*, and complete a certification process composed of a written exam, supervisory evaluations, and professional references.

The MSW degree is awarded by accredited schools or programs of social work to students have who completed the required number of academic hours (usually 60), including field placement and, when required, completion of a research project or thesis (CSWE, 2001).

A *social worker*, then, is a graduate of a social work education program at the bachelor's or master's degree level who uses his or her knowledge and skills to provide social services for clients. These clients may be individuals, families, groups, communities, organizations, or society in general (Barker, 1999).

CONTINUING PROFESSIONAL EDUCATION

The NASW *Code of Ethics* (1996) articulated the ethical responsibility of social workers to participate in continuing social work education:

Social workers should strive to become and remain proficient in professional practice and the performance of professional functions. Social workers should critically examine and keep current with emerging knowledge relevant to social work. Social workers should routinely review the professional literature and participate in continuing education relevant to social work practice and social work ethics. (Standard 4.01(b))

Education for professional practice is considered a lifelong pursuit based on the need for professionals to remain up-to-date with new knowledge in the field and new and evolving practice methodologies throughout their careers. Formal, degree-oriented social work education is seen as providing students with foundation level of knowledge and skills and a beginning level of advanced learning in the profession. Acquisition of the breadth and depth of knowledge required for competent practice throughout a career involves ongoing education to acquaint social workers with new conceptual models and intervention approaches and other innovations (Reamer, 1998).

NASW, in its *Standards for Continuing Professional Education* (1998), set forth the following view:

By consistent participation in educational opportunities beyond the basic, entry level professional degree, social workers are able to maintain and increase their proficiency in service delivery. New knowledge is acquired, skills are refined, and professional attitudes are reinforced. (p. 1)

Continuing education refers to "training taken by social workers and other professionals who have already completed formal education requirements to enter their field" (Barker, 1999,

p. 103). The goal of continuing education is to provide social workers with the opportunity to acquire new and pertinent information; strengthen qualifications for professional credentialing (see discussion below); meet changing career demands, explore potential career paths, or both; and demonstrate—to self and others—a commitment to personal and professional development (NASW, 1998). Forty-eight states require a specific number of continuing education hours for license renewal, generally in the range of 15 to 36 contact hours per one to three years (Maidenberg, 2001).

Unlike degree-oriented education in which there is a prescribed curriculum, continuing education is a self-directed process in which the individual social worker is expected to assume responsibility for his or her own development (NASW, 1998). The areas of continuing education participation are guided by personal choice, although employing agencies may have a say in the selection of content if participation is paid for by the agency or involves time away from work.

Such educational offerings are typically made available by three types of providers: higher education institutions, including schools of social work and their extension divisions; professional associations, such as the National Association of Social Workers; and employers, such as social services agencies (Reamer, 1998; Strom & Green, 1995). There are also a growing number of private (for-profit) providers who offer continuing education as their primary business and their advertisements can often be found in the *NASW News*. Increasingly, continuing education is being offered on the World Wide Web. Examples include the Institute for Alternatives in Continuing Education (http://www.institute4ace.com), the American Society on Aging (http://www.asaging.com), and the Center for Continuing Education (http://www.continuingedu.org).

CREDENTIALING

There are several types of credentials in social work, all designed to assure the profession,

clients, and the public that a practitioner has entry level competence for safe practice (Biggerstaff, 1995). The primary credentialing is the basic academic qualification. Beyond that, there are a variety of voluntary professional credentials as well as those that may be required by a state for legitimate practice.

One form of credentialing is the voluntary certification program. Although state licensing or registration establishes minimum criteria for entry level practice, voluntary professional certification identifies specialty areas of practice (Biggerstaff, 1995).

Voluntary certification programs have been developed by NASW and other professional organizations. The Academy of Certified Social Workers (ACSW), which was established by NASW in 1962 to evaluate and certify the practice competence of social workers at the MSW level, is one such form of voluntary certification. Social workers are eligible for ACSW membership after they have obtained an MSW or doctorate in social work from an accredited school, have two years of supervised full-time or 3,000 hours of part-time practice experience, successfully pass a written examination, and provide three professional behaviorally anchored rating references. NASW membership is required for admission to and continued participation in the academy.

Another example of voluntary certification is the Diplomate in Clinical Social Work. The diplomate is now used as a credential to distinguish advanced-level professional clinical social workers who meet specified qualifications of the sponsoring organization. There are two sponsoring organizations: the American Board of Examiners in Clinical Social Work (ABE) and the National Association of Social Workers. Criteria for diplomate status typically include a graduate degree, postgraduate supervision, 7,500 hours of direct practice experience within a five-year period, fulfillment of requirements for state licensing, and passing an advanced examination (Barker, 1999).

Another form of voluntary certification is the qualified clinical social worker (QCSW), offered through the National Association of Social Workers. The QCSW is intended to recognize social workers who have met national standards of knowledge, skill, and experience in clinical social work practice. Eligibility for this credential also involves an agreement to abide by the NASW *Code of Ethics*, the NASW *Standards for the Practice of Clinical Social Work*, and the NASW *Continuing Education Standards*. Two years or 3,000 hours of postgraduate supervised clinical experience in an agency setting must be demonstrated, and the applicant for the credential must hold a current state social work license or certification or be a current member of ACSW (NASW, 2002).

Each state in the United States, as well as the District of Columbia, Puerto Rico, and the U.S. Virgin Islands, has some form of legal regulation for social work practice. These laws control who can practice social work, the services they can provide, methods they can use, and the titles they can present to the public (Biggerstaff, 1995). Of the more than 150,000 members of the National Association of Social Workers, more than half hold at least one credential (Biggerstaff, 1995). Many public and private social services agencies now require licensing or registration or eligibility for such as a prerequisite for employment.

A licensing law is protective regulatory legislation implemented through state agencies. Such laws regulate the interactions between consumers and providers of services by establishing minimum standards for entry into the profession, including education, training, experience, and supervision (Biggerstaff, 1995). A *licensed clinical social worker* (LCSW) is "a professional social worker who has been legally accredited by a state government to practice clinical social work in that state" (Barker, 1999, p. 276). Qualifications for the license vary from state to state but typically include an MSW from an accredited school of social work, several years of supervised professional experience, and successful passage of a social work licensing exam. A *licensed independent clinical social worker* (LICSW) is the "designation used by some state licensing bodies and some third-party financing institutions to indicate that the practitioner is qualified for independent practice" (Barker, 1999, p. 276). (Readers are referred to the Web site of the Association of Social Work Boards—http://www.aswb.org—for information about licensing and links to the individual state boards of social work.)

Registration laws and statutory certification, also forms of legal regulation, are voluntary statutes that apply only to social workers who wish to use a particular title. These laws also specify minimum requirements that social workers must meet. Such title protection often limits certain areas of professional practice, such as private practice, to those who meet the minimum requirements (Biggerstaff, 1995).

WHAT SOCIAL WORKERS DO

What Social Workers Do seeks to provide a sampler of what social workers do and the multiplicity of roles that they carry out in diverse settings. The goal is to portray the breadth of the social work profession and the richness of opportunities available for those entering or learning about the profession and for currently practicing social workers who may wish to explore new avenues of practice.

REFERENCES

Barker, R. (1991). *Social work dictionary.* Washingon, DC: National Association of Social Workers.

Barker, R. (1999). *Social work dictionary* (4th ed.). Washington, DC: NASW Press.

Barker, R. (2003). *Social work dictionary* (5th ed.). Washington, DC: NASW Press.

Bartlett, H. M. (1970). *The common base of social work practice.* Washington, DC: National Association of Social Workers.

Biggerstaff, M. (1995). Licensing, regulation, and certification. In R. L. Edwards (Ed.-in-Chief), *Encyclopedia of social work* (19th ed., Vol. 2, pp. 1616–1624). Washington, DC: NASW Press.

Bogo, M., Raphael, D., & Roberts, R. (1993). Interests, activities, and self-identification among social work students: Toward a definition of social work identity. *Journal of Social Work Education, 29,* 279–292.

Council on Social Work Education. (2001). *Educational policy and accreditation standards.* Alexandria, VA: Author.

Crouch, R. C. (1979). Social work defined. *Social Work, 24,* 46–48.

Falck, H. S. (1988). *Social work: The membership perspective.* New York: Springer.

Germaine, C. B. (Ed.). (1979). *Social work practice: People and environments—An ecological perspective.* New York: Columbia University Press.

Gibelman, M. (1995). Purchasing social services. In R. L. Edwards (Ed.-in-Chief), *Encyclopedia of social work* (19th ed., Vol. 3, pp. 1998–2007). Washington, DC: NASW Press.

Gibelman, M. (1999). The search for identity: Defining social work—Past, present, future. *Social Work, 44,* 298–310.

Gibelman, M. (2000). The nonprofit sector and gender discrimination: A preliminary investigation into the glass ceiling. *Journal of Nonprofit Management & Leadership, 10,* 251–269.

Gibelman, M., & Demone, H. W., Jr. (Eds.). (1998). *The privatization of human services: Policy and practice issues.* New York: Springer.

Gibelman, M., & Schervish, P. (1997). *Who we are: A second look.* Washington, DC: NASW Press.

Hollis, F. (1970). The psychosocial approach to the practice of casework. In R. W. Roberts & R. H. Nee (Eds.), *Theories of social casework* (pp. 33–75). Chicago: University of Chicago Press.

Horejsi, C. R., & Garthwait, C. L. (1999). *The social work practicum: A guide and workbook for students.* Boston: Allyn & Bacon.

Lowenstein, S. (1964). *Private practice in social casework.* New York: Columbia University Press.

Maidenberg, M. (2001). *Factors which influence social workers' participation in continuing education.* Unpublished doctoral dissertation, Yeshiva University, Wurzweiler School of Social Work, New York.

Merriam-Webster (1999). *The new Merriam-Webster dictionary.* Springfield, MA: Author.

National Association of Social Workers, Commission on Social Work Practice. (1956). Working definition of social work practice. Reprinted in H. L. Lurie (Ed.), *Encyclopedia of social work* (15th ed., pp. 1028–1033). New York: National Association of Social Workers.

National Association of Social Workers. (1973). *Standards for social service manpower, policy statement 4.* Washington, DC: Author.

National Association of Social Workers. (1981). *Standards for the classification of social work practice: Policy statement 4.* Silver Spring, MD: Author.

National Association of Social Workers. (1996). *Code of ethics.* Washington, DC: Author.

National Association of Social Workers. (1998). *Standards for continuing professional education.* Washington, DC: Author.

National Association of Social Workers. (2002). *Qualified clinical social worker.* Washington, DC: Author. Retrieved November 12, 2003, from http://www.socialworkers.org/credentials/qcsw.asp

National Center for Charitable Statistics and the Foundation Center. (1993). *The national taxonomy of exempt entities* (rev. ed.). Washington, DC: Independent Sector.

National Center for Charitable Statistics. (2002). *NCCS frequently asked questions.* Washington, DC: Urban Institute. Retrieved November 12, 2003, from http://ncss.urban.org/FAQs.htm

O'Hare, T., & Collins, P. (1997). Development and validation of a scale for measuring social work practice skills. *Research on Social Work Practice, 7,* 28–39.

Reamer, F. G. (1998). *Ethical standards in social work: A critical review of the NASW code of ethics.* Washington, DC: NASW Press.

Reynolds, B. C. (1942). *Learning and teaching in the practice of social work.* New York: Russell & Russell.

Strom, K., & Green, R. (1995). Continuing education. In R. L. Richards (Ed.-in-Chief), *Encyclopedia of social work* (19th ed., Vol. 1, pp. 622–632). Washington, DC: NASW Press.

Teare, R. J., & Sheafor, B. W. (1995). *Practice-sensitive social work education.* Alexandria, VA: Council on Social Work Education.

U.S. Department of Labor, Bureau of Labor Statistics. (2002). *Tabulations from the current population survey, 2001 annual averages.* Washington, DC: U.S. Government Printing Office.

Weinbach, R. W. (1994). *The social worker as manager: Theory and practice* (2nd ed.). Boston: Allyn & Bacon.

Wellford, W. H., & Gallagher, J. G. (1988). *Unfair competition: The challenge to charitable exemption.* Washington, DC: National Assembly of National Voluntary Health and Social Welfare Organizations.

Chapter Three THE CONTEXT OF SOCIAL WORK PRACTICE

"The times they are a-changin," sang Bob Dylan. And as the times change, so does the profession of social work. The sociopolitical and economic environment at any given point in time has always influenced the goals, priorities, targets of intervention, technologies, and methodologies of the social work profession. The interaction, however, is two sided. The mission of the profession, the motivations and characteristics of the social work labor force, and changes in methodology and technology also serve to expand or contract what social workers do. The relative influence of internal (profession-specific) versus external (societal) forces in defining social work may be idiosyncratic to particular points in time, but their dynamic interaction provides the context in which the growth and development of the profession can be understood.

In the first edition of this book, published in 1995, the context of social work practice focused on a Republican-controlled Congress and the potentiality that the Contract with America would severely curtail society's ability to respond effectively to social problems. Any updating of this situation would have focused on the failed efforts at health care reform and the resulting strong-hold of private market forces on the financing and delivery of and access to health and mental health care. The outcome of the presidential election of 2000, too, would figure prominently in a discussion of the sociopolitical factors likely to influence the face of social work

in the new millennium. These developments are, in fact, reviewed below in terms of their implications for social work practice.

It is necessary, however, to begin "in the moment," and that moment of a changing world was defined on September 11, 2001. As the American public—with the world looking on—watched the terrorist attacks on venerable institutions—the Pentagon and the World Trade Center— live on television complacency became a thing of the past. Individual concerns about diet and exercise, where to go on the next vacation, how to deal with an annoying supervisor, where to obtain Retin-A, whether a face-lift should be considered, and how to find organically grown vegetables at a reasonable price were suddenly replaced with different concerns. These new concerns included the potential for missile attacks; fathers and sons, mothers and daughters going off to a war in a faraway place that most people couldn't spell correctly; deadly toxins that would produce plagues, such as smallpox; whether the mail was any longer safe to open because of anthrax lacing; and a gas mask should be purchased and Cipro be taken as preventive measures.

The Bush administration's domestic agenda was suddenly off the table, as priorities of national security became paramount. But at the same time, there was an unprecedented acknowledgment of the need for mental health services and the obligation of government to make available the personnel and fiscal resources needed for large-scale crisis intervention and counseling (U.S. Department of Health and Human Services [DHHS], 2001). As this book goes to press, the United States is still engaged in its War on Terrorism and the War with Iraq, the American economy remains on shaky ground, and fears grow about the proliferation of nuclear weapons in such countries as North Korea, India, and Pakistan. Within such a context, human services, at least for now, are a lesser concern to public policymakers than might be the case in other times. It is within this context that social workers now function.

SOCIAL WORK'S PLACE IN SOCIETY

Fluidity exists both in regard to how the profession defines itself and the boundaries of what constitute social work practice. Changes in the profession are driven by internal or external forces (Walz & Groze, 1991). The role and function of social workers are, for example, affected by both the larger environmental context in which the profession functions (the economy, social need, culture, political preferences, and so forth) and the stage of development of professional thought, leadership direction, technology, and mission and goals. In fact, the multiple missions of the profession and the nature of social work practice encompass this dual focus. As Hopps and Pinderhughes (1987) commented, "the uniqueness of the social work approach lies in its expertise in acknowledging the interface between intrapersonal and environmental forces" (p. 353).

The course and direction of the profession's development can also be seen as a reflection of social work's location within the social structure. The domain of the profession, according to Rosenfeld (1983), is defined, in part, as the gap between the well-being of people at a particular time and place and the spheres of well-being of individuals for which adequate provision is not provided. Dealing with these discrepancies

between the needs of people and the provision of resources is the specialty of social work. In fact, the very purpose of social work is to reduce such incongruities (Rosenfeld, 1983). However, such incongruities in society are specific to time and place and thus inevitably change over time. Thus, what social workers do changes in response to the changing human condition within the context of the larger environment. Nevertheless, the expertise of social work remains rooted in the discrepancies between need and need fulfillment, no matter what the nature of the need may be over time.

The breadth of social work's domain depends, in part, upon the availability of other professions and institutions to provide the resources that people need. Roles and functions may be assumed by social workers because no other profession is ready to deal with them (Rosenfeld, 1983). Any attempt to "fix" the boundaries of the profession is likely to be unsuccessful, given the constantly changing societal environment and prevailing ideologies. Thus, the domain of social work today is likely to be somewhat different tomorrow; it is a dynamic and evolving profession. The evolution of the profession is also rooted in changing technology and intervention methodology. Our knowledge base continues to grow. Theories are subject to more rigorous testing.

Every profession has its distinct pattern of relationships and behavior, and each moves at its own pace in its professional development (Houle, 1983). One of the hallmarks of a profession, according to Houle (1983), is the concern of its members with clarifying and defining its dominant characteristics and functions. The relative emphasis given to these areas of debate are frequently defined by the prevailing cultural, political, social, and organizational environment. Within this context, social work has also been described as "a residual institution with boundariless areas of concern" (Bar-On, 1994, p. 53). Bar-On (1994) argued that the role of social work can only be deduced from the particular context in which it is practiced; the range of the profession's concerns is reflected in needs not being met by primary needs-meeting institutions of society. Thus, the boundaries of professional concern are defined within the here and now.

The profession grows and changes. Some may argue against the direction of change, but value judgments about the wisdom of the course of the profession's development are, by and large, irrelevant. It would be the unusual group process in which total unanimity was reached. Social workers are not a homogeneous group. Although they share in common a belief in and commitment to the principles of the profession's *Code of Ethics*, their personal beliefs and values are as varied as the population as a whole. Many social workers are politically liberal, but there are also politically conservative social workers. Some social workers identify with the socialist tradition and others have strong convictions about the merits of free enterprise (Ginsberg, 1988). Some favor a one-on-one approach to helping, whereas others believe that social action is the only viable means of affecting change. The composition of the profession reflects the diversity of American society. The definition of social work and its fluidity allows for such diversity within the profession and means that growth and change are possible.

One of the consistent characteristics that sets social work apart from other helping professions is its orientation to the *person-in-environment* perspective. That is, social work views the client as part of an environmental system. This perspective "encompasses the reciprocal relationships and other influences between an individual, the relevant other or others, and the physical and social environment" (Barker, 1999, p. 359). The centrality of the client (be it an individual, group, community, or society as a whole) and his or her interaction with the environment are echoed in the relationship of the social work profession to the larger society in which it functions. The types of jobs available, the priority afforded particular problem areas or populations, the predominant intervention modalities, and the settings in which social workers practice

are all affected by the prevailing sociopolitical philosophy and culture of the times. The same societal forces, exemplified, in part, in the degree to which the prevailing political climate is seen as "conservative" or "liberal," influence the perceptions and preferences of those entering the field of social work. Thus, some degree of congruence between social change and social work change can be found in dominant social thought at any given period of time.

THE ROLE OF GOVERNMENT

The types of problems the clients of social workers confront—problems such as poverty, homelessness, single parenthood, lack of job skills or education, and poor health, to name just a few—are of such magnitude that only the government has the resources and authority to address them in any significant way. Thus, what happens to social programs depends on government ideology and political preferences. In turn, the job market for social workers is affected by the size and type of social programs currently given priority by the government.

The Past as Prelude

The 1960s War on Poverty is an example of externally driven change that was seen by social workers as positive because of its overarching concern with human well-being and enfranchisement of heretofore disenfranchised populations. Although social work theory and practice have always included an advocacy component, the War on Poverty provided an unprecedented opportunity to recruit into the profession and provide job opportunities for those wishing to practice advocacy as a primary function. But the strategies of confrontation and change are less effective today; the issues have changed, as has the sociopolitical environment.

"Reaganomics" posed a new set of challenges for the profession of social work. In the early years of the presidential administration of Ronald Reagan (1981–1988), the social work literature reflected concern about the potential impact of the president's agenda. "Social work's future appears precarious," said one commentator (Getzel, 1983). Anne Minahan, then editor-in-chief of *Social Work*, commented that the Reagan period represented one of the worst of times for social work and our society. She noted, however, "a time of societal crises can create a common recognition of the shared social work perspective, values, and purpose that shape social workers' view of the world" (Minahan, 1982, p. 291). Taubman (1985) similarly noted that a silver lining may shine through the withdrawal of human services resources. In his view, "the profession may come out of the crisis with a clearer definition of priorities, better monitoring and evaluation mechanisms, and more effective and efficient human service organizations" (p. 181).

Others offered suggestions about how social agencies might "do more with less" and develop strategies to deal with retrenchment in human services funding and programs (Turem & Born, 1983). Adaptation was urged. Austin (1984) argued that managing cutbacks involved new role requirements for agency administrators, including strategic planning and "cheerleading" (for example, increasing staff involvement in all levels of decision making). Other commentators cautioned that social workers should not be sanguine about the impact of doing more with less. Taubman (1985), for example, concluded that "minimizing the negative effect of massive budget cuts may lull the profession and its communities and legislatures into the complacency of thinking that less is more" (p. 180). The posture of the profession during the Reagan years was largely reactive and incremental; social work fought to maintain the status quo and protect programs and professional status with modest successes (Schorr, 1988).

The presidency of George Bush in 1989 extended Republican control of the government until 1992 (Hopps & Collins, 1995). The social work literature continued to reflect a concern with survival strategies, cutback management,

holding the line, advocacy, and hope for the future. Social workers took an active role in educating decision makers about the impact of budget cuts and a diminished federal government role in health and human services. Social work did indeed survive, finding ways to stem the tide of cuts and reaching out to embrace new areas of practice to augment or replace practice areas hard hit by retrenchment.

It is not coincidental that, during the 1980s, when social policy resulted in a diminution of social work labor market opportunities in some sectors of traditional practice, there was a substantial increase in the numbers of social workers entering independent practice (Gibelman & Schervish, 1997). What is less clear is whether the labor market defined or reflected social worker preferences. The overall conservative societal bend was no doubt reflected in the sociopolitical attitudes of the entering pool of social workers and similar attitudinal adaptations among the existing social work labor force. We are a product of and reflect, in degree rather than kind, the prevailing values of our society.

A Democrat in the White House

Different times call for different strategies. The election of Bill Clinton in 1992 placed social work, after 12 years, in a position to be heard and to influence. Social workers mobilized to have a say in the development of new social policies, foremost in the area of health care reform (Ewalt, 1994). Yet it was only a short time later—in 1995—that the profession was again defining the sociopolitical context as a "time of singular peril" (Cohen, 1995). The context was the Republican Party's *Contract with America*, the implications of which were far reaching. According to Robert Cohen (1995), then Acting Executive director of NASW:

Programs that for decades have been the bedrock of our social welfare infrastructure are threatened. The very nature of government as most of us have known it is under attack. . . . The refrain is that government, especially the federal government, has failed: Taxes are too high, industry is over-regulated, environmental protection laws are impeding progress, immigration is out of control, crime is rampant, affirmative action is undemocratic and liberals, feminists, gays and lesbians have weakened the "American family." . . . Congressional actions taken this past year and projected for 1996 threaten to unravel the fabric of social legislation that has evolved over the past 60 years. (p. 2)

The Republican-controlled House of Representatives sought to implement its Contract with America and social workers quickly and loudly voiced their opposition to this contract in regard to its potential impact on the most vulnerable in this society and its likely affect on the provision of services by social workers and other helping professionals.

The 1994 midterm elections signified a new bent on the perception that "all is not well" in American society, but this time the system itself was seen as a root cause of the problems. The 1994 election results were a manifestation of a growing distrust in the very institutions of our society—Congress included. Distrust in government remains widespread and the requests on the part of the various interest groups for more funds, programs, and services are now looked upon with suspicion, if not disfavor.

As the history of American social welfare shows, the swinging of the pendulum in regard to the role of government in social welfare is one of the most consistent characteristics of our system. The bleak forecast for social welfare programs under the Contract with America materialized only in very modified form and it was not long before the vocabulary of this contract disappeared except in historical reference. Incrementalism is the hallmark of our governmental system. Government involvement in social welfare has been consistent and strong since the Great Depression, and, even prior to

that time, there had been some successful efforts to define a federal role. The nature and extent of that role, however, fall along a continuum, as affected by and intertwined with sociopolitical philosophy, supported by public opinion. Appropriate public policy responses to identified social problems may be slow in development, but, in general, retrenchment is equally slow once a program has become institutionalized.

The first Clinton administration also signaled another reality of public policy and social work's intertwined relationship with government: the failure to act. Despite yeoman's efforts, the Clinton administration was unable to get health care reform through Congress. This left the problems of health care—the millions of people uninsured; the spiraling costs of treatment, particularly prescription drugs; and the uncontrolled exigencies of the private marketplace on access to and cost of treatment—unaddressed. Thus, the absence of policy has had enormous repercussions for the quality of health and mental health services, as well as access to care and freedom for clients to choose their providers.

Managed care, which gained a stronghold on the unregulated health care system, has had a profound influence on the nature of the services provided by social workers. Psychotherapeutic, long-term treatment has given way to brief therapies, often of a behaviorally oriented nature and emphasizing the documentation of the outcomes of treatment. Social workers have always included brief therapies among their repertoire of interventions and solution-focused clinical practice; continues to gain adherents (O'Neill, 2000). Since identifying interventions that work best with clients has always been a priority for social work practitioners, the managed care movement may have provided a push in a direction already identified as desirable. Still at issue, however, is the impact on the nature of services provided when longer-term interventions are needed, but the health care system disallows such treatment.

Another complicating factor is that managed care organizations (MCOs) have not been the money-making business propositions envisioned, leading to a steady stream of mergers and acquisitions. Industry consolidation, in this case, has squeezed mental health providers even harder, as the financially strapped MCOs seek deeper cuts in operating costs through limitations on services (O'Neill, 1999). As businesses, MCOs are concerned with efficiency and bottom line revenues, not with practitioners or clients. Inpatient mental health treatment has decreased and hospitalizations are for very time-limited periods—usually time to evaluate, stabilize the patient on medication, and refer to outpatient treatment facilities. Outpatient mental health care visits, at least those provided under insurance programs, have also decreased, in large part because of MCO limitations on either the number of allowable visits per year or limits on the actual dollar amount of coverage for practitioner fees per year (O'Neill, 1999). The one positive piece of news, though at the expense of mental health colleagues in related professions, is that MCOs prefer social workers to psychologists or psychiatrists. The reason: cheaper hourly reimbursement rates.

Social workers were, in general, pleased with the Clinton administration (at least relative to the sentiments of many professionals during the Reagan and first Bush administrations), although they were often dissatisfied with specific policies. The optimism related more to the fact that social workers now had access to and a receptive ear from the White House. Nevertheless, through the two terms of the Clinton administration, Republicans were the dominant party in Congress, with control of one or both houses. This meant, from a political point of view, that compromise was the only realistic approach to passage of any social welfare legislation. Prevailing political ideology, backed by public sentiment, supported a less active role for the government. Social workers mobilized— this time in a maintenance mode—through such strategies as educating decision makers by emphasizing the successful outcomes of social

service interventions and highlighting areas of unmet need; creating partnerships with clients, allied professionals, and concerned citizens; and refining skills to enhance effectiveness ("Execs Offer Directions," 1995).

Government's prevailing views about its role in human services financing and delivery thus have a profound impact on the profession of social work. Ginsberg (1988) noted that "social work has been tied to government and politics since its beginning as a profession" (p. 245). More recent laws have had a similar effect in defining the boundaries of the work social workers perform. One noteworthy example of the changing nature of social policies is found in the welfare reform act (Personal Responsibility and Work Opportunity Reconciliation Act of 1996 [PRWORA], P.L. 104-193), which had significant influence on priorities afforded to particular kinds of programs of service and, consequently, the nature of practice carried out by social workers.

Welfare Reform

The economic recession of the early 1990s resulted in more people joining the ranks of the poor and more people on welfare; the welfare rolls grew by 25 percent during this recessionary period (Lens, 2000). The presidential campaign of 1992 embraced the issue of welfare reform and in the years following the election of Bill Clinton, various proposals were offered to solve "the welfare problem." Although there was widespread support in this society that something must be done about welfare, there was substantial disagreement about the content and form of such change.

The abolishment of Aid to Families with Dependent Children in 1996 and its replacement with Temporary Assistance for Needy Families (TANF), subsumed under PRWORA, turned welfare into a highly restrictive block grant program, limiting aid to five years, requiring states to force recipients into the workforce, and mandating penalties against states and recipients if they did not comply (NASW, 1996; Super, Parrott, Steinmetz, & Mann, 1996).

The 1996 law, the reauthorization of which was being debated within Congress in late 2002 and early 2003, employs several strategies to end dependency. Welfare is now considered temporary and transitional, with a five-year lifetime cap on benefits. States may opt to impose shorter time limits. And instead of open-ended federal dollars, states now receive a fixed sum each year for welfare in the form of a block grant. If the money does not cover state expenses, poor families can be denied assistance (Greenberg & Savner, 1996). TANF also transformed welfare into a work program by requiring recipients to work in exchange for receiving benefits within two years of receiving assistance (Lens, 2000). Sanctions, in the form of reduced benefits or loss of benefits, can be imposed for those who do not meet the work requirement.

The new law affected what social workers do in the form of the priority afforded to different kinds of services. Entitlement has ceased to be the operative word for the public welfare system. With greater discretion, states are free to redesign their services systems to reflect local conditions and preferences. Public welfare agencies have had to revamp their procedures and operations to administer an entirely different program, with new rules in regard to eligibility determination, duration of benefits, and enforcement of work provisions and sanctions. In the longer term, such public agencies are likely to curtail some of their operations as drops in the number of TANF recipients come to be realized.

Social workers employed by nonprofit agencies that earlier had provided training, day care, counseling, and financial management programs may have found that their workload has shifted to meet the mandates of the redesigned welfare system. Reducing dependency by helping people to become self-sufficient through employment became the number one (and sometimes only) priority. Self-sufficiency, however, was predicated on an expanding economy and job creation. That scenario had changed substantially between 1996, when the law was enacted, and

2002, when reauthorization of the law was debated in Congress. Congress failed to bring the measure to a vote prior to its recess and decided instead to extend the legislation into the next fiscal year.

The debate about reauthorizing PRWORA occurred within the context of a changed world and a changed economy. On one side are those who argue that the economic prosperity that characterized the time period in which PRWORA, particularly the TANF provisions, was enacted is now gone, and with it the realistic opportunity for welfare recipients to seek, find, and sustain employment. On the other side are those who would prefer no safety net of any type and who tie the receipt of public benefits to a moral litmus test that, if enacted, would push people into marriage as a "solution."

The lifetime limits imposed by the law are now being reached for many people who were eligible for and received benefits in 1996. This means that recipients' benefits will be terminated. These people will need to reapply to be transferred to the safety-net program of their state of residence, as they do not automatically qualify for it (Vallianatos, 2002)—a complicated and confusing process that varies by state and even by case. Welfare recipients who still need benefits when the lifetime limit has been reached may find that their state of residence is no longer able to help. The National Governors' Association and the National Association of State Budget Officers reported in May 2002 that state budgets are in their worst shape in 20 years, with no immediate prospects for improvement in the situation. Forty-eight of the 50 states reported that revenues in 2002 have fallen short of original projections and often by substantial margins (Broder, 2002). States have dipped into their reserves and, much like the federal government's situation, budget surpluses are gone. Some states have decided to risk the political fallout and have raised state taxes rather than cut programs at the same time that Washington enacts even further tax cuts.

NASW, in its recommendations concerning reauthorization of PRWRA, offered a perspective on the state of affairs for those affected by TANF:

> Welfare caseloads have fallen by more than 50 percent since 1993, but in 2000, nearly 40 percent of former welfare recipients continued to live below the federal poverty line. And the percentage of families living in deep poverty, defined as income below 50 percent of the poverty level, has been growing—from 4.9 percent in 1989 to 5.1 percent in 1998. ("Recommendations for the Preauthorization," 2001)

With funding from the Joyce Foundation, a Chicago-based group that supports programs to reduce poverty and violence and improve schools, a report was commissioned that pulled together and analyzed 24 studies conducted by a variety of academic and research organizations. The results showed that the welfare rolls in seven midwestern states were substantially reduced in recent years (by as much as two-thirds), but many of the 2 million former aid recipients from those locales remain in poverty. In five of the seven states, welfare caseloads increased in 2001, further highlighting that the gains made in earlier years were largely attributable to a booming economy rather than to welfare-to-work programs (Wilgoren, 2002). Thus, although the immediate goals of the 1996 welfare reform act were, in large part, achieved, it seems unlikely that this positive state will be long lasting unless means are found to maintain former welfare recipients in jobs in a worsening economy and in capacities in which they can move up the economic ladder. The report concluded that the reauthorization of welfare reform needs to include a safety net to support the working poor, including a larger investment in education and training and added provisions for child care and transportation (Wilgoren, 2002).

The overall economy does not bode well for the welfare-to-work goal. Major transformations have occurred in the workplace. For some citizens, the result is under- or unemployment because they lack the skills that are now required. A new underclass of displaced workers has emerged. Society has less and less need for unskilled labor; people lacking the skills for employment often also have educational deficits that diminish job options even further.

George W. Bush

The election of George W. Bush in 2000 suggested a different mind-set in terms of social welfare programs, budgets, and priorities, many of which were already manifest prior to September 11, 2001. The disputed presidential election of 2000 was, perhaps, both a verification of the strength of democracy and a sign of the occasional weaknesses of the sociopolitical system. That election fueled the public's growing distrust in the institutions of American society. The lack of a mandate for the Bush presidency remains difficult to assess, as the intervening factor of September 11, the War on Terrorism, and the War with Iraq has so significantly altered the political landscape.

In many ways, the Bush administration's agenda resembled that of his earlier predecessors, including Presidents Reagan and his father, George Bush. The theme is "compassionate conservatism," translated to mean a smaller role for government, further movement to give states more decision making and administrative powers in how they use federal dollars, and a new emphasis on the use of faith-based groups to provide human services (Kessler & Goldstein, 2001). Other themes include substantial tax reductions achievable through curtailed spending. Also made clear is the administration's intention to scrutinize programs within DHHS with an eye to budget cutting.

But the larger environmental context in which the profession of social work now functions is less clearly defined. The aftermath of September 11 produced a more "united" United States with an articulated enemy about which there was overall consensus. The shock of the attack on the United States reverberated in an acknowledgment of human frailties—both physical and psychological. Attention to depression, posttraumatic shock, and grief and bereavement made mental health interventions not only palatable to a large proportion of the public, but a need now defined as normative.

When President Bush assumed office in January 2001, it appeared that the budget surplus achieved during the Clinton administration was likely to hold. The first item on the Bush agenda was an across-the-board tax cut, diminishing the dollars available to maintain or increase a budget surplus. Democrats were, by and large, unsupportive of this tax cut because of concern about the continued financial base of the social security system and the priority placed on some type of health care reform, at least in regard to prescription drugs for Medicare-eligible people and insurance provisions of some type for the estimated 37 million people without any form of health coverage. No one anticipated that the War on Terrorism and War with Iraq would occupy either the political agenda or eat away at the budget surplus.

Wars are costly. Paying for national security as well as an overseas war has turned the budget surplus into a budget deficit. This means that the money to pay for publically funded health and human services as they existed prior to September 11, 2001, is open to scrutiny and the prospect for new programs that entail real dollars grows dimmer.

With the beginning of the year 2002, President Bush began to apply pressure on Congress to address domestic issues. High on his list of priorities were education, faith-based legislation, patients' rights, energy independence, and an economic stimulus package (Allen, 2001). Despite prodding, however, little movement has been made as of September 2003. The extent to which these current ideologies and conditions coalesce and how social work responds to such challenges will have major repercussions for the nature of the profession in the coming years. We know less, understandably, about how our profession will respond to these current and future environmental conditions.

THE EVOLVING PROFESSION
Modern Day Influences
Social work's sanction comes from the society of which it is a part. This implies that society recognizes that there are disparities between "what is" and "what should be" and that there is a need to rectify this condition (Rosenfeld, 1983). This recognition on the part of any society that it is "flawed" should not be taken for granted. Social work simply does not exist or is not allowed to exist in some societies in our modern civilization because there is no sanction to address societal incongruities. Simply put, recognition that "all is not well" with some components of a society is a necessary precursor to the development of a systematic and professional response to address the perceived problems. The degree to which society is willing to identify such incongruities depends on the sociopolitical context of the times (Gibelman, 1999).

There is a sizable literature, as evidenced in any issue of *Social Work*, about the negative effect of changing federal policies on the role and function of social workers and, of course, on the well-being of the people social workers serve. Professional roles and relationships underwent substantial transformation during the 1980s, largely resulting from political negativism toward the profession and those it serves. Media perceptions and political rhetoric, perhaps fueling each other, raised questions about the legitimacy of the profession and left social work without a clear sense of direction (Jones & Novak, 1993). But legislative budget cuts are cyclical in nature. Although the Reagan years may have been particularly tough for the profession of social work, the vulnerability of human services programs to the budget ax occurs again and again. Expansion seems to inevitably follow upon a period of contraction. In this regard, past NASW president Ruth Mayden (2001) noted:

> The public is rarely interested in what we do as social workers or in whom we serve until things go wrong—seeking to blame rather than to help, being unrealistic in their expectations and finally, much too often, not being willing to pay the price of undoing the harm that has been done through societal neglect and not being willing to invest in programs that can prevent new and further harm from being done. . . . These realities make for very demanding challenges for us as ordinary human beings, as well as for us as individuals who have chosen social work as our profession. (p. 2)

There is a consistent pattern of expansion and then retraction in social welfare programs. Each fluctuation necessitates changes in the conditions of practice and the nature of social work practice itself. Gearing up for program expansion causes significant disequilibrium for social welfare organizations and their social work employees. Cutbacks, in turn, bring with them significant upheaval—retrenchment, on the one hand, and gearing up for new program initiatives, on the other. This seemingly inevitable state of flux suggests the need for social workers to have flexibility, a longer-term focus, and a repertoire of proactive strategies, including advocacy (Jarman-Rohde, McFall, Kolar, & Strom, 1997).

With each major election at the federal or state level (president, Congress, state legislature), various interests mobilize to analyze the implications for their particular group and issue a "call to action," whether in favor of or against a candidate or party platform on the basis of its salience for and consistency with group interests. Social workers are among the groups that seek to influence the outcome of elections—and later, specific administrative or legislative proposals— in order to further their own agenda and those

of the people represented by them—including the poor, disenfranchised, disabled, or chronically ill. As discussed in Chapter 11, social workers often ally with other groups to increase the influence that can be brought to bear. The alliances, however, depend on the particular issue under consideration.

A review of social welfare trends in the United States suggests that it is the potential of change itself that raises the concern of interest groups. When a different party comes into power, such as with the election of a new president of a different party than his predecessor or a change in the majority party in either house of Congress, groups naturally seek to protect the programs that affect them and to rally against proposals that will harm them and those they represent. But change also occurs even if the same party remains in power, as the platforms upon which candidates seek and win elections almost always suggest the need for something new—be it less government spending or more government programs. "Business as usual" or "more of the same" is not typical of political platforms.

Proposed changes are thus seen as threats to interest groups, including social workers. For example, the *NASW News* reported "Special-Education Law under the Gun," which concerned the opposition of NASW and other groups to any legislative action that would result in a weakening of the provisions of the Individuals with Disabilities Education Act of 1990 (P.L. 101-476), which was up for reauthorization (see Landers, 1995). In a similar vein, another *NASW News* headline, this time in 2000, proclaimed the success of an advocacy effort to forestall budget cuts to a grant program for counseling in elementary schools ("School Counseling Program Saved," 2000). Relating to attempts to deprofessionalize social services in state agencies, yet another headline proclaimed "State Criteria Downgrading Beaten Back" (1999). The headline "Groups Gird to Save Nursing Home Role" also appeared in 1999. That story described efforts to fight to save the role of social workers in skilled nursing homes. These headlines suggest a justified preoccupation on the part of the profession and its members to defuse political efforts to dismantle health and human services initiatives or to deprofessionalize the human services labor force.

The predictability of political change is mediated, to some extent, by the incremental nature of the American political system. But incrementalism should never be taken for granted, and each effort of social workers to anticipate and respond to changing social policies that are potentially harmful to the profession and those it represents is a responsible stance.

Beneficiaries of Public Policy

Although the current political environment suggests that the profession may experience some diminution of its roles and boundaries, at least in the short term, social work has also been the beneficiary of public policy. For example, during the 1960s, social workers were active and successful in pressing state legislatures to enact consumer choice legislation, which recognizes social workers as qualified providers of mental health services and makes them eligible for insurance and other third-party reimbursement for services rendered (Whiting, 1995). These laws stipulate that consumers have the freedom to choose any qualified mental health provider, of which social workers are one category, if their health insurance provides mental health coverage. As a precursor of such legislation, social workers were also successful in gaining legal recognition, in the form of licensing and registration laws, now operative in all states and the District of Columbia. Legal regulation of social work is almost always a requirement for eligibility under state consumer choice or vendorship laws (Whiting, 1995).

Federal policy has also contributed to the expanding boundaries of social work practice. The Omnibus Budget Reconciliation Act of 1989 (P.L. 101-239) included provision for clinical social workers to join the limited class of

mental health professionals who are eligible for reimbursement under Medicare. Final regulations for the Family and Medical Leave Act of 1993 (P.L. 103-3) included clinical social workers as health care providers. Clinical social workers were added to the definition of health care providers following active lobbying by more than 400 practicing social workers, five members of Congress, and 14 organizations ("Family Leave Regs," 1995). Also of significance for social workers was passage of the Mental Health Parity Act of 1996 (P.L. 401-204), which required that lifetime limits on services be the same for mental health as for medical and surgical benefits. This act expired in late 2001 and was on the agenda in the 107th Congress, but was not acted upon. The bill to reauthorize this act included amendments that would remove loopholes that prevented true parity for mental health (O'Neill, 2002).

Many federal policies that have expanded the boundaries of social work's domain concern the establishment of policies and programs to meet the needs of specific populations. Examples include the enactment of such national social welfare policies as the Adoption Assistance and Child Welfare Act of 1980 (P.L. 96-272), which ushered in an emphasis on permanency planning and family preservation; the McKinney Homeless Assistance Act of 1987 (P.L. 100-77), which was the first major federal initiative to approach the problem of homelessness from a multiple problem framework; the Anti-Drug Abuse Act Amendments of 1988 (P.L. 100-690); and the Americans with Disabilities Act of 1990 (P.L. 101-336), which resulted in new and expanded roles for social workers. These and other laws provided a new conceptualization of social problems and the financial wherewithal to develop new programs.

Social workers have always played an important role in planning, implementing, and evaluating new programs and services for our clients. Social workers have an equally long record in seeking to forestall enactment of laws that are perceived to be detrimental to the health and well-being of vulnerable groups or which challenge the concept of social justice. A key example here is social work's opposition to many of the components of the PRWORA of 1996.

The state of the U.S. economy has always been a factor in the growth and nature of the social work profession, particularly as the economy is reflected in employment and unemployment trends. Increasingly, the economic effects on the nature of social work are global rather than national (Reisch & Gorin, 2001). Periods of higher immigration demands on the United States, for example, are often affected by the economic conditions of other nations. Further, within the United States, the continued shrinking of the middle class is reflected in a growing gap between high and low wages and between permanent and temporary employment (Reisch & Gorin, 2001). It is within this disparity between those who have and those who do not that social work finds its niche.

Social policy change is a constant. Each year, Congress reauthorizes and creates new laws to address a large spectrum of social problems. Federal initiatives have their counterpart in the actions of the 50 state legislatures. Further, the annual federal and state appropriation processes expand or contract the funds available to implement the many laws. Every four years a new president is elected or reelected, with his own agenda. The bureaucracies that implement public laws at the federal and state levels also have significant influence on the pattern of human services delivery. One pattern to emerge, legislatively and administratively, in recent years is that of demands for accountability.

Accountability Demands

Distrust of government has led to an ongoing demand that public institutions and those that benefit from public dollars, such as nonprofit social welfare programs, be held accountable. Social workers are, more than ever before, being called upon to document and prove the quality and cost-effectiveness of the services they provide and to demonstrate that these services are effective in changing the lives of people (Almgren, 2002; Cournoyer & Powers, 2002).

Public demand for accountability continues to grow, and human services organizations and their social work employees have not been exempt from these demands. Accountability is broadly referred to as "the extent to which service providers are answerable to their community, the consumers of service, and/or to governing bodies, such as a board of directors, for its processes and outcomes" (Council on Accreditation of Services to Families and Children, 1997, p. 5).

The call for accountability can be seen in the increased emphasis funding bodies are placing on demonstrating the outputs, quality, and outcomes of services. This movement toward an "outcome orientation" is, in large part, a result of managed care dictates and the drive to reduce the cost of health care and services. Performance accountability is now codified in the Government Performance and Results Act of 1993 (P.L. 103-62), and the states have their own set of administrative procedures (Melkers & Willoughby, 1998).

The development of systems and measures for determining the outcomes of social work interventions is a challenging task, as it involves unlinking the processes of delivering care and the results of that care on the persons, groups, or communities affected (Almgren, 2002). Also involved in the development of outcome measures is the need to control for extraneous events—what researchers call intervening variables—that may affect causality between what social workers do and what the results of the interventions are.

The focus on outcomes relates to the demand that tax-funded programs meet the test of cost-effectiveness. Client benefit is not the sole criteria. The client benefit is seen within the context of and measured against the cost of the service and the resources utilized to achieve and maintain the outcomes. Although social workers have made significant strides in measuring outcomes and meeting accountability demands, there are many outstanding issues. On the agenda for the profession is the need to estimate the costs that are avoided for individuals, groups, and society when social interventions are provided (Almgren, 2002).

CYCLICAL TRENDS

The events of September 11, 2001, and their aftermath leave unclear the course government social policy will take. There are, however, some useful indicators. The federal budget is a powerful reflection of political priorities—both in relation to comparisons between budget categories, such as defense, environment, and education, and within budget categories, such as allocations for job-training programs versus allocations for shelters for the homeless. Within the human services, another way to gauge priorities is to look at what is being funded under contractual relationships.

A review of early 2002 federal government grant and contract announcements provides some clues about the thinking of the Bush administration. Plans for the allocation of federal dollars are a concrete manifestation of political priorities. Recent announcements of grant and contract opportunities include the following provisos:

- Request for proposals issued by the U.S. Department of Health and Human Services for early learning grants to develop local child development and school readiness programs included a "tip": "HHS encourages councils [local councils designated by a local government agency] to incorporate strategies to promote involvement of faith-based providers; healthy marriage; services in rural communities and support to families making the transition from welfare to work." (*Federal Grants and Contracts Weekly*, 2002a, p. 2)

- A call for applications from the U.S. Department of Education to implement comprehensive community strategies that create safe and drug-free schools and promote healthy childhood development emphasized the development of performance indicators that link directly to proposed goals and objectives. These indicators are intended as a tool for use by grantees to measure progress in achievement of objectives. (*Federal Grants and Contracts Weekly*, 2002b, p. 2)
- Grant opportunities through the U.S. Department of Education to foster the participation of low-income parents in postsecondary education by providing campus-based child care gives priority to applications that "leverage significant local or institutional resources to support child care activities and use a sliding fee scale." (*Federal Grants and Contracts Weekly*, 2002c, p. 3)
- Grant opportunities through the U.S. Department of Labor to provide support services for homeless veterans entering the labor force included the requirement that "proposals must include an outreach component and show links with other programs and services" (*Federal Grants and Contracts Weekly*, 2002d, p. 6)

Several "buzz words" can be identified from these Request for Proposal requirements:

- an emphasis on joint agency initiatives or collaborations
- preference for the use of faith-based groups, which are now within the pool of eligible providers of many government-funded social welfare programs
- promotion of "morally correct" behavior, such as marriage and sexual abstinence
- measurement of outcomes
- ongoing coordination among all direct and indirect consumers and services providers

- cost-sharing arrangements with states, local governments, nonprofit agencies, and educational institutions in project development and implementation.

Rather than being open ended and requesting program formulation ideas from bidders, grant announcements now include a high level of specificity. For example, one U.S. Department of Education Request for Applications concerned provision of programs that would lead to communicative competency in a foreign language among elementary school students. The department specified what the program design should be: at least 45 minutes of foreign language instruction four days a week throughout the academic year. Such specificity may be seen as one means of monitoring and ensuring accountability. Accountability for the achievement of outcomes is now a requirement of most public or privately funded social welfare programs.

INTERPRETING WHO WE ARE

Part of the professional social worker's job is to consistently interpret for the public who we are and what we do. The very same socioeconomic and political factors that affect the boundaries of the profession and the psychosocial conditions of the clients with whom we work also play a role in defining the general public's view of our work. At varying times in modern American history, the image of social workers has not always been positive.

When the word liberal is branded as bad, social work inevitably suffers by association. Social workers have also been branded as "bleeding hearts" and "do-gooders"—pejorative expressions about those who show concern and compassion for the disadvantaged or who attempt to raise the consciousness of the more advantaged about disadvantaged people (Gibelman, 2000). Stewart (1984) suggested that the values and practice commitments of the profession, which include respect for and pro-

tection of the dignity of *all* people, can place social workers out of the mainstream of public sentiment. Client populations with whom many social workers work are the "unwanted" in American society, those who are weak, sick, unproductive, or unappealing. Such people may be the subject of public scorn and resentment. By association, Stewart suggested, social workers become identified with these populations and the objects of public avoidance, anger, and scorn.

Social workers must be able to interpret for their relevant audiences what they do and how well they do it. The more the public knows about the nature and value of social work services, the less likely misinformation can be successfully communicated. This is not an easy task, as social workers are often stigmatized precisely because they work with stigmatized populations—people, groups, and communities in which poverty, unemployment, mental illness, other disabilities and vulnerabilities, violence, and other social ills are pervasive. It has also been suggested that resistance to acknowledging the contributions of social work to American society relates to the difficulty citizens have with accepting society's problems (Nieves, 1997). Some segments of society may simply resent that tax dollars go to assist vulnerable populations, and see social workers as the vehicle for maintaining people in a dependent state. Although the number of social work jobs continues to rise, public perceptions remain "stuck" in regard to false ideas about who social workers are and what they do.

Improving the image of social work has been a long-term concern of the National Association of Social Workers. NASW has urged, for example, that social workers identify themselves as such, rather than as therapist or clinician or manager. Nieves (1997) cited several model cause-related public relations efforts—smoking, drunk driving, and seat belts, for example—in which the strategic campaign of information, media exposure, and advertising significantly altered people's behaviors and beliefs. These successful campaigns suggest the importance of positive media exposure, some methods of which are explored in chapter 11.

A RECIPROCAL RELATIONSHIP

The substantial change in social workers' functions over the history of the profession relates to social work's integral relationship with the society of which it is a part. The traditional emphasis on practical problems, concrete tasks, and the provision of resources has changed to a focus on more clinical concerns, or a change from "hard" social work functions to "soft" functions (Davis, 1988). This modern day focus on clinical social work is evident in the growing proportion of social workers in private, psychotherapeutically oriented practice (Gibelman & Schervish, 1996).

Change does not imply value judgments about its course, but commentators on the status of the profession inevitably apply such judgments. For example, the shift in focus toward the provision of soft services has been seen as carrying negative consequences for psychiatric patients when social workers are reluctant to perform some of the more concrete service tasks, such as discharge planning, that are essential to clients' well-being. Davis (1988) concluded that this "current mind-set should be challenged and practical functions should be reincorporated into the social worker's repertoire" (p. 373). Similarly, Specht and Courtney (1994) viewed the movement toward a clinical, private practice emphasis within the profession as negative: "We believe that social work has abandoned its mission to help the poor and oppressed and to build communality" (p. 4). In their view, community problems are increasing and social work as a profession is devoting itself more and more to "the psychotherapeutic enterprise." The profession now seeks overridingly to "perfect the individual" rather than acting on the belief in the "perfectibility of society." In this same vein is Jacobson's (2001) admonishment that, although

social work continues to articulate a social justice mission, the profession no longer prioritizes the programs, services, and interventions that are needed to achieve these goals. She argued that the therapeutic orientation of the helping relationship needs to be modified to achieve more power-balanced relationships between services providers and program participants.

These arguments, in fact, are not new; they resurface as the profession's boundaries change and expand and the traditional concepts of what constitutes social work are reopened for scrutiny. Harriet Bartlett (1970) much earlier noted that, with the broadening of social work practice, social work's concerns with individuals and small groups might be sacrificed. She verbalized concern about the potential for sharp separation between the two views of practice (what we would today call micro and macro practice) and the risk that the division would undermine the profession and threaten its unity.

Divisions within a profession are not unusual; in fact, as professions evolve, specialization within the ranks is to be expected. Specialists within a profession are typically able to coexist, as evidenced by the multiple fields of practice represented through the American Medical Association, American Bar Association, and the National Education Association (Gibelman, 1999). Such disparate interests within these professions do not negate the unifying identification of physicians, educators, or lawyers. In some instances, specialty associations have been created to represent very specific professional interests, such as the American Psychiatric Association. Within social work, we have the examples of the National Association of Oncology Social Workers, the National Network for Social Work Managers, and the Association of Community Organization and Social Administration. Social workers frequently join specialty groups in addition to rather than instead of affiliation with the primary professional association, the National Association of Social Workers.

That social workers choose employment in clinical social work is a reflection of the availability of related jobs and the preferences of the social work labor force. It is difficult, if not impossible, to determine the relative weight of market forces over individual choice in tracking the evolution of the profession. For example, the number of social workers in community organization practice has decreased (Gibelman & Schervish, 1997); this may indicate a retrenchment in the number of jobs rather than an abdication on the part of social workers. Supporting data come from the steady erosion in community-oriented activist War on Poverty programs, such as Model Cities, Neighborhood Youth Corps, and the Community Action Program. In turn, such program changes reflected a turnabout in public and political attitudes about the causes of and appropriate interventions to alleviate social problems, cycling back to a more individualistic view of problems and remedies. Funding patterns further reflect the direction of change, with the defunding of community programs. Thus, Specht and Courtney (1994) may have reached the right conclusion—that social work has abandoned communality—but with a faulty explanatory base. The market may have abandoned this component of social work rather than the other way around.

An indeterminate factor is the extent to which social workers share popular societal attitudes about the direction and scope of change. A more modern day scenario of this same nature can be seen in the large-scale entrance of social workers in the 1990s into the for-profit sector, independent practice, or both; this phenomenon likely reflects labor market opportunity as well as individual choice.

Any attempt to determine the boundaries of the profession is likely to be both arbitrary and unsuccessful, given the constantly changing societal environment and prevailing ideologies. Also constraining professional boundary setting is the ambivalence of society about the functions of social work and, by extension, those

who carry out these functions. In prosperous times, society regards social work as openhanded and optimistic, but in hard times, social work is regarded as an unwelcome reflection of society's injustices (Hopps & Collins, 1995). As the political and economic environment shifts, the scope and nature of our work also changes, in part due to concomitant and inevitable alterations in the social work job market and also to the desire on the part of the profession to meet priority social needs at any given point in time. The evolution of the profession is also rooted in changing technology and intervention methodology. It is this dynamic interplay between social work and the sociopolitical environment that molds the profession is an ongoing evolutionary pattern. As the social work knowledge base continues to grow, the profession has more to offer to consumers of human services and to society as a whole.

REFERENCES

Adoption Assistance and Child Welfare Act of 1980, P.L. 96-272, 94 Stat. 500.

Allen, M. (2001, December 9). Bush urges public to pressure Congress on domestic agenda. *Washington Post*, p. A2.

Almgren, G. (2002). Measuring and evaluating outcomes in health care settings. In A. R. Roberts & G. J. Greene (Eds.), *Social workers' desk reference* (pp. 772–776). New York: Oxford University Press.

Americans with Disabilities Act of 1990, P.L. 101-336, 104 Stat. 327.

Anti-Drug Abuse Act Amendments of 1988, P.L. 100-690, 102 Stat. 4181.

Austin, M. J. (1984). Managing cutbacks in the 1980s. *Social Work, 29*, 428–434.

Barker, R. (1999). *Social work dictionary* (4th ed.). Washington, DC: NASW Press.

Bar-On, A. A. (1994). The elusive boundaries of social work. *Journal of Sociology & Social Welfare*, XXI, 53–67.

Bartlett, H. M. (1970). *The common base of social work practice*. Washington, DC: National Association of Social Workers.

Broder, D. S. (2002, May 27–June 2). States in fiscal crisis. *Washington Post National Weekly Edition*, p. 4.

Cohen, R. H. (1995, October). Looking ahead: Time of singular peril is time to act. *NASW News*, p. 2.

Council on Accreditation of Services to Families and Children. (1997). *Behavioral health care standards* (U.S. ed.). New York: Author.

Cournoyer, B. R., & Powers, G. T. (2002). Evidence-based social work: The quiet revolution continues. In A. R. Roberts & G. J. Greene (Eds.), *Social workers' desk reference* (pp. 798–807). New York: Oxford University Press.

Davis, S. (1988). "Soft" versus "hard" social work. *Social Work, 33*, 373–374.

Ewalt, P. L. (1994, January). Visions of ourselves. *Social Work, 39*, 5–7.

Execs offer directions for the profession; urge aggressive advocacy. (1995, February–March). *Currents of the New York City Chapter, National Association of Social Workers*, pp. 1, 9–11.

Family leave regs revision adds clinicians. (1995, February). *NASW News*, p. 1.

Family and Medical Leave Act of 1993, P.L. 103-3, 107 Stat. 6.

Federal Grants and Contracts Weekly. (2002a, April 29). Early learning grants (pp. 1–2). Alexandria, VA: Capitol Publishing Group.

Federal Grants and Contracts Weekly. (2002b, April 29). Performance indicators key in safe schools grants competition (pp. 1, 14). Alexandria, VA: Capitol Publishing Group.

Federal Grants and Contracts Weekly. (2002c, May 6). Healthy child development (p. 2). Alexandria, VA: Capitol Publishing Group.

Federal Grants and Contracts Weekly. (2002d, May 6). Homeless veterans (p. 3). Alexandria, VA: Capitol Publishing Group.

Getzel, G. S. (1983). Speculations on the crisis in social work recruitment: Some modest proposals. *Social Work, 28*, 235–237.

Gibelman, M. (1999). The search for identity: Defining social work—Past, present, future. *Social Work, 44*, 298–310.

Gibelman, M. (2000). Say it ain't so, Norm! A commentary on who we are. *Social Work, 45*, 463–466.

Gibelman, M., & Schervish, P. (1996). The private practice of social work: Current trends and projected scenarios in a managed care. *Clinical Social Work Journal, 24*, 321–338.

Gibelman, M., & Schervish, P. (1997). *Who we are: A second look*. Washington, DC: NASW Press.

Ginsberg, L. (1988). Social workers and politics: Lessons from practice. *Social Work, 33*, 245–247.

Government Performance and Results Act of 1993, P.L. 103-62, 107 Stat. 285.

Greenberg, M., & Savner, S. (1996). *The Temporary Assistance for Needy Families block grant*. Washington, DC: Center for Law and Social Policy.

Groups gird to save nursing home role. (1999, March). *NASW News*, pp. 1, 8.

Hopps, J. G., & Collins, P. M. (1995). Social work profession overview. In R. L. Edwards (Ed.-in-Chief), *Encyclopedia of social work* (19th ed., Vol. 3, pp. 2266–2282). Washington, DC: NASW Press.

Hopps, J. G., & Pinderhughes, E. B. (1987). Profession of social work: Contemporary characteristics. In A. Minahan (Ed.-in-Chief), *Encyclopedia of social work* (18th ed., Vol. 2, pp. 351–366). Silver Spring, MD: National Association of Social Workers.

Houle, C. O. (1983). Possible futures. In M. R. Stern (Ed.), *Power and conflict in continuing professional education* (pp. 252–264). Belmont, CA: Wadsworth.

Individuals with Disabilities Education Act of 1990, P.L. 101-476, 104 stat. 1142.

Jacobson, W. B. (2001). Beyond therapy: Bringing social work back to human services reform. *Social Work, 46*, 51–61.

Jarman-Rohde, L., McFall, J., Kolar, P., & Strom, G. (1997). The changing context of social work practice: Implications and recommendations for social work educators. *Journal of Social Work Education, 33*, 29–46.

Jones, C., & Novak, T. (1993, June). Social work today. *British Journal of Social Work, 23*, 195–212.

Kessler, G., & Goldstein, A. (2001, April 10). First Bush budget makes modest cuts. *Washington Post,* p. A1.

Landers, S. (1995, October). Special education law under the gun. *NASW News,* p. 5.

Lens, V. (2000). *Welfare reform and the media.* Unpublished doctoral dissertation, Yeshiva University, Wurzweiler School of Social Work, New York.

Mayden, R. W. (2001, June). From the president: Social work a choice profession. *NASW News,* p. 2.

McKinney Homeless Assistance Act of 1987, P.L. 100-77, 101 Stat. 482.

Melkers, J., & Willoughby, K. (1998). The state of the states: Performance budgeting requirements in 47 out of 50 states. *Public Administration Review, 58*, 66–73.

Mental Health Parity Act of 1996, P.L. 401-204, 110 Stat. 2874.

Minahan, A. (1982). It was the best of times, it was the worst of times. *Social Work, 27*, 291.

National Association of Social Workers. (1996, August 27). *Personality Responsibility and Work Opportunity Reconciliation Act of 1996: Summary of provisions* (Government Relations Update). Washington, DC: Author.

Nieves, J. (1997, May). Building a better public image. *NASW News,* p. 2.

Omnibus Budget Reconciliation Act of 1989, P.L. 101-239, 103 stat. 2106.

O'Neill, J. V. (1999, June). Profession now dominates in mental health. *NASW News,* pp. 1, 8.

O'Neill, J. V. (2000, February). Solution-focused therapy gains adherents. *NASW News,* p. 6

O'Neill, J. (2002, February). Parity bill stalled for now. *NASW News,* p. 5.

Personal Responsibility and Work Opportunity Reconciliation Act of 1996, P.L. 104-193, 110 Stat. 2105.

Recommendations for the preauthorization of the Personal Responsibility and Work Opportunity Reconciliation Act. (2001, November 30).

Washington, DC: National Association of Social Workers. Retrieved January 17, 2002, from http://www.socialworkers.org/advocacy/welfare /legislative/recommend.pdf.

Reisch, M., & Gorin, S. H. (2001). Nature of work and future of the social work profession. *Social Work, 46*, 9–19.

Rosenfeld, J. M. (1983). The domain and expertise of social work: A conceptualization. *Social Work, 28*, 186–191.

School counseling program saved. (2000, March). *NASW News,* pp. 1, 10.

Schorr, A. L. (1988). Other times, other strategies. *Social Work, 33*, 249–250.

Specht, H., & Courtney, M. (1994). *Unfaithful angels: How social work has abandoned its mission.* New York: Free Press.

State criteria downgrading beaten back. (1999, April). *NASW News,* p. 4.

Stewart, R. (1984, November). From the president. *NASW News,* p. 2.

Super, D. A., Parrott, S., Steinmetz, S., & Mann, C. (1996, August 14). *The new welfare law.* Washington, DC: Center on Budget and Policy Priorities.

Taubman, S. (1985). Doing less with less. *Social Work, 30*, 180–182.

Turem, J. S., & Born, C. E. (1983). Doing more with less. *Social Work, 28*, 206–210.

U.S. Department of Health and Human Services. (2001, September 13). *HHS initiates immediate and long-term steps to address emotional and mental health consequences of terrorist air attacks* (Press release). Washington, DC: Author. Retrieved October 17, 2003, from http://www.hhs.gov/ news/press/ 2001pres/20010913.html.

Vallianatos, C. (2002, February). Welfare limits: Disaster in the making. *NASW News,* p. 3.

Walz, T., & Groze, V. (1991). The mission of social work revisited: An agenda for the 1990s. *Social Work, 36*, 500–504.

Whiting, L. (1995). Vendorship. In R. L. Edwards (Ed.-in-Chief), *Encyclopedia of social work* (19th ed., Vol. 3, pp. 2427–2431). Washington, DC: NASW Press.

Wilgoren, J. (2002, April 25). After welfare, working poor still struggle, report finds. *New York Times*, p. A20.

Chapter Four MENTAL HEALTH

Social workers in mental health focus their efforts on meeting the needs of people with mental illness—those with major mental illnesses and those with less devastating emotional problems—and people vulnerable to mental illness. Although adults are usually thought of as the population with mental illness, there are as many children and adolescents with treatable mental conditions, often who are not properly diagnosed. Data from the National Institute of Mental Health (NIMH) in 2002 show that more than 7 million children and adolescents in the United States have mental disorders. Depression, obsessive–compulsive disorder, phobias, and substance abuse frequently occur in people under 20 years of age.

Mental health refers to "the relative state of emotional well-being, freedom from incapacitating conflicts, and the consistent ability to make and carry out rational decisions and cope with environmental stresses and internal pressures" (Barker, 1999, p. 299). Mental health is a state for which individuals, groups, and communities strive. The work of social workers primarily focuses on mental health lacks or deficits. In this respect, the majority of social work functions in the field of mental health center on mental disorders, defined as

impaired psychosocial or cognitive functioning due to disturbances in any one or more of the following processes: biological, chemical, physiological, genetic, psychological, or social. Mental disorders are extremely variable in duration, severity, and prognosis, depending on the type of affliction. The major forms of disorder include mood disorders, psychosis, personality disorders, organic mental disorders, and anxiety disorder. (Barker, 1999, p. 299)

SOCIAL WORK PRACTICE IN THE MENTAL HEALTH FIELD

Mental health is probably the most popular area of practice within social work, as indicated by the specialized practice areas of concentration selected by social work students (Lennon, 2001) and by available data on the social work labor force, as reflected in the NASW membership (Gibelman & Schervish, 1997). Social work, however, is only one of several mental health disciplines. Accordingly, social workers often work collaboratively with mental health specialists of other disciplines. Some of these other disciplines include marriage and family therapists, counselors, psychiatrists, psychiatric nurses, psychologists, and substance abuse counselors. Each of these disciplines has an educational program, as well as licensing and credentialing criteria and processes.

Federal law recognizes social work as one of the four core mental health professions. Professional social workers are the largest group of mental health providers in the United States, comprising as much as 60 percent of the core mental health professionals (Vallianatos, 2002). In 1999, it was estimated that there were 192,814 clinically trained social workers in the United States compared 33,486 psychiatrists, 73,018 psychologists, and 17,318 psychiatric nurses (O'Neill, 1999).

Social workers perform mental health services in a variety of settings which include community mental health centers, state and county mental hospitals, private psychiatric hospitals, psychiatric units in general hospitals, veterans organizations, and outpatient facilities such as consultation services for schools and housing sites (Lin, 1995).

Political Context

Societal context plays an important role in defining the parameters of social work mental health practice. Managed care figures prominently among these contextual factors, as it affects the level and type of services that can be provided to clients. The absence of comprehensive health care reform on the political agenda suggests that the private market will continue to dominate how and what services are provided and by whom. The War on Terrorism and the War with Iraq mean that available public dollars have been channeled to disaster relief and defense. Advocacy efforts on the part of the social work community to lobby for an expansion of the Mental Health Parity Act of 1996 (P.L. 104-204) stalled. Congress failed to act on reauthorization of this law and the statute expired on September 30, 2001. The 1996 law made it optional for employers to offer mental health care benefits; if they chose to do so, the benefits were to be equal to those for medical and surgical care ("Parity Gets to Work," 1998). The expiration of the law means that when insurance companies rewrite their plans for next year, they can opt to discontinue matching benefits for mental health services ("Congress Fails to Renew," 2001).

The impact is yet to be determined for mental health professionals and for consumers of services. President Bush, in an effort to rekindle his domestic agenda, has indicated that he will endorse legislation requiring employers to expand insurance coverage for psychiatric illnesses (Milbank, 2002). This legislation would be even stronger than the 1996 law. However, as of this writing, the proposal has a long road through Congress before it becomes law and much can happen before then. Nevertheless, the professional community remains optimistic (O'Neill, 2002c).

In recent years, public attitudes about mental illness have begun to change, and stigmatization of those diagnosed with mental illness has lessened. The 1996 Mental Health Parity Act reflected changing attitudes, as did the limited parity laws enacted in a number of states ("Limited-Parity Laws Spreading," 2000). In addition, David Satcher, during his tenure as Surgeon General of the United States during the first George Bush administration, took the bold action of authorizing comprehensive studies about mental illness in America, the result of which was the issuance of several landmark reports. Cumulatively, these reports and the endorsement of them by the surgeon general put the need for accessible and high quality mental health services on the national agenda (O'Neill, 2000).

Defining Clinical Social Work

Casework has traditionally represented the predominant method of social work practice. But in 1980, the question was raised: What is clinical social work? Editors of *Social Work* noted that the term *clinical social work* had emerged in the profession's vocabulary during the 1970s replacing *social casework, treatment-oriented social group work, social treatment, psychiatric social work*, and *direct practice* (Minahan, 1980, p. 171). Barker (1999) defined clinical social work as "a specialized form of direct social work practice with individuals, groups, and families" (p. 82).

Across settings, social workers in mental health share a common focus. After several years of developmental work, NASW adopted a definition of clinical social work in 1984:

Clinical social work shares with all social work practice the goal of enhancement and maintenance of psychosocial functioning of individuals, families and small groups. Clinical social work practice is the professional application of social work theory and methods to the treatment and prevention of psychosocial dysfunction, disability, or impairment, including emotional and mental disorders. It is based on knowledge of one or more theories of human development within a psychosocial context. (NASW, 1989, p. 4)

Clinical social work draws from a multitude of theoretical frameworks, with some practitioners using a single perspective and others using multiple frameworks (Swenson, 1995). However, the perspective of *person-in-situation* is central to clinical social work practice. Clinical social work includes interventions directed to interpersonal interactions, intrapsychic dynamics, life support, and management issues. Clinical social work services consist of assessment; diagnosis; treatment, including psychotherapy and counseling; client-centered advocacy; consultation; and evaluation. The process of clinical social work is undertaken within the objectives of social work and the principles and values contained in NASW's *Code of Ethics* ("Board Adopts Clinical Practice Standards," 1984).

Following adoption of the definition of clinical social work practice, the NASW Board of Directors approved the *Standards for the Practice of Clinical Social Work*, which are to be "considered desirable for all clinical social workers." The standards have the following goals:

- maintain and improve the quality of services provided by clinical social workers
- establish professional expectations so that social workers can monitor and evaluate their own clinical practice
- provide a framework for clinical social workers to assess responsible professional behavior

- inform consumers, government regulatory bodies, and others, such as insurance carriers, about the profession's standards for clinical social work practice. (NASW, 1989)

Clinical social work continues to evolve, along with new theories, intervention strategies, and a more sophisticated, consumer-oriented client population.

SETTINGS OF MENTAL HEALTH PRACTICE

Traditional areas in which social workers deliver mental health services include community mental health centers, family and child services agencies, inpatient psychiatric facilities, industry-based employee assistance programs, private individual or group clinical social work practices, U.S. Department of Veterans Affairs hospitals, and inpatient and outpatient psychiatric units of public and private hospitals. Social workers in these settings work in rural, suburban, and urban locations.

Frequently, social workers in mental health work as part of a team. Barker (1999) defined mental health teams as "professional and ancillary personnel from several disciplines who work together to provide a wide range of services for clients (and the families of clients) who are affected by a mental disorder" (p. 299). Typically, these teams include a psychiatrist, social worker, psychologist, and nurse. In some settings, the team may also include physical and occupational therapists, recreation specialists, educators, guidance counselors, psychiatric aides, volunteers, and indigenous workers (Barker, 1999).

The problems addressed by social workers in mental health include those associated with the stressors of everyday living; behavioral deficiencies; crises brought on by emotional, environmental, or situational occurrences; eating disorders; parent–child problems; marital problems; depression; schizophrenia; bipolar disorders; and other forms of psychopathology.

Veterans Services

The U.S. Department of Veterans Affairs (VA) has estimated that as of September 30, 2000, there were approximately 25.5 million living veterans in the United States (VA, 2003). The VA was established in 1930 to consolidate and coordinate government programs and services affecting war veterans. It is the largest single system of health care for veterans (Becerra & Damron-Rodriguez, 1995; Rothman & Becerra, 1987). The major VA programs include health care delivery, pension and compensation benefits, educational benefits, housing assistance, life insurance, vocational rehabilitation and counseling, and administration of cemeteries and memorials. In addition, the VA offers domiciliary care, nursing home care, hospital-based home care programs, adult health day care centers, respite care, hospice care, and geriatric evaluations (Foster, 1989).

In August 2000, the Veterans Health Administration (VHA) appointed social worker and veteran Jill Manske as director of social work services. In this position, Manske works as part of the Allied Clinical Services Strategic Healthcare Group, advocating for and supporting social workers in the more than 150 VA medical centers across the country. Prior to this appointment, Manske was chief of the social work services department for the Albuquerque VA Medical Center, a 300-bed tertiary-care center that serves 32,000 veterans each year ("Veterans Affairs Names," 2000).

In providing mental health services, social workers often confront members of the veteran population who are dealing with issues ranging from mild stress reactions to chronic mental illness and homelessness. The VHA operates one of the most comprehensive mental health services in the nation and includes special programs such as chemical dependency units, dual diagnosis programs, and posttraumatic stress disorder programs (Becerra & Damron-Rodriguez, 1995).

Social workers who serve veterans generally work as members of interdisciplinary teams and provide a wide range of services including direct clinical care, development of outreach services, development of new methods of treatment, discharge planning, evaluation, and crisis intervention. Social workers working in an outreach or counseling center for veterans play an important role in making referrals to the VA when inpatient care is necessary. In addition, social workers have the responsibility to coordinate community resources, which is critical to providing cost-effective, high-quality care (Rothman & Becerra, 1987).

Social workers providing mental health services to veterans and their families address problems that range from mild stress to chronic mental illness. Posttraumatic stress disorder (PTSD) is one of the most common psychiatric problems for many veterans. PTSD is defined by Barker (1999) as

> a psychological reaction to experiencing an event that is outside the range of usual human experience. Stressful events of this type may include accidents, natural disasters, military combat, rape, and assault. . . . Individuals may react to these events by having difficulty concentrating; feeling emotionally blunted or numb; being hyperalert and jumpy; and having painful memories, nightmares, and sleep disturbances. (p. 369)

Symptoms include repeatedly experiencing the ordeal in the form of nightmares, flashback episodes, or frightening thoughts, especially when the person is exposed to events or objects reminiscent of the trauma (NIMH, 2002). In acute form, PTSD may render the affected person unable to carry out the normal tasks of daily living. PTSD can be extremely disabling. Effective treatment programs have, however, been developed through research supported by NIMH and the VA (NIMH, 2002).

NIMH (2002) estimated that about 5.2 million adults in the United States have PTSD during the course of any given year. About 30 percent of the men and women who have experienced military combat in war zones experience PTSD. One million veterans of the Vietnam War developed PTSD, and it has also been identified among veterans of the Persian Gulf War. As illustrated in the following vignette, PTSD may be accompanied by other illnesses, such as depression, alcohol or other substance abuse, or another anxiety disorder. In addition, physiological ailments, such as headaches, gastrointestinal problems, dizziness, or chest pain, may be part of the PTSD symptomology.

The Legacy of War for One Man

In February 1991, Army serviceman Dave Burton stepped on a land mine and had to have both of his legs amputated below the knee. He returned home from the Persian Gulf War with an honorable discharge and some serious psychological issues to confront. Dave began drinking heavily and was constantly morose and depressed. His wife Debbie was concerned about him and convinced him to go to the San Diego Veterans Administration Medical Center. Dave finally agreed to go, and he met with Jake Adams, a social worker at the medical center.

Jake was interested in working with veterans and he had conducted research on delayed stress response, which was commonly found in veterans of the Vietnam War, and the effect of stressful life events. Stressful life events are those external events that make adaptive demands on a person. The person may successfully make the adaptations, or there may be a period of resistance and psychological or physiological tensions.

Jake interviewed Dave and made a brief assessment of Dave's psychosocial situation. He met with Dave several more times before suggesting that Dave participate in the readjustment counseling service provided by an outreach center of the San Diego VA. The outreach center was community based and specialized in helping veterans like Dave. The service is based

on a model that blends group process, self-help principles, and cognitive–behavioral therapy. Dave agreed to take part in a "rap group" that Jake facilitated which consisted of eight other veterans. Jake also referred Dave to a psychiatrist for a consultation. Studies have shown that medications help ease some of the symptoms associated with PTSD, and Jake thinks that Dave may, benefit from medication.

Dave attended the rap groups every week, and he met with Jake individually every other week. Dave also attended Alcoholics Anonymous meetings on a regular basis. In addition, Jake helped Dave access training in computer science provided by the VA. Dave was then able to get a job with a local accounting firm as a computer programmer. Change did not occur quickly, but it did occur, and Dave slowly accepted and adapted to his new lifestyle.

In this case, Jake provides direct mental health services. However, this scenario exemplifies the many facets of that direct services role. First Jake conducts several interviews in order to assess and diagnosis Dave's psychosocial situation. He then provides counseling, support, and advice in his biweekly sessions with Dave. The therapeutic approach Jake utilizes in the rap group is based on cognitive–behavioral therapy, an approach that research has demonstrated to be effective with people suffering from PTSD (NIMH, 2002). However, Jake's functions as a social worker do not stop there. He also provides referral services by getting Jake involved in Alcoholics Anonymous and the readjustment counseling service. Furthermore, Jake uses his coordination skills to help Dave access other VA programs, such as the computer training and job search services.

Case Management

The increasing emphasis on cost controls and cost-effectiveness in the delivery of health and mental health services has led to shortened inpatient stays and a corresponding reliance on outpatient services. Case management is one approach to the provision of services on an out-patient basis. Case management is multifaceted, as the following definition highlights (Barker, 1999). Case management is

> a procedure to plan, seek, and monitor serv-ices from different social agencies and staff on behalf of a client. Usually one agency takes primary responsibility for the client and assigns a case manager, who coordinates serv-ices, advocates for the client, and sometimes controls resources and purchases services for the client. The procedure makes it possible for many social workers in the agency, or in different agencies, to coordinate their efforts to serve a given client through professional teamwork, thus expanding the range of need-ed services offered. Case management may involve monitoring the progress of a client whose needs require the services of several professionals, agencies, health care facilities, and human service programs. (p. 62)

Key words in this definition illustrate the many components of case management: coordi-nate, advocate, purchase services, monitor. The goal is to ensure access to services and service coordination (Frankel & Gelman, 1998). Case management has also been promoted as a means to produce systems change (Austin, 1993) and as an inherent component of com-munity organizing and managerial practice (Wolk, Sullivan, & Hartmann, 1994). Case managers work to promote benefits for clients collectively—as, for example, for all people with chronic mental illness living within a particular community. Relevant tasks include community education, developing support and self-help groups, and working with other community organizations to promote community change to foster client well-being (Rothman, 2002).

Although there are some variations in the definition of case management, there is general agreement that it is essentially a coordinating approach to services delivery. Case management

is a function that transcends many fields of practice, such as child welfare, developmental disabilities, and gerontology (Johnson & Yanca, 2001). It is considered to be a service for high-ly vulnerable client populations and offers a means to ensure that they receive the help they need from among the varied services systems—health, mental health, housing, public assis-tance, and so forth (Rothman, 2002). It is high-lighted in this chapter on mental health because of the reliance on case management in work with people with chronic mental illness.

Case management has been identified as an effective method to ensure that patients are assisted in the transition from hospital to com-munity with the appropriate supports in place. In addition, case management has increasingly been recognized as an important tool to provide services to the long-term mentally ill popula-tion, thus overcoming the lack of community support, services, and trained personnel which have marred services delivery in the past (Frankel & Gelman, 1998; Kanter, 1987).

Orloff-Kaplan (1990) identified five compo-nents of case management: (1) case identification; (2) assessment and planning; (3) coordination and referral; (4) implementation of services; and (5) monitoring, evaluation, and reassessment. Effective case management requires continuity of care, titrate support, managerial interventions to address various needs, and enablement of client resourcefulness (Kanter, 1987). The tasks range from assessing clients' needs and planning servic-es to therapeutic intervention (provided directly or delivered through another source) and moni-toring and evaluating clients' progress. The social worker sees the client through the entire helping process, as illustrated in the following vignette.

CASE MANAGEMENT IN A RESIDENTIAL SETTING

St. Vincent's offers a variety of programs for people with mental illness, ranging from a self-contained residential rehabilitation center for clients with serious impairments to outpatient vocational training programs and almost everything in between these two extremes. Southwood, the residential rehabilitation program, represents the newest component of the agency. Social workers are at all levels of the hierarchical ladder and perform a variety of functions. This program operates under the auspices of case manager Phyllis Anderson, LCSW.

Phyllis is involved in every aspect of client services. As a case manager, Phyllis interfaces with a variety of people on behalf of Southwood clients. On a typical day, Phyllis may talk to the patient liaison at Aurora State Mental Hospital to facilitate the admission of a new client; the county police to clarify an incident involving Southwood clients at the local shopping center; the pharmacist at the local drug store to double check possible side effects of a client's medication or to determine the protocol for a new client prescription.

Phyllis meets individually at least once a week with the clients assigned to her, typically 15 or more of the residents of Southwood. The purpose of these meetings is to discuss any issues or concerns of clients and to review with them their progress and plans. In addition, Phyllis weekly confers with the consulting psychiatrist about her concerns and observations regarding the clients and provides feedback about their progress on medication, participation in Southwood programs, demeanor, and so forth.

Should a client require rehospitalization, Phyllis communicates with the relevant physicians and the hospital social worker about both the condition of the client and the discharge plan. This plan involves either a return to Southwood or an alternative program, depending on the client's suitability for continued community integration. Part of Phyllis's job involves networking with county and hospital officials to determine the most suitable placement for a client.

In this vignette, the social worker identifies resources needed by clients, coordinates with the relevant systems to obtain cooperation on behalf of clients, and provides the information needed to coordinate services effectively. Phyllis links the clients through both formal and informal methods (Rothman, 2002). For example, she may use her personal network of colleagues to gain access for one of her clients to a job-training program that is officially closed to new applicants, but where exceptions are possible. Regular monitoring is part of the case management function. Phyllis serves as broker and advocate for her clients and monitors clients' status on a regular basis and the degree to which the services provided are meeting their needs. At the agency level, Phyllis coordinates information and services, provides short-term problem-focused therapy, and advocates for resources for her clients.

Case management may be the predominant function carried out by a social worker, or one function among many. The title *case manager* is carried, typically, by those for whom case management is a primary function. Social workers providing clinical social work, however, usually include case management among their functions. Social workers working with people with serious mental illness, such as major depression, bipolar disorder, schizophrenia, and personality disorders, are often required to address client issues related to housing, income support, medical care, job training, social outlets, life skills development, and medication (Walsh, 2002). In this respect, case management can be seen as complementary to and a component of the psychosocial perspective. Here, the social worker intervenes, as needed, in the social environment of the client in order to acquire, coordinate, and monitor care that goes beyond the clinical relationship.

Employee Assistance Programs

Employee assistance programs (EAPs) constitute one arena within the larger category of occupational social work. A variety of strategies have been developed to address the problems faced by employees, including health promotion and wellness programs. In EAPs, professional human services are provided in the workplace through employer-funded programs. The goal is to help employees meet their human and social needs by providing services to deal with emotional problems, social relationships, and other personal problems (Barker, 1999). The concept behind EAPs is that workers who are struggling with personal concerns will have a higher rate of absenteeism and tardiness and a lower level of productivity.

EAPS are defined as "services offered by employers to their employees to help them overcome problems that may negatively affect job satisfaction or productivity" (Barker, 1999, p. 153). A 1999 survey by the Employee Assistance Professionals Association found that about 46 percent of its more than 6,000 members were social workers. Social workers are thus the largest professional group employed by EAPs (O'Neill, 2002b).

With the emergence of EAPs as a new arena of social work practice, NASW commissioned an Occupational Social Work Task Force to address the relevant standards and practices in the occupational field (Stewart, 1984). In 1984, NASW also issued a statement on occupational social work, declaring it "a legitimate field of practice with a developing focus and a body of knowledge that calls for a full range of appropriate skills" ("Social Work, Public Policy," 1984, p. 11).

There are four primary designs for EAP services: internal, external, consortium, and association. An internal program is one in which EAP staff are employees of the organization. An external model is where services are provided by a contractor, usually in an off-site office. The consortium model allows several employers to combine resources and get group coverage. Usually, this is most effective with organizations that have a logical connection or affiliation with each other. Finally, an association EAP serves occupational membership groups such as the National Association of Social Workers or the American Medical Association (Van Den Bergh, 1995).

The roles of social workers employed in EAPs have expanded and changed in recent years, in part as a result of the changing demographics of the American workforce and the restructuring of many American industries. Job loss and the instability of many businesses have emerged as major problems in today's workplace. As unemployment rates took a pronounced upward turn in 2001 and businesses slashed their payrolls, concern about the shaky economy and the fate of newly unemployed workers has grown. Social workers, who lead the majority of EAPs, realize that more layoffs bring a new set of issues to the workplace. They are also in a position to help. Social worker Dale Kaplan, Vice President of Clinical Services at Employee Health Programs, noted:

> Job loss affects not only the employees who are let go, but the managers and co-workers who remain at the company. Social workers are able to provide assistance such as implementation of comprehensive programs to reduce the potential for workplace violence and increase the potential for a smoother transition for the remaining employees. (NASW, 2001a)

Just as individuals confront life events, so do organizations. Due to growing global marketplace competition, corporate downsizing and restructuring are no longer isolated or idiosyncratic occurrences. Downsizing is a euphemism for the termination of employment necessitated by organizational considerations that are not related to employee performance, such as when there is an unanticipated reduction in agency income or elimination of some programs or services.

The aging workforce brings with it several issues needing the intervention of EAP social workers. The increased life expectancy rates and early retirement trends often cause economic hardship for older workers. In addition, the phenomenon of early retirement is occurring concurrent with a diminishing number of youths entering the labor market, the result of which is a shortage of available workers in selective industries and occupations (Mor-Barak & Tynan, 1993). Furthermore, many healthy, older employees wish to continue working in their professions. EAPs can help individuals with financial planning, referral services, education, and support groups. In addition, EAPs can help corporations understand the issues of aging and develop programs to assist older employees so that they can continue to work (Mor-Barak & Tynan, 1993).

With more layoffs expected in corporate America, one group that may be especially hard hit is older workers. Age discrimination may be an issue if a disproportionate number of older workers receive "pink slips." They may also face more problems than younger laid-off workers in finding new jobs (Carlson, 2001). EAP social workers can help such individuals to explore their rights under applicable employment laws and to research sectors of the economy in which their job hunt may be most successful.

The types of intervention offered during times of change range from training supervisors how to manage employees during downsizing—with emphasis on spotting the troubled employee who may have a hard time with loss—to providing individual counseling to the employees who have lost their jobs (NASW, 2001a). EAPs generally help employees cope with job-related pressures or even personal problems that affect the quality of their work. Social workers may provide direct services to individuals and families, such as marriage and relationship counseling or childrearing concerns. Social workers in EAPs can also provide substance abuse treatment and referrals to specialized community programs. Many EAPs also provide referrals for legal or financial problems that can affect productivity. Social workers in EAPs may also consult with managers and supervisors, assist with organizational development, train staff, and help with administration of programs and the analysis of policies.

Some EAP social workers have adopted an organizational focus and have developed programs of dependent care and AIDS education, researched the extent and severity of employee substance abuse problems, and consulted with supervisors about employees who have job performance or behavioral problems (Googins & Davidson, 1993). Due to their training in understanding environmental as well as individual issues, occupational social workers have an opportunity to intervene on a macro level and address organizational issues which may be at the root of many problems that confront individual workers on a regular basis. Indirect EAP services include the social work functions of organizing and planning regular training sessions and educational seminars for employees and supervisors. EAPs generally attempt to provide preventive services before problems arise—such as sexual harassment training and racial and ethnic sensitization seminars (Van Den Bergh, 1995).

One view of the guiding mission of EAPs is that they should "help employees maximize their ability to handle life events and to help corporations anticipate and adapt to changes brought about by the life events of employees and the community" (Googins & Davidson, 1993, p. 480). Life events can be anything from divorce to chemical dependency to caregiving for terminal illnesses. In addition, occupational social workers are uniquely qualified to assist physically disabled employees and their employers. A variety of issues are raised in disability cases for which social work expertise can be applied, including workplace requirements, individual physical and emotional needs, and public policy (Mudrick, 1991). EAPs are also seen as a bridge between the employee and the corporation. They must help employees find solutions to their problems, and at the same time help corporations understand various life events affecting employees (Googins & Davidson, 1993).

Social workers practicing in EAPs face some constraints on their practice unique to that setting. For example, the reason EAPs have been introduced into industry has less to do with humanitarian concerns for employees and more to do with ensuring a healthy and productive workforce. Because of legal protections offered to workers who are ill or disabled, firing workers because of their behavior outside the workplace (even if it affects performance inside the workplace) can be risky and costly for the company. Companies have found it less costly to address the problems of their employees and keep them healthy than to terminate their employment (Green, 1994). Social workers working within EAPs need to understand the corporate value system, with its emphasis on accountability, productivity, and profitability, simultaneously maintaining their focus on the provision of services.

Several issues have been identified that could affect future professional growth within EAPs unless resolved (Akabas, 1995). One major problem that has consistently plagued EAP workers is confidentiality. This is a critical issue, because a violation of confidentiality could result in the client either losing his or her job or being the victim of subtle discrimination and ostracism. Not only must the social worker scrupulously adhere to the NASW *Code of Ethics* in regard to confidentiality, but he or she must also reach an agreement about confidentiality and any limitations to it with the manager of the corporation before ever seeing a client.

Another concern regarding EAP social workers focuses on their role as agents of change. Social work has always focused on serving the individual within the environmental context. Will EAP social workers continue to help individuals or will they serve corporations that view individuals simply as a means of the most effective production (Kurzman, 1987)?

Since occupational social workers are in the unique position of serving both individuals and organizations, many different social work functions are required, including assessment, diagnosis, identification, support, counseling, advocacy, referral, mobilization, exchange, program development, coordination, consultation, and evalua-

tion. The following vignette indicates one of the many situations an EAP worker may encounter.

DOWNSIZING

It seemed that almost everybody who lived in Chickasha, Oklahoma, worked at the Deers Manufacturing Plant. Tommy Merton had worked there for 28 years and his son had worked there for five. Even his youngest daughter was planning to work there after she graduated from high school in June.

The plant was all Tommy had ever known. His father and his grandfather had worked there. His wife knew all the other wives and she was happy. Every day, Tommy punched in at 8:30 A.M. and punched out at 5:00 P.M. It was his life, and he loved it.

Recently, Tommy had been hearing rumors that the company had lost several major customers and was going to have to lay off some workers in order to cut operating costs. Tommy felt bad for the new boys. He knew they would be the first to go. He knew he was safe—he'd been there 28 years. He was almost ready for his 30-year plaque.

On December 12, Tommy was called to the office of the plant manager, Mr. Dorn. Mr. Dorn asked Tommy to sit down and then began explaining the plant's financial situation. He thanked Tommy for all his hard work but told him he was going to be one of the first 100 people let go. Tommy was speechless. Mr. Dorn then asked Tommy to go down the hall and see Mr. Lee, the EAP staff person. Tommy did what he was told. He didn't know what else to do. As he entered Mr. Lee's office, Tommy began to realize what had happened; he had been fired. After 28 years of hard, loyal work—he had been fired. With that thought, he dismissed Mr. Lee with the wave of his hand, stood up, and walked out past the other workers who watched in disbelief and offered shallow words of assurance.

Mr. Lee sat and stared at the empty chair Tommy had left. He took a deep breath and began assessing the situation before him. He knew that after all 100 employees were dismissed, the problems would not be over—they would just be beginning. Mr. Lee knew that the survivors, those that did not lose their jobs, would face feelings and frustrations similar to those felt by survivors of other major traumas.

In the ensuing weeks, Mr. Lee heard the remaining workers talk about their own fears of being fired. They wondered how Tommy—the best worker they knew—could have been laid off. They worried about being the next to go. The layoff was extremely hard because it came right before Christmas. The surviving workers expressed a great deal of guilt. How, they wondered, was Tommy going to celebrate Christmas—what about Sarah Ann, or Jose, or James, or Carter? They had all been fired.

The survivors were angry and frightened as they realized that the company to which they had devoted their lives had no loyalty to them. Mr. Lee realized that individual counseling and referrals, although important, were not going to be enough. He decided to begin a "survivor training program" to help the continuing employees cope with the loss and continue to work productively. Mr. Lee arranged the workers into several different groups that met weekly. He encouraged the workers to talk openly about their feelings of fear and guilt. Mr. Lee then arranged for Mr. Dorn to come to all the group meetings and answer questions honestly. Mr. Lee explained to Mr. Dorn that the workers were afraid of losing their jobs and needed to understand why the cutback had occurred. Mr. Dorn agreed to explain the plant's financial concerns that led to the layoffs and discuss future operating plans.

The survivor training appeared to be helping workers deal with their fears as well as helping them recommit to the organization and their jobs. However, Mr. Lee knew that studies showed companies that downsize once often do

it again. He did not want the workers to be caught unaware if another cutback was necessary so he advised them to be proactive about the situation. He wanted them to feel that they had some control over their lives—even if they did get laid off. He counseled the survivors on the importance of continuing to do quality work. He also suggested they pay close attention to any news about the company's financial status by asking questions and reading the local business paper. Finally, he reinforced the importance of their support for each other.

In addition to working with the employees, Mr. Lee explained to Mr. Dorn the importance of letting the workers know about the positive effects of the cutbacks on the plant's financial stability. He told Mr. Dorn that employees often become cynical if they are not aware of positive changes after such a painful process as downsizing. Mr. Dorn agreed to work with Mr. Lee to produce a quarterly operations statement for all employees so that they would be informed of the plant's progress in dealing with the loss of customers and the increased global competition.

This vignette exemplifies the difficult situations that often confront EAP workers. They must be able to interact effectively with individual employees as well as understand organizational and systemic issues. At Deers Manufacturing, Mr. Lee engaged in individual and group counseling and fulfilled the social work functions of assessment, diagnosis, support, counseling, enabling, referral, program development, coordination, and consultation. Although individual counseling, the survivors' training program, and the quarterly newsletter produced by Mr. Dorn all had positive effects, Mr. Lee knew that if more cutbacks were necessary, the current situation will worsen. Many of the employees who Mr. Dorn had counseled might need ongoing professional social work services in the future. Accordingly, he developed a list of resources in the community and surrounding areas. On his own time, he also put together a booklet on tips for finding a new job. Realistically, many of the employees will need this type of help.

Social workers employed in EAPS have seized the opportunity to develop outreach approaches to meeting the needs of company employees. EAPS now offer a variety of services on the World Wide Web, including:

- education about factors that influence behavior, such as substance abuse, personal problems, work stress, financial problems, caring for an elderly parent, and the like
- chat rooms with counselors on many topics
- telephone (one-on-one) appointments with social workers
- self-assessment tools to identify problems such as depression, anxiety, stress, and substance abuse
- helpful hints about a large range of topics (such as diet and nutrition, anxiety, anger, relaxation) and resources for further assistance.

Online services provide easy access for people who work all day or who may be reluctant to seek a counselor during work hours when they might be observed. Employees have the choice about whether they wish to use the online services. Because EAPs are under company auspices, they are not limited in some of the ways that characterize managed behavioral health services (O'Neill, 2002b). The services provided through an EAP may be much broader than those available through traditional insurance plans, including parent–child and marital issues, addictions, and financial and legal matters.

EAPs have also made significant headway, in comparison with other social work programs and services, in demonstrating the outcomes of interventions. Because worksite-based services are designed to help identify and resolve behavioral, health, and productivity problems that adversely affect employee job performance, outcomes are more easily measurable. Studies have shown that EAP services return from $7.00 to $13.00 for every dollar a company spends on them (Vallianatos, 2000). One evaluation approach is to have managers rank employees before and after EAP services; another approach utilizes a control group—one group of employees have used EAP services and the other group has not. The two groups are then compared in regard to such indicators as absenteeism, accident rates, use of sick leave, and use of medical benefits (Vallianatos, 2000). Client satisfaction is another approach taken in the assessment of outcomes. EAPs, according to the experts, offer a high measure of accountability. They are solution oriented and short term in nature and have the advantages associated with early intervention, which is conducive to improved outcomes.

Community Mental Health

The community mental health movement, which gained momentum following World War II, reflected the recognition of the failings of institutional care. Deinstitutionalization of people with chronic mental illness from hospitals was facilitated by the development of psychotropic medications, which, with proper monitoring, would allow those with serious mental illness to live within the community.

Community mental health centers are partially financed and regulated by the federal government (Barker, 1999). These centers are local organizations that provide a range of psychiatric and social services to people residing in the area. Services include inpatient and outpatient care; partial hospitalization; emergency and transitional services; screening and follow-up care; and programs oriented specifically for special populations, such as older people and children and substance abusers. Within the context of community-based programs, social workers function in a variety of roles, depending on the level of impairment of the specific client and the approach of the agency involved.

Program Management in a Community Mental Health Center

The Nassau Community Mental Health Center is a not-for-profit agency that relies heavily on state and county dollars, as well as third-party reimbursement from Medicaid and Medicare. The agency was started in the mid-1970s when it became evident that, in this affluent community, there was a large number of homeless, chronically mentally ill people who were not receiving any services. The center offers a variety of programs for people with chronic mental illness, ranging from psychiatric consultations and medication dispensing and monitoring to shelter care and vocational training programs.

The shelter program was initiated last year when the center applied for and received a first-time grant under the McKinney Homeless Assistance Act. Ellen Turner was hired as the program manager shortly after the center received notification of funding. The shelter program does more than provide a temporary nighttime residence; its aim is to assist chronically mentally ill people who are presently without an address of their own to locate permanent living situations and to involve themselves in other programs of the center that will assist them in gaining the maximum degree of independent functioning.

As manager of a newly created program, Ellen is responsible for getting it off the ground. During the first few weeks on the job, Ellen spent a lot of time recruiting and hiring staff. She is also responsible for training and supervising the staff. Understaffing is a problem in direct services for people with chronic mental illness, as many professionals prefer to work with a client population with a more positive prognosis for growth and change. But Ellen was able to hire a few energetic, enthusiastic people who are truly committed to working with this population. The staff of the homeless program is small; there are, in addition to Ellen, two full-time social work-

ers, two student interns from a local school of social work, a housing specialist who will assist clients in securing permanent housing, a facilities manager, and several part-time employees who handle concrete tasks, such as cooking meals. The center's staff will also be involved, including the vocational trainers and the psychiatrist who prescribes and monitors medication.

During the first month, Ellen worked in concert with the center's executive director to finalize a lease for the shelter site, arrange for building modifications, and order furniture and supplies. The goal was to have the shelter operational within the first 90 days. With a lot of overtime, Ellen was able to meet this deadline.

By the end of the third month, the smell of wet paint still permeated the building and workmen were putting on the finishing touches, but the shelter was ready to receive referrals, which come from the center's staff. All clients are already known to the center. Some are seen for medication monitoring, although others are seen for consultation following discharge from a psychiatric hospital.

Staff at the center are briefed on the types of clients who might appropriately be referred to the shelter program, and a referral form is prepared for staff use. Criteria include a diagnosis of chronic mental illness, a history of consistent use of medication and follow-through on medical appointments to monitor medication, and a current status of homelessness. In addition, client referrals are encouraged for those who are able and motivated to hold a full- or part-time job.

During the first few weeks in which referrals are accepted, 15 clients are referred to the program. Potential clients are screened by a social worker to determine whether they meet the established criteria for participation. Ellen sits in on several of these screenings to observe the process. She encourages the social workers to ascertain the clients' eligibility for federal benefits, such as Medicaid, Medicare, or Supplemental Security Income. Twelve of the 15 referred are found to be good candidates for the program and are immediately relocated to the facility. Each is given an orientation by one of the social workers; is given specific tasks for which he or she is responsible, such as helping in the preparation of meals; and is encouraged to participate fully in the day-to-day operations and activities of the facility. Meanwhile, the social workers are able to initiate the process of applying for benefits for five of the clients who are considered eligible. Several of the other clients are already receiving benefits.

During this early phase of the program, Ellen meets twice a week with the staff to seek feedback about operations and issues. During these staff meetings, clinical and administrative issues are thoroughly discussed in a roundtable, egalitarian atmosphere geared to brainstorming about any and all components of the program. In one of these meetings, a format is devised for the development of program plans for each of the clients with whom the social workers work, with the active participation and input of the client. This program plan represents the major focus of all staff–client interaction and will be used as a measure against which to assess progress in goal achievement. The plans will include medication compliance, vocational and employment goals and timetables, tasks assigned within the facility, personal hygiene issues, and any interpersonal relationship problems.

In addition to staff meetings, Ellen conducts weekly supervision meetings with all direct services staff on an individual basis. During these sessions, which usually last 45 minutes to one hour, Ellen provides feedback about the employee's performance, listens to any concerns, provides feedback, and entertains specific ideas for program development or implementation.

As the program manager, Ellen interfaces with a variety of people on behalf of center clients. On a typical day, Ellen may talk to the state employment office to check on new job listings for which her clients may be eligible, the public housing office about pending client applications for subsidized housing, the county

police to resolve an incident involving clients at the local shopping center, or a family member of a client who wants to know about the possibility of overnight visitation.

Ellen is pleased with the progress made during the initial months of the program. It is time for her to write her first quarterly report to the U.S. Department of Housing and Urban Development, which administers the McKinney funds that were received, and she has a lot of solid progress to report. She knows that the following months will include many challenges, but the foundation established for the program makes her optimistic about its future.

As a middle-level manager in a satellite program of a community mental health center, Ellen interfaces with administrators, funding agencies, staff, and clients. As the program gets underway, Ellen will have more contact with staff of other agencies as she and her staff seek to locate jobs and housing for clients. The program planning and development functions of the job are paramount for Ellen in this start-up operation. Ellen is responsible for handling logistical arrangements in preparing the facility for its residents. Functions also include personnel management. Ellen must recruit, screen, hire, and train the staff, in collaboration with the center's executive director. Staff supervision is another important component of her job.

As the program becomes fully operational, Ellen's functions will extend to interorganizational coordination, including serving as liaison with the contract agency and participating in contract renegotiations. In addition, Ellen will be responsible for designing and implementing an evaluation plan to show that the program is meeting its intended goals.

Mental Health Services in Rural Areas

The problems experienced by rural Americans often go unrecognized, but they are very real and have been worsening in recent years. Rural Americans account for about one-third of the population of the United States. This population experiences higher rates of unemployment and persistent poverty than urban or suburban areas. Rural Americans also suffer disproportionately higher rates of maternal and infant mortality, chronic illness and disability, and morbidity related to cancer, diabetes, high blood pressure, stroke, heart disease, and lung disease than urban residents (Duncan, 1999; Moore, 2001; Second Harvest, 2003). Homelessness, often thought of as an urban problem, is also increasing in rural areas.

Social workers often enter a rural environment expecting to work with a homogenous group. However, rural communities are diverse in terms of both population characteristics and presenting problems (Davenport & Davenport, 1995; Moore, 2001). People who live in rural areas experience many of the same problems as do urban residents, only without the range of health, mental health, and social services resources needed to prevent or ameliorate these problems. Rural America is diverse in racial and ethnic composition and includes significant numbers of African Americans, predominantly in the south; Hispanics, primarily Chicanos, in the southwest and west; Puerto Ricans, in the east; and Native Americans, who have always been a predominantly rural population ("Rural Social Work," 2003).

The past decade has been one of crisis and change for rural populations. Many farmers, for example, found that they can no longer afford to operate, particularly in the face of mergers and acquisitions which have created corporate farming and timber harvesting industries (Sheafor & Lewis, 1992). Smaller farm auctions and foreclosures have become commonplace, accompanied by the occurrence of huge debts and high emotional tolls. Concurrently, rural manufacturing, which produced low-wage jobs, steadily declined, resulting in wide-scale unemployment (Moore, 2001). Furthermore, employment opportunities are scarcer in rural communities than in urban areas. The resulting stress on rural communities is

reflected in the rising incidence of child abuse and neglect, divorce rates, suicides, and the demand for mental health services (Sheafor & Lewis, 1992). Yet, rural Americans often lack access to the range of services they need.

Rural social workers work as advocates, organizing both on the local level to help communities help themselves and on the macro level to support legislation directly affecting the provision of mental health services to rural communities. Social workers have realized that the economics of rural life must be addressed if any attempt to solve the problems facing this population is to be effective ("Farm Communities Dig In," 1987).

Government and nonprofit social services delivery systems are largely built on urban models. Issues related to distance and time of travel and the absence of public transportation affect the ability of rural residents to utilize social services ("Rural Social Work," 2003). Due to the lack of sufficient facilities or, in some cases, any mental health facilities at all, rural social workers may find themselves as the only line of defense against a mounting array of social ills within this population.

Rural areas face perpetual shortages of mental health workers and facilities. This need has become even more pronounced in recent years, as managed care requirements have meant that area agencies had to hire MSWs. Radford University's social work education program opened an extended campus program in rural Virginia, near the Tennessee border, to encourage students to stay and work in rural America (Vallianatos, 2001). This outreach is consistent with the roots of rural social work, the origins of which include the application of community organization skills ("Rural Social Work," 2003). Community and faith-based social services groups have been created to reach out to the urban poor of all ethnic, racial, and religious groups (Hardcastle, Wenocur, & Powers, 1997).

Programs throughout the midwest have been developed to include rural community outreach, peer-listening training, crisis hotlines, and stress-relief retreats, which subsidize farm families to get away for a weekend to a church camp to alleviate the stress on the family. Groups organized by social workers provide everything from support for recovering addicts to confrontational therapy for wife beaters. According to one rural social worker, "We have to take the self-reliance exhibited by the farm community and use it as a strength. Because we are so few in number, we must train rural residents to help themselves" ("Farm Communities Dig In," 1987, p. 4).

In many rural communities, social workers have helped to recruit and train volunteers and to involve neighbors, families, clergy, and other natural support networks. Other efforts throughout rural communities include helping churches and agencies to better respond to the needs of farmers, organizing farmers for political action, offering crisis hotlines, and conducting community meetings to provide information on available services and encourage supportive networks. The self-reliance of farmers and the stigma associated with mental health services mean social workers need to get out into the community to provide services in a setting that promotes more comfort (Sheafor & Lewis, 1992).

Social workers practicing in rural communities are often employed within the public sector, in public welfare, child welfare, and mental health agencies. Usually, the generalist practice model is the one that is best suited for rural social work practice. This model focuses on the social worker's ability to assess problem situations and identify when and where intervention is needed. Rural social workers must also be able to identify and coordinate resources within and outside of the community, such as with state and local organizations. Social workers must be flexible and able to adapt to their surroundings and the needs of their clients (Davenport & Davenport, 1995).

A mental health social worker in a rural environment may use the functions of assessment and counseling when working with survivors of sexual assault or domestic violence.

The social worker may also engage in organizing and coordinating the development of a support group, organize a task force, or implement an emergency food pantry. In addition, a rural social worker may advocate and lobby legislators for increased funding and services (Davenport & Davenport, 1995). The following vignette illustrates the situations a rural social worker confronts and the diverse range of functions carried out to meet individual, family, and community needs.

MENTAL HEALTH NEEDS IN A RURAL AREA

Rina Williams is a 32-year-old mother of five children. Her husband Dale runs a corn and soybean farm covering 500 acres in northeast Iowa. For the past two years, a drought has ruined a large proportion of their annual harvest. In addition, overhead costs have increased, and crop prices have decreased. The bank is threatening foreclosure and Dale has begun to drink quite heavily. The marriage, too, is falling apart—communication lines have broken down. Jim Walker, a social worker employed at a mental health center serving six Iowa counties, has recently seen several women for first-time appointments with similar complaints of depression, marital problems, and family dysfunction. In addition, there has been an increase in acting-out behaviors among adolescents and teenagers in the community, ranging from petty theft to fistfights.

Recognizing the impact of the farm crisis on these and other rural families, Jim decides to try a community intervention approach. He also knows that farmers can be tough customers. Resistance to mental health services has been long-standing in the community, particularly among the men, and there is little chance of involving these men in family or individual therapy. Therefore, Jim takes a two-pronged approach. First, he organizes a support group to help the wives cope. Next, he organizes the first of what he hopes will be an ongoing series of community meetings to discuss the farm situation and its impact on the community. To gain the participation from the men in the community, Jim invites several of them to serve on a planning committee to identify topics for discussion, hoping that this will help create a sense of ownership and give them a stake in the success of the program.

The first community meeting is held at the local school in an effort to reduce the stigma associated with the mental health center. The topic selected by the planning committee is helping children cope with the financial, social, and emotional impact of the farm crisis. Members of the planning committee and residents attending the meeting agree that there is an increasing number of children suffering from depression or acting out behavior. The residents at the meeting then turn to Jim for help in solving the problem, but Jim simply tells them it is their meeting and asks them what they want to do. In saying this, Jim is attempting to empower the community residents and allow them to solve their own problems.

After several minutes of silence, a woman in the crowd states that her son doesn't have anything to do after school; the area school is much too poor for an athletic program. Other parents begin to echo similar experiences. The kids seem to be bored and, as a result, they are depressed and act out. Some of the teens in the community are at the meeting, so Jim asks them what they think of the situation. Excited to express their opinions, several of the teens offer suggestions. Finally, after hours of discussion, a tentative plan is developed. The teens want to develop a county store—some of the teens want to make carpentry items such as wooden stools, shelves, and benches; others are interested in making jewelry from dried flowers and stone; and still others are interested in learning the business end of running a store, everything from ordering stock to arranging the shelves.

After several more meetings, it is decided that the community will work together to build the store and the youth will work there after school. Special positions such as store manager and accountant will rotate every month among the youth. In addition to providing guidance and facilitation at local meetings, Jim uses his contacts in the town to get a small loan from the bank for supplies and to secure agreements from local merchants to display and sell at least some of the finished products.

In this case, Jim carries out the social work function of assessment to identify the social problems confronting the residents of the community. He also seeks to empower community residents and assist them to develop their own self-help skills. Further, Jim carries out the social work functions of organizing, mobilizing, and coordinating to develop the support group for the wives and to initiate the planning committee for the community meetings. Finally, Jim engages in negotiation and exchange to access resources in the surrounding locality.

The activities in which Jim engages to identify social problems in the community and to develop programs to address them also respond to a larger societal problem termed a "health crisis in this country." In 1999, former Surgeon General Satcher issued the Surgeon General's Report on Mental Health, in which he decried the lack of availability and quality of and access to mental health for America's youth (Satcher, 1999). The report noted that one in 10 children and adolescents suffers from mental illness of such severity as to cause some level of impairment. However, in any given year, fewer than one in five receives needed treatment. The youth depicted in the above scenario show signs of emotional problems, in part a reflection of the difficult and very real circumstances faced by the total community. The children lack constructive and organized activities, which add to the propensity to seek excitement in deviant or illegal activities.

Throughout the United States, emotional, behavioral, and developmental needs are not being met. After the Surgeon General's report was issued, a conference of mental health experts was held to draft a response in the form of a National Action Agenda on Children's Mental Health (O'Neill, 2000), which identified eight goals in the form of a blueprint for change. The agenda emphasized education in assessment, treatment, and prevention for all people involved in the care of children. Also on the agenda was continued research linked to practice.

Private Practice

One of the most profound and far-reaching changes in the profession of social work has been the movement of social workers into independent practice. The private practice of social work has been defined by Barker (1999) as

> the provision of professional services by a licensed/qualified social worker who assumes responsibility for the nature and quality of the services provided to the client in exchange for direct payment or third-party reimbursement. Also, the process in which the values, knowledge, and skills of social work, acquired through sufficient education and experience, are used to deliver social services autonomously to clients in exchange for mutually agreed payment. (p. 377)

In private practice, the social worker is employed directly by the client and is paid by the client either directly or through a vendorship arrangement. Private practitioners usually provide for their own offices, health insurance, pension plan, and billing and record-keeping services.

Private practice is predominantly focused on the direct delivery of clinical social services. The circumstances under which private practice is carried out are influenced by the policies of the state regulating agency, by the standards of professional associations, and by the insurance companies that determine reimbursement rates (Karger & Stoesz, 1998).

A major impetus to independent practice in social work came in 1982. In that year, the Civilian Health and Medical Program of the Uniformed Services Act was amended to eliminate the physicians' role in supervising treatment by clinical social workers. For the first time, social workers had attained vendor status and would be reimbursed directly for psychotherapeutic services (Barth, 2001). Although this policy change concerned eligible services under the military insurance program, it paved the way for changes in other parts of the health care delivery system. The Mental Health Parity Act of 1996, discussed in several chapters of this volume, opened more doors for social workers to receive reimbursement as independent practitioners.

The significant movement within the profession toward the private practice of social work has been explained and justified on the basis of the need of the profession to expand its mission to take into account and reflect the realities of economic and social change (Gibelman & Schervish, 1996; Jayaratne, Davis-Sacks, & Chess, 1991; Saxton, 1988). In reality, the interests of social workers in the private practice of social work converged with licensing and vendorship—external variables—to shape the course of the profession. Social work licensing laws, granting formal government authorization to practice, are now in effect in all 50 states and the District of Columbia. Vendorship is "the practice of providing goods and services for specific fees that are charged either to the consumer or to a third party" (Barker, 1999, p. 508). These third parties may include health insurance companies, government agencies (Medicare and Medicaid), or business organizations. The social worker, then, becomes a vendor—one who is selling a product or service.

The private practice of social work has been controversial within the profession, although it has gained increasing acceptance over time. A major impetus to this acceptance came with social work vendorship. The arguments against private practice have focused on value conflicts with professional ethos, including discrimination against the less affluent and failure to provide services to those who are unable to pay (Barker, 1992; Karger, 1989; Merle, 1962). Other arguments include the potential depletion of social workers in agencies where they are needed and the importance of the norms and standards of the agency for the practice of social work (Barker, 1992).

Counterarguments, of course, have been waged to refute the discrimination claim; it is argued that agencies also select the clients they wish to serve on the basis of ability to pay or some type of means test, on the basis of religion or ethnicity, or on the type of disability or other personal characteristic, such as gender. Less frequently refuted are claims that private practice usually excludes poor people because they do not have geographic, social, or financial access to their services (Barker, 1992). Concerns about depleting the agency-based labor force have not been borne out (Williams & Hopps, 1990).

The debate continues, although with less intensity than in the past. Specht and Courtney (1994) unequivocally viewed this movement within the profession as negative: "We believe that social work has abandoned its mission to help the poor and oppressed and to build communality" (p. 4). In their view, community problems are increasing, although social work as a profession is devoting itself more and more to "the psychotherapeutic enterprise." The profession now seeks overridingly to "perfect the individual" rather than acting on the belief in the "perfectibility of society."

Some social workers have decided to pursue a career in private practice to escape the bureaucratic constraints of many public services jobs. Some want a higher income with more freedom to determine their own schedules and clientele. In addition, many social workers have found that private practice is the only way they can remain in direct practice; if they remain on the clinical staff of a social service agency, they are likely to get promoted to an administrative or supervisory role. Furthermore, cutbacks in funding for social service agencies have greatly reduced the number of available positions, thereby forcing some social workers into private practice simply to remain in their chosen profession (Barker, 1995).

Although there are many positive aspects to private practice, social workers should also be aware of the difficulties. First, the expense of establishing and maintaining a private practice can be large and the income is often unpredictable. Typically, less than half of the money social workers collect from clients is spendable. Much of the income goes for overhead expenses such as taxes, health and other insurance, education, and retirement (Barker, 1995).

In addition to overhead costs, private practitioners often expend considerable time and energy to make their practice succeed. They must devote themselves to activities such as business record keeping and filing, processing insurance forms, and participating in educational activities. Furthermore, the isolation of the private practitioner often facilitates burnout because there is no social and professional support from colleagues. Finally, social workers in private practice often face legal problems with the threat of malpractice litigation constantly looming (Barker, 1995).

Among the range of services provided by social workers in private practice, most tend to be in the "soft services" category. Psychotherapy, for example, is a specialized, formal interaction between a social worker and a client (who may be an individual, family, or group). A therapeutic relationship is established to help resolve symptoms of mental disorder, psychosocial stress, relationship problems, and difficulties in coping (Barker, 1999). Psychotherapy is an umbrella term that encompasses several modalities, including family therapy, supportive treatment, behavioral therapy, transactional analysis, and group psychotherapy.

A SOCIAL WORKER IN PRIVATE PRACTICE

Wendy, a 46-year-old private clinician in Chicago, describes herself as a psychotherapist and clinical social worker. She works in a downtown office, which she shares with three other licensed social workers, and sees only individual, adult patients ranging in age from 18 to 65 years. Her practice consists of long-term, open-ended psychotherapy. Approximately 75 percent of her patients qualify for some type of insurance reimbursement; the remaining 25 percent being private pay clients. She charges $110 for a 50-minute session and spends anywhere between 30 and 35 hours per week seeing clients.

Reflecting her personal choice, her office hours begin at 7:30 A.M. and end at 3:30 P.M. Her downtown office ensures easy access for most of her clients, who are either within walking distance or a short subway ride away. From her perspective, location is a critical variable in the success of her practice. Referrals from clients and other clinicians constitute the major source of her practice, and in her 14 years of practice she has managed to maintain a full schedule. She sees most of her patients once or twice a week. In the initial one to five sessions, she evaluates the client and determines the parameters of the therapy, including whether or not a referral to a psychiatrist for possible medication is appropriate, the frequency of visits, the specific problems to be addressed, and the fee arrangement.

To fine-tune her skills as a private practice clinician, Wendy has participated in postgraduate training at an analytic institute and has attended professional conferences on a regular basis. In the past, she has also served as a supervisor for social workers in training. Wendy has concerns about the future of her practice, particularly in light of the managed care movement. She feels that client choices about providers are becoming very limited. Several of her clients have had to terminate therapy because of limitations imposed by their insurance companies on the number of visits allowed. Wendy is also concerned about stories she has been hearing that managed care companies are canceling provider contracts when the practitioner has been advocating on behalf of a health care member, appealing a managed care organization (MCO) decision, or requesting a review or challenging a termination decision.

Although Wendy is aware that recent court rulings have required MCOs to modify their "no cause" termination clauses, she is also aware that compliance is another matter ("Firm to Modify Contracts," 2001). She fears that, in the future, cost-containment efforts will result in a very altered practice picture for her and others like her.

Private practice continues to be a popular form of practice. The enthusiasm for private practice among social workers has been attributed to several factors, including the prestige and income that private practitioners enjoy in relation to their salaried and agency-based counterparts. In addition, salary potential for private practitioners is generally higher than for agency-based social workers in direct practice (Gibelman & Schervish, 1997). Private practice also offers a degree of autonomy that is not available to social workers employed in traditional agencies, including a level of specialization that is individually determined (Karger & Stoesz, 1998). The case of Neil, a 36-year-old computer analyst, is an example of the broad scope of the private practitioner's role. Intrapsychic as well as psychosocial and environmental factors are considered in assessment and treatment.

PRIVATE PRACTICE: NOT JUST PSYCHOTHERAPY

Neil, who is of Anglo-European background, is an ivy-league college graduate. He is described by his social worker, Amy, as tall, unkempt, disheveled, with poor personal hygiene. Neil sought out Amy for therapy after attending a practice-building seminar she had presented on the subject of relationships at his place of employment.

Neil's presenting problem is his "lack of a meaningful relationship" in his life. He reported that he had never been on a date and had never had a sexual relationship. On the few occasions he has attempted to approach women he has been rebuffed. He is feeling hopeless about ever finding a suitable partner, although he has a list of criteria that such a woman would need to meet.

Neil reported that he had been in therapy before but was vague about when, where, or with whom, and would not give Amy any details or consent to send for his records. It appears that he had not stayed with any treatment or therapist over any length of time. Amy wondered out loud what he hoped this therapy would provide for him that previous therapies had not. He indicated that he had liked what Amy said in the seminar and hoped that he could learn something from her to help him find a girlfriend.

During the first few sessions, Amy attempted to take a psychosocial history. She learned that Neil's father was a college professor who had always been critical of his son. His mother was a businesswoman whom Neil perceived as nonnurturing. He felt little affection had been given him by either of his parents, who divorced when he was 12 years old. He has one married brother with three children, but there is little relationship or contact, and the brother lives several hundred miles away. He speaks to his parents occasionally and sees them a few times a year. There is no extended family, no family gatherings, and Neil describes himself as very socially isolated. He has a few acquaintances at work, but basically no social life. His spare time is spent working on the computer. Holidays are spent alone.

Neil describes his health history as good but explains that he was in an auto accident at 10 years of age and sustained a head injury.

Although he reported that he had been told there were no neurological findings, he felt that all of his problems began at that time. He was no longer able to concentrate, began to do poorly in school, had difficulty making friends, and felt that other kids teased and made fun of him. Although Neil had tested in the gifted range on IQ tests, he said he did about average work in school and performed below his potential. School for him was lonely and he does not remember joining anything or having more than one good friend.

Upon further exploration, Neil told Amy about his long-standing depression, broken occasionally by periods of high energy and enthusiasm when he would get many projects completed and accomplish a lot at work, clean house, and work in the yard. The rest of the time he lacked energy, felt sluggish, depressed, and sometimes had suicidal thoughts. Neil further said that he missed work at times because he could not get himself together or organized enough to get there. He also collected things like old magazines, newspaper articles, and old radios that he described as "overtaking his house." He admitted to having been on psychotropic medications in the past but did not remember which ones or what diagnosis had been given.

At this point, Amy faces a dilemma. The client presented requesting help in forming relationships, but shows evidence of one or more major mental health diagnoses. Following the principle of client self-determination, should she focus on relationship skills or tell him what her assessment really is? Compounding her concern is that fact that Neil's insurance is through a managed behavioral health care plan that requires short-term cognitively based treatment, written treatment plans, diagnoses, homework, and evidence of patient involvement. For Amy to focus on his desire to improve his relationship skills and to fail to refer him for a medication evaluation would have been poor care and would not meet medical necessity criteria. However, Amy also knew he would protest the recommendation that he see a psychiatrist, as he had done before and had not felt that he had been helped. Amy did not think that Neil would respond well to a cognitive or an insight-oriented approach, but believed that what he could really benefit from was a long-term supportive relationship. This is not the type of treatment usually covered by managed care plans.

Amy decided to do both—attempt to make a connection with him by helping him work on forming relationships, but also tell him that she believed there was help for some of the other things that bothered him and hoped that, at some point, he would consult with a psychiatrist colleague of hers to see what could be done for his mood swings, disorganization, and compulsiveness. Neil didn't reject the latter recommendation but said that he would think about it and see how things went in treatment.

Amy first needed to advocate for her client with his insurance company to ensure that treatment would be covered. She asked for a clinical consultation with a care manager and explained the presenting problem and symptoms. She further elaborated that without treatment the client would probably deteriorate and possibly need hospitalization, and his level of insight and awareness of his problem was limited. The insurance company agreed to extend sessions as long as Amy kept them informed about his progress.

When Neil's parents came to town to visit, Amy invited him to bring them in for a family session. She was able to obtain some information from them and arouse their concern about Neil so that they would stay in closer touch with him.

To work on relationship building, Amy referred Neil to a local seminar on communication skills and called a colleague who ran a support group for singles at a nondenominational church. Amy arranged to have Neil meet the colleague to help him feel more comfortable and then to attend the group to see if he liked it, which he did. He developed an interest in a female group member, which kept him attend-

ing for some time and provided him with some social outlets other than the computer.

Using bibliotherapy, Amy developed a reading list for Neil that included books on relationship skills as well as on mood disorders, treatment with psychotropic medication, and other psychological issues. She downloaded a "mood chart" from an Internet site on bipolar disorder and asked him to keep track of his moods so they could discuss them. After consulting with a psychiatrist colleague on the case, she herself researched some literature on the comorbidity of attention deficit disorder with bipolar disorder. Eventually, trusting their relationship, Neil agreed to see the psychiatrist and begin a trial of medication. Neil continued in therapy with Amy for several years, with the focus on maintenance rather than problem resolution or cure.

In order to help this client, Amy goes beyond the functions of assessment, diagnosis, and treatment. Amy also identifies community resources, networks with colleagues, refers Neil for supportive social activities, and involves the client's family. Amy also seeks professional consultation, negotiates with the managed care company, utilizes the Internet for research and therapeutic aids, develops a bibliography specifically for the client, refers Neil to a psychiatrist for a diagnostic and medication evaluation, and maintains contact with the psychiatrist to coordinate care. Each of these functions is performed with the purpose of achieving the same goal: to enhance the problem-solving, coping, and developmental capacities of the client (NASW, 1981).

There are some less evident skills implicit in this vignette. Amy's pro bono workshop for the company's employees was part of a systematic plan to market her private practice. Community outreach seminars are one means of informing the public about mental health issues and services in general. She has obtained some referrals from conducting these workshops. Amy also stays in contact with other professionals in the area in order to network. In addition, she applied for and became credentialed on several insurance panels. To build and sustain a private practice, such outreach is often a necessity.

Amy budgets a portion of her time to marketing and promotion. Related strategies include preparation of brochures, person-to-person contacts with other health and mental health providers, and visits to referral sources, including churches, community centers, and businesses. Visibility is extremely important in bringing in business.

The social worker has a broad range of skills to bring to the role of therapist, whether in private or agency-based practice. The concept of the person-in-environment, the importance of the psychosocial history, and the broad scope of related skills that are developed in formal social work education and in practice experience represent the unique contributions that are offered by the clinical social worker. The scope of practice of the social worker–therapist is much broader than just psychotherapy.

Private practitioners also treat people in groups. The following vignette describes a private practitioner's group approach for people who are afraid of flying. The group intervention described below illustrates that a behavioral approach, combined with the support of group members in similar circumstances, can be an effective tool in addressing fears that impact upon human behavior.

DEALING WITH FEAR OF FLYING THROUGH GROUP THERAPY

Marsha's job requires that she travel out of town at least once a month. Some of these trips are to distant cities, and flying is the only feasible way of getting to the various destinations. Marsha has never liked to fly.

As a child she grew up near LaGuardia Airport outside of New York City. One day, when she was 10 years old, she was walking home from a birthday party with several friends.

It was dusk. All of a sudden the sky lit up, as if there were fireworks going off. There was a horrible noise that followed. Once home, Marsha learned what she had witnessed: an airliner, on takeoff, had exploded over Jamaica Bay, killing all passengers aboard.

It is 20 years later and Marsha has flown all over the world, but never happily. Understandably, takeoffs are moments of acute anxiety for her. She jokes that she is responsible for holding up the plane with her knees. And by the time she gets to her destination, she is always exhausted. Going straight to a business meeting is difficult; she really needs 24 hours of solid sleep. Marsha has tried all types of things to deal with her fears—tranquilizers, liquor, even hypnosis. Nothing seems to work.

Nancy Marks is a social worker who has established a for-profit behavior therapy center. She specializes in working with phobic disorders. Just recently, she has noticed a large increase in the number of phone calls coming in following the crash of an American Airline's flight shortly after takeoff from New York City's JFK Airport. So many phone calls come in that Nancy decides to form a short-term group for those diagnosed as phobic about flying. A number of the calls come from residents of Belle Harbor, NY, where the plane crashed, killing several victims on the ground. Working with people with a fear of flying is not new for the social workers at the center, but interventions have generally been on a one-to-one basis.

In the group, Nancy encourages people to talk about their specific fears, their experiences with flying, and what they think was happening in their lives when they first became aware of their phobia. Then Nancy helps the group members to plan a plane trip, which will take place at the last session of the group—kind of a "graduation" send off. Members discuss where they will go, how they will purchase the tickets, how much time they will need to allow to get to the airport, and other such practical matters. Then, in subsequent sessions, Nancy guides the group members in psychodrama—playing out the flying experience using imagery and relaxation techniques. These techniques include exercises for the group members to challenge negative thinking, control obsessive thinking, and become more comfortable in their environment.

At the fourth of seven sessions, Nancy takes the group of eight on a field trip to one of the city's major airports. With the cooperation of a major airline company, arrangements are made to board an aircraft, talk to the pilot and crew, and learn as much as possible about the mechanics of flying. At the next session, the group thoroughly "debriefs" about this experience. Finally, it is the seventh and final session.

Marsha and the other group members show up as scheduled on April 20 for their graduation flight. The tickets are provided free of charge by the airline; they will take off, fly to a cruising altitude for an hour, and then land back in their city of origin. They all go together, sit in seats they had selected for themselves on the earlier airport visit, and listen to Nancy's final instructions. All goes well; the group members are able to use the techniques they have learned for a successful flight.

The fear of flying shared by many people is an outgrowth of the shock felt by the public when it hears about so many deaths occurring at one time, and in a manner that is totally outside of personal control. In the aftermath of the September 11 terrorist attacks in 2001, in which commercial aircraft were used as weapons of destruction, these fears have taken on new dimensions. Ongoing media stories about breaches in airport security and the relatively poor state of the art of explosive-detection technology keep the fears alive for a number of would-be travelers (Firestone, 2002).

Other factors include difficulty understanding how planes work and fear of the unknown. The fear may be about crashing, but it may also center on claustrophobia, the fear of confined spaces. Some people feel a slight apprehension about flying, although others will not board a plane under any circumstances. To varying degrees, this phobia can be disabling. Experiences with the kind of group described above have shown high success rates.

In this example, the social worker, Nancy Marks, carries out several different professional functions. For example, she engages in assessment, identification, support, and counseling when working with group members. She must listen carefully to what they are saying about themselves and how they respond to each other. In addition, the social worker also exhibits organization and coordination skills as she works with airlines to arrange a practice flight for group members. Finally, the social worker uses her skills to enable the group members to help themselves and, ultimately, to overcome their fear of flying.

At any point in time, practitioner interests are both shaped by and help to shape the future of the profession. The growth of the private practice of social work was made possible by a permissive and enabling economic and political climate. An increasing number of consumers wanted the service and could afford to pay for it themselves or had insurance that would cover all or part of the expense (Barker, 1992).

Managed Care

As with other social work practice areas, the socioeconomic and political context of American society will affect the future of social work in private practice. The demand for private practitioner services in social work and allied professions may be diminishing because of changing demographics, values and priorities, and cost factors.

Managed care has been defined by the U.S. Department of Health and Human Services (DHHS) as "an organized system of care which attempts to balance access, quality, and cost effectively by using utilization management, intensive case management, provider selection, and cost containment methodologies" (Moss,

1995, p. 1). The term refers to a variety of arrangements by which to control, coordinate, and monitor the delivery of health care to control the cost of care and services through the use of third parties (beyond physician or caregiver and patient or client). The overall objective of this system is to ensure that clients receive the care they need in the most cost-effective manner.

According to Gibelman (2002), the different types of MCOs share in common

- active supervision of the financing of medical care delivered to members
- active management of the "delivery system"—who gives care, where it is provided, and so forth
- a central gatekeeper—usually a primary care physician
- limitations on medical services to control costs. (p. 17)

Social workers in mental health practice, particularly private practice, have had to learn quickly the business of managed care, including its technicalities, reimbursement systems, and legal and regulatory requirements. Rather than a direct relationship between the human services organization and the client, there is now an intermediary. Intervention methods are dictated by the limits on reimbursable care, often manifest in limitations on the number of visits that are covered. Long-term, open-ended therapies have been replaced by short-term, behaviorally oriented interventions. In addition, MCOs have begun to introduce standardized preferred practice guidelines and protocols that indicate the practices or interventions to use to address a particular client problem (Mitchell, 1998), effectively limiting the freedom of practitioners to tailor services. Nevertheless, it is the practitioner's skill and professional judgment, based on a careful assessment of the client's situation, which should guide practice ("Law Note Aids," 2000).

Social workers also face a host of ethical dilemmas deriving from managed care arrangements. One such dilemma occurs when an MCO denies an extension in the number of authorized visits but the social worker determines that more care is needed. Although the social worker may appeal the decision, this takes time. In the interim, does the social worker continue to see the client until the payment issue is resolved? And what if the appeal is turned down?

Some practitioners have found that contracts with managed care companies lack consistency and predictability over time, since they are subject to change or even cancellation. A recent example concerns CIGNA Behavioral Health, a large nationally based managed care company with major operations in Massachusetts. CIGNA made a unilateral decision in 2001 to reduce its reimbursement rates by $2 per session for social workers, but not for psychiatrists or psychologists, and to reduce the number of authorized initial sessions from six to four (Vallianatos, 2002). With the intervention of the Massachusetts NASW Chapter in the form of dialogue and negotiation, CIGNA restored its original rate for a psychotherapy session from 45 to 50 minutes and further agreed to restore initial authorization to six sessions, with a consecutive six-session authorization upon request (Vallianatos, 2002). Despite these gains, the Massachusetts NASW Chapter leadership feel there is more work to be done. In the words of Chapter President Rita Van Tassel and Executive Director Carol Brill:

So, first CIGNA deviates from industry standards with a micro-managing style that just serves to alienate the clinicians it says it wants to partner with. Then it rewards the most cost-effective clinicians by lowering their rate to the lowest in the industry. This is bad practice, bad public relations and counter to fostering a "partnership" relationship. (cited in Vallianatos, 2002, p. 1)

Another effect of managed care is the increased competition for access to the few available slots on provider panels. Practitioners must apply for provider status, sometimes blanketing in all of their eligible employees by category (for example, those with an MSW and who are licensed) if permitted by the MCO, or otherwise meeting specific MCO requirements to be authorized as services providers. When the MCO provider panels are full—that is, when the MCO does not require any more practitioners to whom to refer clients—new applicants are closed out.

Social workers have had to develop and fine-tune their negotiating skills to deal with managed care companies. Business savvy is necessary (Gibelman & Whiting, 1999). Also needed is some knowledge of the legal issues attendant to contracting with managed care companies. Expertise in conflict resolution also emerges as a required skill, particularly in mediating between the interests of the client and those of the MCO and between the dictates of ethical professional practice and the requirements of MCOs (Galambos, 1999; Strom-Gottfried, 1998).

In recognition of the disequilibrium between managed care companies and individual practitioners, NASW has prepared a "law note"— *Social Workers and Managed Care Contracts*— about information social workers need to know before signing with an MCO. Social workers are urged to read and understand provider agreements before signing them. They are also urged to do homework about the MCO, utilizing the experience of other social workers and network providers, including gathering information about number of expected annual referrals from the company, accreditation status, grievance procedures, membership composition, company marketing strategies, and record of payment of claims ("Law Note Aids," 2000).

Managed care has brought with it heightened demands for accountability, with particular emphasis on documenting the successful outcomes of service. Requirements to demonstrate

the effectiveness of treatment and achievement of planned outcomes are now a component of most, if not all, MCO contracts, as these companies look for results-oriented data. Therefore, tracking or monitoring case progress in regard to treatment plan milestones has become an imperative component of practice (Gibelman & Whiting, 1999). Franklin (2001) specified three types of measures clinicians need to perform: (1) proof of program efficiency (such as cost savings and fewer sessions); (2) evidence of client–patient satisfaction; and (3) satisfactory clinical outcomes (such as number of goals met, cessation of certain behaviors, and so forth).

Evidence-based practice (EBP) is one attempt to meet outcome and evaluation demands. EBP refers to

the process of utilizing a variety of databases (for example, research reports and systematic case studies) to guide interventions that foster client change. The central goal of EBP is to increase the empirical basis and effectiveness of social work practice by helping clinicians choose the best approaches to care. . . . EBP can also be used in the areas of program evaluation, policy development, and administration. (Vandiver, 2002, p. 731)

The premise of EBP is straightforward: practice must be guided by the best available science. Ethical, cost-efficient, and outcome-oriented practice is facilitated by the selection of psychosocial interventions that possess scientifically credible evidence of effectiveness (Thyer, 2002).

EBP encompasses three approaches. The first is the use of practice guidelines—systematically compiled and organized statements and recommendations for care based on research findings and practitioner consensus (Vandiver, 2002). The guidelines are intended to provide the base for social workers to find, select, and use interventions that have been shown to be most effective and appropriate within the context of a specific presenting problem, situation, and desired outcome. The second approach involves expert consensus guidelines that are identified from a broad-based survey of expert opinion. Here, too, the emphasis is on the practical, as the end result is a compilation of recommendations for the treatment of major psychiatric disorders. This compilation is intended to augment the information identified through research findings (Vandiver, 2002). The third approach—the self-directed approach—is intended for use in situations in which practice protocols or guidelines are not available (Cournoyer & Powers, 2002).

Although EBP approaches are not always accepted in mental health settings, they are increasingly used by practitioners as they provide a concrete, practical approach to meeting accountability demands (see, for example, American Psychiatric Association, 1997; Corcoran, 2000; Howard & Jensen, 1999). These approaches build upon social work practice principles. For example, the beginning point for EBP is psychosocial assessment, diagnosis, and treatment planning. At the point of diagnosis, the social worker using EBP would select specific practice guidelines and modify these to an even greater level of specificity as the treatment plan is developed (Vandiver, 2002).

The implication for social work practitioners, particularly those in solo or small group private practice, is that treatment effectiveness and cost containment must go hand in hand. The model of short-term, problem-focused therapy fits best with these dual-operating principles. Demonstrating the effectiveness of treatment and achievement of planned outcomes will be increasingly stressed as managed care companies look for hard data to determine who can treat what types of problems best.

Independent social workers practicing solo or in small groups have been cautioned that they are at a disadvantage in negotiating with MCOs. Information on working within managed care contracts provided by NASW includes the sobering fact that "absent significant legislative change, the climate for solo practitioners will remain tenuous" ("Law Note Aids," 2000, p. 8). As one private practitioner recently remarked:

> There aren't enough hours to earn more money at managed care rates, and the type of contract I used to have with the doctors doesn't really exist anymore, so the options are to lower overhead, find options for medical insurance, or pay off debt with assets, and I am working on all of them. But I love what I do—I work very hard and no one but managed care tells me what to do. I have hired a billing person to have my collections improve.

Nevertheless, interest in private practice remains strong among those entering the profession of social work. Clearly, the profession needs to monitor the impact of managed care on private social work practice over time.

DISASTER RELIEF

Disaster relief encompasses crisis interventions that are initiated because of natural or other disasters and includes both health and mental health components. Environmental or natural disasters such as earthquakes, floods, and fires can be financially, emotionally, and physically devastating for the affected individuals, families, and communities.

Many social workers are represented among local and state crisis response units and among the volunteer crisis teams of the American Red Cross or state emergency response units. Social workers, in fact, provide 40 percent of the disaster-relief mental health services offered by the Red Cross ("Social Workers Heed the Call to Volunteer," 1999). The following are some examples of disaster relief provided by social workers:

> On January 8, 1998, a severe ice storm hit the far northeastern United States. Although most people were at home or in emergency shelters, Sam Conant, a social worker in pri-

vate practice and Red Cross mental health coordinator for Vermont's Grand Isle County, ventured out to provide assistance. The first night, Mr. Conant checked the local shelters and worked with shelter coordinators to meet specific and immediate needs. One of the shelters accommodated 600 people, many of whom were elderly. In that shelter, efforts were focused on making the seniors as comfortable as possible and ensuring that they received their medications.

The havoc wrought by the ice storm meant that the emergency shelters had to be used for four to five days. At that point, the shelter coordinators also needed some attention, a need Conant attempted to meet. ("Ice Storm Spawns Heroes," 1998, p. 6)

In September 1998, Hurricane George left people in Puerto Rico, as well as other islands, with substantial infrastructure damage, including damage to electric and water supplies. The wreckage caused by the storm also resulted in damage to schools, businesses, homes, and agriculture. In the aftermath of the hurricane, NASW's Puerto Rico Chapter reconstituted and expanded its disaster committee and members immediately began meetings with political and human services officials to develop a plan to provide assistance to those most severely affected. Efforts included participation in a televised appeal for money, food, medicine, and clothes for victims in the Dominican Republic and visits to isolated villages to distribute food, assess needs, and provide follow-up services. ("Chapter Aids in Aftermath of Hurricane," 1999, p. 6)

Hurricane Floyd struck North Carolina in the fall of 1999. At least 49 people died, most as a consequence of floods, and more than 1.1 million farm animals perished. A state of emergency was declared in 60 counties. Under an agreement between NASW and the American Red Cross to mobilize association members in natural disaster and crisis situations, social workers were called upon to deliver family services, casework, and mental health counseling. Social workers and students in the devastated areas of North Carolina, as well as social workers from across the country, volunteered to help as many displaced people as possible, doing whatever needed to be done. Interventions ranged from crisis services, to work in emergency shelters, to resource identification. Social workers also collected and distributed donated clothes and food and walked through neighborhoods to reach out to people in need. Dot Bonn, head of social work and professional development at North Carolina's health and human services department, coordinated teams of clinical social work volunteers. The North Carolina NASW Chapter raised $3,000 in emergency relief funds, recruited Red Cross volunteers, and fielded donations from across the United States. (Beaucar, 2000, p. 5)

Nature continues its periodic ravaging of land and people's lives. When tornados, earthquakes, hurricanes, or other acts of nature strike, social workers are among the first to the front to participate in disaster-relief efforts. In these situations, social workers engage in the functions of assessment, support, and counseling to mediate the short- and long-term emotional impact of such tragedies. Equally important is the social work role in organization, mobilization, and exchange that makes it possible for different agencies in the community to interact and share resources in a time of need. Finally, extensive planning and supervision may be needed to avoid duplication of services and to make sure that all needs are being met.

September 11, 2001

The role of social workers in disaster relief was never so apparent as in the aftermath of September 11, 2001. Social workers were in the forefront in responding to the attacks, many in a volunteer capacity. Since 1997, NASW has had a formal agreement with the American Red Cross for close cooperation in the delivery of mental health services to victims of disaster, rescue workers, military personnel and their families, and refugees (O'Neill, 2001d). More specifically, the agreement called for NASW to assist in the development of a national network of Red Cross-trained, licensed, or certified social workers to be mobilized in times of disaster. At least six NASW chapters have formal agreements with local Red Cross units, and many others have informal agreements (O'Neill, 2001d). On September 11 and in the ensuing months, social workers came through.

Ilia Rivera-Sanchez, a member of a Red Cross disaster mental health team in Alexandria, VA, was on the scene at the Pentagon a few hours after the American Airlines flight crashed into the building. She provided water, food, iced towels, and encouragement to firefighters and to military personnel and other rescue workers. Later that day, she worked with military chaplains to provide support to rescue workers who had begun to search for victims. In the following days, Ms. Rivera-Sanchez was assigned to the morgue to work with those bringing bodies out of the building. (O'Neill, 2001b)

NASW Hawaii social worker Ken Lee, who serves as part of the American Red Cross Air Incident Response Team, was deployed to New York City to help survivors, families, and friends of victims and fire, law enforcement, and emergency personnel cope with the traumatic event ("Social Work in the Public Eye," 2002a). Lee described the experience: "Just outside [of Ground Zero] the

Red Cross set up one of their two kitchens to feed this army of dedicated but exhausted workers. The pain, fatigue, and blank stares reflected in the faces of the workers I encountered said it all." ("Social Work in the Public Eye," 2002a, p. 15)

At the NASW national office in Washington, DC, Senior Staff Associate Rita Webb worked with Red Cross National Headquarters personnel to process a request for disaster-trained volunteers to staff a nationwide information and assistance hotline. Over 1,000 social workers were contracted through state NASW chapters. (O'Neill, 2001a)

Lisa DeDue, a Red Cross volunteer from Iowa, was detailed to the Washington, DC, area a few days after the attack as a mental health coordinator for the Pentagon site. In her words:

My job is to coordinate teams that are providing debriefings to groups that are having difficulty returning to work. We give them basic education to help them understand their symptoms and tell them how they can help their children. Children are affected on many levels. (O'Neill, 2001b, p. 8)

Social work volunteers were in front of Bellevue Hospital in New York City to meet people searching for family members and friends. They offered support and comfort. One volunteer was Barbara Dane, professor of social work at New York University and a trained Red Cross volunteer. She spent two days at Bellevue Hospital and the medical examiner's office reaching out to people who came searching for news of loved ones. She also coordinated a seven-day-a-week, 6 P.M. to midnight group of volunteers at the New York University Medical School to serve meals to hundreds of rescue workers. (O'Neill, 2001c, p. 10)

In New York, social services agencies sent their workers to talk to people in local grocery stores, churches, and beauty salons ("Chapter Convenes Roundtable Discussion," 2002). These social workers distributed informational flyers about community resources available to help. Social workers also engaged people in discussions about their experiences and reactions to 9/11. Community residents were invited to informal drop-in groups held daily, evenings, and on Saturdays, convened by local agencies (Bryant, 2002).

Safe Horizon is an agency dedicated to providing support, preventing violence, and promoting justice for victims of crime and abuse, their families, and communities. Beginning on September 14, staff at Safe Horizon began issuing emergency relief checks on a same-day basis. And within a week of the attacks, Safe Horizon staff worked with other community agencies to develop a comprehensive resource referral guide for immediate and ongoing use by social services agencies to direct clients to emergency assistance and longer-term support. The guide, the production of which was supported by the September 11th Fund, has been regularly updated to provide the most current information on benefits and services to those affected by the disaster.

Several NASW chapters, particularly those in neighboring regions to the attacks on New York City and the Pentagon, mobilized to get more people trained in crisis intervention. Such efforts to increase the number of social workers trained in disaster response are ongoing (O'Neill, 2001b).

In the Aftermath of Crisis

The world in which we live, sadly, is marked by many tragedies that are rooted in interpersonal and intergroup conflict. Terrorism is no longer an isolated event. And its impact on the collective American spirit and psyche is pronounced. In the days following the September 11, 2001, terrorist attacks on New York City and Washington, DC, Americans anxiously anticipated the possibility of more attacks. As the days stretched into weeks, the entanglements of everyday life took hold again, but the anxiety easily erupted with new attack alerts or, for some, even with the sound of police sirens. One commentator, addressing the atmosphere in New York City, noted:

> Throughout the city, an unrelenting fear persists in the recesses of many people's minds that something else bad is going to happen. A car bomb. A chemical attack. More planes. Will it be today? Tomorrow? In the night? (Kleinfield, 2001)

The lingering problems associated with trauma fall under the rubric of posttraumatic stress disorder (PTSD)—a psychological reaction to experiencing an event that is outside the range of usual human experience (Barker, 1999). Although PTSD is thought to afflict primarily those who personally experience life-threatening danger, the unprecedented nature of the September 11 attacks leaves many unanswered questions about PTSD. For example, what was the emotional impact for Americans who watched the attacks unfold live on television and who now feel personally threatened? Experts in PTSD acknowledge that there are a number of factors that affect the duration and intensity of emotional reactions to trauma. These may include proximity to the disaster, emotional vulnerability, and availability of social and family supports (Vedantam, 2002).

Each person reacts differently; there is a range of responses to a disaster of any size. Emotional responses can manifest themselves immediately or sometimes months later. Common responses include:

- disbelief and shock
- fear and anxiety about the future
- disorientation, apathy, and emotional numbing
- irritability and anger
- sadness and depression
- feelings of powerlessness
- over- or undereating
- difficulty making decisions
- headaches and stomach problems
- difficulty sleeping
- excessive drinking or drug use
- crying for no reason. (National Mental Health Association, 2002)

In the following vignette, Laurie manifests many of these symptoms.

THE NIGHTMARES DON'T STOP

It was a beautiful late summer day. Laurie had thought about calling in sick—it was just too wonderful a day—her birthday—to spend in her office cubicle on the 50th floor of Tower 1 of the World Trade Center. But she had several meetings that day and plans to meet her sister for dinner that night for a special treat at Windows on the World, at the top of the World Trade Center.

Laurie emerged from the subway at exactly 8:48 A.M. She will never forgot that moment. Her eyes were looking upward as she climbed the subway steps—upward to get a clear view of the ball of fire emanating from the first jet plane that slammed into the World Trade Center. People around her screamed and then began to run—some to the Tower, some away from it. It seemed like Laurie was frozen in place; she kept staring in disbelief. She turned away after what seemed like minutes but was really far less time, and started to walk. And walk. She ended up in midtown Manhattan at the office of her brother, Larry. By this time, the second tower had been hit and one of the buildings had collapsed. Larry had been frantic with worry. He had spent the

hour prior to Laurie's unexpected arrival on the phone with Laurie's husband and mother.

With her brother's help, Laurie eventually made it back to her apartment that night, once the subways were again running. She didn't cry. She didn't do much of anything. She felt dazed. But when Laurie's husband Sam was finally able to get home, Laurie began to sob and shake and could not stop. In the background, the television was on. The estimates of the number of people reported killed continued to rise. Laurie could have been one of them.

For the next few days, Laurie refused to leave the apartment. Sam stayed home with her, fielding telephone calls from worried friends and relatives. Laurie couldn't eat or sleep; she complained of constant nightmares that were a reliving of the scene when she emerged from the subway. During the day, she cried for no reason. Sam didn't know how to help. He couldn't tell her "everything will be alright." Forty of Laurie's coworkers had been killed.

Sam was reading the newspaper when he came across a notice that employees of the financial management company where Laurie worked should call a hotline number to report in. The company had, in fact, set up an emergency crisis intervention service for employees. Sam placed a call. A social worker, Eleanor, answered the phone, and Sam, in response to her queries, provided information about the symptoms Laurie was exhibiting.

Eleanor asked Sam if Laurie would be willing to get on the phone. With some coaxing, Laurie agreed. Eleanor explained who she was and why her employer had established this service. Eleanor asked Laurie some open-ended questions—encouraging her to talk about her feelings. The phone conversation lasted for over an hour. Laurie talked, listened, and cried. Eleanor reassured her that her feelings were perfectly normal but that help was available. By the end of the conversation, Laurie and Eleanor had an agreement. Laurie would make an appointment with her internist for the following day. Eleanor also said she would give Sam the names of some mental health experts in the community who could help Laurie deal with her feelings.

Prior to terminating the telephone conversation, Eleanor asked Laurie to put Sam back on the line. She discussed with Sam the agreement reached and provided him with a list of mental health agencies as well as two social workers in private practice who were experienced in dealing with trauma and its aftermath. She also made some concrete suggestions—that he and Laurie go out for walks, visit with relatives and other friends, and schedule activities that Laurie finds relaxing and soothing. Eleanor also suggested that Sam be on the lookout for and avert Laurie's use of alcohol or any prescribed drugs that may be in the house.

The problems and symptoms Laurie exhibits are normal reactions to abnormal events (O'Neill, 2001e). Some people may experience only relatively short-lived problems—intense worries and bad memories, for example—that diminish with counseling, emotional support, and time. Others may experience what can be long-term and debilitating problems including depression, anxiety, hopelessness, stress disorders, and even suicidal thoughts. Anniversaries of the event also can trigger symptoms and related problems in functioning (DHHS, 2001).

The company for which Laurie works had the foresight to arrange for crisis intervention services for its employees. This step was taken immediately after 9/11 in recognition of the fact that few disaster survivors seek mental health assistance. Outreach is necessary (O'Neill, 2001e). In addition to the hotline telephone number, the company advertised over radio and television, and mental health personnel were provided with lists of employees, who were contacted directly.

The details provided by Sam and Laurie enabled Eleanor, the social worker, to identify that the symptoms were all consistent with trauma. Although many of these symptoms will abate with time, there is no guarantee that this will happen; and immediate intervention, in Eleanor's assessment, was needed. The physical manifestations of trauma—loss of appetite and sleep, for example—suggested that short-term medication might be helpful. The internist could provide a workup and, if the physician thought Laurie needed medication beyond sleeping aids or mild tranquilizers, Laurie might be referred to a psychiatrist. A referral was also in order to a mental health specialist, preferably one who utilizes cognitive—sbehavioral therapy treatment (Vedantam, 2002).

During their hour-long conversation, Eleanor was able to provide some hope that the pain Laurie was feeling would subside with time and that help was available to her. Eleanor also encouraged Laurie to take care of herself and, in a follow-up discussion with Sam, Eleanor emphasized the need for nurturing. The pieces were now in place for Laurie to receive the physical and psychological support she needed.

The functions performed by Eleanor included a rapid assessment and a preliminary diagnosis of posttraumatic stress disorder. Eleanor provided immediate intervention on the telephone. She listened and provided support. She provided information about PTSD and some concrete, as well as emotional, help. She then provided a referral and enlisted the help of Laurie's husband to ensure that Laurie would seek and receive the kind of treatment she needed. Telephone counseling of this nature is time limited and crisis oriented. It involves the need to rapidly assess and respond to the precipitating crisis. In the days after September 11, a great many such calls for help were made.

Professional Burnout

Among those who have been affected by the terrorist attacks on September 11 are the relief workers. They may find it hard to let go and rebuild their own lives. Rescue workers may face special emotional challenges. Usually they spend most of their time rescuing people who are alive; much of their professional identity is based on this fact. For them, this experience in which they have had to recover many dead victims may seem to be a personal failure (DHHS, 2001).

As the above examples show, social workers responded in the immediate aftermath of the attacks on the World Trade Center and the Pentagon with grief counseling and crisis intervention. They carried out these functions in work sites, hospitals, community mental health centers, schools, and as part of the many Red Cross and Salvation Army emergency assistance teams (NASW, 2001b). The work of social workers—in volunteer as well as staff roles—was emotionally demanding even for those who had extensive experience counseling trauma clients. Volunteers worked eight- to 12-hour shifts with little relief from constant grief, pain, and anguish.

At the Northside Center for Child Development in upper Manhattan, the initial response of administrators was to assess the impact of 9/11 on their staff and to identify ways in which the agency could be supportive of them. Staff expressed the desire to meet on an individual or group basis to talk about their feelings and experiences and to exchange information about coping strategies upon which they could draw. Daily opportunities for formal and informal sharing were organized and refreshments provided (Bryant, 2002). In addition, the agency provided training about the effects of trauma on adults and children and treatment strategies. Staff were also encouraged to participate in training offered by the Federal Emergency and Management Agency. Staff also sought opportunities to contribute to the community directly affected by the attack. Administrators encouraged staff to volunteer at the Family Assistance Center set up by the city to address the concrete and psychosocial needs of people affected (Bryant, 2002). These responses were oriented to both the needs of staff and the needs of the constituencies served by the agency and community. The responses related to the social work functions of advocacy and enabling, support and assistance, and program and staff development.

It is important for social workers working with those affected by the events to stay engaged with others, including work associates and social work colleagues, and to use these support networks, as well as family and friends (Miller, 2001; NASW, 2002). Such supports provide the nurturing, perspective, and emotional support needed to enable social workers to continue their important work.

Legitimizing Mental Health Services
The terrorist attack unified the United States in many important ways, including a shared sense of anger and grief and a resolve for the future. It also legitimized mental health services in an unprecedented manner.

On September 13, 2001, the U.S. Department of Health and Human Services issued a press release: "HHS Initiates Immediate and Long-Term Steps to Address Emotional and Mental Health Consequences of Terrorist Air Attacks." Excerpts from the press release follow:

HHS Secretary Tommy G. Thompson today announced steps the department is taking to respond to the immediate and long-term emotional and psychological impact of the loss of life and damage caused by terrorists in New York, Washington, D.C., Pennsylvania and throughout the nation. The Secretary, in New York today to tour health and emergency facilities, acted in response to concerns about mental health consequences expressed by local and state officials.

These devastating aerial attacks have shocked the nation into the realization that acts of massive, random, criminal violence cannot be relegated to some place "over there," the Secretary declared.

The emotional and psychological wounds from the human-caused tragedies of September 11 will be deeper and take much longer to heal than those from events of similar scope caused by natural forces.

"Because the size and scope of this attack and the potential for serious traumatization is unprecedented in this country, the HHS commitment is long-term," Secretary Thompson said. The need for crisis mental health services will extend into the foreseeable future. "Crisis counseling is all the more critical today," the Secretary said. "The fact that this was a human-caused disaster, not a natural one, affects the emotional healing of survivors. The fact that the targets were among the nation's landmarks, the perpetrators international terrorists, deeply affects every American. Everyone of every age may have unanticipated feelings and reactions over the coming days, weeks, months and even years.

The more devastating and terrifying the trauma is, the more vulnerable individuals are to develop emotional or psychological symptoms. The lack of warning, extent of injuries and death, exposure to horrifying events, and possibility of recurrence—all hallmarks of the events of Tuesday September 11 and the days to follow—make the likelihood of emotional repercussions all the more challenging for adults and, particularly, for children.

Social workers face the challenge of adapting their skills to help themselves, the public, and clients cope with the changed world (O'Neill, 2002a). Social workers in mental health are helping clients deal with their reactions and fears using cognitive techniques. Such techniques include relaxation exercises and biofeedback. They are also using their skills to rally support by helping individuals, families, and groups extend and use their personal and community networks (O'Neill, 2002a). Further, an important component of the social work response is the identification of people at increased risk for emotional problems because of their proximity to the terrorist attacks (Clark, 2002). Children who lost a parent on September 11 are one at-risk group. The death of a parent is always devastating for a child, but in this instance the cause

of the loss is on constant public display (Levine & Ly, 2002).

Suzanne Adelman, a social worker and crisis program coordinator for the Jewish Social Services Agency of Metropolitan DC, commented that "if people can learn the facts about the actual scale of the threat, they may be able to diminish their fears, especially if they learn that the chances of something happening to them and their loved ones is small" (as cited in O'Neill, 2002a, p. 3). The fears of some clients are helped by limiting their exposure to news accounts, adhering to their usual schedule and routine, and diverting their attention to something that gives them pleasure—such as movies or television, exercise, and get-togethers with friends.

MILITARY SOCIAL WORK

Social workers work in the military in two capacities—as members of the armed services or as civilians.

A CASUALTY OF WAR

It was a scene reminiscent of many movies Brenda had seen. The doorbell rang and there stood a priest accompanied by two soldiers in dress uniform. They had come to tell her that her husband Bruce had been killed in a helicopter accident in Iraq. Brenda watched the news constantly. She knew that her husband, a pilot, was flying search missions over Bagdad. Earlier that day, tuned in as always to CNN, Brenda had learned that an Army helicopter had been lost. She had a feeling, but heard nothing until the visitors arrived at her door. She knew before they said a word. Bruce was dead.

The next few days went by in a blur. The army, of course, took care of transporting the body back home. Family and friends arrived and helped to plan the funeral. Brenda did not have much time to think, as her first concern was with the reactions of her two young children to the news of their father's death. She felt numb—as if she were just walking through the motions of what needed to get done.

A few days after the funeral, Brenda received a telephone call from a military social worker who asked if he could stop by to see her. He explained that he was available to assist the family in whatever way needed. Although wary, she agreed to have Lt. Wilson, the social worker, visit the following day.

Lt. Wilson arrived as scheduled. He had to coax Brenda to talk. She said she didn't want to talk about Bruce—it was too difficult for her. She just wanted to wake up from this nightmare and find that it had not happened—that Bruce would be coming home. Lt. Wilson indicated that Brenda could talk about whatever she wanted—perhaps she might tell him about how she was getting along— was she sleeping, eating? Lt. Wilson wanted to get an idea of Brenda's physical state and how she was handling her grief. It was already apparent that the emotions were being internalized and that she was purposely trying to deny the reality.

Brenda admitted to having no appetite and to not sleeping well. Lt. Wilson suggested she contact her personal physician and see if he might be able to prescribe something that would help her sleep. Lt. Wilson indicated that it was important that she get rest and take care of herself—the children needed her now more than ever. Lt. Wilson also tried to access Brenda's support network and determine whether family and friends were available for her, perhaps even to come and stay for a period of time. Brenda indicated that her mother had offered to stay, but that she had refused. Lt. Wilson softly suggested that Brenda might want to reconsider this offer—even if only for a few days.

Lt. Wilson knew that it was not yet time to begin to address the many practical issues and questions that lay ahead for Brenda and her children. But he did want to begin to establish a relationship so that, in the future weeks, he could provide more services to Brenda. However, he did tell her during this first visit about the Tragedy Assistance Program for Survivors, Inc. (TAPS), a national nonprofit military survivor peer support network, which offers grief counseling referral, case worker assistance, and crisis information to help families and military per-

sonnel cope and recover. He provided her with the telephone number (1-800-959-TAPS).

In the future, Lt. Wilson plans to help Brenda identify some of the concrete details to which she will need to attend—applying for survivor's benefits, dealing with insurance, and so forth. He knows that she will eventually need to think about where she wants to live. The military housing she currently occupies will only be available to her for a few more months. But first things first— Brenda needs to deal with her grief and that of her children.

Lt. Wilson has been through this scenario with many other families. He knows the devastation that these families experienced. He has learned to take it slow—to "start where the client is" and to offer services as the family is able to accept them. His initial role is to provide support. He makes himself available to Brenda in whatever capacity she needs during these initial days. He knows that the concrete planning will take time and a level of readiness, and he does not push.

David L. Kennedy is one military social worker who has achieved the rank of captain in the U.S. navy and is believed to be the first social worker to attain that rank ("Social Work in the Public Eye," 1998). Kennedy was first commissioned in 1980 as a social work officer in the U.S. Navy Bureau of Medicine and Surgery. During his military career, he has also served as manager of the U.S. Navy Medical Department Family Advocacy Program and as head of the social work department at the National Naval Medical Center in Bethesda, MD. He was also deployed with a navy hospital ship during the Gulf War.

Some social workers who are members of the U.S. armed services seek to educate the public about America's role abroad. Chief warrant officer and military social worker Joseph Murphy talked to fourth grade students at a school in Rye, New York, about the significance of Veterans Day and the War on Terrorism. A former member of the Rye school board, Murphy served in both the navy and marine corps and was responsible for establishing the Junior Reserve Officer Training Program at Rye High School. Many of the young people in this program went into the service and earned college scholarships ("Social Work in the Public Eye," 2002b).

The U.S. armed forces have employed active-duty, professional social workers for more than 50 years. Social workers serve in every branch of the military as commissioned officers and as civilian employees (Garber & McNelis, 1995). In the military arena, social workers are called upon to provide intervention in diverse areas such as military family policy, child welfare, health care, substance abuse, mental health, hostage repatriation, and humanitarian relief. Most of the people served by military social workers are active-duty personnel and their families, veterans and their eligible family members, or civilian populations who are eligible for special military assistance (Garber & McNelis, 1995).

In providing this wide range of services, social workers in the military practice on both micro and macro levels. Micro interventions include direct services counseling, advice, assistance, and referral in cases such as child neglect or substance abuse. However, macro skills are also developed as a result of military training in leadership, administration, and management (Garber & McNelis, 1995). Military social workers may find themselves using their macro skills to develop special programs such as child care for active-duty members or providing input in regard to U.S. Department of Defense policy for families of the military reserve.

Although social work in the military setting can be a richly rewarding experience, there are some drawbacks. A typical military career usually includes multiple assignments that are often decided by organizational need rather than by personal or professional choice. Although civilian social workers serving military families are generally less mobile than those who are on active duty, some flexibility regarding work location and special assignments is usually needed. Such tours of duty, particularly for social work

military officers, may entail work in isolated areas or overseas. In addition to logistics of assignments, social workers in the military system must also deal with the often overwhelming influence of the larger command on individual service members and their families (Garber & McNelis, 1995).

In addition to actual employment with the military, social workers may serve this population through a limited number of private organizations. For example, the American Red Cross includes within its mission to serve the men and women of the armed forces and their families. The goals of the Armed Forces Emergency Services Division of the American Red Cross are to provide members of the U.S. military and their families with timely and reliable emergency communications and case management services, 24 hours a day, worldwide. Specifically, the Red Cross has developed an emergency communications division that is equipped with the highest technology and a 24-hour staff in order to provide emergency messages to American military personnel stationed at installations around the world and on ships at sea (American Red Cross, 1995).

The Red Cross also provides casework services such as financial assistance for emergency travel when a family member needs to go to the bedside of a seriously ill serviceman or servicewoman. Also, the Red Cross provides members of the U.S. military and their families with timely and reliable information and referral services when Red Cross services do not address their specific needs (American Red Cross, 1995). The Red Cross also employs social workers in the role of caseworkers and program directors. For example, a social worker may be in charge of a chapter's emergency services division that includes services to the armed forces. In this role, the social worker would carry out the functions of organizing, exchange with other community services agencies, administration, program development and evaluation, and supervision.

THE FUTURE

Mental health practice in the future will be substantially impacted by the nature of potential health care reform legislation. Although initial reform initiatives failed in the mid-1990s during the Clinton administration, the debate about reform continues, with particular attention to prescription drug costs and the over 43 million Americans who are uninsured. The key question emerging in this debate for social workers is whether and to what extent mental health will be part of the package and whether social workers will be recognized as care providers. NASW has taken an active role in arguing for health care reform that includes mental health and substance abuse benefits and recognizes social workers as qualified (and reimbursable) providers of these services. The profession of social work maintains its commitment to provide quality mental health services to all individuals without regard to race, color, religion, national origin, gender, age, sexual orientation, or disability (Mental Health Bill of Rights Project, 2002). In collaboration with nine participating national groups, including the American Counseling Association, American Nurses Association, and four supporting national groups, NASW has issued a Mental Health Bill of Rights. The document focuses primarily on consumers of services, but, in detailing the rights of consumers, incorporates expectations about professional performance, ethical conduct, and the scope of service provision. Highlights of this bill of rights include:

- *Benefits.* Individuals have the right to be provided information about the nature and extent of their mental health and substance abuse treatment benefits, including details on procedures to obtain access to services, on utilization management procedures, and on appeal rights.
- *Professional expertise.* Individuals have the right to receive full information from the potential treating professional about

that professional's knowledge, skills, preparation, experience, and credentials. Individuals have the right to be informed about the options available for treatment interventions and the effectiveness of the recommended treatment.

- *Contractual limitations.* Individuals have the right to be informed by the treating professional of any arrangements, restrictions, or covenants established between third-party payers and the treating professional that could interfere with or influence treatment recommendations. Individuals have the right to be informed of the nature of information that may be disclosed for the purpose of paying benefits.
- *Appeals and grievances.* Individuals have the right to receive information about the methods they can use to submit complaints or grievances regarding provision of care by the treating professional to that profession's regulatory board and to the professional association and the right to be provided information about the procedures they can use to appeal benefit utilization decisions to the third-party payer systems, to the employer or purchasing entity, and to external regulatory entities.
- *Confidentiality.* Individuals have the right to be guaranteed the protection of the confidentiality of their relationship with their mental health and substance abuse professional, except when laws or ethics dictate otherwise.
- *Choice.* Individuals have the right to choose any duly licensed and certified professional for mental health services. Individuals have the right to receive full information regarding the education and training of professionals, treatment options (including risks and benefits), and cost implications to make an informed choice regarding the selection of care deemed appropriate by the individual and professional.

- ***Determination of treatment.*** Recommendations regarding mental health and substance abuse treatment shall be made only by a duly licensed and certified professional in conjunction with the individual and his or her family as appropriate. Treatment decisions should not be made by third-party payers. The individual has the right to make final decisions regarding treatment.
- ***Parity.*** Individuals have the right to receive benefits for mental health treatment on the same basis as they do for any other illness, with the same provisions, copayments, lifetime benefits, and catastrophic coverage in both insurance and self-funded–self-insured health plans.
- ***Discrimination.*** Individuals who use mental health and substance abuse benefits shall not be penalized when seeking other health insurance or disability, life, or any other insurance benefit.
- ***Benefit usage.*** The individual is entitled to the entire scope of the benefits within the benefit plan that will address his or her clinical needs.
- ***Benefit design.*** Whenever both federal and state law or regulations are applicable, the professional and all payers shall use whichever affords the individual the greatest level of protection and access.
- ***Treatment review.*** Individuals have the right to be guaranteed that any review of their mental health and substance abuse treatment shall involve a professional having the training, credentials, and licensure required to provide the treatment in the jurisdiction in which it will be provided.
- ***Accountability.*** Treating professionals may be held accountable and liable to individuals for any injury caused by gross incompetence or negligence on the part of the professional. The treating professional has the obligation to advocate for and document necessity of care and to advise the individual of options if payment authorization is denied. Payers and other third parties may be held accountable and liable to individuals for any injury caused by gross incompetence or negligence or by their clinically unjustified decisions.

Important issues confront our nation and our profession in the evolution of a managed health care system, including access to quality care and the availability of mental health services. Rationing of certain types of expensive, specialized care is already occurring, and the demands for controls on health care expenses, including mental health, will continue to dominate the provision of services. But it is not just a self-serving matter of reimbursement rates for social work services or length of allowable treatment by insurance companies. The heart of the health care debate concerns the escalation of costs of maintaining a system that has failed many Americans who receive no care, inadequate care, or inappropriate care. Social work advocacy is a vital component of the social work role in mental health to increase access to and affordability of mental health care.

President Bush, in the second year of his administration, issued an executive order establishing a New Freedom Commission on Mental Health as a component of a newly announced mental health initiative. Among its charges, the commission will conduct a comprehensive study of the mental health services delivery system and identify innovative mental health treatments, services, and technologies that have demonstrated effectiveness and can be replicated in other settings. The initiative also includes support for pending legislation to increase access under insurance plans to mental health treatment on a par with physical treatment. This initiative, in fact, is an update of the Mental Health Parity Act of 1996, which expired in 2001. No new mental health grant programs are on the horizon ("Briefing," 2002).

CAREER OPPORTUNITIES

The job listings that follow represent a range of employment opportunities for social workers in the services area of mental health. The purpose is to illustrate the types of responsibilities social workers maintain in mental health and the qualifications employers in the current market seek from applicants. Although they are based on actual classified advertisements in the *NASW News*, these do not represent current job listings. For this reason, details about the actual location of the job may be absent, as well as application procedures.

Program Manager (Crisis Intervention Unit, Mental Health Specialist 5)

Douglas County Mental Health Division is seeking a program manager for its crisis and evaluation unit, supervising 12 professional staff. This challenging, fast-paced position also includes front-line clinical duties of intake assessment, psychological evaluations, after-hours crisis coverage, child custody evaluations, medication management services, crisis intervention and counseling, crisis case management, medication monitoring, and protective services intervention. The ideal candidate will possess demonstrated competence in the team management approach, community mental health and managed care management, and quality monitoring. Qualifications include a master's degree in psychology, social work, or related field and five years postmaster's experience in a community mental health setting, which includes two years supervisory or program management experience or satisfactory equivalent combination of experience and training. Oregon professional licensure preferred. A preference may be given for prior experience managing mental health crisis services. (*NASW News*, November 2000, p. 24)

Clinical Social Work Director

Experienced and talented social work clinician with leadership skills sought to direct 18-person department. Southwestern Virginia Mental Health Institute, located in the beautiful mountains of southwest Virginia, is a 176-bed certified and accredited, full-service psychiatric facility. Strongly prefer LCSW with treatment and rehabilitation experience with seriously mentally ill inpatients and demonstrated ability to supervise social workers and lead a dynamic social work department. (*NASW News*, January 2002, p. 24)

Director of Clinical Services

Located in Portland, ME, on beautiful Casco Bay, two hours north of Boston and one hour east of the White Mountains of New Hampshire, Community Counseling Center has an immediate opening for a director of clinical services. The clinical director is responsible for all agency clinical practices, supervision of program directors and senior supervisors, coordination of program services with community resources, development of agency Child Quest International program, and assistance in program development. The successful candidate will have a master's degree in social work and LCSW; will be computer literate; will possess strong verbal and written communication skills; and 10 years of clinical experience, including five years of successful supervisory experience. Previous experience as a director of clinical services is preferred. (*NASW News*, February 1999, p. 20)

Licensed Clinical Social Worker

One of the largest and most well-established private practice groups in the greater Memphis area is searching for a full-time, Tennessee-licensed clinical social worker for immediate hire. Looking for a well-trained individual who is highly motivated, flexible, and works well within a group practice, with two-year postdegree experience and interest in working with individuals, couples, and families. We offer a competitive compensation package and provide a great opportunity to develop as a practitioner within a group of highly respected psychologists and LCSWs in the Memphis area. (*NASW News*, March 2002, p. 24)

Employee Assistance Program Manager

Motorola, Ltd., currently has a challenging position available in Sendai, Japan. We are seeking multicultural candidates who are fluent in both Japanese and English and possess the ability to interact with individuals at all levels. The EAP manager will provide assessment, referral, and follow-up for employees. These services will be provided for both self-referrals and management referrals. Ability to coordinate with human resources and benefits department is a necessity. The EAP manager will provide training for management and employees on the use of EAPs, alcohol and drug awareness, and the psychological aspects of business change. The EAP manager will provide consultation to management regarding individual employee problems as well as organizational assessments and interventions. Requirements include master's degree in behavioral science with licensing and certification as required by profession, law, or geographical location of practice. LCSW is preferred. Clinical knowledge and skills in EAP, mental health, chemical dependency, and crisis intervention preferred. Ten years EAP or clinical experience in mental health and chemical dependency; prior experience with case management; knowledge and understanding of confidentiality laws and regulations; crisis intervention experience; ability to present training and educational materials and to operate independently within a professional framework, but also to participate as a team member in a matrix-management system; and strong administrative and organizational skills are preferred. Computer experience and knowledge is desired. We provide competitive compensation and complete benefits. (*NASW News*, October 2000, p. 16)

Chief Executive Officer

Kings View Mental Health System (KVMHS), a Mennonite-sponsored not-for-profit organization, seeks a visionary chief executive officer with strong financial acumen to lead its multisite organization in central California. KVMHS provides a broad range of outpatient behavioral health services, social services, and residential services for adolescents from 20 locations in a 10-county area. Minimum candidate requirements are active Christian individual involved in local congregation, appreciate Mennonite–Ana-Baptist heritage, master's level education, eight years of senior management experience, and strong interpersonal skills. Preferred candidate will have extensive health care and multisite management experience. (*NASW News*, January 2000, p. 18)

Psychiatric Social Workers

Advance your career with the Los Angeles County Department of Mental Health, a diverse and dynamic mental health system dedicated to making our community better by providing world-class mental health care. Psychiatric social workers are invited to apply for positions in adult and child outpatient programs, children's residential and detention facilities, and mental health services at the Twin Towers Correctional Facility. Minimum requirements for unlicensed social workers: master's degree in social work, registration within 30 days of appointment with the state board; licensed social workers: master's degree in social work, LCSW license from the California Board of Behavioral Examiners, two years of social work experience in a social services agency, clinic, hospital, or day treatment center, with one year of specific mental health experience. (*NASW News*, January 2002, p. 16)

Psychiatric Social Workers

Altascadero State Hospital, a nationally known accredited forensic mental health hospital, is accepting psychiatric social worker applications. Qualified individuals are encouraged to apply for several new positions resulting from the opening of a 258-bed hospital expansion. Salary range: $3,487 to $3,942 per month plus monthly recruitment and retention bonus ($600 a month for licensed, $400 a month for unlicensed). Benefits package valued at additional

30 percent. MSW required. If not California state licensed, supervision available. Social workers are an integral part of interdisciplinary teams. Duties include assessments, social histories, groups, and working with community agencies. On-site child care available. (*NASW News*, February 2002, p. 14)

Mental Health Adult and Family Therapist

Regional medical center in northwest Wisconsin has an opening for a master's level mental health clinician working as an adult–family therapist in an outpatient setting. Our behavioral health center is certified for inpatient, outpatient, and day treatment services for both mental health and substance abuse. Candidates must have a Wisconsin license and be eligible for third-party reimbursement (requires 3,000 hours of postgraduate supervision). Previous outpatient mental health experience working with adults, adolescents, and families is also required. Benefits include relocation assistance, continuing education, health insurance, and so forth. (*NASW News*, March 2002, p. 23)

Vietnamese-Speaking Clinician

Part-time master's level clinician sought to provide clinical services, psychoeducation, and outreach to the Vietnamese community Cross-Cultural Counseling Center. Requirements include master's degree or doctorate in psychology, social work, or related field; licensure or certification; fluent in English and Vietnamese. One day a week to start. Some evening hours are possible. Salary is commensurate with experience. (*NASW News*, October 2000, p. 21)

Social Workers

Social workers are needed for Advice Hotline, the Feel Good Phone Call, a national call-in service. Work from home; set your own hours (both part-time and full-time positions available). BSWs, MSWs, and social work interns with training or experience in human relations needed. We are an exciting new company that provides advice about a variety of personal problems troubling our diverse American public. We are seeking candidates who possess strong interpersonal skills, including warmth and the ability to engage others, sensitivity to people and their problems, good listening skills, a pleasant telephone voice, and comfort working with various client populations on the telephone. A solution-focused orientation is essential, that is, the ability to ask appropriate questions, synthesize and conceptualize succinctly, and intervene quickly while encouraging sustained client contact. Candidate must possess a dedicated telephone and computer (Internet connection preferred) and be able to receive calls in a quiet setting without interruptions. Candidate can work extremely flexible hours from home. Telephone service provides 24-hour service, which allows logging in based on candidate's schedule. We offer competitive compensation and part-time flexibility. Current liability insurance a plus. Company will assist candidate in obtaining liability insurance if needed. (*NASW News*, May 2002, p. 19)

Executive Director

Samaritan Counseling Center of Greater Sacramento, providing counseling that integrates mind, body, and spirit, seeks an executive director who can take it to the next level of growth. Applicants should be experienced in pastoral counseling, therapy, or clinical social work, possess the relevant California license, and present superior aptitude for all facets of executive leadership and administration, including financial planning and oversight; staff recruitment and training; policy development and implementation regarding both clinical services and office management; relationship building with clergy, congregations, and other referral sources; and collaboration with the board of directors. An affiliate of the Samaritan Institute, the center was founded in 1994 by two local congregations (Presbyterian and Episcopalian). Continuing referrals from these congregations and high client satisfaction provide the foundation for expanded services. (*NASW News*, November 2001, p. 17)

Fee for Service

Nonprofit therapy center looking for therapists experienced in working with lesbian issues. We also serve the lesbian, gay, bisexual, and transgender community. Minimum two years postgraduate supervised clinical experience; malpractice insurance required. Free supervision provided. Volunteer supervisory positions also available. (*NASW News*, May 2002, p. 16)

Crisis Response Mental Health Professional

Crisis response professional needed to provide mobile crisis interventions, clinical assessments, and stabilization services to adults, children, and families. Join our quality culture and work in picturesque rural waterfront community between Olympic National Park and the Strait of Juan de Fuca. Requires registered nurse or master's degree in behavioral sciences, nursing sciences, or related field, and two years subsequent treatment of mentally ill or emotionally disturbed people. Competitive salary and benefits, with opportunities for additional "on call" compensation. (*NASW News*, November 2001, p. 24)

Executive Director

Unique community-based system of care for emotionally disturbed children and adolescents in Utica, NY, seeks chief executive officer. Responsibilities include program and staff development and supervision. Excellent verbal and written skills required. Ability to interact with community stakeholders and develop creative programming to address community needs. Master's degree, related supervisory and administrative experience are necessary. (*NASW News*, July 2001, p. 18)

Licensed Clinical Social Workers

LCSWs sought in the following cities for federal EAP law enforcement contracts: Altanta, Boston,

Chicago, Denver, Hartford, Houston, Miami, New York, San Diego, San Francisco, San Juan, Seattle, St. Louis. Must have minimum five years experience with law enforcement personnel in areas of clinical treatment (including families), trauma response, and management consultation. Experience with delivery of training to law enforcement personnel is especially desirable. (*NASW News*, September 2000, p. 18)

Clinical Social Worker

New Directions, a comprehensive rehabilitation program for homeless veterans, is seeking part-time and full-time marriage and family therapist and MSW or LCSW interested in working with chemically dependent and dually diagnosed veterans. (*NASW News*, January 2002, p. 18)

Chief, Mental Health Services

Lexington, KY, Veterans Affairs Medical Center is seeking a chief for mental health services. The VA facility is a complex two division medical facility affiliated with the University of Kentucky. The mental health service offers a wide variety of programs including a 19-bed acute care inpatient unit and outpatient mental hygiene services including posttraumatic stress disorder and substance abuse treatment clinics. Applicants must meet qualification standards, licensing requirements, be U.S. citizens with proven administrative, clinical, and academic skills. Candidates must be eligible for academic appointment with the University of Kentucky College of Medicine. (*NASW News*, June 2001, p. 18)

EAP Counselor

Marshfield Clinic, a 600-physician, 4,300+ employee multispecialty clinic, has a full-time EAP counselor opportunity available. This position is primarily located in Marshfield, WI, but will also include outreach to other regions on a regular basis. Responsibilities are to provide confidential assessment, short-term counseling, and referral services to employees and families, accomplished through individual consultation, conflict resolution, training, and outreach. Master's degree in social work or counseling and guidance from an accredited program. State certification or certified employee assistance professional and a current (valid) Wisconsin driver's license required. Minimum of five years experience in clinical work with varied populations. EAP experience preferred. (*NASW News*, September 2000, p. 25)

Behavioral Health

Nationally recognized community mental health center located in Milwaukee, WI, has immediate openings for bilingual (Spanish–English) psychotherapists. One full-time and one part-time position available. Duties include promoting healthy personal and family relationships through education, exploration of relationship dynamics, and therapeutic interventions. Qualifications include 3,000 hours postmaster's degree for third-party billing, Wisconsin state license or eligibility, minimum of two years experience working with children, adults, and families with a wide range of behavioral health issues as well as the ability to relate well to people from diverse ethnic and cultural backgrounds. (*NASW News*, June 2001, p. 20)

Military

Full-time positions working with victims of child and spouse abuse at U.S. Army Health Center, Ft. Bragg, NC (Fayetteville). Use your clinical skills with the U.S. Army Family Advocacy Program to provide assessment, crisis, case management, and group services. Essential requirements: MSW, two years postdegree with two years recent experience working with this population; LCSW (any state) and CPR certification. (*NASW News*, March 2001, p. 17)

Social Worker

The Southwest Guidance Center, a licensed, nonprofit community mental health center, is seeking a social worker, licensed or licensable in the State of Kansas, to engage in individual,

marital, group, and family therapy in an outpatient mental health setting. Bilingual–bicultural Hispanic background preferred, but not necessary. Knowledge and experience in the area of sexual abuse treatment and prevention are preferred. Salary for this position will be commensurate with the clinician's experience. (*NASW News*, March 2001, p. 16)

Director of Clinical Services

Cunningham Children's Home, a recognized leader in child welfare for over 100 years, serves a diverse population of behavioral and emotional disordered children and adolescents. Our 32-acre campus is located in Urbana, IL, home of the University of Illinois and one of the midwest's most vibrant university communities. Immediate opening for director of clinical services. Responsibilities include providing clinical direction to the therapeutic treatment of agency residents; provide clinical consultation to director and coordinator level staff; work closely with the director of residential services, intake–admissions coordinator, and director of education, as well as the assistant directors in residential services. Minimum requirements are as follows: a master's or doctoral degree in the human services from an accredited university or college. A current license as a licensed clinical professional counselor, licensed clinical social worker, or a licensed clinical psychologist. Applicants must have at least five years of direct clinical work with children and adolescents. At least five years of experience in human services (preferably residential treatment) with three years of supervisory and administrative duties. Highly competitive salary and benefits package. Salary commensurate with education and experience. (*NASW News*, February 2002, p. 15)

Executive Director

Jackson Hole Community Counseling Center, a small mental health center serving Teton County, WY, is seeking an executive director. Necessary qualifications are master's or doctoral degree in a mental health profession; licensure for independent practice in Wyoming at the time of taking the position; at least three years of demonstrated, postdegree experience in the direct provision of mental health treatment services in a mental health setting; and at least two years of demonstrated relevant experience in mental health management or administration. Documented interest and skill in financial and business management; fundraising; grant writing and program development; overseeing clinical operations and developing clinical teams; networking and building alliances with other human services provider organizations; and strong commitment to ethical standards in the delivery of mental health services. (*NASW News*, March 2001, p. 20)

Clinical Social Worker

Full-time position for MSW with two years supervised postmaster's clinical experience. Licensed by current state required. Full-time private practice, $30,000 to $35,000 plus benefits. Practice located on Maryland's Eastern Shore of the Chesapeake Bay. Clinical opportunities include work with children, families, women, men, and groups. Multidisciplinary team approach consisting of psychologists, psychiatrist, and social workers using predominantly cognitive approach to therapeutic intervention. Highly motivated population. (*NASW News*, March 2001, p. 16)

Clinical Social Worker

Psychotherapy Associates, a Lincoln, NE, private practice, is actively recruiting a license-eligible clinical social worker to provide outpatient psychotherapy to survivors of acute and chronic trauma. Preference given to candidates with training and experience in treatment of complicated PTSD, dissociative disorders, borderline personality disorders. Compensation options, including associate and salaried status, dependent upon individual qualifications. (*NASW News*, March 1999, p. 21)

Emergency Services Provider

Immediate opening for full-time evening emergency services provider. Responsibilities include evaluation and disposition of emergency cases at a rural community mental health center. Master's degree in social work, psychology, or counseling with outpatient emergency services preferred. (*NASW News*, March 2000, p. 15)

Licensed Clinical Social Workers

All Care Consultants, Inc., in conjunction with Etherapy.com currently have wonderful opportunities for licensed social workers to provide therapeutic services on the Internet. This concept, although not new, has been taken to the next technological level by Etherapy.com. Etherapy.com is creating a Web site that far surpasses any of the current online therapy sites. One thing that makes Etherapy unique is that it offers the social worker, at NO COST, the opportunity to build an online virtual practice. Therapists can choose their own hours, make their own fee schedules, and even see their clients offline without any fees or penalties. All Care is a staffing and placement firm specializing in mental health services. We are owned and operated by social workers, so we understand your professional needs. (*NASW News*, April 2000, p. 14)

Telephone Therapists

All states. My Therapy Network LLC seeks additional certified, insured, practicing therapists for its national intrastate network. There is no cost to apply. (*NASW News*, March 2001, p. 14)

Kaiser Permanente Seeking
Adult IOP Case Manager

Working collaboratively, this adept communicator will provide diagnosis, treatment, and crisis intervention for members with acute or chronic psychiatric disorders. You will develop treatment programs, provide outpatient psychotherapy, chart treatment and progress, and make referrals to community services and resources. Must be a

California-licensed clinical social worker with an MSW and at least two years of experience in the use of psychosocial assessment and psychotherapeutic methods. Thorough knowledge of state regulations and professional board standards is vital. On-call rotation required.

Patient Evaluation Coordinator

For this position, you will perform DSM-IV diagnoses of a wide range of adult patients, as well as provide crisis management, hospital consultation, and short-term psychotherapy. Must be a California-licensed clinical psychologist, social worker, or marriage and family therapist with a PhD in clinical psychology or a master's degree in counseling psychology. Background should include exposure to a wide range of psychosocial problems. Familiarity with psychopharmacological interventions is a strong plus, as are bilingual (English–Spanish) skills.

Adult Mental Health Professional Therapist

Performing DSM-IV diagnosis of adult patients, this patient-focused professional will provide crisis management and intervention, emergency room and hospital consultation, and short-term psychotherapy. Must be licensed clinical psychologist, clinical social worker, or marriage and family therapist with a PhD or doctorate in psychology (clinical) or master of science or master of arts degree in counseling psychology or social work. Required experience must include psychological testing, brief psychotherapy, and psychopharmacological interventions. Thorough knowledge of cognitive behavioral therapy is vital. (*NASW News*, July 2002, p. 12)

REFERENCES

Akabas, S. H. (1995). Occupational social work. In R. L. Edwards (Ed.-in-Chief), *Encyclopedia of social work* (19th ed., Vol. 2, pp. 1779–1786). Washington, DC: NASW Press.

American Psychiatric Association. (1997). Practice guidelines for the treatment of patients with schizophrenia. *American Journal of Psychiatry, 154* (Suppl.), 1–63.

American Red Cross. (1995). *Armed forces emergency services handbook*. Washington, DC: Author.

Austin, C. D. (1993). Case management: A systems perspective. Families in Society: *Journal of Contemporary Human Services, 74*, 451–459.

Barker, R. L. (1992). *Social work in private practice* (2nd ed.). Washington, DC: NASW Press.

Barker, R. L. (1995). Private practice. In R. L. Edwards (Ed.-in-Chief), *Encyclopedia of social work* (19th ed., Vol. 3, pp. 1905–1910). Washington, DC: NASW Press.

Barker, R. L. (1999). *Social work dictionary* (4th ed.). Washington, DC: NASW Press.

Barth, M. C. (2001). *The labor market for social workers: A first look* (Prepared for the John A. Hartford Foundation). Retrieved May 2, 2002, from http://www.icfconsulting.com

Beaucar, K. O. (2000, January). Volunteers aid Floyd's victims. *NASW News*, p. 5.

Becerra, R. M., & Damron-Rodriguez, J. (1995). Veterans and veterans services. In R. L. Edwards (Ed.-in-Chief), *Encyclopedia of social work* (19th ed., Vol. 3, pp. 2431–2439). Washington, DC: NASW Press.

Board adopts clinical practice standards. (1984, September). *NASW News*, p. 18.

Briefing: Mental health initiative focuses on removing barriers. (2002, May 13). *Federal Grants and Contracts Weekly*, p. 11.

Bryant, P. (2002, February). Northside Center for Child Development's comprehensive approach to 9/11. *Currents of the New York City Chapter, National Association of Social Workers*, p. 4.

Carlson, E. (2001, April). You're going to have to fight. *AARP Bulletin*, pp. 2, 10.

Chapter aids in aftermath of hurricane. (1999, March). *NASW News*, p. 6.

Chapter convenes roundtable discussion to focus on long-term impact of 9/11. (2002, February). *Currents of the New York City Chapter, National Association of Social Workers*, pp. 1, 11.

Clark, E. J. (2002, January). From the director: Needs compete, not our mandates. *NASW News*, p. 2.

Congress fails to renew Mental Health Parity Act. (2001, November). *NASW News,* p. 5.

Corcoran, J. (2000). Evidence-based social work practice with families. New York: Springer.

Cournoyer, B. R., & Powers, G. T. (2002). Evidence-based social work: The quiet revolution continues. In A. R. Roberts & G. J. Greene (Eds.), *Social workers' desk reference* (pp. 798–807). New York: Oxford University Press.

Davenport, J. A., & Davenport, J., III (1995). Rural social work overview. In R. L. Edwards (Ed.-in-Chief), *Encyclopedia of social work* (19th ed., Vol. 3, pp. 2076–2085). Washington, DC: NASW Press.

Duncan, C. M. (1999). *Worlds apart: Why poverty persists in rural America.* New Haven, CT: Yale University Press.

Farm communities dig in for the long haul. (1987, February). *NASW News,* p. 4.

Firestone, D. (2002, March 10). Air travel fear fades, but experts still worry. *New York Times,* p. A1.

Firm to modify contracts. (2001, July). *NASW News,* pp. 1, 8.

Foster, Z. (1989). Mutual help groups for emphysema patients: Veterans Administration Medical Center. In T. S. Kerson & Associates (Ed.), *Social work in health settings: Practice in context* (pp. 177–193). New York: Haworth Press.

Frankel, A. J., & Gelman, S. R. (1998). *Case management: An introduction to concept and skills.* Chicago: Lyceum.

Franklin, C. (2001). Developing effective practice competencies in managed behavioral health care. In A. R. Roberts & G. J. Greene (Eds.), *Social workers' desk reference* (pp. 3–10). New York: Oxford University Press.

Galambos, C. (1999). Resolving ethical conflicts in a managed care environment. *Health & Social Work, 24,* 191–197.

Garber, D. L., & McNelis, P. J. (1995). Military social work. In R. L. Edwards (Ed.-in-Chief), *Encyclopedia of social work* (19th ed., Vol. 2, pp. 1726–1736). Washington, DC: NASW Press.

Gibelman, M. (2002). Social work in an era of managed care. In A. R. Roberts & G. J. Greene (Eds.), *Social workers' desk reference* (pp. 16–23). New York: Oxford University Press.

Gibelman, M., & Schervish, P. (1996). The private practice of social work: Current trends and projected scenarios in a managed care environment. *Clinical Social Work Journal, 24,* 321–338.

Gibelman, M., & Schervish, P. (1997). *Who we are: A second look.* Washington, DC: NASW Press.

Gibelman, M., & Whiting, L. (1999). Negotiating and contracting in a managed care environment: Considerations for practitioners. *Health & Social Work, 24,* 180–190.

Googins, B., & Davidson, B. N. (1993). The organization as client: Broadening the concept of employee assistance programs. *Social Work, 38,* 477–484.

Green, S. A. (1994, October 2). When it's cheaper not to let people go down the drain. *Washington Post,* p. H6.

Hardcastle, D. A., Wenocur, S., & Powers, P. R. (1997). *Community practice: Theories and skills for social workers.* New York: Oxford University Press.

Howard, M., & Jensen, J. (1999). Clinical practice guidelines: Should social work develop them? *Research on Social Work Practice, 9,* 283–301.

Ice storm spawns heroes. (1998, March). *NASW News,* p. 12.

Jayaratne, S., Davis-Sacks, M. L., & Chess, W. (1991). Private practice may be good for your health. *Social Work, 36,* 224–232.

Johnson, L. C., & Yanca, S. J. (2001). *Social work practice: A generalist approach* (7th ed.). Boston: Allyn & Bacon.

Kanter, J. (1987). Mental health case management: A professional domain. *Social Work, 32,* 461–462.

Karger, H. J. (1989). Private practice: The fast track to the shingle. *Social Work, 34,* 566–567.

Karger, H. J., & Stoesz, D. (1998). *American social welfare policy: A pluralistic approach* (2nd ed.). New York: Longman.

Kleinfield, N. R. (2001, September 24). Disquiet in New York: A siren's wail can bring shudders. *New York Times,* p. A1.

Kurzman, P. A. (1987). Industrial social work (occupational social work). In A. Minahan (Ed.-in-Chief), *Encyclopedia of social work* (18th ed., Vol. 2, pp. 899–910). Silver Spring, MD: National Association of Social Workers.

Law note aids in practitioner contracts. (2000, September). *NASW News,*, pp. 1, 8.

Lennon, T. (2000). *Statistics on social work education in the United States: 1999.* Alexandria, VA: Council on Social Work Education.

Levine, S., & Ly, P. (2002, May 18). Heirs to a nation's pain. *Washington Post,* p. A1.

Limited-parity laws spreading. (2000, February). *NASW News,* p. 9.

Lin, A.M.P. (1995). Mental health overview. In R. L. Edwards (Ed.-in-Chief), *Encyclopedia of social work* (19th ed., Vol. 2, pp. 1705–1711). Washington, DC: *NASW* Press.

Mental Health Bill of Rights Project. (2002). *Joint initiative of mental health professional organizations: Principles in the provision of mental health and substance abuse treatment services—A bill of rights.* Washington, DC: National Association of Social Workers. Retrieved November 7, 2003, from http://www.socialworkers.org/practice/behavioral_health/mental.asp

Mental Health Parity Act of 1996, P.L. 104-204, 110 Stat. 2874.

Merle, S. (1962). Some arguments against private practice. *Social Work, 7,* 12–17.

Milbank, D. (2002, April 25). Bush plans to endorse mental health "parity." *Washington Post,* p. A1.

Miller, M. (2001). Creating a safe frame for learning: Teaching about trauma and trauma treatment. *Journal of Teaching in Social Work, 21*(3/4), 159–176.

Minahan, A. (1980). What is clinical social work? *Social Work, 25,* 171.

Moore, R. M. (Ed.). (2001). *The hidden America: Social problems in rural America for the twenty-first century.* Teaneck, NJ: Fairleigh Dickenson Press.

Mitchell, C. G. (1998). Perceptions of empathy and client satisfaction with managed behavioral health care. *Social Work, 43,* 404–411.

Mor-Barak, M. E., & Tynan, M. (1993). Older workers and the workplace: A new occupational challenge for occupational social work. *Social Work, 38,* 45–55.

Moss, S. (1995). *Purchasing managed care services for alcohol and other drug treatment* (Technical assistance publication series, No. 16, Vol. III, Publication No. SMA 95-3040). Rockville, MD: U.S. Department of Health and Human Services.

Mudrick, N. R. (1991). An underdeveloped role for occupational social work: Facilitating the employment of people with disabilities. *Social Work, 36,* 490–495.

National Association of Social Workers. (1981). *NASW standards for the classification of social work practice* (Policy statement 4). Silver Spring, MD: Author.

National Association of Social Workers. (1989). *NASW standards for the practice of clinical social work.* Washington, DC: Author. Retrieved October 19, 2003, from http://www.socialworkers.org/practice/ standards/clinical_SW.asp

National Association of Social Workers. (2001a, May 9). *Social workers, through employee assistance programs, help ease stress on the job* [Press release]. Washington, DC: Author. Retrieved October 2, 2003, from http://www.socialworkers.org/pressroom/2001/050901.asp

National Association of Social Workers. (2001b, October 10). *Social workers say trauma of September 11 creates long-term effects for many* [Press release]. Washington, DC: Author. Retrieved October 19, 2003, from http://www. socialworkers.org/pressroom/2001/101001.asp

National Association of Social Workers. (2002, March 11). *Six month anniversary of 9–11 brings a host of unexpected emotions* [Press release]. Washington, DC: Author. Retrieved March 30, 2002, from http://www.socialworkers.org/pressroom/2002/ 031102.htm

National Institute of Mental Health. (2002). *What is post-traumatic stress disorder?* Bethesda, MD: U.S. Department of Health and Human Services, National Institutes of Health. Retrieved December 5, 2002, from http://www/nimh.nih.gov/anxiety/ptsdri4.cfm

National Mental Health Association. (2002). *Coping with disaster: Tips for adults.* Retrieved October 21, 2003, from http://www.nmha.org/reassurance/ adulttips.cfm

O'Neill, J. V. (1999, June). Profession dominates in mental health. *NASW News,* pp. 1, 8

O'Neill, J. V. (2000, February). Surgeon General's report lauded. *NASW News,* pp. 1, 6

O'Neill, J. V. (2001a, October). NASW responds to terror attacks. *NASW News,* pp. 1, 10.

O'Neill, J. V. (2001b, November). Social workers heed call after attacks. *NASW News,* pp. 1, 8, 10, 14.

O'Neill, J. V. (2001c, November). University at "ground zero." *NASW News,* p. 10.

O'Neill, J. V. (2001d, November). Red Cross, NASW have pact. *NASW News,* p. 8.

O'Neill, J. V. (2001e, November). Two terrorist acts: The past is prologue. *NASW News,* p. 3.

O'Neill, J. V. (2002a, January). Coping with the fear-filled new reality. *NASW News,*p. 3.

O'Neill, J. V. (2002b, January). EAPs offer multitude of internet services. *NASW News,* p. 14.

O'Neill, J. V. (2002c, May). Parity prospects bright. *NASW News,* p. 7.

Orloff-Kaplan, K. (1990). Recent trends in case management. In L. Ginsberg (Ed.), *Encyclopedia of social work* (18th ed., 1990 Suppl., pp. 60–77). Silver Spring, MD: NASW Press.

Parity gets to work. (1998, March). *NASW News,* pp. 1, 10.

Rothman, G., & Becerra, R. M. (1987). Veterans and veterans' services. In A. Minahan (Ed.-in-Chief), *Encyclopedia of social work* (18th ed., Vol. 2, pp. 809–817). Silver Spring, MD: National Association of Social Workers.

Rothman, J. (2002). An overview of case management. In A. R. Roberts & G. J. Greene (Eds.), *Social workers' desk reference* (pp. 467–467). New York: Oxford University Press.

Rural social work. (2003). *Social work speaks.* Retrieved October 19, 2003, from http://www.socialworkers.org/resources/abstracts/abstracts/rural.asp.

Satcher, D. (1999). *Mental health: A report of the Surgeon General.* Washington, DC: U.S. Government Printing Office. Retrieved November 19, 2002, from http://www.surgeongeneral.gov/library/mentalhealth/home.html

Saxton, P. M. (1988). Vendorship for social work: Observations on the maturation of the profession. *Social Work, 33,* 197–201.

Second Harvest. (2003). *Issue paper 2: Rural hunger.* Retrieved November 7, 2003, from http://www.secondharvest.org/site_content. asp?s=152.

Sheafor, B. W., & Lewis, R. G. (1992). *Social work practice in rural areas: The Appalachian experience.* In A. T. Morales & B. W. Sheafor (Eds.), *Social work: A profession of many faces* (6th ed., pp. 419–447). Needham Heights, MA: Allyn & Bacon.

Social work in the public eye. (1998, May). *NASW News,* p. 13.

Social work in the public eye. (2002a, January). *NASW News,* p. 15.

Social work in the public eye. (2002b, March). *NASW News,* p. 17.

Social work, public policy stands okayed. (1984, October). *NASW News,* p. 11.

Social workers heed the call to volunteer. (1999, January). *NASW News,* p. 4.

Specht, H., & Courtney, M. (1995) *Unfaithful angels: How social work has abandoned its mission.* New York: Free Press.

Stewart, R. (1984, October). From the president. *NASW News,* p. 2.

Strom-Gottfried, K. (1998). Applying a conflict resolution framework to disputes in managed care. *Social Work, 43,* 393–401.

Swenson, C. R. (1995). Clinical social work. In R. L. Edwards (Ed.-in-Chief), *Encyclopedia of social work* (19th ed., Vol. 1, pp. 502–513). Washington, DC: NASW Press.

Thyer, B. A. (2002). Principles of evidence-based practice and treatment development. In A. R. Roberts & G. J. Greene (Eds.), *Social workers' desk reference* (pp. 739–742). New York: Oxford University Press.

U.S. Department of Health and Human Services. (2001, September 13). *HHS initiates immediate and long-term steps to address emotional and mental health consequences of terrorist air attacks* [Press release]. Washington, DC: Author. Retrieved November 7, 2003, from http://www.hhs.gov/news/press2001/ pres20010913.html

U.S. Department of Veterans Affairs. (2003). *A brief description.* Retrieved October 30, 2003, from http://www.va.gov/vetdata/demographics/Vetpop2001adj/specialtopics/abriefdescription.doc

Vallianatos, C. (2000, September). Social work steps onto proving ground. *NASW News*, p. 3.

Vallianatos, C. (2001, July). Appalachian grads aid area. *NASW News*, p. 12.

Vallianatos, C. (2002, February). CIGNA cut reversed. *NASW News*, p. 1.

Van Den Bergh, N. (1995). Employee assistance programs. In R. L. Edwards (Ed.-in-Chief), *Encyclopedia of social work* (19th ed., Vol. 1, pp. 842–849). Washington, DC: NASW Press.

Vandiver, V. L. (2002). Step-by-step practice guidelines for using evidence-based practice and expert consensus in mental health settings. In A. R. Roberts & G. J. Greene (Eds.), *Social workers' desk reference* (pp. 731–738). New York: Oxford University Press.

Vedantam, S. (2002, March 17). After Sept. 11, psychic wounds slow to heal. *Washington Post*, p. A3.

Veterans affairs names new social work chief. (2000, November). *NASW News*, p. 4.

Walsh, J. (2002). Clinical case management. In A. R. Roberts & G. J. Greene (Eds.), Social workers' desk reference (pp. 473–376). New York: Oxford University Press.

Williams, L. F., & Hopps, J. G. (1990). *The social work labor force: Current perspectives and future trends*. In L. Ginsburg, S. Khinduka, J. Hall, F. Ross-Sheriff, & A. Hartman (Eds.), *Encyclopedia of social work* (18th ed., 1990 Suppl., pp. 289–306). Silver Spring, MD: NASW Press.

Wolk, J. L., Sullivan, W. P., & Hartmann, D. J. (1994). The managerial nature of case management. *Social Work, 39*, 152–159.

Chapter Five CHILDREN AND FAMILIES

The problems that families and children experience result from—and are intertwined with—other areas of living: housing, employment, income, health, and mental health. Dramatic increases in child poverty, homelessness, substance abuse, and violence are exacerbating the strains on families. As a result, the need for services is expanding. So are the costs—to the families, children, and society. In 1998, states spent at least $15.6 billion on child welfare services ("Reform's Effect on Families Studied," 2002).

The profound change that the American family has experienced over the course of the past 50 years is evident in the disparity between the "ideal" family type—a husband, wife, and two or more children at home, with the husband as the sole breadwinner—and the reality (Johnson & Wahl, 1995). A majority of U.S. families represent exceptions to the ideal. According to data on children compiled and analyzed by the Children's Defense Fund (2001):

- 1 in 2 will live in a single-parent family at some point in childhood
- 1 in 3 is born to unmarried parents
- 1 in 3 will be poor at some point in childhood
- 1 in 4 lives with only one parent
- 1 in 24 lives with neither parent
- 1 in 3 is behind a year or more in school
- 1 in 5 was born poor
- 1 in 6 is poor now

- 1 in 6 is born to a mother who did not receive prenatal care in the first three months of pregnancy
- 1 in 5 is born to a mother who did not graduate from high school
- 1 in 7 has a worker in their family but still is poor
- 1 in 15 lives at less than half the poverty level
- 1 in 8 lives in a family receiving food stamps
- 1 in 8 never graduates from high school
- 1 in 8 is born to a teenage mother
- 1 in 12 has a disability
- 1 in 12 was born with low birth weight
- 1 in 7 has no health insurance
- 1 in 139 will die before their first birthday
- 1 in 1,056 will be killed by guns before age 20.

In January 2001, the National Action Agenda on Children's Mental Health, issued by the Office of the Surgeon General, revealed that one in 10 children and adolescents suffers from mental illness of sufficient severity to cause some level of impairment. However, in any given year, fewer than one in five youths receives treatment (O'Neill, 2001). According to former Surgeon General David Satcher, "growing numbers of children are suffering needlessly because their emotional, behavioral, and developmental needs are not being met by the very institutions and systems that were created to take care of them" (as cited in O'Neill, 2001, p. 12).

Changes in lifestyles and values have also impacted upon the types of problems clients of social workers experience. Examples are plentiful. The diversity of the American family is seen in the increase in same-sex parenting. Social workers have advocated for the rights of gay men and lesbians to enter into second-parent adoptions—the legal adoption of a child by the partner of the biological or adoptive parent (Vallianatos, 2002). With developments in modern technology and a more accepting social climate, surrogate parenting is now a potentially more accepted form of family creation for infertile and involuntarily childless couples (Blyth, 1993). Gay and lesbian adolescents have been identified as a group negatively stigmatized and one that requires social support and intervention at the family and societal level (Morrow, 1993). Because of increased life expectancy, more generations are likely to exist in family or kinship networks that may include spouses and former spouses, in-laws, children, and stepchildren (Johnson & Wahl, 1995).

Many of these emerging social issues reflect new knowledge, changing values, and progressive technology that transcend geography and cultures. The experiences of other countries provide both context and useful insights into the policies, programs, and services for children and families from a cross-national perspective. Information about such policies and programs is readily available. An example is the Clearinghouse on International Developments in Child, Youth and Family Policies established by Columbia University's Institute for Child and Family Policy (http://www.childpolicyintl.org).

The varieties of situations that define the modern American family suggest the broad range of services families may need to survive and thrive. Current trends are likely to continue and new trends will emerge that profoundly impact on family dynamics and require new types of supports and services from social services agencies and social workers.

SOCIAL WORK WITH CHILDREN AND FAMILIES

The National Association of Social Workers, in gathering data about the areas of service in which its members work, classifies children and families as distinct areas of practice. Child services rank second among primary practice areas (following mental health) at 16.3 percent of responding NASW members. Family services rank fourth among the primary practice areas, with 11.4 percent of NASW members citing families as their primary practice area (Gibelman & Schervish, 1997).

Child and family services is an extremely broad arena of social work practice, reflecting the breadth and depth of problems encountered by families and children today. Social workers may specialize on the basis of type of problem, population, or service area. Specializations may include adoption, child protective services, runaway and homeless youths, homeless families, foster care, adoption, day care, family violence, rape crisis services, resettlement–immigration, child prostitution and pornography, teen pregnancy, children with AIDS, teen suicide, family life education, and juvenile justice. Of course, the problems encountered by families also crosscut other arenas of social work practice. For example, teenagers may have substance abuse problems, and families may require mental health counseling.

Social workers in family and child services carry out a number of roles in diverse practice settings, addressing a broad range of societal problems. In providing direct services, social workers assess the presenting situation, offer counseling and assistance, and coordinate the family's access to services in the community. In addition, social workers may participate in legal proceedings related to the determination of child abuse and neglect or, alternatively, may provide family reunification or family preservation services to enable families to stay together. Social workers may also use their supervisory and administrative skills to develop and administer programs, departments, or entire agencies. Social workers in this service area also bring their skills to the surrounding community and help local groups organize to improve social institutions, systems, and practices through advocacy efforts (Liederman, 1995).

Historical Perspective

Child and family services, as an area of practice, dates back to the origins of social welfare in this country and to the birth of the profession of social work. Federal, state, and local laws and regulations govern many of the services within this broad category that are oriented to the care, protection, and healthy development of children. The overall goal is to ameliorate conditions that put children and families at risk; strengthen and support families so that they can successfully care for their children; protect children from future abuse and neglect; address the emotional, behavioral, and health problems of children; and, when necessary, provide permanent families for children through adoption or guardianship (Barker, 1999).

The focus on the child and the family has waxed and waned over time, depending on changing psychosocial perspectives about problem causation and amelioration and available intervention methodologies. The earliest child welfare services centered on child protective services and foster care. Now, child welfare encompasses, among other areas, family preservation, services to homeless families and runaway youths, and early intervention and prevention.

Federal and state laws have periodically been revamped to address the burgeoning needs associated with families and children in today's complex society. The Adoption Assistance and Child Welfare Act of 1980 (ACWA) (P.L. 96-272); for example, signified a new thrust in child welfare. The AACWA spurred the permanency planning movement, the goal of which was to return children in foster care to their natural families or free them for adoption if families were unable to assume care within a reasonable period of time (Brissett-Chapman, 1995). No definition was provided of "reasonable effort" to achieve permanency. Nevertheless, the AACWA substantially altered the way child welfare organizations provided services to children and families, with permanency planning replacing the more open-ended reunification goals of the past. Programs were redesigned to reflect this new emphasis. Despite this new focus in child welfare, 17 years after its enactment the number of children in foster care remained unacceptably high (Pecora, Whittaker, Maluccio, & Barth, 2000).

The Adoption and Safe Families Act of 1997 (P.L. 105-89; ASFA) modified the landmark 1980 AACWA. The ASFA was enacted in response to the perceived weaknesses of the AACWA. Under the ASFA, reasonable efforts are no longer required under certain circumstances, such as when the separation has occurred because of abandonment, torture, chronic abuse, or sexual abuse (Blanchard, 1999). The new goal became that of promoting adoption of children in foster care, with a main tenet of the law that of the primacy of the child's health and safety. The change of goals once again created a need to reorient program foci.

The ASFA affords substantial latitude to the states. For example, it is largely up to each state to define "reasonable efforts." The definition used by each state, in turn, affects the way in which organizations approach the scope of work involved in carrying out ASFA mandates. The ASFA also reduced the time frame for the first permanency hearing from 18 months under AACWA to 15 of the previous 22 months in order to move children in foster care more quickly into permanent homes—specifically, adoptive homes. Agencies, in fact, may be encouraged to seek an adoptive placement for a child concurrent with the efforts to reunite a child with the natural family (Blanchard, 1999). Time limits potentially intensify worker contact with all involved in the case and demand rapid implementation of the case plan.

In late 2001, the Promoting Safe and Stable Families Amendments (P.L. 108-36) were passed by Congress and reauthorized ASFA for five years with additional funding to meet the act's four main purposes: family preservation services, community-based support services to help prevent abuse and neglect, time-limited family reunification services, and promotion and support for adoption. The reauthorized law, however, did away with guaranteed funding levels.

As these examples show, each public policy shift alters the nature of the tasks and responsibilities delegated to both public and nonprofit human services organizations under purchase of services arrangements and, in turn, to the social workers employed by them. Child and family services, agencies are also subject to annual legislative budget allocations, which may forestall or enhance the types of resources needed to serve client populations.

CHILD WELFARE PRACTICE IN PUBLIC SETTINGS

Due to the linkage between the investigative function and the social services function in child protective services, social workers serve as agents of the state, and investigations have a quasi-law-enforcement function. Once a determination of child abuse or neglect has been made and the investigative role is concluded, the public agency may directly provide services or purchase selected services from other public, voluntary, or proprietary agencies (Gibelman, 1995).

At a time when public social services agencies are required to do more, often with fewer resources, they have endured a host of problems that have hampered their effectiveness, including caseload size, insufficient personnel and financial resources, staff turnover, and lack of community awareness and support (Beaucar, 1999; Pecora et al., 2000; Rycraft, 1994). Problems of professional status, recruitment, retention, and social worker "burnout" have long been identified with the public social services

ices and the ability to correct these work conditions has been hampered by the resulting negative reputation afforded this arena of practice (Duncan & Chase-Lansdale, 2002; Pecora et al., 2000). Identified problems include vacant or frozen staff positions as a result of budget cutbacks, caseload size ranging from 60 to 200 children per worker, and too little time and too few personnel resources spent on legally freeing children for adoption and recruiting adoptive families. Too often, insufficient staff, both in numbers and experience, hinders the ability of public agencies to emphasize prevention services for troubled families and, ultimately, can lead to a failure to provide adequate protection for those children in care. For many social workers in the field of child protective services, the commitment to work versus the conditions of work present an emotional dilemma—to stay or to leave (Beaucar, 1999).

The problems in public child welfare practice have been consistently reiterated ("Child Welfare Panel Seeks," 1987; "Feds Told about Child Welfare Morass," 1990; "Staff Called Key," 1993; "System Overload Endangers Kids," 1991). High caseloads, low salaries, and lack of training opportunities continue to threaten the capability of child welfare agencies to prevent and ameliorate child abuse and neglect. In fact, studies have concluded that children are being harmed not only by their parents, but also by the public welfare system established to ensure their protection. In a number of states, including Connecticut, Kansas, Missouri, and New York, federal and state supreme court decisions have held states responsible for rectifying the conditions of their child welfare systems, but responses have been slow and sometimes inadequate (Beaucar, 1999). Budget constraints figure prominently in preventing compliance with caseload standards and in hiring social workers with the requisite education and skills.

Nationwide, public social services agencies continue to report difficulties in hiring and retaining public child welfare caseworkers, despite the ever-growing need for professionals within this sector and past and current efforts to attract more social workers to this area of practice. There have been problems maintaining an adequately large and culturally diverse workforce that reflects the clientele being served (Liederman, 1995). Child welfare services experience the highest turnover and vacancy rates of any social work practice area (Beaucar, 2000).

Despite more progressive laws that broaden the array of services that can be provided, emphasize family preservation, family reunification, or both, and establish timetables for achieving permanence for the child, outcomes remain questionable. Children continue to be maintained in foster care or other temporary arrangements for longer than necessary because services are fragmented, management information systems are lacking, and there are few financial incentives for agencies to provide better services that will lead to permanence ("Child Welfare Changes Eyed," 1999).

The New York Times columnist Nina Bernstein (2001) eloquently documented the systemic failures of the child welfare system in her book, *The Lost Children of Wilder: The Epic Struggle to Change Foster Care*. Bernstein followed the threads of the life of a 12-year-old girl, Shirley Wilder, as she entered the child welfare system in New York and the son born to her when she was 14 years old. In 1973, the American Civil Liberties Union filed a class action lawsuit on behalf of Shirley Wilder and other children in the foster care system alleging that the New York City foster care system was unconstitutional because it gave private religious agencies control of publicly financed foster care services. These religious agencies, it was alleged, gave preference to white Catholic and Jewish children, whereas all other children received lesser care in inappropriate institutions. The lawsuit is as compelling as the situation with which it dealt; it took 26 years to wind through the judicial process.

A 2002 incident in the State of Florida exemplified some of the continued problems that plague the child welfare system. A five-year-old girl, Rilya, in foster care disappeared and was missing for 15 months without the knowledge of the state's child welfare agency. The foster mother reported that the child had been taken away for evaluation by a child welfare worker. It was only when the media reported that a five-year-old girl had been found dead in another state that the foster mother called authorities, but the deceased child turned out not to be Rilya. State workers were supposed to make monthly visits to the foster home but clearly had not done so. Two caseworkers were identified in the press as deceiving the state's child welfare system by submitting paperwork that indicated that Rilya was being visited regularly (Associated Press, 2002a, 2002b). Questions were also raised about the suitability of the foster mother, questions that should have been resolved prior to Rilya's placement with her.

Efforts to improve the system have been ongoing. In New York, a broad consortium comprised of the social work education community, the state Office of Children and Family Services, and the county child welfare agencies has been initiated to strengthen and reprofessionalize child welfare practice (O'Neill, 2002). The consortium has divided the state into six planning regions in which the educational and agency partners identify the most pressing needs in their areas. Areas identified for attention include

- accessing social work education for child welfare workers through scholarship and stipend programs
- promoting faculty-supervised field instruction to help evaluate the level of practice in child welfare agencies
- promoting distance learning, including satellite courses
- initiating a workforce study to examine factors that induce child welfare workers to stay on the job
- promoting best-services strategies that can be documented empirically

- examining core training of children welfare workers at agencies to see if the training qualifies for academic credit as a means to interest workers in social work graduate education. (O'Neill, 2002)

There is empirical evidence to support the efforts to professionalize public child welfare services. Dhooper, Royse, and Wolfe (1990), for example, found that employees with social work degrees are better prepared to perform their jobs than are those without such education. There is both need and opportunity for social workers in public child welfare services.

CHILD ABUSE AND NEGLECT

Child maltreatment is the primary reason why parents and children are referred or reported to child welfare agencies for service. Although there is no universal definition of child maltreatment in the United States, five major categories are consistently used to codify such cases: physical abuse, sexual abuse, physical neglect, educational neglect, and psychological maltreatment (Pecora et al., 2000). Efforts to accurately portray the incidence of abuse in the United States have been mandated by Congress. The Third National Incidence Study of Child Abuse and Neglect (NIS-3) is the most comprehensive source of information about child abuse and neglect in the United States and provides insights about the incidence of child abuse and neglect longitudinally. The NIS-3 data (National Clearinghouse on Child Abuse and Neglect Information [NCCAN], 2001), which examined changes in incidence between 1986 and 1993, revealed that

- there have been substantial and significant increases in the incidence of child abuse and neglect since the last national incidence study was conducted in 1986
- the total number of children seriously injured and the total number of endangered both quadrupled during this time

- children of single parents had a 77 percent greater risk of being harmed by physical abuse, an 87 percent greater risk of being harmed by physical neglect, and an 80 percent greater risk of suffering serious injury or harm from abuse or neglect than children living with both parents
- children from the lowest income families were significantly more likely to be sexually abused, educationally neglected, and more likely to be seriously injured from maltreatment than children from higher income families
- the estimated number of physically abused children rose from 311,500 to 614,100 (a 97 percent increase)
- the estimated number of sexually abused children increased from 133,600 to 300,200 (a 125 percent increase)
- the more recent estimate of the number of emotionally abused children was 183 percent higher than the previous estimate (188,100 in 1986 versus 532,200 in 1993)
- the estimated number of physically neglected children increased from 507,700 to 1,335,100 (a 163 percent increase)
- the estimated number of emotionally neglected children nearly tripled in the interval between the studies, rising from 203,000 in 1986 to 585,100 in 1993 (a 188 percent increase).

The growing burden for public child welfare agencies is to somehow manage the recent increase in the number of reported and substantiated child maltreatment cases without an equal increase in staff and resources. It would appear that the child protective services (CPS) system has reached its capacity to respond to the maltreated child population (NCCAN, 2001). The increasing workload for the CPS system and the failure to expand the labor force providing services in proportion to the growth in caseload shed light on why children may "fall through the cracks." The CPS investigations were found to extend to only slightly more than one-fourth of the children who were seriously harmed or injured by abuse or neglect (NCCAN, 2001).

Child Protective Services Practice

Child protective services refer to those interventions by social workers and other professionals on behalf of children who may be in danger of harm from others. Social workers are usually employed by a public agency, such as a state, county, or local department of social services. They may also work for the courts or law enforcement agencies. Their primary job is to investigate situations in which a child may be at risk. The goal is to help ameliorate the situation, minimize further risk, and arrange for alternative placements and resources for the child at risk (Barker, 1999; DeVita & Mosher-Williams, 2001).

Social workers in CPS engage in a variety of social work functions, drawing on many different skills. For example, during the initial interview the social worker will use his or her assessment and diagnostic skills to determine, first, whether the child is at risk of further abuse, and second, to determine an appropriate treatment plan for both the child and the family (Brissett-Chapman, 1995). The primary goal in cases of abuse and neglect is to protect the child by helping the parents to recognize and change behavior that is harmful to their child. In doing this the social worker will often carry out the social work functions of advice, counseling, enabling, referral, and support.

After providing the initial services, the social worker must then determine if the detrimental conditions have been corrected. If the situation has not improved, the social work agency may initiate action, either with parental cooperation or by a petition to the court to mandate appropriate services or substitute care for the child (Brissett-Chapman, 1995).

The decision that a child is in danger and should be removed is ultimately a legal one, and CPS social workers routinely provide testimony to the courts about case facts and recommenda-tions. Social workers must be prepared, effective, and professional in presenting case information, as highlighted in the following vignette.

A DAY IN COURT

Joanie Clay is a social worker for the Spring Valley Department of Social Services outside of Chicago. This is her first job; she received her MSW eight months ago. She works in child protective services and carries a caseload of almost 90 children. One of her more troublesome cases has been a seven-year-old boy named Joshua. His mother has a serious problem with alcohol and drug abuse. His father works the night maintenance shift at the Spring Valley Hospital and spends the days at the local bar or sleeping. Joshua's next door neighbor frequently feeds him, and she reported the situation to CPS.

During the past month, Joanie has been trying to work with the family to improve care for Joshua. However, on a recent icy, winter day, Joanie visited and found no heat in the house. Joshua was sitting huddled on his bed in only his underwear and he had not eaten since yesterday morning when the neighbor had given him a sandwich. He did not know where his mother or father was. Joanie knew Joshua was being badly neglected and that this could not be allowed to continue. She consulted with her supervisor, and they decided to get a court order to remove Joshua from the home and put him in foster care. Without voluntary parental consent, Joanie would have to testify in court about her observations and actions in the case and receive court authorization to remove the child.

Joanie's supervisor works with her about her forthcoming court appearance and explains the importance of being prepared, precise, and informed. Joanie also knows the importance of maintaining a professional manner in both her appearance and her testimony. She has observed other social workers testifying as expert witnesses during her training with the department. However, this is her first time on the witness stand. As an expert witness, Joanie is allowed to answer hypothetical questions posed by lawyers and offer her own professional opinion.

Before the hearing, Joanie visits the court-room alone to get a feel for the room's layout. She also prepares 3 x 5 index cards document-ing her own educational and professional expe-rience. She plans to take these cards with her into the witness box so that she can refer to them when citing her qualifications. In addi-tion, Joanie reviews the case notes thoroughly before the hearing.

On the day of the hearing, Joanie feels relaxed and confident. She knows that she will have to use precise and descriptive words and body language to help the judge see and hear what she has witnessed. Joanie's supervisor warned her about the cross-examination process, which can often put social workers on the defen-sive. For example, she told her not to answer more than what was asked. She also told her to be prepared for negative questions about herself and any previous decisions she has made. Finally, Joanie's supervisor advised her to answer all questions truthfully.

The nature of CPS work often requires the social worker to present testimony in court; skills in such presentations are vital to protect the best interests of the child. As an expert witness, the social worker engages in the functions of consul-tation and advocacy to improve the plight of the child at risk. As an expert witness, the social worker must let the full truth be known with objectivity and clarity (NASW, 1990).

In this instance, Joanie represented CPS in the agency's capacity to offer advice and coun-sel to the court to assist in judicial decision making. There are times, however, when a social worker may be called upon to testify in which the confidentiality of the social worker–client relationship is at issue. The granting of client privilege is decided on a case-by-case basis, although privileged communication clauses may be included in state licensing laws.

Social workers may not be granted privileged communication status. The exigencies about privileged communication depend on state licensing laws, judicial interpretation about the role and function of the CPS worker, and state precedents, among other factors.

The actual determination that a child has been abused or neglected is a judicial decision. Should there be a legal determination that the child has, in fact, been abused, the foster care worker becomes the primary provider of servic-es to the entire family.

FOSTER CARE

A child is placed in foster care when a determi-nation is made that the parent or caretaker is unwilling or unable to care for the child. The term foster care encompasses single-family homes, group homes, and residential settings (Pecora et al., 2000). The intent is to provide for the physical care of children in a family environ-ment on a temporary basis when the children are not able to live with their natural parents or legal guardians (Barker, 1999). The placement is tem-porary while a permanent plan is made and implemented.

In actuality, "temporary" has too often turned into "long-term," and many children linger in foster care or are switched from one foster home to another. The number of children in foster care continues to rise. An estimated 547,000 children were in foster care as of March 31, 1999—a 35 percent increase since 1990. Approximately 117,000 of these children are waiting for permanent adoptive families (Children's Defense Fund, 2002).

The social worker in foster care conducts assessments of children and their families to assist in determining the need for placement; evaluates potential foster homes, through a home-study process, as to appropriateness for placement; monitors the foster home during placement; works with the biological family to enable reunification to take place; and helps determine when it is appropriate to return the child to the biological family (Barker, 1999). In addition, social workers' evaluations of the children and their families are used by legal authorities to determine the need for placement in the first instance and, later, to determine when it is appropriate to return the children to their natural families. Aspects of the process are delineated in the following vignette.

RYAN NEEDS A HOME

Ryan is a five-year-old African American boy who was abandoned by his mother in a train station. Ryan was found by the police curled in a corner—dirty and hungry. The police called the intake division of the state's department of human services (DHS) and a social worker, Sue Williams, came to get Ryan. She first took Ryan to the local hospital for an examination. Their next stop was a McDonalds restaurant. Ryan was withdrawn and frightened. He would nod his head in response to questions but was not willing to talk. Sue took Ryan back to the DHS office, where her supervisor had already begun the search for an immediate foster care placement for Ryan until his family could be located or other more permanent plans could be made for him. Both Sue and her supervisor wanted to ensure that the foster parents selected for Ryan would be able to offer him the emotional support he most desperately needed following his abandonment. Fortunately, such a home was identified—the McKinleys.

By phone, Sue provided the foster parents with as much information as she had about Ryan and his situation. During this time Ryan was kept busy with crayons and a coloring book in the agency's playroom. The McKinleys, who already had one adopted and two foster children living in their home, agreed to Ryan's placement with them. The social worker attended to the paperwork necessary to obtain a clothing voucher, and she and Ryan stopped at the local Wal-Mart to buy Ryan a change of clothes, sleep wear, and toiletries. Then they went straight to the McKinley home. Sue remained with Ryan and the McKinley foster family for 90 minutes, easing Ryan's transition into yet another unfamiliar surrounding and updating the foster parents about his situation. Sue promised Ryan that she would return the next day to check on him.

Several visits were scheduled to the foster home in the days following Ryan's placement. Sue discussed with the foster parents the need to enroll Ryan within the week in the local public school; he would be entering kindergarten. The possible adjustment reactions Ryan might have to a new school were also reviewed. Back at the office, Sue processed the necessary requisitions to obtain an emergency clothing allowance for Ryan, made application on his behalf for Medicaid, and referred Ryan to Dr. Evans, a child psychiatrist, for the purpose of conducting a complete psychiatric evaluation. Sue was able to locate an address for Ryan's family as they had previously been known to the agency. She attempted to reach them by phone, but the number had been disconnected. The earlier case record showed a pattern of substance abuse on the part of Ryan's mother. The father had been in and out of the picture and also was known to be a drug abuser who had also been imprisoned for selling drugs. Since Sue was unable to locate the parents, she prepared and mailed a certified letter to their previously known address asking that they contact her as soon as possible. She was not optimistic about hearing from them.

The children coming into the foster care system have been abused or are at risk of physical, sexual, or emotional abuse. Consequently, the initial focus of the social worker's attention is on crisis intervention—ensuring a safe and secure environment for the child. Thus, Sue's first task is to ensure that Ryan is physically unharmed and then to find him a temporary home. She consoles Ryan and provides reassurance to him. She assesses the psychological trauma of the abandonment and arranges for a psychiatric consultation.

For many children who are placed in the foster care system, the ultimate goal is to strengthen the family unit to overcome the problems that led to the need for temporary out-of-home care. The prospect of family reunification, however, is dim in Ryan's case. He was abandoned intentionally, and the likelihood of locating his parents is poor. If Ryan's mother is located, a judge might order that she receive detoxification and then aftercare substance abuse services; these services then become part of the service plan. If Ryan's parents are not located, the case becomes one of abandonment and permanency plans may include termination of parental rights and eventual adoption.

Sue's interventions with and on behalf of Ryan highlight the concrete and practical tasks involved in foster care work. Emergencies are the norm in this field of practice, and the unexpected must be anticipated. After the immediate crisis is addressed, the foster care social worker is responsible for preparing a services plan for the child and the family, as applicable. Implementing the services plan involves the foster care worker in the functions of information and referral and case management. Parent education, substance abuse counseling, individual and family therapy, psychiatric evaluations for the mother and child, job training, and other services that may be recommended to promote the reunification of the family are provided by an array of community agencies, depending on the case circumstances.

The foster care worker must oversee that referrals are made to appropriate agencies, that there are follow-up reviews to ensure that the services are in place and being used, and that the services provided to children and their families are coordinated. The social worker also will arrange family visits, if the court so orders, and make periodic and scheduled appearances in court to report about case progress.

The removal of children from their homes and their subsequent placement with foster families involve substantial trauma. Even if the home situation was abusive, children have difficulty separating from their parents. Sometimes, a child may "act out" in foster placement due to preexisting psychosocial problems or difficulty adjusting to the changed circumstances. The following vignette highlights a placement that does not work out for the child or the foster family. Here, alternatives to foster care are considered.

AN UNSUCCESSFUL PLACEMENT AND THE SEARCH FOR OPTIONS

Joanne Medley is a social worker in the out-of-home placement unit of Family and Child Services in Chicago. Under contract with the Cook County Department of Social Services, Family and Child Services, a not-for-profit agency, is responsible for providing intensive services to children in out-of-home placement.

On Monday morning, Joanne receives a phone call from the foster mother of nine-year-old Joseph Smith asking that Joseph be removed from the home immediately. The previous evening, Joseph had a violent outburst. He was verbally abusive to the foster mother and hit a younger foster child in the home over the head with a baseball bat. The younger child had to be taken to the emergency room where he received 10 stitches in his forehead.

Joanne immediately files a request to use an agency car to visit the home of the foster parent. While she awaits approval, she reviews the case record.

Background
Joseph has serious emotional, social, and academic problems. He consistently uses profane and sexual language and exhibits aggressive behavior toward his peers and open defiance toward directives given by most authority figures. He came into foster care a little over a year ago. He and his three siblings were left alone for several hours and the two youngest children were found by a neighbor locked in a room with the door tied shut. The children

had only attended school sporadically. The home was filthy and in disarray and crack cocaine was found on the premises.

Following the removal of the children from the home, the mother disappeared and has not been located. The identity of Joseph's father has not been revealed. The only known relative is the maternal grandmother, who is recuperating from a stroke and is unable to care for Joseph or his siblings. A termination of parental rights hearing is scheduled in two months; pending the outcome of that hearing, Joseph may be legally free for adoption.

Joseph had been placed in five different foster homes in little over one year. He exhibited adjustment problems in all of these foster homes, including hitting other children and using profanity and sexually explicit language. In one foster home, the foster parent had, in her words, "gone beyond the breaking point" and had whipped Joseph with a belt. Subsequently, Joseph was removed from that home and then experienced three more unsuccessful placements. He had been in the current foster home for two months. The several changes in foster homes had also meant changes in schools. Joseph is very far behind in school and has already been left back one grade. He was scheduled to begin weekly therapy sessions but refused to go.

Immediate Intervention

The issue is clear—the foster mother has exhausted her personal resources and patience, and another placement must be found for Joseph today. Joanne calls the social worker at Home for Boys, a residential care facility in Chicago, to see if it will take Joseph on an emergency basis. The Home for Boys social worker, Mary, says that she will need to speak with the facility director and will call back that afternoon. Joanne then drives out to the foster home.

When Joanne arrives at the foster home, Mrs. Elkin, the foster mother, informs her that Joseph has taken off on his bicycle and she has no idea where he has gone. She had told him to

go to his room to await Joanne's arrival, but he had used profanity and left abruptly. On a hunch, Joanne calls Mrs. Cheddar, the foster parent of two of Joseph's siblings. Yes, Mrs. Cheddar responds, Joseph is there visiting with his preschool-age twin sisters. Mrs. Cheddar had tried to reach Joanne at the agency just a short time ago.

Joanne talks with Mrs. Elkin to ascertain whether there is any possibility that she would consider having Joseph continue in her home. Not surprisingly, the answer is negative. Mrs. Elkin explains that she cannot risk the potential danger to the other children in the home. She is afraid that something even more serious will happen next time. It is clear that Mrs. Elkin is emotionally distraught about the events of the previous evening and that her assessment of potential danger is realistic. Joanne speaks with Mrs. Elkin for several minutes to reassure her about her decision and to thank her for her real efforts in working with Joseph. Joanne then suggests that Mrs. Elkin pack up Joseph's things, which she will pick up later.

Joanne then drives over to the home of Mrs. Cheddar. Joseph is not aware that she is coming. Joanne and Joseph have a good relationship, stemming from the several outings they have gone on together, including a recent trip to the zoo. Joanne asks to speak with Joseph alone, and they go to the kitchen to talk. Joanne asks Joseph about the events of the previous evening. As is his pattern, Joseph externalizes all responsibility and blames the younger child for initiating the fight. He feels that his actions were justified. Joanne then calmly but firmly reminds Joseph of their past discussions about the use of profanity and violence and the consequences of this behavior. She explains that Mrs. Elkins is so fearful of more harm to the other children in the home that she cannot have Joseph return.

Joseph's response is surprising. Instead of playing the tough guy role—his usual stance— he quietly sheds a few tears. Joanne hugs him, which he allows. Joanne then explains that she *will be taking Joseph back to the office and they will work to find a place for him to stay while investigating longer-term possibilities.*

When they arrive back at the office, there is a phone message from Mary, the Home for Boys social worker, saying that the facility can accept Joseph, but only for a 30-day period. Joanne is relieved but realizes that a lot of work will be needed to find an appropriate long-term placement for Joseph. Beginning tomorrow, psychological tests will be scheduled, along with a full psychiatric evaluation at the local psychiatric hospital. Joanne had previously spoken with her supervisor about the possibility of a residential treatment center placement for Joseph should this latest foster care arrangement with Mrs. Elkin fail to work.

Joanne takes Joseph to MacDonald's restaurant for lunch so that she can tell him about the Home for Boys and what will happen next. Joseph has again adopted his tough guy stance and shows no visible emotion at the news of yet another placement. Joanne again brings up the subject of therapy with Joseph, explaining how important it is that he have someone he can talk to about things that bother him. She asks that he think about it some more.

The Plan

Joanne arranges for an aide to have Joseph's clothes picked up from Mrs. Elkins' home and delivered to the Home for Boys. She then drives Joseph to the facility and introduces him to Mary. Before departing, Joanne talks with Joseph about immediate plans: Joseph will attend school on the premises, a visit with his brother and sisters will be arranged for the weekend, and appointments to see some special doctors will be scheduled. Joseph doesn't ask about these doctors, which is out of character, but he is clearly distracted by his new surroundings and is eager to break away.

Once back in the office, Joanne makes a list of the arrangements that must be made for Joseph. These include referrals for psychological

and psychiatric testing and initiating the process to find a residential treatment facility that might be able to take Joseph within the next 30 days. Joanne arranges for a conference with her supervisor to discuss this case and to seek direction on possible residential placements. She then turns her attention to the stack of phone messages awaiting her attention.

In this case scenario, Joanne works with both Joseph and the foster care parents. Assessment skills are employed to determine the nature and extent of the presenting problem, and support and counseling are then offered to Joseph and the foster family. Information and referral are also important skills, as evidenced by the social worker's use of psychological and psychiatric referrals to obtain further evaluative information about Joseph for use in locating a long-term placement and other services. Crisis intervention is again a necessary mode of intervention. Finally, the social worker must engage in coordination and negotiation to access other community services that are necessary for her client, such as the Home for Boys.

Because of Joseph's history of behavioral problems and the number of failed placements he has experienced, residential care appears to be the best option. Finding such a placement—and one that is appropriate for Joseph—will be time consuming. There are far too few residential facilities for youths in the vicinity, and there may be a waiting list. Joanne wishes there were other options. However, unlike many other youths with whom Joanne has worked, Joseph does not have any relatives who are able to provide a home for him.

Placement with a relative—what is known as kinship care—is often preferable to foster care because the child lives in a home with relatives with whom he or she is familiar. Studies have shown that children are more successful in living situations in which they can maintain a strong connection to their family of origin (Walton, 2002). Barker (1999) defined kinship care:

The full-time nurturing and protection of children by adult relatives other than parents; these adults may have family ties or other important bonds, such as being members of their tribes or clans, godparents, or stepparents. When the child must be separated from parents, kinship care may be provided informally—that is, without state involvement— by kinship caregivers or kinship foster parents under formal arrangement with the public child welfare system. (p. 264)

More than 2.5 million families are maintained by grandparents who may have one or more grandchildren living with them (Hegar, 1999). Although placement in kinship care can be a much easier adjustment for children, not all states recognize care by relatives as eligible for financial reimbursement (Anderson, 2001). In such situations, relatives may be unable or unwilling to care for the children.

Foster care is a temporary situation when efforts to maintain the family unit have failed or when there is a crisis, such as abandonment or abuse. Family preservation services, discussed below, focus on interventions that seek to prevent the need to remove children from their homes.

FAMILY PRESERVATION SERVICES

Intensive family preservation services have emerged as one of the most widely used models in family-based services to prevent out-of-home placement of children and preserve and strengthen the family unit (Bath & Haapala, 1993). *Family preservation* is defined by Barker (1999) as

planned efforts to provide the knowledge, resources, supports, health care, relationship skills, and structures that help families stay intact and maintain their mutual roles and responsibilities. (p. 169)

Family preservation services are based on the assumption that many children can remain at home and not have to enter the foster care system if services are provided earlier and more intensively (Tracy, 1995). Although in-home services oriented to preserving and strengthening the family have a long history in social work, the use of this approach was given significant impetus by the Adoption Assistance and Child Welfare Act of 1980, which mandated that reasonable efforts be made to prevent the removal of children from their homes (Reed & Kirk, 1998).

Intensive family preservation services are predicated on core values—keep families together; believe in the ability of families to change; respect the family; identify and build on family strengths; and foster family resourcefulness (Sallee & Lloyd, 1991). Different programs have different foci but most are family centered, intensive, and relatively short-term (from 60 days to 90 days); are available 24 hours a day; combine clinical and concrete services; are flexible; focus on limited objectives, such as stabilizing families in crisis; and are delivered by social workers who carry small caseloads (Kinney, Haapala, & Booth, 1991; Walton, 2002).

Family preservation services are intended to stabilize the family at risk, alleviate dangerous conditions, strengthen the family's ability to function in the community, and improve the family's problem-solving and coping skills (Walton, 2002). Frequently, families who are referred for preservation services have multiple and complex problems involving child abuse, child neglect, sexual abuse, alcohol and other drug abuse, and delinquency, as the following vignette illustrates.

STRENGTHENING A FAMILY'S FUNCTIONING
Denise, a recent MSW graduate, works in the family preservation unit at Northern Virginia Family Services. She usually carries a caseload of three families at a time and primarily engages in short-term, crisis intervention. She recently

closed a case and was assigned a new family—the Santiago family. Ms. Santiago is from El Salvador, and she is a single mother with three boys, ages eight, five, and three. Mr. Santiago still resides in El Salvador, and they are legally divorced. He provides no child support.

The family was referred by the five-year-old's teacher who said she suspected child abuse and neglect. The boy is often dirty, and she has recently noticed a large bruise on his right leg and one on his right arm. Denise calls Ms. Santiago on the phone, explains that the agency has been contacted because of concern for the family and that she would like to visit with them. Ms. Santiago speaks little English, and Denise switches to Spanish, a language in which she is fluent. Ms. Santiago is initially wary of arranging an appointment and claims that everything is fine. However, Denise explains that once a complaint has been received by the agency, it is her responsibility to follow through. With reluctance, Ms. Santiago agrees to the home visit, which is scheduled for the next day.

Upon arrival, Denise notices that the home is sparsely furnished, but that it is neat and clean. The children are all home. Denise notices bruises on the arm of the five year old, but does not immediately question the mother about them. Instead, her initial goal is to make Ms. Santiago feel at ease and to establish the beginnings of a relationship with her. Denise talks with Ms. Santiago and the children to get an idea of their living situation. She finds out that Ms. Santiago works two full-time jobs to support her family. Therefore, she is rarely home and often leaves her children to care for themselves, with the eight-year-old child in charge.

Denise recognizes the hurdles Ms. Santiago has overcome to provide a decent home for her family. She comments that Ms. Santiago seems to have a lot to contend with and that perhaps the agency might be of some help. At that point, Denise mentions her observation of bruises on the child's arm. Ms. Santiago responds that the child bruises easily and must have bumped into some-

thing. Denise arranges to come back the next day. Although she is concerned about the bruises, the children do not seem to be at immediate risk.

During her next session with Ms. Santiago Denise asks her about leaving the children home with an eight-year-old child. Ms. Santiago appears confused and explains that this is very common in El Salvador, where an eight-year-old child is generally considered old enough to care for his or her siblings. Denise pursues the subject of the Salvadoran culture and how it differs from American culture. In subsequent sessions, Denise talks with Ms. Santiago about the general method of discipline in a family. This time, Ms. Santiago admits that the bruise marks on her son's arm happened when she grabbed him to break up a fight between him and his older brother.

From her talks with Ms. Santiago and the children, Denise learns that this is not a typical child abuse case. Rather, Ms. Santiago is struggling to make a living in this country and she is simply using the child care methods that are acceptable in El Salvador. The mother explains that she would like to spend more time with her children but that she cannot afford to work only one job. Ms. Santiago is adamant about not receiving public support despite Denise's encouragement. However, Denise does learn that Ms. Santiago's sister is in the area. She contacts the sister with the phone number provided by Ms. Santiago and arranges a meeting. At the meeting the sister indicates her desire to help and agrees to come over in the afternoons and evenings so that she can be with the children after school.

Denise then talks with the mission director of the local church that Ms. Santiago attends. She explains the situation and the mission director agrees that the Santiago family is qualified for the adopt-a-family program at the church. This program matches families that are financially stable with younger families that are struggling to make ends meet. Assistance comes in the form of weekly meals, as well as help with child care and even some financial donations.

Finally, with the client's agreement, Denise arranges for Ms. Santiago to attend a working mothers' support group on Saturday mornings at the local library. A play group for children under the age of six years meets at the same time under supervision. Also, children six years and over participate in their own facilitated group to deal with their emotions about their mothers' absences from the home and to learn ways to help make the situation easier.

In this situation, Denise engages in short-term, family-centered interventions. Through personal interviews with the client family, Denise performs the function of assessment and identification of any environmental problems. She is sensitive to and takes into consideration cultural differences that affect childrearing practices. Denise helps the family to build a network of resources that can be sustained over time; she does this through information gathering and brokering. This network includes both formal and informal resources. For example, the referral to and involvement of the family's church utilizes the resources of the community and provides a bridge between professional helpers and faith-based groups (Walton, 2002).

The interventions employed by Denise are based on a strengths perspective in which the focus is on the client family's personal strengths and resources. In addition to providing concrete assistance, Denise links Ms. Santiago and her children to available services, such as the support group and the adopt-a-family program at the church. In pursuing these creative sources of support, Denise carries out the social work functions of referral and service coordination.

Family preservation services are reserved for only those families at imminent risk of having a child placed in the foster care system. Generally, these families have multiple problems and are often involuntary clients for example, they have not sought services and may be resistant to what can be perceived as interference. Therefore, social workers must work to engage the client in a trusting relationship. They do this by using active listening skills and empathic communication during the assessment stage to establish a nonjudgmental tone. Upon completion of the psychosocial assessment and formulation of a case, the social worker carries out support, advice, counseling, and referral functions to help the family overcome its sense of failure, hopelessness, and hostility (Tracy, 1995).

Perhaps one of the strongest contributions of this approach is that of empowerment—recognizing and using the resources and personal strengths of the family members (Tracy, 1995). However, the primary goal of family preservation is the child's well-being, and there are times when the child is simply not safe in the home and must be placed in a safe and nurturing environment. For this reason, family preservation services should be viewed within a continuum of child welfare services that includes both preventive work before a crisis evolves as well as long-term, supportive services, a range of temporary out-of-home placements, family reunification services, and adoption and postadoption services (Hartman, 1993).

ADOPTION

Adoption is both a legal and a child welfare function and process, in which a person, usually an infant or child, is taken permanently into a family and, with the legal transfer of the individual from the birth parents to the adopting parents, the child is treated as though born into the adoptive family, with all rights and privileges therein (Barker, 1999).

Although adoptions occur through a variety of means, there are generally four adoption categories: stepparent, independent, relinquishment or agency, and intercountry. Stepparent adoptions refer to the adoption of a child by the spouse of a parent. Independent adoptions occur when parents place children directly with adoptive families of their choice without an agency as an intermediary. Agency or relinquishment adoptions are overseen by public or private agencies and occur when there are a voluntary or involuntary legal termination of parental rights to the child. Finally, intercountry adoptions involve adoption of foreign-born children by U.S. families (Barth, 1995).

Most social workers in the field of adoption provide direct services to all parties concerned with the adoption process. Social workers offer nondirective counseling services to pregnant women on their options: abortion, retention, or placement of the infant. The social worker also links a pregnant woman with the medical, educational, housing, and financial services she may require. In addition, social workers conduct home studies of the potential adoptive parent or parents to evaluate the family and the physical and emotional environment for the child who is to be placed. As part of the assessment process, the social worker explores with the applicant family such issues as infertility, openness to adoption, willingness to accept a special-needs child, level of preparation the parents are willing to undertake in regard to their new responsibilities, and dealing with adoption issues over the child's lifetime. If the home study results in approval of the prospective adoptive family, the adoption process proceeds to match a child with the prospective parents.

When a prospective match is made, depending on the age of the child and circumstances, the social worker assists in preparing the child and adoptive parents for their initial and follow-up meetings. Information is provided to the parents about the child, and the adoptive parents may be encouraged to join a parent support group.

Adoption has been described as a "lifelong experience" that may require a range of support services (Landers, 1993). A key role for social workers is to prepare adoptive parents to help children deal with their struggle over identity and loss. In fact, postadoption services are a growing component of adoption practice as older adoptees deal with identity, loss, and self-esteem issues; medical and educational problems that may have a genetic or hereditary basis; and potential contact with birth parents.

Heretofore, adoption services typically ceased after the child was placed in the adoptive home and the adoption was finalized. Even today, postadoption services are not always available. Social workers are increasingly recognizing the need for such services, especially in light of the growing number of families who are adopting older and special-needs children—those with mental, emotional, or physical disabilities. Similarly, the increasing number of international adoptions has created a need for families to understand and deal with different cultures and backgrounds (Groza, 1997). Social workers in adoption and family services agencies have responded to these new developments by establishing support groups for adoptive families, as well as offering individual counseling. In addition, some agencies have established outreach programs for postadoption families, and social workers often visit the homes of adoptive families to gather information about how well the adoption process has worked for the particular family (Landers, 1993).

Many of the children in the foster care system who are eligible for adoption have special needs. These special needs may relate to demographic, physiological, psychological, or developmental conditions. Barker (1999) defined *special-needs adoption* as

> adoption of children who have extenuating conditions or circumstances (such as older children; siblings; children of color; or children who have special physical, emotional, or developmental needs). Each state establishes its own definition of children with special needs. (p. 461)

Subsidized adoption is one mechanism that has been used to encourage and facilitate the adoption of special-needs children. Here, public financial assistance is made available to families who adopt. The criteria used to determine eligibility for subsidy arej that the child is legally free for adoption and that adoptive placement without a subsidy has already been attempted unsuccessfully because of the child's physical or emotional condition or racial or ethnic background (Barker, 1999). The following vignette concerns special-needs adoption.

LOVE AT FIRST SIGHT

Anne Casey, 32 years old, has recently been laid off from her job as a computer analyst. With time on her hands, she decides to volunteer at a local residential child care facility for infants and very young children who have no place else to go. Many of these children are "boarder babies"—children who have been abandoned by their parents at birth. One of the infants to whom Anne is assigned is a three-month-old boy named Terrence. Terrence was born HIV positive.

After several weeks of volunteering, Anne realizes that she has developed a strong attachment to Terrence. She thinks about him all the time and wants to make him a permanent part of her life. She talks with staff at the child care facility about adoption. Social workers there are honest with her about the questionable long-term prognosis. Although the immune systems of some HIV-positive babies are able to "self-correct," others develop full-blown AIDS. It was too early to tell with Terrence, but the risks were certainly there.

Anne was not deterred. She wants to adopt Terrence. One of the social workers at the facility refers her to the county department of social services to begin the adoption application process. A home study will need to be conducted for this single-parent adoption.

Madelyn Smith, the public child welfare agency's social worker assigned to this case from the adoption resource branch, referred Terrence for a determination of eligibility for subsidized adoption, based on his at-risk or special-needs status. Subsidies are available to families that adopt special-needs children (including older children and children with disabilities) without a means test, although their financial situations are taken into account. The subsidy agreement specifies the amount of the assistance payment, the types of services or other assistance to be provided, and the duration of the agreement.

Madelyn meets with Anne several times to conduct the home study and to prepare the subsidy application. She also obtains financial information from Anne in order to determine if Anne is financially stable, a situation compounded by her recent job loss. Fortunately, Anne has been offered another full-time, salaried position at another company that she has accepted. Anne also agrees to attend a weekly adoption course for parents of children with special needs as well as monthly informational sessions on the HIV virus and its progression. Madelyn is impressed with Anne and her willingness to put the necessary energy into providing a quality home environment for Terrence. After consulting with her supervisor and the medical professionals on the multidisciplinary team at the residential facility, Madelyn determines that Anne will be allowed to adopt Terrence and receive a subsidy to help with his care.

In this case scenario, Madelyn carries out the social work function of assessment as she attempts to determine Anne's emotional and financial stability to parent a young infant with HIV. Madelyn also must identify future problems and use information and referral and coordination skills to ensure that proper resources and supports are in place to help Anne meet these challenges. Examples of such resources include referral to the weekly adoption classes and HIV information sessions and arrangements for the subsidy. Madelyn also offers Anne support and counseling in making this major decision to adopt a special-needs child. The social worker consults with her supervisor for feedback and guidance about this potential adoption. Once Anne has been approved as an adoptive parent, Madelyn utilizes her skills in counseling and support to assist the client in preparing for her parenting role of a special-needs child.

In the United States, adoptions includes children who come not only from the child welfare system, but also from other countries. These international adoptions represent about 10 percent of all U.S. adoptions (Barth, 1995). Such adoptions have increased over the years, in part because of the abandonment or displacement of children in times of war or political upheaval in different parts of the world (Groza, 1997). These private adoptions are typically handled by specialized nonprofit or for-profit agencies that match adoptive families with children who are born outside the United States.

Many of the children available for adoption in the United States have special needs, largely come from ethnic or racial minority groups, or both. For families that can afford the costs and desire to adopt a child who is white or of Asian descent, international adoption offers the best opportunity. However, many of these children also have special needs, as the overwhelming majority of them have lived in institutional or group care arrangements for a period of time. There are inherent risks to a child's development when the child has been institutionalized early in his or her life (Groza, 1997), as shown in the following vignette.

EMILY JOINS THE FAMILY

Harriet and Bob Nelson were biologically unable to have children. They had tried everything, including in vitro fertilization. It was time to consider options, as both very much wanted to have a family. First, they applied to a sectarian adoption agency in their area but found that the waiting list was long and the prospects of adopting a white child were slim. Although Harriet and Bob prided themselves on being "liberals," they were not prepared to deal with interracial adoption. They very much wanted the grandparents to have an active role

with their grandchildren; a child of another race or an interracial child would not, they believed, be accepted into the family.

The Nelsons had heard about a private agency that handled overseas adoptions, particularly of children from Romania and the former Soviet Union. They made an appointment and were seen by Diane Nader, a social worker who specializes in international adoptions. Diane's role in this initial interview was to acquaint Harriet and Bob with the procedures involved in international adoption, respond to their questions, and establish a timetable and plan to conduct a psychosocial assessment to determine the family's suitability for parenting an adopted child.

Adopting a child from overseas can be expensive, and this issue, Diane knows, must be addressed from the outset of the process. First, private agencies (particularly for-profit agencies) charge fees for their services that may be based on what the market will bear. In addition, the family will be responsible for travel costs and arrangements in the host country.

At the conclusion of the first meeting with Diane, Harriet and Bob have a lot of information to digest. This process was much more complicated, expensive, and time consuming than they had envisioned. However, they want to proceed, and a second appointment is arranged to begin the home study process. At home, they begin to calculate what the actually costs might be and come up with a staggering figure of $20,000 or even more. And this is just to get the baby home! The Nelsons are not rich, but they do have savings. This is what they have been saving for.

The processing of their application takes about two months. Reference letters are needed. The agency also wants a physician's statement about their health status. Some initial payments are made to cover agency expenses in this process. But it is a matter of "hurry up and wait." With the process completed, the Nelsons now have to await word that a child has been located for them. Diane has given the Nelsons a lot of reading materials about international adoption, including information related to some of the special issues that may arise. Diane has also suggested that they enroll in a group run by the agency for parents about to adopt from overseas. This group focuses on cultural issues and helping the child to build an identity associated with his or her ethnicity and culture.

The Nelsons attend once a week group sessions and learn a lot about what to expect when they go to Romania or Russia as well as the issues they will need to address when they arrive back in the United States. They know that when they receive a call, they will need to make immediate plans to travel abroad and to stay for several weeks to handle the arrangements required by the host country. Their passports are in order and advance notice has been given to each of their employers.

Two months later, the call came—an eight-month-old girl who had been abandoned at birth and has been living in an institution in Moscow was to be theirs. Two weeks later, Harriet and Bob are on an airplane. The agency had helped with arrangements in Russia, including reservations at a hotel near the orphanage. They have the name of a lawyer in Russia who will handle the paperwork on that end. They decided that their baby would be named Emily.

On their arrival in Moscow, things at first seem to be going well. The Nelsons were able to contact the lawyer within a day of their arrival. They had some difficulty communicating, as the lawyer's English was not very good. The lawyer suggested that he arrange for an interpreter for them during their stay, foremost when they visited the orphanage. The Nelsons gave the go-ahead to hire the interpreter. This was the first of a long list of unexpected costs.

Two days later, with the lawyer and interpreter present, the Nelsons have their first opportunity to meet Emily, who is now nine months old. But when they look at this little

bundle in the crib, it is difficult to believe that she is more than a month or two old—she's so tiny and frail looking. However, Emily responds to being held, searches the faces of these new people, and delights at the stuffed toy the Nelsons have brought her.

Each day the Nelsons visit the orphanage. The lawyer said that the paperwork to have Emily transferred to their custody and to leave the country was "in process." It would only be a short time now. But then a full week goes by, and then another week. The Nelsons were becoming concerned that there were problems about which they were not being informed. They were also frustrated because even with access to an interpreter, communication proved to be more than a matter of language. It was difficult to get questions answered. The elongation of the process was getting expensive for them, and they were also concerned about how much more time they could take from their jobs. They also learned that they would have to pay a hefty fee to the orphanage for its part in processing Emily's papers, although the U.S. agency had said this would not happen. The good news was that Emily seemed more and more responsive each day.

The week or so in Russia proved to be a month or so. It was a time of ups and downs for Harriet and Bob, accompanied by a high degree of tension. But they were on their way home with Emily to what they hoped would be a happy life for all of them.

The Nelson's story does not end with their arrival back in the United States. Emily was taken to a pediatrician as soon as an appointment could be made. He confirmed what they suspected—she was underweight and not at the appropriate developmental level for a nine month old. The pediatrician, Dr. Westin, asked a lot of questions about Emily's early days and her parent's health history. The Nelsons had anticipated the need for this information, but had been unable to secure it. Dr. Westin has treated a number of children who were adopted from other countries and who had lived in insti-

tutions. He concluded that Emily displayed some of the characteristics associated with early institutionalization—below normal weight and height, delays in fine and gross motor skills, a level of passivity, and extreme cautiousness around new people (Groza, 1997). Dr. Westin suggested a special enrichment diet for Emily and close medical follow-up examinations in the following weeks, as the risk of opportunistic infections was high. He also recommended that the Nelsons continue their participation in the agency's group for adoptive parents.

Harriet and Bob have some mixed feelings about returning to the adoption agency because the experience they encountered differed significantly from what they had been told to expect. However, they decide to rejoin the group. There they learn, over time, to anticipate a number of problems related to Emily's earliest months and that they will need practical and emotional help and support along the way. They also learn that they are lucky. Emily appears to be thriving in the home environment.

CULTURALLY SENSITIVE SERVICES

Much has been written in the social work literature about the importance of culturally sensitive practice. Barker (1999) defined *culturally sensitive practice* in social work as

the process of professional intervention while being knowledgeable, perceptive, empathetic, and skillful about the unique as well as common characteristics of clients who possess racial, ethnic, religious, gender, age, sexual orientation, or socioeconomic differences. (p. 113)

Data from the U.S. Bureau of Labor Statistics (as well as NASW membership data) consistently show that social workers are predominantly white. The demographics of the client populations with whom social workers work, however,

fall within the broad category of disenfranchised populations, including a disproportionate number of people of color. These demographics—in which there is a discrepancy between the composition of the social work labor force and the demographic profile of many client groups—have led the profession to identify and emphasize the need for social workers to develop competence in culturally and ethnically sensitive practice. Such sensitivity encompasses an understanding of the role of ethnicity, race, religion, gender, age, and other demographic variables on psychosocial functioning. Culture, language, and even geographic location of residency may also have implications for diagnosis and treatment planning for individuals, groups, and communities. The special capabilities, distinct cultural histories, and unique needs of people of various backgrounds must be identified and understood if successful interventions are to result.

The following vignette represents a real social worker of Native American heritage who chose to advocate for and work on behalf of American Indian causes. The work of Russell Redner was highlighted in a 1998 *NASW News* article ("Protector of Kids and a Culture") and is reprinted here in its entirety.

PROTECTOR OF KIDS AND A CULTURE

When Russell Redner was hired about a year and a half ago by the Pyramid Lake Paiute Tribe as director of Pyramid Lake (Nevada) Social Services, the Native American social worker found a lot to keep him busy.

He reports a caseload of 300 child welfare cases, 300 general assistance cases, and 30 Indian child welfare cases.

In late summer (1998), Redner also began working with the families of several American youths charged in connection with the August beating death of a 25-year-old Hispanic man. Redner sought to minimize hostile confrontations between the Native American and Hispanic communities, as both held rallies and marches during September. He spoke at a joint prayer meeting held by the two groups before a court hearing for 12 of the defendants, who range in age from 14 to 24.

"What we're trying to do here is unite these two communities who are divided on this case," Redner told the Reno Gazette-Journal in an article headlined, "Social Worker Battles for Indian Rights." Redner joined with a representative from the Hispanic community in urging both groups to see that justice is done and further violence avoided.

Advocating Indian causes for more than 25 years, he was a member of the American Indian Movement (AIM) long before he became a social worker and explains that he has participated in all demonstrations since Native Americans took over Alcatraz in 1969.

Redner sees his memberships in AIM and NASW as "a fitting combination since both organizations are working for and saving people."

Redner teachers a course in American Indian activism at Western Nevada Community College American and he told the Gazette-Journal that his work on behalf of the Indian defendants and their families represents the "modern face of activism." He is also working with the Paiute tribal counsel to put into operation a six- to eight-bed therapeutic group home for children who must now be placed in out-of-state homes, some as far away as Oregon. The existence of a group home on the reservation was also seen as a budget-trimming measure, since about $300,000 was spent over two years on child placement.

The tribe has already purchased an existing home, described by Redner as a "dream house" with a swimming pool, tennis court and beautiful location beside a river. He expects to employ traditional Native American methods of healing with standard social work treatment techniques learned at the University of Nevada–Reno. "We have already brought the drum and some of the more ceremonial items into the group home," Redner said. Elders, who

are revered members of the tribe, will also be involved in treatment, he noted, possibly relating the history of the Pyramid Lake tribe to the children in their native language.

Redner expects the home, believed to be the first therapeutic group home on a reservation, to open in about six months. "Native American social workers are much like the early social workers," Redner related in correspondence with NASW. "We do this work," he stated, "as an attempt to, literally, save our culture." (p. 12)

Russell Redner was able to secure a position that allowed him to provide individual, group, and systemically oriented services to the Native American community with which he identified. Many—perhaps a majority—of social workers, however, provide services to a highly diverse group of people who represent the spectrum of ethnic, racial, and religious differences that characterize the U.S. population.

Cultural competence is a "must" in the practice of social work, as the United States has increasingly become a multicultural society. In some locales, such as Chicago, Houston, Los Angeles, and New York City, social workers' caseloads may be overwhelmingly composed of people of color or people for whom English is a second language. Immigrant communities of people who came from Central and South America, Mexico, Viet Nam, Korea, China, and Thailand, among other nations, may require social services, including acculturation services, job training, and language skills development. Sometimes they require family and child welfare services. It is thus imperative that social workers have knowledge of specific cultural groups and the ability to provide services with sensitivity to differences. The use of culturally grounded interventions has been identified as a core skill in culturally competent practice (Hurdle, 2002).

Several terms are used in social work to refer to the knowledge and skill base needed to work with people of diverse backgrounds and ethnicities: culturally sensitive practice, ethnic-sensitive practice, and social work with ethnic minority groups (Barker, 1999; Hurdle, 2002). The common thread is the need to understand the dimensions of culture and to apply them to practice. As Hurdle (2002) noted: "Cultural competence is not a static process of acquiring ability but rather an ongoing process of attuning oneself to the ever-changing cultures of various client groups" (p. 185).

DOMESTIC VIOLENCE

For many years, social workers have been working with the victims of domestic violence in such settings as the courts, shelters, and hospital emergency rooms. Domestic violence is the primary cause of injury to women in the United States—across ethnic, religious, and socioeconomic boundaries (Barnett, Miller-Perrin, & Perrin, 1997). However, precise statistics are lacking because so many incidents go unreported and sources of data are limited to official reports, clinical studies, and self-reports (Corcoran, Stephenson, Perryman, & Allen, 2001). Even today, there are some segments of society that still believe that domestic violence is a private issue that typically occurs within the sanctity of marriage and that government should refrain from involvement. A component of the argument is that if the situation was so bad, the woman would leave; her failure to do so is seen as complicity and perhaps evidence of masochism (Grana, 2001). Concrete data, however, suggest that the victim-centered views are ill informed.

Under the auspices of the National Institute of Justice and the Centers for Disease Control and Prevention, a survey, consisting of telephone interviews with a nationally representative sample of 8,000 U.S. women and 8,000 U.S. men, was conducted about their experiences with intimate partner violence (Tjaden & Thoennes, 2000). Among the major findings, the study revealed:

- Intimate partner violence is pervasive in U.S. society. Nearly 25 percent of surveyed women and 7.5 percent of surveyed men said they were raped or physically assaulted by a current or former spouse, cohabiting partner, or date at some time in their life times; 1.5 percent of surveyed women and 0.9 percent of surveyed men said they were raped or physically assaulted by a partner in the previous 12 months. According to these estimates, approximately 1.5 million women and 834,732 men are raped or physically assaulted by an intimate partner annually in the United States.
- Stalking by intimates is more prevalent than previously thought. According to estimates, 503,485 women and 185,496 men are stalked by an intimate partner annually in the United States.
- Women are significantly more likely than men to report being victims of intimate partner violence.
- Rates of intimate partner violence vary significantly among women of diverse racial backgrounds. Asian and Pacific Islander women and men tend to report lower rates of intimate partner violence than do women and men from other minority backgrounds; African American, American Indian, and Alaska Native women and men report higher rates.
- Violence perpetrated against women by intimates is often accompanied by emotionally abusive and controlling behavior.
- Most intimate partner victimizations are not reported to the police.

In response to the recognition of domestic violence as a significant social problem, Congress passed the Violence Against Women Act of 1994 (P.L. 103-322), which was reauthorized in 2000. In addition, there may be state laws to protect victims of domestic violence and to provide services to them under the Victims of Trafficking and Violence Protection Act of 2000 (P.L. 106-386).

The Violence Against Women Act of 1994 provides authorization and funding for a number of programmatic responses to the problem of domestic violence. The Safe Streets for Women Program, for example, addresses penalties for repeat offenders, provides for mandatory restitution for sex crimes, and authorizes funds for victims' counselors. Also of relevance to the social work profession are provisions regarding authorization and funding for education and prevention, training programs, battered women's shelters, community programs on domestic violence, and research. Through this act, the National Domestic Violence Hotline was established (1-800-799-SAFE; U.S. Department of Justice, 2002). The Violence Against Women Act reauthorization includes incremental changes to provide funds to coordinate the law enforcement, judicial, and social services systems that respond to domestic violence; to extend eligibility for Section 8 housing certificates for those escaping domestic violence; and to increase training for judges, social workers, teachers, and others.

The fact that battered spouses frequently remain in abusive relationships may seem incomprehensible. However, feminists explain that women are often held captive by their own sense of powerlessness. Many women are socialized to accept the belief that they are solely responsible for their marriage and their children. The fear that if they leave they will have to care for themselves and their children without assistance shackles many women with a sense of hopelessness and despair (Davis, 1995). It may be dangerous for a woman to leave her abuser. If the abuser is the major breadwinner and controls economic resources, leaving can cause additional problems for the woman. Leaving can also mean living in fear, facing the possibility of losing child custody, and experiencing harassment at work (National Coalition Against Domestic Violence [NCADV], 2002b).

During the past 20 years, a network of services has developed under public and private auspices across the country to address the problems of domestic violence. Grassroots coalitions have played an important role in services provision; these coalitions have also been instrumental in prodding public agencies to make use of available public funds to expand programs and services (Davis, Hagen, & Early, 1994). Alliances at the community level have also been formed between police departments and social workers. A prototype of these programs was developed in the late 1960s on an experimental basis in New York City, the goal of which was to prevent family violence with arrest used only as a last resort (Corcoran et al., 2001). Police officers trained in mediation and crisis intervention were encouraged to make referrals to social services agencies.

This concept was adopted by a local police department in Rhode Island in the mid-1970s, with the creation of a crisis team composed of one police officer and one social worker. This team approach provided victims with an immediate range of social services. Several other cities picked up on this approach. A recent evaluation of a domestic violence response team comprised of police and human services personnel in a suburban area of a southwestern state sought to assess the program from the police perspective (Corcoran et al., 2001). Findings revealed that the coordinated response of police and social workers to the provision of comprehensive services is effective.

People who have been the victims of domestic violence require a continuum of services to improve their economic and psychological independence. Shelters offer temporary protection in a safe environment where women can learn that the abuse they have suffered is not due to their own failures. Shelters also help women to develop confidence in their ability to live on their own, away from their abuser. In terms of economic support, women may turn to Temporary Assistance for Needy Families (TANF) for temporary assistance; however, they also need education and training to assist them in obtaining a permanent source of employment (Davis, 1995). Finally, battered women may need affordable housing and legal assistance to help them in the often long and contentious process of separation, divorce, and child custody arrangements, as the following vignette suggests (Davis, 1995).

A BATTERED WOMAN FINDS A SAFE HAVEN
Becky is 30 years old and has two young boys, ages three and five years. She has been married for seven years and, for three out of the seven years, her husband Sam has beaten her. It started when her husband lost his job at the railroad company. He began collecting unemployment and drinking to excess. Sam now drives a taxicab and comes home at all hours of the night, usually after having several drinks. The young children are often asleep when he comes home, but Becky waits up even though she knows what will probably happen. She tries to make everything perfect so that he won't get angry, but there is always something that sets him off. Two nights ago, Sam came home at midnight and was furious that she had left the light on at the end of the driveway. He yelled at her that she was wasteful and ungrateful, and he began pushing and hitting her. Finally, the five-year-old boy ran downstairs and tried to stop the beating only to be pushed into the wall by his father who then stormed out the door and drove off into the night. Becky was horrified that he had pushed their son, so she gathered up the two boys, packed a small bag, and drove to Safe Haven.

Safe Haven is a small battered women's shelter that accepts children. Becky had learned about Safe Haven when she visited the department of social services last month. Estelle, the social worker at the shelter, welcomed Becky and her children. She gave them one of the two empty rooms and a key to a locker where they could put their belongings. For the next two

days, Estelle let Becky and her boys just relax and stay together in safety. She met with Becky for an hour every day and with each of the boys for about half an hour. Estelle then arranged for the boys to get transportation to and from school and alerted their teachers and the principal that the boys were not to be allowed to go home with their father if he attempted to pick them up.

Estelle then began working with Becky who had very little education or training other than a high school diploma. Residents are generally allowed to stay at the shelter for six months; therefore, Estelle was working with Becky to develop goals and life skills so that she could maintain a job, find an apartment, and care for her two boys after she had to leave the shelter.

Estelle helped Becky apply for TANF for short-term financial assistance. Estelle then signed Becky up for local computer training courses at the library where Safe Haven had developed a working relationship. In addition, there was a subsidized housing complex to which Safe Haven had sent many previous clients. The apartments were located in another town, and the boys would probably have to change schools, but both Becky and Estelle thought that might be for the best. Estelle liked the apartment and, since she was with Safe Haven, the management agreed to hold it for her until she had the first month's rent or until six months had passed.

In addition to her computer courses, Becky participated twice a week in a support group that was held at Safe Haven. Becky learned that it wasn't her fault that her husband was abusive, and that it was his problem rather than hers. Her two sons also participated in a support group for children that helped them understand the situation and to learn that violence is not an appropriate way to deal with frustration and anger.

After five months of training and counseling, Becky saved enough money to make the first month's rent on an apartment, and she had secured a job as a secretary at the telephone com-

pany. However, before she moved, Estelle helped Becky contact a lawyer who worked with Safe Haven and specialized in abuse cases. The lawyer agreed to assist Becky for a minimal fee. Once in her new home, with her new job, Becky and her sons finally felt free.

In this case, the social worker carried out the functions of assessment, identification, support, and counseling as she interacted with Becky and her two sons. The social worker also used coordination and linkage skills with many agencies with which she had already developed relationships, such as the local library and the subsidized housing complex. Furthermore, by helping Becky get training, employment, TANF benefits, and legal assistance, Estelle carried out the social work functions of referral, case management, and advocacy. Although all social work functions are important, advocacy is one area in which social workers must get involved—especially in the realm of domestic violence. With their special training and focus on the person-in-environment, social workers are able to "frame the problem of woman abuse within the larger social context and to advocate at a national level for policies that truly empower all women" (Davis, 1995, p. 787). Such interventions include advocating for more comprehensive social policy, maintaining and increasing funding levels for domestic violence programs, and documenting the nature of the problems affecting victims and their children and the outcomes of social work interventions.

The social worker was able to help Becky to locate permanent, affordable housing. But in some situations, financial stability and permanent housing are difficult goals to achieve. A 1999 study conducted by the U.S. Conference of Mayors found that domestic violence was a primary cause of homelessness (NCADV, 2002a). Other studies reveal that a large proportion (up to 50 percent) of women who receive TANF cite domestic violence as a factor in their need for assistance (NCADV, 2002c).

HOMELESS FAMILIES

In the past, the public's conception of a homeless person was a white, alcoholic male. However, this is no longer accurate. Homelessness is a condition that affects men, women, and children of all races and ages (U.S. Conference of Mayors, 2001). For a growing number of families for whom the ravages of poverty, lack of affordable housing, or unemployment have diminished life options, home may be a shelter, welfare hotel, or the streets. In fact, families are the fastest growing segment of the homeless population (U.S. Conference of Mayors, 2001). A "typical" homeless family is comprised of a single parent and two or three children, often under school age. Most are not substance abusers or mentally ill; they have simply fallen through society's safety net.

The official definition of homelessness comes from the Stewart B. McKinney Homeless Assistance Act of 1987 (P.L. 100-77), as amended:

> A person is considered homeless who: lacks a fixed, regular, and adequate night-time residence; and has a primary night-time residency that is
> (a) a supervised publicly or privately operated shelter designed to provide temporary living accommodations . . .
> (b) an institution that provides a temporary residence for individuals intended to be institutionalized, or
> (c) a public or private place not designed for, or ordinarily used as, a regular sleeping accommodation for human beings. (National Coalition for the Homeless [NCH], 1999c)

There are problems with this definition as it includes only those people who are literally homeless—on the streets or in shelters—and people who face imminent eviction (within a week) from a private dwelling or institution and have no resources to obtain housing. This literal definition applies more to urban dwellers than to those in rural areas, who may be taken in by relatives or live in overcrowded or substandard housing (NCH, 1999c).

Dissatisfaction with the legislative definition of homelessness, however, has not led to a consensus about how homelessness should be defined. Although many people agree that homelessness refers to not having a place to live that is either owned or rented, there is less agreement about those who live with others for long periods of time or who reside in single-room occupancy hotels (First, Rife, & Toomey, 1995). Definitions of homeless families are also unclear. People are usually counted as part of a homeless family only if they have dependent children who are homeless with them. If their children are staying with someone else, the parents are classified as single adults, which ignores the devastating effects of homelessness on the family (First et al., 1995).

The high mobility of the homeless population and the difficulty of locating them make it impossible to arrive at a precise count of the number of homeless people in the United States. Various studies have identified widely different estimates of the incidence of homelessness—for example, 500,000–600,000; 700,000 per night and 2 million per year; 7 million; 3 percent of the U.S. population (NCH, 1999b). Almost every study or report presents a different statistic; however, there is agreement that the number of homeless people is steadily increasing (First et al., 1995; NCH, 1999b). One way of measuring the rate of homelessness is the utilization of shelter beds. A review of research conducted in the decade between 1987 and 1997 in 11 communities and four states found that shelter capacity more than doubled in nine communities and three states during that time period (NCH, 1999b).

Why are so many people homeless? Several generally accepted explanations for homelessness have been offered, including mental illness, lack of adequate housing, lack of community resources, poverty, and a decrease in federal sup-

port programs (Karger & Stoesz, 1998; NCH, 1999a, 1999c, 1999d; Rossi, 1994). The NCH attributes the rise in homelessness to two major trends over the past two decades: a growing shortage of affordable rental housing and a concurrent increase in poverty. Homelessness and poverty are inextricably linked (NCH, 1999a).

The problems associated with poverty are interrelated and cyclical. For example, unemployed persons or low-wage earners are usually unable to purchase medical insurance and, therefore, an illness of a family member may force them into extreme poverty. Their homelessness inevitably denies them a network of supportive relationships that is essential to any person's maintenance of physical and mental health.

Also related to the rise in homelessness is the decline in the availability of public assistance based on the Personal Responsibility and Work Opportunity Reconciliation Act of 1996 (P.L. 104-193). In some communities, former welfare families appear to be experiencing increased rates of homelessness (NCH, 1999a).

Other factors account for homelessness. Domestic violence may force battered women to choose between abusive relationships and homelessness. About 20 percent to 25 percent of the single adult homeless population suffers from some form of severe and persistent mental illness (NCH, 1999e). Often these people are excluded from programs for the homeless because they are mentally ill, and they are excluded from services for the mentally ill because they are homeless.

For families with children, the cost of housing has been a major contributor to homelessness. Housing policy experts say that the real estate boom in the 1980s resulted in increasing housing costs and decreasing low-income affordable rental options (Karger & Stoesz, 1998). Urban renewal, which is sweeping many areas of the country, replaces older, low-cost, inner-city dwellings with downtown shopping malls and other development. In the following vignette, the effect of a downward trend in the economy takes its toll on a family.

A FAMILY ON THE STREETS

Greg was 22 years old when he married Jenny. She was 20 years old—and five months pregnant. Greg had a job as a construction worker for Burlington Works helping to build the new Central Bank building for $12 an hour. They had a small, substandard efficiency apartment, but at least it was a roof over their heads.

Two months after their marriage, Burlington Works cut Greg's pay to the minimum wage of $5.75 an hour. Jenny began to skip her obstetrician appointments to save money. Two weeks later Greg was fired. The construction foreman explained that the bank job was almost finished and no more new construction in Vermont was anticipated until next year at the earliest. Greg and Jenny were scared. They could not afford to pay their rent. There were no family resources to call upon; Jenny's mother was deceased and her father was an alcoholic with whom she had purposely lost contact several years back. Greg, whose parents lived in Missouri, had not spoken to them since he moved out when he was 15 years old. They had no other relatives and few friends in the area, so they moved into the only place they had—their old, rusted station wagon.

When it came time for Jenny to give birth, they went to the emergency room of the county hospital. Fortunately, the baby was healthy, although slightly underweight. Greg told the social worker at the hospital that they had no home and had been living in their car. The social worker talked to Greg and Jenny about their options and then referred them to the Streetwork Project in Burlington that provides year-round assistance to homeless families.

When Jenny, Greg, and their new baby arrived at Streetwork, they were assigned a social worker, Ms. Marks. Ms. Marks met with Jenny and Greg. She learned that Greg had a high school education and some experience in construction and auto repair. Jenny needed one more year to earn her high school diploma. Ms. Marks

was aware that the young family needed immediate shelter and, fortunately, there was an available room in the emergency shelter at Streetwork. However, she knew they needed more long-term assistance and she arranged to meet with them daily to help Greg find employment and to help Jenny get her GED. Ms. Marks also arranged for their new baby to receive immunizations and a complete health assessment.

As Ms. Marks counseled Jenny and Greg she became aware of their troubled past and she urged them to go to self-help groups. She suggested Adult Children of Alcoholics for Jenny and a fathering group for Greg. Ms. Marks believed that these opportunities would allow them to develop their socialization skills and form a support network of peers. Ms. Marks also advised Jenny and Greg on the importance of family planning. Ms. Marks arranged for Jenny and Greg to meet with a Planned Parenthood counselor who came to Streetwork every two weeks.

Ms. Marks enjoyed working with Jenny and Greg. They were young and had fallen into the trap of homelessness and poverty, but they were motivated to change their circumstances.

Some of Ms. Marks's clients had been homeless for so long that they had given up hope, but Jenny and Greg actively participated in counseling sessions with Ms. Marks and attended the group meetings she suggested. Shortly after their arrival, Greg began working in auto repair at the service center for county automobiles. Ms. Marks helped them to establish a banking account, and with guidance and support they were on their way to self-sufficiency.

Social workers who work with the homeless population use a variety of skills. On the direct services level, as presented in this vignette, the social worker counsels and advises homeless families on ways to decrease stress and alleviate crises situations. Social workers also provide referral services when necessary as exemplified when Ms. Marks arranged for Greg and Jenny to meet with the Planned Parenthood counselor and attend group support meetings. Ms. Marks also carried out the social work function of enabling by helping Greg and Jenny to maximize their independence through employment for Greg and a GED for Jenny.

Ziesemer, Marcoux, and Marwell (1994) outlined the key tasks of social workers involved in the arena of homelessness. Social workers must help those who are already homeless, and they must also work to change conditions and prevent an increase in the numbers of poor and homeless people in the future. To do this social workers take on advocacy roles and work to help homeless families deal with the multiple stressors in their lives. Some changes that may help to improve the plight of the homeless are keeping shelters open all day, providing day care and preschool programs to homeless children, allowing homeless families to stay together, and providing support services during a shelter stay as well as follow-up services after departure from the shelter.

In addition to providing direct services, social workers can also get involved in program planning and community organizing to benefit and empower the homeless population. For example, many more shelters are needed for short-term, immediate emergency needs, and there is a longer-term need for low-cost housing options.

THE FUTURE

Social workers in the field of family and children's services are cognizant of the changing demographics of the clientele with whom they work. Increasingly, the population is becoming more multicultural, and children who are members of racial and ethnic groups are disproportionately represented in the child welfare system (Liederman, 1995). In addition, the drug abuse epidemic that has ravaged the country in recent years has had a tremendous impact on the child welfare system. Familiar safety nets are simply no longer adequate to handle cases in which

substance abuse and addiction are involved. The human immunodeficiency virus (HIV) and acquired immune deficiency syndrome (AIDS) have also increasingly affected children, adolescents, and their families (Liederman, 1995).

A constant issue for social workers in the field of family and children's services is that of funding. Although there is substantial public support for programs that protect children and foster their growth and development, this does not always translate into the use of tax dollars for such purposes. Highlighting the need for ongoing advocacy in the public arena is the very important distinction between legislative authorizations and actual appropriations. One example is the Violence Against Women Act, which was reauthorized in 2000. In that act, Congress authorized $3.3 billion over a five-year period, with $677.3 million for FY 2001. However, in the FY 2001 budget, only $468.4 million was appropriated (NCADV, 2002c).

The task of child welfare work is best understood as a combination of policy, research, and practice. Practice research and, as important, utilization of research findings to inform practice are now considered essential keys to the future of the profession (O'Neill, 2000; Thornton, 2001). Social workers in the arena of child welfare services are examining the impact of TANF and how it has affected the children and families who need services. Child welfare advocates, including social workers, have been advocating primarily for programs that promote parenting, encourage self-sufficiency, include quality child care, emphasize the prevention of adolescent pregnancy, and provide access to health care and affordable and safe housing (Liederman, 1995). Social workers are utilizing the growing body of research that documents the outcomes of TANF and other laws in terms of legislative goals and the often unanticipated consequences of social policy to inform renewed public debate about welfare reform and its impact on families and children. This aspect of practice is discussed in detail in chapter 11.

CAREER OPPORTUNITIES

There is a broad range of career opportunities in the field of family and children services, examples of which are listed below. However, the new conservative thrust of government has threatened massive restrictions and elimination of many family and child programs. It is essential for social workers in this arena to bring their skills, knowledge, and experience to the debate and to be actively involved in the formation of public policy.

Center for Family and Youth Coordinator

City of Long Beach, CA, seeks a clinical services coordinator for a family preservation program, including supervising program staff and providing counseling. Requirements are a valid mental health professional license and one year of related professional experience. Desirable are three years of total experience, including development of written and verbal communication skills. (*NASW News*, March 2001, p. 14)

President and Chief Executive Officer

Growing Home, an innovative family services agency operating in Minnesota and South Carolina, seeks nominations and applications for the position of president and chief executive officer. Our mission is to help children, youths, and families who are at risk of institutionalization or homelessness realize their potential and contribute to the community. The position will report to the board of directors and has the responsibility for directing the overall activities of the agency, including the supervision of the chief financial officer, state program executives, vice president for communications and marketing, vice president for fund development, director of youth development, and others. The president and chief executive officer must have an MSW degree, plus experience in supervising staff, writing proposals, developing budgets, and implementing programs. A commitment to leadership development, teamwork, cultural competency, and a strengths-based perspective is essential. Previous experience in child welfare and juvenile

corrections is preferred. Flexibility is required. Growing Home has 52 staff people and serves over 300 youths and families. It is an active member of the Foster Family-Based Treatment Association and is accredited by the Council on Accreditation. (*NASW News*, March 2002, p. 21)

Social Worker, Heritage Camp Director

Holt International has provided Heritage Camps for young international adoptees for 18 years. We are currently seeking a director and mentor for the Heritage Camp program beginning in 2002. This full-time position will also provide other postadoption services supporting adoptive families, adoptees, and birth parents. The ideal candidate will be an international adoptee with a master's degree in social work and five years experience in a social services setting with a social work focus. Camp experience is preferable. Position requires ability to work well with children and proven skills in cultural competency and program management. (*NASW News* July 2001, p. 15)

Program Supervisor

Choices, a domestic violence prevention program, needs a program supervisor for therapist coordination and supervision; correspondence with court and legal system; direct services to clients; participation in development and implementation of program. MSW degree plus two years experience preferred. Must be license eligible. Must have strong organizational, writing, and speaking skills; and supervisory experience of staff and interns. Knowledge of domestic violence and the Prevention of Domestic Violence Act preferred. Competitive salary; excellent benefits. (*NASW News*, November 2001, p. 21)

Executive Director, Social Worker

Maple Star Nevada, Inc., a private foster and group home care provider in Nevada, is seeking to fill the position of executive director. The executive director is responsible for directing the activities of the agency, recruiting and hiring staff, supervising staff, managing agency finances, developing and implementing family care programs, obtaining necessary contracts and licenses, and nurturing relations with state and county officials. Competitive compensation and benefits. Qualifications: Candidates must have experience in foster care, program management, and staff supervision; an MSW degree; and a license (or eligibility for) to practice social work in the State of Nevada. (*NASW News*, September 2000, p. 25)

Social Workers

For Love of Children (FLOC) seeks adventurous social workers interested in utilizing best-practice techniques to join an innovative, strengths-based, solution-focused approach to family work designed to transform the child welfare system. FLOC is a critical partner in a revolutionary project addressing family and child issues that has the potential to finally make child welfare work productive and rewarding for both families and social workers. If you are a licensed general social worker (LGSW) or licensed independent clinical social worker in DC or Maryland and have child welfare and family systems experience, send your resume to FLOC. (*NASW News,* March 2001, p. 15)

Administrator for Child Protective Services

The New Hampshire Division for Children, Youth and Families is searching for an administrator for the bureau of child protective services. Position is responsible for managing all aspects of 12 district offices and 175 field workers. MSW and seven years of social work experience to include at least four years of managerial experience are required for consideration. Reimbursement for graduate MSW loan is negotiable. (*NASW News*, September 2000, p. 22)

Clinical Positions in Supervisory and Direct Services

Positions available with growing agency that serves children and families with both residential and day treatment programs. Be a part of a dynamic Joint Commission on Accreditation of Healthcare Organizations psychiatric treatment center that is on the cutting edge, increasing numbers and types of programs in a continuing effort to provide the best services possible. Come grow with us. Located in the beautiful Willamette Valley, near beaches, mountains, skiing. Outstanding benefits, pleasant surroundings, rewarding work. (*NASW News*, January 2002, p. 2)

Social Worker

Wisconsin Department of Health and Family Services, Bureau of Milwaukee Child Welfare is currently looking for dynamic individuals interested in working on the cutting edge of child welfare reform. Duties include performing child welfare intake; conducting initial assessments (investigations) of alleged child abuse and neglect referrals in Milwaukee County; implementing appropriate intervention strategies; preparing written and oral testimony for children's court; and maintaining documentation of caseloads. Job requirements include possession of a State of Wisconsin certified social worker credential (temporary certificates will be accepted) and computer skills. (*NASW News*, March 2001, p. 18)

Vice President, Treatment Services

FamiliesFirst, one of California's premier child welfare–mental health agencies with $50+ million budget, seeks a seasoned professional to assume overall responsibility for programs and services. Based in Davis, the vice president will report to the executive director and collaborate with the senior management team striving for high quality, continuous agency growth, and leadership in determining state policy. Qualifications include solid management experience, extensive knowledge of children–families services and nonprofit agency operations, vision, entrepreneurial spirit, leadership, high value on teamwork, and mutual learning. (*NASW News*, September 2000, p. 19)

Assistant Director of Treatment Services

Position is a unique opportunity for individual with good clinical skills who wants to grow and develop professionally. The Children's Home, Inc., in Tampa, FL, a 105-year-old multifunction child welfare agency, operates a psychodynamically oriented long-term residential treatment program using the primary caretaker model of therapy. Candidates must have a minimum of four years of children's residential treatment or foster care experience, some supervisory experience and appropriate clinical training, and be comfortable working within a psychotherapeutic model. Duties include program development, individual supervision, and training for clinical and child care staff. Must have MSW and be license eligible. (*NASW News*, May 1998, p. 15)

Psychotherapist

Enjoy hiking, skiing, fishing, camping, rafting, and the serenity of the Rocky Mountains? Montana Academy, a coeducational therapeutic boarding school for troubled adolescents located on a ranch in the mountains of rural northwest Montana, currently seeks adolescent therapist to provide individual, group, and clinical leadership within our treatment team. Requirements: master's degree in counseling or related field; experience with adolescents; prefer chemical dependency experience or certification. (*NASW News*, January 2002, pp. 20–21)

Child Protective Service Specialists

Arizona Department of Economic Security has direct services and administrative positions available throughout Arizona in the state's children services agencies. BSW or MSW is preferred; related fields will be considered. (*NASW News*, February 2002, p. 14)

Child Therapist

Opening for a full-time position in a private practice servicing children, adolescents, and their families. Join a strong team of professionals in a growing practice. Special consideration will be given to candidates with expertise in the assessment and treatment of abuse or eating disorders. Training and experience with child or adolescent therapy required. Must have a licensed clinical social work degree. Licensure or licensure eligibility in Maryland required. Cognitive–behavioral orientation preferred. (*NASW News*, September 1998, p. 22)

Clinical Supervisor

Wilmington, DE, needs clinical supervisor to be responsible for supervision of 14 clinicians in a state-contracted crisis program for adolescents. The position assures compliance with state contract requirements, liaison to contractor; monitors records and documentation; organizes work, activities, and human resources programs. Experience in crisis services and staff clinical supervision required and experience in individual, family, children, or adolescent counseling necessary. Master's degree in social work or related field and clinical license required. (*NASW News*, September 2000, p. 20)

Clinical Supervisor, Family Therapists or Counselors, Case Managers

Escape the rat race and relocate to the beautiful coast of Maine. Clinical supervisor is needed in our Bangor office for the Intensive Home-Based Family Preservation Program that provides in-home, team-delivered family therapy. LCSW and a minimum of two years of supervisory experience required. Also needed are family therapists or counselors in our Bangor, Ellsworth, and Machias offices for the Home-Based Family Preservation Program providing short-term, team-delivered therapy and intervention. Must be eligible for licensure at bachelor or master's level. Case managers are needed for community intervention program in our Machias office, providing case management and family support to child protective referrals. BS required. Outpatient therapist for our Machias office is needed, providing therapy to children, adults, and families in an outpatient setting, with occasional school setting. Licensed clinical social work degree required. All candidates must be creative, flexible, and able to think outside of the box. Excellent salaries, great benefits with clinical supervision provided. (*NASW News*, June 2001, p. 18)

Associate Director
Boy's Village, a private multiservice treatment organization for troubled children and their families, is seeking an associate director to oversee all direct services programs, including day treatment, residential treatment, foster care, an alternative school, and outpatient counseling. This individual will provide supervision and leadership to over 200 employees and foster parents. The job entails policy, program, and budget development, along with maintaining excellence in treatment standards services to over 275 adolescents and children. Specialized treatment populations include sexual offenders and chemically dependent and behaviorally disordered youths. Position requires a master's degree or doctorate in counseling, social work, or psychology and immediate independent license eligibility in the State of Ohio. Applicants need at least five years of experience in management and five years of experience in out-of-home care services for children and adolescents. A visionary individual with strong demonstrated leadership and public relations abilities is needed. Prefer individuals with knowledge and practice in managed care and Medicaid and mental health. We have an excellent starting salary and fringe benefits package. (*NASW News*, March 2000, p. 18)

Program Supervisor
A treatment foster care program in Roswell, NM, is seeking a program supervisor. Candidate must have a master's degree and two licenses (LISW, LPCC, or PhD) with two years prior experience working with seriously emotionally disturbed children. Supervisory experience preferred. Requires excellent organizational, written, and oral communication skills. Will provide

clinical supervision as part of a multidisciplinary treatment team and will be required to manage workload independently. The supervisor oversees and supports the treatment coordinators and therapist as leader of the treatment team. Training provided in attachment and bonding intervention and developmental play therapy. Foster families are located in Chavez County. We offer competitive salary and excellent benefits. (*NASW Newss*, February 2002, p. 17)

Home Visitor, Social Worker
The New Parent Support Program is a joint effort between the U.S. Marine Corps and Children's Hospital, San Diego, CA. The program provides child abuse prevention services to Marine Corp families. Professional teams of social workers use a home-visiting model to provide therapeutic support services, perform psychosocial assessments, and individualized outreach. Minimum qualifications include knowledge of military system and community resources. Proof of current state-licensed MSW or state-licensed master's degree in family and child counseling (MFCC) is required. Previous experience: minimum two years postgraduate experience in community organization and prevention of child–spouse abuse or minimum two years postgraduate experience delivering clinical therapy with dysfunctional couples or families experiencing stress, domestic violence, or abuse. Proof of valid driver's license and proof of current automobile insurance are required. Positions available in Palms, CA; Okinawa, Japan; Camp Pendleton, CA; Yuma, AZ; and MCRD/Miramar, CA. Must meet qualification requirements as defined by Federal Contract Guidelines. (*NASW News*, January 2000, p. 20)

Director of Community Services
The director of community services is responsible for providing direction for the overall development and administration of the community services division. The director will manage, supervise, and coordinate the program compo-

nents to ensure contract compliance. The director will take an active role to initiate collaboration with agencies, community organizations, and key public and community figures; director must demonstrate knowledge and experience in management of social services programs, including program administration, contract compliance, fiscal management, fund development, personnel management, and quality assurance. Must have five years prior supervisory experience, three years of direct agency administration–coordination. Master's degree in social services and excellent organization skills to handle many community meetings and planning sessions with grantors. Must have flexible schedule and the ability to make contacts with key community, government, and political figures. (*NASW News*, June 2001, p. 16)

REFERENCES

Adoption Assistance and Child Welfare Act of 1980, P.L. 96-272, 94 Stat. 501-535.

Adoption and Safe Families Act of 1997, P.L. 105-89, 111 Stat. 2115.

Anderson, G. (2001). Formal and informal kinship care: Supporting the whole family. In E. Walton, P. Sandau-Beckler, & M. Mannes (Eds.), *Balancing family-centered services and child well-being: Exploring issues in policy, practice, theory, and research* (pp. 179–198). New York: Columbia University Press.

Associated Press. (2002a, May 14). Police testing foster child's DNA. *New York Times.* Retrieved May 14, 2002, from http://www.nytimes.com/aponline/national/AP-Missing-Girl.html

Associated Press. (2002b, May 27). Panel finds deception in case of missing girl. *Washington Post*, p. A5.

Barker, R. L. (1999). *Social work dictionary* (4th ed.). Washington, DC: NASW Press.

Barnett, O., Miller-Perrin, C., & Perrin, R. (1997). *Family violence across the lifespan.* Thousand Oaks, CA: Sage Publications.

Barth, R. P. (1995). Adoption. In R. L. Edwards (Ed.-in-Chief), *Encyclopedia of social work* (19th ed., Vol. 1, pp. 48–59). Washington, DC: NASW Press.

Bath, H. I., & Haapala, D. A. (1993). Intensive family preservation services with abused and neglected children: An examination of group differences. *Child Abuse & Neglect, 17,* 213–225.

Beaucar, K. O. (1999, May). Case overload compounds children's peril. *NASW News,* p. 3.

Beaucar, K. O. (2000, March). What's more important than a child? *NASW News,* p. 3.

Bernstein, N. (2001). *The lost children of Wilder: The epic struggle to change foster care.* New York: Pantheon Books.

Blanchard, C. (1999). *Relationship of services and family reunification in New Jersey.* Unpublished doctoral dissertation, Yeshiva University, Wurzweiler School of Social Work, New York.

Blyth, E. (1993). Children's welfare, surrogacy and social work. *British Journal of Social Work, 23,* 259–275.

Brissett-Chapman, S. (1995). Child abuse and neglect: Direct practice. In R. L. Edwards (Ed-in-Chief), *Encyclopedia of social work* (19th ed., Vol. 1, pp. 353–366). Washington, DC: NASW Press.

Child welfare changes eyed. (1999, February). *NASW News,* p. 5.

Child welfare panel seeks to attract social workers. (1987, January). *NASW News,* p. 8.

Children's Defense Fund. (2002). *The state of America's children yearbook,* 2002. Washington, DC: Author.

Corcoran, J., Stephenson, M., Perryman, D., & Allen, S. (2001). Perceptions and utilization of a police–social work crisis intervention approach to domestic violence. *Families in Society, 82,* 393–398.

Davis, L. V. (1995). Domestic violence. In R. L. Edwards (Ed.-in-Chief), *Encyclopedia of social work* (19th ed., Vol. 1, pp. 780–795). Washington, DC: NASW Press.

Davis, L. V., Hagen, J. L., & Early, T. J. (1994). Social services for battered women: Are they adequate, accessible, and appropriate? *Social Work, 39,* 695–704.

DeVita, C. J., & Mosher-Williams, R. (Eds.). (2001). *Who speaks for America's children: The role of child advocates in public policy.* Washington, DC: Urban Institute.

Dhooper, S. S., Royse, D. D., & Wolfe, L. C. (1990). Does social work education make a difference? *Social Work, 45*, 57–61.

Duncan, G. J., & Chase-Lansdale , P. L. (Eds.). (2002). *For better and for worse: Welfare reform and the well-being of children and families.* New York: Russell Sage Foundation.

Feds told about child welfare morass. (1990, May). *NASW News*, p. 13.

First, R. J., Rife, J. C., & Toomey, B. G. (1995). Homeless families. In R. L. Edwards (Ed.-in-Chief), *Encyclopedia of social work* (19th ed., Vol. 2, pp. 1330–1346). Washington, DC: NASW Press.

Gibelman, M. (1995). Purchasing social services. In R. L. Edwards (Ed.-in-Chief), *Encyclopedia of social work* (19th ed., Vol. 3, pp. 1998–2007). Washington, DC: NASW Press.

Gibelman, M., & Schervish, P. (1997). *Who we are: A second look.* Washington, DC: NASW Press.

Grana, S. J. (2001). Sociostructural considerations of domestic feticide. *Journal of Family Violence, 16,* 421–435.

Groza, V. (1997). Adoption: International. In R. L. Edwards (Ed.-in-Chief), *Encyclopedia of social work* (19th ed., 1997 Suppl., pp. 1–14). Washington, DC: NASW Press.

Hartman, A. (1993). Family preservation under attack. *Social Work, 38*, 509–512.

Hegar, R. (1999). The cultural roots of kinship care. In R. Hegar & M. Scannapieco (Eds.), *Kinship foster care: Policy, practice, and research* (pp. 17–27). New York: Oxford University Press.

Hurdle, D. E. (2002). Native Hawaiian traditional healing: Culturally based interventions for social work practice. *Social Work, 47*, 183–192.

Johnson, G. B., & Wahl, M. (1995). Families: Demographic shifts. In R. L. Edwards (Ed.-in-Chief), *Encyclopedia of social work* (19th ed., Vol. 2, pp. 936–941). Washington, DC: NASW Press.

Karger, H. J., & Stoesz, D. (1998). *American social welfare policy: A pluralistic approach.* New York: Longman.

Kinney, J. M., Haapala, D. A., & Booth, C. (1991). *Keeping families together: The homebuilders model.* Hawthorne, NY: Aldine de Gruyter.

Landers, S. (1993, May). After adoption: Aid ends, needs don't. *NASW News*, p. 3.

Liederman, D. S. (1995). Child welfare overview. In R. L. Edwards (Ed.), *Encyclopedia of social work* (19th ed., Vol. 1, pp. 424–433). Washington, DC: NASW Press.

Morrow, D. F. (1993). Social work with gay and lesbian adolescents. *Social Work, 38*, 655–660.

National Association of Social Workers. (1990). *The professional as witness: Testifying with authority, video presentation.* Silver Spring, MD: NASW Insurance Trust.

National Clearinghouse on Child Abuse and Neglect Information. (2001, April). *Third national incidence study of child abuse and neglect.* Available through the National Data Archive on Child Abuse and Neglect, Family Life Development Center, College of Human Ecology, Cornell University, Ithaca, NY. Data sets are available online at http://www.ndacan.cornell.edu/NDACAN/Databases_list.html

National Coalition Against Domestic Violence. (2002a). *Facts on women's housing & domestic violence.* Retrieved October 22, 2003, from http://www.ncadv.org/publicpolicy/housing.htm.

National Coalition Against Domestic Violence. (2002b). *Why do women stay?* Retrieved November 10, 2003, from http://www.ncadv.org/problem/ why2.htm

National Coalition Against Domestic Violence. (2002c). *Violence against women appropriations fact sheet.* Retrieved October 22, 2003, from http://www.ncadv.org/publicpolicy/approp2002.htm

National Coalition for the Homeless. (1999a). *Why are people homeless?* (NCH Fact Sheet No. 1). Retrieved October 22, 2003 from http://www.nationalhomeless.org/causes.html

National Coalition for the Homeless. (1999b). *How many people experience homelessness?* (NCH Fact Sheet No. 2). Retrieved October 22, 2003, from http://www.nationalhomeless.org/numbers.html

National Coalition for the Homeless. (1999c). *Who is homeless?* (NCH Fact Sheet No. 3). Retrieved October 22, 2003, from http://www.nationalhomeless.org/who.html

National Coalition for the Homeless. (1999d). *Employment and homelessness* (NCH Fact Sheet No. 4). Retrieved October 22, 2003, from http://www.nationalhomeless.org/jobs.html

National Coalition for the Homeless. (1999e). *Mental illness and homelessness* (NCH Fact Sheet No. 5). Retrieved October 22, 2003, from http://www.nationalhomeless.org/mental.html

O'Neill, J. V. (2000, June). Practice–research sync "crucial for survival." *NASW News*, p. 3.

O'Neill, J. V. (2001, March). Report says youth aren't receiving adequate care. *NASW News*, p. 12.

O'Neill, J. V. (2002, February). Plan aims to professionalize child welfare. *NASW News*, p. 11.

Pecora, P. J., Whittaker, J. K., Maluccio, A. N., & Barth, R. P. (2000). *The child welfare challenge: Policy, practice and research* (2nd ed.). New York: Aldine de Gruyter.

Personal Responsibility and Work Opportunity Reconciliation Act of 1996, P.L. 104-193, 110 Stat. 2105.

Promoting Safe and Stable Families Amendments of 2001, P.L. 108-36, 117 Stat. 800.

Protector of kids and a culture. (1998, November). *NASW News*, p. 12.

Reed, K. B., & Kirk, R. S. (1998). Intensive family preservation services: A short history but a long past. *Family Preservation Journal, 31*(1), 41–57.

Reform's effect on families studied. (2002, January). *NASW News*, p. 5.

Rossi, P. H. (1994). Troubling families: Family homelessness in America. *American Behavioral Scientist, 37*, 342–395.

Rycraft, J. R. (1994). The party isn't over: The agency role in the retention of public child welfare caseworkers. *Social Work, 39*, 75–80.

Sallee, A. L., & Lloyd, J. C. (1991). The challenge and potential of family preservation services in the public child welfare system. *Protecting Children, 10*, 5.

Staff called key to child welfare reform. (1993, June). *NASW News*, p. 6.

Stewart B. McKinney Homeless Assistance Act of 1987, P.L. 100-77, 101 Stat. 482.

System overload endangers kids, study says. (1991, March). *NASW News*, p. 16.

Thornton, A. (Ed.). (2001). *The well-being of children and families: Research and data needs.* Ann Arbor: University of Michigan Press.

Tjaden, P., & Thoennes, N. (2000). *Extent, nature, and consequences of intimate partner violence: Findings from the National Violence Against Women Survey.* Washington, DC: U.S. Department of Justice, National Institute of Justice. Retrieved October 22, 2003, from http://www.ojp.usdoj.gov/nij/pubs-sum/181867.htm

Tracy, E. M. (1995). *Family preservation and home-based services.* In R. L. Edwards (Ed.-in-Chief), Encyclopedia of social work (19th ed., Vol. 2, pp. 973–983). Washington, DC: NASW Press.

U.S. Conference of Mayors. (2001). *A status report on hunger and homelessness in America's cities.* Retrieved October 22, 2003, from http://usmayors.org/uscm/news/press_releases/documents/hunger_121101.asp

U.S. Department of Justice, Violence Against Women Office. (2002). *Violence Against Women Act of 1994.* Retrieved October 22, 2003, from http://www.ojp.usdoj.gov/vawo/laws/vawa/ vawa.htm

Vallianatos, C. (2002, January). Gay parents' rights backed. *NASW News*, p. 5.

Victims of Trafficking and Violence Protection Act of 2000, P.L. 106-386, 114 Stat. 1464.

Violence Against Women Act of 1994, P.L. 103-322 108 Stat. 1796.

Walton, E. (2002). *Family-centered services in child welfare.* In A. R. Roberts & G. J. Greene (Eds.), *Social workers' desk reference* (pp. 285–289). New York: Oxford University Press.

Ziesemer, C., Marcoux, L., & Marwell, B. E. (1994). Homeless children: Are they different from other low-income children? *Social Work, 39*, 658–668.

Chapter Six SOCIAL WORKERS AND HEALTH CARE

Many social workers are employed in a variety of settings the chief purpose of which is to provide health care, not human services. These include hospitals, hospices, medical clinics, health maintenance organizations, and nursing homes. What these practice settings have in common is that they are oriented to the prevention, amelioration, and cure of physical illness. Human services are a means to an end or an adjunct, facilitative aspect, rather than the mission or focus of the work of the sponsoring organization.

These settings of practice fall under public, not-for-profit, and for-profit auspices. Nursing homes are seldom under public auspices; traditionally, they have been not-for-profit but increasingly are for-profit. Hospitals and medical clinics may be under public, not-for-profit, or for-profit auspices. Hospices are often under not-for-profit auspices, whereas health maintenance organizations, such as Kaiser Permanente, are for profit.

Under these different auspices of practice, social workers carry responsibilities in many different program areas. These program areas include AIDS, child immunization, family planning, maternal and child health, genetics, discharge planning, emergency room care, hospice, and support groups related to specific diseases, such as multiple sclerosis.

Although there are distinct settings of health practice, such as hospitals, the problems of patients that social workers address in these settings are by no means confined to the physiological. They may range from the practical needs of patients for aftercare services to the emotional crisis facing a family with the death of a child. Similarly, social workers often work with the families and friends of people with health problems. For example, social workers employed in a hospice setting may primarily work with elderly or younger terminally ill people (such as those suffering from AIDS), but they also offer services to the families, friends, and significant others of these patients.

Teen pregnancy is not only a health issue, but also a family and child services concern and, frequently, a focus of attention of social workers practicing in school settings. Similarly, HIV/AIDS is a devastating and as yet incurable disease, but AIDS is also associated with the social problems of discrimination as the populations affected include homosexuals, intravenous drug users, and prostitutes. People with HIV/AIDS often need assistance with housing, employment, and family and social relationships in addition to their medical regimes.

Social workers in nonhealth settings also need to be attuned to the interplay between physiological and emotional problems, such as the effects of medication, the impact of chronic illness on the patient and his or her family, and the psychosocial and economic consequences of debilitating disease. Thus, social workers in all areas of service are concerned with the health of their clients.

Although social workers primarily deliver direct services to patients and their families in health settings, functions also include macro-level interventions. Some social workers in health care occupy administrative positions, such as a director of social services in a hospital. Others may engage in research under the auspices of organizations concerned with health issues, such as research centers affiliated with universities (for example, schools of public health and social work) or "think tanks" such as the Urban Institute. Still others may work for private organizations that have largely information and referral or linkage functions, such as matching those with home health care assistance needs with appropriate providers. Social workers who carry out policy functions may work to promote access to health care—here, social workers may be employed by advocacy groups. Social workers in the health care field share a common concern about the number of people in the United States who have no health insurance. An Urban Institute report on "Snapshots of America's Families II," for example, found that rates of uninsured people remained largely unchanged between 1997 and 1999, with 26.5 million adults (16 percent) and 9.6 million children age 18 and younger (12.5 percent) uninsured ("Reports: Uninsured Rate Steady," 2001).

SOCIAL WORK PRACTICE IN HOSPITALS

Social work practice in the hospital is oriented to facilitating good health, preventing illness, and aiding physically ill patients and their families to address and resolve the social, financial, and psychological problems related to the illness. Hospital social work involves, according to Barker (1999),

the provision of social services in hospitals and similar health care centers, most often within a facility's department of social services or social work. The services provided include prevention, rehabilitation, and follow-up activities, as well as discharge planning and information gathering and providing. Other services include assisting patients with the financial and social aspects of their care and counseling patients and their families. (p. 221)

Hospital social work is practiced in a variety of public and private, sectarian and nonsectarian settings including general and specialized acute care medical centers; psychiatric hospitals; rehabilitation centers; long-term care facilities, such as nursing homes and adult day care programs; primary-care settings, such as health maintenance organizations; ambulatory clinics; and home health programs.

Historical Developments

Hospital social work practice has a long history. Ida M. Cannon initiated the first hospital social work department in 1905 at Massachusetts General Hospital for the primary purpose of helping patients make a smooth transition from the hospital to the community. Richard Cabot, the physician who directed the hospital in 1905, recognized the importance of psychosocial care in comprehensive treatment and the importance of continuity of care and, therefore, included social workers as home visitors in his clinic at Massachusetts General. These goals continue to guide present-day hospital social workers as they strive to ensure that progress made in the acute medical care arena is maintained when the patient returns to his or her community (Oktay, 1995; Rossen, 1987).

Social work practice in hospital settings boomed following the enactment of Medicare and Medicaid in the 1960s because hospitals were able to build social work charges into their routine daily costs and receive reimbursement for these services. As Medicare caseloads increased, so did the number of hospital social workers. The typical client was usually an elderly patient over 65 years of age and his or her family. Although elderly people continue to be a large proportion of patients, the role of hospital social workers has expanded to include many different types of clients and settings.

In 1966, the American Hospital Association established the Society for Hospital Social Work Directors. This organization strengthened the credibility of hospital social workers by facilitating their participation in the hospital industry and by establishing professional accountability standards (Rossen, 1987).

In 1984 the Deficit Reduction Act (P.L. 98-369) developed a prospective pricing system for Medicare through the creation of diagnostic-related groups, a federally mandated prospective payment mechanism designed to control the costs of medical and hospital care for Medicare recipients (Barker, 1999). Under this system, hospitals maximize their profits by decreasing the time patients spend in the hospital. For the social worker in a hospital setting, this means that attention is focused on the efficient use of patients' stays in the hospital and more timely discharge.

Under the Balanced Budget Act of 1997 (P.L. 105-33) and the Medicare Benefits Improvement and Protection Act (BIPA) of 2000 (P.L. 106-554), prospective payment systems were developed for hospital outpatient, skilled nursing facility, and home health systems.

Social Work Functions

The functions performed by social workers in direct practice vary according to the level of care and the type of health setting. For example, acute care settings require social workers to be involved in high-risk screening, discharge planning, collaboration, information, and referral (Poole, 1995). However, in a health care setting that focuses on health promotion and prevention, such as a neighborhood clinic, social workers may be involved in needs assessment, education, coordination of services, advocacy, and community and program development (Poole, 1995). The social worker, depending on the cir-

cumstances, may use crisis intervention, short-term individual psychotherapy, family therapy, and information and referral techniques to help the patient and family members understand the options, work through feelings, and take appropriate actions.

Discharge planning responsibilities are a growing and major component of social work practice in hospitals. *Discharge planning* has been defined as "a social service offered in hospitals and other institutions that is designed to help patients or clients make timely and healthy adjustments from care within the facility to alternative sources of care or to self-care when the need for service has passed" (Barker, 1999, p. 132). Functions include helping the client and relevant others to understand the nature of the problem and its impact, facilitate his or her adjustment and adaptation to a new role, and help arrange for postdischarge care (Barker, 1999).

Discharge Planning

Mary is a 76-year-old widow who has been living by herself in an apartment in Arizona since her husband died three years ago. Her son, who is 50 years old, lives in Los Angeles and visits her twice a year. Yesterday, while taking her daily walk, Mary fell and fractured her hip. She underwent emergency hip replacement surgery and now needs physical therapy and six days of hospitalization before she can go home. Once home, she will need continuing help with daily activities and the adjustment to a new lifestyle. Mary's only income is her monthly social security check of $615. Lying in bed after the surgery, Mary is frightened and unsure of her future. She wishes someone were there to help her.

There is someone to help. Based on her age, health, living status, and income, Mary is designated as a high-risk patient by the hospital intake staff and referred to the hospital social services department. A social worker is then able to assist Mary in many ways.

The basic social work functions of assessment, support, referral, and coordination include the following interventions:

- helping Mary understand what happened to her hip and the medical implications for her future daily activities
- helping Mary work through her fear and frustration at losing some of her independence
- working with Mary to evaluate her eligibility for needed services and ongoing care
- arranging for the appropriate services to assist Mary for a certain period of time after she leaves the hospital so that she can make a smooth transition to living alone
- helping Mary to adjust to her new lifestyle and dependence on others
- facilitating communication between Mary, her son, and members of the hospital team to ensure quality care that includes psychosocial aspects.

A study on postdischarge implementation found that discharge plans frequently failed to be carried out in full, with some but not all services delivered or fewer services delivered than planned (Simon, Showers, Blumenfield, Holden, & Wu, 1995). The role of the hospital social worker must extend beyond the point of patient discharge to ensure that the after hospital care needed by the patient is, in fact, provided.

Hospital social workers use many of the same skills and encounter many of the same issues as social workers in other settings. However, there are some unique aspects to hospital social work including the short-term setting, the physical and medical components, and the collaboration with a health care team (Rossen, 1987). Social workers in hospitals work as members of interdisciplinary teams toward the goal of providing comprehensive, coordinated care to patients in health settings (Abramson, 2002). Interdisciplinary teams refer to a group of professionals from different disciplines who work together with a common purpose. Roles are assigned on the basis of expertise. Each team member contributes his or her perspective in decision making. A high degree of communication, coordination, and interaction is needed to make teamwork successful (Faulkner, Schofield & Amodeo, 1999).

Hospital social work has become increasingly specialized. Social workers in medical settings are frequently assigned to specific units and focus their work on patient needs based on different age groups, gender, diagnosis, or point along the continuum from diagnosis to treatment problems. Oncology is one such specialization. Here, social work roles include counseling, such as working on illness-related psychosocial problems and dealing with problems involved in rehabilitation, recovery, and reentry into normal life; problems related to terminal illness, planning for the future, discharge planning, relaxation, and stress-reduction therapy; and grief counseling. Other roles include helping with tangible resources, such as transportation, financial aid, and housing, and providing information about and referral to self-help groups and community resources. And with the enormous advances in biomedical technology, new specializations have emerged, as illustrated in the following vignette. In this instance, the social worker, Ilene Gelman, is an actual person who occupies a management position at Columbia Presbyterian Medical Center.

A SOCIAL WORKER ASSISTS A HEART TRANSPLANT PATIENT AND HIS FAMILY
Ilene Gelman is a social work manager at Columbia Presbyterian Medical Center, New York Presbyterian Hospital, where she has worked for 12 years. Her job involves overseeing four transplant services—heart, kidney, liver, and lung. Six social workers are assigned to these transplant units.

Mr. Hunt, age 64, was admitted to the hospital last night with congestive heart fail-

ure. He desperately needs a new heart to live. A resident of Hartford, CT, Mr. Hunt arrived in New York City yesterday, accompanied by his 63-year-old wife and two daughters, ages 29 and 33. They are all here to participate in the hospital's five-day evaluation program. Because of the vacation schedule of the social worker assigned to the heart transplant unit, Ilene is handling this case directly.

Initially, Ilene seeks to determine, from a psychosocial perspective, if Mr. Hunt is an appropriate candidate for the extremely delicate and complicated heart transplant procedure. Through interviews with the patient and the family, Ilene assesses whether this patient can and will comply with the demanding medical regimen that must be followed after the surgery. His track record in medication compliance and keeping appointments needs to be determined, as well as his overall attitude, and that of his family, toward the idea of transplant. Heart transplant, after all, involves the use of an organ donated by a person now deceased. To make such a determination, Ilene needs to gain an understanding of Mr. Hunt's past behavior and how his beliefs may affect his current health care. In this assessment process, Ilene considers issues of culture and ethnicity as these factors may have an impact on Mr. Hunt's ability to understand and comply with the medical regime.

In addition to the issue of medical compliance, Ilene attempts to determine if the patient has a strong support system and a solid understanding of the complex transplant process. One complicating factor that frequently occurs in the assessment process is that the patient does not speak English. This is not the case with Mr. Hunt. But with other patients, Ilene and her staff need to make sure that someone is present to help with translation and to assess patients' level of understanding of what has happened—and will happen—to them.

The cost of surgery and follow-up treatment is also an issue that must be addressed.

Even before Ilene meets with Mr. Hunt and his family, he had an appointment with a representative of the hospital's finance department. In that interview, the finance person reviewed Mr. Hunt's medical insurance plan to make sure that it will cover the full cost of not only the surgical procedure, but also the lifelong medication regime to follow. Medication costs can be as much as $2,000 a month. If the insurance plan does not cover medications, the finance officer needs to determine if the family can pay for medicine over the long haul.

After several meetings with Mr. Hunt and his wife and daughters, Ilene concludes that he is a good candidate for the procedure, a recommendation she will make at a team selection meeting in which all members of the team participate—the psychiatrist, the physician, the nurse, and the social worker. At these selection meetings, each patient is presented from the perspective of the different disciplines involved—the facts are communicated along with a recommendation and justification. Not all patients are accepted into the transplant program. Sometimes, as is the case with Mr. Hunt, the team is unanimous in its decision. At other times, there may be disagreements from a medical or psychosocial perspective that need to be hashed out within the case conference.

With the team's decision to accept Mr. Hunt into the transplant program, Ilene's role changes from that of psychosocial assessment to that of educating the Hunt family and "emotionally immunizing" them in preparation for the rigorous medical procedures involved in heart transplantation and recovery. She meets with the Hunt family before their return to Connecticut. Some patients accepted into the program may opt to go home to wait—others, who may live at a considerable distance from the hospital, arrange for temporary housing nearby. In addition to helping the family cope during the waiting period, Ilene prepares them for the very real possibility that medical efforts *will fail and a new heart will not arrive in time or will be rejected by the patient's body. This is a difficult, yet essential, part of Ilene's work with the family. About 20 percent of those waiting for a transplant will die before a donor organ is located. It is not a matter of "first come, first served." Blood type and organ size must be matched.*

Now, as Ilene has seen in so many cases, the family enters perhaps the most stressful time of the procedure—the wait. With the current shortage of donors, the wait could be many months or even years, and the stress often brings out family problems that have gone unaddressed for years. During this period, Mr. Hunt returns to the hospital for periodic check-ups to monitor his condition. Ilene arranges to see Mr. Hunt and family members, if they accompany him, in conjunction with these medical appointments. She also maintains regular contact with the family by phone— answering questions about their father's illness, addressing unresolved family issues, and help-ing them to understand the transplant process.

Finally, a new heart is available. Mr. Hunt, who is available at all times by cell phone, receives the call, and he and his wife immediately get into the car for the two-hour trip to Manhattan. Within a few hours, Mr. Hunt is on his way to surgery.

The procedure is long and difficult; how-ever, after six stressful hours, the surgery is over. Mr. Hunt has a new heart and he is doing well. In one postoperative meeting with the family, Mr. Hunt tearfully tells Ilene of his gratitude to the donor family. He realizes that the donor family has experienced the loss of a loved one and he is committed to taking care of his heart—for their sake as well as for his own. After 10 days of follow-up medical care, he and his wife return to their home to face a new lifestyle with hope, joy, fear, and a refreshed desire to live for the present. Mr. Hunt will be on medication for the rest of his life, a reality he readily accepts.

Ilene Gelman's work with Mr. Hunt high-lights some of the following specific functions of hospital social work.

Functions of Hospital Social Work

FUNCTION	EXAMPLE
Assessment	Determine Mr. Hunt's ability to comply with the medical requirements
Support	Assist Mr. Hunt by maximizing his family support network— facilitate support groups and refer to community caregiver groups
Advice and Counseling	Counsel Mr. Hunt and his family
Appropriate Referrals	Make referrals to support groups and to needed services such as the hospital financial department
Coordination	Facilitate communica-tion between Mr. Hunt, his family, and the medical team
Education	Reinforce prescribed medical regime— medication, diet, exercise; provide information about what to expect

In this vignette, Ms. Gelman specializes in work with transplant patients. Lee Suszycki, past president of the National Clinical Network for Social Workers on Heart Transplant Programs, described the excitement of working "where social work skills are so badly needed to human-ize this entire experience and make it real"

("Heart Transplants," 1987, p. 3). Ilene Gelman agrees with this assessment and claims she "wouldn't want to do any other kind of work."

Social work with transplant programs is only one example of the many social work opportunities in a hospital. In addition to working with transplant patients, there are opportunities for hospital social workers to provide services in almost every area of treatment including medical–surgical, pediatric, psychiatric, obstetric–gynecologic, intensive care, rehabilitation, and emergency services.

Social Work Practice in the Emergency Room
Visits to the emergency room involve severe physical conditions or trauma, which may also be accompanied by emotional trauma for patients and their families. There also may be a number of practical matters that require attention that are beyond the ability of the ill person to address, such as making temporary arrangements for children when a single mother needs to be hospitalized. Because of the crisis nature of many emergency room situations, many hospitals have a social worker on call or assigned full-time to the emergency room.

Children and adolescents are one age cohort that is susceptible to risk behaviors that may lead to medical emergencies. Each year, 16 million children and adolescents are seriously injured and are rushed to the emergency rooms of hospitals for treatment. Many of these injuries result from risk-taking behaviors, such as drug overdose, attempted suicide, high-speed driving or driving while intoxicated, or physical altercations among youths, sometimes involving gang "warfare." Given the nature of many of these emergencies, effective treatment includes a mental health component to help prevent future risk taking and to forestall the development of more severe behavioral, cognitive, or affective impairments ("In the E.R.," 1998). The following vignette illustrates the crisis a family experiences when a child inexplicably falls ill and the immediate intervention the social worker provides.

WHERE DO WE TURN
"My baby is dying!" Jay Scranton cried out to someone as he crashed through the emergency room doors of Northtown Hospital in Gainsville, GA, carrying his six-year-old daughter who lay limp in his arms. Nurses and doctors rushed to him as he ran aimlessly down the hall, looking for help. The doctors took his daughter, and a nurse gently guided him back to the waiting area where his wife sat with tears streaming down her face. The nurse then paged Lisa Green, the social worker, who came to talk with Mr. and Mrs. Scranton.

As they waited to hear the diagnosis, Lisa was able to get a fairly clear understanding of what had happened. Apparently, their daughter, Caroline, had fallen asleep on the couch when she suddenly started shaking uncontrollably. Her parents did not know what was happening as they tried to control her thrashing arms and legs. Her jaw was clamped shut and her eyes were rolled back into her head. By the time they arrived at the hospital, Caroline had stopped convulsing and had passed out completely. From the description, Lisa believed that Caroline had had an epileptic seizure, but she waited to talk with the doctors before sharing her perspective.

Hours and many tests later, a diagnosis of epilepsy was confirmed, and although the Scranton's were thrilled that Caroline was not going to die, they really had no idea what epilepsy was or what was involved in caring for their daughter. Lisa briefly educated them about epilepsy's onset and treatment. Caroline would be admitted to the hospital for a few days for more tests and to stabilize her on medication. However, Lisa knew that the family needed more than her brief description so she arranged a referral to the hospital's support group for parents of children with neurological and developmental disabilities.

In the meantime, Lisa continued to assist the family as Caroline was being monitored in the hospital and the physicians attempted to determine the best type of medication to control Caroline's seizures without severe side effects. Although these tests were necessary, the Scranton's were a poor family, and what little insurance they had was used almost immediately. However, Lisa was able to help them access federal benefits under the Supplemental Security Income program and referred them to the state agencies responsible for providing services for which they were eligible and how they could access them. When Caroline was stabilized and ready for discharge, Lisa provided one more referral for the family—the local chapter of the Epilepsy Foundation. There, Lisa knew, the family would have consistent access to information and support.

In her work with the Scranton family, Lisa uses a crisis intervention framework. The functions of assessment, diagnosis, and identification are carried out to determine the psychosocial issues that need to be addressed. In addition, Lisa offers support and counseling, and she works with the Scranton's to enable them to access community resources and benefits. Lisa also refers the family to the state agency responsible for administering the Developmental Disabilities Assistance and Bill of Rights Act of 1990 (P.L. 101-496) to determine the services for which the family would be eligible (DeWeaver, 1995). She also carries out the social work function of referral when she helped the family to connect with the hospital parental support group and, later, the Epilepsy Foundation. She also engages in coordination and consultation in her interactions with the interdisciplinary team at the hospital and with the social work staff of the Epilepsy Foundation.

Because hospitalization usually is sudden and requires major personal adjustments, much of hospital social work requires crisis intervention. Unlike social work in any other setting, hospital social workers usually have only five to 10 days to accomplish their intervention goals.

The importance of timely social work interventions on behalf of families in the emergency room has been recognized by the Health Resources and Services Administration Maternal and Child Health Bureau. With the administration's funding, NASW has developed guidelines to help emergency room staff provide crisis services to families of dying children. The guidelines identify several stages to address service provision in the emergency room. These include establishing protocols and procedures and training staff to prepare emergency room personnel to help the family of a child who dies; reaching out to families as they arrive in the emergency room; informing parents promptly, compassionately, and privately about the death of the child; and following up with families at home after the death of a child. Also included in the guidelines are coping mechanisms for staff after a childhood death in the emergency room (NASW, 2000a).

Throughout the years, hospital social workers have exhibited creativity and success in managing various functions. "Social workers are the only health professionals in hospitals whose responsibilities are closely tied to social health problems, yet disconnected from physical care of patients" (Ross, 1995, p. 1369). Some serve in clinical roles, whereas others serve as managers for specific programs administered by the hospital in areas such as mental health, aging, and community outreach. Social workers must be able to assess, diagnose, and evaluate the patient's situation. The social worker must also be able to work with the individual and the family to develop a care and evaluation plan (Ross, 1995).

Outpatient Services

With selective cuts to social work staff in hospitals within the larger context of a shift from inpatient to outpatient care, some social workers are using their medical social work background within community clinics and physician group practices. Research has shown that 50 percent of randomly sampled primary-care patients suffered from some degree of depression or anxiety

(Levenson, 1998). Studies have also revealed that primary-care physicians often overlook common psychosocial problems and treat symptoms inappropriately. At the same time, medical practitioners prescribe 70 percent of all psychotropic medications and 80 percent of all antidepressants (Levenson, 1998).

Social worker Kari Knutson-Bradac, in her role as manager of community initiatives and social services at Seattle's Medalia HealthCare Providence and Franciscan Health Services, is responsible for a program in which social workers train primary-care physicians to identify stress, grief, depression, and panic disorders among their patients. Physicians are also taught to make appropriate referrals. Social worker Leslie Lieberman is the northern regional coordinator for a Kaiser Permanente program, Early Start. Here, social workers in primary-care clinics help identify pregnant women who abuse drugs and steer them to appropriate services. During the first prenatal visit to participating clinics, women complete questionnaires that provide clues about possible drug and alcohol use. Women suspected of abusing drugs or alcohol are referred to a social worker for evaluation and counseling. Social workers also consult with physicians and teach parenting classes (Levenson, 1998). These two programs are examples of a slowly growing trend to integrate primary and behavioral health care.

The Future

Challenges to the stability, if not very future, of hospital social work are ongoing. There is now widespread acknowledgment that health care expenditures have grown out of control. And social work departments have increasingly come to be seen as "nonessential" to the primary mission of the hospital. In recent years hospital closures of social work departments have become more frequent. Also pervasive is the reorganizing of social work departments within hospitals. The move from a traditional social work department to a decentralized model in which social work staff is reassigned to other departments has raised questions about proper supervision and the quality of treatment for patients (Globerman & Bogo, 2002). Reorganization has also meant, in some cases, replacing department directors with non–social work personnel.

During this time of uncertainty and change, hospital social workers must redefine the profession's role in the new medical environment and develop accountability standards to ensure professionalism that is critical for future support and expansion. Clearly, there will be continued emphasis on containing costs through controlled length of hospital stays and other means.

AIDS

AIDS is an infectious, chronic disease with no cure. Ten years ago, a diagnosis of AIDS was a death sentence. Today, with advances in pharmacology, AIDS has become increasingly manageable, and many people with AIDS have been helped to live longer. Elongation of life with AIDS has had an effect on quality-of-life issues ranging from medication side effects to impaired earning capacity.

AIDS is caused by the human immunodeficiency virus (HIV). It attacks and destroys the immune system of the infected person, making him or her vulnerable to a wide variety of cancers, nervous system degeneration, and opportunistic infections caused by other viruses or bacteria (American Medical Association [AMA], 2002). Although opportunistic infections are not ordinarily life threatening in a healthy individual, they can be deadly to a person with AIDS whose immune system has been weakened by HIV (Lloyd, 1995).

HIV disease is transmitted by unprotected sexual intercourse when one of the partners is infected with HIV; through exposure to infected blood through transfusions, blood-contaminated needles, infected donated body organs, or infected semen; and when an infected mother passes the virus to the fetus or infant before, during, or a short time after birth (AMA, 2002; Lloyd, 1995). Initially, the AIDS epidemic in the United States largely affected the population of gay and bisexual men, who account for 65 percent of all diagnosed cases since 1981. AIDS quickly spread to intravenous drug users, their heterosexual partners, and women who engaged in unprotected sex. Also affected are children and adults suffering from hemophilia (Poindexter, 1999). Today, rates of infection are growing fastest among women and minority groups, as well as young homosexual men, drug users, and adults over age 50 (U.S. Department of Health and Human Services [DHHS], 2002b). As of January 2000, total deaths in the United States from complications related to AIDS numbered 430,441 (Centers for Disease Control and Prevention [CDC], 2002).

By June 30, 2001, 793,026 cases of AIDS had been reported to the CDC (2002). Forty thousand new cases of HIV infection are diagnosed each year (DHHS, 2002b). In 1999, an estimated 320,282 people in the United States were living with AIDS and from 650,000 to 900,000 U.S. residents were living with HIV infection (AMA, 2002). Declines in the incidence of and deaths from AIDS are associated with the widespread use of antiretroviral therapies (CDC, 2000b).

As the demographics of people with HIV/AIDS have changed over the years, public attitudes have shifted. Children, who may be born to a mother with AIDS or become infected through a transfusion of contaminated blood, are now among the affected population. Fifty percent of all new HIV infections occur in young people under age 25 (CDC, 2002). Elderly people, too, are now counted among those with HIV/AIDS, primarily because of the misperception that when a person no longer needs contraceptive protection, that person is no longer susceptible to sexual transmission of the disease (Williams & Donnelly, 2002).

As dismal as these data are, equally as compelling are the strides that have been made. New

AIDS cases reported to the CDC declined 12 percent between 1996 and 1997, and this trend continues (AMA, 2002). Although AIDS is now the fifth leading cause of death in the United States among people ages 25 to 44, there is an enormous increase in the number of people with AIDS who are surviving (AMA, 2002). AIDS-related deaths dropped 67 percent between 1995 and 2000 (CDC, 2002). As the survival rates continue to increase, so do the needs of this population for health, financial, social, psychological, and other types of services.

Legislative Responses

Although the United States was slow to recognize and respond to the AIDS crisis, by 1990 several important legislative initiatives had been passed by Congress. These include the Ryan White Comprehensive AIDS Resources Emergency (CARE) Act of 1990 (P.L. 101-381) and the Americans with Disabilities Act (ADA) of 1990 (P.L. 101-366).

The Ryan White CARE Act seeks to address the health care and services needs of people with AIDS and their families. Programs under this act, which was reauthorized in 1996, include HIV testing and counseling, outpatient health care, early intervention, and comprehensive support services, including case management, housing assistance, and home health and hospice care. It is estimated that more than 500,000 individuals use services under this act each year (DHHS, 2002a).

The ADA is far reaching in the populations that come under its provisions, but has important implications for people with AIDS. Individuals with disabilities are protected under the ADA. People with HIV, whether they have outwardly manifested symptoms or not, are considered to have physical impairments that substantially limit one or more major life activities. Therefore, the ADA covers them. The ADA gives federal civil rights protection to individuals with disabilities. It also guarantees equal opportunity in public accommodations, employment, transportation, state and local government services, and telecommunications (NASW, 2002).

Social Work and AIDS

Social workers are engaged in helping people with AIDS, their families, lovers, spouses, friends, and colleagues in many different settings. They work in hospitals, state and county social services departments, community health clinics, and nonprofit organizations specifically serving the AIDS population. Social workers' engagement with people with AIDS and their families relates directly to enabling federal legislation, which authorizes and funds a variety of initiatives in states, cities, and communities across the country.

From the very beginning of the epidemic, social workers have played a significant role both in pushing for appropriate government responses to the crisis and providing the labor force necessary to do the difficult work of caring for the sick and educating those at risk. Social workers continue to play a vital role in community-based AIDS organizations providing case management, information and referral, services coordination, financial management, education, and advocacy and support services, among others (Williams & Donnelly, 2002).

The professional values of social workers, which reflect the inherent worth of individuals and their right to self-determination, represent an important counterbalance to the oftentimes prejudiced and discriminatory judgments about AIDS victims. Social workers advocate for clients in the legal system by assisting them in discrimination cases through legal referrals and ongoing support and acting as case managers to direct people to concrete services. Social workers also work in hospice care to ensure provision of comfortable care at home for patients in end-stage AIDS.

The Gay Men's Health Crisis (GMHC), a nonprofit organization, was formed in the early 1980s by members of the gay population who felt that the medical and social services available at that time were not responding to the crisis of AIDS. A group of gay professionals developed GMHC; however, as the caseload grew and became increasingly complex, social workers and other professionals joined GMHC (Getzel, 1989). Other nonprofit AIDS organizations have similar stories of how social workers came to be involved. Social workers now play an integral role in this area of service, as exemplified in the following vignette.

JASON'S STORY

Jason Jackson is 30 years old. He is a midtown reporter for a New York newspaper. He does volunteer work at a nursing home. He likes to jog and write poetry. He likes to travel and play basketball. And Jason has AIDS.

He sits in the window of his 10th floor apartment overlooking the city and thinks about how this all started. A few weeks ago, he went to his doctor because he had been tired and had the flu for almost two weeks. He also had a sore throat and diarrhea. His physician prescribed some antibiotics and then asked if Jason had reason to believe he may have contracted HIV. Jason said that he was gay and had had unprotected sex, but he was in a monogamous relationship. The doctor said he would have to do some tests to find out if Jason had HIV, but before doing that, the doctor referred Jason to the GMHC to get counseling about the HIV testing procedure and consequences.

Jason went to GMHC where he met with a social worker, Janet Deer. He explained his concerns to her and told her about the physician's recommendation that he have an HIV test. Ms. Deer had been at GMHC for almost six years and she was a very skilled worker. She took a detailed personal and sexual history from Jason. Ms. Deer attempted to assess Jason's previous experience in handling crisis situations. She then helped Jason determine his degree of risk. It appeared to be reduced because he was in a monogamous relationship, but Ms. Deer contin-

ued to counsel Jason because she knew it was important for people considering testing to be fully informed about HIV and AIDS. Jason had the test done, and two days ago he found out that he tested positive for AIDS. He did not believe it at first; there had to be a mistake. But there was no mistake. Jason called his lover who admitted to having an affair earlier in the year. Jason was furious. He hated his lover—and he hated himself. He was angry and frightened. He has been sitting in the window ever since the telephone encounter—thinking and crying.

He makes an appointment to see Ms. Deer at GMHC. He has nowhere else to turn. His father is a retired Navy captain and has no idea Jason is gay. Jason believes neither his father nor his mother will ever accept the fact of his homosexuality. His older brother is in the Army and is living in Germany. Jason feels completely alone.

Ms. Deer's psychosocial perspective is essential in helping Jason come to terms with his diagnosis as well as the relationship issues that he will inevitably have to face when he informs his parents of his illness. She knows that Jason will experience intense stress and probably some amount of social isolation. As Jason begins to develop the physical symptoms of the virus, his isolation will increase. Ms. Deer is aware that Jason will initially be in denial and may isolate himself. This is necessary to some extent yet becomes dangerous when denial contributes to depression, dependency, and despondency. The assessment of the role of denial is a critical task for social workers in this practice area. As the virus begins to weaken Jason's body, necessary lifestyle changes will cause resentment. Ms. Deer knows that people with AIDS may experience depression, delirium, and dementia which can alter impulse control, thus putting a person at risk to self and others. She must be cognizant of these issues and recognize such behavior immediately.

As an initial intervention, Ms. Deer counsels Jason independently on the issues he will face

such as coping with and expressing the anger he feels toward his lover and his parents. She helps Jason share his "secret" of homosexuality with his parents and prepares him for their possible reaction. She also starts Jason in group therapy for people with HIV/AIDS. The group therapy gives Jason a chance to see how others with HIV/AIDS deal with certain experiences in their personal relationships as well as in their medical treatments.

Jason continues to see Ms. Deer on a regular basis over several months. As Jason's physical condition deteriorates and his death becomes imminent, Ms. Deer suggests that he have a GMHC volunteer crisis worker visit him daily at home because Jason does not want to die in the hospital. This volunteer worker concentrates on being with Jason during times of stress and helps Jason plan for his future.

In this example, Ms. Deer carries out the basic social work functions of assessment, support, counseling, enabling, referral, and coordinating. Social workers who serve people with AIDS must have special knowledge of the epidemiology of HIV and AIDS, prevention techniques, and obstacles to behavior change. Social workers in this practice area must also be aware of cultural reactions to HIV and AIDS, homophobia, stereotypes of drug users, and social attitudes about people infected with HIV (Lloyd, 1990).

The basic social work intervention focuses on helping the infected person remain active and productive and as fully integrated as possible, both socially and emotionally. To achieve this goal, social workers must be knowledgeable about medical resources, self-help and support groups, case management services, home health care organizations, and inpatient treatment facilities.

To effectively work with people with AIDS/HIV, social workers often intervene with family members, significant others, social services agencies, social security, public assistance programs, health care, home care, and hospice services. Social workers must be skilled in direct practice, group work, case management, and resource utilization (Lloyd, 1990). In addition, social workers disseminate educational information, promote prevention techniques, and inform the community about the often-misunderstood facts of HIV and AIDS (Taylor-Brown, 1995).

This case example takes place in a specialized HIV/AIDS services setting; however, there is an ongoing debate over the best place to administer HIV/AIDS medical and social services. Many social workers promote treatment through primary-care centers based on the belief that medical and psychosocial needs should be conveniently located to ensure provision of holistic services. However, other social workers promote specialized HIV services settings based on the premise that all health care workers providing services to this population must have specialized knowledge and training (Lloyd, 1995).

The issues that have been discussed apply to social work with AIDS/HIV patients regardless of age, sex, race, or color. However, there is one population that warrants special attention: children with AIDS.

Children with AIDS

During the early 1990s, an estimated 1,000 to 2,000 infants were born HIV positive each year (National Center for HIV, STD, & TB Prevention [NCHSTP], 1998a). Medical advances have dramatically decreased these numbers; clinical trials showed that HIV-infected women could reduce the risk of transmitting the virus to their babies by as much as two-thirds by administering zidovudine (AZT) during pregnancy, labor, and delivery, and by direct administration to babies during the first six weeks after birth. Despite the progress made in reducing perinatally acquired AIDS, less progress has been made among African American and Latino children (NCHSTP, 1998b). African American children represent nearly two-thirds of all pediatric AIDS cases (CDC, 2002).

MY NAME IS CHRIS

My name is Chris. I am a social worker at Beth Israel Hospital in Los Angeles. I specialize in pediatric AIDS. I love my work, and I hate my work. When I see the children come in, I feel completely powerless. I know they will die before they have even have a chance to live. I also know that there is probably more than one member in the child's family who has HIV or AIDS. Many of the families are poor and minority and have problems of finances and discrimination in addition to the AIDS diagnosis. These children are dying alone. They are stigmatized and excluded. The fear, misunderstanding, and ambivalent feelings toward children with HIV/AIDS are exhibited by teachers, playmates, medical personnel, and even morticians.

Most of the children I work with contracted the disease from their mothers at birth. Some are severely ill and are in the hospital, others live at home or in foster care. I don't just work with the children—I can't. The whole family needs help in coping with their own denial, sorrow, and guilt at having passed on the disease. The family needs to be assisted in their grief and then mobilized to support and care for the child. Often the mother is also dying, so I try to help the parents make appropriate custody arrangements. I also attempt to change high-risk behavior in the parents and obtain income support, medical care, and housing assistance for them when necessary.

In my work, I am forced to constantly reevaluate my own attitudes and bias toward my clients. I must try to understand their culture and what beliefs, values, and life circumstances have contributed to their situation. I constantly strive to promote education and prevention about HIV/AIDS to do whatever I can to reduce the number of children born with AIDS. People ask me how I can work every day with clients who are dying. Sometimes I wonder the same thing. But every day these children humble me by their own strength and vulnerability, and I know that if I am not there for them, who will be?

Social workers were among the first professionals to offer services to children who were affected by HIV and their families (Wiener, Fair, & Garcia, 1995). Social workers who work with children with AIDS may experience feelings of powerlessness because of the dire prognosis. Social workers must address a range of problems affecting the child and his or her family and use the range of social work interventions, from counseling to advocacy. In the early stages of the disease and even through its progression, social workers are called upon to help affected families meet their most basic needs for housing, food, and transportation. In addition, social workers often act as case managers by facilitating access to services and coordinating hospital, home, and community care (Wiener et al., 1995). Social workers often provide mental health services, such as support and advice, to the client as well as the immediate and extended family (Wiener et al., 1995).

Tapping family support is particularly crucial because the family often faces stigma and condemnation, resulting in a lack of extended family and community support. The hysteria that can accompany community knowledge that a child has AIDS was made obvious in the case of Ryan White, a 15-year-old hemophiliac who contracted AIDS from a blood transfusion (and for whom the 1990 law was named). The family was harassed, and Ryan was expelled from school and readmitted only after legal intervention.

In addition to actively working with the affected families and children, social workers are involved in community education and prevention services. An example of the power of community organization and advocacy is the development of the New York State Standby Guardian Law. The law was developed in response to the growing number of children who were being orphaned by parents who had AIDS. In an effort to prevent a huge influx of children into the foster care system, social workers played an essential role in planning the Orphan Project, a research study designed to explore policy options to meet the needs of HIV-affected and HIV-infected children. Social workers also used the skills of coordination and organization to bring together public and private organizations such as Mothers of Children with AIDS, Lincoln Hospital, St. Vincent's Hospital, the New York City Department of Health, the Rose F. Kennedy Center, and many others to use their knowledge and influence in ensuring the bill's passage. The result was the formation of a policy with the specific objective of facilitating the appointment of standby guardians, thus reducing the numbers of children placed in the foster care system (Letteney, 1995).

Social workers are active in identifying long-term needs of families and children associated with the AIDS crisis. They help parents cope with denial, depression, and guilt; family support is mobilized to care for the child and, often, the parent; arrangements are made for child custody; and practical assistance is offered to obtain needed medical care, income support, and housing assistance.

Social workers also intervene at the societal level to advocate for and support legislation promoting the rights of people with AIDS and, at the community level, to monitor compliance with existing laws and regulations. NASW highlighted the strength of discrimination on people with AIDS:

> Discriminating against people who are infected with HIV/AIDS or anyone thought to be at-risk of infection violates individual human rights and endangers public health. Every person infected with and affected by HIV/AIDS deserves compassion and support, regardless of the circumstances surrounding their infection. Education is crucial in getting this message out. (NASW, 2002)

The epidemic of AIDS has now spanned almost two decades. Although substantial progress has been made in the diagnosis and treatment of this disease, there remains no cure.

People with AIDS can now live many years beyond their initial diagnosis. Although finding a cure remains a paramount priority, the prolongation of life for people with AIDS has created a host of new social concerns and problems. Many people with AIDS are affected by multiple psychosocial problems, some of which, such as substance abuse, may have led to exposure to the HIV virus in the first place. In years past, transitional housing was sufficient to address the housing needs of who were not expected to live beyond this period. Now, permanent housing is needed. However, living independently in the community means that the gamut of psychosocial problems affecting this subset of the AIDS-affected population must be addressed. The case of Pedro illustrates the range of problems that affect people who live with HIV/AIDS.

LIVING WITH AIDS

Pedro, 26 years of age, was born in El Salvador and migrated to the United States in 1996. He speaks little English. His main reason for emigrating was the persecution he experienced as a homosexual in a Catholic country in which such "deviance" was not tolerated. He wanted to be able to live his life without fear.

Pedro settled in New York and took a job as a janitor in an apartment building. He obtained a green card and was adjusting well to his new country. Pedro also had an active social life but, unfortunately, did not practice safe sex. With many partners, Pedro became a statistic— he tested positive for HIV.

Pedro was initially seen at the Gay Men's Health Center. After the diagnosis, he was referred to an internist who specialized in treating people with HIV/AIDS. Although Pedro had some health insurance through his job, this did not include prescription drugs. The new physician immediately prescribed what is known as a "cocktail"—several different drugs, including AZT, which have been found to be

successful in warding off, or at least delaying, the onset of AIDS. The cost of the prescriptions, however, left Pedro with no money for living expenses. In addition, he did not respond well to the drugs and often was so sick from them that he was unable to work. After about two months, Pedro quit his job. One of the perks of his job was a free apartment. Pedro had to find another place to live.

Pedro sought help through the case manager at the health center, Bill. Bill first conducted a thorough psychosocial assessment. Pedro needed ongoing monitoring to ensure medication compliance. He also needed financial assistance, as he was now unemployed. Bill thought that Pedro might qualify for disability benefits. He also needed immediate shelter while a search was underway to find longer-term housing. Bill knew that finding appropriate housing might take time. First, the affordable housing supply in the New York metropolitan area is extremely limited. Second, Pedro's debilitating physical status suggested the need for special housing. People with HIV/AIDS may have less strength to open doors, and they may tire more easily when walking or climbing stairs. They may use a wheelchair, electric scooter, or other device for mobility purposes. Although Pedro was ambulatory, he was extremely weak. There was no way to assess his future needs. But it was prudent to select housing that could accommodate the eventuality of further debilitation. Bill was aware, however, that finding suitable housing would be difficult. First, there is the issue of affordability. Another issue concerns that of discrimination—landlords are often unwilling to rent to people with an illness or disability, despite the law.

Depending on the extent to which the medication side effects could be controlled, Pedro might be able to seek employment elsewhere, at least on a part-time basis. This possibility would need to be monitored over time. But for the moment, there are other priority needs—medical stabilization, housing, and activation of a support network for Pedro.

*Bill's assessment also included explo-
ration of Pedro's support network. It was very
limited. Pedro had few friends in the area
and no relatives. He was somewhat isolated,
a situation made worse by his physical condition and the fear of those around him that
they might "catch" AIDS even without sexual contact.*

*Bill's first task was to identify transition-
al housing for Pedro. The Fair Housing
Amendments Act of 1988 (P.L. 100-430)
prohibits housing discrimination against people with disabilities, including people with
HIV/AIDS. This act is enforced by the Fair
Housing and Equal Opportunity Office.
However, enforcement takes time, and Pedro
didn't have much time to locate housing. This
was when Bill used his collegial network. His
friend, Vera, worked for the city agency
responsible for coordinating transitional
housing programs for people with HIV/AIDS.
If there were any vacancies in transitional
housing, Vera would know. Bill was able to
reach Vera by phone and, as he hoped, she
knew of one opening—if Bill can act fast.*

*A few phone calls later, Pedro has a tem-
porary home. Bill is relieved, as the temporary
housing crisis is resolved. But Bill also knows
that finding permanent housing will be even
more difficult.*

The case of Pedro highlights the vital role of
social workers in health care in coordinating
with many different kinds of services providers.
In Pedro's case, a physical condition—HIV-positive status—was accompanied by a host of
practical problems, such as housing, finances,
and unemployment. In addition, Pedro is
socially isolated and understandably depressed.
The initial problem is a health crisis—the diagnosis of HIV-positive status and the need to
begin a medication regime. But as the immediate health crisis is addressed, the social worker's
role expands to help Pedro with his psychosocial
and concrete needs.

In 1998 the Supreme Court in *Bragdon v.
Abbott* ruled that people infected with the AIDS
virus but do not yet exhibit symptoms of the disease are protected from discrimination by the
ADA ("HIV Is a Disability," 1998). Under the
ADA, all people with disabilities, including those
with AIDS and now HIV-positive status, are
given equal opportunity to use or enjoy a public
accommodation's goods, services, and facilities.
Public accommodations include restaurants,
hotels, theaters, doctors' offices, dentists' offices,
hospitals, retail stores, health clubs, museums,
libraries, private schools, and day care centers. An
example of discrimination would include a doctor or a dentist who categorically refuses to treat
people with HIV/AIDS (NASW, 2002).

Under the provisions of this law, a landlord
could not refuse to rent an apartment to Pedro
because of his HIV-positive status. However, discrimination does not cease just because a law is
passed. The law must be enforced, and this takes
time and money for all parties concerned, including the government, the person with HIV/AIDS,
and social and legal services agencies.

FAMILY PLANNING

Family planning has been defined as "making
deliberate and voluntary decisions about reproduction" (Barker, 1999, p. 168). Such planning
between a couple involves decisions about the
number and timing of pregnancies based on
such factors as individual choice, economics,
age, and other considerations. Purposeful family planning usually involves choices about the
use of contraception.

Social workers in family planning engage in
many different functions, from clinical counseling and assessment to program design and evaluation. They can work with teenagers, young
adults, or middle-aged clients. They can work in
a health department, neighborhood clinic,
school-based clinic, or Planned Parenthood.
They may deal with the acute needs of an
unwed, pregnant teenager, or they may help a

young adult female decide on the most appropriate form of contraception.

The majority of family planning services in the United States are provided by state and local health departments, neighborhood health clinics, school-based clinics, and Planned Parenthood. Social workers in family planning may work in any of these settings. The Planned Parenthood Federation of America is a private, nonprofit agency with affiliates throughout the country that provide medical services ranging from birth control counseling to vasectomies. The organization also offers education and training programs for a variety of issues including sex education, natural family planning, and services for the handicapped.

For more than 100 years, family planning has been a controversial topic. In the past, sexuality was not discussed, and knowledge was lacking regarding human reproduction. The medical profession contributed to the public's ignorance by considering birth control to be a social rather than a medical issue. It was not until 1965 that the federal government recognized the importance of family planning services by providing financial resources. Title X of the Public Health Service Act of 1970 (P.L. 91-572) is administered by the U.S. Department of Health and Human Services Office of Population Affairs and is the only federal program specifically directed toward family planning services (Planned Parenthood, 2002b).

As the social and political acceptance of birth control services increased, so did the technology. Unfortunately, no contraceptive is 100 percent reliable and safe. All have some detrimental side effects and some degree of risk (Planned Parenthood, 2002c). Therefore, one of the primary functions of a social worker in family planning is to help clients understand the pros and cons of the different contraceptives and decide on the most suitable method for each individual's circumstances.

Social workers in family planning who work in health clinics review patient charts and interview those admitted to the clinic to identify high-risk patients, such as those who are unmarried or who have a physical or mental disability. Carrying out the social work functions of assessment and counseling, the social worker must then attempt to determine the client's current knowledge base and ability to make rational decisions regarding contraception and family planning. Factors to be considered are the client's ability to appropriately care for herself, the availability of an adequate support system, and the knowledge of available resources. After assessing the client's base of information, the social worker—who must be knowledgeable about prenatal and perinatal issues—counsels the client on health education, contraception, and family planning. However, in order for the new information to be useful to the client, the social worker must use his or her skills to communicate clearly in a manner that the client understands. Social workers also offer support and counseling to the client and others involved, enable the client to access appropriate resources, and provide referrals when necessary.

Teen Pregnancy

Although social workers involved in family planning work with clients of all ages, the rate of teenage pregnancy in the United States, which is reaching near epidemic proportions, points to the need for expanded services to the teen population. Each year, approximately 1 million teens in the United States become pregnant, and about 40 percent of American women become pregnant before age 20 (Annie E. Casey Foundation, 1998; Planned Parenthood, 2002a, 2002b). Although the national teen pregnancy rate has been falling, with a 17 percent decline between 1990 and 1996, the rate of teenage childbearing in the United States is the highest in the developed world. Reasons for lower rates of childbearing outside of the United States relate to mandatory, medically accurate sex education programs, easy access to contraception and other forms of reproductive health care, and public health media campaigns concerning information and services (Berne & Huberman, 1999).

As the rate of teenage pregnancy escalates, social workers in family planning increasingly encounter teens who understand the need for contraception but do not know what kind to use or how to access it. Many of the teens who do use contraceptives do so only casually and ineffectively (Annie E. Casey Foundation, 1998). As researchers persevere in their studies of problems encountered by pregnant teens, there continues to be a lack of information in regard to epidemiology and effective intervention techniques (Alan Guttmacher Institute, 1998). It is clear, however, that adolescent pregnancy carries significant risks to the health of both the pregnant adolescent and the child.

Teen pregnancy and early childbearing are associated with a host of lifelong financial, social, and psychological issues. Studies have consistently documented that teenage mothers are more likely to drop out of school and live in poverty and that their children frequently experience health and developmental problems. Nearly 80 percent of teen mothers eventually go on welfare. The estimated financial burden to society is $7 billion per year (Annie E. Casey Foundation, 1998; Hoffman, 1998). There are also negative health, economic, and social consequences for the children born to teen mothers. It is estimated that one-third of pregnant teens do not receive adequate prenatal care, resulting in low birth weight babies, childhood health problems, and more frequent hospitalizations that those born to older mothers (Alan Guttmacher Institute, 1998; Planned Parenthood, 2002a). These children are also more likely to perform poorly in school and are at greater risk of abuse and neglect. Further, the sons of teen mothers have been found to be significantly more likely to end up in prison and daughters more likely to become teen mothers themselves than is the case for children born to nonteen mothers (National Campaign to Prevent Teen Pregnancy, 2002). Such data highlight the need to emphasize prevention services.

TEENAGE DADS

Becky is a school social worker in San Francisco. She is busy with several different cases ranging from a ninth grade boy whose parents are divorcing to an 11th grade girl who is anorexic. She is interrupted by a telephone call. It is Martha Crow, a social worker with the Ford Foundation in New York. The San Francisco public schools had previously worked with the Ford Foundation to implement and evaluate a drug prevention program, and Becky had gotten to know Martha in their work together on that project.

Martha explains to Becky that the foundation has joined with other organizations to fund programs in major cities targeting teenage pregnancy. She explains that they are already sponsoring several programs for teenage mothers and are interested in programs targeting teenage fathers. She wants to know if Becky's school would be interested in serving as a demonstration site for this project.

"Teenage fathers?" Becky asks. Martha explains that contrary to the common stereotypes, many of the young men want to contribute and be a part of the lives of their children, but they often lack resources and need a great deal of assistance. Becky tells Martha that she will talk to her colleagues and the school principal and call back within the next week.

Becky sits at her desk and considers the proposal. She knows that Brackton South is an urban school with a large population of low-income students. She also recalls that she has worked with six pregnant teenage girls in the last year. Of the six, three of the fathers dropped out of school to make money for child support.

In the next week Becky conducts a great deal of research, talks with her colleagues, and explains the opportunity to the principal. They all agree teenage pregnancy is a school and a community problem. However, the principal asks Becky why they should spend time working with the teenage fathers. If the pregnancy has already occurred, why not dedicate resources to the mother? Becky presents her research findings and explains that oftentimes, the young men may want to help but don't know how. As a result, they may drop out of school to support the child or go to the opposite extreme and offer absolutely no assistance. After Becky's presentation, the principal concurs that support for teenage fathers is needed. Becky agrees to work full-time on developing a program, and the other human services professionals in the school agree to take Becky's share of new cases. The decision to proceed is made, and Becky calls Martha with the news.

Becky begins to review case files regarding past work with pregnant teenagers. She finds many cases in which the teenage father dropped out of school to provide financial support for the child. Although this indicates responsible intentions, Becky knows that the program she designs will have to address how these fathers can immediately contribute financially and at the same time remain in school so they can eventually improve their employability and earnings potential. Becky's plan is to have school social workers counsel teenage fathers who want to drop out about the consequences of a future of minimum-wage jobs. The social worker will assess the teenage father's situation and, if possible, help him get a part-time job while remaining in school. As a result of taking an extra job, the social worker may also have to help the teenager reduce his class load or receive tutoring if necessary.

In addition to financial concerns, a number of the cases Becky finds show teenage fathers who are depressed and who have no hope for their future. They are often condemned by their own family as well as the family of the teenage mother. In her program, Becky plans to have social workers facilitate communication between the teenage mother and father and the grandparents to ease the tension in an already stressful situation.

Teen fatherhood, Becky learns, has negative consequences. Teen fathers are more likely to

engage in delinquent behaviors, including alcohol abuse or drug dealing, and they complete fewer years of schooling than their childless counterparts. A study conducted under the auspices of the Annie E. Casey Foundation (1998) followed teen fathers over the course of 18 years following the birth of their first child. Findings revealed that the fathers of children born to teen mothers earned about $3,400 less per year than the fathers of children born to mothers who were 20 or 21 years old.

Becky feels that her program will address the situation early, with social workers encouraging expectant mothers from the beginning to bring expectant fathers to meetings and counseling sessions. In addition, the same social workers will work with the teenage parents throughout the pregnancy, delivery, and the postpartum stages. This continuous service, Becky assesses, will eliminate a "gap period" when the young parents may feel alone and confused and lose the benefits of program participation that they have achieved.

Becky also plans to offer services that include child care, health and sex education, individual and group counseling, parental training, career assistance, childbirth preparation, paternity establishment assistance, and a healthy meal program, including breakfast and lunch. This will involve hiring a new social worker specifically for the program, but she anticipates that the Ford Foundation will support this new hire.

Becky decides that she will be pleased with the program if it has the following results:

- reduces repeat births to the same teenage parents
- increases school retention among both teenage mothers and fathers
- raises infant birth weights (Many teenagers' babies are underweight).

With her proposal complete, Becky arranges a meeting to review her ideas with her colleagues and the principal before sending the plan to Martha at the Ford Foundation.

In the case described here, Becky carries out the social work functions of mobilization, exchange, program development, coordination, and grant writing. She also uses her research skills to identify findings that support particular program approaches. After the program is implemented, Becky will also have to monitor service delivery and conduct an outcome evaluation to determine if the original goals have been achieved. Ongoing coordination in the form of interorganizational relationships will need to take place between the school and the Ford Foundation.

Although family planning has been widely accepted in society, a controversy currently blazes in regard to dispensing birth control in school-based health clinics or even information about contraception. Such clinics have multiplied in the last several years, and many are in low-income, urban areas with inadequate health care and transportation services. These clinics generally operate in junior and senior high schools and are funded by government or private agencies rather than through the school budget. Some clinics actually dispense contraceptives, whereas others may write prescriptions.

Social workers in the field are not unified in their opinions. Some believe that family planning, sex education, and health services must complement the distribution of contraceptives to decrease teenage pregnancy. However, others believe that such education will not affect the pregnancy rate because teenagers get pregnant for other reasons, such as low self-esteem, sexual identity, peer pressure, loneliness, and other inner needs. Those holding this view see the solution as lying in a more comprehensive strategy than family planning alone.

Sexually Transmitted Infections

Sex education is only one of several issues that confront the social worker, as part of the health team, in working with teens, young adults, and even older adults. Sexually transmitted infec-

tions (STIs), often referenced as sexually transmitted diseases (STDs), are among the most common infections experienced by people in the United States, yet their prevalence is vastly underestimated, and most men and women of reproductive age do not comprehend their own personal risk (Planned Parenthood, 2002b). Planned Parenthood recommends use of the term STI rather than STD, as it is more accurate medically. Many STIs are not diseases. Also STIs can evidence no symptoms and therefore go undetected (Planned Parenthood, 2002d).

It is estimated that more than 15 million new cases of STIs are diagnosed each year in the United States, approximately one-fourth of which occur among teenagers (Cates, 1999; CDC, 2000a). Over 65 million people are estimated to be infected with an STI other than HIV (NCHSTP, 1998a). Despite this alarming prevalence—more than one in five Americans—many people delay getting treatment or do not even recognize that they may have an STI. This is because many of these infections are asymptomatic. Also, the social stigma attached to STIs discourages men and women from seeking treatment, leading to what has been termed a "hidden epidemic" (Eng & Butler, 1997).

Social workers, because of their assessment skills and strengths in encouraging open communication, provide an important link between the patient and the physician. The Guidelines for Women's Health Care of the American College of Obstetricians and Gynecologists recommend that all women under age 65 receive evaluation and counseling on STIs as part of their routine examinations. Of the 15 million people who contract STIs each year, about one-quarter or 3,750,000 are teenagers (Kaiser Family Foundation, 2001). These statistics suggest the need for prevention and early intervention. For teenagers, school-based clinics provide one important means of access to such services.

GENETICS

In recent years, technological developments have made it possible to identify and, in some cases, treat genetic disorders. The completion of the first mapping of human DNA has brought with it both opportunities and mandates for social workers and social scientists to examine the ethical, legal, and social implications of this knowledge explosion (Vallianatos, 2000).

The success in the human genome mapping has already produced a knowledge explosion about the causes of and possible interventions into disease. With this knowledge, however, come new and far-reaching practice-related as well as ethical questions. In the not-too-distant future social workers, along with the full spectrum of health care professionals and ethicists, will need to explore the implications of the next stage of scientific advancement: cloning. Genetic links have been identified in bipolar disease, mental retardation, sickle cell anemia, Alzheimer's disease, as well as an array of physical maladies ranging from diabetes to arthritis and cancer. Social workers are often positioned to deal with the impact of the genetic links on families (Clark, 2002; Stoesen, 2002). Even the biopsychosocial assessments routinely conducted by social workers should now include a genetics history.

There are 3,000 known genetic disorders, and there are vast ethical, psychological, and physiological issues that are involved in the occurrence or risk of occurrence of a genetic disorder in a family. Psychosocial services for families with genetic disorders are now recognized as a vital component of the interdisciplinary team approach to treatment. Genetic testing and improved medical technology have led to new populations of clients, complicated choices for them, and unprecedented psychosocial issues (Rauch & Black, 1995). As a result, social work involvement with people needing genetic services is growing. As we learn more and more about the human genome and how genes and the environment affect mental health as well as the physical health of the client, the social work role is likely to continue to expand.

As the nation's largest provider of mental health services, social workers face an array of issues relating to genetics. Issues of informed consent and confidentiality arise, as do issues of discrimination, self-determination, and the immediate benefits of genetic test results. Social workers need to communicate to the client the limits of protection of confidentiality under federal and state law; strengths and limitations of the test itself; availability of prevention, treatment, and cure; and potential risks of stigmatization, discrimination, and psychological distress, including risk to intrafamilial relationships (Clark, 2002; NASW, 2000b). In addition, social workers need to help clients and their families identify genetic resources and work through privacy and confidentiality as well as insurance concerns.

Social workers work directly with the families, taking detailed family histories and offering information and referral, supportive counseling, and concrete information (Rauch & Black, 1995). Social workers also participate as part of study teams. For example, a social worker who is part of a team studying Huntington's disease within family units may be asked to help locate family members. This process is likely to involve extensive phone work and hours of research in court document rooms and libraries locating birth, death, and marriage certificates. Once located, it is also the social worker's job to explain the study to family members and gain their participation in a blood comparison test of affected and unaffected people.

People who have a genetic disorder must deal with a variety of life-affecting tasks. For example, they may have to learn more about the disease, they may have to modify their plans to have children, and they may have to alter their lifestyle to adhere to medical protocols. Such adjustments do not come easily, and social workers must use the functions of assistance, advice, and enabling to help clients cope with the inevitable changes (Rauch & Black, 1995).

Social workers generally apply crisis intervention at the time of diagnosis, whenever exacerbations of illness occur, hospitalizations, and during dying and bereavement stages. Important social work skills in this arena include familiarity with specific disorders and the burdens that accompany them; understanding of the psychological and familial effects; and competent assessment skills (Rauch, 1988). Referral and case management are also used both in times of crisis and after stabilization has been achieved (Rauch & Black, 1995). After the initial crisis has abated, the social worker is also instrumental in linking the family with support services. One example of a support network is the Alliance of Genetic Support Groups, an organization founded by social worker Joan Weiss. This organization, known as the Genetic Alliance, is a coalition of organizations and support groups specifically for individuals and their families who suffer from a range of genetic disorders (Stoesen, 2002).

The Genetic Alliance seeks to promote healthy lives for all people living with genetic conditions, in part by working for rapid translation of medical research into practice. Membership includes individuals with genetic conditions and more than 600 advocacy, research, and health care organizations (Genetic Alliance, 2003).

As in many other areas of social work, advocacy is also an important aspect of social work practice in the field of genetics. There is documented evidence that, in addition to genetic disorders, environmental agents and birth defects are significantly related. Therefore social workers in this field should advocate for programs such as those that prevent maternal drug and alcohol abuse during pregnancy and those that promote obtaining protection from damaging chemicals or radiation in workplaces and communities (Rauch & Black, 1995). Further, social workers need to ensure that genetic testing is accessible to all populations and is affordable (Stoesen, 2002). Here, social work skills of lobbying, mediating, and negotiating on behalf of clients with insurance companies, hospitals, and government officials (in the case of Medicaid and Medicare) are critical. Advocating for legislation that protects the privacy and confidentiality of genetic information is another aspect of macro interventions in this field.

In recent years, biomedical advances have led to the development of a test for Huntington's disease, which has its onset at midlife and which causes early death. Those who are tested will have the answer to "Will I develop Huntington's?" However, advances in genetic testing are accompanied by many unimagined dilemmas. Social workers must use their skills and resources to make sure the new medical advances are used responsibly and beneficially (Rauch & Black, 1995). The emotional and ethical issues surrounding the decision of whether to be tested are illustrated in the following vignette.

DO I WANT TO KNOW

Judy Epstein was 11 years old when her father died. She only vaguely remembers when he first became ill, but she remembers all too keenly how quickly he went from being a vibrant, healthy man to a bed-ridden invalid racked with convulsions and pain—a shell of a man, really. It was the kind of slow death she thought must be the vengeance of a hateful God. After her father's funeral, when the relatives and friends returned to their house, Judy remembers her relatives whispering about who might be next.

Judy is now 26 years old and has met a man she plans to marry. Bill wants to have a large family; children, he says, are "what it's all about." Judy knew this about Bill from almost the first moment they met. And now, as the prospect of marriage looms, she must consider the consequences of not having told him about the cause of her father's death. All her efforts to suppress her fears that she may fall victim to Huntington's disease no longer work. She is unable to sleep or eat; Bill wants to set a wedding date.

Only recently, Judy learned that there is a test that can determine whether she carries the gene that will, if present, eventually mean that she will develop the disease. Does she want to know? Could she deal with it? And if she doesn't find out, how can she proceed with her marriage plans? She could be dooming her children to an early death sentence.

Judy decides to seek out a therapist. She calls the Huntington's Society national office in New York to obtain a referral to a therapist who specializes in working with families faced with chronic illness. She is informed that there is a social worker on their staff, Anne Milner, who would be available to meet with her. Anne makes an appointment to see Judy and then reflects on the impact of the new genetic testing that is available. Most of Anne's cases used to be depression cases, either with the sick individual or with his or her spouse or other family members. Occasionally, Anne also worked with people who had expressed suicidal ideation. However, recently she had begun to see more and more people who are struggling with the issue of whether to submit to the genetics test.

Anne understands the difficult decision that faces these clients, and her primary mode of intervention is empathic listening and communication. Anne usually meets with the individual client for at least two to three sessions when she gathers history and information regarding the current social support structure. Generally, in these sessions, Anne assesses the situation and makes an initial diagnosis. She then identifies areas of need and offers support and counseling. However, Anne never makes the decision for a client. She strongly believes in self-determination and the importance of letting the client decide if he or she wants to have the test.

Often, Anne invites other family members to later sessions if they need support or assistance. Anne also frequently refers clients and family members to support groups in the area composed of people who are facing or have already faced similar difficult decisions about genetic testing

for themselves or their family members and loved ones. Generally, Anne does not provide long-term counseling, which is considered to be more than eight sessions. As a national association, the Huntington's Society has an extremely large client base which requires it to provide short-term, crisis intervention counseling and offer referrals if further help is needed.

After meeting with Anne twice, Judy decides that she must tell Bill about her father's death and the implications that it holds for their future together. Judy and Bill both come to counseling sessions for the next two weeks and share their concerns and anxiety about having the test performed to determine whether Judy carries the Huntington's gene. In addition to offering support and assistance, Anne refers them to a local support group for people with genetic diseases who are struggling with similar issues. After meeting with Anne and attending the support group, Bill and Judy decide to have the test performed. Anne wishes them luck and tells them to contact the organization if they need help in the future.

In this case scenario, most of Anne's work is focused on the provision of direct services. She performs assessment and diagnosis upon her initial contact with Judy and Bill. She also identifies areas of need and offers support and counseling to both of them. Anne also carries out the social work function of referral when she helps Judy and Bill get involved in a local support group. Finally, Anne provides information about the disease and the testing procedures and encourages and enables Judy and Bill to make their own, well-educated decision about which path they wish to follow.

Although Anne primarily carries out direct practice functions, social workers in similar organizations will often engage in macro activities such as planning, administration, and supervision. One of the most important social work functions in such arenas is that of program development and evaluation. An essential component of social work practice is identifying needs in a specific population or a community and developing and administering a program or service to meet that need.

Anne engages in social work practice within a nontraditional setting. The primary mission of the Huntington's Society is not related to the provision of social work services. National voluntary health agencies, such as the Huntington's Society, typically have as their purposes to combat a particular disease, disability, or group of disabilities and to improve the health of a particular group of people. Many have local affiliates to provide community or individually oriented educational and support services and to raise money; many of these local efforts are of a self-help nature. In general, national voluntary health agencies provide five types of services: public education, patient services, professional education, research, and community services such as health screening and promoting improved health practices (Gibelman, 1990). However, in recent years, a number of local affiliates and even some national organizations have begun to hire social workers in recognition of the psychosocial and emotional needs of those affiliated with the disease or disability.

A survey conducted under the auspices of the Human Genome Education Model Project of six national health professional organizations, including NASW, found that a majority of their members worked with clients with genetic conditions but few had confidence in their ability to provide genetic services and most had little or no education in genetics (Vallianatos, 2000). NASW, in collaboration with the Council on Social Work Education, has been working to establish practice policy, which will include accessibility of genetic screening for those who desire it, protection of the rights of people who participate in screening, preservation of the rights of the client to determine for himself or herself whether to be screened, guarantee of confidentiality; and use of data for planning and developing services delivery.

As the implications of the Human Genome Project become more accessible to professionals and the public, social workers will need to develop basic competency in genetics. A document entitled "Core Competencies in Genetics Essential for All Health-Care Professionals" was developed by the National Coalition for Health Professional Education in Genetics in 2001. This document sets forth skills and attitudes for health professionals and suggests that, at a minimum, professionals should be able to (1) appreciate the limitations of their expertise; (2) understand the social and psychological implications of genetics services; and (3) know how and when to make a referral to a genetics professional (Clark, 2002).

In 2003, NASW published *Standards for Integrating Genetics into Social Work Practice* under the leadership of social worker Joan O. Weiss, founding director of the Genetic Alliance.

EATING DISORDERS

The interplay between physical and emotional illness is particularly apparent in the range of problems that fall under the category of "eating disorders." Eating disorders refer to maladaptive or unhealthy patterns of eating and ingestion which are usually first evident in childhood or adolescence (Barker, 1999). There are several types, the better known of which are anorexia nervosa, bulimia nervosa, and binge eating disorders (Anorexia Nervosa and Related Eating Disorders [ANRED], 2002a).

Anorexia nervosa is an eating disorder most often encountered in girls and young women. This condition may be life threatening and is related to a disturbed body image and an exaggerated fear of becoming obese (Barker, 1999). Anorexia nervosa has been called "the relentless pursuit of thinness" (ANRED, 2002a). People suffering from this disease refuse to maintain normal body weight for their age and height and weigh 85 percent or less than what is considered appropriate for them. Symptoms include weight loss (sometimes extreme) and for women cessation of menstrual periods, and for men a drop in sex hormone levels. Psychological symptoms are also prevalent, including depression, irritability, withdrawal, compulsive rituals, and strange eating habits. Those affected tend to deny the dangers of low weight, are terrified of gaining weight and becoming fat, and report feeling fat even when very thin (ANRED, 2002a).

The weight–height formula that is used by insurance companies indicates a diagnosis of anorexia nervosa if an individual has lost at least 25 percent of his or her average body weight. The other measurement tool, the average body weight table of women ages 15 to 69 indicates anorexia nervosa when a person weighs less than 75 percent of his or her average body weight (Logan, 1995).

Bulimia nervosa is one of the eating disorders in which a "pathologically excessive appetite with episodic eating binges is sometimes followed by purging. The purging may occur through such means as self-induced vomiting or the abuse of laxatives, diet pills, or diuretics" (Barker, 1999, p. 56). The disorder is also characterized by a compulsive preoccupation with food and a compulsive need to keep the behavior secret. Although bulimics are similar to anorexics in that they are concerned with body weight, and are overly concerned with gaining weight, they tend to maintain a more normal body weight and some may even be obese (Logan, 1995). This is because of the fact that frequently bulimics will go on extremely long binges, ingesting huge amounts of high caloric foods that are impossible to completely purge (ANRED, 2002a).

The binge–purge cycle of bulimia is as, if not more, dangerous than the starvation practices of anorexics. Binging and purging can upset the body's balance of electrolytes that can cause fatigue, seizures, muscle cramps, irregular heartbeat, and decreased bone strength and density. Furthermore, the repeated vomiting can damage the esophagus and stomach and can cause the swelling of glands, the receding of gums, and the eroding of tooth enamel (Logan, 1995).   .

Here, too, psychological problems are often manifest. Bulimics may be depressed, lonely, ashamed, and feel empty inside. Impulse control may be a problem, and there is a high occurrence of shoplifting, promiscuity, alcohol and drug abuse, and other kinds of risk-taking behavior (ANRED, 2002a).

In addition to anorexia and bulimia, compulsive overeating is another food-related addiction that is referred to as a binge eating disorder. Although bulimics may compulsively overeat, they tend to purge afterward. On the other hand, compulsive eating is generally described as uncontrollable binge eating that is not accompanied by starvation or purging methods (Logan, 1995). Even when not hungry, people with this eating disorder often overeat and feel a loss of control about their food intake and, here too, tend to be depressed. They may also feel guilty and ashamed of their eating, have a history of diet failures, and be overweight (ANRED, 2002a).

About 1 percent of female adolescents are estimated to have anorexia, but reliable figures are lacking for younger children and older adults (ANRED, 2002b). Bulimia nervosa is thought to affect about 4 percent of college-age women, but is rare in children. Approximately half of those people who have been anorexic develop bulimia or bulimia patterns (ANRED, 2002b). These eating disorders occur overwhelmingly—about 90 percent—in women.

In response to the growing recognition of the pervasiveness and seriousness of eating disorders, a new, nationwide prevention and advocacy organization was formed in 2001 as a result of a merger of several smaller organizations—the National Eating Disorders Association (NEDA) (ANRED, 2002c). NEDA offers information and referral, supports research, and advocates for relevant social policies, among other activities. Information about this nonprofit association is available on their Web site: http://www.nationaleatingdisorders.org.

There a number of different theories and models that attempt to explain the etiology of various eating disorders. Social workers must attempt to assess, identify, and diagnosis the core psychopathology of the disorder. In dealing with this complicated condition, social workers must be concerned with assessing the common secondary pathologies of eating disorders, as well. For example, there may be family and interpersonal problems, personality disorders, substance abuse, depression, or any combination of these problems (Logan, 1995).

Social workers in this specialty area who practice in hospitals and other institutional settings will generally handle a fair number of clients who are noncompliant and involuntary. Oftentimes, as in other areas of social work, the person refuses to acknowledge or admit that there is a problem (Logan, 1995). In treating eating disorders, there has been a general trend toward a multidisciplinary approach including social workers, physicians, and nutritionists. Usually, clients with eating disorders are treated first for physical symptoms to ensure their medical stability before progressing to psychosocial and supportive issues (Logan, 1995).

Social workers will not only carry out the functions of assessment and diagnosis, but also frequently engage in referral and coordination as part of the multidisciplinary approach (Logan, 1995). And, once again, social workers are encouraged to advocate for societal changes that will cast aside the worship of thinness and focus on self-acceptance in the socialization of young women.

People with eating disorders often resist treatment and behavior changes. They see a happier life if only they can lose enough weight. However, eating disorders are treatable. Those people with the best prognosis are treated with a combination of medical and psychosocial interventions (ANRED, 2003). The process starts with a medical evaluation. Components of treatment may include the following:

- hospitalization to prevent death, suicide, and medical crisis
- weight restoration to improve health, mood, and cognitive functioning
- medication to relieve depression and anxiety
- dental work to repair damage and minimize future problems
- individual counseling to develop healthy coping mechanisms
- group counseling to learn how to manage relationships effectively
- family counseling to alter old patterns and create new and healthier family interactions
- nutrition counseling to overcome food myths and design healthy eating patterns
- support groups to overcome isolation and alienation. (ANRED, 2003)

University-based counseling centers are an important source of help, as the following vignette illustrates.

CASSIE'S STORY

Cassie is an 18-year-old college freshman at William and Mary College. She is originally from Wilmington, VT, and her parents and brother still live there. Cassie was an all-around athlete in high school where she won numerous state and regional athletic honors in soccer, volleyball, and basketball. However, Cassie decided not to pursue her athletic career in college because she told her mother she "wanted to be a normal girl without big muscles and with lots of dates." When she arrived at William and Mary, Cassie decided to go on a diet. She wanted to be prettier and thinner than all the other girls. She began running five miles every morning, and then she would have only an apple for breakfast. After her first two classes, she would go swimming. She often skipped lunch, and if she did eat, she ate only a rice cake with a piece of fat-free cheese. She then went to an aerobics class from 4:30 to 5:30 and ran from 5:30 to 6:30.

Cassie began to lose weight very quickly. By Christmas she had lost 15 pounds. By March of the next year, she had lost 45 pounds, and her five-foot seven-inch, 90-pound frame was nothing more than a skeleton.

Cassie was forced to leave school for medical reasons, and she returned home to Vermont. Her mother was extremely worried about her, but her father could only verbalize his frustration through anger. "Why don't you just eat?" he would yell. Finally, Cassie entered the local hospital as an inpatient. Her weight had dropped to 85 pounds and the doctor said her body would soon begin to use the heart muscle for fuel. Cassie began to meet with Barbara, a social worker at the hospital, who specialized in eating disorders.

Barbara worked with Cassie every week. They would talk about everything from Cassie's family, to sports, to boys, to school. Barbara also referred Cassie to a support group that met at the hospital once a week. At these meetings Cassie was able to see people like herself who had lost so much weight they were now in the hospital being fed by tubes inserted in their arms. Cassie was shocked at how sick they looked, and she slowly realized that she looked the same way. She also saw people who had fought their disease of anorexia or bulimia and won. They looked so happy and free. Cassie wanted to be that way—she didn't want to have to worry about everything that touched her lips and she didn't want to obsess about exercising after every meal. She began to realize that the happiness she was trying to achieve did not relate to her size and that being ultra-thin didn't bring her love and joy. Cassie told this to the social worker and Barbara secretly breathed a sigh of relief. Cassie had taken the first step—she had recognized and admitted the problem. And she had decided to fight back.

In this vignette, Barbara engaged in assessment and diagnosis to determine the best way to treat Cassie and communicate with her. The

psychosocial interventions are planned in tandem with medical treatment. The social worker also coordinated with the doctors and participated as part of the interdisciplinary hospital team. Finally, the social worker effectively used referral skills by encouraging Cassie to attend the group meetings where she could see and talk with others who were in a similar predicament. In this way, Barbara was able to help Cassie escape her self-imposed isolation and recognize that there was hope.

PREVENTION

Many of the scenarios described above to illustrate the work of social workers in the field of health care involve services to ameliorate the concrete and psychosocial needs of people suffering from physical ailments. There is also a preventive side to social work practice in health care. A case in point is the Screen Adherence Follow-Up (SAFe) program, a health education counseling and case management intervention designed for culturally diverse, high-risk women who have had an abnormal mammogram or Pap smear exam.

Funded for four years by the Centers for Disease Control and Prevention to the Institute for the Advancement of Social Work Research, the principal investigator of the grant is Kathleen Ell of the University of Southern California. The underlying concern that this program addresses is that low-income women from minority groups have not availed themselves of follow-up assessment and treatment after abnormal screens, or even after a preliminary diagnosis of cancer (O'Neill, 2001). The program was piloted at medical facilities in Los Angeles and New York.

The program has several components, including interactive health education and counseling intervention by telephone after a woman has an abnormal screening; assessment of level of risk for problems in the woman's life that affect her ability to follow medical recommendations; a structured protocol for frequency and type of follow-up counseling, including telephone contact to reinforce the need for follow-up care and to address specific barriers to follow up; and psychological screening and counseling to enhance self-management skills regarding health care (O'Neill, 2001). The intensity of counseling and case management services provided to participants is established according to the level of risk determined through the assessment phase.

At the Los Angeles site, a social worker and three bilingual peer counselors sought to intervene with a very mobile population, including undocumented aliens. Initial evaluation findings revealed that those enrolled in this program achieved a 94 percent compliance rate, compared with a 76 percent compliance rate among the control group of those not enrolled. The final step of the program is to replicate the design and to develop a final version of a training manual detailing the methods used.

LOOKING AHEAD

The role of social workers in health care settings is undergoing change. A variety of social policy initiatives, such as Medicaid and Medicare, have influenced how and to what extent social workers are part of the health care team. Perhaps equally as important as legislation extending health care benefits has been the failure to enact major health care reform in the 1990s. This means that the private market exercises substantial control over the nature of our health care system.

Managed care, a movement that gained force through the private market, is about cost control. The role of the hospital social worker, as discussed earlier in this chapter, has become increasingly more focused on discharge planning. Service provision is, in the main, oriented to getting patients out of the hospital either to their homes or to less costly rehabilitation or step-down medical facilities. Many hospital-based social services departments have, over the last decade, been reorganized, shut down, or

streamlined. In some instances, social workers have been replaced by nurses who serve as both staff and managers of discharge planning units.

At the same time that hospital-based work has been affected by the cost containment movement, new and burgeoning roles for social workers have emerged. These include roles related to genetics counseling that may be based in a hospital or in clinics or even in the offices of private physicians. As the population ages, more and more people need long-term care arrangements in assisted living facilities, nursing homes, and in their own homes, through home health services. The role of social workers in capacities related to the provision of long-term care services has grown. Given the aging of the American population, home health programs and nursing homes are likely to expand their use of social workers, as discussed in Chapter 8.

Another area of potential growth for social workers concerns research, demonstration projects, and training for health care professionals aimed at reducing disparities in care and outcomes among minority groups. Shortly before leaving office, President Clinton signed the Minority Health and Health Disparities Research and Education Act of 2000 (P.L. 106-525). This law focuses on decreasing the disparities in the incidence of disease and health care outcomes among racial minorities when compared to the overall population ("Minority Health Bill Enacted," 2001). The act provides over $150 million to create a National Center on Minority Health Disparities at the National Institutes of Health; increases funding for research on race and health disparities through the Agency for Health Care Research and Quality, creates a new program to attract researchers into the field, and supports training for health care professionals on reducing health disparities through the Health Resources and Services Administration ("Minority Health Bill Enacted," 2001).

From a policy perspective, health care reform still looms for social workers and the people they serve as a major need. Despite heretofore inconceivable advances in medical care—ranging from transplants to genetic engineering—the health care system is open to some people but closed to many others. For millions of Americans, access to and choice about health care remain illusive.

Health insurance is typically available through the workplace. For those who work in seasonal jobs or are "downsized" and unemployed, there may be no health coverage available. For example, more than 529,000 laid-off employees lost medical coverage in the first three months after the terrorist attacks of September 11, 2001 (Nicholson, 2002). When these people reenter the job market, some may find themselves ineligible for insurance that covers preexisting conditions. The explosion in the costs of health insurance has also been passed along to consumers, causing some to drop their coverage. Of the millions of working Americans who have no insurance, many do not seek or receive medical care until an illness, such as cancer, diabetes, HIV, or hypertension, becomes too serious to ignore (Connolly, 2002).

From a social justice perspective, even when "all things are equal," people of color do not receive the same care. A study by the Institute of Medicine found that racial and ethnic minorities receive lower-quality health care than do whites, even if their income and health insurance coverage are the same. Earlier studies had documented—repeatedly—that there is differential access to care. The Institute of Medicine study was the first to look at racial disparities in care among people who have health insurance (Stolberg, 2002a).

More than 40 million Americans are uninsured, and of these nearly 85 percent work or live with families in which someone works (Connolly, 2002). Current trends suggest that the number of uninsured will approach 47 million by 2005 (Clark, 2001). Being uninsured, in turn, can lead to financial hardship and increased medical risk (Nicholson, 2002). A study conducted by the American Association of Retired People (AARP) revealed that nine out of 10 respondents who did not have health insurance failed to consult a physician when needed, or had a family member who did not seek needed treatment (Nicholson, 2002). Eight out of 10 have forgone necessary treatments or purchase of prescription drugs. Nearly 9 percent were forced to declare bankruptcy because of medical debts. Another study commissioned by the National Academy of Sciences supported the AARP findings and revealed that the lack of health insurance leads to delayed diagnosis, life-threatening complications, and about 18,000 premature deaths each year (Connolly, 2002).

Also at risk are the thousands of women and families currently enrolled in the Temporary Assistance to Needy Families (TANF) program. When they find employment or are terminated from TANF, they may find themselves in part-time jobs or low-pay full-time employment in which health benefits are either not offered or are offered at too high a cost. Thus, the uninsured population is likely to grow in the immediate future from among those now covered by Medicaid through their TANF status. Social workers need to understand the health care system to advocate effectively for their clients and to assist clients to obtain benefits that may be available to them. (One information source about health insurance on a state-by-state basis is a Web site maintained by the Georgetown University Institute for Health Care Research and Policy located online at http://www.health-insuranceinfo.net.)

Also within the advocacy mandate is HIV/AIDS. Enormous progress has been made, but there is still no cure for the disease. Advocacy for financial allocations to research new drugs and treatment protocols, as well as preventive approaches, remains high on the agenda. Further, the obligation of the social work community around such advocacy extends beyond the borders of the United States. Dr. Jeffrey D. Sachs, chair of a World Health Organization panel to examine the economic impact of AIDS, observed, "it took tens of millions of people being infected and dying before our political system woke up to those realities" (as cited in Stolberg, 2002b). Because AIDS now extends its impact to children, it has become easier for politicians to embrace it. Dongressman Richard Gephardt (D-MO), the House Minority Leader, had been among the cautious in terms of the U.S. obligation to assist other nations with the pandemic. But then he visited Africa, where AIDS is now the leading cause of death and where 6,000 young people ages 15 to 24 and 2,000 children under 15 years are infected with HIV every day. The experience, Mr. Gephardt said, was "life changing" (as cited in Stolberg, 2002b). Even the conservative senator Jesse Helms (D-NC) has come out in favor of more money for global AIDS. The actual and potential role for social workers in this wide arena of health concerns is enormous.

CAREER OPPORTUNITIES

Social workers who are considering entering the field of health care should be cognizant of the expected trends. For example, the present form of managed care will probably give way to more selective contracting and networks of providers. In addition, there will most likely be an increase in fiscal management of care rather than clinical management (Edinburg & Cottler, 1995). In the new health care arena, clinical social workers will still be called upon to provide inpatient and outpatient services in medical, rehabilitation, and psychiatric settings. In all settings, social workers will have to deal with the insurance companies' case managers in care issues such as discharge planning and type of service (Edinburg & Cottler, 1995).

Social workers are increasingly taking on administrative, supervisory, and case management functions. Social workers are assuming the role of advocate for patients in families who are dealing with the managed care system. These clients need help in understanding their benefits and how to access services. In addition to advocating within the managed care system, social workers must be major players in shaping health care policy to ensure adequate and affordable coverage for all citizens (Edinburg & Cottler, 1995).

Within the health arena, there are a large variety of job opportunities available to social workers. These jobs, a sample of which appears below, range from population specific (teen mothers, people with HIV, people with cancer) to setting specific (hospital, hospice), in which the social worker works with many different populations. Again, these jobs are based on actual classified ads but do not constitute opportunities available at this time.

Licensed Clinical Social Worker

Rush-Presbyterian-St. Luke's Medical Center is seeking a LCSW in the Child Psychology Department. The LCSW will be the psychotherapist responsible for the treatment of individuals, families, and groups. Additionally, he or she will provide social work services to enact community resources for the child and family. The primary focus of this role is to ensure excellent clinical care and manage a caseload that includes interfacing with other community agencies, particularly schools. Requires IL state license and a master's degree in social work from an accredited university. (*NASW News*, March 2002, p. 21)

Senior Clinical Social Worker

Children's Hospital and Regional Medical Center, Pulmonary Division. Our team of talented health professionals find a daily dose of fulfillment as they meet the needs of children and their families. Recently ranked one of the best children's hospitals in the nation, Children's Hospital and Regional Medical Center in Seattle, WA, knows that supporting its staff translates into good patient care. You will be part of an environment where miracles are made each and every day. We are currently seeking a full-time senior social worker for the pulmonary division. This position will provide clinical social work services to inpatients and outpatients with acute and chronic pulmonary conditions, including psychosocial assessment, counseling, bereavement, and risk assessment for possible child maltreatment. This also includes being the social work faculty member to the Pediatric Pulmonary Leadership Training Center Grant, clinical faculty appointment with the Washington School of Social Work, and supervising a graduate student in social work each year. Must have experience in and a commitment to working with children with chronic health care needs and experience in diverse communities. Experience working as part of a multidisciplinary team and working with graduate students is essential. Requires an MSW from a Council on Social Work Education approved program (a joint MSW–MPH is preferred), four to five years experience, leadership experience, and Washington state licensure or be license eligible. Prior experience working with maternal child health programs is preferred. (*NASW News*, March 2002, p. 25)

Social Worker

The Children's Hospital of New Jersey at Newark Beth Israel Medical Center, Pediatric Cardiology department, has an excellent part-time opening for an experienced social worker (LCSW). As a member of the pediatric team, you will work with a diverse group of children and young adults with cardiac disease. In this challenging position, you will provide psychosocial assessment, individual and family counseling, advocacy, and follow-up review to ensure patient compliance. Candidates must possess strong knowledge of community resources and entitlements. Exceptional problem solving, leadership, and communication skills are required. LCSW supervision provided. Experience within a hospital setting is preferred. (*NASW News*, April 2000, p. 17)

Social Worker

Mayo Clinic, Department of Medical Social Services has an exciting opportunity available for a social worker. The successful candidate will provide social work services for facilitating solutions to the medically related psychosocial–environmental problems of patients and families. Provides assessment of the patient's and family's psychosocial functioning. Social worker must have current Minnesota license. Prefer master's degree in social work from an accredited school of social work with at least one year of supervised practice in a medical setting or a BSW or BA with a major in social work and four or more years of related experience. (*NASW News*, November 2001, p. 19)

Medical Social Worker

San Leandro Hospital proudly celebrates its anniversary—40 years of improving the quality of life in our community. Come join our team! We have an immediate opportunity for a full-time MSW to provide discharge planning and psychosocial assessment–intervention for a primarily geriatric acute care population. Requires medical social work and discharge planning experience; LCSW preferred. We offer a professional work environment, excellent compensation and benefits, free parking, and a $2,000 sign-on bonus. (*NASW News*, January 2002, p. 16)

Management, AIDS Project, Los Angeles

An exciting management opportunity in the mental health program. The program includes individual, couple, and family counseling in English and Spanish, addictive behavior services, support group program, psychotherapy provided by volunteer licensed mental health professionals, and a graduate intern clinical training program. Share grant writing and grant monitoring responsibilities with other AIDS project staff, develop and update mental health policies and procedures, and develop and maintain a quality assurance program as required by regulatory bodies. Requires a doctoral degree in psychology or a master's degree in social work, psychology, or counseling; four years clinical practice beyond receipt of licensure; four years supervisory experience. Experience in a group or agency practice preferred. Experience with gay and ethnic minority clients, substance abuse (alcohol and drug) issues, clinical skills in diagnosis and treatment of mental illness and multiple diagnosed clients; and experience with group, conjoint, marital, and family therapy preferred. Knowledge of current psychosocial diagnostic and treatment procedures; use of the DSM-IV; project and program management; quality assurance techniques; standard clinical record-keeping methods; basic medical and psychosocial aspects of HIV/AIDS; behavioral theories; basic mental health needs of people experiencing a chronic or life-threatening illness or bereavement; and program planning and evaluation. (*NASW News*, May 2002, p. 14)

Rehabilitation Social Worker

Frye Regional Rehabilitation Center, Hickory, NC, accredited by the Commission on Accreditation of Rehabilitation Facilities, is a unique 29-bed inpatient facility within Frye Regional Medical Center. We provide interdisciplinary, comprehensive inpatient services for individuals with traumatic brain injuries, spinal cord injuries, amputations, strokes, arthritis, and other neurological and orthopedically related disorders. This position provides primarily discharge planning with a small counseling component included. Master's degree in social work required. (*NASW News*, January 1997, p. 30)

Medical Clinical Social Worker

Sutter Merced Medical Center, a nonprofit, 174-bed facility located in California's thriving Central Valley, has been providing comprehensive health care to our patients for 120 years. And in our ideal location—only a short drive from the wonders of Yosemite, Monterey, and San Francisco—you'll experience the perfect setting in which to grow your career. We currently have

an opportunity for an experienced professional to plan, organize, and implement social work services to patients of all ages and their families. You will also plan for discharge and aftercare, as well as maintain contact with referring agencies and with community resources used for referral. Requires a master's degree, CA LCSW license, and three years full-time social work casework experience in a public or private institution or private services agency, with one plus years in an acute care hospital. We keep up with the market, offering a competitive salary and benefits package. (*NASW News*, March 2001, p. 16)

Hospice Care Services

Vitas HealthCare Corporation, the nation's leading provider of hospice care services experiencing rapid growth and expansion, has exciting career opportunities for LCSWs to work out of our Miami, FL, location. Please consider joining our health care team where your input will be valued, appreciated, and where your work enhances the quality of life for our patients and families. Candidates should possess two or more years of social services experience in a health care setting and currently licensed in the State of Florida. Hospice or oncology experience would be a plus, as well as experience with the geriatric population. We offer a competitive salary, excellent benefits, and a wonderful work environment. (*NASW News*, January 2002, p. 19)

Eating Disorders, Psychiatric Social Worker

Part-time. Eating disorders and hospital experience preferred. Master's degree in social work and current New York license required. We offer excellent salaries and comprehensive benefits, tuition reimbursement, a scenic environment, and free parking. (*NASW News*, May 2002, p. 16)

Psychotherapists

Harlem United Community AIDS Center, Inc., the largest provider of comprehensive AIDS services in Central Harlem, has the following positions available in its continuum of care: The Adult Day Healthcare Center has an excellent opportunity for two psychotherapists interested in becoming part of our growing dynamic interdisciplinary care team. Responsibilities include completing assessments and providing group and individual supportive psychotherapy. The primary focus of one clinician will be working with mothers in our women and children's program. Requirements are an MSW or CSW or licensed clinical psychologist with minimum three years experience in mental health, substance abuse (harm reduction), or AIDS; bilingual a plus. The above positions offer excellent salary and benefits in a supportive environment of experienced professionals. (*NASW News*, October 2000, p. 21).

Social Worker, Care Manager

Dana Farber Cancer Institute needs a social worker to provide psychosocial assessment, psychoeducation, clinical intervention, and care coordination services to patients and families throughout all phases of inpatient and outpatient treatment and follow up. Other responsibilities include identifying high-risk psychosocial factors of patients that may have an impact on bone marrow transplant course and discharge planning; helping staff understand the influence of psychosocial factors upon patient's care; assessing adaptation of patients and families to treatment, prognosis, and future care; providing individual, couples, or family intervention and crisis intervention as needed; supporting group facilitation within the bone marrow transplant program. Must have MSW, LICSW. Hematology or oncology experience preferred. (*NASW News*, May 2001, p. 16)

Medical Social Worker

St. John Medical Center is seeking a medical social worker for a full-time position in our care management department. Candidate must have MSW from an accredited school of social work. Prefer CSW with hospital experience. Person will contribute to the development and imple-

mentation of cost-effective, appropriate health care plans by assisting members with locating alternate living arrangements or home care assistance, assessing community resources, preadmission and postdischarge planning. Also will contribute to optimal health outcomes of health plan members by assessing and intervening in psychosocial–economic problems. Interventions may include medically oriented individual, family, or group counseling, case management, system coordination, and so forth. (*NASW News*, July 2001, p. 18)

REFERENCES

Abramson, J. S. (2002). Interdisciplinary team practice. In A. R. Roberts & G. J. Greene (Eds.), *Social workers' desk reference* (pp. 44–50). New York: Oxford University Press.

Alan Guttmacher Institute. (1998). *Facts in brief: Teen sex and pregnancy*. Retrieved November 7, 2003, from http://www.agi–usa.org/pubs/fb_teen_sex.html.

American Medical Association, HIV/AIDS Resource Center. (2002). *HIV/AIDS statistics*. Retrieved March 2, 2003, from http://www.ama–assn.org/special/hiv/support/aidstat.htm

Americans with Disabilities Act of 1990, P.L. 101-336, 104 Stat. 327.

Annie E. Casey Foundation. (1998). *Kids count special report: When teens have sex: Issues and trends*. Baltimore, MD: Author.

Anorexia Nervosa and Related Eating Disorders, Inc. (2002a). *The better known eating disorders*. Retrieved November 10, 2003, from http://www.anred.com/defswk.html

Anorexia Nervosa and Related Eating Disorders, Inc. (2002b). *Statistics: How many people have eating disorders?* Retrieved November 10, 2003, from http://www.anred.com/stats.html

Anorexia Nervosa and Relating Eating Disorders, Inc. (2002c). *Who we are*. Retrieved November 10, 2003, from http://www.nationaleatingdisorders.org

Anorexia Nervosa and Relating Eating Disorders, Inc. (2003). *Treatment and recovery.* Retrieved November 10, 2003, from http://www.anred.com/tx.html

Balanced Budget Act of 1997, P.L. 105-33, 111 Stat. 251. Barker, R. L. (1999). *Social work dictionary* (4th ed.). Washington, DC: NASW Press.

Berne, L., & Huberman, B. (1999). *European approaches to adolescent sexual behavior and responsibility.* Washington, DC: Advocates for Youth.

Cates, W. (1999). Estimates of the incidence and prevalence of sexually transmitted diseases in the United States. *Sexually Transmitted Diseases, 26,* S2–S7.

Centers for Disease Control and Prevention. (2000a). *Tracking the hidden epidemic: Trends in STDs in the United States 2000.* Retrieved August 8, 2003, from http:www.cdc.gov/nchstp/dstd/Stats_Trends/Trends2000.pdf

Centers for Disease Control and Prevention. (2000b). *HIV prevention strategic plan through 2005.* Retrieved August 8, 2003, from http://www.cdc.gov/hiv/partners/PSP/How_to_use.htm

Centers for Disease Control and Prevention. (2002). *HIV/AIDS: Basic statistics.* Retrieved February 12, 2003, from http://www.ced.gov/hiv/stats.htm

Clark, E. (2001, October). From the director: Unequal burden: Care disparities. *NASW News,* p. 2.

Clark, E. J. (2002, May). From the director: We share in the genetics world. *NASW News,* p. 2.

Connolly, C. (2002, May 22). Study: Uninsured don't get needed health care. *Washington Post,* p. A3.

Deficit Reduction Act of 19834, P.L. 98-369, 98 Stat. 494.

Developmental Disabilities Assistance and Bill of Rights Act of 1990, P.L. 101-496, 104 Stat. 1191.

DeWeaver, K. L. (1995). Developmental disabilities: Definitions and policies. In R. L. Edwards (Ed.-in-Chief), *Encyclopedia of social work* (19th ed., Vol. 1, pp. 712–720). Washington, DC: NASW Press.

Edinburg, G. M., & Cottler, J. M. (1995). Managed care. In R. L. Edwards (Ed.-in-Chief), *Encyclopedia of social work* (19th ed., Vol. 2, pp. 1635–1642). Washington, DC: NASW Press.

Eng, T., & Butler, W. (Eds.). (1997). *The hidden epidemic: Confronting sexually transmitted diseases.* Washington, DC: National Academy Press.

Fair Housing Amendments Act of 1988, P.L. 100-430, 102 Stat. 1619.

Faulkner Schofield, R., & Amodeo, M. (1999). Interdisciplinary teams in health care and human services settings: Are they effective? *Health & Social Work, 24,* 210–219.

Genetic Alliance. (2003). *About the Genetic Alliance.* Retrieved October 22, 2003, from http://www.geneticalliance.org/members/aboutus.html

Getzel, G. S. (1989). Responding effectively to the crisis of a gay man with AIDS. In T. S. Kerson (Ed.), *Social work in health settings: Practice in context* (pp. 247–266). New York: Haworth Press.

Gibelman, M. (1990). National voluntary health agencies in an era of change: Experiences and adaptations. *Administration in Social Work, 14,* 17–32.

Globerman, J., & Bogo, M. (2002). The impact of hospital restructuring on social work field education. *Health & Social Work, 27,* 7–17.

Heart transplants: Waiting for new life. (1987, March). *NASW News,* p. 3.

HIV is a disability, high court rules. (1998, September). *NASW News,* p. 6.

Hoffman, S. D. (1998). Teenage childbearing is not so bad afterall . . . or is it? A review of the new literature. *Family Planning Perspectives, 30,* 236–239, 243.

In the E.R., prevention is vital key. (1998, November). *NASW News,* p. 10.

Kaiser Family Foundation. (2001). *Sexually transmitted diseases.* Retrieved October 22, 2003 from http://www.kff.org/content/2001/20010801a/summaryoffundings.pdf

Letteney, S. (1995, January 14). *Policies affecting women and children in a time of AIDS: New York State's standby guardian law.* Unpublished manuscript, Yeshiva University, Wurzweiler School of Social Work, New York.

Levenson, D. (1998, November). Primary care: Social work is moving in. *NASW News,* p. 3.

Lloyd, G. A. (1990). AIDS and HIV: The syndrome and the virus. In L. Ginsberg et al. (Eds.), *Encyclopedia of social work* (18th ed., 1990 Suppl., pp. 12–50). Silver Spring, MD: NASW Press.

Lloyd, G. A. (1995). HIV/AIDS: Overview. In R. L. Edwards (Ed.-in-Chief), *Encyclopedia of social work* (19th ed., Vol. 2, pp. 1257–1290). Washington, DC: NASW Press.

Logan, S. L. (1995). *Eating disorders and other compulsive behaviors.* In R. L. Edwards (Ed.-in-Chief), *Encyclopedia of social work* (19th ed., Vol. 2, pp. 805–815). Washington, DC: NASW Press.

Minority health bill enacted. (2001, February). *NASW News,* p. 1.

Minority Health and Health Disparities Research and Education Act of 2000, P.L. 106-525, 114 Stat. 2512.

National Association of Social Workers. (2000a, April 10). *NASW develops bereavement guidelines for emergency rooms* (Press release). Retrieved September 6, 2001, from http://www.socialworkers.org/pressroom/2000/041000.htm

National Association of Social Workers. (2000b, August 30). *Social workers and genetics education important for the future* (Press release). Washington, DC: Author.

National Association of Social Workers. (2002). *Discrimination and HIV/AIDS: A fact sheet for practitioners.* Retrieved January 3, 2003, from http://www.socialworkers.org/practice/hiv_discrimination.htm

National Association of Social Workers. (2003). *Standards for integrating genetics into social work practice.* Washington, DC: Author.

National Campaign to Prevent Teen Pregnancy. (2002). *General facts and stats.* Retrieved November 2, 2002, from http://teeenpregnancy.org/resources/ data/genlfact.asp

National Center for HIV, STD, & TB Prevention. (1998a). *Critical need to pay attention to HIV prevention for women: Minority and young women bear greatest burden.* Retrieved March 21, 2001, from http://www.cdc.gov/nchstp/hiv_aids/pubs/facts/hivrepfs.htm

National Center for HIV, STD, & TB Prevention. (1998b). *Trends in the HIV/AIDS epidemic.* Retrieved March 21, 2001, from http://www.cdc.gov/nchstp/hiv_aids/stats/trends 98.pdf

National Commission on AIDS. (1993). *AIDS: An expanding tragedy: The final report of the National Commission on AIDS.* Washington, DC: Author.

Nicholson, T. (2002, February). *Life on the edge— Without insurance. AARP Bulletin,* pp. 3, 10–11.

Oktay, J. S. (1995). Primary health care. In R. L. Edwards (Ed.-in-Chief), *Encyclopedia of social work* (19th ed., Vol. 2, pp. 1887–1894). Washington, DC: NASW Press.

O'Neill, J. V. (2001, March). Social work aids in medical adherence. *NASW News,* p. 3.

Planned Parenthood Federation of America. (2002a). *Adolescent sexuality* (Fact sheet). Retrieved March 14, 2002, from http://www.plannedparenthood.org/library/factsheets.htm

Planned Parenthood Federation of America. (2002b). *America's family planning program: Title X* (Fact sheet). Retrieved March 14, 2002, from http://www.plannedparenthood.org/library/FAMILY– PLANNINGISSUES/TitleX_fact.html

Planned Parenthood Federation of America. (2002c). *Pregnancy and childbearing among U.S. teens* (Fact sheet). Retrieved March 14, 2002, from http://www.plannedparenthood.org/library/TEEN–PREGNANCY/teenpreg_fact.html

Planned Parenthood Federation of America. (2002d). *Sexually transmitted infections* (Fact sheet). Retrieved March 14, 2002, from http://www.plannedparenthood.org/library/STI/STI_fact.html

Poindexter, C. C. (1999). Promises in the plague: Passage of the Ryan White Comprehensive AIDS Resources Emergency Act as a case study for legislative action. *Health & Social Work, 24,* 35–41.

Poole, D. L. (1995). Health care: Direct practice. In R. L. Edwards (Ed.-in-Chief), *Encyclopedia of social work* (19th ed., Vol. 2, pp. 1156–1167). Washington, DC: NASW Press.

Public Health Service Act of 1970, P.L. 91-572, 84 Stat. 1504.

Rauch, J. B. (1988). Social work and the genetics revolution: Genetic services. *Social Work, 33,* 389–395.

Rauch, J. B., & Black, R. B. (1995). Genetics. In R. L. Edwards (Ed.-in-Chief), *Encyclopedia of social work* (19th ed., Vol. 2, pp. 1108–1117). Washington, DC: NASW Press.

Reports: Uninsured rate steady. (2001, March). *NASW News*, p. 7.

Ross, J. W. (1995). Hosptial social work. In R. L. Edwards (Ed.-in-Chief), *Encyclopedia of social work* (19th ed., Vol. 2, pp. 1365–1377). Washington, DC: NASW Press.

Rossen, S. (1987). Hospital social work. In A. Minahan (Ed.-in-Chief), *Encyclopedia of social work* (18th ed., Vol. 1, pp. 816–821). Silver Spring, MD: NASW Press.

Ryan White Comprehensive AIDS Resources Emergency Act of 1990, P.L. 101-381, 104 Stat, 577.

Simon, E. P., Showers, N., Blumenfield, S., Holden, G., & Wu, X. (1995). Delivery of home care services after discharge: What really happens. *Health & Social Work, 20,* 5–14.

Stoesen, L. (2002, May). Genetics: Science takes on a human face. *NASW News*, p. 3.

Stolberg, S. G. (2002a, March 21). Minorities get inferior care, even if insured, study finds. *New York Times*. Retrieved April 4, 2002, from http://nytimes. com/2002/03/21/health/21RACE. html

Stolberg, S. G. (2002b, May 12). With convert's zeal, Congress awakens to AIDS. *New York Times*. Retrieved May 15, 2002, from http://www. nytimes.com/2002/05/12/politics/12IMMU. html

Taylor-Brown, S. (1995). HIV/AIDS: Direct practice. In R. L. Edwards (Ed.-in-Chief), *Encyclopedia of social work* (19th ed., Vol. 2, pp. 1291–1305). Washington, DC: NASW Press.

U.S. Department of Health and Human Services, Health Resources and Services Administration, HIV/AIDS Bureau. (2002a). *Ryan White Care Act*. Retrieved November 12, 2002, from http://www.hab.hrsa.gov

U.S. Department of Health and Human Services, National Institutes of Health, Office of AIDS Research. (2002b). *HIV/AIDS statistics* (Fact sheet). Retrieved November 12, 2002, from http://www.niaid.nih.gov/factsheets/aidsstat.htm

Vallianatos, C. (2000, October). Social workers prepare for the genetics era. *NASW News*, p. 10.

Wiener, L., Fair, C. D., & Garcia, A. (1995). HIV/AIDS: Pediatric. In R. L. Edwards (Ed.-in-Chief), *Encyclopedia of social work* (19th ed., Vol. 2, pp. 1314–1324). Washington, DC: NASW Press.

Williams, E., & Donnelly, J. (2002). Older Americans and AIDS: Some guidelines for prevention. *Social Work, 47,* 105–111.

Chapter Seven SOCIAL WORK PRACTICE IN THE SCHOOLS

School social work is that social work specialty "oriented toward helping students make satisfactory school adjustments and coordinating and influencing the efforts of the school, the family, and the community to help achieve this goal" (Barker, 1999, p. 426). It involves the provision of social work services in the setting of an educational agency by credentialed or licensed school social workers (NASW, 2002).

Social workers serve as a link between the home, school, and community, linkages that educational reformers believe are vital to improving educational outcomes (Gibelman & Lens, 2002). School social workers typically are called upon to help students, families, teachers, and even educational administrators deal with a range of problems that affect students. These include truancy, depression, withdrawal, aggressive or violent behavior, rebelliousness, and the effects of physical or emotional problems. Students with disabilities, who comprise about 11 percent of the public school population, also require special services. The largest group within this category of children with disabilities has some form of emotional disturbance (Landers, 1995).

Social workers represent a growing force within the field of education (NASW, 2000). The *24th Annual Report to Congress on the Implementation of the Individuals with Disabilities Education Act* (U.S. Department of Education, 2002) lists 14,988 school social workers involved in providing special education and related services for children and youths ages three to 21 years for the 1999–2000 academic year. The School Social Work Association of America estimates that school social workers now number over 17,000 throughout the 50 states (Randy A. Fisher, personal communication, October 30, 2003).

CREDENTIALING AND STANDARD SETTING

To address the special nature of social work practice within the schools, NASW first developed *Standards for School Social Work Services* in 1978. The standards were revised first in 1992 and again in 2002 to reflect changing policies and practices. Because of the importance of these standards in guiding social work practice in the schools, they are summarized here.

Standard 1. A school social worker shall demonstrate commitment to the values and ethics of the social work profession and shall use NASW's *Code of Ethics* as a guide to ethical decision making.

Standard 2. School social workers shall organize their time, energies, and workloads to fulfill their responsibilities and complete assignments of their position with due consideration of the priorities among their various responsibilities.

Standard 3. School social workers shall provide consultation to local education agency personnel, school board members, and community representatives to promote understanding and effective utilization of school social work services.

Standard 4. School social workers shall ensure that students and their families are provided services within the context of multicultural understanding and competence that enhance families' support of students' learning experiences.

Standard 5. School social work services shall be extended to students in ways that build students' individual strengths and offer students maximum opportunity to participate in the planning and direction of their own learning experience.

Standard 6. School social workers shall help empower students and their families to gain access to and effectively use formal and informal community resources.

Standard 7. School social workers shall maintain adequate safeguards for the privacy and confidentiality of information.

Standard 8. School social workers shall advocate for students and their families in a variety of situations.

Standard 9. As leaders and members of interdisciplinary teams and coalitions, school social workers shall work collaboratively to mobilize the resources of local education agencies and communities to meet the needs of students and families.

Standard 10. School social workers shall develop and provide training and educational programs that address the goals and mission of the educational institution.

Standard 11. School social workers shall maintain accurate data that are relevant to planning, management, and evaluation of school social work services.

Standard 12. School social workers shall conduct assessments of student needs that are individualized and provide information that is directly useful for designing interventions that address behaviors.

Standard 13. School social workers shall incorporate assessments in developing and implementing intervention and evaluation plans that enhance students' abilities to benefit from educational experiences.

Standard 14. School social workers, as systems change agents, shall identify areas of need that are not being addressed by the local education agency and community and shall work to create services that address these needs.

Standard 15. School social workers shall be trained in and use mediation and conflict resolution strategies to promote students' resolution of their nonproductive encounters in the school and community and to promote productive relationships.

Standard 16. School social workers shall meet the standards for practice set by NASW.

Standard 17. School social workers shall possess knowledge and understanding basic to the social work profession.

Standard 18. School social workers shall understand the backgrounds and broad range of experiences that shape students' approach to learning.

Standard 19. School social workers shall possess knowledge and understanding of the organization and structure of the local education agency.

Standard 20. School social workers shall possess knowledge and understanding of the reciprocal influences of home, school, and community.

Standard 21. School social workers shall possess skills in systematic assessment and investigation.

Standard 22. School social workers shall understand the relationship between practice and policies affecting students.

Standard 23. School social workers shall be able to select and apply empirically validated or promising prevention and intervention methods to enhance students' educational experiences.

Standard 24. School social workers shall be able to evaluate their practice and disseminate the findings to consumers, the local education agency, the community, and the profession.

Standard 25. School social workers shall possess skills in developing coalitions at the local, state, and national levels that promote student success.

Standard 26. School social workers shall be able to promote collaboration among community health and mental health services providers and facilitate student access to these services.

Standard 27. School social workers shall assume responsibility for their own continued professional development in accordance with the NASW Standards for Continuing Professional Education and state requirements.

Standard 28. School social workers shall contribute to the development of the profession by educating and supervising school social work interns.

Standard 29. State departments of education or other state entities that license or certify educational personnel shall regulate school social work practice.

Standard 30. State departments of education or other state entities that license or certify educational personnel shall employ a state school social work consultant who is a credentialed and experienced school social worker.

Standard 31. School social work services shall be provided by credentialed school social workers employed by the local education agency.

Standard 32. Local education agencies shall employ school social workers with the highest level of qualifications for entry-level practitioners.

Standard 33. Social workers in schools shall be designated "school social workers."

Standard 34. Salaries and job classifications of school social workers shall be commensurate with their education, experience, and responsibilities and be comparable to qualified professionals employed by the local education agency.

Standard 35. The administrative structure established by the local education agency shall provide for school social work supervision.

Standard 36. The administrative structure of the local education agency shall delineate clear lines of support and accountability for the school social work program.

Standard 37. The local education agency shall provide a professional work setting that allows school social workers to practice effectively.

Standard 38. The local education agency shall provide opportunities for school social workers to engage in professional development activities that support school social work practice.

Standard 39. The goals, objectives, and tasks of a school social work program shall be clearly and directly related to the mission of the local education agency and the educational process.

Standard 40. The local education agency shall involve school social workers in developing and coordinating partnerships with community health, mental health, and social services providers linked with or based at school sites to ensure that these services promote student educational success.

Standard 41. All programs incorporating school social work services shall require ongoing evaluation to determine their contribution to the educational success of all students.

Standard 42. The local education agency shall establish and implement a school social worker to student population ratio to ensure reasonable workload expectations.

For many school systems, these standards reinforce current practices. For others, they provide a challenge and a goal to be achieved. For school social workers, they both validate the uniqueness and diversity of school social work as a specialty practice area and affirm the value of school social work in enabling children to achieve maximum benefits from their educational experiences.

In 1994 NASW initiated the School Social Work Section, the organization's first specialty practice section to serve the diverse interests of the members. The section decides the program directions under its own steering committee. The formation of this section is seen as a way to achieve a stronger national voice for school social workers, including greater opportunity to network, share practice innovations, and promote the use of school social workers (Hiratsuka, 1994).

In October 1999, the School Social Work Specialist Certificate was inaugurated by NASW based on education, experience, and references.

Evaluation of the individual applicant by a supervisor and a social work colleague along the newly established criteria replaces the earlier written examination that had been required (O'Neill, 2000a). The school social work specialist credential identifies social workers who have met rigorous national standards for education and experience in school social work practice.

Eligibility criteria for the specialist credential include an MSW from an accredited school of social work; at least two years or 3,000 hours of supervised school social work experience (one year of which may come from graduate practicum experience in a school setting); supervisory evaluations and professional references; and successful passage of the school social work section of the National Teachers Exam.

In recent years, recognition of the rights of persons with disabilities; changes in the family unit; and the effects of increasing social, economic, and academic pressures on children are some of the forces that have significantly shaped social work services in schools. The value of school social work intervention has increasingly been recognized through legislative initiatives.

ENABLING LEGISLATION

Since passage of the Education for All Handicapped Children Act of 1975 (P.L. 94-142), social workers have played an important role in the schools. This legislation, later codified as the Individuals with Disabilities Education Act of 1990 (IDEA) (P.L. 101-476), and its successive amendments mandate the provision of appropriate free educational resources for handicapped children (Dane, 1985); the educational system is required to provide services in the "least restrictive environment." These resources address issues of equal access, supportive services, and procedural protections for children with disabilities. Services include special testing, remedial lessons, counseling, and tutoring (Barker, 1999).

The handicapped children's act has been the primary law to address early intervention and special education for infants, toddlers, children, and youths with disabilities (Stoesen, 2002). The Education for All Handicapped Children Act of 1986 (P.L. 99-457) established a foundation for an early intervention system for infants and toddlers with special needs (DiMichele, 1993). Services may include psychological assessment, parent and family training, counseling, and transition services to preschool programs. The Hawkins-Stafford Elementary and Secondary School Improvement Amendments Act of 1988 (P.L. 100-297) also expanded the role of school social workers in its provisions for preventive interventions to high-risk children and youths (Freeman, 1995).

Passage of the IDEA in 1990 and its subsequent amendments further improved the original 1975 legislation to ensure the best education for students with special needs. Improvements were aimed at increasing access for students and their families to needed services. Social work services were explicitly added to the definition of early intervention services. The last update of IDEA occurred in 1997 (Stoesen, 2002).

The IDEA was again up for reauthorization in 2003. Social workers are working collaboratively to ensure that the range of services they can provide under IDEA are clearly spelled out in the law (Stoesen, 2002). NASW, working in concert with the School Social Work Association of America, has presented proposed changes to the law to the U.S. Department of Education. Key among these proposed changes is new language "to ensure school personnel consult with and are trained by experts, such as school social workers, to ensure that strategies and supports are effectively implemented" (Stoesen, 2002, p. 5). Other recommendations include the addition of a case manager to the individualized education program teams, hiring additional trained personnel, and funding new research to address emotional and behavioral disorders.

When President William "Bill" Clinton signed the Improving America's Schools Act of 1994 (P.L. 103-382), reauthorizing the Elementary and Secondary Education Act, the role of school social workers, among other pupil-services personnel, in helping children succeed in school was further expanded. For example, under Title I of the act, Compensatory Education, social workers must be consulted in the development of state plans to help disadvantaged children. Pupil-services personnel are also to be part of state school-support teams that assist schools to develop and evaluate programs and identify problems. In addition, social workers are part of state school-support teams, the role of which is to assist schools in developing and evaluating programs and identifying problems ("School Act Boosts,"1995).

Another feature of this legislation, the Elementary School Counseling Demonstration Act of 1994 (ESCDA; P.L. 103-382), provides grants for schools to initiate or expand comprehensive elementary school counseling programs. Programs are required to use school social workers, school counselors, and school psychologists. Under the demonstration act, a *school social worker* is defined as "an individual who holds a master's degree in social work and is licensed or certified by the state in which services are provided or holds a school social work specialist credential" ("School Act Boosts," 1995, p. 14).

Although the act was passed in 1994, funds were first appropriated in fiscal year 2000. The expansion of social work services was immediately apparent. The DeKalb County Schools in Georgia were awarded funds to hire five new school social workers; Allendale County School District in Allendale, SC, received funds to provide intensive in-home and community-based counseling services utilizing the expertise of a guidance counselor and school social worker; and the Milwaukee Public Schools received a grant to hire a school social worker, guidance counselor, and school psychologist (Vallianatos, 2000). At the close of the 106th Congress in 2000, a consolidated appropriations bill was passed that included a $10 million increase in the ESCDA, up to $30 million ("Funds Hiked," 2001).

Under the No Child Left Behind Act of 2001 (P.L. 107-110), the ESCDA was reauthorized as Title V, Part D, Subpart 2, the Elementary and Secondary School Counseling Program. The school counseling component was expanded to include secondary schools. Further, the law authorized the use of school social workers and other providers to provide in-service training for teachers and other school personnel to assist in early identification and intervention for students who needed services ("School Counseling, Stable Families," 2002). The reauthorization also provided that recipients of these funds must show progress toward meeting ratios of professionals to students recommended by the American School Health Association—1:800 for school social workers, 1:250 for school counselors, and 1:1,000 for school psychologists. These ratios are less rigorous than those proposed by NASW. Also reauthorized is the Safe and Drug-Free Schools Program in which mental health services are an allowable use of program funds.

Between 1986 and 1996, the total number of students served under IDEA rose 29 percent. The number of children with disabilities between the ages of six and 21 years who spent at least 80 percent of their day in regular classrooms has, in this same time period, more than doubled—from 1.1 million to 2.3 million. Of these children who met the IDEA requirements, 51 percent had learning disabilities, 20 percent had speech or language impediments, 1 percent were children with mental retardation, and 9 percent were children with emotional disorders (Beaucar, 1999).

As with most of social work practice, social policy is the driving force in what services are provided in the schools, to whom, and how often or intensive such services can be. A consistent theme is that each time a law that affects school social work practice is up for reauthorization, there is a certain level of precariousness. Will the law survive? What changes will be made?

Legislation defines some of the boundaries of professional practice, often extending these borders. In implementation of laws, however, restrictive boundaries may become manifest, particularly pertaining to the delegation of roles. Interpreting and negotiating one's role within the school setting may be hampered when there is little collegial support, as the following vignette illustrates.

No One To Talk To

Jacqui is a school social worker. She is lonely in her work setting. She is one of five social workers in the school district; her colleagues, however, are assigned to different schools, and their offices are in other locations.

One of the hardest aspects of the job for Jacqui is that the supervisor to whom she reports is not a social worker. Jacqui has not yet received her advanced clinical license and needs 3,000 hours of supervised practice by an MSW in order to qualify. Thus, she has had to pay out of pocket to receive social work supervision. Her supervisor at work construes the supervisory role as administrative only. She spends time with Jacqui going over the details of work assignments, but there is no discussion about the qualitative aspects of her work—how well she is doing and what she might do differently to improve her performance. Jacqui knows that this lack of supervision violates established standards for social work practice in the schools, but there seems to be no way around this reality.

The isolation sometimes gets to Jacqui. To make matters worse, there have been rumors that the school district is looking carefully at how the budget might be cut, and support services seem to be particularly vulnerable. There is a chance Jacqui's job will be eliminated. There are three school psychologists and two counselors also on staff, and tensions have risen as the various helping professionals see themselves in competition for jobs and job security. Because administrators have written job descriptions, they do not reflect the special knowledge and skills of each professional and the unique contributions of each. Rather than working together to secure all of their jobs, the professionals see themselves in competition. Each seems to be claiming that they can handle the job responsibilities of the other. Morale is terrible.

Jacqui has begun to question how long she can last on this job. The private supervision is costing her a lot of money. She could get the needed supervision in a social services agency setting. In such an environment, she thinks, perhaps she could grow as a professional and be better able to assist her clients.

Jacqui's situation is not uncommon in host settings. Administrators and supervisors who are unfamiliar with the professional training and expertise of social workers may have preconceptions about their role and function within the school setting. In Jacqui's case, the supervisor had a very narrow view of the social work role. Role assignments, as well as the value placed on the professional role, are influenced by the degree to which educational administrators understand what social workers do (Tower, 2000).

In a work environment that contrasts sharply with professional expectations, it is not surprising that Jacqui would experience disillusionment. For a new social worker, working alone and with no professional direction can quickly lead to burnout. Potential allies, such as the school psychologists and counselors, were concerned about protecting their own jobs and had little time or energy to help Jacqui.

This negative experience need not be normative. Social workers may be the head of pupil-services personnel, in which case there is greater understanding of the social work role and supervision is expected and provided. Even when non–social workers are in charge, collaboration among the professionals of various disciplines comprising the pupil-services team can provide professional stimulation.

INTERDISCIPLINARY PRACTICE

School-based social work practice involves interdisciplinary coordination. The need for and commitment to teamwork and cooperation among the pupil-services disciplines was codified in 1990 with the issuance of a joint statement: "Pupil Services Essential to Education," which stands today. The statement is a product of the work of a task force composed of representatives of the National Association of Social Workers, the American Association for Counseling and Development, the American School Counselors Association, and the National Association of School Psychologists. The need to have all of these mental health disciplines in the schools is recognized, as each offers a unique perspective and service required to meet the needs of children in a comprehensive way. The team concept is emphasized in the statement, which reads, in part:

Our purpose is to support the efforts of counselors, psychologists, social workers and other pupil service professionals in providing a coordinated delivery system designed to serve this country's school-aged youth. . . . The complex needs of students demand the comprehensiveness implied by uniting the skills of trained professionals. Through teamwork, school psychologists, school social workers, school counselors and other pupil services providers work together to provide coordinated services for students and their families. ("Groups Support Team Approach," 1990, p. 12)

Despite agreement among the helping professionals working within the schools about the essential need for teamwork, the organizational setting may create conditions in which collaboration gives way to competition. Obstacles to effective interdisciplinary work include unequal status of participants, role blurring or lack of role clarity, differential professional socialization processes, unclear responsibility for team leadership, lack of shared professional language and technologies, and role competition or "turf" issues (Abramson, 2002).

As our school social worker Jacqui discovered, pupil-services personnel may sometimes be in competition with each other when school districts, strapped for funds, consider or make personnel cuts. As the guest in the school, the social worker, along with other helping professionals, may have less job security than teachers. School boards and school administrators are primarily concerned with ensuring the fiscal integrity of the core school function—education. Selective states have sought to cut social work positions in budget-cutting moves, sometimes retaining school psychologists and making a choice between the helping professions. For example, with many states strapped for funds, social work jobs in public settings are now vulnerable. The Detroit school board, in February 2002, announced that 49 school social workers would be laid off as of March 5. The social work community organized and lobbied, and the day before the cuts were to take effect, 30 of the layoffs were rescinded and five more social workers were later reinstated ("Detroit, Mississippi Layoffs Spotlighted," 2002).

Competition between professionals is largely the result of financial issues (Canter, 1998; Gibelman, 1993). In some cases, schools are replacing pupil-services personnel entirely and instead are contracting out with mental health care providers on a case-by-case basis (Beaucar, 1999). This precarious situation suggests that social workers in the school setting have an ongoing responsibility to interpret and promote their roles and to define themselves within the system (Goren, 1981). It cannot be assumed that the contributions of the social worker in the school setting are widely known or understood.

Collaboration among pupil-services personnel is more the rule than the exception. School social workers possess a unique set of skills and a systems perspective that they bring to the assessment and diagnosis of children's needs. As team leaders or members, school social workers plan, develop, and implement activities to overcome institutional barriers and gaps in services, and they do so in conjunction with their colleagues of other disciplines (NASW, 2002).

RANGE OF PRACTICE ROLES IN SCHOOLS

In some communities, schools have been identified as the logical location for one-stop services," including those oriented to health and mental health. School-based clinics, many of which are located in low-income urban areas, have expanded rapidly in recent years. They provide comprehensive services ranging from mental health counseling, to sports physical examinations, to alcohol and drug abuse counseling, to nutrition and weight reduction information. These clinics are generally located in junior or senior high schools and are operated and funded by government or private agencies rather than by the schools.

School-linked services gained popularity with the rise in child poverty and other social problems such as drug addiction and HIV/AIDS. The concept of services integration in schools has been promoted at different times throughout history but most recently re-emerged in the late 1980s as an attempt to counteract the fragmentation of the social services and the school system and the inability to meet pressing social needs (Hare, 1995).

School social workers have recognized that many outside barriers such as poverty or lack of housing have a tremendous effect on the educational achievements of students. School-linked services were proposed and have gained increasing acceptance as a means to foster collaboration between schools and communities in order to improve the education of today's youths (Hare, 1995).

The growing services integration movement is based on three major goals (Hare, 1995):

(1) to improve the coordination and efficiency of programs by reducing waste and duplication

(2) to improve legal access to comprehensive services by modifying legislative requirements for eligibility through mechanisms such as waivers and pooling separate funding streams

(3) to improve the quality and effectiveness of local services by providing comprehensive and well-coordinated services in one easily accessible location.

Social workers in the past have often been more focused on psychotherapeutic clinical work or have become overburdened in the public system and have thus left the development of services integration to other professionals (Hare, 1995). However, social workers must take an active role in the future development of services integration. Their skills in functions such as planning, mobilizing, coordinating, program development, and evaluation are essential in ensuring the most effective services delivery system.

Social workers have been called upon to play an active role in increasing educators' understanding of requirements for detecting and reporting child abuse and providing support services in the schools for abused children. Social workers, in many states, are obliged to personally report the abuse to public authorities or see that it is reported (O'Neill, 2000b). Providing consultation and training to school staff, assisting in educational and curriculum planning, serving as community liaisons, developing support systems, and supporting individual and family therapy for abused children have been identified as roles social workers can and should assume in intervening with victims of abuse (Graham, 1993).

In current practice, school social workers tend to emphasize services that address educational needs and other issues that may interfere with the student's academic achievement (Sanders &

Satir, 1995). Other functions include coordination between home and school, educational counseling, and advocacy to enable families to make use of community resources. In addition, social workers are involved in program development and planning in an effort to promote preventive services, cultural diversity, and community development (Allen-Meares, 1994).

In a position statement on school services, NASW (2000) included the following roles for school social workers:

- assessing and intervening in the social and emotional needs of students in relation to learning
- understanding, evaluating, and improving the total environment of pupils and thus contributing to a positive school climate
- strengthening the connections with home, school, and community
- building mutual communication and support among all participants in the school system
- developing preventive and remedial intervention programs for systemic problems
- providing meaningful and relevant consultation and in-service programs to teachers and school administrators concerning student needs
- providing group and individual counseling for students and, when necessary, for the family
- ensuring that students with disabilities receive appropriate educational services. (pp. 91–92)

In some jurisdictions, school social workers are tackling some of the emerging problems that afflict children and youths in schools and in their communities. These include programs and services to address date rape and violence among youths. Pilot programs, for example, have been implemented at the junior high and high school levels and focus on attitudes and popular myths that surround dating activity of young people through an experiential learning format (Nightingale & Morrissette, 1993). Social workers not only intervene in problem situations but also are instrumental in developing prevention efforts (Sanders & Satir, 1995).

School social workers have also joined with other pupil-services personnel to devise and implement plans to respond more effectively to the AIDS epidemic. This initiative comes out of the recognition that social workers will increasingly be called upon to help students experiencing stress over AIDS-related issues, including HIV testing, loss of family members to the disease, stigmatization, and sexuality in the age of AIDS. Identifying the barriers to services delivery related to AIDS and developing strategies to overcome these barriers are part of the school social worker's job.

Homelessness is another problem that confronts school social workers on a regular basis. A major problem resulting from the increase in homeless children is that of education. A substantial proportion of homeless children do not attend school. When they do attend, homeless youths may be shunned or ridiculed by the other students (Hall, 1990).

To address these and other issues, school social workers have developed and implemented innovative techniques to facilitate school attendance for homeless children. For example, school social workers have worked with school administrators to develop flexible criteria for the transfer of records and proof of residency, organized an appropriate transportation system, provided free breakfast and lunch programs, offered free or discounted school supplies, and provided a safe place for the student to keep his or her belongings. In addition, school social workers have helped homeless youths by developing buddy programs and assisting the students to develop social supports (Ziesemer, Marcoux, & Marwell, 1994). Social workers have also been active in developing school and community awareness programs that address and help eliminate myths and stereotypes about homelessness.

Another population that often needs the services of school social workers is that of gay and lesbian youths, who face social, emotional, and cognitive isolation and ostracism from peers. Gay and lesbian youths have a higher rate of suicide, alcohol and drug abuse, and HIV infection than do "straight" students, not because of their sexual orientation, but because of their feelings of worthlessness and isolation caused by the reactions of others to their homosexuality (Hiratsuka, 1993). Social workers work with teachers to help infuse information about homosexuality into the curriculum and help parents accept children who are homosexual. Portland, Oregon, area schools now mandate services to lesbian and gay youths. And in other school systems throughout the country, social workers are taking the initiative to expand programs and information and referral to this population of youths.

SCHOOLS AS THE MODERN MELTING POT—CULTURALLY SENSITIVE PRACTICE

More than ever, social workers need to develop and use skills for culturally competent practice (Fellin, 2000). Today, issues of ethnic, racial, and religious conflict fill the daily news—Jews and Arabs, Indians and Pakistanis, Catholics and Protestants. Following the terrorist attacks of September 11, 2001, there was a rising trend of anti-Semitism globally (Pincus, 2002). In France synagogues were defaced and torched. In the United States, government warnings of potential future acts of terrorism, often including potential acts of terror by foreign tenants in apartment buildings, caused landlords and neighbors to look with suspicion at Arabs living at the same address. Youths of Muslim descent in the United States became the target of backlash.

The complexities associated with cultural diversity in the United States, particular in times of heightened tension, require social workers to deliver culturally competent services to a broad range of clients (NASW National Committee on

Racial and Ethnic Diversity, 2001c). In recognition of the role of social workers in promoting cultural sensitivity and tolerance within society and its institutions, including schools, NASW (2002) issued the following press release about an article by Hodge in *Children & Schools*:

ADDRESSING RELIGIOUS CONFLICT

In the January issue of Children & Schools, *a publication from NASW, David R. Hodge, MSW, MCS, a Rene Sand doctoral fellow at the George Warren Brown School of Social Work, Washington University, explored the ways in which social workers can offer solutions for conflicts between Islamic and secular discourses, as well as possible value conflicts in the school setting.*

Muslims constitute a significant and growing percentage of American youths. A basic understanding and awareness of Islam in the school setting could help reduce value conflicts and peer pressure to socialize into Western secular values. School social workers can serve as a bridge between Muslims and school officials to broker solutions that address the needs of all parties.

According to Hodge, the first step is for social workers to have a background in Islamic faith, to understand the five pillars that constitute the common core of the religion. These pillars are the declaration of faith, the daily performance of five ritual prayers at set times throughout the day, almsgiving, the yearly sunrise to sunset fast during the month of Ramadan, and a one-time pilgrimage to Mecca.

As a result of elevated rates of immigration, conversions to Islam, and high birth rates, Muslims may either soon become or already have become the second largest religious population, after Christians, in the United States. Muslim youths are an increasingly vibrant component of the nation's multicultural mosaic.

There are also several values and practices that are most pertinent for Muslim youths—

family, community, modesty, morality, and nutrition. Many Muslim parents fear that children will be socialized into Western secular values that they believe will do little to advance their children's well-being. Most Muslim youths want to retain their Muslim values even if they are different from Western values and culture.

However, according to Hodge, the desire of many Muslim youths to exercise their religious faith can result in conflict, especially in U.S. public schools. Prayer and fasting may be difficult without the assistance of school officials. Hodge notes that teachers may be reluctant to excuse students from class or other events when prayers should occur. Muslim youths may also experience a significant degree of peer pressure because of their beliefs. Muslim youths may be ridiculed or worse for failing to follow secular values.

Social workers who work with Muslim youths, especially in the school setting, can be instrumental in helping Muslim students exercise their religious rights. Many problems can be alleviated by dispelling misinformation. Problematic peer interactions and lack of understanding of Islam by adults in school settings suggest a need for raising awareness about Islamic beliefs and values. (NASW, 2002)

Culture refers to "the integrated pattern of human behavior that includes thoughts, communications, actions, customs, beliefs, values, and institutions of a racial, ethnic, religious, or social group" (NASW National Committee on Racial and Ethnic Diversity, 2001c). This term encompasses race, ethnicity, and religion and goes further to include people with disabilities and people who are gay or lesbian. The NASW *Code of Ethics* (1996) clarifies the social work mandate: "Social workers are sensitive to cultural and ethnic diversity and strive to end discrimination, oppression, poverty, and other forms of social injustice" (p. 1). The practice implication that derives from this code is that social workers have a responsibility to promote sensitivity to and knowledge about oppression and cultural and ethnic diversity. To practice effectively in this regard, social workers must be culturally competent. The NASW *Standards for Cultural Competence in Social Work Practice* (2001c) identify five elements that contribute to becoming culturally competent: (1) valuing diversity, (2) having the capacity for cultural self-assessment, (3) being conscious of the dynamics inherent when cultures interact, (4) institutionalizing cultural knowledge, and (5) developing programs and services that reflect an understanding of diversity between and within cultures.

In today's world of ethnic and religious tensions, the social worker can be an important influence in promoting educational programs about different cultures and creating a school environment of acceptance of difference. Cultural competence is the basis for working effectively in the cross-cultural situations that characterize schools today.

EPIDEMIC OF VIOLENCE

The violence that plagues American society is also felt in the nation's schools. Gang fights erupt in lunchrooms. Teachers fear being harmed by their own students (Landers, 1995).

The word "Columbine" has come to signify the most notorious incident of school violence in U.S. history. On April 20, 1999, two students at Columbine High School in Littleton, Colorado, opened fire in a shooting spree that resulted in the death of 12 classmates and one teacher. Educators, parents, and helping professionals, in the weeks and months following this incident, sought to understand this and other acts of violence by children. What became evident was a "culture" within Columbine and other schools in which students who did not conform to what was considered "cool" were ostracized. Athletes, for example, were found to exhibit behavior that was tolerated for them, but not for others, including bullying and even sexually harassing behavior (Adams & Russakoff, 1999). The homecoming king was a football player on probation for burglary. Eric Harris and Dylan Klebold—the two boys who staged the shooting rampage—were at the wrong end of the social acceptance continuum. As the conditions which led to the rampage were analyzed, it became clear that Harris and Klebold sought vengeance against athletes against whom they felt powerless (Adams & Russakoff, 1999).

In the aftermath of Columbine, school social workers agreed that there are no guarantees that another Columbine will not happen. But they also agreed that the chances can be reduced. Consistent themes are the need for individual contact with at-risk students and their families; programs available to all students that instill respect for each other; and tools, such as anger control and mediation, to resolves differences before they escalate into violence (Beaucar, 1999; NASW, 2001d). Parental involvement in the schools is also seen as critical. However, one school social worker, Sharon Scheffler of Goddard, KS, noted, "parents are a lot less accessible than 10 or 20 years ago. Parents are busier; mothers are working. They are both hesitant and inaccessible for working as a team in a crisis-intervention situation" (as cited in Beaucar, 1999, p. 3).

School social workers recognize the interplay between home and community life and students' adjustment and progress in school. Such factors as broken homes, poverty, substance abuse, and neglect provide little stability for children and this is reflected in their school performance and behavior (Beaucar, 1999). Social workers also acknowledge the lack of resources in many communities to deal with these issues and the fact that children in need of mental health care may have no place to get the assistance they need.

The two boys involved in the Columbine attack were not special education students. They were students with emotional problems made worse by ostracism, ridicule, and bullying by their peers. Although they were at risk and, perhaps, in hindsight there were signs of trouble brewing, these signs were not heeded.

Various strategies have been attempted from a safety point of view. To ensure safety for students and educators, suspension and expulsion offer one immediate solution. (Note, however, media reports of students, once suspended or feeling mistreated, going back to the school to commit a violent crime.) The federal Improving America's Schools Act of 1994 (P.L. 103-382) requires a one-year suspension for any student found with a gun on school property. These "get-tough" policies address violence after the fact, and do so from a law and order point of view. Violence in the schools presents a thorny dilemma for administrators, teachers, and helping professionals. Although "zero tolerance" for threats of or actual violence is understandable, there are many students—an unknown proportion of whom have one or more disabilities—who are not able to conform to disciplinary codes (Landers, 1995). Are they all to be expelled? And then what happens to them? Unemployment, poverty, and perhaps continued acts of violence.

A complicating factor is that, under IDEA, students cannot be expelled for behavior that can be attributed to their disability (Landers, 1995). There is also a time limit (10 consecutive days) for suspension from school of a special education student without a court order. The 1994 amendments to IDEA expanded the penalties for students with disabilities that apply to cases when a gun is brought to school. In addition to a 10-day suspension, they may be placed in alternative settings for up to 45 days. Thus, there are limits, under the law, to the penalties that may be imposed for dangerous behavior. These limits point to the need for social workers and other helping professionals in the schools to plan and implement conflict resolution and other programs to mitigate against violence in the schools. In addition, pupil-services personnel work to ensure that the individualized education programs for children with disabilities adequately address behavior problems.

School social workers have assumed an important role in promoting schools free of violence. With the surge of violence and substance abuse among young people, school social workers are using their skills to recognize possible causal factors and create comprehensive prevention programs. These skills include reaching out to and building upon community resources and cooperation of parents, local churches, police, mental health centers, and others. Several themes have been and continue to be pursued, including gun control, creation of more after-school programs, and classes in parenting and conflict resolution (Loose & Thomas, 1994; Vallianatos, 2001). The following vignette exemplifies how social workers can take on the challenge of developing a safer environment in our nation's schools.

AN APPROACH TO VIOLENCE PREVENTION

Laura Nelson is one of four social workers in the Howard County school system. She is assigned to two elementary and one intermediate school in this largely working class suburban community. As an experienced school social worker, Laura has an extensive network of colleagues and friends who work in inner-city, suburban, and rural school districts. At a recent statewide symposium on violence in the schools, Laura had the opportunity to learn about violence prevention strategies being initiated on an ad hoc basis in numerous school districts. The notion of "prevention" stuck with her as the only approach that made sense. Given the incidence of physical assaults and even the use of weapons in other schools, it seemed only a matter of time before Howard County fell prey to the same epidemic.

When Laura returned home from the conference, she decided to take action. She spoke with the Director of Pupil Personnel Services for the county, Ms. Dickson, who wholeheartedly supported Laura's desire to develop a violence prevention program. Ms. Dickson cautioned, however, that it was probably wise to think in terms of a pilot program in one school, thoroughly evaluate the results, and then determine whether the county or perhaps a private source would fund a countywide effort. The rationale for a pilot approach was that the school system was in a budget crunch, and the board of education was not inclined to support new initiatives that had a price tag attached. On the other hand, if Laura could show promising results in one school, perhaps enthusiasm could be generated for a larger scale effort. Ms. Dickson did promise to inform the principals throughout the county, as well as members of the board of education, about the pilot program to be developed, as Laura had indicated she might need their input.

From everything that Laura had read and heard about prevention programs, the first step was to thoroughly understand the scope of the problem to be addressed and how people with a stake in the issue viewed the problem—students, teachers, administrators, parents, police, community residents, and others. In conducting a needs assessment, Laura decided to use a nominal group approach. This approach is basically a workshop atmosphere that brings together selected participants from various interested groups. The goal is for participants to share their views about the problem being addressed (that is, school violence), offer feedback on possible solutions, and identify barriers that may be encountered (Siegel, Attkisson, & Carson, 1995).

Laura actively sought out interested student leaders, teachers, administrators, parents, police personnel, community residents, and religious leaders. They met together over the course of four consecutive weeks to discuss the issue of rising youth violence and the need for prevention in the schools.

During the last meeting, the group developed a tentative list of goals for a violence prevention program. Laura then solicited input from several principals throughout the county as well as members of the board of education and brought their suggestions back to the group.

The final goals agreed on were as follows:

* create a change in the institutional environment
* build a better school climate that is based on respect rather than power
* provide student and faculty training in conflict resolution and mediation
* develop a peer mediation and counseling program
* provide training to students and faculty in problem-solving skills.

After agreeing on these five major goals, objectives needed to be defined. Laura could set objectives by herself. However, she wanted to continue to receive input from the community and school participants in order to maximize their "buy in" to the program. Therefore, the group selected one member from each population represented (for example, students, teachers, parents, and so forth). These members then joined Laura to form a planning committee. It was decided that they would meet once a week and would be joined by the school principal and representatives of the board of education once a month.

The planning committee outlined its agenda for the upcoming meetings. The committee would first attempt to develop operational objectives for each of the goals, so that instead of vague ideas and concepts, they would have a concrete action plan. The next step was to prioritize the goals and objectives in the order of importance as related to the goal of violence prevention. In addition, an evaluation measure would have to be developed to determine the success or failure of the program. Although there was still a substantial amount of work to be done in developing and implementing a violence prevention program, Laura felt good about the input of the planning committee and the planning process. She was confident that this program would be an important step in preventing the occurrence of violence in the schools.

In this case example, Laura engaged primarily in macro social work functions. Through her interaction with other professionals, she identified the problem of youth violence and recognized its devastating effect on the school environment for all students. She then consulted with her supervisor about developing a prevention program. Upon receiving approval, Laura engaged in the functions of organizing, coordinating, and managing to develop a group forum. She then carried out the functions of planning and program development to shape goals and objectives. When the time came for implementation, Laura also had to engage in the function of mobilization to encourage and empower students and faculty to carry out the program specifics. Finally, Laura had to evaluate the program so that its outcomes could be studied and possibly duplicated in other schools.

Even more common than extreme acts of violence in schools is "bullying" behavior, which may take the form of name calling, insults, and pushing and shoving. This type of behavior has been found to be very responsive to conflict resolution programs.

Social worker Debra Woody offered an empirically validated model of conflict resolution to address this bullying problem. This model included schoolwide participation spanning an entire school year. Ongoing training in conflict resolution methods was found to increase the likelihood that students actually internalized the skills and, therefore, maximized the long-term effects of managing anger and resolving conflict (NASW, 2001a).

Woody said that although there were other models of conflict resolution being taught, what made this model successful was that it included everyone. "It's a systematic approach; the principal of the school made it mandatory training. Every student, every teacher, every administrator and every secretary received the training and were required to use the skills" (NASW, 2001a).

The conflict resolution program included three phases. The first phase encompassed a four-hour training segment with no more than 20 students at a time. They were taught skills in communication enhancement and conflict resolution through negotiation. Acceptance of and appreciation for diversity were emphasized in training. The second phase included training of both faculty and staff. They received the same conflict resolution training as students but were also taught how to utilize this training on a daily basis. Phase three consisted of daily follow-up training. In homeroom, teachers reviewed and facilitated discussions about a particular concept presented in the training and each day students received a daily "booster." All new students, faculty, and staff received mandatory training as well.

At the end of the school year, students were tested on resolution skills and the ability to apply these skills. In evaluating the program, Woody found that training about conflict resolution increased students' knowledge of nonviolent means to resolve conflict; facilitated a more positive attitude about nonviolent conflict resolution methods; and reduced the frequency of violent confrontations in the school (NASW, 2001a). "The next phase," she said, "is to add parents into the loop. While some problems are school related, there is a component that has roots at home. Parents would learn the skills and be able to offer resolutions based on the same skills they learn at school" (NASW, 2001a).

Violence is a way for youths to seek or maintain power. Thus, any effort to intervene to break the cycle of violence or to prevent it altogether must provide youths with empowering alternatives (Mattaini, 2001; Vallianatos, 2001). Programs need to take in the totality of the youths' environment, including teachers, administrators, parents, peers, and the social and cultural networks in which children and youths interact.

Social worker Dr. Mark Mattaini introduced the peace power initiative in his book, *Peace Power for Adolescents: Strategies for a Culture of Nonviolence* (2001). This is a program that seeks to construct and maintain a "new way of life" for all of those involved in a child's world in an interlocking system composed of the family, school, peer, and community cultures. The goal is to reduce violence and initiate a sense of belonging for everyone (NASW, 2001c).

Peace power is predicated on four principles: recognizing contributions, acting with respect, sharing power in community, and making peace. These principles form the foundation for a flexible strategy to achieve cultural change based on what is known about effective prevention of and intervention in youth violence. The peace power programs help youths learn to communicate with each other and with adults with respect for everyone involved. Avoidance of coercive behaviors, such as threats, punishment, and needless hurt, such as bullying, is stressed (NASW, 2001c).

Social workers also intervene at the macro level to address the problem of bullying. NASW has partnered with the National Education Association (NEA) and other national organizations concerned with school services to support NEA's National Bullying Awareness Campaign. This effort is geared toward reducing and eventually eliminating bullying in America's schools (Vallianatos, 2002). Part of the initiative is to educate organizations and communities about the harmful effects of bullying, publicize the issue within the social work community, including modes of intervention, and inform key decision makers about the need for changing the environment, culture, and climate in the schools that allow bullying to continue.

How much has changed since Columbine? Were lessons learned? Statistics on school violence wax and wane. In New York City, for example, the numbers are not good. Statistics show increases in several crimes that directly affect the safety of students. Comparing 2000 with 2001, reports of sex offenses have risen 7 percent, weapon offenses are up 1 percent, and misdemeanor assaults, such as fistfights, are up 34 percent. In 2001, there were 741 incidents of such assaults compared to 553 the previous year

(Baker, 2002). These and other lesser crimes increased 11 percent overall in 2001. Major crime in the schools has increased 6.6 percent over the same period in 2000 (Baker, 2002).

ALTERNATIVE PROGRAMS

Social workers have taken important leadership roles in identifying alternative educational programs for students in special circumstances. One such example is the Harvey Milk School in New York, an alternative school for gay and lesbian youths (although the school is open to anyone regardless or orientation). The school is run from and under the auspices of the Hetrick-Martin Institute, a social services organization, and is sanctioned by the New York City Board of Education.

Social worker Steve Ashkinazy conceived of the school as a solution for openly gay and lesbian youths who drop out of school or are chronically truant. These students, who had not made a secret of their homosexuality, had been ridiculed by teachers, other students, and sometimes even rejected by their parents. Several had tried to commit suicide; others had gotten into trouble, including prostitution and drug abuse ("Troubled Gay Youth," 1985).

The school opened in the spring of 1985 in a Greenwich Village church with 20 students enrolled. The New York city Board of Education agreed to pay the costs of an instructor and some class materials; the Institute for the Protection of Lesbian and Gay Youth (IPLGY) paid the remaining costs. The philosophy of IPLGY is that the youths it seeks to serve suffer the effects of systematic discrimination and that a learning environment free from harassment might lure them back into school. The premise is to offer students more than an education. Within a supportive environment, they receive nurturing and the chance to observe positive role models, both straight and gay. Students participating in the program receive individual and group therapy after school.

Critical stories ran in the *New York Times* and one tabloid featured the headline, "School for Scandal." The board of education, however, strongly maintained its support. Then chancellor of schools Nathan Quinones told reporters that "these are youngsters who, in most instances [due to their behavioral problems], would never have been allowed to remain in a high school setting previously" ("Troubled Gay Youth," 1985, p. 12). The school continues to flourish. Referrals come in from other New York City schools requesting "safety transfers" because the home–school environment is unsafe for the gay or lesbian youngster who has "come out." About half of Harvey Milk's 50 students transferred from other schools because they felt unsafe or because the atmosphere was so hostile that chronic truancy and other acting out behaviors resulted (Evans, 2002).

Gay and lesbian students may face ostracism and bullying in their regular schools, but there may not be an alternative school available. Pupil-services personnel have made strides in some school districts to promote a more accepting culture and provide support to gay, lesbian, and bisexual students. In Massachusetts, for example, about half of the high schools have established gay–straight alliances. This initiative followed passage, in 1993, of the Safe Schools Initiative in that state. Advisors meet with students who have identified as gay or lesbian or who may have questions about their sexual identity in small groups where their sexuality issues are discussed (Boes & van Wormer, 2002). These groups are led by teachers who may be openly gay or lesbian or by adult members of the community, with the purpose of providing peer support.

Boes and van Wormer (2002) identified some of the strategies social workers can pursue within the school setting to promote acceptance of sexual and other differences:

- help institute programs to prevent bullying and verbal abuse of students who are thought to be "different"

- challenge homophobic practices in the school setting
- share stories of personal growth and resilience in individual counseling sessions
- help open the door to new support systems in the community
- help students discover their own identities and avoid premature labeling
- work with the school librarian to make sure that information is available about homosexuality and homophobia
- provide teacher workshops on homophobia and school bullying
- organize gay and lesbian panels from a nearby college to address the school each year
- connect with the group Parents, Families, and Friends of Lesbians and Gays, which has implemented a nationwide program to work with parent–teacher associations and engage in speaker panels. (pp. 621–622)

In promoting acceptance of difference, specific activities may involve documenting the problems, presenting the problems to the appropriate people in the local education agency or community, and promoting decision making and action among educators, other professionals, and citizens.

CRISIS INTERVENTION

Crisis intervention is a social work function that transcends most fields of practice. In chapter 4, the social work role in disaster relief was discussed in detail. Crisis work also extends to practice within the school setting, as the following vignette illustrates.

TWO FRIENDS DIE

It was a beautiful spring night. Sixteen-year-old Emily Williams and 17-year-old Denise Fowler had been at a party at the home of a friend, Bill. Bill's parents were out of town for the weekend and, against his parents' explicit instructions, Bill had decided it was an opportune time to "party." An older friend of Bill's had been willing to purchase a keg of beer, and Emily and Denise were among those who had a considerable amount to drink.

It was after midnight when Emily and Denise left the party. Denise had use of the family car; she had recently gotten her driver's license. She knew that she was feeling a little tipsy but thought that she was in good enough shape to drive home. As they were leaving, Jim, a neighbor who was also at the party, hopped in the car for a ride home.

No one will ever know exactly what happened. The police, on a routine patrol, found the smoldering vehicle with the front end embedded in a tree. The impact was so great that the front end of the car resembled melted and jumbled steel. Emily and Denise had been killed instantly. Jim had been thrown from the car and was clinging to life.

The lead story on the morning news told the gruesome tale. Cheryl Williams, the social worker in Sun Valley High School, was listening to the news as she dressed to go to work. As the report about the accident reached her consciousness, Cheryl became dizzy and nauseated. The few minutes of immobilization gave way to a sense of urgency—she needed to get to school.

Cheryl arrived at school a half hour earlier than usual and headed directly to the principal's office. The school psychologist and assistant principal were already there, though no meeting had been called. The principal asked the administrative assistant to notify the other six members of the special services unit to come to her office upon their arrival in the building.

The focus of immediate attention was on the development of a crisis plan. The students of Sun Valley High had also heard the news reports or, if not, the informal communication network would soon be activated. By the time the students got to school, within an hour, they would be at a high level of upset. Of particular concern were the close friends of Jim (in critical condition), Emily, and Denise. However, Cheryl and her colleagues were also concerned about the emotional reaction of all Sun Valley students. Death—sudden and tragic death—was not within the framework of most of their life experiences.

Within 15 minutes, the rough outline of a plan was in place, and Cheryl knew what she had to do. Students would be arriving shortly for the start of the school day, and there was little time to put the plan in place. The first step was implemented when the principal made an announcement over the public address system asking all teachers to immediately report to the auditorium. The principal conveyed the factual information that was known and then turned the meeting over to Cheryl. Cheryl correctly anticipated that she must first acknowledge and deal with the feelings of the teachers, allowing them time to ask questions and express their own upset. Because of time constraints that morning, Cheryl suggested that the teachers get together at the end of the day to talk further about their own reactions, what transpired during the day, and how they dealt with it. Cheryl then provided the teachers with information about what reactions they might expect from their students, how to encourage them to express their feelings, what responses are appropriate, and how to identify those students who need special attention (and referral to the social worker). Cheryl indicated that she would be available in her office throughout the day and that any student who seemed more upset than the others should be sent to her.

The teachers then returned to their classrooms. Cheryl and the principal conferred briefly about other issues they anticipated would arise during the day: calls from parents and contacts from the media, some by phone and some in person. The principal decided to contact central administration to prepare a statement about the accident; in addition to the tragedy itself, there was the issue of alcohol involvement.

During the day, Cheryl saw eight students, most of whom were close friends of Emily and Denise. Cheryl also checked with the hospital about Jim's condition. There was good news. Although his injuries were very serious, he would survive.

The following day, the special services team again met with the principal to debrief on the events of the previous day and to continue planning. It was decided that the principal would contact the families of Emily and Denise, offer condolences, and obtain details about the funeral. It was a difficult call to make. Ms. Peterson, the principal, correctly anticipated the overwhelming grief being experienced by the girls' parents. Ms. Peterson considered that, in the weeks to come, she would want her special services team to involve the parents in substance abuse program planning for the students in the school.

Both sets of parents decided on a small and closed funeral for family members and close family friends. When Ms. Peterson relayed this news back to the special services team, Cheryl suggested that the school hold a memorial service so that the girls' friends and other students would have a chance to say goodbye and to express their grief in an open and accepting atmosphere. Ms. Peterson decided to wait a few days, until after the funerals, to invite the families to participate in the memorial service.

The days passed slowly. Some of the students had responded to the initial news with a kind of numbness that was now wearing off and turning to outward expressions of grief. Cheryl continued to counsel students individually throughout the week. The teachers had responded well to the request to identify and refer students who seemed to be having difficulty. Cheryl also recognized that the teachers continued to react strongly to the deaths of their students, and she spent extra time in the teachers' cafeteria talking informally with them.

Ms. Peterson sent a memo to all staff asking for volunteers to help plan the memorial service. Cheryl suggested that several of the close friends of Emily and Denise also be asked to participate in planning the service. The nondenominational service was scheduled for the following Friday. Both Emily and Denise's parents attended the service and several of the girls' friends spoke about their lives with Emily and Denise and about the need to prevent a similar tragedy.

Although the service went well, Cheryl recognized the need for long-term intervention in the form of an alcohol and drug prevention program. The following week, she spoke with Emily and Denise's parents. Both families were very interested in participating in planning the prevention program. Cheryl also recruited student and teacher participants. Together, the group discussed how they could give something back to Emily and Denise by developing a program to prevent this type of tragedy in the future.

The teachers and pupil-services personnel, as well as the parents involved, all tossed out ideas for a long-term substance use prevention campaign. However, one of the female students spoke up and said she was scared about the prom next month. It was decided that the prom would be the kickoff for the entire program. Although there is already a rule against alcohol at the prom, many of the kids drink heavily before and after the prom. The students and the teachers decided that there was no way to prevent drinking, but that they could launch a campaign that actively promoted an alcohol-free evening.

Cheryl then worked with the students and the parents to have T-shirts designed and printed for the prom that promoted a no-alcohol evening. Cheryl also made arrangements with a local taxicab company to provide free transportation at any time in the evening for students who had been drinking. The taxicab number was posted throughout the school and stickers, supplied by the cab company, were given to all students with their prom tickets. If the prom night was successful, the cab company had exhibited interest in developing a more permanent partnership. In addition, special student trainings were organized to share information *about alcohol and drug use, and peer support groups were arranged once a week after school. Cheryl was also coordinating a visit from a local automobile distributor who had designed a car that simulated driving while intoxicated. Students could directly experience the lack of control and the decreased reaction time that result after even one or two drinks.*

The planning committee continued to meet and pursue a coordinated, long-term alcohol and drug prevention program. Hopefully, the program will help to prevent another tragedy.

In this vignette, Cheryl carried out both micro and macro social work functions. In the immediate aftermath of the accident, she assessed needs and provided support and counseling to assist both teachers and students to work through their emotions about the deaths of Emily and Denise. Following the initial period of crisis intervention, Cheryl organized and supervised a planning committee of students, faculty, and parents to develop, first, a memorial service and, for the longer term, a prevention program. With the help of the group members, Cheryl engaged in planning and program development. She also used the social work skills of coordination and exchange when she accessed the services of the taxicab company and the automobile distributor. Cheryl will also need to develop an evaluation tool to monitor the success of the prevention program so that the outcomes can be shared with other schools.

Cheryl's efforts to address the problem of substance abuse over the longer term takes into account what she has learned about the deleterious and sometimes fatal consequences of alcohol and drugs. A study, "Teen Tipplers, America's Underage Drinking Epidemic," conducted under the auspices of the National Center on Addiction and Substance Abuse of Columbia University (2002) found that 5 million high school students, or 31 percent, engaged in binge drinking (five or more drinks in a row) at least once a month. Although alcohol consumption

by teenagers dropped in the 1980s, this decline has level off since the mid-1990s (Lewin, 2002). In a recent school-based survey, 41 percent of the girls and 40 percent of the boys reported drinking alcohol in the last month. Teenage girls' drinking habits now mirror that of boys, a change from earlier patterns (Lewin, 2002).

Project SUCCESS (Schools Using Coordinated Community Efforts to Strengthen Students) is a model prevention program that was initially funded in 1996 by the U.S. Department of Health and Human Services Center for Substance Abuse Prevention and is now funded by the New York State Office of Alcoholism and Substance Abuse Services and participating schools. The program is administered to alternative high school students by Westchester, NY, social worker Ellen Morehouse and is designed to prevent and reduce substance use and abuse among high-risk adolescents. The program operates out of six alternative schools and involves four different interventions carried out by social workers from area alcohol and drug abuse agencies. First is a series of workshops presented to participants on such topics as being an adolescent; information about alcohol, tobacco, and other drugs; family pressure and problems; and skills for coping. Second, participating students receive individual assessments. Third, social workers lead focused counseling groups for adolescents at risk of substance abuse. Fourth, if students need additional help, they are referred to outside agencies. The program includes an evaluation component, which has thus far demonstrated a 37 percent reduction in the rate of use by participating youth compared to nonprogram youth ("Social Work in the Public Eye," 2001).

TEENAGER SUICIDE

For youths between the ages of 15 and 24, suicide is the third leading cause of death, behind unintentional injury and homicide (Surgeon General, 1999). In 2001, former Surgeon General Dr. David Satcher released a National

Strategy for Suicide Prevention, which included 11 goals and 68 measurable objectives to prevent suicides and suicide attempts (NASW, 2001b). This strategy included specific goals related to youths and incorporated and expanded upon the 1999 Surgeon General's Call to Action to Prevent Suicide (Surgeon General, 1999). These objectives included the following:

- implementing integrated suicide prevention programs that include life skills, beliefs and values, and connections to family and community
- increasing the number of professional and volunteer groups that integrate suicide prevention into their ongoing activities
- improving suicide prevention education and training for health care professionals, counselors, clergy, teachers, and other community "gatekeepers." (NASW, 2001b)

Various reasons have been attributed to the increasing number of adolescents and teens who consider or attempt suicide, including high levels of stress, alcohol and drug abuse, academic failure, and the difficulties of normal development, including the desire for independence and the need for acceptance. Risk factors for attempted suicide in youths include depression, alcohol or other drug use disorder, and aggressive or disruptive behaviors (Surgeon General, 1999). (For more information about teenage suicide, contact Centers for Disease Control and Prevention, National Center for Injury Prevention and Control online at http://www.cdc.gov, or the National Institute of Mental Health, Suicide Research Consortium online at http://www.nimh.nih.gov/research/suicide.htm.)

How to Help a Friend

Mark doesn't know what to do. His best friend, Bill, has been acting weird lately. He seems distracted all the time, hasn't been taking good care of himself in terms of personal hygiene,

and just the other day said that he didn't think life was worth living. All this began about two weeks ago, just after Bill's girlfriend Beth told him that she didn't want to date him anymore.

At first, Mark figured that Bill was just experiencing some bad days because of the rejection. But here it is two weeks later, and Bill is sounding more and more despondent. The threat of suicide scares Mark. He had heard that one guy in the 12th grade had actually attempted suicide. Mark has tried to be a good friend. He has spent a lot of time with Bill these past two weeks and has tried to listen and understand. But it is more than he can handle.

This morning, Bill shows Mark an essay he has prepared for English class about his visions of himself in the future. In it, Bill writes that he doesn't have a future, that there is no point in living because things just get worse and worse. Mark can't think of a response. But he knows that he has to do something. As Mark walks to class, he passes the school social worker's office. He stops, looks in, and sees that Ms. Cleary, the social worker, is sitting at her desk. He continues down the hall, turns back again, and then stands in place wrestling with himself about whether he should go in. Ms. Cleary spots Mark standing by the door, smiles, and motions him to come in. He enters.

Mark sits down in the chair by Ms. Cleary's desk, and she inquires how things are going. She and Mark had talked once a year or so ago, when his grades had briefly fallen. His response "Okay, I guess," leads Ms. Cleary to prod a bit further. "I guess?" she says, "that sounds like you're not sure." It didn't take much encouragement for Mark to blurt out "I don't know if I should squeal on a friend. I just don't know what to do."

Ms. Cleary and Mark then talk for a little while about circumstances under which "squealing" is the sign of a good friend, not a bad person. Mark hesitates for only a few minutes; he has received the permission he needs to unload the heavy burden he feels. Mark tells Ms.

Cleary that he has this good friend who has changed a lot lately and has started to say scary things—things he intends to do to himself. Ms. Cleary responds by asking if Mark means suicide. Mark nods his head in affirmation. Ms. Cleary then asks if this friend is a student at the school. Mark nods in affirmation again.

"Look Mark," says Ms. Cleary, "I want to talk to you more—a lot more—about your feelings about squealing. But right now there is something important you need to tell me. When people talk about suicide, we have to take that seriously. I want to help your friend, and to do that, I need to know who he is." Mark still hesitates. "You won't tell him I told you?" "No," Ms. Cleary assures him, "this is between you and me." Very quietly Mark says "Bill Graybar." "Thank you, Mark," says Ms. Cleary. "I know how difficult it was for you to tell me but you've done the right thing. You are a good friend to Bill. He needs help. Let me see what I can do. In the meantime, let's talk again tomorrow."

With the promise that Mark would stop in tomorrow, he leaves to go to class. Ms. Cleary sits at her desk for a few minutes trying to figure out the best approach to talk with Bill. She looks up his schedule and decides to walk to his classroom; classes would be changing soon and she thinks she can catch him. She had met Bill on a few occasions, but had never talked with him at any length.

When Bill walks out of class—the last to do so— he looks very downcast and distracted. Ms. Cleary intercepts him at the door and asks if she can speak with him. Bill is surprised, but agrees to accompany Ms. Cleary to her office.

Once in her office, Ms. Cleary tells Bill that she understands his girlfriend has broken up with him. She also tells Bill that she has heard he is upset and has spoken about hurting himself. She asks him if this is true. At first, Bill is furious at Mark. He knows Mark must have talked to Ms. Clearly, because Mark is the only person Bill has spoken to about his feelings. Even though Ms. Cleary had promised she would not

reveal that Mark had told her, she expected that Bill would guess. She tells Bill that his friends care about him very much and that they simply don't want anything to happen to him.

Bill settles down and shrugs his shoulders. He talks briefly with Ms. Clearly about his depression and desire to end the pain. Ms. Cleary listens intently and offers support. However, she tells Bill that she is going to have to call his parents because all threats of suicide must be taken seriously. Ms. Cleary has Bill wait in her office with her until his parents arrive. When they do arrive, Ms. Cleary invites them in to meet with her and Bill. They had no idea how much Bill was hurting and they are obviously scared. Ms. Cleary gives them a referral to a mental health clinic, and they immediately make an appointment.

Ms. Cleary touches base with Bill's parents the next day and asks them to have Bill sign a release of information form from the psychiatrist so that Ms. Cleary can monitor Bill's progress and coordinate appropriate services. Bill returns to school after a week and a half and meets regularly with Ms. Cleary for short-term counseling concerning issues such as his return to school and the reactions of the other students. Ms. Cleary also meets with Mark to help him resolve his own feelings of guilt and to encourage his friendship with Bill.

In this vignette, Ms. Cleary engages in assessment and diagnosis when she first talks with Mark and Bill. She determines that the threat of suicide is real and she must intervene. Ms. Cleary then discusses appropriate services with Bill and his parents and carries out the function of referral to the mental health center. Finally, Ms. Cleary offers support and counseling to all those involved: Bill, his parents, and Mark. A follow-up session with Mark will address feelings of guilt he may have about betraying his friend's confidence.

The contact with Bill's parents without his explicit authorization raises ethical considerations. School social workers must be familiar and comply with the various legal mandates related to confidentiality. Confidentiality is a major component of any therapeutic relationship, starting from the initial contact with the client. However, there are important exceptions to confidentiality, foremost when there is the potential that a person will harm himself or someone else. The often-cited case of *Tarasoff v. Board of Regents of the University of California*, decided by the California Supreme Court in 1976, illustrates the limitations of confidentiality. Here, the court ruled that

> when a therapist determines, or pursuant to the standards of his profession should determine, that his patient presents a serious danger of violence to another, he incurs an obligation to use reasonable care to protect the intended victim against such danger. . . . We conclude that the public policy favoring protection of the confidential character of patient–psychotherapist communications must yield to the extent to which disclosure is essential to avert danger to others. The protective privilege ends where the public peril begins. (551 P.2d 344 at 336–337)

Threats of suicide are taken seriously by mental health professionals. Bill fits the profile; the risk for suicide among young people is greatest among young white males (Surgeon General, 1999). However, between 1980 and 1996, the sharpest increases in suicide have been among young black males, where the suicide rate quadrupled among those from ages 10 to 14. The increase in the suicide rate among white females ages 10 to 14 also experienced a sharp increase (Squires, 1995; Surgeon General, 1999).

Social workers have recognized the need to actively reach out to at-risk teens and to educate teachers, school staff, parents, police, and youths about early warning signs and suicide prevention. Teaching young people about warning signs is particularly important, as teens turn to their friends before parents and professionals.

Strategies to prevent youth suicide include training teachers and school officials to identify those at highest risk for suicidal thoughts and attempts, establishing referral programs and suicide crisis hot lines, and educating young people about suicide (Boes & van Wormer, 2002; Squires, 1995).

School social workers play an important role in developing suicide prevention programs. For example, in a school where there are several "copycat" attempts after an actual suicide, the social worker may set up an awareness and prevention program designed to train school personnel in prevention strategies, involve parents in the program planning process, and coordinate with other agencies in the community.

PREVENTING SCHOOL DROPOUT

The national dropout rate refers to the percentage of youths from 16 through 24 years of age who are not enrolled in school and have not obtained a high school diploma or a high school equivalency certification. Dropout rates within this age group vary considerably by region and ethnicity. Dropout rates, for example, are higher in the south and west than in the midwest and northeast regions of the United States. Dropout rates are also considerably higher for Hispanics than for other ethnic groups, particularly among those born outside the United States (U.S. Department of Education, 1996; U.S. General Accounting Office [GAO], 2002). A recent report by the GAO (2002) found that there had been little change in national dropout rates between 1990 and 2000. Between these years, the dropout rates fluctuated between 10.9 percent and 12.5 percent.

A range of factors has been found to be associated with school dropout, and often multiple factors in combination account for this phenomenon. First are factors associated with the family. Students from low-income, single-parent, and less-educated families are more likely to drop out than other students, in part because they come to school less prepared than children from more affluent homes and better-educated families. The second factor relates to benchmarks that occur for children within the school. These factors include academic failure, absenteeism, disciplinary problems, being retained for one or more grades, and changing schools. In later years, other behavioral predictors become evident, including substance abuse, pregnancy, criminal behavior, and immediate economic need. Dropping out of school has been found to be a long-term process of disengagement that begins in the earliest grades and continues until the time the student ceases to attend school (GAO, 2002).

A variety of state, local, and private programs have been initiated to assist youths at risk of dropping out of school, ranging from small-scale supplemental services (such as mentoring or counseling on an individual level) to comprehensive school system restructuring efforts to improve educational opportunities for all students (GAO, 2002). Examples include the privately funded Coca-Cola Valued Youth Program, which supports a program in which older children tutor younger children, and Project GRAD, which is a comprehensive school reform model that offers integrated programs for kindergarten through 12th grade students. A new program—the Dropout Prevention Demonstration Program—was first funded in fiscal year 2001 at $5 million (a relatively small sum) and is specifically targeted to dropouts (GAO, 2002).

As the following vignette illustrates, social work interventions may range from psychosocial assessments to advocacy for broad system changes. Strategies include educating school administrators, teachers, and other school personnel about the characteristics of at-risk youths. School social workers can directly provide crisis intervention, management, and support services for students in the school setting and link students at risk of dropping out to other needed services, including mental health evaluations, screening, and treatment beyond the scope of the school. School social workers can also assist in establishing linkages with community services providers to develop more comprehensive and accessible services in the areas of psychological and social functioning for youths prone to dropping out of school (Franklin, 1992).

A GROUP TREATMENT APPROACH TO PREVENTING SCHOOL DROPOUT

Peter Ownings is the only social worker in a school district of 6,500 students. The district is a bedroom community of Indianapolis and includes a minority population of about 30 percent and neighborhoods ranging from very affluent to very poor. Peter has worked in this school district for 15 years, beginning as an elementary school teacher. His teaching experience made him realize that he wanted to help his students in a different kind of way, and he enrolled in Indiana University's MSW program as an extension student. After four years of part-time study and with his MSW in hand, Peter applied for and was hired as the district's social worker in 1992.

One of Peter's concerns is the increasing number of students who leave school before graduation. For many of these students, Peter realized, it was too late—they were so disinterested in school that little could be done. Perhaps, he hoped, they would return to get their GED when they realized the importance of education in directing the course of their lives. Peter concluded that the best approach was to address the dropout problem from a prevention standpoint, believing that kids can be turned around if they are reached at an early age.

Peter spent many hours talking with teachers and school administrators, getting their views on why students drop out and how they might be helped. He decided to target middle school children, those in the sixth, seventh, and eighth grades, who had poor academic records, discipline problems, or evidenced general maladjustment in school. Peter reviewed the literature on successful dropout programs and, when he attended the Indiana NASW chapter's symposium that year, talked with other school social workers about their approaches to the problem. Then he began to formulate ideas for a prevention program in the form of a support group that focuses on issues that are important in achieving academic success.

With the program model in place, Peter turned his attention to recruiting students. He prepared a brochure for distribution to all sixth, seventh, and eighth graders with information about the program. Students were asked to contact Peter if they were interested in participating; the goal of this first effort was to have students identify themselves as volunteers. A week after the brochures were distributed, Peter had 15 students who wanted to participate. After talking with each of them and their teachers, all but one was considered appropriate for the support group.

At the first meeting, students were asked to enter into a "contract" in which realistic attendance and behavioral expectations for the school term are laid out on an individual basis (that is, an individualized contract was prepared for each of the 14 students). For example, Dean, one of the participants, had received four "F" and two "D" grades on his previous report card. Goals were set for Dean to bring two of the grades up to passing. Another student, Amy, had missed 14 days of school the previous term, and few of these absences were related to illness. Her goal was to reduce absences by one-third.

Group meetings were scheduled twice a week, with the students having a chance to decide in advance what would be discussed. Topics included vocational planning, alcohol and drug abuse, teen suicide, and teacher "attitudes." Throughout the 30-minute sessions, Peter kept coming back to the theme: these students can succeed in school.

The students were willing participants. They enjoyed the special attention and interest in them. Their teachers began to comment on the changes they witnessed in the students. At the end of the school year, more than half of the participating students had fully fulfilled their contracts. The remaining half had made substantial improvements.

With the success of this program, Peter was able to obtain a grant through the NEA's Operation Rescue to expand the number of participants for the following year. His hope was to establish a group for more middle school children and to initiate similar support groups for children in the ninth grade. Peter knew that behavior problems tend to increase due to poor adjustment to high school and the growing lure of alcohol and drugs.

Peter's work highlights a number of important social work functions. As the school social worker, Peter identifies the dropout rate as a serious problem that must be addressed. He then carries out the functions of coordination, research, and exchange to conduct an informal needs assessment by gathering information from other professionals and reviewing the literature. After the needs assessment is completed, Peter carries out the social work functions of program planning and development to initiate a support group for students at risk. Peter also constructs an evaluation tool to measure the outcome of the program so that he can secure additional funding from the NEA.

School dropout remains a serious concern. A report on school dropout conducted by the GAO (2002) recommended several ways to address this ongoing problem. One recommendation is to create a single source of comprehensive information about promising dropout prevention practices and programs. Other recommendations include evaluating the quality of existing dropout prevention research; determining how to best encourage or sponsor the needed level of evaluation of promising prevention programs and practices; and determining how best to disseminate information about successful programs. Social workers have much to contribute in all of these recommended areas to stem the tide of school dropout.

LEARNING DISABILITIES

Nearly 4 million school-age children in the United States have learning disabilities. A learning disability, according to Barker (1999), is "a descriptive term for children of normal or above-normal intelligence who experience a specific difficulty in school, such as dyslexia (reading difficulty), dysgraphia (handwriting difficulty), or dyscalculia (math or calculation difficulty)" (p. 272). A learning disability is thus a broad term that covers a range of possible causes, symptoms, treatments, and prognoses. Because learning disabilities can be manifest in many different forms, they are often difficult to diagnose (National Institute of Mental Health [NIMH], 2002).

Learning disabilities are hidden handicaps that can be lifelong conditions that affect a person's school or work life, daily routines, family life, and even friendships. Some people may have only one isolated learning disability, whereas others may have overlapping learning disabilities (NIMH, 2002).

The criteria and characteristics for diagnosing learning disabilities are detailed in the *Diagnostic and Statistical Manual of Mental Disorders IV-TR* (American Psychiatric Association, 2000), where they are divided into three categories: developmental speech and language disorders; academic skills disorders; and "other," a category which includes certain coordination disorders and some learning problems that are not covered by the other categories. Under each of these three categories are subcategories that provide greater description and specificity.

The causes of learning disabilities remain unknown. Research suggests that most learning disabilities do not stem from a single, specific area of the brain, but from difficulty in linking or bringing together information from various brain regions (NIMH, 2002).

A large proportion of affected children—mostly boys—display symptoms of hyperactivity, which may present as an inability to sit still, blurting out answers, and interrupting (Children and Adults with Attention Deficit Hyperactivity Disorders [CHADD], 2002a; NIMH, 2002). However, not all children with attention deficit disorder manifest hyperactive behavior. When hyperactivity is not present, teachers and pupil-services personnel may overlook the condition to explain a child's difficulty in school. Attention disorders, whether or not hyperactivity is present, are not considered learning disabilities in themselves. Attention problems seriously interfere with school performance and thus usually accompany academic skill disorders (NIMH, 2002), as illustrated in the following vignette.

ATTENTION DEFICIT HYPERACTIVITY DISORDER

Winston, an African American child eight years of age, moved to Kansas City with his family in late August, just in time to begin the new school year. He was placed in Mr. Davis's third grade class. Winston's school records had not yet arrived from his previous elementary school in Philadelphia, where the family had lived before, so there was no information available yet about his past school performance or any problems.

By the second day of school, Mr. Davis knew he had a difficult situation on his hands. Winston could not sit still for more than a few minutes; he was rough in his contacts with the other kids, and Mr. Davis feared that the one or two pushing incidents could easily turn into something worse.

Mr. Davis referred Winston to the director of special education for a special education evaluation. Winston's case was then passed on to a school social worker, Alicia. Alicia's first step was to contact Winston's previous school. The social workers and teachers at that school said that no evaluation had been performed but that Winston had demonstrated many behavioral problems and had very few friends. Alicia then referred Winston to the school psychologist for comprehensive testing.

While waiting for the results, Alicia used the time to observe Winston's behavior in the classroom, interview Mr. Davis, review past records, talk with his parents, and take a complete social history through interviews with both Winston and his parents. Alicia also had Winston's parents complete a behavioral checklist to determine specific areas of the child's difficulties. The extensive psychosocial history facilitates the identification of specific behaviors—such as fidgeting, interrupting, or talking excessively—that have occurred over time and may help in the diagnostic process. Alicia also referred Winston for a complete physical and neurological exam.

After considering all of this information, along with the results of the psychological and physiological testing, Winston was diagnosed with attention deficit hyperactivity disorder (ADHD). Alicia spoke with the family physician about Winston's diagnosis and the possibility of medication to alleviate some of the symptoms. The medication Ritalin was prescribed, and Alicia worked extensively with Winston's parents to educate them about the disorder and the effects of the medication. In addition, Alicia worked with Winston on a regular basis to establish a self-monitoring behavioral system, which has been shown to change classroom behavior over time. Alicia also worked with Mr. Davis, Winston's teacher, to develop and implement a reward system to reinforce Winston's positive behaviors.

Alicia is aware that diagnosis is only the first stage in a helping process that may span Winston's school career. Creating a plan and modifying it until it is right for the child is not a one-time occurrence. And because ADHD affects the child and the family in so many different ways, Alicia is prepared to offer direct help or referral over the long term in regard to educational, medical, emotional, and practical issues.

As this vignette suggests, there are a range of manifestations indicative of learning disabilities. In Winston's case, ADHD was identified

after an extensive assessment process that includes a psychosocial assessment, testing, and a physical and neurological examination. Sometimes the diagnosis of ADHD is deduced from ruling out other possible explanations. This is because some of the symptoms of ADHD overlap those of other learning disabilities. ADHD may also coexist with other disorders, such as mood disorders, anxiety disorders, tics and Tourette's syndrome, and depression (CHADD, 2002c).

In her school social work role, Alicia engages in assessment and diagnosis to determine the presenting problems. She then uses her coordination and organization skills as she interacts with the professionals at Winston's previous school as well as with Mr. Davis, Winston's current teacher. Alicia further engages in the functions of advice and counseling as she helps Winston's parents understand more about the disorder and the medications. For example, Alicia provides the parents with information about local support groups for parents of children with ADHD and tells them about the resources of the National Information Center for Children and Youth with Disabilities and its Web site (http://www.nichcy.org). Finally, she carries out the function of referral in her work with the psychologist and physician to determine the reasons for Winston's behavior.

The services provided by Alicia with and on behalf of Winston and his family are possible because learning disabilities fall under the purview of the Individuals with Disabilities Education Act of 1990 (P.L. 101-476) and Section 504 of the Rehabilitation Act of 1973 (P.L. 93-112). The provisions of these laws guarantee children with ADHD and other learning disorders a free and appropriate public education and, further, require that they be educated to the maximum extent appropriate with children who do not have disabilities (CHADD, 2002b). In the case of Winston, it was his transfer to a new school and the observations of his behaviors that precipitated the intervention of the social worker and other pupil-services personnel. Parents, too, who suspect that their children may have a learning disability may also contact the school and initiate an assessment process.

SOCIAL WORK PRACTICE IN HIGHER EDUCATION SETTINGS

The role of social workers in higher education is often overlooked. Many colleges and universities in the United States have counseling centers available to their student population, and social workers are among those employed in such settings. Such work, and the settings in which the work takes, place also fit the definition of school social work. However, here the population of students is older. Nevertheless, social workers in higher education settings also collaborate with members of other professions and disciplines and deal with many of the same presenting problems as do practitioners working in kindergarten through the 12th grade.

When social workers are employed in college or university counseling centers, the focus of their work is more on the psychosocial functioning of the individual student who, typically, seeks service. Referrals are less frequent than in K–12 grade. Also, it would be unusual for a social worker in a college setting to interact with the students' parents because most students are over age 18. However, the treatment setting is that of education, and many of the problems students experience may be a result of academic, adjustment, or behavioral issues—much as is the case for the kindergarten through 12th graders.

Students entering college may experience a difficult adjustment. They have left the protective environment of their family, friends, and community. Some students are away from home for the first time and find the adjustment to independent living difficult. Others experience academic difficulty and fear that they will flunk out. They may need help with study skills and require referral to the university's learning center.

Some students are disappointed with their academic progress. At one time they had been at the top of the class; now there is a higher level of competition. Social relationships grow more complex. Serious romantic relationships may end and leave a student in turmoil. They may find that many of the values to which they adhere are out of step with those of their new friends. Such values—and their behavioral manifestations—may include more liberal sexual behavior and drug and alcohol use. The conflict may arise for students between their own sense of right and wrong and peer pressure to be one of the crowd.

College students may also face different normative behavior than they have experienced in the past. For example, many college students have the idea that drinking hard is a ticket to social normalcy, because they have bought into the myth that regular heavy drinking is how most students socialize and become cool. Most campus cultures still promote the myth that heavy drinking is a normal, even necessary, college rite of passage (Mendelson, 2000).

Aggregate reports about drinking on college campuses have shown that about 1,400 college students die and about 500,000 are injured each year in accidents related to alcohol use. The impact of alcohol also extends to students who do not drink. Research has revealed that more than 600,000 college students are assaulted annually by other students who have been drinking, and more than 70,000 are victims of alcohol-associated sexual assaults or date rapes (Okie, 2002).

Helping students to resist the campus culture typically involves interventions at the individual level. There are also prevention efforts that have been initiated, albeit often ineffectually. Most have been administrative (policies and sanctions to limit student drinking), medical (identifying high-risk drinkers and getting them into treatment), or educational (informing students of alcohol's dangers). The Task Force on College Drinking of the National Institute on Alcohol Abuse and Alcoholism concluded that most efforts by colleges to reduce high-risk drinking have failed. Reasons include a focus on individuals rather than on the entire community. Educating students about alcohol does not work without trying to change a campus culture that encourages heavy drinking (Okie, 2002).

TACKLING CAMPUS DRINKING

Social worker Gerry Tornello works in the counseling center of Western University, where she provides both individual and group counseling. Gerry is alarmed by what she sees as a growing trend toward weekend alcohol binges. She learns about these weekend forays from the young men and women in her "coping" group—a group that is for students who are having difficulty adjusting to college life.

The details conveyed by group members fit with research reports Gerry has recently come across. According to the findings of a study conducted under the auspices of the National Institute on Alcohol Abuse and Alcoholism, roughly 40 percent of college students are binge drinkers (Morgan, 2002). The new data show that the consequences of heavy drinking by students are greater than previously realized. For example, about 31 percent of college students responding to a national survey in 1999 met accepted criteria for a diagnosis of alcohol abuse. Young Americans between the ages of 18 and 24 have the highest rates of periodic, heavy drinking of any age group, and college students drink more heavily than people of similar ages who are not in school (Okie, 2002). The researchers calculated that there are approximately 1,100 alcohol-related motor vehicle crash deaths and approximately 300 alcohol-related fatal injuries among college students annually.

Some of the members in Gerry's group own up to their own weekend binges. Some have sworn off of alcohol because of how bad they felt the day after. To Gerry's surprise, those who talked about participating in heavy drinking

included a fairly representative number of women. In Gerry's mind, alcohol was a "guy thing." Other members of the group verbalized disdain for the behavioral manifestations of alcohol. One person said, "It's not a lot of fun to be kept up half the night with the sound of my roommate vomiting." Gerry asks the group about their knowledge of the consequences of intoxication. They offer a variety of such consequences—including death, injury, assault, unprotected sex, drunk driving, vandalism, suicide, and academic problems. They also discuss how most people know about these risks, but it doesn't seem to make any difference in terms of their behavior. Gerry digests all that she has heard. At the next session of the group, she reflects back on the discussion about drinking. She wonders aloud if the group's goals might be expanded to deal with issues around drinking, particularly the pressures they may feel to participate in binging. As this theme fits well with the purposes of the group—adjusting to college—the group members are amenable.

Gerry begins to read all she can find about the best approaches to reduce drinking among high-risk students: programs that combine alcohol education, behavioral skills training, and motivational enhancement. One promising method for getting past young people's defenses is sometimes called the "social norms" approach. Gerry found a detailed report, "A Call to Action: Changing the Culture of Drinking at U.S. Colleges," from the National Institute on Alcohol Abuse and Alcoholism (2002). This approach is predicated on the assumption that most young people desire to be "normal," to fit in.

Social normalcy highlights the gap found on most campuses between what students perceive to be the normal levels of alcohol consumption (large quantities) and most students' actual consumption (moderate to none). Students are informed of the actual alcohol consumption on their campuses, usually on average from zero to three drinks at parties, to let students know that they are in fact normal. Abnormal, in this case, applies to those who drink in excess (Morgan, 2002).

Gerry tries this activity with the group at its next session. She asks the students to write down on a slip of paper how many drinks, on average, they think the most popular people on campus consume on a Friday night; then how many their close friends consume; and finally, how many they consume. Two people are put in charge of tallying the responses. Gerry then reads them. "Popular" students are rated as consuming eight to 10 drinks on a Friday night; their friends, five to six drinks per night; and themselves, one to three drinks per night.

Gerry then provides them with the facts about drinking patterns on campus. According to the social norms model, when students realize that most of the other students actually drink only moderately, if at all, they can begin to let go of the false belief that they will be more normal—more cool—if they drink excessively (Morgan, 2002). Gerry goes one step further. She suggest that on the next Friday evening, they observe and count how many drinks the most popular person in the room consumes and count, also, their own drinks and that of their friends.

This approach contrasts with traditional scare tactics, such as information campaigns that advertise the dangers of binge drinking. These tactics may at first cause alarm, but students tend to "blow them off" as untrue or not significant. Social norms messages, on the other hand, probably work because they speak to students as fellow adults, not as children needing to be lectured (Morgan, 2002).

When the students report back the following week on their "counts" of drinking, there is a collective "wow!" Their perceptions about drinking in excess as normative behavior were ill founded. Gerry notes with satisfaction, and some relief, that the lesson appears well learned; perhaps she should try this same approach later on with regard to drug use.

In this vignette, the focus of attention is on problem drinking, but the approach used could also be applied to any behaviors that place students at risk. Gerry, our social worker, has kept up with the literature and is therefore aware of and sensitive to binge drinking on campus. Since Gerry is already running a group for students who are having difficulty adjusting to college, she realizes that this forum would be an appropriate venue for addressing the potential or actuality of binge drinking behaviors. Thus, Gerry uses the modality of group work to educate members and to use the power of the group to redefine normal behavior.

A number of colleges and universities have established programs to address drug and alcohol use. The Center for Science in the Public Interest, with grant funds, has tested an advertising advocacy project at the University of North Carolina at Chapel Hill, Cornell University, and the University of Arkansas at Little Rock. The project is based on the premise that heavy drinking diminishes the quality of life for everyone on the campus. In addition to encouraging individual students to make safer drinking choices, the approach seeks to empower the less visible, but numerical majority of low-risk drinkers and abstainers and help them create for themselves a healthier campus environment. Student activists are helped to devise ways to stimulate peers to think and talk about healthier drinking and socializing. For example, the student group at Cornell, named Renaissance, helped create Slope Fest, an alcohol-free festival, directly alongside the traditional, booze-soaked, end-of-year party Slope Day. For the two years Slope Fest has existed, the number of injuries and incidents requiring police intervention has declined.

Rather than focusing on alcohol's primary effects on binge drinkers, the emphasis is on secondary effects on friends and neighbors (Mendelson, 2002). Ultimately, the goal is to shift the definition of what is considered "cool."

CHALLENGES TO SCHOOL-BASED PRACTICE

Schools continue to be an important arena of social work practice. Nevertheless, in the past several years, there have been challenges to school social work on a selective state-by-state basis due to fiscal cutbacks. Some states have sought to cut social work positions in budget-cutting moves, or may have to make a choice between retaining social workers or psychologists. In some states, prompt action on the part of social workers has saved jobs.

Because most pupil services are authorized by federal, state, and local legislation, these services are also subject to changes in political climate, often related to budget constraints. For example, the U.S. Department of Education sought to institute mandatory across-the-board budget trimming in response to the spending cuts mandated in 2000 by the Consolidated Appropriations Act. The effect would have been to diminish the dollars available to local educational agencies by $3 million (out of $20 million appropriated in 1999). With extensive lobbying on the part of school social workers and other pupil-services personnel, the cuts were forestalled ("School Counseling Program Saved," 2000).

Contracting out school-based mental health services has also been a strategy more recently employed to keep the cost of services lower (Canter, 1998). The result has been a growing emphasis on evaluating children to determine their eligibility for federally funded program participation and a decrease in direct and ongoing intervention.

The practice of school social work is further hindered by factors such as large caseloads, multibuilding assignments, and the unreasonable expectations of other professionals (Allen-Meares, 1994). Because many local education agencies have insufficient support staff, priorities must be established on the basis of their impact on children's well-being, the availability of other resources, and the social worker's professional skills.

As exemplified in the vignettes presented in this chapter, school social workers engage in both micro and macro functions. School social workers may provide direct counseling and supportive services to students, parents, and staff. They may be involved in program planning, development, and evaluation. They may also be called upon to advocate on behalf of pending legislation, legislative reauthorizations, and funding allocations. The context of practice is constantly changing and, therefore, all social workers—including those who work in schools—must be vigilant in monitoring legislative and judicial actions.

The career opportunities listed below are examples of typical school social work positions. However, regardless of their job description, social workers in this arena must become more involved in leadership and policy making in order to clearly define the profession's role in the educational system (Allen-Meares, 1994).

CAREER OPPORTUNITIES

The listings below, as in the other chapters, do not represent actual jobs available at this time. Rather, they highlight the position descriptions and qualifications listed in recent years for social work positions in schools.

Clinical Social Worker, School-Based Clinic

You will provide individual, family, and group treatment using a variety of modalities. Responsibilities include conducting comprehensive psychosocial assessments and evaluations, administering care management, home visits, and clinical groups; developing peer counseling and other programs; providing consultation to public school faculty and staff; and collaborating with the health center team and others to evaluate and develop treatment plans and measure overall effectiveness. Qualified candidates will have an MSW degree with current Connecticut LCSW and from three to five years broad-based clinical social work experience with a diverse adolescent population. Extensive clinical experience in a school-based clinic is strongly preferred. The regular schedule for this full-time position is Monday–Friday. (*NASW News*, January 2000, p. 21)

School Social Worker

Social workers are sought for work in Bethel, AS. The Lower Kuskokwim School District has a total of 23 village-based schools and five schools in Bethel. An MSW is required for a Social Worker II. The position entails work with students, parents, and staff in offering services to support and enhance students' educational programs and adjustments. These positions require extensive travel to remote locations. The school social worker will live and work in a cross-cultural, rural Alaskan environment. Candidate should have experience working with children, adolescents, and adults and an independent working style. Knowledge of the Yup'ik language and culture is preferred, but not required. This is a permanent position for a 10-month year. (*NASW News*, June 2001, p. 14)

School Social Worker

Bachelor's degree or foreign equivalent in social work or social welfare required. Under close supervision, the following work is closely monitored: aid adolescents and young adults with behavioral, mental, emotional, or physical problems related to life stresses. Practical and theological counseling emphasizing spiritual life and growth consistent with Presbyterian Church doctrine. Lead group counseling sessions; liaison between home, school, church, and community resources. Aid parents with counseling related to children's behavioral problems. Located in Denver, CO. (*NASW News*, March 2001, p. 15)

Clinical Social Worker

Counseling and psychological services, University of Kansas. Full-time unclassified position. Required qualifications are master's degree in social work from a Counsel on Social

Work Education accredited program; licensed for independent practice in Kansas at the LSCSW level or license eligible within one year; two years supervised clinical social work experience beyond the master's degree; strong written and oral communication skills. (*NASW News*, April 2000, p. 15)

Coordinator of Mental Health Services

Brigham and Women's Hospital is seeking a coordinator of mental health services for a school-based teen health center located in Jamaica Plain. Affiliated with the Brookside Community Health Center, the teen health center is seeking a clinical social worker to coordinate counseling and mental health services for a culturally diverse student population. In conjunction with the program manager, this position is responsible for the administrative, management, and clinical activities of the mental health component of school-based services. MA, LICSW, five years of direct services experience, three years of clinical and administrative supervisory experience, and experience with adolescents, school systems, and multicultural interventions. Bilingual (Spanish–English) preferred. (*NASW News*, January 1999, p. 24)

Senior Counselor

University of Michigan, Ann Arbor, MI. The University of Michigan Counseling and Psychological Services is a multidisciplinary and multicultural counseling center. Currently we are seeking qualified MSW/ACSW candidates to fill an open senior counselor position. Duties will include short-term individual psychotherapy; group counseling; crisis intervention and supervision in our intern training program. Other duties include design and delivery of workshops, consultation with faculty and staff, and outreach services. The candidate should have experience in one or more of the following areas: counseling Asian American, Native American, African American, Latina or Latino, international, lesbian, gay, bisexual, or transgender individuals; women's issues; and eating disorders. Qualified candidates will possess demonstrated abilities to provide a wide range of clinical services. State of Michigan certification or other state licensure eligibility is expected. Clinical experience in a college or university mental health setting is preferred. Other relevant clinical experience will also be considered. The position is a full-time, 12-month appointment. (*NASW News*, February 2001, p. 20)

Part-Time Social Worker

The Foote School in New Haven, CT, an independent kindergarten through ninth grade school with a diverse population, is seeking an experienced social worker to work 25 hours per week serving children and families individually and in groups. Candidate must have a master's degree, extensive experience in a school setting, be an effective communicator, and skilled at collaborating with appropriate professionals. (*NASW News*, November 2000, p. 17)

Director, Sexual Assault Prevention and Awareness Center

The University of Michigan Division of Student Affairs is seeking an experienced professional to administer the development, planning, and coordination of educational, counseling, crisis intervention, and referral programs and services related to sexual assault prevention and awareness for students; and to administer consultative, referral, and educational services for faculty and staff. Responsibilities: develop, plan, and implement policies and procedures for the center; develop, plan, and coordinate educational workshops, crisis intervention, counseling services, and referral programs for students, staff, faculty, and university departments; provide assistance in the design of appropriate research, programming, surveys, and grant writing; participate in the coordination of university responses to concerns about sexual assault issues; refer students, faculty, and staff to community agencies, organizations, and individuals to meet the needs relat-

ed to sexual assault; serve as advocate for survivors of sexual assault; represent the unit to student groups, university operating units, academic departments, and community organizations; promote and maintain good working relationships with key offices, including but not limited to Department of Public Safety, University Medical Center, Office of Student Conflict Resolution, and Counseling and Psychological Services; serve as consultant and coordinate staff training programs; and exercise functional and administrative supervision over professional, support, and student staff. Qualifications: a master's degree is required; a PhD is preferred; considerable experience in student services; considerable knowledge regarding the concerns and issues of sexual assault; considerable experience in developing, creating, and supervising a program. (*NASW News*, November 2001, p. 19)

Therapist, Team Leader

Montana Academy, a coeducational therapeutic boarding school for troubled adolescents, seeks a full time therapist, team leader. Montana Academy is on a beautiful 300-acre ranch in the Rocky Mountains of northwestern Montana. The academy includes an alternative high school and a therapeutic treatment program. Duties will include individual, group, and family therapy. Master's degree in social work, counseling, or related field required. Three years experience working with adolescents preferred. License eligibility required. (*NASW News*, January 2000, p. 27)

Staff Therapist, Counseling Center

The Syracuse University Counseling Center is recruiting three full-time, 11-month staff therapists to provide services to a large, diverse undergraduate and graduate population. Responsibilities include: providing short-term individual and group therapy, diagnostic assessment and triage, crisis intervention, outreach, consultation, and after-hours on-call services. Also responsible for implementing special projects and will act as a liaison with other university services and academic departments. Experience and expertise working with a diverse population is desired. Requirements include a doctorate in clinical or counseling psychology or a master's degree in social work from a duly accredited program, New York State licensure or state certification or license eligibility in respective profession is desired. Salary commensurate with education and experience. (*NASW News*, May 2002, p. 16)

REFERENCES

Abramson, J. S. (2002). Interdisciplinary team practice. In A. R. Roberts & G. J. Greene (Eds.), *Social workers' desk reference* (pp. 44–50). New York: Oxford University Press.

Adams, L., & Russakoff, D. (1999, June 12). Dissecting Columbine's cult of the athlete. *Washington Post*, p. A1.

Allen-Meares, P. (1994). Social work services in schools: A national study of entry-level tasks. *Social Work, 39*, 560–565.

American Psychiatric Association. (1994). *Diagnostic and statistical manual of mental disorders (4th ed.-TR)*. Arlington, VA: Author.

Baker, A. (2002, March 26). Crime is up in city schools, mostly in assault category. *New York Times*, p. B4.

Barker, R. L. (1999). *Social work dictionary* (4th ed.). Washington, DC: NASW Press.

Beaucar K. O. (1999, June). The violence has come home to roost. *NASW News*, p. 3.

Boes, M., & van Wormer, K. (2002). Social work with lesbian, gay, bisexual, and transgendered clients. In A. R. Roberts & G. J. Greene (Eds.), *Social workers' desk reference* (pp. 619–623). New York: Oxford University Press.

Canter, A. (1998). Purchasing school psychological services. In M. Gibelman & H. W. Demone, Jr. (Eds.), *The privatization of human services: Case studies in the purchase of services* (Vol. 2, pp. 123–150). New York: Springer.

Children and Adults with Attention Deficit Hyperactivity Disorders. (2002a). *The disorder named AD/HD* (CHADD Fact Sheet No. 1). Retrieved December 5, 2002, from http://www.chadd.org/fs/fs1.htm

Children and Adults with Attention Deficit Hyperactivity Disorders. (2002b). *Educational rights for children with AD/HD* (CHADD Fact Sheet No. 4). Retrieved December 5, 2002, from http://www.chadd.org/fs/fs4.htm

Children and Adults with Attention Deficit Hyperactivity Disorders. (2002c). *AD/HD and co-existing disorders* (CHADD Fact Sheet No. 5). Retrieved December 5, 2002, from http://www.chadd.org/fs/fs5.htm

Dane, E. (1985). Professional and lay advocacy in the education of handicapped children. *Social Work, 30*, 505–510.

Detroit, Mississippi layoffs spotlighted. (2002, June). *NASW News*, p. 12.

Dimichele, L. (1993). The role of the school social worker in early childhood special education. *School Social Work Journal, 18*, 9–16.

Education for All Handicapped Children Act of 1975, P.L. 94-142, 89 Stat. 773.

Education for All Handicapped Children Act Amendments of 1986, P.L. 99-457, 100 Stat. 1145.

Elementary School Counseling Demonstration Act of 1994, P.L. 103-382, 108 Stat. 3518.

Evans, R. (2002, April 29). Growing up gay. *New York Magazine*, pp. 28–34.

Fellin, P. (2000). Revisiting multi-culturalism in social work. *Journal of Social Work Education, 36*, 261–278.

Franklin, C. (1992). Family and individual patterns in a group of middle-class dropout youths. *Social Work, 37*, 338–344.

Freeman, E. M. (1995). School social work overview. In R. L. Edwards (Ed.-in-Chief), *Encyclopedia of social work* (19th ed., Vol. 3, pp. 2087–2099). Washington, DC: NASW Press.

Funds hiked for school counseling. (2001, March). *NASW News*, p. 6.

Gibelman, M. (1993). School social workers, counselors, and psychologists in collaboration: A shared agenda. *Social Work in Education, 15*, 45–53.

Gibelman, M., & Lens, V. (2002). Entering the debate about school vouchers: A social work perspective. *Children & Schools, 24,* 207–221.

Goren, S. (1981). The wonderland of social work in the schools: Or how Alice learned to cope. *School Social Work, 6*(1), 19–26.

Graham, T. L. (1993). Beyond detection: Education and the abused student. *Social Work in Education, 15,* 197–206.

Groups support team approach in pupil service. (1990, September). *NASW News,* p. 12.

Hall, J. A. (1990). Homelessness in the United States. In L. Ginsberg et al. (Eds.), *Encyclopedia of social work* (18th ed., 1990 Suppl., pp. 159–174). Silver Spring, MD: NASW Press.

Hare, I. (1995). School-linked services. In R. L. Edwards (Ed.-in-Chief), *Encyclopedia of social work* (19th ed., Vol. 3, pp. 2100–2109). Washington, DC: NASW Press.

Hawkins-Stafford Elementary and Secondary School Improvement Amendments Act of 1988, P.L. 100-297, 102 Stat. 140.

Hiratsuka, J. (1993, April). Outsiders: Gay teens, straight world. *NASW News,* p. 3.

Hiratsuka, J. (1994, June). First specialty section set to go. *NASW News,* p. 1.

Hodge, D. R. (2002). Working with Muslim youth: Understanding the values and beliefs of Islamic discourse. *Children & Schools, 24,* 1–64.

Improving America's Schools Act of 1994, P.L. 103-382, 108 Stat. 3518.

Individuals with Disabilities Education Act of 1990, P.L. 101-476, 104 Stat. 1142.

Landers, S. (1995, October). Special-education law under the gun. *NASW News,* p. 2.

Lewin, T. (2002, February 27). Disturbing finding on young drinkers proves to be wrong. *New York Times.* Retrieved February 27, 2002, from http://www.nytimes.com/2002/02/27/national/27ALCO.html

Loose, C., & Thomas, P. (1994, January 2). "Crisis of violence" becoming menace to childhood. *Washington Post,* pp. A1, A19.

Mattaini, M. (2001). *Peace power for adolescents: Strategies for a culture of nonviolence.* Washington, DC: NASW Press.

Mendelson, E. (2000, October 20). Emphasis on social norms can help curb drinking. *Chronicle of Higher Education,* p. B13.

Morgan, R. (2002, April 9). Report on alcohol use criticizes "culture of drinking" on campuses. *Chronicle of Higher Education.* Retrieved April 12, 2002, from http://chronicle.com/daily/2002/04/2002040903n.htm.

National Association of Social Workers. (1996). *Code of ethics.* Washington, DC: Author.

National Association of Social Workers. (2000). Education for children and youths. In *Social work speaks: National Association of Social Workers policy statements, 2000-2003* (5th ed., pp. 89–95). Washington, DC: Author.

National Association of Social Workers. (2001a, April 13). *Conflict resolution training found to curb school violence* (Press release). Retrieved September 7, 2002, from http://www.socialworkers.org/pressroom/2001/032301b.asp

National Association of Social Workers. (2001b, May 2). *Suicide: Social workers agree, it's a national public health issue* (Press release). Retrieved September 7, 2002, from http://social workers.org/pressroom/2001/050201b.htm

National Association of Social Workers, National Committee on Racial and Ethnic Diversity. (2001c). *NASW standards for cultural competence in social work practice.* Washington, DC: Author.

National Association of Social Workers. (2001d, June 25). *Ready for back-to-school—A how-to guide for living nonviolently* (Press release). Retrieved September 9, 2001, from http://socialworkers.org/pressroom/2001/062501.htm

National Association of Social Workers. (2002). *NASW standards for school social work services.* Washington, DC: Author.

National Center on Addiction and Substance Abuse at Columbia University. (2002, February 26). *Teen tipplers: America's underage drinking epidemic.* Retrieved December 4, 2003, from http:// www.casacolumbia.org/absolutenm/templates/articles.asp?articleid=247&zoneid=31

National Institute of Mental Health. (2002). Learning disabilities. Retrieved November 4, 2002, from http://www.nimh.nih.gov/publicat/learndis.htm

Nightingale, H., & Morrissette, P. (1993). Dating violence, attitudes, myths, and preventive programs. *Social Work in Education, 15*, 225–232.

No Child Left Behind Act of 2001, P.L. 107-110, 115 Stat. 1425.

Okie, S. (2002, April 10). Study cites alcohol link in campus deaths. *Washington Post*, p. A2.

O'Neill, J. V. (2000a, January). School credential has new criteria. *NASW News*, p. 6.

O'Neill, J. V. (2000b, June). Aid offered on reporting of child abuse. *NASW News*, pp. 1, 8.

Pincus, H. W. (2002, June 14). *Anti-semitism is "right here." Jewish Standard*, p. 7.

Rehabilitation Act of 1973, P.L. 93-112, 87 Stat. 355.

Sanders, D., & Satir, V. (1995). School social work overview. In R. L. Edwards (Ed.-in-Chief), *Encyclopedia of social work* (19th ed., Vol. 3, pp. 2087–2099). Washington, DC: NASW Press.

School counseling program saved. (2000, March). *NASW News*, pp. 1, 10.

School counseling, stable families measures pass. (2002, February). *NASW News*, p. 4.

Schools act boosts social workers' role. (1995, January). *NASW News*, pp. 1, 14.

Siegel, C., Attkisson, C., & Carson, L. G. (1995). Assessment. In J. E. Tropman, J. L. Erlich, & J. Rothman (Eds.), *Tactics and techniques of community intervention* (3rd ed., pp. 10–34). Itasca, IL: F. E. Peacock.

Social work in the public eye. (1999, January). *NASW News*, p. 17.

Social work in the public eye. (2001, July). *NASW News*, p. 13.

Squires, S. (1995, May 9). Sharp rise reported in youth suicides. *Washington Post*, Health, p. 5.

Stoesen, L. (2002, May). IDEA reauthorization proposals offered. *NASW News*, p. 5.

Surgeon General's Call to Action to Prevention Suicide. (1999). *At a glance: Suicide among the young*. Retrieved March 21, 2001, from http://sur geongeneral.gov/library/calltoaction/fact3.htm

Tarasoff v. Board of Regents of the University of California, 33 Cal. 3d 275 (1973), 529 P. ed 553 (1974), 17 Cal. 3d 425 (1976), 551 P. 2d 334 (1976), 131 Cal. Rptr. 14 (1976).

Tower, K. (2000). Image crisis: A study of attitudes about school social workers. *Social Work in Education, 22*, 83–94.

Troubled gay youth find help in school. (1985, September). *NASW News*, p. 12.

U.S. Department of Education, National Institute on the Education of At-Risk Students. (1996, March). *High school dropout rate*. Retrieved August 12, 2000, from http://www.ed.gov/pubs/OR/ ConsumerGuides/ dropout.html

U.S. Department of Education. (2002). *24th annual report to Congress on the implementation of the Individuals with Disabilities Education Act*. Retrieved November 1, 2003, from http://www. ed.gov/about/reports/annual/osep/2002/ index.html

U.S. General Accounting Office. (2002, February). *School dropouts: Education could play a stronger role in identifying and disseminating promising prevention strategies* (Report No. GAO-02-240). Washington, DC: Author

Vallianatos, C. (2000, November). Additional schools get grants. *NASW News*, p. 1.

Valliantos, C. (2001, July). Programs keep the peace among teens. *NASW News*, p. 3.

Vallianatos, C. (2002, January). Anti-bullying effort mounted. *NASW News*, p. 9.

Ziesemer, C., Marcoux, L., & Marwell, B. E. (1994). Homeless children: Are they different from other low-income children? *Social Work, 39*, 658–668.

Chapter Eight AGING

Social workers work with elderly people in hospitals, nursing homes, hospices, retirement communities, family services agencies, state departments of aging, area agencies on aging, and other related public and private entities. Within these settings, social workers provide services that pertain to long-term care, health and mental health, recreation and quality of life, intergenerational issues, death and dying, nutrition, housing, and at-home supervision and assistance. Social workers carry out functions such as individual and family counseling and support, empowering clients to access community resources, and developing programs to strengthen links between formal and informal service providers.

To understand what social workers do in working with older citizens, it is essential to first understand the unique characteristics of the population. Accordingly, this chapter includes a brief review of the demographics of and issues affecting older citizens. A description of the current federal, state, and local frameworks for providing aging services is then provided. Finally, vignettes illustrating the range of social work involvement are presented within the context of several of the major subcategories of social work practice in this service area.

THE POPULATION
In 1900 there were 3 million Americans, or 4.1 percent of the population, age 65 years and older.

The current population 65 years and over is about 34.7 million, or 13 percent of the population. In 1999, there were 4.2 million Americans age 85 and older, about 1.5 percent of the population. The number of people 65 years of age and older in the United States is expected to double over the next three decades to nearly 70 million, or 20 percent of the population (National Council on Aging [NCOA], 2002).

The demographic profile of older Americans points to a number of potential physical, social, and psychological vulnerabilities:

- Women live longer. In 1998, there were 143 older women for every 100 older men.
- Because women, as a group, outlive men, men ages 65 and over are more likely to be married than women of a similar age.
- In 1998 the median income of older people was $18,166 for men and $10,054 for women.
- About 10 percent of older Americans were poor in 1998—about the same proportion as the adult population under age 65.
- The old–old population is soaring. The population ages 80 and over is projected to grow to 14.9 million, or 4.4 percent (from the current 9.2 million, or 3.35 percent) by the year 2050. (NCOA, 2002)

The growing number of older people in the United States is leading to an increased demand for health and social services oriented to enhancing or restoring their capacity for optimal social functioning. The increasing need for social workers in the field of aging is directly related to the absolute and proportional growth of this population in American society.

The elongated life expectancy of people has led to the identification of three groups who make up the aged population: (1) the young old or those ages 65 to 74, (2) the aged or those ages 75 to 84, and (3) the old-old or those 85 years and older (Barker, 1999). The term "frail elderly" refers to "older men and women who suffer from or are vulnerable to physical or emotional impairments and require some care because they have limited ability or opportunity to provide entirely for their own needs" (Barker, 1999, p. 181).

There are a number of problems that a sizable proportion of the older population experience in the United States. These include decreased income, physical illness, frailty, how to use leisure time, altered familial relationships, physical and psychological abuse, alcohol-related problems, living arrangements, and crime victimization (Karger & Stoesz, 1998). In addition, age discrimination—unfair treatment of people on the basis of age—has affected the ability of the aged to obtain and retain employment or be considered for promotions. Ageism, stereotyping, and generalizing about people on the basis of their age also have widespread repercussions for older people. Some of these problems are exacerbated for the minority elderly, with statistics confirming that this group has a much higher incidence of poor education, poverty, substandard housing, ill health, and malnutrition. The delivery of services to minority elderly is often impeded by language and cultural differences, physical isolation, and lower income. The quickly growing populations of older adults have special needs that must be understood and met in order to allow them to maximize their independence and quality of life (National Association of Area Agencies on Aging [NAAAA], 2002a).

POLICIES AND PROGRAMS

The Social Security Act of 1935 (42 U.S.C. 301 et seq.) included two key systems: federal social insurance for people who have been connected to the workforce, and federal/state categorical assistance. The term "social security" has come to be associated primarily with the social insurance component that seeks to provide old age, survivors, and disability insurance benefits to workers and their families. The act established the Old Age and Survivors and Disability Insurance (OASDI) program. OASDI provides monthly benefits to retired people, families whose wage earner died, and workers who become unemployed due to accident or illness. Workers qualify for these benefits by having been employed for a minimum amount of time and by having contributed to the program. The intent, as the name suggests, is to provide security by protecting individuals from unforeseen catastrophes. Once an individual has qualified for protection, certain other family members are also eligible for benefits. Financial need is not a requirement. Unlike welfare, which is a categorical assistance program administered by the states, social security benefits are paid to an individual or his or her family at least in part on the basis of the person's employment record and past contributions to the system (AARP, 2002). These contributions are in the form of a tax that is deducted from workers' payroll checks. The system is administered by the Social Security Administration.

The Social Security Act is considered to be the foundation for later legislation to expand the types and scope of benefits and services for older Americans. Medicare Part A and Part B, Medicaid, and the Supplemental Security Income programs are among the important additions to early legislative provisions for the aged population (AFL-CIO, 2003; Torres-Gil & Puccinelli, 1995).

Throughout the years there has been a shift from simply providing a minimum subsistence level of income to actual income replacement. This goal was actuated through Title XVI of the

Social Security Act, commonly known as Supplemental Security Income (SSI). Basically, SSI is a monthly cash payment to people who are aged, blind, or otherwise disabled and who are living at or below subsistence levels. Today, SSI provides a significant portion of income for most retirees in the lower and middle income levels. Many people also receive pensions, income from other assets, or part-time wages.

In 1965 Medicare (Parts A and B) and Medicaid were enacted to assure medical services without subjecting citizens to the catastrophic costs of acute care. Social security, SSI, Medicare, and Medicaid have had a positive impact on the overall status of older Americans. Since 1966, the poverty rate for the elderly has fallen from 28.5 percent to 11.7 percent in 1994 and about 10 percent in 1999 (Choudhury & Leonicio, 1997; NCOA, 2002). However, the future of these programs remains an open question.

Older Americans Act

The current framework for aging services finds its basis in the Older Americans Act of 1965 (OAA) (P.L. 89-73), which created a national network of federal, state, and local agencies to serve the elderly population. Its purpose is to ensure minimum standards for programs and services for older Americans by providing guidelines for and categorical funding in response to the diverse needs of older people (Laureano, 1999). Amendments to the act in 1978 and 1981 introduced targeted initiatives for ethnic and racial minorities and other measures to make the OAA more responsive to the diverse economic and social situations of older people (Binstock, 1995).

On the federal level, OAA established the Administration on Aging (AoA), which is under the auspices of the U.S. Department of Health and Human Services. There are 57 state offices on aging and, at the local level, more than 655 area agencies on aging. In addition, the act provides funding to more than 190 Native American tribal organizations in an effort to target the most vulnerable elderly Native American

Indian population (AoA, 2002a). Title III of the OAA appropriates federal funds to states and territories based on the size of their population over 60 years of age. The states then make grants to local area agencies on aging to administer a wide range of services for the elderly.

The OAA was reauthorized in 2000 and maintains the original 10 objectives aimed at preserving the rights and dignity of the nation's older citizens (AoA, 2002a). The 2000 amendments retain the targeting provisions for low-income minorities and add a new focus on older individuals residing in rural areas. The amendments also retain several priority services, including access, in-home, and legal services. A new feature of the 2000 amendments is the National Family Caregiver Support Program to address the needs of caregivers. Finally, a new part of Title VI, Grants to Native Americans, authorizes a program to support caregivers of Native American elders (AoA, 2002b).

Fiscal allocations to support programs for older Americans have increased. For fiscal year 2002 there were significant increases in funding for the OAA and other programs to benefit seniors and their families, including:

- $357 million for supportive services, an increase of $32 million over the preceding fiscal year
- $141.5 million for the National Family Caregiver Support Program, an increase of $16.5 million
- $390 million for congregate meals, an increase of over $11.6 million
- $176.5 million for home-delivered meals, an increase of $24.5 million
- $445.1 million for the Title V Senior Community Service Employment Program, an increase of about $5 million
- $893.4 million for the National Institute on Aging, an increase of $107 million
- $2 billion for the Low Income Home Energy Assistance Program, an increase of $300 million. (NCOA, 2001)

Unmet Needs

Older Americans constitute an increasingly powerful political force. AARP for example, boasts a membership of 35 million; advocating for and on behalf of older Americans is among the major goals of this organization (AARP, 2002). The ARRP and NCOA (among other national advocacy organizations) establish public policy agendas and strategies to effect policy change, utilizing their networks of members and organizational affiliates to lobby, provide testimony, and monitor the progress of legislation. These groups work to meet the unmet needs of older people and to improve their quality of life.

Many issues remain on the agenda, including access to and cost of health care. The channeling of Medicare recipients into health maintenance organizations (HMOs) was intended to promote comprehensive care at lesser cost. Despite such promises, the elderly who are served through Medicare HMOs were found to use an average of nearly 50 percent more of their own money for medical care in 2001 than they did three years earlier. Those in poor health paid even a larger proportion for out-of-pocket care (Freudenheim, 2002). Findings of a study conducted by researchers at Mathematica Policy Research revealed that out-of-pocket costs rose 62 percent in 2001 for those in poor health, due primarily to spending for prescription drugs, premiums, and other services not fully covered by Medicare.

The AARP has identified a "prescription drug crisis" and has intensified its campaign for a Medicare drug benefit (Novelli, 2002a). Older adults, who rely on prescription drugs more than any other age group, increasingly find themselves uninsured or with limited medical coverage. The current Medicare program does not cover most outpatient prescription drugs (NAAAA, 2002b). Social workers are collaborating with advocacy groups for the elderly (that is, NAAAA, NCOA, and AARP) to lobby for the inclusion of a prescription benefit through the Medicare program.

Another major policy concern is the very future of the social security system. For several years, various government departments and special commissions have debated the future of social security, which is the major public program to ensure some level of financial security for older Americans. It is predicted that the social security fund will run dry when the baby boomers age into the system. One recurrent theme is to privatize social security—using the power of Wall Street and the investment savvy of individuals to establish investment accounts (see, for example, Duka & Carlson, 2002). However, privatization has lost steam, particularly with the stock market plunge of 2001–2002, in which many Americans who invested in individual retirement accounts (IRAs) found that their "nest eggs" had suffered a severe blow (Krugman, 2002).

Also on the policy agenda is regulation and monitoring of the nursing home industry; questions have been raised about the breadth and quality of psychosocial services provided by nursing homes. The U.S. Department of Health and Human Services' Office of Inspector General initiated a study to explore nursing home conditions and services. One part of the investigation concerned the legality and consequences of hiring social work "designees." Such designees usually have little or no training or formal professional education but nevertheless are hired to perform social services functions in skilled nursing facilities (O'Neill, 2002).

At issue is compliance with the Nursing Home Reform Act, a component of the Omnibus Reconciliation Act of 1987 (P.L. 100-203). The law requires skilled nursing facilities to provide "medically related social services to attain or maintain the highest practicable physical, mental and psychosocial well-being of each resident." Other provisions of the act require that "the services provided or arranged by the facility must meet professional standards of quality" (O'Neill, 2002, p. 6). Social workers had earlier lobbied successfully to postpone a ruling by the Health Care

Financing Admini-stration that social workers could no longer provide clinical services to patients in skilled nursing facilities and independently bill Medicare. Had the ruling gone into effect, the result would have been to end case-by-case mental health consultation care by clinical social workers to frail elderly and disabled people living in nursing homes (Nieves, 1999; O'Neill, 1999b). However, this issue is postponed, not resolved.

There are also gaps in existing social policies that may adversely affect the elderly. For example, it is estimated that approximately 7 million Americans age 65 and older will need long-term care in the year 2002 and that this number will nearly double to 12 million by 2020 (Roper, 2001). A study conducted under the auspices of AARP found that Americans age 45 years and over are relatively uninformed about long-term care services and the attendant costs. Further, Americans in this age group believe they have long-term care coverage when they probably do not (Roper, 2001).

Most people age 65 and over live with family members, and of these about two out of three live with spouses or other family members. Twenty percent of men age 65 or above live alone compared with 42 percent of women within the same age group (NCOA, 2002). The two groups most likely to live alone are those over 75 years of age and those with the lowest incomes—the same groups most likely to suffer serious health deterioration or loss of income, leaving them in a housing crisis (AARP, 2002). Despite the chance of health or income emergencies, more than half of older Americans have done very little, if any, planning for the future.

There is a direct relationship between current social policy provisions and the types of programs of services provided by social workers in a variety of settings established to meet the needs of older Americans. Gaps in social policy also result in unmet needs and gaps in social provision.

SOCIAL WORK PRACTICE IN THE FIELD OF AGING

Despite the important roles for social workers in the field of aging, a relatively small proportion of social workers are involved in the provision of services to older people. There is consensus that the profession of social work has failed to address the need for adequately trained social workers to work with the elderly. The National Institute on Aging projected a need for between 40,000 and 50,000 geriatric social workers by the year 2000. But barely 10 percent of that number is available (O'Neill, 1999a).

The need for a stronger social work presence in the field of gerontology has been consistently echoed. An earlier report published by the Association for Gerontology in Higher Education, "Social Work and Gerontology: A Status Report," concluded that social work education is not turning out a sufficient number of practitioners prepared to work with the growing elderly population ("Too Few Trained for Aging Work," 1991). Since issuance of that report, the situation has not appreciably changed. Reasons for this gap in the social work labor force specializing in the field of aging may relate to historic hiring patterns, which have favored paraprofessionals and BSW level workers, as well as relatively low salaries in this field (Barth, 2001; Gibelman & Schervish, 1997).

To address the need for a larger social work presence in the field of aging, the Hartford Foundation, in 2000, provided funding for two grants totaling more than $8 million to further the development of education in social work to improve the number and training of social work educators and students in gerontological social work. One grant funded a fellowship program for doctoral dissertation research in the field. The second grant funded a faculty scholars program to provide career development and support research on improving geriatric outcomes in community-based health settings. The grants are administered by the Gerontological Society of America ("$8 Million Goes," 2000).

The NASW has also sought to encourage and promote the interest of social workers in the field of aging. In 1998, NASW initiated a special member section for social workers working in gerontological settings ("NASW Establishes Section," 1998). This section seeks to enhance communication and information sharing among social workers in the field of aging and to keep members informed about new developments in the field.

THE CONTINUUM OF CARE

The aging process often means a decrease in some cognitive and physical capabilities. Diminution of capacity may be very mild, such as needing help to reach items on the top shelf of a cabinet, to severe, at which time an individual may need help with the gamut of tasks of daily living, from dressing to bathing to eating. The range of needs has its counterpart in a continuum of services. Some service needs may be met informally through family and friends. Some services needs may involve the use of care systems for a few hours a day. Other service needs may be met by alternative living environments. Several of these alternative care services, which fall along a continuum from assistance in one's home to nursing home care, are discussed in the following sections.

Case Management Services

As the baby boom generation moves into middle age, their parents become senior citizens with extended life expectancies and complicated care issues ranging from physical health to depression. There has been a decrease in the average number of children per family, and as a result, there are fewer familial caregivers for parents as they grow older. Nevertheless, it is estimated that over 80 percent of people in need of long-term care rely upon family members and friends to provide uncompensated caregiving. The estimated value of such care, if purchased, is $196 billion per year (NAAAA, 2002a).

Individuals in midlife with significant family and work responsibilities find themselves sandwiched between the care demands of their children and those of their parents, leading to coinage of the term "the sandwich generation." The proportion of Americans age 60 with a least one living parent has risen dramatically—from 7 percent in 1900 to 13 percent in 1940 to 24 percent in 2000 (NCOA, 2002). Forty years ago, 14 percent of Americans age 50 still had both parents living. That proportion has almost doubled to 27 percent (Uhlenberg, 1996).

The situation is further complicated by the increasing mobility of society, often resulting in long-distance caregiving of older relatives; older people may be visited only once or twice a year. Such visits can be jarring, as the impact of the aging process hits home. The adult child may realize that the father is no longer practicing good hygiene; he is no longer steady on his feet and is afraid that he will fall in the shower. Or the parent may exhibit signs of dementia, such as repeating the same story or asking the same question over and over (Crowley, 2001; Marcell, 2000). These situations cause a great deal of stress for both younger adults as well as older adults who need services but do not want to leave their homes for a more protective environment.

Case management services are increasingly considered to be important in evaluating and monitoring the services needed by and provided to older adults. Barker (1999) offered a definition of the case management function:

A procedure to plan, seek, and monitor services from different social agencies and staff on behalf of a client. . . . [A case manager] coordinates services, advocates for the client, and sometimes controls resources and purchases services for the client. . . . Case management may involve monitoring the progress of a client whose needs require the services of several professionals, agencies, health care facilities, and human services programs. It typically involves case finding, comprehensive multidimensional assessment, and frequent reassessment. . . . Social workers and nurses are the professional groups most often called on to fulfill this function. Case management is seen as an increasingly important way of limiting problems arising from fragmentation of services, staff turnover, and inadequate coordination between providers. (p. 62)

The five basic social work functions involved in case management include identification of clients; assessment of needs; services or treatment planning; referral to appropriate services; and monitoring case progression and services delivery (Garner, 1995; Rose & Moore, 1995), as illustrated in the following case example.

Case Management Services for the Elderly

Mary Bartow is 78 years old and has lived in Bismarck, ND, for the last 60 years. Her husband died two years ago and their only child, Matthew, lives in Colorado Springs with his wife and two teenage daughters. Matthew worries about his mother. She seems depressed and she rarely leaves the house. She refuses to try the local senior center activities and she won't hear of moving to Colorado. She said that she would just stay in Bismarck until she died, and she didn't think that would be too much longer.

Matthew didn't know what to do so he went to see the employee assistance social worker at his place of work. The social worker suggested a case manager for his mother and gave him a name and number of a case management agency in the Bismarck area. Before calling the agency, Matthew spoke with his mother to tell her about his plan. He decided to be firm with her and not ask permission. He knew she would probably negate the idea. As expected, Mary indicated that she had no need for any outside help. However, she finally agreed to see a case manager to make Matt "happy." Matthew then called the agency and

explained the situation. He was told about the agency and its services and fees. Written information was also sent to him.

Matthew was informed that Dana Forkner, a social worker, would follow through directly with his mother. Because Mrs. Bartow would be the primary client, it was also explained to Matthew that discussions with his mother would be confidential unless she agreed that Dana could share the information or unless there appeared to be imminent risk to Mrs. Bartow.

When Dana first arrived she spent more than an hour talking with Matthew's mother and recognized her depression and loneliness. After meeting with Mrs. Bartow a second time, Dana identified three major issues: (1) she needed to establish contact with other people to reduce her loneliness; (2) she needed to get a checkup and a new prescription for her eyeglasses; and (3) she needed to get at least one nutritionally sound meal a day.

Dana went back to her agency and first contacted Mrs. Bartow's doctor to arrange an appointment. She then called the local transportation company with which her agency contracted and arranged transportation to take Mrs. Bartow to and from the appointment. Dana then contacted a church near Mrs. Bartow's home where congregate meals are served every evening to a group of senior citizens who come together to eat and socialize. There are often activities before or after the meals that are sponsored by the local senior center. There was room for another person, so Dana arranged for Mrs. Bartow to attend Monday through Friday. She thought this would allow Mrs. Bartow not only to get a good meal, but also to interact with other people. Perhaps, Dana thought, after seeing some of the activities offered by the senior center, Mrs. Bartow might eventually agree to go there during the day. Dana then had to recontact the transportation company to arrange for daily transportation for Mrs. Bartow to and from the church where the evening meals are served. Of course, before con-

firming any arrangements, Dana had explicit approval from Mrs. Bartow to proceed.

After the initial plan was put into place, Dana called Matthew. She reassured him that important steps had been taken to address his mother's needs. Dana urged Matthew to be in touch with his mother by phone so that she could tell him the details of her new experiences. Dana plans to monitor Mrs. Bartow's progress and to encourage her to participate more fully in the programs available to her.

In this scenario, Dana first assessed Mrs. Bartow's situation and needs. She then offered brief counseling to Mrs. Bartow to help her develop an initial understanding of her situation and the options available to her. She used this counseling opportunity to encourage and facilitate a medical appointment for Mrs. Bartlow and her enrollment in the meals program. With Mrs. Bartow's agreement, Dana also coordinated with providers of transportation services. Dana construes these interventions as preliminary; she plans to monitor Mrs. Bartow's progress, continue to offer her services, and reassess the client's needs based on information that becomes available.

Matthew's concerns about his mother were justified. Such concerns are also shared by many baby boomers who discover that roles can reverse—that children become caregivers to their parents. Matthew was not in a position to assist his mother directly. But he was resourceful. Through such services as the Eldercare Locator (800-677-1116 or http://www.n4A.org), Matthew was able to contact a local agency and, through it, obtain social work services to assess his mother's status and put into place the supports she needed.

Opportunities for social workers in the provision of case management services to older Americans are on the increase. In early 2002, $128 million in grants to states was released under the National Family Caregiver Support Program, which is administered by AoA. This program, created under the 2000 amendments to the OAA, helps family members provide care for the elderly at home. The grant money is used to support programs that provide critical home and community-based services to help families maintain their caregiving roles (U.S. Department of Health and Human Services, 2002). Services provided under these grants include information and assistance, counseling, support groups and training, respite services to provide short breaks for caregivers as needed, and supplemental services that complement care provided by informal caregivers.

As the population ages, social workers have increasingly recognized the need for greater collaboration between professionals and families, both because families have needs of their own and because families often provide much of the care for their aging relatives. Therefore, many social work interventions include the goal of empowering families and helping them to develop and use their own strengths and skills (Hooyman & Gonyea, 1995).

Social workers have sought to bring public attention to the availability of caregiving services and to the needs of elderly people. For example, Scarsdale, New York, social worker Joseph Ilardo has made several appearances on NBC's *Today* show and on radio shows about elder care and caring for ailing parents or other family members. In a recent *Today* show interview, Mr. Ilardo spoke about how to help parents without taking over, even if they are not functioning well. He also coauthors a regular column—"Dilemma Doctors"—in the magazine *Today's Caregiver* and has published advice columns in popular magazines and online ("Social Work in the Public Eye," 2002).

Community-Based Services

Aging in place has been identified as a primary desire among many older Americans, and 85 percent of the respondents to an AARP survey said that they wanted to stay in their own homes and never move (AARP, 2002). Services such as home-delivered meals, homemaker services, and respite care help people to remain independent in their own communities (NAAAA, 2000). The NAAAA, the umbrella organization for the nation's area agencies on aging, has been a strong advocate for community-based services.

Adult senior centers focus on providing social, physical, religious, and recreational activities for older people. Such centers are usually publicly funded, although there are some privately funded facilities. These centers may also provide or refer clients to congregate meals, which ensure a nutritious meal for a group of older people at a group facility; legal assistance programs, which assist the elderly in legal issues ranging from wills to pension problems; and employment services, which help older citizens by providing preretirement counseling as well as training, education, and job placement, if appropriate (NAAAA, 2002a).

In the following case, a social worker reaches out to a senior citizen to assess needs and offer services. In this case, the agency and social worker are "real"; the client situation represents a composite of situations that characterize the clientele of the agency.

REACHING OUT TO THE ELDERLY

Robin Kahan is director of social services at the Jewish Community Council (JCC) in New York City. The JCC was started in 1973 by a coalition of 40 local Jewish organizations as an umbrella agency to preserve the community and service its residents. At that time, middle-class families had fled the neighborhood for the more affluent suburbs, leaving behind a disproportionately high elderly population. The community has changed substantially in the ensuing years. Some of the Jewish immigrants have stayed and have aged in place, but there has been a large influx of immigrants from the former Soviet Union and the Dominican Republic. The JCC has sought to attract Russian immigrants to the neighborhood to help preserve the

Jewish community and has developed a full gamut of refugee resettlement services for them.

Robin is one of two social workers employed by the JCC. There are also four case aids who conduct friendly visits to the agency's clients; one of them speaks Russian. About 120 elderly clients are registered with the JCC for daily services. A far larger number of clients receive concrete services, such as access to the food pantry, provision of weekend meals, case management assistance, English as a second language classes, transportation service, and housing assistance.

Robin's job is multifaceted. The broad area of her concern is with services to the elderly, who are often homebound and isolated. She supervises the case aids and also attends community board meetings, writes grants, gives presentations to community agencies about JCC services, and provides direct services.

Case assessment is also an important aspect of Robin's job. Recently, Robin received a phone call from a neighborhood landlord about a tenant in the building who is constantly overflowing her bathtub and causing damage to her own apartment and to the apartment below her. Robin immediately realized that this tenant was at risk of eviction or, possibly, intervention by the city's adult protective services. Robin first called around to the other agencies in the neighborhood to determine if the tenant was receiving services elsewhere. She was not. The landlord, however, was unable to provide Robin with the tenant's phone number because the spelling of the last name was not correct and Robin could not obtain the number from directory assistance. No other action was taken in response to this call, except that Robin encouraged the landlord to get back in touch with her if there were any further problems.

About a week later the landlord called back to tell Robin about another flood. This time he had obtained the tenant's phone number from a neighbor and provided it to Robin. Robin immediately called Mrs. W, introduced herself, and told her a little about the services of the

JCC. She did not mention the flooding problem during this initial contact. Mrs. W agreed to have Robin come and visit her and an appointment was set up for the following day.

Mrs. W seems cautious when she opened the door for Robin but invited her into the living room. Robin told her about the JCC and found that Mrs. W had heard of the agency from neighbors. She seemed to have a positive impression about the agency. Robin further explained her role as a social worker and the desire of the agency to help senior citizens in the neighborhood by providing services that may help make life a little easier. Robin did not refer to the call from the landlord.

Robin observed that Mrs. W is a small woman, about 80 years of age. She came to the United States from Russia in the late 1930s with her parents and settled into the neighborhood. She has never lived anywhere else. She married someone also from Russia, but Mr. W died of a heart ailment over 30 years ago. They had no children. Since then, she has lived on her own. She worked for a number of years as a seamstress but stopped working when her eyesight began to deteriorate.

At first, Mrs. W was not very talkative, and she tended to answer Robin's questions in monosyllables. But after a while, she became visibly more relaxed. Robin was able to learn that Mrs. W shops and makes her own meals. She is proud of her independence. However, when asked about friends and relatives, it became clear that Mrs. W is isolated. In fact, she described herself as a "hermit." She does have one niece who visits occasionally, although Mrs. W seemed disappointed that the visits were not more often. Most of her friends have died. She reads a lot and watches television. She would not disclose information about her finances but indicated that she was "okay" in terms of having enough money to pay her rent and eat.

Robin asked if she could see the apartment to see if any repairs were needed. Robin was able to determine that the apartment was clean.

However, the bathroom was in need of grouting, and there were no safety bars in the tub.

Mrs. W admitted having some recent issues with memory and gave the example of forgetting to turn off the water in the tub. Robin asked Mrs. W whether any problems has resulted from the tub overflowing. With this opening, Mrs. W admitted that the landlord was very unhappy with her and had threatened possible eviction if it happened again. Mrs. W said that she had just put this threat out of her thoughts—who would evict an "old lady"? Robin responded that the landlord might have the right to evict if there was repeated damage to her apartment or any other apartment. A startled Mrs. W asked, "What will I do? I don't flood the bathroom on purpose."

This was the opening Robin had sought. Robin asked directly whether Mrs. W would like to come to the JCC and participate in its programs. Robin also indicated that there were other services that could be arranged for Mrs. W, such as a homemaker. Mrs. W refused the offer of services but agreed that Robin could call her and "perhaps" come visit again some time. She also agreed to have Robin speak with the landlord about installing safety bars in the bathroom and to have the tub grouted. Further, she would think about having a "friendly visitor," a person who will periodically visit her at home.

A few days later, Robin received a telephone call from Sarah Wells, Mrs. W's niece. Robin discovered that Sarah lives in Pennsylvania. She tries to visit Mrs. W at least once a month, but she has her own family to take care of and a job. At one point, Sarah had tried to convince her aunt to move to an assisted living facility, but Mrs. W flatly refused to consider a move.

Sarah indicated that she was pleased that the agency had reached out to her aunt and expressed concern about how long Mrs. W could continue to live alone. She encouraged Robin to intervene and see if Mrs. W might eventually accept some of the services the agency could offer.

Robin's agency helps to make it possible for older community residents to continue to live independently and receive services as needed. Referrals are handled largely on an informal basis; this is possible because of the outreach work of Robin and other staff to form and maintain relationships with neighborhood business people, particularly landlords and building superintendents. It is the landlords and superintendents who are likely to first recognize any problems. The relationship is reciprocal. They inform the JCC about people in need of services. The agency responds quickly, thus helping landlords maintain tenants. Periodically, the JCC housing coordinator conducts workshops for landlords and members of the community board to keep them informed about JCC services and any new programs in the works. This ongoing dialogue offers an opportunity for community members to provide input about service needs and, as well, to learn how the JCC can respond to identified needs.

The functions Robin performs are an example of community-based practice. Here direct social work services are integrated with the skills traditionally associated with community organization and development (Barker, 1999). The work of the JCC includes efforts to enhance the social bonds among members of the community. The JCC uses both professionals and volunteers to reach out to senior citizens. The concept of the *friendly visitor*, first introduced by the Charity Organization Societies in the late 1800s and early 1900s, is evident in the home visits and social supports offered by volunteers.

Robin's initial interventions focus on case assessment. As Mrs. W is not initially inclined to accept agency services, Robin addresses her concrete needs—such as home repairs. Robin leaves the door open for follow-up and plans to call Mrs. W in a few days. Because Mrs. W is presently able to live at home, but needs supports, Robin has formulated a longer-term plan and hopes to work with the client to accept JCC assistance. Robin concludes that Mrs. W

would benefit from a homemaker, perhaps three times a week. The homemaker could assist Mrs. W to bathe, clean, shop, and cook. If Mrs. W cannot afford to pay for the homemaker, Robin would find a source to subsidize the service. Right now, Robin does not feel that Mrs. W is in imminent danger. Robin intends to concentrate on relationship building with Mrs. W. Also, Robin will be in touch with the landlord to get the repairs done and to assure him that the agency will stay involved.

In-Home Services

In-home services are a subcategory of community-based services designed to assist older people to remain in their homes and to live as independently as possible. Home delivered meals, for example, provide nutrition for elderly citizens who can no longer cook for themselves. Home health services, another example, are often provided by a nurse or physician and include skilled nursing care, health monitoring, and often distributing medications. Other examples of in-home health services include homemakers, chore services, telephone reassurance, friendly visitors, energy assistance and weatherization, and respite care for caregivers (NAAAA, 2000).

Although Medicare covers most of these home health services, a similar service often called home attendant service is not covered by Medicare. Home attendant services generally include assistance with activities of daily living, such as bathing or feeding, that do not require skilled nursing care (NAAAA, 2002a). This service is often needed by people whose only alternative would be nursing home care. This gap in federal policy continues despite evidence that the most cost-effective form of long-term care is home and community-based services (NAAAA, 2000).

Various private services have been developed to make it possible for older people to remain in their homes and to ease the burden on family caregivers. For example, an advertisement in the February 2002 issue of the *NASW News* featured a "patient care at home" agency, which offers nonmedical, in-home companion care. This same agency offers an around-the-clock medical and emergency monitoring service. Another example is the Expanded In-Home Services Program in New York that provides case management and home care for seniors who fall above the Medicaid level. Most clients are considered to be "near poor." The aging services network provides a continuum of care, depending on client needs. Services available include multiservice senior centers, meals-on-wheels, transportation, adult day services, case management, home care, mental health, and housing (Sackman, 2002).

Respite Care

Respite care has been recognized as one means of supporting caregivers. Respite care is "the temporary assumption of responsibilities of a person who provides for the home care of another. . . . The goal is to give the caregiver a break from the responsibility so that tensions are minimized, the caregiver can have some other interests or take care of personal crises, and the client can stay out of institutional care" (Barker, 1999, p. 412). Social workers can arrange for respite care as case managers or perhaps organize a registry or list of respite caregivers for citizens in need of such services.

CAREGIVERS NEED HELP, TOO

Carol is 82 years old. She is legally blind in her left eye and partially blind in her right eye. She is paralyzed from the waist down as a result of an earlier stroke, and she remains in a wheelchair. She also has an ileostomy bag, a drainage bag or container designed to receive feces discharged after a surgical procedure to remove all or part of the intestines (Fasthealth, 2003), which needs to be emptied regularly. However, Carol does not want to go to a nursing home, and she can remain at home if there is someone to provide care by cooking her meals, helping her

bathe, and being available in case of emergency. Carol's sister Margaret provides this assistance.

Margaret is a 76-year-old widow who has been living with Carol and taking care of her for the past four years. Carol and Margaret both enjoy this arrangement. However, Dave, the county social worker who has been involved with the case, has begun to worry about Margaret's health. She frequently appears tired, and she can no longer sleep through the night because Carol has been having severe leg cramps and often calls for her sister. Dave tries to encourage Margaret to take a vacation and visit her son, who lives in Dallas. However, Margaret is afraid to leave Carol.

Dave begins investigating respite care options and finds that the care that Carol can afford is limited and does not offer the medical services she requires. Carol needs to have someone there at night in case there is an emergency. Fortunately, Dave is able to find several nursing homes that will accept Carol for a weeklong stay. Dave then takes Carol to visit these nursing homes so that she can determine which one she likes best.

Carol is initially very unhappy about having to go to a nursing home and Margaret feels quite guilty, but Dave works with them both to explain the necessity of Margaret taking a vacation in order to rejuvenate and restore her own health so that she can continue to care for Carol.

In this case scenario, Dave carries out the functions of assessment and diagnosis to determine the problems that need to be addressed. Dave then uses the skills of enabling, organizing, and coordinating to locate an appropriate provider of respite care. Finally, he carries out support and counseling functions to help both Carol and Margaret understand the need for Margaret to take a vacation.

Elder Abuse Prevention Programs

Elder abuse prevention programs are another form of community service and are generally offered through state or local departments of social services. These programs are designed to identify and alleviate situations of abuse, neglect, or self-neglect. Elder abuse refers to the "mistreatment of older people and relatively dependent people . . . [which] may be inflicted by the older person's adult children or other relatives, legal custodians, or other care providers" (Barker, 1999, p. 150). Abuse can take the form of battering, neglect, exploitation, and psychological harm. When such abuse does occur, adult protective services are usually involved in providing assistance.

Adult protective services consist of social, medical, legal, residential, and custodial care that are provided for adults who are unable to provide such care for themselves or do not have a family member, friend, or other person who can provide it. Those in need of adult protective services are often incapable of acting judiciously on their own behalf and are consequently vulnerable to being harmed or inflicting harm on others. In such instances, the courts may intervene to assign responsibility for care and decisions about care to a social agency or other care facility (Barker, 1999).

DELIVERING ADULT PROTECTIVE SERVICES
Mark is a young social worker in the adult services division of the department of social services in Queens, NY. He has a caseload of 25 older adults who are functionally impaired. However, he has one case that is especially troubling, that of Mrs. Nowles. Mrs. Nowles is 68 years old and diabetic. She has had two strokes and has gone into a diabetic coma on one occasion. She has numerous gastrointestinal problems and takes six different medications. Mrs. Nowles lives with her daughter, Brenda, who is 45 years old, and her 14-year-old nephew, who is diagnosed with severe learning disabilities. Brenda does not work and has a record of drug and alcohol abuse. She is currently on parole for attempting to sell drugs.

Mark's primary concern is about Mrs. Nowles, who is often so depressed that she talks of killing herself and ending her misery. Mark worries about the administration of her insulin and the chance of another diabetic coma that could take her life. Brenda insists that she gives her all required daily medications, but Mark recently found out that Brenda went away for three days, leaving no one to care for Mrs. Nowles. Mark is treating this as an adult protective services case, and he knows that he must be able to show true neglect and abuse in order to remove Mrs. Nowles from the home. Complicating the matter further is Mrs. Nowles's assertion that she does not want to leave and that her daughter takes care of her as good as anyone else could.

This case exemplifies the dilemmas that face social workers in many abuse cases. Mark must call on a variety of social work skills in order to handle the case effectively. He must be able to assess the situation and diagnose the presenting problem. He must also give advice and counseling to all family members. He must support Brenda and help her understand the consequences of neglecting to give her mother the proper medication. Mark must constantly reevaluate the situation, coordinate services with physicians and other health care professionals, and be ready to take decisive action if the circumstances deteriorate further.

Facilitated Living Arrangements

Assisted living arrangements constitute a midway point between living independently and living in a nursing home. The older person usually needs daily assistance but not continuous medical care. Senior housing services provide a safe and secure residential environment but do not offer the skilled medical care or assistance of nursing homes or assisted living arrangements. Senior housing is usually in the form of rental apartments or group residences. Many such programs offer transportation services, congregate meals, and social and recreational activities (NAAAA, 2002a).

Continuing care retirement communities are one of the newer developments in long-term care. These communities offer a long-term contract that basically assures continuous care as a person ages. There are several different types of facilities offering a range of care from simple safety and support to highly skilled nursing services. Social workers employed in these environments provide direct services such as assessment, diagnosis, support, and counseling. They are also involved in planning, developing, and evaluating programs for the residents.

Adult foster care is a form of residential care provided for those who cannot live independently and are placed in the private homes of nonrelatives. The foster family, or caregiver, provides room and board and assistance in daily living in exchange for a monthly payment (Barker, 1999). People who may benefit from adult foster care include those suffering from mental illness or mental retardation, or frail elderly people. Social workers employed by such agencies as the U.S. Department of Veterans Affairs or the adult protective services division of a state or city department of social services are charged with the responsibility to find foster homes; match them with appropriate adults in need; provide ongoing information and referral, concrete services, and counseling to adult clients; and supervise the foster care arrangement. Adult foster care is often a way to avoid institutionalization while allowing continued opportunities for social interaction.

FRANK STAYS IN THE COMMUNITY

Frank is a 69-year-old man with moderate retardation. He had been living with his daughter but she recently had twins and her husband lost his job. They can no longer afford to care for Frank, so the daughter called the adult services division of Montgomery County's department of social services.

Frank's case was presented at the morning staff meeting. Staff reviewed the intake report

from the assessment center and then discussed whether foster care would be an appropriate option. There was agreement that this option should be pursued. MaryAnn, a social worker in the adult foster care division, was assigned to the case. She immediately contacted Frank's daughter and arranged to meet with her, her husband, and Frank.

Mary Ann first attempted to explain the foster care system and the benefits that Frank may be able to get from living in a home rather than an institution. Frank's daughter and son-in-law agreed that this is a good opportunity. Frank was nervous about meeting a new family.

MaryAnn took some time to talk alone with Frank. She told him that there would be another person, a 72-year-old man, also living with the foster family. She explained that she would set up a time for Frank to meet the family and maybe he could first spend a week with them. If he didn't like it there, he certainly did not have to stay. Frank readily agreed to this plan and was somewhat excited about meeting the other man, as he did not have many friends.

Mary Ann then met with the foster family who had been approved by the department. The family agreed to take Frank for a trial period of one week. MaryAnn met with Frank and the caregiver two times during the trial period, which concluded with Frank excited about his new surroundings, the caregiver happy with Frank, and Frank's family pleased about Frank's new home.

However, adult foster care does not simply end with arranging an acceptable placement. Mary Ann now had to begin the task of working with Frank and the foster care family. For example, Mary Ann helped Frank get a part-time job and set up a savings account. She also worked with the foster family to provide an understanding of Frank's special needs. After one year in adult foster care with regular monthly visits from Mary Ann, Frank was thriving in his new surroundings.

In this case, MaryAnn first conducted a psychosocial assessment, the result of which was to substantiate the initial plan to consider Frank for adult foster care placement. She also had to assess the caregiver's lifestyle to determine if Frank would be a good fit. In addition, MaryAnn carried out the social work function of counseling for Frank, his daughter and her husband, and the caregiving family. She also assisted Frank to develop the skills he needed to live in a new environment and referred him for appropriate services.

MaryAnn worked for a public agency. Community-based care and alternative living situations are also arranged by social workers in private practice. This form of private practice is significantly different than that discussed in Chapter 4, Mental Health. An article in the NASW News (O'Neill, 2000b) detailed the work of a social worker who has become an "entrepreneur" in the field of aging in order to mold and manage social workers' systems of care.

Entrepreneurship and Work with the Elderly

Social worker Constance Kilgore of Dallas built her business, which offers services to the elderly, from scratch.

Kilgore raised a family prior to getting her MSW at the University of Texas in Arlington in 1978. While an intern at Dallas Psychiatric Associates, she saw how a private company explores and takes advantage of opportunities. Upon graduating, she stayed with this agency and was soon developing inpatient programs for hospitals and running the Dallas Psychiatric Social Work Department.

While a graduate student, Kilgore had taken courses in gerontology, and in her postgraduate work she used this knowledge to provide services to the elderly. She saw that these older clients needed much more than psychotherapy if they were to live independent lives or adjust to other circumstances.

Kilgore was nervous about the prospect of setting up her own practice but took the plunge in 1984. Initially, her practice focused on clinical work. But in 1987, she took the next step of moving to what she described as "plain old social work" with the elderly and young people with chronic illnesses. She established a business—alone—to find the services that would enhance the lives of the elderly and clients with chronic disabilities and allow them to live as independently as possible. Finding clients involved marketing herself to trust departments of banks, physicians, accountants, attorneys, clergy, and hospital discharge personnel. She joined national networks and began to advertise. Those who contacted her wanting services were often adult children of the elderly. She began by conducting an assessment of many factors, including physical (contacting physicians), legal (power of attorney, will), spiritual, clinical (including possible dementia), and family.

If the assessment showed that the client was able to remain in his or her own home, Kilgore might find caregivers, such as cooks and housecleaners, to go with the client to appointments with physicians, make sure the client's physicians are aware of what other medical services the client is receiving and that they are available 24 hours a day for medical emergencies, and contract for needed modifications or repairs to the client's home. Other interventions might include arranging for meals-on-wheels or ensuring that special dietary needs are met. She educates family members and caregivers about diseases such as Parkinson and Alzheimer's. When family members or friends are out of town, Kilgore also provides close monitoring of the client.

Sometimes clients need to move, perhaps to an assisted living facility. In such cases, Kilgore works with them and their families to identify facilities that offer the level of care needed, takes them to visit the facilities, and works with the entire family to reach a decision.

Kilgore's philosophy is that no matter who pays the bill, the frail elderly person with dis-

abilities is the client and his or her wishes are what count. This may involve conflict resolution with adult children.

As her caseload steadily increased, she hired four master's level social workers and a certified accountant to help staff the business. Kilgore and her four social work associates cover seven counties of the Dallas–Fort Worth area and work primarily from their own homes. The accountant oversees bill paying, bookkeeping, and Medicaid-related matters. Her employees are paid well, at least in relation to what a social worker in a nonprofit agency who carries similar job responsibilities would earn. In Kilgore's view, the work is hard and takes a tremendous amount of good judgment and character.

Part of her work in recent years is to act as a paid mentor to others around the country who are starting similar businesses. (Adapted from "Social Workers Risk Running Businesses" by J. V. O'Neill, 2000, NASW News, October, p. 3)

Social workers are becoming private case managers for elderly people whose immediate family members are unavailable to provide the necessary care due to geographic distance or other pressing responsibilities. Some private case managers also identify services and providers in distant communities, utilizing their collegial networks. The emergence of private case management as a distinct field of practice has been attributed to the growth in the elderly population, rising services costs, increasing complexity of the services system for the elderly, inability of public programs to meet all care-coordination needs, and the entrepreneurial initiative of human services professionals ("MSWs Lead in Private Case Management," 1988). These case managers and management firms tend to be independent and self-managed and operate on a for-profit basis. The services provided by the social work staff include family and client counseling; housing and nursing home placement; functional, social, and financial assessments;

referrals to and monitoring of services; client evaluation for community-based care or institutional placement; and assistance with eligibility forms and other paperwork associated with eligibility for and receipt of human services.

Nursing Homes

Because of the overwhelming preference of older people to "age in place," nursing homes are low on the possible list of options. However, in cases where older people are unable to care for themselves and community resources are insufficient to meet needs, nursing homes are a viable choice. Examples include people suffering from dementia or Alzheimer's disease who are unable to live safely on their own.

There are now 17,000 nursing homes in the United States, with 1.6 million residents (O'Neill, 2002). Nursing homes vary in size, funding, and level of care provided. Generally, they can be distinguished by the type of care they provide, with the three most common being skilled nursing facilities, intermediate care facilities, and custodial care (Hancock, 1990). All nursing homes must meet specific state guidelines in order to receive a license, and an increasing number of states are requiring preadmission screening. These screening programs are used to evaluate applicants and ensure that placements are necessary. Furthermore, a preadmission screening is often required before Medicaid will reimburse nursing homes (NAAAA, 2002a).

Although there is often a reluctance to work in a nursing home due to the aura of hopelessness, social workers are much needed and can make a tremendous positive impact (Hancock, 1990). In a nursing home, a social worker works as part of an interdisciplinary team with other health care professionals. The social worker provides assessment, diagnostic, and counseling services to residents who may be having problems with depression or lifestyle adjustment. Social workers in this area of service also coordinate communication between family members and patients and encourage and enable a family to take an active role in a patient's care. Social workers use their creativity and skills to plan, develop, administer, and evaluate programs to better serve the residents.

A NURSING HOME RESIDENT

Clara is 95 years old and has been a resident of Northwest Health Care Center, a skilled nursing facility, in Topeka, KS, for more than 10 years. Her husband and all of her children have died. She has only two granddaughters still living, and they are not able to visit her often. Clara is frequently depressed and lonely. As a result, she concentrates excessively on her own physical ailments and is convinced that her own death is imminent.

Kim is the director of social work at the nursing home. She has spoken with Clara's social worker, Tom, on several occasions. Tom tells Kim that he is worried about Clara, but, with all of his other clients, he cannot spend as much time with her as he would like. He is aware of her loneliness and depression. He believes that she needs to increase her level of social interaction in order to take her mind off of her own illnesses.

Kim suggests that Tom get Clara involved in floor activities. However, Tom claims that Clara refuses to join the other residents in the day room for any scheduled activity. Kim considers Clara's situation and recognizes that there are important mental health issues involved.

Kim is aware that mental health services for the elderly are inadequate, as reflected in the fact that only 1 percent of nursing home residents can access psychological or psychiatric treatment. Often surrounded by loss and fear, some older citizens look to end their own suffering which is represented in the disproportionately high suicide rates among the elderly population. In an effort to address the mental health needs of the elderly, Kim recently spoke with a geriatric counseling firm, which offered

to provide services to residents at the nursing home. The counselors accept Medicare and Medicaid so clients do not have to pay for services. Kim explains the geriatric services to Tom and suggests that he talk to Clara about his concerns and ask her if she would be willing to talk to a counselor.

Clara agrees to meet a counselor once as a trial. Tom then calls Clara's granddaughters and explains the situation to them and invites them to meet the counselor with Clara. Tom believes that even if Clara can meet with the counselor just once a week, she will have someone to count on and someone with whom she can share her feelings. Perhaps, after she begins to trust the counselor, she may feel more comfortable interacting with the other residents.

In this case, Tom carries out the social work functions of assessment, diagnosis, and referral. He then facilitates communication with Clara's granddaughters and coordinates referral services with the geriatric counselor. In addition to Tom's role in the case, the social work supervisor, Kim, also carries out several important social work functions. She, too, assesses the client's situation, bringing to bear her advanced knowledge about depression in elderly people. She provides Tom with appropriate supervision and guidance in the best way to handle the case and opens up the possibility of approaches and resources he had not considered. To provide Clara with geriatric counseling services, Kim plans, coordinates, and negotiates with the counseling organization to reach an agreement for services.

In addition to nursing home case management and supervision, social workers can also coordinate and plan resident activities. Incorporating knowledge of both physical and emotional factors of aging, social workers can develop and administer programs such as reminiscence groups which help older people conduct life reviews to affirm their own existence and resolve any conflicts. Using the ecological perspective, their knowledge of human needs, and their skills in planning, organizing, and coordinating, social workers have also been instrumental in understanding the importance of intergenerational programs that allow young children to spend time with older adults. For example, some nursing homes have initiated special programs with the Boy Scouts and Girl Scouts. Here, the children come to the nursing homes to help celebrate the birthdays of the residents. The adults share their wisdom and experience, while the children bring freshness and vivacious. Interactions such as these allow the older residents to once again feel needed and alive.

Terry Tirrito, a social work educator and aging expert, detailed some of the advantages social workers offer in nursing homes (as cited in O'Neill, 2000a). These include social workers' understanding of mental health problems and the role of families as helpers or barriers in working with nursing home residents. The psychosocial assessments conducted by social workers of family and residents provide a firm base for determining what interventions are needed. Social workers' skill in managing groups is an important aid in working with interdisciplinary health care teams. Social workers are also trained to understand and use available community resources for family members, including caregiving groups and access to Medicare and Medicaid benefits. Their skill in advocacy for clients promotes more optimal conditions for people living in nursing homes.

The use of trained health care professionals is associated with the quality of care offered through nursing homes. But the use of untrained personnel in nursing homes is an ongoing issue. Untrained social services designees often carry out social work functions in nursing homes. The Health Care Financing Administration has permitted untrained social services personnel, some without any training whatsoever, to act as medical social workers in nursing homes even though federal law requires professional services when payment is through Medicare and Medicaid (O'Neill, 2000a).

Other problems plague nursing homes. There have been, and continue to be, complaints about nursing home abuse of residents physically, emotionally, and materially. In September 1999, the National Coalition to Protect America's Elders declared that the mistreatment of residents in nursing homes had reached "a state of emergency" (as cited in Beaucar, 2000, p. 15). A recent GAO study on this subject found that 90 percent of the nation's 17,000 nursing homes are inadequately staffed (Fleck, 2002). Various proposals to remedy the situation have been proposed, including video surveillance, more frequent government inspections, and strengthening the penalties for noncomplying facilities. All of these proposals are costly to implement.

The U.S. Department of Health and Human Services requires all states to have ombudsman services. Ombudsman workers are charged with monitoring the implementation of federal, state, and local laws pertaining to nursing home administration as well as investigating and resolving complaints made by or on behalf of individual residents. Typical complaints may include food service, financial issues, and medical treatment issues (NAAAA, 2002a), but sometimes the complaints can be far more serious. Social workers serving in the ombudsmen role must effectively advocate to insure that the rights of patients are upheld.

Nursing homes conditions have received widespread media attention, and the impetus for change has grown. The federal government took initial steps through a pilot program in six states to develop a rating system for nursing homes. A guide, "How Do Your Local Nursing Homes Compare," is available to professionals and consumers on the Internet (http://www.myziva.net) and in newspapers. Information includes the track record of nursing homes in regard to nine quality measurements, including a record of the use of physical constraints and a record for treatment of pain and infection (Connolly, 2002).

Social workers employed within nursing

homes are well equipped to assist in identifying individual cases of abuse, to provide aggregate and trend data about their caseloads and those of colleagues, and to take action through appropriate channels (agency administration and boards, regulatory boards, "watchdog" agencies). In almost all instances, the beginning point for change is at the agency level.

Because of the demographics of the growing aging population, social work roles in the provision of long-term care will increase dramatically in the coming years. In addition, residents of nursing homes are likely to be older and more severely disabled (Garner, 1995). Therefore, social workers in this arena will face great challenges, but they are well equipped with the skills to provide efficient, effective, and caring treatment. Social workers in this area of service must continue to utilize their advocacy skills to promote policies and programs that benefit and protect the nation's elderly population (Garner, 1995; O'Neill, 2000a).

ALZHEIMER'S DISEASE

Senile dementia, Alzheimer's type, is the single most prominent irreversible organic brain disease. At this time there is no known cause or cure for Alzheimer's, in which memory, language ability, and rational thinking decline over time. This decline interferes with the ability of individuals to function autonomously and to engage in social relationships (Eastman, 2002).

Warning signs of Alzheimer's disease include memory loss, difficulty performing familiar tasks, problems with language, disorientation of time and place, poor or decreased judgment, problems with abstract thinking, misplaced things, changes in mood or behavior, changes in personality, and loss of initiative (Alzheimer's Association, 2002c). Experts predict that, without a cure, about 14 million Americans will have Alzheimer's by the year 2050, up from the 4 million people currently diagnosed (Eastman, 2002). The predicated

increase in the number of people afflicted Alzheimer's has been termed to be of "epidemic proportions" (Pear, 2002).

It has been estimated that one in 10 people over 65 years of age and nearly half of those over age 85 have Alzheimer's disease. A person with Alzheimer's disease lives an average of eight years and as many as 20 years or more from the onset of symptoms (Alzheimer's Association, 2002a). Although Alzheimer's is marked by memory impairment, there are no definite characteristics that indicate the presence of the disease. Rather, Alzheimer's is diagnosed by exclusion of all other causes of intellectual impairment. Physicians today are able to provide a tentative diagnosis of early Alzheimer's through the use of standard tests, such as the Mini-Mental State Examination, which evaluates memory and reasonable abilities (Eastman, 2002), as well as through a comprehensive evaluation, including a complete health history, physical exam, CAT scan (or MRI), and blood work. Diagnoses are "probable" or "possible." Confirmation can be made at this point in time only through examination of brain tissue at autopsy (Alzheimer's Association, 2002b).

The normal progression of Alzheimer's disease can be further complicated by the presence of depression or paranoia. Depression often co-occurs with medical, psychiatric, and substance abuse disorders, though it is frequently unrecognized and untreated. Untreated depression can interfere with the patient's ability to follow the necessary treatment regimen or to participate in a rehabilitation program. It may also increase impairment from the medical disorder and impede its improvement (National Institute of Mental Health [NIMH], 2002a, 2002b). When these other illnesses are combined with Alzheimer's disease, the patient experiences severe impairment. A social worker can concentrate on alleviating the depression or the paranoia, which will lessen the clinical impact of the Alzheimer's disease.

Despite the poor prognosis for people suffering from Alzheimer's, some important biomedical advances have been made. When diagnosed at an early stage, medications are now available that slow the degenerative brain disease in its initial phases and enable patients to lead normal lives longer. Medical and social management of the disease is possible. There are now four drugs approved by the Federal Drug Administration for the treatment of Alzheimer's disease—tacrine, donepezil, rivastigmine, and galantamine—with several others in clinical trials (Alzheimer's Association, 2002b). Studies have shown that drugs such as donepezil, which boosts a chemical in the brain that affects coherent thinking, delay the average time between diagnosis and entrance into a nursing home by 21 months (Eastman, 2002).

Treatment of Alzheimer's symptoms, however, has been thwarted by Medicare reimbursement regulations. Because treatment was believed to be futile, Medicare claims for the costs of mental health services, hospice care, or home health care for people with Alzheimer's were routinely denied (Pear, 2002). However, in March 2002, the Bush administration authorized Medicare coverage for the treatment of Alzheimer's disease. Clinical studies, supplied to the government by the Alzheimer's Association and the American Bar Association's Commission on Legal Problems of the Elderly, among other patient advocacy groups, provided scientific evidence that psychotherapy, physical and occupational therapy, and other services can stave off the worst effects of the disease and prolong a relatively normal life (Pear, 2002).

This change in policy and the scientific evidence upon which it is based have important implications for social workers who treat people with Alzheimer's and their families. Patients with mild-to-moderate forms of the disease have been shown to benefit from psychotherapy. Mental health treatment helps them cope with loss of memory and with feelings of depression and anxiety.

Social Work Interventions

Robyn Yale, a clinical social worker in San Francisco, was recently featured in AARP's Bulletin (Eastman, 2002) about her pioneering work in early-stage-Alzheimer's patient support groups. Mrs. Yale noted that people in the beginning stages of Alzheimer's are often able to participate in decisions about the kind of treatment they want, where they want to live when they need more care, and how they want financial, legal, and medical issues to be handled in the event they become incapacitated. Individual and group therapy can offer such decision-making opportunities. Support groups also provide important social opportunities, ranging from outings and art projects to volunteering, which help those affected stay involved and engaged in life (Eastman, 2002). The groups are also a source of information. Participants can be helped to deal with such issues as when to stop driving a car or paying bills.

Support groups are premised on the belief that Alzheimer's disease affects an entire family. Not only does the afflicted individual suffer serious impairment and eventual death, but also the person or people charged with caring for the patient with Alzheimer's disease must cope with increasing dependence on them and, thus, enormously elevated personal stress levels. Many Alzheimer's caregivers report high levels of depression as well as stress, and social workers have come to realize that the caregiver is also in need of intervention from a mental health professional (Alzheimer's Association, 2002a).

Support groups can help the family identify and understand lapses in thinking and behavior and thus be prepared to take steps to keep the individual safe and functioning as long as possible. Families can also be helped to prepare for the eventual, but inevitable, decline in their loved ones' ability to deal with anger, anxiety, and feelings of isolation.

Social workers have also organized respite programs to provide the primary caregiver with temporary relief. More than seven out of 10 people with Alzheimer's disease live at home, and almost 75 percent of home care is provided by family and friends (Alzheimer's Association, 2002a). Social workers either arrange for alternative care within the community or, in some cases, provide the care themselves. One resource for locating such groups is the Eldercare Locator (800-677-1116), which provides information about services and programs by geographic area. In other areas of the country, social workers have organized support groups for primary caregivers, allowing these individuals to vent their grief, frustration, sense of loss, and concerns over the deteriorating state of their charges, as well as offering practical suggestions for coping with extremely difficult, long-term situations.

Social workers also help the primary caregivers determine when they can no longer provide the necessary care to their ill relatives. Once this difficult decision is made, the social worker can assist the caregiver in selecting a nursing home or arranging for some form of alternative care. In many cases, the caregiver also needs grief counseling in dealing with the gradual loss of a loved one.

A social worker can also assist the caregiver or family with the economic issues of long-term health care. Medicare and Medicaid regulations are complicated and confusing, especially when coupled with the already overwhelming responsibility of caring for an Alzheimer's patient.

Alzheimer's Disease: Family Impact

Leigh Hunter has been the social work supervisor of the Alzheimer's wing at Willow Run Nursing Home in Newport News, VA, for almost 10 years. She supervises five other social workers in the wing and provides regular consultation during weekly meetings with each worker. There are 50 patients in the wing at any one time—10 per social worker.

This morning, Leigh meets with Annie, one of her most experienced social workers. Annie told Leigh she had received a phone call from

the son of a patient. The patient is an 81-year-old man named Charles. His wife Chris is 78 years old. Charles is in the latter part of the second stage of Alzheimer's disease. He has severe memory impairment and has lost some motor skills. He has also become increasingly agitated and combative. Chris has been caring for her husband at home, but as he gets progressively worse, she and her children are frightened that he will hurt himself or Chris.

Finally, Chris's children talked her into admitting Charles to Willow Run so that he can get the care he needs. Although now Charles is getting the appropriate care, Chris has become extremely depressed and guilt ridden. Her son reports that she rarely leaves the house and is not eating or sleeping properly. He is very concerned about her.

Considering the case, Leigh recognizes that Charles is technically the patient. However, she has always treated the patient and the immediate caregiving family as one, strongly believing that the mental health of one greatly affects the mental health of the others. Therefore, she urges Annie to invite Chris to meet and explore ways to understand and cope with her grief. She also suggests that Annie research support groups in the area and encourage Chris to get involved. Finally, Leigh recommends that Chris be made more of an active part of Charles' care plan so that she will not feel as if she abandoned him in his time of need.

In this scenario, Annie is the direct services social worker who will assess the situation and provide assistance, advice, and counseling services to Chris. She will also carry out the function of referral by helping Chris to get involved in a local support group. As a supervisor, Leigh also had to assess the situation. She then carried out her management, supervision, and consultation roles in helping Annie determine the best course of action.

Social workers working with Alzheimer's patients have access to up-to-date information about resources and psychosocial treatment approaches. Such resources include the Alzheimer's Association (httpo://www.alz.org), which offers both information and referral to support groups; the American Academy of Neurology (http://www.aan.com/public/practiceguidelines/patient_info.htm), which offers tips for families of patients with earlier Alzheimer's; and the National Institute on Aging's Alzheimer's Disease Education and Referral Center (http://www.alzheimers.org).

HOSPICE CARE

When people think of hospice care, they often think of a place or a hospital, but hospice care is a concept rather than a place. Barker (1999) defined hospice as "a philosophy of caring and an array of programs, services, and settings for people with terminal illness" (p. 221). Such services are generally provided outside of a hospital setting and, instead, in homelike facilities that provide for the health, homemaker, and social services needs of people who are terminally ill. In recent years, many hospice care programs have added "palliative care" to their names to reflect the range of care and services provided. The goal of palliative care is to address not only physical pain, but also emotional, social, and spiritual pain. The emphasis is on care rather than cure.

The major national organization representing the hospice movement is the National Hospice and Palliative Care Organization (NHPCO). This organization represents hospice and palliative care programs and professionals (including social workers) in the United States. The NHPCO is committed to improving end-of-life care and expanding access to hospice care toward the goal of enhancing the quality of life for people who are dying and for their loved ones (NHPCO, 2002). Among its activities, the NHPCO advocates for the terminally ill and their families, develops public and professional education programs and materials to increase understanding and availability of hospice and

palliative care, provides technical information to its members, and conducts research.

To address the full array of individual and family needs, hospice care almost always involves a team-oriented approach that includes expert medical care, pain management, and emotional and spiritual support as appropriate to and in line with the patient's wishes (NHPCO, 2002).

The National Hospice Foundation (NHF), a 501(c)(3) subsidiary of the NHPCO, was created in 1992 to increase understanding of hospice care through research and education. The foundation informs the public about the quality end-of-life care that hospice provides. The NHF is committed to providing opportunities for people, at the end of life, to maintain their dignity and self-respect, live their final days pain free, have the involvement and support of loved ones, and access the highest quality care available through hospice (NHF, 2002).

Although U.S. hospice care is rooted in home-based care, hospice programs can also be found in hospitals. Some hospice programs are called scattered bed programs, which is when hospice patients are scattered throughout the hospital in various wards and a hospice team makes daily rounds to visit each patient. Other hospice programs may be on a specific ward or floor of a hospital that is set aside for hospice care. Nevertheless, the majority of hospice programs are still home-based care programs (Richman, 1995).

Hospice care is differentiated from standard home health care, hospital care, and nursing home care in its extensive use of volunteers. Some hospice programs may be run entirely by volunteers and others are staffed by a combination of volunteers and paid employees. Hospice social workers often serve as administrators for volunteer programs. Social workers may also supervise volunteers who have to handle intense relationships with the families they are serving (Proffitt, 1987). Despite these different models for hospice programs, the basic concept of care remains the same: palliative and supportive care for the patient and the family and bereavement care for the family after the patient's death.

Hospice care is available 24 hours a day, seven days a week. However, hospice care is only for terminally ill patients with an expected life span of three to six months. Generally, hospice care is available to all terminal patients regardless of their ability to pay. The Medicare hospice benefit was passed in 1982 as part of the Tax Equity and Fiscal Responsibility Act (P.L. 97-248). Therefore, Medicare hospital insurance can help pay for hospice care if a doctor certifies the need for it and the care is provided by a Medicare-certified program. In addition, some private insurance companies have begun to pay for hospice care.

A hospice social worker has responsibilities to the patient, the family, the community, and the hospice care team. Social workers in the field of hospice care generally perform functions in five major areas: (1) provision of information and financial assistance; (2) interaction and coordination with the community; (3) administration and management of agencies; (4) performance of clinical work and counseling with individuals and families; and (5) advocating for the acceptance of the hospice philosophy by patients, the health care system, and society (Richman, 1995).

Social work responsibilities in regard to caring for the patient may include making the initial visit to the patient in order to assess the needs of the patient and family and to develop a plan of care. Hospice social workers also help patients and families to identify and take advantage of available community resources. Finally, social workers join with other members of the hospice team to assist the patient to handle unfinished business such as an unresolved quarrel, an unpaid debt, a relationship to be mended, and any legal actions that need to be finalized such as a will or a power of attorney (Hancock, 1990).

The role of the social worker does not end with the patient's death. Rather, one of the social worker's primary responsibilities is to counsel family members before and after the patient's death. In addition to helping patients and families, hospice social workers often conduct workshops for fellow colleagues and volunteers to assist them in understanding and dealing with their own grief at the repeated losses they experience as hospice workers.

FACING THE DEATH OF A SPOUSE

Will has been my husband for 50 years. Five months ago we celebrated our anniversary. I try to tell myself that a miracle will happen and we will be together for another 50 years, but I know that is not the case. Will is dying. He has inoperable prostate cancer. The doctor recently said Will has two months to live.

Will is trying to be upbeat. He doesn't want me to be upset. But he is in so much pain. When he doesn't think I am looking, he bites his lip and grimaces in pain. My neighbor is a nurse at our community hospital and she gave me the number of an organization called Oyster Bay Hospice Care. She said they would help Will to live the rest of his life at home without such excruciating pain.

I called the hospice care center and made an appointment with a social worker, Marie, to come and meet with us. Marie came to our home and talked with us about Will's illness, our family and friends in the area, our involvement in the church, Will's current medication regime, and other needs that we have, such as special food preparation to accommodate Will's particular needs and desires. Marie was very supportive and listened to our concerns without telling us what we should do. She explained the hospice care concept and answered all of our questions. I was relieved to hear that I could get assistance in caring for Will at home so that he would not have to die in a hospital. Marie helped me to transport Will to the hospital for one day so that the hospice team physicians and therapists could determine the best medical treatment to alleviate Will's pain while still allowing him to be mentally alert.

Will has been much happier now that he is no longer in agonizing pain. In addition, Marie has helped me to get involved in a spousal bereavement group composed of women whose husbands are dying as well as those who have already lost their spouses.

Marie has also helped us maintain our religious activities. Our church and Sunday worship sessions have always been very important to us and since Will has been sick we have had to stop going to church. Marie arranged for the hospice team pastor to visit us weekly to pray with us and guide us in our religious cares and concerns. The pastor's visits have been a wonderful source of inspiration for both of us.

Since we first became involved in the hospice program, I have been caring for Will at home, administering all of his medications. It is much closer to Will's death now and I can see him growing weaker everyday. However, we are both so grateful that these last few months have been a time of treasured enjoyment rather than a time of unending agony. I am still scared. I do not know how I will continue without him, but I am strengthened by the knowledge that Marie and the rest of the hospice care team will be there to support me even after Will's death.

In this case scenario, the social worker, Marie, in her first several visits with Will and his wife, conducts a psychosocial assessment to determine the environmental, family, and personal supports of the patient and his wife and children. Marie will continue the assessment process throughout her work with this family, and she will update the care plan as necessary. Marie educates the family about hospice care and, once the family has agreed to enroll in the program, acts quickly to make the necessary referrals, including medical assessments. Marie also provides support and assistance to address their emotional and concrete needs.

The function of advice and counseling is evident in Marie's work with Will's wife as she attempts to help her through the bereavement

process. Finally, Marie continues to carry out the social work function of referral in her work to help Will's wife access the spousal bereavement support group and to arrange for regular pastoral visits.

END-OF-LIFE DECISIONS

Death has become a prolonged process for many people. Medical advances have led to the elongation of life. Technology, such as ventilators, may allow people to linger in physical states that lack any meaningful quality of life. Extending life through technological means involves substantial financial and human costs, particularly to the immediate families affected. However, American society has become enamored of the miracles of such technology, which may forestall death but create emotional and ethical dilemmas of heretofore unknown proportions. At issue are the values of self-determination and quality of life (Hardwig, 1997) or, as the title of a play and later movie posed the issue, "Whose life is it anyway?"

The quandary over quantity versus quality of life has crystallized as the population ages and medical advances make choices available. The right to refuse medical treatment has been clearly established in law, the most significant of which is the Patient Self-Determination Act of 1990 (P.L. 101-508), included as part of the Omnibus Reconciliation Act of that year. This law requires that any physician or facility receiving public funds inform patients about their right to refuse or terminate medical treatment and their right to complete advance directives in the form of living wills or health care proxies.

The unequivocal nature of the law, however, pertains only to the right to refuse medical treatment. There are other end-of-life decisions that may fall outside the law but nevertheless may be real considerations for the patient, his or her family, and the physician. These alternatives include suicide, assisted suicide, and active euthanasia. Physician-assisted suicide came to public attention through the media reports and subsequent trial of Dr. Jack Kevorkian who assisted in over 100 suicides. The ambivalence of the general public to assisted suicide was highlighted when three juries refused to convict him (Erlbaum-Zur, 2001). Physician-assisted suicide is defined as "a patient's use of a medical doctor's drugs, instruments, and expertise to consciously and deliberately take his or her own life" (Barker, 1999, p. 362).

To date, Oregon is the only state to have enacted a law to address end-of-life decisions. The Oregon Death with Dignity Act (1997) requires an evaluation of candidates for physician-assisted suicide for sound decision making (Farrenkopf & Bryan, 1999). Social workers who work with older people in long-term care settings are in a position to contribute to this assessment process (Erlbaum-Zur, 2001). Social workers, with their empathic understanding of the psychosocial issues involved, should be actively involved in the planning and policy development process that is currently taking place in this arena (Kaplan, 1995).

A TIME TO DIE

Mollie, age 74, suffers from advanced-stage lung cancer. At the time of her diagnosis seven months ago, Mollie had agreed to undergo treatment in the form of chemotherapy and radiation. Mollie was severely debilitated, as she also had emphysema, the result of a lifetime of smoking.

Mollie has two adult daughters—one, Nancy, who lives about 250 miles away and the other, Judy, who lives on the other side of the country. Both work and have families of their own. They received the news about the diagnosis from a friend of the family. The daughters then spoke to the physician by a conference call; he suggested that, while Mollie is briefly hospitalized, they coordinate with the hospital social worker concerning treatment and care planning.

Isabel is the social worker in the hospital's oncology department. She explained to Nancy and Judy that the chemotherapy and radiation treatment protocol will span a six-month period. She also mentioned something the physician failed to discuss with them—there is a poor prognosis for those with this form of lung cancer. This caught the daughters by surprise, and they asked a number of questions. The physician had not mentioned "no treatment" as an option. Isabel was not in a position to respond to the technical questions, but suggested that the daughters speak again with the physician and check out the Web site of the National Institutes of Health for up-to-date information about lung cancer diagnosis and treatment. She also suggested that when Nancy and Judy visit their mother, they arrange a time to meet. Isabel realized the daughters were dealing with new information—their mother was dying. In the interim, there were a number of concrete arrangements to be made in order for Mollie to begin chemotherapy the next week.

The protocol required that she stay overnight in the hospital one night every two weeks. Someone had to be with her. This was not going to be easy to arrange, and the social worker again proved to be a valuable resource. Mollie lives in a rural area; the hospital is located 50 miles away, and some type of transportation service needed to be arranged.

Isabel researched the options and put the daughters in touch with two different services. The more difficult issue, however, concerned identifying people who could stay with Mollie in the hospital during her treatments. Mollie, who had lost her husband 10 years ago, had grown quite critical of her friends and didn't want to have anyone doing her any favors. The daughters worked out a schedule to at least get through the chemotherapy appointments for the first three months. This was accomplished with the assistance of Isabel, who was able to arrange for private 24-hour nursing aide care for the time periods when the daughters could not be there.

Mollie did not respond well to the chemotherapy. She had always been somewhat overweight, but now she could not keep any food down. Her weight quickly dropped—and continued to fall. Her hair fell out. Her depression level grew. Just getting through the day was an ordeal. Clearly, home help was needed, but Mollie was again resistant.

Over the next few months, the daughters watched their mother waste away. Still, the treatment continued. Nancy had begun to do some research and learned that treatment was, at best, a long shot. Although radiation and chemotherapy might reduce the size of the main tumor and therefore make breathing easier, the only hope was a small increase in life span. The quality of life, however, was gone.

Many people don't prepare for death; this is something that happens to someone else. Mollie had not completed a medical proxy nor did she have a living will. She had grown compliant— never questioning or refusing treatment—only intervening on her own behalf in terms of location of the treatment. Nancy and Judy talked about discontinuing treatment, but they had no right to intervene, as Mollie was conscious and was legally competent. Mollie didn't even realize that she had options. Nancy wanted to discuss with her mother the possibility of discontinuing treatment and, instead, receive hospice care, which would control the pain and keep her comfortable. Judy, however, was opposed.

One evening, Mollie was rushed to the hospital. She was so weak that she had fallen and was badly bruised. Her blood count was dangerously low. The pain emanating from her fall also left Mollie unable to sleep. She was skin and bones—now weighing in at 100 pounds. The bruising meant that there was no position in which she could get comfortable.

The physician came to the room to talk with Mollie; both daughters and the grandchildren were present. The doctor indicated to Mollie that if she remained unable to sleep, he could give her some medication. However, the medication would suppress her breathing and this might mean that she would not wake up. He asked Mollie if, under these circumstances, she would want the medication. Mollie, too weak to speak, nodded her head in affirmation. The physician asked her again if she understood the possible consequences of the medication. Mollie again nodded.

The medication that would help her sleep might also hasten her death. Although there would be no overdosage, any medication to help Mollie sleep would easily put her into cardiac arrest. Nancy and Judy left the room and went to find Isabel. Nancy felt that Mollie's wishes had been made clear. Judy indicated that even if this was the case—and she wasn't so sure—that it was wrong. Judy, a practicing Catholic, believed that death must only be natural; that intervening with God's plan was unacceptable. Isabel listened and then acknowledged their feelings, their difference in views, and the dilemma they faced. Isabel also clarified that perhaps the real issue for them was whether the decision to take the medication was premature. What was the reality of Mollie's condition, and what was the degree of her suffering? Isabel urged Nancy and Judy to talk directly to Mollie about end-of-life wishes in the absence of an advanced directive to satisfy them that she understood the implications of her decision. Judy agreed that, if satisfied that Mollie comprehended, she would honor her mother's wishes.

In this scenario, the social worker, Isabel, recognized that the daughters had experienced a very common communication breakdown with their mother. They had not discussed death. Adults are uncomfortable discussing death, and, according to the findings of a study conducted by the NHF (1999), more than one out of every four American adults is not likely to discuss with their parents issues related to death, even if a parent is terminally ill and has less than six months to live. Mollie, too, was one of the majority of Americans who had not communicated her wishes about how she would liked to be cared for at the end of her life, nor had she put these wishes in writing.

The disagreement between the daughters about end-of-life decisions echoes society's debate, which touches on deeply rooted religious and philosophical beliefs about the sanctity of life. Diversity of viewpoints on this issue is evident, as well, among religious leaders, physicians, nurses, and other health care professionals. Although health care professionals, supported legislatively by the Patient Self-Determination Act, encourage the communication of end-of-life wishes, studies have revealed that even when there is an advance directive, there is often disregard for the patient's wishes (Moskowitz & Lindemann, 1995). Recent study findings reveal that more than a third of seriously ill patients who requested that their physicians ease their discomfort instead of prolonging life had their wishes overlooked (Nagourney, 2002b).

The physician's actions in this case also raise questions about ethical boundaries. Palliative care is widely accepted and perfectly legal. The physician offered Mollie a remedy for her sleeplessness. But the medication had the potential to hasten death in that any sedation would affect Mollie's respiration. The physician revealed this risk, ensuring that Mollie understood. Was he, in fact, offering to assist her in suicide? It is not so clear. Miller and Brody (1995) argued that physician-assisted death in such situations is compatible with the doctor's duty to practice competently. If death is imminent and discomfort extreme, the question of options remains unclear. In this case, the social worker played an ancillary role, although "whistle blowing" was a potential action she might have taken. Instead, Isabel sought to help the daughters resolve their own ambivalence and to urge communication with Mollie that might aid them in reconciling the issues for themselves.

Many social workers are cognizant of the need to become more familiar with the practical and ethical issues involved in end-of-life care. A Social Work Summit on End-of-Life and Palliative Care was held in March 2002 at Duke University to explore the role of social work in end-of-life care. Toby Weismiller, Director of Professional Development and Advocacy at NASW and a summit participant, noted that although the focus on medical needs of people at the end of life has increased, there has been less attention paid to the psychosocial aspects. It is in this latter arena that social workers can make a major contribution (Stoesen, 2002). Summit participants developed the acronym PEG (palliative care, end-of-life care, and grief work) to encompass and integrate the psychosocial aspects of care. This concept also incorporates symptom relief earlier in the course of an anticipated death and the intervention required to address traumatic and catastrophic deaths, and it involves patients and their families, caregivers, support networks, and communities. The term "grief" was used rather than bereavement because social workers engage in grief work before the end of life and throughout the dying process (Stoesen, 2002). The goal of the summit was to draft an agenda for social workers to improve the care of the dying and those affected by death ("Social Workers Set Goal," 2002).

DEPRESSION IN OLDER ADULTS

Although most people ages 65 and older feel satisfied and happy with their lives, the risk of depression among older citizens is four times greater than in the general population (Henry, 1995). An estimated 6 percent of Americans age 65 and older in a given year, or approximately 2 million of the 34 million adults in this ages group in 1998, had a diagnosable depressive illness (major depressive disorder, bipolar disorder, or dysthymic disorder). In contrast to the normal emotional experiences of sadness, grief, loss, or passing mood states, depressive disorders can be extreme and persistent and can interfere significantly with an individual's ability to function. There is evidence of comorbidity and interaction between mental illness and physical illness, particularly depression, in later life ("Surgeon General's Call," 1999). A link has also been confirmed between depression and the ability to ward off disease. A recent study suggests that even mild depression can weaken the immune system. The immune system generally declines as people age. As a result, older people are more vulnerable to disease. Depression can accelerate that deterioration (Nagourney, 2002a).

Older Americans are disproportionately more likely to commit suicide. Making up only 13 percent of the U.S. population, people age 65 and older accounted for 20 percent of all suicide deaths in 1997. The highest rate was for white men age 85 and older: 64.9 deaths per 100,000 people in 1997, about six times the national U.S. rate of 10.6 per 100,000 (Nagourney, 2002a; "Surgeon General's Call," 1999).

Mental health in later life is a growing concern in service provision to the elderly and substantial unmet mental health needs among this population have been identified (Gatz, 1995; Rosen & Persky, 1997). Meeting the mental health needs of the elderly was the third highest priority identified during the 1995 White House Conference on Aging (Saltz, 1997). Mental illness in older adults is often not recognized or treated. In addition, mental health services are underutilized or used only in crisis situations, at which time there is an overreliance on inpatient treatment. Prevention, early intervention, and community-based mental health care services for the elderly are often not accessible to those who need them (Saltz, 1997).

The causes for depression are numerous. However, there are some primary causes of depression that are particularly important to recognize among older people. First, long-term, sudden, or fatal illnesses can cause or aggravate depression. Poor physical health has also been associated with depression, and this is even more apparent in the older population because as

health declines there is an increased need to depend on others (Hancock, 1990).

Risk factors are different from those confronting youth and younger adults. Older people are more socially isolated, have more physical illnesses, and suffer from depression disproportionate to their numbers in the population. Some contributing factors that are particularly important, especially among older people, are:

- *Other illnesses.* Long-term or quick onset illnesses can bring on or aggravate depression. Strokes, certain types of cancer, diabetes, Parkinson's disease, and hormonal disorders are examples of illnesses that may be related to depressive disorders.
- *Medications.* Some medicines cause depressive symptoms as side effects, such as certain drugs used to treat high blood pressure and arthritis. In addition, different drugs can interact in unforeseen ways when taken together.
- *Genetics and family history.* Depression often runs in families. Some people probably have a biological predisposition that makes them particularly vulnerable. ("Surgeon General's Call," 1999; NIMH, 2002a, 2002b)

Depression can also be brought on by abrupt changes in lifestyle. A common "land mine" for many older Americans is retirement. Retirement is associated with the cessation of working—withdrawal from the workplace. The abrupt change—from worker to retired—can involve loss of identity for some people. Others have not planned well how to use their time, or they expected they would enjoy sitting on the front porch and playing with the grandchildren. Instead, they find that they feel like a discarded old tire.

Retirement is a rapidly changing concept. Those who retire at age 65 may expect to live for 10, 20, or even 30 years longer. Some people are electing to work—but in a new career or business. For example, a retired insurance salesman has always wanted to be a teacher. This is his opportunity, particularly given the nationwide teaching shortage. Other retirees are using their time to travel, take classes, master the computer, and volunteer. It is estimated that the volunteer work of older Americans today is the equivalent of 1.1 million full-time workers (Novelli, 2002b). The postretirement options are many and can be combined.

As with any major life change, planning is an essential component. Retirement can signal a beginning, not an ending (Novelli, 2002b).

Retirement Isn't All Tom Expected It to Be

The day had finally come. Tom was retiring, after 35 years, as a high school biology teacher. He and his wife Ellen looked forward to moving from their home outside of Detroit, MI, and relocating to Tampa, FL. They had purchased a condominium last year in Tampa as part of their long-term retirement planning.

Tom had been a committed teacher, putting in many more hours per week at the job tutoring students who needed extra help, organizing field trips, and providing an ear to anyone who needed to talk. He was also active in his community and church. Tom and Ellen have two children, both of whom are grown and married. They have five grandchildren, all of whom live in the Detroit area, and Tom is a devoted grandfather. This year, he built a tree house for his grandson.

The day of the big move arrives. Neighbors, family, and friends gathered to throw a big retirement–moving party for the couple the night before. The moving truck was due momentarily. Tom walked through his home and noted all of the work he had put into making it a great place to live. He would miss it. But the fish were calling, the golf course awaited him, and he was confident that he would meet new friends.

Several months after the relocation to Tampa, Ellen spoke to Tom about her growing concerns about him. He seemed to have grown listless and had no interest in even going out of the house. He claimed that he didn't like the people who lived in the condo and had nothing in common with them. "And," he said, "you can't go fishing everyday." Tom's interest in learning to play golf had also been thwarted when he badly twisted his ankle and found it difficult to get around.

Tom shrugged off his wife's concerns. But the situation did not improve. He spent more and more time in front of the television but seemed not to be paying attention to what was on. He had lost considerable weight and was not interested in eating even his favorite dishes. He commented that he missed his grandchildren, yet rarely responded to their phone calls with any enthusiasm. The cheerful, enthusiastic, and energetic husband seemed to be gone.

Although Tom was reluctant to go for a physical exam, he agreed when Ellen insisted that he do so. The physician had not met Tom before and took an extensive history prior to beginning the examination. The physician, who specializes in geriatric medicine, recognized that Tom exhibited many of the classic symptoms of depression, which include the following:

- *a persistent sad, anxious, or "empty" mood*
- *loss of interest or pleasure in ordinary activities, including sex*
- *decreased energy, fatigue, feeling "slowed down"*
- *feelings of hopelessness or pessimism*
- *sleep problems (insomnia, oversleeping, early-morning waking)*
- *eating problems (loss of appetite or weight, weight gain)*
- *difficulty concentrating, remembering, or making decisions*
- *feelings of guilt, worthlessness, or helplessness*

- *thoughts of death or suicide—a suicide attempt*
- *irritability*
- *excessive crying*
- *recurring aches and pains that don't respond to treatment.*

Tom then receives a full physical workup. He is, in the words of the physician, "the picture of health." Since there was no medical condition that might explain the listlessness and loss of weight, the physician concluded that the problem was depression. As a first step, the physician prescribed Zoloft, an antidepressant medication. However, as he explained to Tom, medication was not a panacea, and it was important for Tom to get to the cause of the depression with an experienced mental health professional. The physician referred Tom to a social worker in private practice who works primarily with older citizens, many of whom have experienced mild to severe adjustment problems associated with their retirement.

Tom called the social worker and arranged for an appointment. He had never been to a mental health professional before and was pleasantly surprised about how easy it was to talk to her. He had expected to lie down on a couch and talk about his childhood! This was not at all the case. He found the social worker to be direct and goal oriented. She asked Tom what he wanted to get out of therapy, and they identified several goals. Then they "contracted" for an initial three months of visits, once per week. Short-term therapies (usually from 12 to 20 sessions) to treat depression focus on the specific symptoms of the depression.

After a few weeks on the antidepressant medication and the therapy sessions, Tom began to enjoy his retirement as much as he had expected. With treatment, even the most seriously depressed person can start to feel better, often in a matter of weeks, and return to a happier and more fulfilling life.

People in Tom's age group often experience numerous difficult and life-changing losses such as the loss of a spouse, loss of friends, loss of home, loss of community, loss of employment, loss of income, and loss of status. These losses can contribute to an eroding sense of security and can cause or aggravate depressive symptoms (NIMH, 2002b). Tom suffered many losses simultaneously: the loss of his identification as a teacher, the loss of his neighbors and friends brought on by physical relocation, and the distance between himself from his children and grandchildren. The plan for retirement in which Tom and Ellen had engaged did not include consideration of the potential impact of such losses, and Tom, in particular, was ill-equipped to deal with them.

There are three major types of treatment for clinical depression: psychotherapy, medication, and, in some cases, other biological treatments. At times, these treatments may be used in combination. Most doctors agree that patients who exhibit symptoms of depression should first undergo a complete physical examination to rule out any physical causes (Henry, 1995). In Tom's case, physical problems were ruled out, and medication and psychotherapy were the recommended treatments.

The three types of drugs most often used in the past to treat depression are tricyclic antidepressants, monoamine oxidase inhibitors, and lithium. Now, selective serotonin reuptake inhibitors are also widely used. All medications alter the action of brain chemicals to improve mood, sleep, appetite, energy levels, and concentration. Different people may need different medications, and sometimes more than one medication is needed to treat clinical depression. Improvement usually occurs within weeks (NIMH, 2002a). Psychiatrists can prescribe antidepressant drugs because they are physicians. Other mental health specialists, however, often work with physicians to ensure that their patients receive the medications they need.

Social workers in this arena may work as primary therapists, or they may be part of a health care interdisciplinary team. Most of the social work assistance will be in the form of crisis intervention in an attempt to restore the person to his or her predepression activity level (NIMH, 2002a). The social worker will usually conduct a thorough assessment and gather information pertaining to any past problems and coping mechanisms. The assessment also explores physical health, medication, nutrition, and income level. After the assessment, the social worker may determine that other support systems for the client need to be located or created. Senior centers, which were discussed earlier in the chapter, are often useful to proivide socialization opportunities. The key is not to let depressed people feel alone or unsupported (Hancock, 1990). The good news is that nearly 80 percent of those with clinical depression can be successfully treated (Henry, 1995).

Tom had the support and encouragement of his wife, family, and friends. Many older people, however, do not have such supports, as highlighted in the case of Amy.

A Beloved Pet Dies

One Saturday morning, Dr. Ross, a veterinarian, received a phone call from Amy Richards, a 78-year-old widow. Dr. Ross had been aggressively treating Mrs. Richards' 14-year-old golden retriever for several weeks following an episode of severe seizures. Dr. Ross had been honest with Mrs. Richards about the prognosis. Jaime was dying, and it was only a matter of days or maybe weeks. Dr. Ross had also told Mrs. Richards that a natural death for Jaime might not be pain free for the dog.

Mrs. Richards did not have any children, and her husband died 12 years ago. Since that time, Jaime has been Mrs. Richards's primary companion. Mrs. Richards was remarkably fit for a woman of her age, in part because of her exercise program with Jaime and her overall sense of well-being.

When Dr. Ross took the call from Mrs. Richards, it was with a sense of foreboding. Since the seizures, he had treated Jaime several times, and her condition was rapidly deteriorating. Mrs. Richards, in a strained voice, told Dr. Ross that she had decided to "put Jaime to sleep"— that the dog was clearly in pain and she could not stand to see her suffer. An appointment was made for the following day and Dr. Ross said that he would come to the house to get Jaime. He suggested that she think about whether she wanted to be with Jaime when she received the injection, and if so whether there was a friend she might ask to be with her at that time.

The next morning, as planned, Dr. Ross came to the house. Jaime was in the backyard; she had somehow managed to get herself up and out that morning without assistance, causing Mrs. Richards to question whether this was really the time. She asked Dr. Ross directly if he was sure that the time had come. He responded affirmatively. She then told Dr. Ross that she wanted to be with Jaime when she was euthanatized and that she would come to the animal hospital shortly, but alone. She couldn't think of anyone to ask to be with her.

At the animal hospital, Dr. Ross left Mrs. Richards alone with Jaime, who had been mildly sedated, in the examining room. When he reentered, Mrs. Richards was crying softly while talking to the dog. Dr. Ross explained what he would be doing and what Mrs. Richards should expect. He then proceeded to administer the lethal injection. During this short period of time, Mrs. Richards caressed Jaime's head and continued to talk to her. As Jaime entered her permanent sleep, Dr. Ross put his arm around Mrs. Richards and talked with her about their happy memories of the dog and the mischief she used to get into as a puppy. He then told her she could stay in the room with Jaime for as long as she wanted.

Later that evening, Dr. Ross called Mrs. Richards to see how she was doing. He became concerned by her flat voice and lack of emo-

tion. It seemed as if the energy had been drained from her. Dr. Ross paused for a moment to consider what he should do. He then asked Mrs. Richards if it would be okay if he had an associate of his, Sandy, call on her the next day. He briefly explained that Sandy is a social worker with whom he frequently consults. Mrs. Richards agreed.

Over the years, Dr. Ross had observed the crushing psychological impact of the loss of a pet on his clients. About a year ago, he decided to hire a social worker on a part-time basis to provide bereavement counseling when appropriate. He knew this was unusual, although he had heard that a few other vets had added social workers to clinic staff. Dr. Ross knew that if someone has recently experienced a loss, feelings of sadness and even depression may be part of a normal grief reaction. But, if the feelings persist with no lifting of the mood, the person may need professional help.

Sandy, the social worker, loves animals; she has several cats and dogs of her own. In her opinion, the relationship between people and their pets deserves a lot more attention in social work practice. During the past year, Sandy and Dr. Ross had both developed a respect for the important role in helping people adjust to the loss of a pet. Not all of her work concerns bereavement; sometimes she helps families decide to give a pet up for adoption or talks with families about the potential impact on the children of adopting a pet.

The next day, Dr. Ross asked Sandy to get in contact with Mrs. Richards. Sandy said she would follow up immediately. Mrs. Richards answered the phone after seven rings. Sandy immediately noticed the flat lack of emotion evident in her voice. Upon questioning, Mrs. Richards said that she was doing fine. But further probing revealed that she had not eaten, had slept poorly, and had resisted the efforts of her friends to offer comfort; clearly, Mrs. Richards was suffering from the depression that often is a part of the grieving process. Sandy sug-

gested that she stop by to see Mrs. Richards later that day, an offer that was accepted but with little enthusiasm.

The home visit confirmed Sandy's suspicions about the depth of Mrs. Richards' depression. Sandy did not shirk from the subject at hand. She invited Mrs. Richards to talk about Jaime and in the process acknowledge how significant the dog had been to her and the grief that she was feeling. Mrs. Richards began to cry as she related a story about the first time she had seen Jaime as a puppy and how they had bonded immediately; Jaime, one of eight puppies, had come up to her and licked her hands.

In the two weeks following Jaime's death, Sandy paid several visits to Mrs. Richards. Sandy encouraged Mrs. Richards to grieve openly. Jaime had been cremated; they talked about finding a headstone (perhaps a statute of a dog) that Mrs. Richards could place over the ashes that would be buried. Mrs. Richards began to shop around at neighborhood stores looking for an appropriate statute. She also, at Sandy's urging, looked through her many photos of Jaime and selected one to have enlarged and framed. Finally, Sandy learned that Mrs. Richards had been an English teacher before retirement and enjoyed writing. She suggested that Mrs. Richards commit to paper her feelings about the dog.

Several weeks after Jaime's death, Mrs. Richards handed Sandy an "ode" she had written to her dog. It went as follows:

Lessons from Jaime

I learned so much from you . . .

How to communicate directly about what you want and need . . .

In your case, it was barking when you wanted to go out, positioning yourself where you wanted to be scratched, sitting under the counter by the cookie jar when it was time for a snack.

Perhaps, thinking of you, it will be easier for me to ask others for what I need.

Not to be ashamed of emotion . . .
You quivered all over when I walked in
the door.
Your expression of joy at seeing me made
me glad to be home.
In fact, it helped make the house a home.
Love can be unconditional . . .
That the presence and strength
of unabashed love elicits the same feelings
in turn;
it was so easy to love you.
Relationships can be so simple, and yet
so profound and meaningful.
You taught me that life's pleasures can be
as easy as the throw of a tennis ball;
a game of catch could make the day for
both of us.
You taught me about loyalty; there could
be none greater than you showed me.
You showed me about dignity in aging; you
never complained, never showed your pain.
You brought peace and contentment to
my life.
You gave total acceptance, devotion,
and love.
I hope I gave to you nearly as much
and what you needed.
You will always be in my heart and thoughts.
I will miss you and be ever grateful that
you were in my life.

---

*Mrs. Richards indicated that it had taken
several days to compose the poem and that she
had wept through every sentence of it. But with
its completion, she felt that she had finally said
a proper goodbye to her companion and that she
had accepted that Jaime was gone. She now felt
that she would be able to manage and perhaps
someday she would consider getting another dog.*

*Sandy plans to continue to visit with Mrs.
Richards periodically and, when the time seems
right, will help her make the decision about
another pet—not to replace Jaime, for clearly
that could never be, but to provide a new companion and faithful friend.*

Sandy exemplifies a social worker providing
social services to older people (and others) in a
nontraditional practice setting. Her major role is
to provide bereavement counseling concerning
the loss of a pet, an event that can precipitate
grief and mourning, as well as anxiety, depression, and anger (Sable, 1995). Sandy's interventions are based on a theoretical framework of
attachment, in this case specifically focused on
the relationship between people and their pets.
Theories concerning the affectional bonds
between people, such as Bowlby's ethological
framework, provided Sandy with insights about
the strength and durability of Mrs. Richards's
bond with Jaime (Sable, 1995). Sandy's review
of the pertinent research has led her to understand that pet attachment is particularly important among divorced, never married, childless
couples, and widowed people. An article Sandy
came across emphasized this point:

> Because the substitute attachment of a pet
> provides closeness, touching, and a chance to
> feel worthwhile and needed, it may have spe-
> cial value for elderly people, who are apt to
> experience disruptions in relationships with
> familiar people, places, and things, as well as
> declining health, physical incapacity, and lim-
> ited financial resources. The loss of a pet may
> compound distress. (Sable, 1995, p. 338)

In recent years, attention to the human–animal bond has expanded. Social workers have
been among the professionals exploring the
meaning and depth of this bond. Social workers
have also been involved in creating and implementing programs that involve pets. Animals
have been used as adjuncts to the clinical process
to relieve the anxiety of clients. Services have
been initiated to bring animals to nursing homes
to provide stimulation and companionship for
the elderly and, in some instances, one or more
animals have become residents of facilities.
Animal companionship has been found to minimize loneliness, and tactile stimulation has been

shown to have a positive affect on the cardiovascular system (Netting, Wilson, & New, 1987). Any pet owner will confirm that a family dog or cat enriches the quality of life (Sable, 1995).

Programs involving pets are continuing to evolve. Correctional facilities have used companion animals with inmates with positive results. Guide dogs for the blind, of course, have provided a level of independence for the owners, and recently "hearing ear dogs" have been trained to respond to doorbells, alarms, and telephones and "handidogs" assist people in wheelchairs, making it possible to live independently (Netting et al., 1987).

Social workers can contribute their knowledge and skills to helping people deal with the loss of a pet through individual counseling, support groups, and consultation with veterinarians. They can also help to educate the public about the importance of pets in people's lives (Sable, 1995).

CONCLUSION

The vignettes in this chapter highlight some of the issues and situations that confront social workers in this field of practice. In order to provide continuous quality services, social workers must increase their own knowledge of issues related to the aging process (Zuniga, 1995). Knowledge development includes recognizing one's own feelings and attitudes toward the elderly, how membership in a particular age cohort affects elderly individuals, the variability among elderly individuals, and how gender and ethnic minority status affect the aging experience (Toseland, 1995). Social workers must sensitize themselves to the issues of aging and "avoid the stereotypes and negative images that interfere with effective helping" (Toseland, 1995, p. 158).

Social workers in this practice arena carry out the general functions of assessment, diagnosis, counseling, information and referral, advocacy, coordination, supervision, and policy analysis (Bellos & Ruffolo, 1995; Toseland, 1995). A related and essential social work function is that

of empowerment and enabling older citizens and their families to develop and retain a sense of competence (Zuniga, 1995).

Social workers in the field of aging also carry out important roles in managing agencies, planning and developing programs, researching the outcomes of different types of interventions, and intervening at the macro level to influence social policy. Social workers also address the mental health needs of older Americans through their community organizing, managing, and research roles. Social workers in all settings may refer to or collaborate with advocacy organizations to promote public awareness; provide clients with resources, such as support groups; and promote effective policies to meet current and emerging needs of older people.

As is the case with virtually all human services, the nature and breadth of programs of services available to older people depend on political currents. As noted earlier in this chapter, older Americans are a powerful—and growing—political force. Nevertheless, in anticipation of significant decreases in federal funds, some states and cities have already made selective budget cuts that affect programs for this population. However, as one author termed it, "the future is aging" (Takamura, 2001, p. 3). Attention to some of the major policy issues that affect the health and well-being of the elderly are likely to command attention if only because of the sheer size of this population. These issues include the future of the social security system, the adequacy of coverage under Medicare, the need for community care, and nursing home conditions.

There is agreement within the profession that the numbers of trained and experienced social workers are insufficient to provide the range of services needed for older people and their families. Although there has been significant intraprofessional dialogue about how to address this shortage, personal interests and career track preferences of social workers have remained consistent over time, without impacting on the critical shortage in the field of aging. This means that professionals from other disciplines, combined with paraprofessionals, make up a sizable proportion of the gerontological workforce.

CAREER OPPORTUNITIES

Despite the call for more social workers with expertise in the field of aging, the classified ads in the NASW News between 1998 and June 2002 reflect very few opportunities for social workers in gerontology, particularly in comparison with job openings in the fields of child welfare, health, mental health, and education. Any interpretation of this phenomenon is, at best, speculative. The lack of ads may reflect a perception within the gerontological field that there is little interest or expertise among social workers who are members of NASW in this practice area or that there are other advertising venues that will lead to more fruitful application pools.

Clinical Social Worker

Hospice of Baltimore, an affiliate of Greater Baltimore Medical Center, is seeking full-time and part-time clinical social workers. Responsibilities include conducting psychosocial assessments, supportive services to the patient and family unit of care, counseling to assist with adjustments to illness and grief, and assisting in resolving financial and environmental difficulties. Flexibility regarding periodic evening and weekend on-call work is essential. A master's degree in social work and current Maryland license are required. A valid driver's license is necessary. Experience in medical social work or community home visits desired. (*NASW News*, June 2001, p. 18)

Geriatric Therapist

Lewis-Gale Clinic's department of psychological medicine is seeking a LCSW or PhD psychologist specializing in the assessment and treatment of geriatric patients. Applicant must be licensed or license eligible in Virginia. Experience working in extended care facilities and outpatient settings is preferred. Must be able to market services and serve as liaison between extended care facilities and medical practices. Excellent benefits and working environment are offered. Lewis-Gale Clinic provides exceptional primary and specialty health care services at the main clinic in Salem, VA, and in 15 satellite offices throughout the Roanoke Valley and surrounding communities. (*NASW News*, April 1999, p. 20)

Coordinator of Geriatric Mental Health Programs

Located in Portland, ME, on beautiful Casco Bay, two hours north of Boston and one hour east of the White Mountains of New Hampshire, Community Counseling Center has an immediate opening for a coordinator of geriatric mental health programs. The coordinator is responsible for management of the clinical practices of the agency's geriatric day treatment program; home-based geriatric mental health assessment and treatment program; nursing home education, consultation, and training program; and the geriatric case management program. The successful candidate will have an MSW, be computer literate, possess strong verbal and written communication skills, and have five years of clinical experience, including three years of successful supervisory experience. Experience in geriatric social work is required. Community Counseling Center offers a competitive salary and excellent fringe benefits. (*NASW News*, July 1999, p. 17)

Full-Time Social Workers or Counselors

At LifePath Hospice, compassionate professionals like you are making a difference in the quality of life for hospice patients and their families. Currently, we have the following career opportunities available: Full-time social workers or counselors are needed to provide home-based counseling and case management to hospice patients and survivors. Positions available in Polk, Hardee, Highlands, and Hillsborough Florida Counties. MA or MS required. MSW or LCSW preferred. (*NASW News*, May 2000, p. 15)

Director, Homemaker Services

Design, develop, implement, and oversee para-professional home care services for elderly individuals living independently. Network with other social services and health care providers within field of aging, that is, geriatric care specialists, for referrals. Developing pricing structure for programs. Recruit, hire, and train home care staff. Oversee quality assurance. Direct collection, analysis, and interpretation of program statistics. Prepare annual budget. MS in social services or gerontology plus one year of experience in similar job or as a health care manager required. Prior experience must include recruiting and training home care staff, quality assurance for elderly care programs, and networking with other social services and health care providers in field of aging. Applicants must show proof of legal authority to work in the United States. (*NASW News*, March 2001, p. 15)

Program Coordinator

National Center on Grandparents Raising Grandchildren is seeking highly motivated individual with experience in not-for-profit agencies; fund raising in private and public sectors; program development and implementation; and policy and public relations. Master's degree or equivalent experience required. Salary commensurate with experience. (*NASW News*, June 2002, p.15)

Social Worker

Home & Hospice Care of Rhode Island, the premier hospice in the area, invites you to join our team of caring experts as we meet the growing needs of the community. Master's degree social worker with experience in a home, hospice, long-term care, or hospital setting preferred. We offer competitive compensation and benefits including Blue Cross health and dental coverage, life insurance, and retirement plan. (*NASW News*, May 2002, p. 16)

Alzheimer's Behavioral Program Consultant

National long-term health care organization (nursing home, assisted living, and senior housing) is seeking a qualified person to provide leadership with the Alzheimer's behavioral program. The chosen person should possess a master's degree in social work or therapeutic recreation and have experience in Alzheimer's programming, program development, and training. Duties include developing and maintaining policies and procedures to ensure regulatory compliance and provide training and consultation including workshops, in-house services, telecommunication, computers, and on-site visits. Sixty percent national travel required. (*NASW News*, May 2000, p. 18)

REFERENCES

Administration on Aging, U.S. Department of Health and Human Services. (2002a). *The Administration on Aging and the Older Americans Act.* Retrieved January 19, 2003, from http://www.aoa.gov/aoa/ pages/aoafact.html

Administration on Aging, U.S. Department of Health and Human Services. (2002b). *Older Americans Act Amendments of 2000.* Washington, DC: Author. Retrieved January 19, 2003, from http://www.aoa.gov/aoa/status/summary.html

AFL-CIO. (2003). *What social security and Medicare mean to all of us.* Retrieved November 20, 2003, from http://www.aflcio.org/issuepolitics/social security/meaning/index.cfm

Alzheimer's Association. (2002a). *General statistics/demographics.* Retrieved June 7, 2002, from http://www.alz.org/hc/overview/stats.htm

Alzheimer's Association. (2002b). *Diagnosing Alzheimer's.* Retrieved June 7, 2002, from http//www.alz.org/hc/overview/symptoms.htm

Alzheimer's Association. (2002c). *Symptoms.* Retrieved June 7, 2002, from http//www.alz.org/hc/overview/symptoms.htm

American Association of Retired Persons. (2002). *Setting a public policy agenda.* Washington, DC: Author. Retrieved December 14, 2002, from http://aarp.org/legipoly.html

Barker, R. L. (1999). *Social work dictionary* (4th ed.). Washington, DC: NASW Press.

Barth, M. C. (2001, February). *The labor market for social workers: A first look.* New York: John A. Hartford Foundation.

Beaucar, K. O. (2000, January). Elder abuse is a crisis, group says. *NASW News*, p. 15.

Bellos, N. S., & Ruffolo, M. C. (1995). Aging: Services. In R. L. Edwards (Ed.-in-Chief), *Encyclopedia of social work* (19th ed., Vol. 1, pp. 165–173). Washington, DC: NASW Press.

Binstock, R. H. (1995). A new era in the politics of aging. *Generations, 19*(3), 68–74.

Choudhury, S., & Leonicio, M. V. (1997). Life-cycle aspects of poverty among older women. Social *Security Bulletin, 60*, 17–36.

Connolly, C. (2002, April 7). U.S. to unveil ratings of nursing homes. *Washington Post*, p. A6.

Crowley, S. L. (2001, April). A daughter's ordeal sheds light on caring. *AARP Bulletin*, pp. 3, 11–13.

Duka, W., & Carlson, E. (2002, February). Privatization wouldn't be cheap. *AARP Bulletin*, pp. 3, 10–11.

Eastman, P. (2002, March). Keeping Alzheimer's at bay: Early diagnosis keeps patients functioning longer. *AARP Bulletin*, pp. 14–15.

8 million goes to gerontology infrastructure. (2000, November). *NASW News*, p. 12.

Erlbaum-Zur, P. (2001). *Attitudes of social workers toward physician-assisted suicide.* Unpublished doctoral dissertation, Yeshiva University, Wurzweiler School of Social Work, New York.

Farrenkopf, T., & Bryan, J, (1999). Attitudes of Oregon psychologists toward physician-assisted suicide and the Oregon Death with Dignity Act. *Professional Psychology: Research and Practice, 30*, 235–244.

FastHealth. (2003). *Ileostomy.* Retrieved October 30, 2003, from http://www.fasthealt.com/dictionary/i/ ileostomy.php

Fleck, C. (2002, April). Nursing home care is found wanting. *AARP Bulletin*, pp. 3, 16–17.

Freudenheim, M. (2002, February 14). Personal costs for Medicare H.M.O.'s rise. *New York Times.* Retrieved February 20, 2002, from http://www.nytimes.com/2002/02/14/health/ 14CARE.html

Garner, J. D. (1995). Long-term care. In R. L. Edwards (Ed.-in-Chief), *Encyclopedia of social work* (19th ed., Vol. 2, pp. 1625–1634). Washington, DC: NASW Press.

Gatz, M. (1995). Questions that aging puts to preventionists. In L. A. Bond, S. J. Cutler, & A. Grams (Eds.), *Promoting successful and productive aging* (pp. 36–50). Thousand Oaks, CA: Sage Publications.

Gibelman, M., & Schervish, P. H. (1997). *Who we are: A second look.* Washington, DC: NASW Press.

Hancock, B. L. (1990). *Social work with older people* (2nd ed.). Englewood Cliffs, NJ: Prentice Hall.

Hardwig, J. (1997). Is there a duty to die? *Hastings Center Report, 27*, 34–42.

Henry, S. (1995, February 12). America's hidden disease. *Washington Post Parade Magazine*, p. 4.

Hooyman, N. R., & Gonyea, J. G. (1995). Family caregiving. In R. L. Edwards (Ed.-in-Chief), *Encyclopedia of social work* (19th ed., Vol. 2, pp. 951–959). Washington, DC: NASW Press.

Kaplan, K. O. (1995). End-of-life decisions. In R. L. Edwards (Ed.-in-Chief), *Encyclopedia of social work* (19th ed., Vol. 1, pp. 856–868). Washington, DC: NASW Press.

Karger, H. J., & Stoesz, D. (1998). *American social welfare policy: A pluralistic approach.* New York: Longman.

Krugman, P. (2002, March 5). Breaking the contract. *New York Times.* Retrieved march 10, 2002, from http://www.nytimes.com/2002/03/05/opinion/05KRUG.html

Laureano, E. (1999). *Successful aging among older latinas.* Unpublished manuscript, Yeshiva University, Wurzweiler School of Social Work, New York.

Marcell, J. (2000). *Elder rage or take my father . . . please! How to survive caring for aging parents.* Irvine, CA: Impressive Press.

Miller, F. G., & Brody, H. (1995). Professional integrity and physician assisted suicide. *Hastings Center Report, 25*, 8–16.

Moskowitz, E. H., & Lindemann, N. J. (1995). The best laid plans: The lessons of SUPPORT. Hastings Center Report, *Special Supplement, 25*, S3–S8.

MSWs lead in private case management. (1988, January). *NASW News*, p. 16.

Nagourney, E. (2002a, February 12). Aging: Mild depression and eroding immunity. *New York Times*. Retrieved February 13, 2002, from http://www.nytimes.com/2002/02/12/health/aging/12MENT.html

Nagourney, E. (2002b, March 12). Patterns: Comfort vs. longevity: Who decides? *New York Times*. Retrieved March, 20, 2002, from http://www.nytimes.com/2002/03/12/health/12PATT.html

NASW establishes section on aging. (1998, March). *NASW News*, p. 6.

National Association of Area Agencies on Aging. (2000). *Long term care*. Retrieved December 6, 2002, from http://www.n4a.org/longtermcare2000.cfm

National Association of Area Agencies on Aging. (2002a). *Home and community-based services*. Retrieved December 6, 2002, from http://www.n4a.org/hacbservices.cfm

National Association of Area Agencies on Aging. (2002b). *Medicare prescription drug benefit*. Retrieved December 6, 2002, from http:// www.n4a.org/medicarerxdrugbenefit.cfm.

National Council on the Aging. (2001). *NCOA public policy update*. Retrieved January 18, 2002, from http://www.ncoa.org/advocacy/ppupd/ppud_12101.html

National Council on the Aging. (2002). *Facts about older Americans*. Retrieved February 1, 2002, from http//www.ncoa.org/press/facts.html

National Hospice Foundation. (1999). *NHF public opinion research: Baby boomers fear talking to parents about death*. Retrieved January 4, 2003, from http://www.hospiceinfo.org/public/articles/index.cfm

National Hospice Foundation. (2002). *The Medicare hospice benefit*. Retrieved January 4, 2003, from http://www.hospiceinfo.org/public/articles/index.cfm.

National Hospice and Palliative Care Organization. (2002). *About NHPCO*. Retrieved January 4, 2003, from http://www.nhpco.org/public/articles/index. cfm.

National Institute of Mental Health. (2002a). *If you're over 65 and feeling depressed: Treatment brings new hope*. Retrieved December 19, 2002, from http:/www.nimh.nih.gov/publicat/over65.cfm

National Institute of Mental Health. (2002b). *Older adults: Depression and suicide facts*. Retrieved January 4, 2003, from http://www.nimh.nih.gov/publicat/elderlydepsuicide.cfm

Netting, F. E., Wilson, C. C., & New, J. C. (1987). The human–animal bond: Implications for practice. *Social Work, 32*, 60–64.

Nieves, J. (1999, March). Activism, redoubled and vigilant. *NASW News*, p. 2.

Novelli, W. D. (2002a, February). A Medicare drug benefit: Our top priority for 2002. *AARP Bulletin*, p. 18.

Novelli, W. D. (2002b, March). As we see it: Reinventing retirement. *AARP Bulletin*, p. 20.

Older Americans Act of 1965, P.L. 89-73, 79 Stat. 218.

Omnibus Reconciliation Act of 1987, P.L. 100-203, 101 Stat. 1874.

O'Neill, J. V. (1999a, February). Aging express: Can social work keep up? *NASW News*, p. 3.

O'Neill, J. V. (1999b, March). Providers, nursing home residents face barrier. *NASW News*, p. 3.

O'Neill, J. V. (2000a, April). Least skilled treating neediest patients. *NASW News*, p. 3.

O'Neill, J. V. (2000b, October). Social workers risk running businesses. *NASW News*, p. 3.

O'Neill, J. V. (2002, January). HHS investigates alleged service breaches. *NASW News*, p. 6.

Oregon Death with Dignity Act, 1997, Or. Rev. Stat. 127.800 et seq.

Patient Self-Determination Act of 1990, P.L. 101-508, 104 Stat. 1388.

Pear, R. (2002, March 31). In a first, Medicare coverage is authorized for Alzheimer's. *New York Times*. Retrieved March 31, 2002, from http://www.nytimes.com/2002/03/31/politics/31MEDI.html.

Proffitt, L. J. (1987). Hospice. In A. Minahan (Ed.-in-Chief), *Encyclopedia of social work* (18th ed., Vol. 1, pp. 812–816). Silver Spring, MD: National Association of Social Workers.

Richman, J. M. (1995). *Hospice*. In R. L. Edwards (Ed.-in-Chief), Encyclopedia of social work (19th ed., Vol. 2, pp. 1358–1364). Washington, DC: NASW Press.

Roper, A. (2001, December). *The costs of long-term care: Public perceptions versus reality*. Retrieved February 15, 2002, from http://research.aarp.org/health/ltc_costs_1.html

Rose, S. M., & Moore, V. L. (1995). Case management. In R. L. Edwards (Ed.-in-Chief), *Encyclopedia of social work* (19th ed., Vol. 1, pp. 335–340). Washington, DC: NASW Press.

Rosen, A. L., & Persky, T. (1997). Meeting mental health needs of older people: Policy and practice issues for social work. In C. S. Saltz (Ed.), *Social work response to the White House Conference on Aging: From issues to action* (pp. 45–54). Binghamton, NY: Haworth Press.

Sable, P. (1995). Pets, attachment, and well-being across the life cycle. *Social Work, 40*, 334–341.

Sackman, B. (2002, May). *Budget cuts impact aging and social work services*. Currents of the New York City Chapter, National Association of Social Workers, pp. 3, 9.

Saltz, C. S. (Ed.). (1997). *Social work response to the White House Conference on Aging: From issues to actions*. Binghamton, NY: Haworth Press.

Social Security Act of 1935, Ch. 531, 49 Stat. 620.

Social workers in the public eye. (2002, March). *NASW News*, p. 17.

Social workers set goal to strengthen care for the dying and bereaved. *Project on Death in America Newsletter*. Retrieved October 30, 2003, from http://www.soros.org/death/newsletter10/social_workers.html

Stoesen, L. (2002, May). Role in end-of-life care examined. *NASW News*, p. 4.

Surgeon General's Call to Action to Prevent Suicide. (1999). *At a glance: Suicide among the elderly*. Office of the Surgeon General. Retrieved February 15, 2002, from http://www. surgeongeneral.gov/library/calltoaction/fact2.htm

Takamura, J. C. (2001). The future is aging. *Social Thought: Journal of Religion in the Social Services, 20*, 3–16.

Tax Equity and Fiscal Responsibility Act of 1982, P.L. 97-248, 96 Stat. 585, 591.

Too few trained for aging work, reports contend. (1991, February). *NASW News*, p. 10.

Torres-Gil, F. M., & Puccinelli, M. A. (1995). Aging: Public policy issues and trends. In R. L. Edwards (Ed.-in-Chief), *Encyclopedia of social work* (19th ed., Vol. 1, pp. 159–164). Washington, DC: NASW Press.

Toseland, R. W. (1995). Aging: Direct practice. In R. L. Edwards (Ed.-in-Chief), *Encyclopedia of social work* (19th ed., Vol. 1, pp. 153–159). Washington, DC: NASW Press.

Uhlenberg, P. I. (1996). Mortality decline over the twentieth century and supply of kin over the life course. *Gerontologist, 36*, 681–685.

U.S. Department of Health and Human Services. (2002, February 7). HHS awards $128 million in grants to help family caregivers. *HHS News*. Retrieved December 14, 2002, from http://www. aoa.gov/pressroom/PR2002/NFCSPfunding02.html

Zuniga, M. E. (1995). Aging: Social work practice. In R. L. Edwards (Ed.-in-Chief), *Encyclopedia of social work* (19th ed., Vol. 1, pp. 173–183). Washington, DC: NASW Press.

Chapter Nine SUBSTANCE ABUSE

ubstance abuse is a major concern in American society and has been referenced as the nation's number one health problem (O'Neill, 1999). Social workers share this societal concern about the continued impact of chemical dependency on individuals, families, and children. Substance abuse is defined broadly as a "maladaptive pattern of using certain drugs, alcohol, medications, and toxins despite their adverse consequence" (Barker, 1999, p. 470). Substance dependence refers to the "continued use; craving; and other cognitive, behavioral, and physiological symptoms that occur through the use of certain drugs, alcohol, medications, and toxins" (Barker, 1999, p. 470). Substance dependence interferes with day-to-day functioning. Symptoms may include preoccupation with the substance, persistent efforts to control its use, reduced work or social activities, and continued use despite recognition of its consequences. Disorders that result from taking drugs of abuse, alcohol, medication, or toxin include substance-induced psychotic disorders, mood disorders, anxiety disorders, sleep disorders, and sexual dysfunction (Barker, 1999).

Although some social workers specialize in work related to substance abuse treatment and prevention, a much larger proportion of social workers address related concerns in their work in other fields or settings. For example, as noted in Chapter 7, alcohol use among high school and college students has become "epidemic." Social workers employed in school settings often provide services to address such abuses. Similarly, social workers in employee assistance programs deal with the manifestations and consequences of substance abuse on the health and mental health of employees. Social workers who work with homeless people often address the comorbidity problems attendant to chronic mental illness and substance abuse. Thus, substance abuse crosscuts a number of areas of social work practice and is intertwined with a range of psychosocial problems, whether as the precipitating problem or as a consequence of other problems.

In this chapter, the focus is on the problem of substance abuse and its treatment within specialized practice settings. However, it is acknowledged that social workers in all settings of practice serve as "gatekeepers" in identifying, treating, and referring clients for specific substance abuse services.

SOCIAL WORK PRACTICE IN THE FIELD OF SUBSTANCE ABUSE

Despite the pervasiveness of substance abuse problems in American society today, only a relatively small proportion of social workers are involved in the provision of substance abuse services as a primary practice area. In 1991, 4.6 percent of responding NASW members indicated that their primary practice area was substance abuse (Gibelman & Schervish, 1993). Because of the small representation of members in the field of substance abuse, in ensuing years NASW combined substance abuse into the category of "other" (Gibelman & Schervish, 1997).

Over the years, there has been consistent concern expressed about the lack of presence of social workers in this field. For example, Magura (1994) urged a greater interest and involvement of social workers in work in chemical dependency treatment, arguing that social workers' commitment and skill are vitally needed.

Inadequate attention to alcohol abuse in social work education programs and lack of knowledge about research-based practice in this field have been identified by the National Institute on Alcohol Abuse and Alcoholism (NIAAA) in 2002. To address this problem, NIAAA funded a faculty development initiative aimed at preparing faculty in schools of social work to teach about research-based practice and to encourage social work faculty to conduct more alcohol research studies ("Alcohol Curriculum Pilot-Tested," 2002). In early 2002, pilot tests were begun on a social work curriculum developed under NIAAA auspices concerning the prevention and treatment of alcohol abuse disorders.

Federal funds have also been used to promote research on substance abuse, one emphasis of which is the extent and nature of drug abuse in minority populations. An expected byproduct of this research is to encourage social workers to develop the expertise to conduct epidemiological research on drug abuse among people of color and vulnerable populations and to gain a greater understanding of risk behaviors ("Substance Abuse Study Funded," 2000). Such research, in turn, will provide a basis for new intervention and prevention strategies.

NASW has also sought to cultivate the interests of and resources for social workers in the field of substance abuse. In 1995, the NASW board of directors granted full membership status to a speciality practice section on Alcohol, Tobacco and Other Drugs ("Sub-stances Section Wins Full Status," 1995). The section

seeks to meet the needs of those who encounter alcohol- and drug-related issues in their practice, not just those who work in this specific area of service.

DIMENSIONS OF THE PROBLEM

Substance abuse affects the young and old, people of all socioeconomic groups, and crosscuts racial, ethnic, and religious lines. Current information on the prevalence, patterns, and consequences of illicit drug, alcohol, and tobacco use in the United States for those 12 years of age and older comes from the National Survey on Drug Use and Health in 2002, a project of the Substance Abuse and Mental Health Services Administration (SAMHSA). Data are based on information obtained from approximately 70,000 people per year. Highlights of that report pertaining to use of illicit drugs are given below (SAMHSA, 2003a). The dimensions of the problems of alcohol and tobacco abuse are then provided.

- In 2002, an estimated 19.5 million Americans were current illicit drug users, meaning they had used an illicit drug during the month prior to the interview. This estimate represents 8.3 percent of the population aged 12 years and older.
- Among youths aged 12 to 17 in 2002, 11.6 percent were users of illicit drugs.
- Among youths who were heavy drinkers in 2000, 65.5 percent were also current illicit drug users. Among nondrinkers, only 4.2 percent were current illicit drug users. Similarly, among youths who smoked cigarettes, the rate of the past month illicit drug use was 42.7 percent, compared with 4.6 percent for nonsmokers.
- An estimated 17.4 percent of unemployed adults were current illicit drug users in 2000.
- In 2002, of the 16.6 million illicit drug users aged 18 years and older, 12.4 million

(74.6 percent) were employed full-and part-time.

- An estimated 11 million people reported driving under the influence of an illicit drug at some time in the past year.

These data provide a perspective on the prevalence of drug use in the United States among all age groups and both men and women. The at-risk behaviors in which drug users engage, such as driving while under the influence of drugs, are also highlighted. The majority of adults who use illicit drugs are employed, putting themselves and perhaps their coworkers at risk, depending on the nature of the work and the industry. Those people abusing substances were also found to have poor employment records—skipping from one employment setting to another. These substance abusers do not constitute some hidden others, but rather coworkers and colleagues.

Factors ranging from the deterioration of the family to the glamorization of drug use by various entertainment media have been identified as partially responsible for the substantial use of drugs in today's society. Regardless of the specific cause, the problem of substance abuse affects people of all social classes. The costs of pervasive drug abuse are enormous in both law enforcement and social measures. In the District of Columbia, for example, about half of the 26,000 criminal cases handled by the DC Superior Court involved drugs or alcohol. Data from the DC Pretrial Services Agency showed that 47 percent of the adults arrested in Washington, DC, during a one-month period tested positive for cocaine, phencyclidine hydrochloride (known as PCP), or opiates. Eighty-five percent of foster care placements in the city involved substance abuse. District officials estimate that the dollar cost of drug and alcohol abuse is about $1.2 billion annually (Kovaleski, 2002). This does not include the cost to life and quality of life for the individuals and families affected.

PRACTICE SETTINGS

Social workers involved in the prevention and treatment of substance abuse work in a variety of settings, including health facilities, inpatient and outpatient substance abuse treatment centers, mental health centers, schools, and in the workplace.

Two types of programs categorize live-in treatment—those that operate treatment programs within facilities and those that provide a supportive and safe living environment to residents who receive treatment services in other settings. Generally, the first category includes inpatient rehabilitation programs in hospitals or separate facilities, and the second group consists of residences, halfway houses, and recovery homes (Smyth, 1995). Outpatient programs focus on helping clients to change their addictive drug abuse behaviors without the use of methadone maintenance programs or other similar substitute drug products.

Managed care, the impact of which affects virtually all areas of social work practice, also has influenced the nature of substance abuse treatment. Inpatient treatment is generally limited to 30 days, during which time the focus is on detoxification and cognitive–behavioral therapy. On release to an outpatient program, clients may concurrently receive mental health treatment, case management for purposes of monitoring behavior, and participation in a 12-step program.

There is little agreement about the interventions most likely to lead to successful outcomes among clients with substance abuse problems. For example, there are conflicting viewpoints about the wisdom of pharmacotherapy as an adjunct to psychosocial treatment. The argument is that one drug is being substituted for another (the abused drug). Methadone maintenance is the most widely known pharmacological approach to longer-term treatment, but other treatments have been developed for alcohol and opiate dependence that are not addictive, such as naltrexone, which serves to reduce craving. Another medication, disulfiram (Antabuse), discourages drinking by making the person feel sick if alcohol is consumed (NIAAA, 2002). These medications are used in conjunction with other therapies and are not, in and of themselves, a "cure." Social workers need to have some knowledge about these pharmacotherapies in order to refer clients appropriately (McNeece & DiNitto, 2002).

Social workers are involved in many aspects of substance abuse treatment, including planning and program development, diagnosis and assessment, information and referral, counseling, and program evaluation, as highlighted in the following vignette.

SUBSTANCE ABUSE TREATMENT IN AN OUTPATIENT CLINIC

Max recently received his MSW and is employed as a social worker in the substance abuse treatment clinic at Middleton Community Health Center in Overland Park, KS. Currently Max is involved as a leader for a group of parents who are experiencing various difficulties with their children who are either experimenting with or are addicted to an illegal substance.

One afternoon Max received a call from Jean, a woman in the group. Jean is in her late 40s and has three children. Jean entered the group because she was having problems with her 18-year-old son Charlie. Charlie's behavior, in the mother's opinion, was out of control. He was not working, was unresponsive to limit setting, and was undergoing personality changes. She suspected he was using drugs, alcohol, or both, and he refused to consider treatment for substance abuse despite the urging of his family. The telltale signs included a glazed look in his eyes, an "out of it" demeanor, and behavior the mother found frightening—he had become loud, rude, and seemed to be constantly on the verge of losing his temper to the point of violence. In addition, she had caught him lying several times, something Charlie had not done before.

One day, Jean called Max and indicated that it was an "emergency." She was clearly distraught as she relayed that Charlie had just tried to assault her and had threatened her with a kitchen knife. She was able to grab her two daughters and run to a neighbor's house. She did not want to call the police, but she wanted Charlie to get help. Max consulted with his supervisor and then arranged to meet the mother at her house so that he could talk with Charlie directly.

When he arrived at the home, Max found Jean on the front lawn with her daughters. Charlie was standing in the doorway looking out at them, still holding the knife. However, Charlie appeared to be more confused than angry. Max approached the door and introduced himself to Charlie. He then indicated that he was a social worker and asked to come inside and talk with Charlie. The boy agreed, and Max asked him to put the knife away. Charlie complied with this request.

Once they were both inside and seated at the kitchen table, Max commented that the situation appeared to have gotten out of hand and that everyone was frightened. Charlie nodded and dropped his head, although Max noticed the tears in Charlie's eyes. Max continued to try to talk to Charlie, but he was unresponsive. Finally, Max suggested that it might be best for Charlie to be examined at a hospital. At first Charlie appeared angry, but then he shrugged his shoulders and again dropped his head. Max asked if he could call the emergency room at the community hospital to alert them that Charlie would be coming. Finally, Charlie nodded in agreement, and the call was made. Max told the hospital personnel the reason for the call and his suspicion of drug involvement as well as possible psychiatric problems. Max then went outside and brought Jean back into the house so that she could provide her support and forgiveness.

Max then took Charlie to the hospital and stayed with him while a psychiatrist interviewed him. Max was able to provide informa-

tion on Charlie's family as Charlie was not particularly responsive during the interview. Max told Charlie that he would come and visit him if that was okay. Max then returned to Jean's house and told her what had happened. He offered to visit Charlie with her. Max also told Jean that he would try to establish a relationship with Charlie in case the Middleton Community Health Center was determined to be part of Charlie's discharge plan.

In this vignette, social worker Max runs a group for parents of youths who are using drugs or are at risk. It is not unusual for Max to receive an emergency call such as that made by Jean. Working with parents and youths when drugs are involved means to expect the unexpected. The community health center allows its staff to intervene outside of the center's "walls" by going into the community. This is because of the special needs and circumstances of the population with which Max and other staff work. Doing so, however, can entail some risk to the social worker, and in some cases, Max has called the police and requested assistance from them.

After receiving the phone call from Jean, Max first has to assess the safety risk to himself and to the family members. After all, Charlie is wielding a knife. However, Jean and her two daughters are now at a neighbor's house and Max cautions that they are not to let Charlie in. Max respects Jean's decision not to call the police, but he has a cell phone with him should it become apparent that the situation warrants police intervention.

Max first attempted to ensure the personal safety of Jean and her two daughters. After doing this, he turned his attention to Charlie, who by this time—although still holding the knife—was in a subdued state. His role was active, as there are several concrete goals to be accomplished in a short period of time. In his talk with Charlie, Max determined that the boy was under the influence of drugs and was having a psychotic reaction to whatever he had taken. Max tried to gain some information about how much of what

Charlie had consumed. This information-gathering function was essential to determine whether there was imminent risk to Charlie. Max utilized his counseling skills and employed active referral techniques in encouraging Max to go to the hospital. Finally, Max coordinated with the hospital staff to gain Charlie's admission and informed them about the situation. Max offers ongoing support and assistance to Charlie and his family.

In addition to their direct services role in preventing and treating substance abuse, social workers also carry out supervisory and administrative roles in this field of practice. The following vignette indicates some of the administrative issues that can arise within an agency and in the agency's relationship to other organizations and also highlights some of the ethical dilemmas that can arise.

MEDIATING INTERORGANIZATIONAL ISSUES
Jonathan Singer has been executive director of a nonprofit, outpatient community-based substance abuse treatment center for five years. During this time, the organization has expanded rapidly, including a contract relationship with the county department of drug and alcohol abuse and a working agreement with the county parole and probation department. At the present time, 15 probationers are being seen by the agency for outpatient substance abuse treatment; this treatment is a requirement of their probation. The agreement with the agency specifies that the social workers providing services are to report any "slips" among the parolees, that is, should they be found to be using drugs or alcohol, this would be considered a probation violation, and the social workers are expected to report it. Probationers participating in this program are required, as a condition of their probation, to waive their rights to confidentiality in that they give permission for the agency to share any and all information with their probation officer.

In reviewing the monthly progress logs of the social workers, Jonathan notices that there are a surprisingly low number of reports being made to the probation and parole department about slips. He knows that treatment for substance abuse rarely goes smoothly; that two steps forward are often accompanied by a step backward.

At the weekly staff meeting with the social workers, eight in all, Jonathan brings up the issue of slips and inquires as to whether the failure to report is a sign of unusually dramatic progress or if there is another explanation. His close working relationship with his staff, built on trust, allows the social workers to "fess up" to their failure to report. They explain, with some indignation, that even though the probationers are informed about the limits of confidentiality and the reporting requirement, they feel that to report is to compromise the treatment process. The end result might be that the probationer is reincarcerated even though he or she might be making substantial progress.

Jonathan, in fact, agrees with this line of reasoning. He had not been happy about incorporating the reporting clause into the agreement but had yielded to the pressure of the county because the agreement marked an important beginning for the agency to reach a targeted population. It was his hope that in future agreements, and once the agency had proven the effectiveness of its services, the reporting requirement could be eliminated.

But here Jonathan finds that he is faced with a dilemma. He is responsible for ensuring contract compliance. He is also responsible for supervising the social work staff and assisting them in providing the services of the agency. On the other hand, the real or potential compromise to treatment and the social workers' resistance to carrying through on reporting slips are issues that need to be addressed.

Jonathan discusses the dilemma openly with his staff, noting that he could not condone their sidestepping the regulations about reporting. In addition to county relationship issues, Jonathan

reminds them of their responsibility to support the agency, including its rules. He asks that, henceforth, they come to him with issues before any covert or overt actions are taken. Here, one staff member interrupted and reminded Jonathan that the staff had indeed come to him about this issue. Jonathan patiently clarified that he had responded to their concerns during that first meeting about the reporting requirement in terms of plans to bring the topic up during negotiations next year, but there had been no discussion about circumventing the reporting requirement—this was a step the staff had decided upon without discussion or authorization.

Jonathan then acknowledged the strong feelings of the social workers about reporting slips and asked whether the sentiment was so strong that the agency should consider withdrawing from its agreement to serve probationers. The eight social workers were stunned by this possibility and indicated that this would be a great disservice both to the clients and to the agency. One person also voiced what many of the others were thinking—termination of the agreement with the probation department could mean the end of their jobs.

Jonathan summed up the sentiments of the staff—the agency should continue with the agreement. "But what about our obligation to report slips," he asked. "How are we going to address this?" After a lengthy discussion of options, one stood out as the most viable: meet with the contract officers from the probation department and try to either amend the conditions of the agreement or reach an informal agreement that slips would be handled differently.

Jonathan called the county contact person, Jeff Daniels (a probation supervisor), and explained the nature of the problem. He indicated that a useful approach might be to have a joint meeting with himself, his staff, Mr. Daniels, and the probation officers who were supervising the agency's clients. After checking with the deputy commissioner, Mr. Daniels called back to arrange a time and place for the meeting. The meeting was scheduled in conjunction with a regular agency staff meeting to ensure that all workers would be present.

Jonathan began the meeting with remarks intended to create a climate in which the discussion would be open and honest. The social work staff expressed their concerns that accurate reporting might result in premature violations. They indicated a lack of trust in the probation officers' abilities to recognize when treatment was working in spite of a couple of slips. The probation officers were able to express their concerns that social workers tend to "coddle" clients and that clients would be able to "get over on them."

The open yet respectful discussion resulted in a compromise agreement that no probationer would be violated for up to two slips without the consent of his or her social worker. This outcome satisfied the social workers in that it gave them an important measure of control over the decision-making process. It also satisfied the probation officers who felt that, ultimately, the decision was in their hands if their probationers continued to slip. Most important, Jonathan felt that the process had created a more effective working relationship between the agency and the probation department. The staffs of both agencies began to take back some of the stereotypical feelings they had of each other and replace them with new understanding and respect for differences.

In this case, the social worker is in a management position. However, he still draws on his assessment skills to determine the extent of the problem (that is, lack of required reporting by staff), only he is applying these skills at a different level of social work intervention. Once the problem is identified, Jonathan uses interorganizational, negotiation, and coordination skills to arrange a meeting with the contract officers and the social workers. Jonathan also makes excellent use of his managerial and supervisory social work skills as he exhibits a supportive yet guiding influence for his staff. Finally, Jonathan is confronted with the inherent ethical dilemmas that can arise in practice, particularly when clients are seen involuntarily, such as a condition of probation or parole. Jonathan identifies and acknowledges these ethical issues and mediates clinical, ethical, legal, and agency concerns.

NEW PROGRAM APPROACHES

Substance abuse may be associated with a number of other physiological and psychosocial problems, including homelessness, mental illness, unemployment, poverty, and crime. Many youths and adults who abuse substances end up in the criminal justice system on felony drug offenses or other crimes associated with the drug epidemic. For example, among youths 12 to 17 years of age, a positive relationship was found between drug use and serious fights, carrying a handgun, selling illegal drugs, and stealing or attempting to steal something worth $50 or more (SAMHSA, 2003c).

In California, a social work supported initiative—Proposition 36—was approved in 2000. This initiative seeks to provide drug treatment services as an alternative to incarceration for all first- and second-time nonviolent drug possession offenders. Excluded, however, are those people involved in the distribution or sale of drugs and those with a previous conviction for a violent felony, unless they have been out of prison for at least five years (Vallianatos, 2001).

According to Janlee Wong, the NASW California chapter executive director, Proposition 36 "signifies the public's belief that people with addictions should be treated and rehabilitated, not punished and jailed" (as cited in Vallianatos, 2001, p. 12). Ms. Wong also noted that the proposition's implementation will lead to more jobs for social workers.

The state Legislative Analyst's Office estimates that 35,000 to 40,000 Californians a year will be diverted from incarceration to drug treatment as a result of the initiative. Further, it is estimated that the state will save from $100 million to $150 million a year, and an additional $50 million for counties, because of the reduced costs of prison and jail operations (Vallianatos, 2001).

In recent years, attention has been focused on the importance of addressing the problem of substance abuse early through various prevention programs. The recognition of the importance of prevention is evident in the increasing number of schools, both public and private, that are instituting curriculum on the dangers of drug and alcohol abuse.

Investing in treatment services is economically prudent even though addiction is chronic and may require several episodes of treatment. The following vignette illustrates the role of social workers in substance abuse prevention.

A SUBSTANCE ABUSE PREVENTION PROGRAM

Thomas is a 15-year-old, Hispanic male who lives with his mother and is the oldest of four children. Thomas has had several run-ins with the police, who have found him hanging around with people who use drugs. The police have also caught Thomas in acts of vandalism.

One evening Thomas was at the local park hanging out with his friends. The police were notified of suspicious activity in the park and when they arrived, the boys scattered. However, the police found crack cocaine and a pipe, so they rounded up the youths and took them to police headquarters.

This particular precinct works in cooperation with an inner-city multipurpose community-based agency. The agency has received city funds to establish a prevention program in conjunction with local police precincts. The program consists of an outreach worker at each precinct as well as two social workers who provide substance abuse counseling. Generally, the clients are youths who are referred to the program in an effort to prevent further abuse or involvement with the criminal justice system.

In this case, the outreach worker, Bruce, called Thomas's mother to ask her to contact the program's social worker so that they could bring Thomas home and then discuss his situation. The mother agreed. The outreach worker then contacted Scott, a white male in his early 30s, who is a recent MSW graduate. Scott met Bruce and Thomas at Thomas's apartment. Bruce's job of coordinating services was complete. It was now up to Scott to fulfill the social work functions of assessing the situation, identifying problem areas, and developing a trusting, helping relationship with Thomas.

Scott proceeded with Thomas to the apartment where he lived; the apartment was small, in a dirty and unsafe building. Thomas' mother Jackie, in her late-30s, greeted them at the door. None of the other children were home—Scott, Jackie, and Thomas were able to sit at the kitchen table and talk. There was a sense of awkwardness as both Thomas and his mother avoided eye contact with Scott. Scott took responsibility for conducting the interview and began by first explaining a little about his agency, the services provided, and the specific prevention program. Scott explained that this program was viewed as an alternative to prosecution through the criminal justice system. The purpose of his visit was to determine what services were needed by Thomas and if the agency could provide them. Throughout this time, Thomas and his mother remained quiet.

Scott then wanted to get information about Thomas's life at home and at school. Scott asked Thomas a few questions to elicit information, but Thomas said there was nothing to tell. He denied any involvement with drugs and said the police were simply picking on the black kids in the neighborhood. Scott then asked Thomas about his performance in school, to which Thomas responded that he did "fine" and had passed "almost" all of his classes. He declined to show Scott a copy of his report card.

Scott asked about previous encounters with the police. Thomas denied that he had ever been arrested. Scott then turned to Jackie and asked her about Thomas's behavior. Jackie indicated that Thomas was basically a good boy, although he was occasionally mischievous. She refused to say anything else and claimed that they did not need any services. Scott recognized that the interview was not going well; there were barriers of race, mistrust, and fear. He decided to discuss these barriers with Thomas and Jackie directly. They seemed surprised at Scott's openness, finally establishing eye contact. The dialogue, however, remained essentially one way. Scott then explained how counseling worked. He said that Thomas would come to see him once a week so that they could get to know each other better and talk more freely. He also explained that the discussions during counseling would be confidential. Neither Thomas nor his mother seemed convinced, and Jackie asked if Thomas would have to go to court if he did not go to counseling. Scott responded that this decision was up to the police but that the police looked favorably upon youths who participated in counseling and this participation was taken into consideration when determining whether to adjudicate.

Jackie turned to Thomas and told him he should go to see Scott every week. Thomas protested. Scott recognized Thomas's resistance and admitted that Thomas may not need any help but he would appreciate it if Thomas would simply try counseling. Thomas finally, but very reluctantly, agreed. Since Thomas usually played basketball after school, they arranged to meet after the basketball game on Mondays at 5:30 PM. Scott then gave Jackie his card and told her to call him if anything occurred to her that might be useful for him to know or if she ever needed to discuss anything.

This case exemplifies the social worker's role in assessment and problem identification. Scott conducted the interview with sensitivity to the client's lifestyle and culture, part of the diagnostic process. Scott was aware of the basic distrust exhibited by Thomas and Jackie, acknowledged

it, and addressed "up front" the issue of racial difference. This direct confrontation of a difficult subject helped break the silence. By no means, however, was the issue of trust resolved. This would have to occur over the longer term. Scott also offered preliminary assistance and arranged for ongoing counseling through referral to the community agency.

On a macro level, the cooperative relationship between the social services agency and the police precinct exemplifies the functions of coordination, organization, and exchange so that resources can be used in the most effective manner. This relationship also highlights the creativity that can result from interdisciplinary collaboration.

Another form of prevention is found in drug-free workplace programs. Such programs create an expectation and climate to discourage alcohol and drug abuse and encourage treatment and recovery. In addition to the basics—a written policy, employee education, and supervisor training—certain characteristics have been identified with effective drug-free workplace programs. These include:

- active, visible leadership and support of the program by the employer
- employee and union involvement in program development
- access to treatment and follow-up for employees who are having abuse problems
- methods of identifying alcohol and drug abusers, including drug testing, to enforce the policy and to provide the opportunity for treatment, recovery, and return to work. (SAMSHA, 2003b)

ALCOHOLISM

Data from the 2000 National Survey on Drug Use and Health also highlight the nature and prevalence of alcohol use in the United States (SAMSHA, 2003c). Highlights of that report pertaining to alcohol use are as follows:

- Over half of Americans age 12 and older reported being current drinkers of alcohol in the 2002 survey (51.7 percent). This translates to an estimated 120 million people.
- Heavy drinking was reported by 6.7 percent of the population age 12 and older, or 15.9 million people; binge drinking was reported by 54 million people (22.9 percent).
- About 10.7 million people age 12 to 20 reported drinking alcohol in the month prior to the survey interview in 2002 (28.8 percent of this age group).
- Among all youths age 12 years and older, 10.7 percent were binge drinkers, and 2.5 percent were heavy drinkers.
- About one in seven Americans age 12 years and older in 2000 (22.3 million people) had driven under the influence of alcohol at lease once in the 12 months prior to the interview.
- Among young adults ages 18 to 25, 19.9 percent had driven under the influence of alcohol in 2000.

A study conducted by Columbia University's National Center on Addiction and Substance Abuse in 2002 found that alcohol abuse is of epidemic proportions among youths and that it is interrelated with behaviors that are deadly to self or others:

America has an epidemic of underage drinking that germinates in elementary and middle schools with children from nine to 13 years old and erupts on college campuses where 44 percent of students binge drink and alcohol is the number one substance of abuse—implicated in date rape, sexual harassment, racial disturbances, dropouts, overdose deaths from alcohol poisoning, and suicides. Teenagers who drink are seven times likelier to engage in sex and twice as likely to have sex with four or more partners than those who do not.

Such behavior can lead to unprotected sex with the increased risk of AIDS, sexually transmitted diseases, and pregnancy.

Drinking in U.S. culture has long been viewed with ambivalence. On the one hand, Americans view drinking as an acceptable way to escape from the stresses of everyday life; on the other hand, they view it as a sign of weakness and a mode of self-indulgence. Further, parents are often responsible for introducing their children to alcohol directly or by tolerating it when it occurs simply as a "rite of passage" for youths.

The fact that the purchase of liquor by adults is legal, that it is so widely accepted in conjunction with activities ranging from a toast to the new bride and groom to a beer at the ball game, and that moderate drinking of some liquors has been shown to have health benefits all muddy the picture. There is ambiguity about drinking that has affected society's response. When, for example, does one cross the line between social drinking and alcoholism? Is it a physiological illness or a psychosocial problem?

Alcoholism as a Disease

Alcoholism is a disease. The craving for alcohol can be as strong as that for food or water. Alcoholics will continue to drink despite the employment, family, health, or legal problems that may result. The disease of alcoholism is chronic and even when sobriety has been achieved, the person remains "an alcoholic." Although alcoholism cannot be cured, it can be treated. The risk for alcoholism is affected by a person's heredity, genetics, and lifestyle (NIAAA, 2002).

People who abuse alcohol may experience an array of behaviors that are secondary to their addiction but inflict extreme pain and hardship on self or others. For example, drivers who are drunk are blamed for the loss of as many as 25,000 lives in highway crashes each year and hundreds of thousands of severe injuries (Argetsinger, 2002). Other problems related to alcohol abuse include violent crimes, problems with families and friends, financial and job problems, and aggressive behavior.

People who abuse alcohol and drugs may be able to hide their addiction—for a time. Nevertheless, the consequences of substance abuse inevitably affect the individual's health, mental health, social relationships, and ability to maintain employment. Family life becomes a casualty of drugs and alcohol, as do friendships. Maintaining a job may become difficult; finances are strained. Take the case of Edna.

COMING TO TERMS WITH ADDICTION

Edna has a good life. At age 50, she is the mother of a teenage, high-achieving daughter. She has been divorced for several years but has been dating a man, and it is a meaningful relationship. She has a career, is economically secure, and has a supportive extended family and good friends.

But all is not well. In the past two years, Edna has lost two jobs. She has easily found employment elsewhere because of her specialty field, but she is now at risk of losing the third job. The immediate problem is that she has taken a lot of time off from work. And often, on the job, she has engaged in confrontational behavior with coworkers so that she has earned the reputation of a "time bomb." Coworkers feel that they must tiptoe around Edna for fear that a wrong remark will trigger a tirade. But Edna is slow to recognize how people are responding to her. She externalizes—the problem is with her boss, her coworkers, the company. At the time she was fired from the first two jobs she felt she was lucky to be out of the terrible work environment. Others had done this to her; she accepted no responsibility.

Within a three-month period, Edna had several minor car accidents. They were minor only because she lives in a large city with a lot of traffic congestion. Had she been going at a faster speed, she might have been seriously hurt or hurt someone else. She paid for the damage in two of

the accidents without going through the insurance company, as she was fearful that she would lose her insurance.

It's difficult for Edna to identify the exact time she came to terms with what was happening. Perhaps it was the last car accident. Her daughter had been in the car that time. Or she may have overheard something said about her at work. Or perhaps her daughter asked what was going on. Edna took a hard look at herself. And then she made a phone call.

The call was to a friend, Lisa, who is a social worker. Edna said, "I have a drinking problem and I need help." She conveyed that she has tried to stop drinking, but she can't. Lisa asked several questions and discovered that the problem was not alcohol alone. Edna was also abusing prescription drugs. The combination was potentially lethal and made the effects of alcohol all the more potent. Edna finally asked: "What do you think?"

Lisa was direct. First, she told Edna that this did not come as a surprise. Lisa did not see Edna all that often socially, but she had noticed that whenever they dined out, Edna ordered a drink—usually several drinks—even if no one else did. Lisa then told Edna that recognizing that there is a problem is an essential first step. But there are several important "next steps" that must be taken in order to achieve successful change. Lisa explained that dealing with substance abuse is a lifelong issue—there is no quick fix and maintaining sobriety is often as challenging as overcoming the addiction.

Lisa provided several concrete suggestions. First, she provided the name of an internist; Edna needed a physical exam and an assessment as to whether she might be a candidate for pharmacotherapy. The second referral was to a mental health center that specialized in the treatment of substance abuse. The third referral was to Alcoholics Anonymous.

Edna promised that she would follow-up on these referrals. She asked Lisa to help her as a friend. She needed to be able to talk about the recovery process she was about to enter. She needed the support of her friends.

Lisa also knew that although Edna had taken an important first step, a degree of self-motivation must be sustained for her to move on to sobriety. Lisa made a commitment to be there for Edna, but as a friend, not a social worker. Lisa was clear about the boundaries and careful not to mingle friendship and a professional relationship.

Adult Children of Alcoholics

People who have been raised in the stressful environments created by the alcoholism of their parents have been termed adult children of alcoholics (ACOAs). Many ACOAs have emotional disorders in common, including anxiety, depression, low self-esteem, and anger. In addition, they have a predisposition toward alcoholism and substance abuse problems (Barker, 1999). Many ACOAs have sought help through self-help groups or other support groups specifically oriented to their problems.

IN HIS FATHER'S SHADOW

Lenny is 27 years old and happily married. He has a good job and good friends, with whom he enjoys going out after work and having a few drinks. However, one drink soon turns into two, which becomes three or four and sometimes five drinks. His wife Carol is very worried. However, Lenny gets angry when she brings up the subject, and Carol doesn't know what to do.

Lenny's father was an alcoholic. Every night he came home from work and had two stiff drinks before dinner, two with dinner, and two more after dinner. By the end of the night he was angry and irritable and he often lashed out at Lenny and his sister with verbal insults and criticisms. Lenny hated to come home after school and after dinner he tried to get to his room as quickly as possible. He remembers his childhood as a nightmare—never knowing what to expect and never being comfortable at

home. No one ever confronted his father about his drinking. When Lenny asked his mother she just said that he worked hard for the family, and she didn't want to upset him more by bringing up the issue. Lenny's father died two years ago from liver disease. His mother is still alive.

Lenny didn't usually start drinking with the desire to get drunk. He just planned to have one beer and head home, but it never seemed to work that way. Lately, with added pressure at work, he has been drinking more. When he comes home, he often is in a bad mood and takes to criticizing Carol and losing his temper over little things. Finally, after one particularly bad scene between them, Carol calls Lenny's sister Marilyn, who has recently quit drinking completely. Marilyn suggests that Lenny go to the local community mental health center, which sponsors a group for ACOAs. Carol calls the community center and talks with the intake social worker, Judy, who facilitates the group. Judy encourages Carol to firmly and consistently urge Lenny to make an appointment. She also offers to see Carol individually or with Lenny, but Carol decides to wait.

One evening after the office happy hour, Lenny was driving home when he lost control of his car. That incident frightened him; he began to think that perhaps he is turning into the father about whom he has so much ambivalence. He discusses these feelings with Carol the next morning. She has already mentioned the group to him (which he rejected out of hand), but this time he agrees to make an appointment at the center.

An intake appointment with Judy is set for later that week. Lenny is surprised about how easy it is to talk with Judy. He relays to her his family background and the precipitating incident driving his car that prompted him to make this appointment. He also acknowledges that he knows how concerned his wife has been about him and that he has not been a good husband lately. Judy, based on her many years of clinical experience, made the connection between

Lenny's background and behavior and the alcoholism to which he had been exposed through his growing-up years. Judy asked Lenny if he had ever heard of adult children of alcoholics. Lenny recalled vaguely reading something about ACOAs in a magazine but otherwise did not know much about them. Judy explained briefly the meaning of the term and told him that there were quite a number of people with problems of adjustment, marriage, and other issues that seemed connected in some way to the family alcoholism that had permeated their youths. Although not all ACOAs have the same problems, there is an important commonality: the alcoholism of one or both parents.

Judy then told Lenny about the group that was run at the center for ACOAs and asked if he would like to participate. Lenny is initially eager—perhaps he could begin to get his life back in order. But he is also aware of how difficult it was to get to this first intake appointment. Nevertheless, he agrees to give it a try.

The group meets each Thursday evening from 8:00 PM to 10:00 PM and he can begin next week. First, Judy explains, the group leader, Michelle, needs to discuss with the group that a new member would be beginning with them and what this means for them.

The following week, with his wife's urging, Lenny attends the group meeting, but with some trepidation. Is he doing the right thing? Will he see it through? Isn't his problem different than those of others? When Lenny enters the room, Michelle considers greeting him but decides to wait to see if someone from the group would take the initiative. Joe, a 29-year-old group member, said, "Welcome. We were expecting a new member tonight. My name is Joe." Lenny feels awkward but mumbles, "Hi, I'm Lenny," and sits down in an empty chair in the group circle.

There was a moment of awkward silence, and then Michelle suggested that perhaps each person could introduce himself or herself. Six of the seven ongoing group members were present. Fran began by saying, "Hi, I'm Fran; welcome

to the group. We're all here tonight except Margot; she had to go to an open school night for her daughter." Jean was next. "I'm Jean. I want you to know that we all know how difficult it is to begin in group and we all went through it. You try to relax and we'll try to make it as comfortable as possible." Each member had a turn. Shirley, another member, explained that this group takes responsibility for its own process. Some groups are very structured, and others are driven more by the participants and their agenda.

Michelle then introduced herself and complimented the group on their efforts and initiative in welcoming Lenny. She also acknowledged the difficulty in beginning, both for the new member and the group. She then suggested another go-around, with each person telling Lenny and retelling each other what brought him or her to the group, how it was going, and what he or she hoped to get out of it. Michelle also welcomed Lenny to share what had brought him to the group and what he hoped to get from it.

Lenny realized that his nervousness was gone. As he listened to each group member tell the story of what brought him or her to the group, he began to realize that everyone there was like him. They all had alcoholic parents and although they had different day-to-day problems, many of their problems related to their ACOA status.

From that moment, Lenny committed himself to the group. After several weeks of attending, he also began to see another social worker, Tom, individually, and sometimes Carol came to these sessions. Carol promised to help Lenny learn ways to avoid the temptations he felt so that he would not turn to alcohol as a solution to problems.

In this case scenario, there are three social workers. Judy is the intake worker—Lenny's first contact with the agency. Her job is to conduct an assessment and, on the basis of an evaluation of the client's situation, offer the support and assistance of the agency. During this initial meeting, Judy also builds rapport with Lenny and makes him feel that there is help available for his problems. Judy is also the referral agent; she arranges for Lenny to become a member of the ACOC group. Michelle is the social worker who facilitates the ACOA group. She is also an enabler, assisting group members to develop self-help skills and recognize their own strengths. Advice and counseling are also functions carried out by Michelle, as she helps clarify feelings and interactions and supports group members in experimenting with problem-solving strategies. As a therapist, Tom engages in the direct services functions of assessment, diagnosis, support, and counseling and sees Lenny both individually and with his wife.

An important feature of this vignette is the role that the family plays in the treatment of alcohol or drug dependency. Family members also need education and support to deal with the addiction, to understand the consequences of the addiction on the family unit, and to promote and sustain recovery (McNeece & DiNitto, 2002).

TOBACCO

For over 30 years, the federal government, through the offices of the Surgeon General, the National Institute of Mental Health, and other agencies, has waged an ongoing campaign to educate the public about the health risks associated with cigarette smoking. Warning labels went from vague references to potential dangers to outright statements that cigarette smoking kills. The cumulative evidence was clear in the growing number of cases of lung disease, lung cancer, and respiratory, heart, and circulatory problems. Smoking is also linked to premature birthweight and other health problems in babies born to mothers who smoke.

An estimated 71.5 million Americans age 12 and older (30.4 percent) reported current use of a tobacco product in 2002. About 61.1 million (26 percent) smoked cigarettes, 12.8 million (5.4 percent) smoked cigars, 7.8 million (3.3 percent) used smokeless tobacco, and 1.8 million (0.8 percent) smoked tobacco in pipes (SAMSHA, 2003c). The proportion of males age 12 years and older who smoked cigarettes in 2002 was higher than females (28.7 percent versus 23.4 percent).

There are racial and ethnic disparities in rates of smoking, with a high of 37.1 percent among American Andeans/Alaska natives to a low of 17.7 percent for Asian Americans (SAMSHA, 2003c).

SMOKING TO DEATH

Emma is 40 years old and smokes over a pack of cigarettes a day. She is a "closet" smoker. It has become so unacceptable in her social group to smoke that most of her friends are not aware that she "lights up" whenever she is alone.

Emma knows all the facts. She watched her mother succumb to lung cancer; her mother had smoked over two packs of cigarettes a day for much of her adult life. She also knows that although lung cancer is not hereditary, there is a genetic predisposition to this form of cancer. She knows that the cost of cigarettes is eating a hole in her pocketbook.

Emma sprays her house with disinfectant. She brushes her teeth several times a day. She always has a breath mint available so that people will not know she is a smoker. She tried to stop smoking after her mother died. Though she herself thought it morbid, she kept the X-ray of her mother's lungs. Surely that would be a visual reminder of what smoking does. She got down to one or two cigarettes a day—close enough to cessation, she thought. But then the number of daily cigarettes started to rise again. She keeps playing games with herself—buying a pack at a time instead of a carton, so that she doesn't have to admit that she is addicted. But she is. Even knowing that it will probably kill her.

For Emma, cessation of smoking will necessitate getting help. She will need the assistance of her physician. She also needs the help and support of a therapist to deal with her addiction.

Cigarette smoking is legal (for adults), as is consumption of alcohol. Sale of cigarettes or alcohol to minors is illegal. Use of illicit drugs is illegal, as is abuse or misuse of prescription drugs. The array of laws governing use of substances that can be abused and the mixed messages contained in many of these laws send a confusing message. Even when the dangers of the substance are well known to the users, this may not be enough for a person to take steps to overcome the addiction. An addict cannot be forced to get help, unless treatment is court ordered or a medical emergency. This is why so many addictions are "intractable" as well as reoccurring.

THE FUTURE

Social workers in all the areas of service are dealing with the manifestations and effects of substance abuse. We know that treatment works for many people. However, there are varying levels of success; some people have long periods of sobriety or remain clean of drugs and then relapse (NIAAA, 2002). It is this cycle that may dissuade some social workers from a career in substance abuse treatment. Despite the scope of the problem and the efficacy of treatment, the proportion of social workers with a primary area of practice in substance abuse is relatively small. Recognizing the profound need for a skilled labor force in this field, social work educators and practitioners have collaborated to develop curriculum materials on drug and alcohol abuse for use in core undergraduate and graduate social work courses. These materials, available through NASW and the Council on Social Work Education, include learning modules to infuse into existing courses such as research, policy, human behavior and the social environment, and practice in the hope of stimulating greater knowledge among all social workers and higher interest in career opportunities in this field.

CAREER OPPORTUNITIES

The field of substance abuse is a difficult, yet often rewarding, arena of social work practice. Social workers who decide to enter the field of substance abuse can choose from a variety of career paths. The career opportunities listed below serve as examples of the range of opportunities within this specialization.

Clinical Counselor

The counseling center at the University of Illinois at Urbana-Champaign needs a clinical counselor. This position combines generalist counselor duties with a significant subspecialty in alcohol and other drug assessment and intervention. Along with the generalist counselor responsibilities described below, this person will serve in the alcohol and other drug office and its intervention team. This counselor will also assume primary responsibility for training, supervising, and consulting with other counselors and interns about alcohol and other drug intervention. As a generalist, the clinical counselor will share with other counselors responsibilities for carrying out the multifaceted mission of the counseling center. The center's mission places a high value on creatively serving a large, diverse student population. The center provides a variety of services to help students with psychological, educational, social, and developmental concerns. The center also has an approved American Psychological Association predoctoral internship program. The successful candidate will be a well-rounded energetic professional who works comfortably both individually and as a team member in providing effective programs. Women and minority candidates are especially encouraged to apply. Qualifications include a master's degree in social work or a doctorate in clinical or counseling psychology or related field; previous experience in college counseling center preferred, but not essential; demonstrated interest, expertise, and experience in the area of alcohol and other drug intervention. Must have demonstrated ability to function at a high level as a generalist counselor in a setting with both diverse clients and staff colleagues; must be licensed in Illinois (or license eligible) as a psychologist, social worker, counselor, or marriage and family therapist. (*NASW News*, March 2001, pp. 15–16)

Addiction Social Worker

The Center for Behavioral Health in Bloomington, IN, has an opening for a full-time LCSW to provide clinical services to alcohol and drug abuse clients and their families. Services include individual and group therapy, consultations, and crisis intervention. Candidate must be two years free of substance abuse if a recovering person. Some evening hours required. Requirements are experience with this population and LCSW with ability to meet provider panel standards. Compensation: positions offer salary commensurate with experience and also a comprehensive benefit plan including health, dental, and wellness benefits, retirement, and generous paid leave. We employ 300 staff in multidisciplinary teams. We have a continuum of outpatient, day treatment, residential, and detox services. (*NASW News*, May 1999, p. 15)

Substance Abuse Assistant Director

A position for clinical and administrative oversight for the director is open; person will report to the director of substance abuse services at the Community Mental Health Center. Candidate will provide clinical supervision for the division, assess needs, and conduct program planning. Supervises program directors clinically and programmatically; sets direction for programs. Responsibilities include assisting with budget preparation and monitoring, grant writing, and monitoring all quality assurance functions. Individual will attend state meetings representing agency and interface with agencies in the community. Knowledge of state-of-the-art substance abuse programming needed; prefer a master's degree with two years experience in substance abuse setting, track record in clinical supervision, and program development. Must have adminis-

tered a complex residential or outpatient program in a clinic delivering substance abuse or mental health programs. Must have excellent writing skills. Must have certification in the candidate's profession. (*NASW News*, March 1999, p. 22)

Clinical Supervisor

Rehoboth McKinley Christian Health Care Services is seeking a clinical supervisor at our behavioral health unit in Gallup, NM. Under the general direction of the unit director, the supervisor will be responsible for the overall supervision and clinical supervision of the addictions program, including staff scheduling, administrative documentation, evaluations, hiring, training, and management of resources. Will also maintain a partial caseload of clients providing individual, marital, family therapy, and group therapy to adult, geriatric, and adolescent patients and their families with alcohol, substance abuse, psychosocial, emotional and behavior problems, and psychological or neurological impairments. Will also function as a clinic supervisor of the vocational rehabilitation program in coordinating and marketing of program. Master's degree in counseling, social work, or related field and experience in the field of alcohol and substance abuse required. Must be licensed to practice in the State of New Mexico or possess a provisional license to practice independently in New Mexico. Two years experience in supervision and six years experience in clinical capacity required. Must agree to a criminal records check, fingerprinting, and meet clearance requirements of Rehoboth McKinley. Must be eligible to drive agency vehicles. (*NASW Newss*, March 2001, p. 17)

Addictions Counselor

Candidate will provide individual and group counseling services in the substance abuse program to assist individuals in achieving more effective personal, social, and educational adjustment in dealing with various addictions, including addictions to controlled substances and non-controlled substances, such as alcohol beverages. Will collect data concerning individuals through interviewing, case history, and observational techniques. Will administer tests and interpret individual abilities. Will conduct individual counseling and group counseling or therapeutic interviews to assist individuals to gain insight into personal problems and to plan goals. A 40-hour week, 2:00 PM to 10:00 PM. Requirements: four years of college, with a bachelor degree in behavioral science, pedagogy, psychology, or social work counseling; two years experience in relevant work. Also requires a certificate from Illinois for addictions counselor as required by the state licensing body. Must speak, read, and write English and Polish languages. Must have proof of legal authority to work permanently in the United States. (*NASW News*, October 1998, p. 20)

Master's-Level Clinician

Seeking master's-level clinician to join an intensive outpatient drug and alcohol treatment team. We provide integrated mental health and substance abuse services to diverse residents of the Bering Straits region of Alaska. Must be an excellent team player and be adventurous enough to live and experience the Alaskan bush country. Cultural sensitivity and a willingness to learn from the local culture are indispensable. License or license eligible in the State of Alaska required. Experience in both substance abuse and mental health counseling is a necessity. (*NASW News*, January 2002, p. 18)

Adolescent Substance Abuse Counselors

Science Applications International Corporation (SAIC) has been providing behavioral health care services to U.S. Army families for the past 10 years. Currently, we are seeking professionals to work in Alaska, Hawaii, Korea, Japan, Belgium, Germany, and Italy. Requirements include a master's degree in social work, psychology, or related field; alcohol and other drugs certification; and three years of full-time clinical

adolescent substance experience. Candidates must be creative and skilled in prevention and education, community referral agreements, and program marketing. SAIC and its subsidiaries have estimated revenues of nearly $4 billion and more than 35,000 employees at offices in over 150 cities worldwide. We are the largest employee-owned company in the United States. SAIC offers a comprehensive compensation package including cost-of-living allowance, comprehensive leave, 401(k) and employee stock purchase plans, along with professional development and training. (*NASW News*, February 1999, p. 17)

Marriage and Family Therapy (MFT) and MSW or LCSW

New Directions—a comprehensive rehabilitation program for homeless veterans—is seeking part-time and full-time MFT and MSW or LCSW individuals interested in working with chemically dependent and dually diagnosed veterans. (*NASW News*, January 2002, p. 18)

Counselor, Social Workers

Phoenix Houses of California, a leading substance abuse organization, has these exciting opportunities open in its facilities throughout southern California. Counselor: Responsible for the general safety of all adolescent clients by providing discipline, communicating rules, and overseeing encounter groups. Must have excellent communication skills, be a positive role model, and work effectively on a team. One of the following required: two years experience working in adolescent treatment center, 12 months sobriety and completion of drug or alcohol program, or 60 units completed Associate in Arts or Associate in Science degree. Social workers: Responsible for the treatment of youths and families enrolled in Phoenix House system. LCSW and two years experience or MFT required. Licensure or waiver as a social worker, Marriage and Family Counseling Certificate, or psychologist preferred. (*NASW News*, October 2000, p. 18)

Licensed Alcohol and Drug Abuse Counselor (LADAC)

The Division for Children and Families of New Hampshire is recruiting for two LADAC professionals to work with adolescents and families in our juvenile justice system. This is an exciting new program that is working collaboratively with the court system. Possession of a bachelors degree with at least 36 credit hours in the behavioral sciences is a must. Master's degree in social work or the equivalent is preferred with at least four years of experience in social work, parole, substance abuse, or juvenile justice. (*NASW News*, May 2001, p. 18)

REFERENCES

Alcohol curriculum pilot-tested. (2002, March). *NASW News*, p. 14.

Argetsinger, A. (2002, April 16). Students finds alcohol learning curve a deadly one. *Washington Post*, p. B1.

Barker, R. L. (1999). *The social work dictionary* (4th ed.). Washington, DC: NASW Press.

Gibelman, M., & Schervish, P. (1993). *Who we are: The social work labor force as reflected in the NASW membership*. Washington, DC: NASW Press.

Gibelman, M., & Schervish, P. (1997). *Who we are: A second look*. Washington, DC: NASW Press.

Kovaleski, S. F. (2002, June 3). *Addicts seeking help find line instead*. Washington Post, p. B1.

Magura, S. (1994). Social workers should be more involved in substance abuse treatment. *Health & Social Work, 19*, 3–5.

McNeece, C. A., & DiNitto, D. M. (2002). Chemical dependency treatment. In A. R. Roberts & G. J. Greene (Eds.), *Social workers' desk reference* (pp. 598–604). New York: Oxford University Press.

National Center on Addiction and Substance Abuse. (2002). *Teen tipplers: America's underage drinking epidemic*. New York: Columbia University. Retrieved May 4, 2003, from http://www.casacolumbia.org/newsletter1457newsletter_show.htm

National Institute on Alcohol Abuse and Alcoholism. (2002). *FAQ's on alcohol abuse and alcoholism*. Bethesda, MD: Author. Retrieved October 10, 2002, from http://www.colledrinkingprevention.gov/facts/q-a.aspx

O'Neill, J. V. (1999, July). Substance abuse: The common thread. *NASW News*, p. 3.

Smyth, N. J. (1995). Substance abuse: Direct practice. In R. L. Edwards (Ed.-in-Chief), *Encyclopedia of social work* (19th ed., Vol. 3, pp. 2328–2338). Washington, DC: NASW Press.

Substance Abuse and Mental Health Administration, Office of Applied Studies. (2003a).

Highlights of findings from the 2002 National Survey on Drug Use and Health. Retrieved May 5, 2003, from http://www.samhsa.gov/centers/clearinghouses.html

Substance Abuse and Mental Health Administration, Division of Workplace Programs. (2003b). *Drug free workplace programs*. Retrieved may 5, 2003, from http://www.workplace.samhsa.gov/M_Level2.asp?Level1_ID=2

Substance Abuse and Mental Health Administration, Office of Applied Studies. (2003c). *National Survey on Drug Use and health: Overview of findings* (Series H-22, DHHS Publication No. SMA 03-3836). Rockville, MD: Author.

Substance abuse study funded. (2000, January). *NASW News*, p. 18.

Substances section wins full status. (1995, October). *NASW News*, pp. 1, 10.

Vallianatos, C. (2001, March). Voters approve drug-treatment plan. *NASW News*, p. 12.

Chapter Ten A POTPOURRI OF OTHER AREAS OF SERVICE

There are several areas of social work practice in which relatively few professional social workers work but are still, individually and collectively, important areas of social work concern. Given the broad range of these other areas of services in which social workers work, the focus in this chapter is on a select few. These include criminal justice and corrections, public welfare, developmental disabilities, mediation, housing, international relief, and practice in faith-oriented community settings.

There is a relatively small social work presence in these areas of service when viewed individually. Nevertheless, together they constitute about 12 percent of the areas of practice of NASW members and an unknown proportion of the larger social work labor force (Gibelman & Schervish, 1997). Social workers learn about these other areas through on-the-job training and experience and exposure to these practice settings in formal social work education (see, for example, Young & LoMonaco, 2001).

Many of these smaller areas of social work practice are carried out in host settings, which refer to arenas in which social workers practice, but the organizations are dominated by people from other professions (Dane & Simon, 1991). The primary mission of these organizations ranges from the provision of health care (as discussed in chapter 5) and education (as discussed in Chapter 6) to the incarceration of criminals.

In these settings, social work is a secondary or ancillary profession. It is physicians, teachers, or correctional officers who carry out the major activities associated with the mission of these employing organizations.

There is general agreement that social workers in host settings face a unique set of problems and challenges (Dane & Simon, 1991; Goren, 1981). In host settings there may be a discrepancy between the professional's perception of his or her role and that of significant others in the organization, termed "role incongruity" (Compton & Galaway, 1999). For example, the prison administrator may perceive that the social worker's job should focus primarily on behavior control within the institutional setting, whereas the social worker may conclude that rehabilitation is the appropriate goal. In some instances, the administrators in host settings may have little understanding of the knowledge and skills possessed by social workers. Commentators have pointed to the need for social workers to define themselves within the system and to document their contributions to the host setting. To varying degrees these challenges pervade the nature of practice in these other services areas.

CRIMINAL JUSTICE

Work in the criminal justice system falls within the category of forensic social work practice. Barker (1999) defined *forensic social work* as the practice specialty in social work that focuses on the law, legal issues, and litigation, both criminal and civil, including issues in social welfare, custody of children, divorce, juvenile delinquency, nonsupport, relatives' responsibility, welfare rights, mandated treatment, and legal competency. (p. 179)

In this discussion, forensic social work primarily concerns work in the criminal and juvenile justice systems. These systems address children, adolescents, and adults who have violated social norms and corresponding laws, are at risk of such behaviors, or are victims of such behaviors. The settings in which social workers provide services include the courts, correctional institutions, probation and parole departments, and juvenile detention facilities. Social workers may work with those accused or found guilty of crimes (such as in a correctional setting) or with victims of crime, in which case they may work in a battered women's shelter, a hospital, or in the court's social services division. Social workers may also be on call with local police departments to assess the needs of victims of violent crime and refer them to community services (Suppes & Wells, 2000). In addition, as a person acquainted with the circumstances of the case and the impact of the crime on the client, the social worker may be called upon to provide testimony when the case goes to trial.

Roberts and Rock (2002) identified a number of professional functions of the forensic social worker:

- risk assessments of mentally ill and substance-abusing offenders, with particular focus on their risk of future violence and repeat criminality
- assessment and treatment of mentally ill offenders in the criminal justice system and forensic mental health units
- assessment of degree of danger posed among convicted sex offenders

- mental health assessment to determine whether an alleged offender is competent to stand trial and assessment of mental status in regard to responsibility standards in criminal cases
- presentence reports for juvenile court and criminal court judges
- child custody evaluations and assessments to determine whether parental rights of people with mental illness, convicted felons, and abusive parents should be terminated
- assessment and treatment of involuntary offenders. (p. 661)

The relatively small number of social workers employed in criminal justice may mean that they encounter misunderstandings about their special skills and potential contributions. There are also value dilemmas that confront social workers practicing in this setting. The role orientation of the host setting is that of punishment, surveillance, and control. Social workers, on the other hand, perceive their role as that of helper. Social workers employed in the criminal justice system often see themselves as "covert agents of law enforcement" (Miller, 1995, p. 657). Issues of control, power, and communication frequently arise; these must be discussed and resolved if social workers are to work together effectively in this setting (Treger, 1995).

Social workers employed in the criminal justice system are typically public employees (that is, they work under the auspices of the federal, state, or local government). Many work in an institutional setting—the prison or jail—although some social workers are employed in probation or parole units that are community based.

Social Work and Corrections

The field of corrections is not typically associated with rehabilitation but rather with punishment. A major concern for social work is to protect the rights of individuals within the context of society's response to deviant behavior.

This concern includes both the perpetrators and the victims of illegal behavior (Garvin & Tropman, 1998; Suppes & Wells, 2000). Criminal justice systems draw from various philosophies, including retribution, restitution, general deterrence, special deterrence, treatment, incapacitation, and "just desserts" (Netherland, 1987). In addition, a wide variety of programs have been tested and used in the United States as alternatives to incarceration. Some of these programs include probation; parole; fines; partial confinement that typically involves work or educational release; and special treatment programs for drug and alcohol abuse, mental illness, and sex offenses (Netherland, 1987). Although some of these alternatives have gained in popularity, it is difficult to attract and maintain qualified staff that can develop and enhance such programs. Nonetheless, the quickly growing inmate population will eventually cause a crisis due to lack of prison and jail capacity. As a result, there has already been a dramatic increase in the use of alternatives to incarceration (McNeece, 1995).

Statistics show that both the number of individuals incarcerated and the rate of incarceration are at an all-time high in the United States (Bureau of Justice Statistics [BJS], 2002; McNeece, 1995). Almost 5 percent of adult males and 1 percent of adult females in the United States were under some form of correctional supervision in 1997 (BJS, 2002). The number of adult men and women under the jurisdiction and supervision of federal, state, and local correctional systems reached 6.3 million in 1999, a figure that represents one in 32 adults residing in the United States (Bonczar & Glaze, 2000). African Americans and Hispanics are overrepresented in arrests and convictions. In 1997 about 9 percent of the African American population in the United States were under some form of correctional supervision compared with 2 percent of the white population and about 1 percent of other races (BJS, 2002). People of color are also overrepresented as victims.

Although there has been controversy in the past about the role and effectiveness of social workers in corrections, it is generally accepted that social workers do carry out an important function. General social work tasks in corrections include intake, screening, diagnosis, classification, supervision, treatment, and release planning (Netherland, 1987). Social workers also bring essential advocacy skills to the field of corrections. In this arena, social workers are called upon to not only participate in the legal system, but also actively advocate for their clients in order to ensure fair legal proceedings (Lynch & Mitchell, 1995). Advocacy is an important social work tool to encourage adult and juvenile courts to consider alternative and more constructive treatments such as substance abuse counseling or employment preparation (Gabel & Johnston, 1995). By advocating for supportive rather than punitive programs, social workers can help to improve the physical and mental health of male and female offenders, their children, and other family members that in turn will break intergenerational cycles of reactive behavior, crime, and incarceration (Gabel & Johnston, 1995).

In a correctional setting, social workers attempt to establish a meaningful relationship with clients and help them to recognize maladaptive behaviors and make appropriate changes. Social workers also help clients develop learning skills and methods of problem solving that will be necessary in other areas of life. Perhaps most important, social workers play an active role in helping inmates with release issues such as finding a job, food, housing, clothing, transportation, and relating to others. Social workers often work within the community to coordinate a support system for the clients after release from prison (Netherland, 1987).

More recent social work efforts in the correctional system have included education and training for inmates on issues such as parental responsibilities, self-esteem, and substance abuse. Social workers also offer counseling services in such areas as health and domestic violence (Gabel & Johnston, 1995). One area of social work services in corrections that is relatively undeveloped is that of family reunification. Social workers are able to support reunification and strengthening of the family through support of parent–child visitation and appropriate placement, if necessary, of prisoners' children (Gabel & Johnston, 1995). In addition to working with inmates, social workers counsel families in handling psychological, social, and economic issues associated with the client's incarceration. Frequently, the family will also need assistance in adjusting to the client's return home after release from prison.

Alternative Sentencing Programs

After serving a prison sentence, a person is frequently released with few skills or resources needed to re-enter life outside institutional walls. Overcrowded prisons, costs associated with incarceration, and soaring crime rates are causing policymakers to look more closely at alternative sentencing programs. Social workers and other professionals involved in alternative sentencing programs are sometimes called sentencing consultants or mitigation specialists and are responsible for devising practical alternatives to long prison sentences and for influencing judges and juries to accept their recommendations.

To devise sentencing proposals, social workers examine an offender's life history and what treatment services are needed. They interview the offender, his or her family members, conduct assessments and psychosocial histories, prepare reports including sentencing recommendations, and discuss strategies and options with defense attorneys (Hiratsuka, 1993). These sentencing consultants may be employed independently or work for organizations such as legal aid societies or public defender services (operated under the federal Legal Services Corporation). Alternative sentencing takes into account the protection of society, provision of treatment, and rehabilitation services; restitution to crime victims; and

often some form of punishment, such as restrictions on the offender's freedom or a period of incarceration followed by probation.

Probation and Parole

Social workers may also be employed by probation departments to work with parolees, a population that includes those adults conditionally released to community supervision whether by parole board decision or by mandatory conditional release after serving a prison term. They are subject to being returned to jail or prison for rule violations or other offenses. Nearly 4.6 million adult men and women were on probation or parole at the end of 2000 (BJS, 2002). Probationers include adult offenders who courts place under community supervision as an alternative to incarceration.

Social workers are hired to work in probation and parole departments because of their ability to provide case management services to former inmates or probationers. The social worker is well positioned to identify the community services needed by the probationer or parolee, services that may include job training and placement, family counseling, parenting skills, financial management, and educational programs.

Social Work Practice in the Judicial System

Social workers also practice within the judicial system; in this case, the organizational setting may be courts or law firms. Social workers are employed in defender services programs such as the New York Legal Aid Society, where they work hand in hand with attorneys to protect the legal rights of the people served.

WORKING IN A DEFENDER
SERVICES PROGRAM
Linda is a social worker in the defenders services program, a unit of the criminal defense division of the state legal aid society. The program uses social services and paralegal staff to complement the work of the defense attorney in an

effort to obtain a favorable disposition for the client. The staff are composed of master's level social workers, paraprofessional case aids, and paralegal staff. Linda, in discussing her work setting and functions, highlights the diverse components of her practice.

Requests for defender services can occur at arraignment, plea negotiations, pretrial, post-conviction, and presentence phases of court case development. Social work interventions are oriented to enable the attorneys to negotiate more effectively and to advocate for their clients both in and out of the courtroom. Social work staff provide information, share resources, prepare reports, and sometimes provide crisis intervention and short-term counseling, as needed, to clients. Staff also assess client needs and follow-up by locating and making referrals to direct services programs, such as vocational and educational counseling, medical assistance, psychiatric intervention, and addiction services. Direction and assistance are also provided to those seeking public assistance or public shelter.

Staff are sometimes called upon by attorneys for immediate intervention to stabilize a difficult defendant or to help in preparing a defendant for court appearances. Defender services staff also act as liaisons between the clients who are being detained, their attorneys, and other defender services staff involved in the case. Written reports are an important part of the job. The written material may be in the form of a letter or memo to the court or a comprehensive psychosocial assessment for referral purposes. Such reports require extensive interviews with the clients, their families, and community contacts.

A social worker's clinical evaluation of the client often is conveyed in court and provides additional aid for the defense. A client-centered plan is developed which utilizes a comprehensive and holistic approach to the defense strategy. This avenue acknowledges that psychosocial circumstances impinge on the client and affect his or her responses to the environment. The ultimate goal of using a holistic services plan is to reduce recidivism and criminal activity by providing clients with positive options that address their underlying problems. (Adapted from Legal Aid Society, 1998)

This description highlights both the essential role of the social worker in legal proceedings and the relationship between the social worker and the attorney. The social worker "assists" in the accomplishment of the major organizational mission: to obtain a favorable legal disposition for the client. The services provided by the social worker are at the request of attorneys and can occur at any point in the criminal process. The social worker responds but does not initiate the intervention. The staffs of different disciplines work as a team, with each one cognizant of the importance of collaboration to achieve the organization's goals and objectives. However, the attorney in charge of the case establishes these goals and objectives.

The role of social workers in criminal court proceedings has been rather minimal and is often inappropriately judged as an effort to excuse criminal behavior. However, social workers have played a much more active and appreciated role in civil proceedings, such as child custody cases (Isenstadt, 1995). The role of social workers in criminal court proceedings is to bring awareness of the systemic features of the defendant's environment, rather than solely focusing on the person's mental state (Isenstadt, 1995).

Some social workers work outside the system to advocate for system change or reform. David Protess, a journalism professor at Northwestern University and a trained social worker, has, along with his journalism students, helped free three inmates on death row and two serving life sentences. In reinvestigating these cases, they found crucial new evidence that exonerated the people convicted.

One of the cases overturned as a result of Mr. Protess's reinvestigation was that of Anthony Porter, who had spent 16 years under a death sentence for a double murder. He was within two days of execution when the Protess team discovered evidence that led another man to confess (Slavin, 2000). Their work is now carried out more systematically under the new Center for Wrongful Conviction and the Death Penalty at Northwestern University. Protess sees his social work education as a valuable asset in his work. Specifically, he cited the importance of his interviewing skills in listening and hearing what the inmates have to say, even looking for body language cues. He feels that his training in community organization helps him understand the power structure and how to cultivate sources. His approach to investigations includes the prisoner, of course, but also extends to empowering residents to solve a serious community problem—the imprisonment of innocent people while the guilty go free (Slavin, 2000). According to Mr. Protess, social work and investigative journalism both seek "to document, expose and remedy social conditions" (as cited in Slavin, 2000, p. 9).

On occasion, social workers may also be represented on the bench. In 1998, social worker Kathleen Blatz was appointed as chief justice of the Minnesota Supreme Court and was reported to be the first woman in Minnesota and the 11th nationwide to attain that position. She was named to this position by former Governor Arne Carlson because of her ability to pay close attention to emerging youth and children's issues. Prior to this appointment, Blatz served as an associate justice, a trial court judge, an assistant county attorney, and, for 15 years, a state representative. In this latter capacity, she drafted laws to improve the state's child protection and criminal justice systems. She also created the Children's Trust Fund to support child abuse prevention programs ("Social Work in the Public Eye," 1998a).

Working with Victims of Crime

Victimology, defined as the study of assistance to victims of crime, is a relatively new specialty specifically devoted to providing aid to crime victims. In the 1970s there were very few victim and witness assistance programs; however, this trend began to change with recognition that the criminal justice system was treating victims worse than convicted felons. Today there are more than 6,000 such programs (Roberts, 1995).

The primary objective of victim and witness assistance programs is to help witnesses cope with their own personal grief and overcome the fear of testifying in court so that they can assist in the prosecution of criminal cases (Roberts, 1995). Services for victims of crime are not as common as witness protection programs, and where they do exist, they are usually found in police departments, hospitals, probation departments, or social services agencies (Roberts, 1995). The field of crime victim assistance has been expanding, in part because of the availability of funds from the Victims of Crime Act of 1984 (P.L. 98-473) and an increased public awareness that the victim is often overlooked (O'Neill, 2000a). Through funding from the U.S. Department of Justice, crime victims in every state are eligible to receive mental health services. The funds to establish programs grew from $100 million in 1985 to $500 million in 1999 (O'Neill, 2000b).

Social workers involved in such programs may provide many services including crisis counseling; assistance with victim compensation applications; emergency financial assistance; food and clothing vouchers; transportation to court, shelters, or hospitals; and referral to mental health centers and social services agencies when long-term counseling and psychotherapy are necessary (Roberts, 1995). Social workers can assist the victim to provide the police with the best possible report of the incident. This may involve employing initial techniques to calm the victim. As the case goes through the criminal justice system, the social worker can keep the victim informed about developments in the case and important times, dates, and places regarding the case.

Police–Social Work Collaboration

As discussed in Chapter 5, one emerging role for social workers is in the area of domestic violence response teams. Alliances at the community level have been formed between police departments and social workers. The premise is that law enforcement is usually the first point of contact for family violence victims, whose needs may go beyond the scope of police work. Coordination of services through the police department system provides access to immediate and comprehensive services. Social work services provided in such collaborations include counseling the victim while the police officer questions the suspect, helping the victim complete emergency protective orders; providing referrals for counseling, and linking the victim with the battered women's shelter and providing transportation to the site (Corcoran, Stephenson, Perryman, & Allen, 2001).

Paul Furukawa, a retired Army social worker, helped establish a victim-assistance program at the San Antonio, Texas, police department. Here, teams of social workers and police officers respond to incidents of violence after police have handled the 911 situations. The teams have worked so well that there is now a staff of 30 people who work in victim services. The staff provide crisis intervention and case management, make educational presentations, and engage in violence prevention work in the community (O'Neill, 2000a).

Social worker Kathi West, of Austin, Texas, is victim-assistance coordinator for the U.S. Attorney's Office, covering 40 counties in west Texas. Assistance is provided for victims of federal crimes, such as fraud, gun violations, and kidnapping. Earlier she worked with the Austin police department to deliver services to victims of family violence. There her work included explaining protective orders and the criminal justice system; recommending shelters, as appropriate; and informing families about how to relocate if necessary (O'Neill, 2000a).

Working with victims of crime involves skills of assessment, crisis intervention, and information and referral, among others. Also involved is the need to work in concert with law enforcement officials. Specialized training beyond the social work degree is beneficial. For example, the U.S. Department of Justice sponsors the National Victims Assistance Academy, which provides an intensive, week-long summer training program at six universities across the country (O'Neill, 2000b). This type of work is not for all social workers. There is ongoing exposure to human cruelties and the impact of violence on families and children. Vicarious traumatization is one of the risks associated with this line of work. Self-care is particularly important for practitioners working with victims of crime.

Juvenile Justice

Like the adult correctional system, the goal of the juvenile justice system is to help prevent and control crime and to adjudicate, incarcerate, and rehabilitate youths engaged in illegal behavior (Barker, 1999; Garvin & Tropman, 1998). There are, however, substantial distinctions between the juvenile justice system and the criminal justice system. At the core of these differences is the underlying premise that youths are developmentally different from adults and that their behavior can be shaped and channeled into acceptable form. This premise is the basis for a system in which rehabilitation and treatment are considered primary goals, along with that of community protection (Office of Juvenile Justice and Delinquency Prevention [OJJDP], 1999).

Youths coming into the juvenile justice system receive a detailed psychosocial assessment in order to devise a plan to address their specific needs and circumstances. There is a hearing to decide the appropriate course of action rather than a trial. Case disposition involves consideration of the social history as well as legal factors (OJJDP, 1999). A juvenile offender is judged to be "delinquent" rather than "guilty."

Empirical investigations have substantiated the need to examine the psychosocial history of youths, particularly in regard to sentencing options. Youths who exhibit either delinquent or problematic behavior are often either abused, neglected, removed from home, suspended, expelled, or arrested depending on the nature of the problem and the location (Barton, 1995). For example, we know that children who have been subjected to abuse or who have witnessed domestic violence are at risk of externalizing their traumas through aggressive actions, delinquency, and noncompliance with parental and school rules (Friend & Mills, 2002).

Under the auspices of the Office of Juvenile Justice, a long-term Program of Research on the Causes and Correlates of Delinquency was initiated in 1986 to improve understanding of delinquency, violence, and drug use among youths. There are three coordinated longitudinal projects: the Denver Youth Survey, the Pittsburgh Youth Study, and the Rochester Youth Development Study, each of which is examining how youths develop within their social environment—family, schools, peers, and community (OJJDP, 2002).

A clear relationship between the drug epidemic and youth violence has long been recognized. One teen reported that he began to sell drugs at age 14 and lost several friends to drug deals gone wrong. In his words, "If you weren't selling drugs, you weren't nobody. If you sell drugs, you had anything you wanted—any girl, any friend, money, status. If you didn't, you got no girlfriend, no friends, no money. You're a nothing" (Wilkerson, 1994, p. B12).

In addition to drug use and the easy access to guns, a "critical lack of parenting" has been blamed for the high incidence of youth violence. A family division judge explained that many of the children "have been bounced from family member to family member, without the love and discipline and guidance that children need. They have no anchor or security. They are literally children who are raising themselves" (Loose & Thomas, 1994, p. A19). The consequences

can be seen in the statistics: juvenile courts processed more than 1.7 million delinquency cases in 1997. These offenses would have been considered crimes, rather than delinquent acts, if committed by adults. Two thousand of these cases were for criminal homicides, 6,500 for forcible rapes, 67,900 for aggravated assaults, and more than 180,000 for drug-related offenses (Frontline, 2002). Of those judged to be delinquent, the vast majority are male, and a disproportionate number are African American and Hispanic youths. This overrepresentation may reflect discrimination within the police and justice systems or the relationship between crime and poor housing, poor education, and lower incomes—situations that disproportionately affect inner-city minority youths.

Although rehabilitation continues to be the focus of the juvenile justice system, the sometimes horrific crimes perpetrated by youths have led to changing views about treatment versus punishment. For example, juveniles were involved in approximately 25 percent of all serious violence victimizations (excluding murder) committed annually over the past 25 years (Frontline, 2002). It has become easier in many states to try juveniles in adult criminal court. The Violent Crime Control and Law Enforcement Act of 1994 (P.L. 103-322) authorized that youths may be tried in adult court for certain criminal activities, such as those involving controlled substances or firearms. Between 1992 and 1997, 44 states and the District of Columbia passed laws to facilitate the transfer of juveniles to the adult justice system. The wisdom of adjudicating youths as adults has been questioned. Findings from a 1996 Florida study revealed that youths transferred to adult prisons had about a 30 percent higher recidivism rate than youths who stayed in the juvenile system (Frontline, 2002).

Despite a movement to subject at least some youth offenders to the adult justice system, the juvenile justice system remains "individualized," in the sense that the disposition of any case is based on the offender's history as well as the severity of the offense. Sentencing may fall within a range of options from community-based to residential; the disposition can be for an unspecified period of time, such as until rehabilitation is achieved or the youth reaches the age of majority (OJJDP, 1999). Prevention advocates are pursuing several other programmatic themes, including gun control, creation of more after-school programs, and classes in parenting and conflict resolution (Loose & Thomas, 1994). Within this context, social workers carry out roles ranging from direct services to planning, development, and program administration.

One example of a preventative approach is found in an innovative program underway in Albuquerque, NM. In that city, social workers are working out of the police department, Bernalillo County sheriff's department substations, and the juvenile detention center in a coordinated effort to provide counseling and intervention to meet the needs of troubled youths. Funded through a federal Juvenile Accountability Incentive Block Grant Program, one social worker is located in the intake area of the juvenile detention center and makes the determination whether a child should be released to parents. The location of social workers in the settings in which youths enter the detention system allows for on-the-spot assessments. The goal is to provide services to the child at the soonest opportunity (Vallianatos, 2000).

Collaboration between social workers in the police station and the detention center is seen as the key to program success. The police refer children who need help to social workers. Social workers, in turn, visit the children's homes and decide whether individual or family counseling is needed. Families have the option of whether they wish to take advantage of the services offered by the social worker.

The Albuquerque program is modeled after a successful police–social work collaboration in Boston. The Boston program began in 1996 with one social worker. By 2000, 13 social

workers were employed in this program, intervening through counseling, substance abuse treatment, and other interventions and reaching more than 1,500 youths (Vallianatos, 2000). Services range from crisis intervention to long-term family therapy. Linking children with appropriate services is a major emphasis.

SOCIAL WORK PRACTICE WITH JUVENILE DELINQUENTS

Betsy Smith is the supervisor of one of the youth services units in Philadelphia. Betsy supervises five other licensed social workers, and also carries a limited caseload herself. The social workers in Betsy's youth services unit work with juvenile delinquents and their families; however, they do not usually provide therapy. The social workers primarily do case management, such as connecting families with the necessary resources by negotiating to purchase services for individuals and families or referring the families to community agencies. In addition, the social workers frequently provide reports to and testify in court to provide the juvenile court judges with their recommendations on the disposition of specific cases.

Most youths coming to the attention of the youth services unit are in a crisis state. If a youth commits a crime in Betsy's jurisdiction, he or she may be sent to the local maximum security detention center. If so, one of the five social workers will contact the youth and, based on a preliminary assessment of the situation, offer the child and family appropriate services. Such services may include arranging for an agency to provide counseling or setting up tutoring sessions for the youth. If the youth commits a crime but is not sent to the maximum security detention center, a social worker will work with the child and family and may place the child in a community program such as a regular group home, a therapeutic group home that provides limited services, a shelter, or a residential placement.

Although residential placements are a last resort, they are sometimes necessary. If a social worker from Betsy's unit refers a child for residential placement, he or she must be extremely well prepared to justify the referral. Betsy often works with and advises the social workers on the best way to present the case.

Recently, Betsy has become frustrated with the lack of community alternatives for juvenile delinquents. She believes that more programs are needed beyond the basic group homes and residential placements. Therefore, Betsy has been actively working with the department of social services, the local detention centers and correctional facilities, and community leaders in the youth services field to develop community-based program options.

In this case scenario, Betsy and the social workers she supervises carry out a variety of social work functions. At the direct services level, functions include assessment, diagnosis, and identification of major problems and issues confronting the child within the context of his or her family and social environment. Since case management is the primary function of this unit, information and referral are frequent tasks. In supervising the social workers in the unit, Betsy engages in the administrative functions of supervision, consultation, evaluation, and staff development. Finally, as Betsy participates in activities to broaden the range of high quality programs available to meet the needs of delinquents, she carries out the social work functions of policy analysis, planning, coordination, and program development.

Effective social work practice in this arena involves a mindset—to bring hope, promise, and progress to the criminal justice system and especially to juveniles in trouble. Social workers carry out the functions of planning, management, and advocacy to bring about fundamental changes in the system (Miller, 1995). Most important, "social workers must continue to contribute to and influence the juvenile justice system to ensure that the system remains not only juvenile, but just" (Gothard, 1987, p. 9).

Providing Expert Testimony

The functions of the forensic social worker also include providing expert testimony or assisting other social workers to provide testimony in courts of law. For example, mental health professionals played a prominent role in the capital murder trial of Andrea Yates, charged with the drowning of her five young children. The defense argued that her actions were the result of severe mental illness, diagnosed as psychosis and postpartum depression. Mrs. Yates pleaded not guilty by reason of insanity (Yardley, 2002), but was convicted in which testimony on the part of mental health experts was a major component of the proceedings. The expert witness status is based on significant educational credentials and professional experience. Social workers may act as expert witnesses either during the trial or during the sentencing process (Isenstadt, 1995).

Qualifying to render expert diagnosis and testimony during a trial is usually decided on case-by-case judicial rulings. In September 2000 a Maryland court of appeals upheld the right of clinical social workers to diagnose mental illness and provide diagnostic expert testimony. This ruling had national implications. The petitioner challenged the right of Dr. Carlton Munson, a clinical social worker and professor at the University of Maryland, to provide expert testimony under Maryland law. The claim was that Dr. Munson's testimony would amount to the "practice of medicine" and that he should have been allowed to diagnose only after referral from a physician, which was not the case. The Washington County Department of Social Services argued that under the language of the Maryland statute, licensed clinical social workers should be permitted to diagnose mental and emotional disorders ("Validity of Social Workers' Testimony Upheld," 2000). The state court of appeals agreed, stating:

It is plain from the statutory language that the legislature deems licensed clinical social workers capable of rendering diagnoses such as those made by Dr. Munson based on DSM-IV. Removing the physician referral requirement and at the same time creating a new clinical social work license is strong evidence of legislative intent. ("Validity of Social Workers' Testimony Upheld (see p.302)," 2000, p. 1)

At least 33 states now have statutes defining social work or clinical social work as including diagnosing or evaluating mental disorders. Such legislation or judicial interpretation, as in the Maryland case, suggests that the qualifications of social workers as expert witnesses are increasingly acknowledged in judicial proceedings.

Practice Issues

The opportunities for social work practice in the field of corrections are substantial. But there are special issues in this field of practice that help explain why social workers are not better represented. First, clients in the correctional system are involuntary; resistance to change is normal ,and some offenders do not change (Netherland, 1987). Social workers employed in corrections are often viewed by society, by the system, and by the clients as agents of control rather than helpers (DiNitto & McNeece, 1990).

Second, it taxes the professional's ability to suspend personal judgments when working with citizens who have committed heinous crimes, such as rape and murder. The current prison environment has been characterized as "violent, depressing, regimented, boring, and dehumanizing" (Netherland, 1987, p. 358). It is a difficult environment in which to work.

There is also the potential of turf struggles and different orientations and values that arise from practice in an interdisciplinary setting. In addition, two-thirds of all correctional officers are male, whereas the overwhelming majority of social workers are female. The officers generally receive short, on-the-job training focused on security issues, weapons, riot control, and so forth, There is often a subculture and behavior code among correctional facility staff that emphasizes security and control, keeping a social distance from prisoners, being tough and dominating, and—unfortunately—not listening to social workers (Netherland, 1987).

One example of a social worker employed in a correctional setting is Nancy Gautreau, one of 12 corrections workers honored in 1999 as the "Best in the Business" by the American Correctional Association. Gautreau earned this distinction as director of mental health at Elayn Hunt Correctional Center in Louisiana, the state's acute psychiatric facility. She was earlier recognized for her work in the facility's suicide prevention program, which was recognized nationwide as a model ("Social Work in the Public Eye," 1999). Her other roles include serving as state director of mental health for the Department of Public Safety and Corrections (DPSC), chairing the Louisiana DPSC Suicide Review Committee, coordinating the department's mental health plan and substance abuse services, and serving as a member of the attorney general's Drug Policy Board.

MEDIATION

Social workers are playing an increasing role in the relatively new practice area of mediation. Mediation has been defined as "intervention in disputes between parties to help them reconcile differences, find compromises, or reach mutually satisfactory agreements" (Barker, 1999, p. 295). A more detailed definition can be found in the NASW *Standards of Practice for Social Work Mediators* (1991):

> Mediation is an approach to conflict resolution in which a mutually acceptable, impartial third party helps the participants negotiate a consensual and informed settlement. In mediation, decision making rests with the parties. Reducing the obstacles to communication, maximizing the exploration of alternatives, and addressing the needs of

those who are involved or affected by the issues under discussion are among the mediator's responsibilities.

The mediator is responsible to the system of people or groups involved in a decision-making process. The mediator must provide this system with the structure and tools to make mutually acceptable decisions under difficult circumstances. In this sense, the mediator's role is to empower the system so that it does not have to resort to outside parties, such as the courts or arbitrators, to make the decision. (pp.1–2)

Increasingly, social workers and other professionals have chosen or been asked to play the formal role of mediator, that is, a neutral third party who helps people or groups in conflict arrive at mutually acceptable solutions. Social workers mediate issues such as divorce and postdivorce disputes, parent–child conflicts, child welfare issues, and disagreements concerning care of elderly people. In addition, they mediate community conflicts, and personnel issues. As the use of mediators in a variety of circumstances has increased, a concomitant development has taken place regarding the conceptual framework and skill set within which mediators function. Mediation is viewed increasingly as a powerful intervention tool distinct from, although informed by, other approaches to client services.

Social workers intervene in many types of interpersonal, group, and social conflicts. In their role as facilitators of person-to-person, person-to-group, person-to-institution, and institution-to-institution interactions, social workers address the resolution of conflict as an ongoing component of their professional activities. The role of social workers in these conflicts has been variously described as advocate, negotiator, and mediator.

Divorce mediation is one specialized type of mediation in which social workers are involved. Here, mediation refers to "a procedure used by social workers, lawyers, and other professionals to help settle disputes between divorcing couples outside the courtroom adversarial process" (Barker, 1999, p. 295). Depending on the state, mediation may occur under court auspices or as a private service. Goals include aiding couples to make acceptable compromises, understand the nature of their marital difficulties, make custody arrangements for children, and agree on an equitable distribution of assets and possessions (Barker, 1999).

The skills of the social worker are well suited to mediation work, as illustrated in the following case example. Social workers often engage in enabling and empowerment to assist clients to resolve conflicts and to learn personal mediation skills, which may be used in future conflict situations (Parsons, 1991).

THE SOCIAL WORKER AS MEDIATOR

Jane holds an MSW and a JD. She sought a career that would allow her to utilize both her legal background and her social work skills. Divorce mediation was it. Jane originally affiliated with a law firm and devoted all of her time to mediation cases, many of which were referred to her by other associates of the firm. Eventually, she built a repetition in the midwestern city in which she lives and went into independent practice.

Ed and Marie St. Victor made an appointment with Jane for divorce mediation. Jane began the first session explaining what mediation was all about, the need to set an agenda, and the need to stay outcome focused. To clarify her role, Jane asks both Ed and Marie to sign an agreement to mediate. This step is taken early in their first session in the form of a contract. The agreement includes the provision that only mediation will be provided and that if the parties need legal, psychotherapeutic, or financial advice, they should seek help elsewhere. This document also includes a fee agreement and provisions of the applicable state law regarding privileged communications (Lemmon, 2002). Not all feelings could be aired or resolved; that was not the purpose of mediation. However, Jane further explains that she needs to know the facts of their situation and where they are in their decision making concerning the dissolution of their marriage.

Marie began by saying, "that's simple, he wants a divorce and I don't." She still loves Ed and, she said, she had made a commitment to him that meant she would stay with him no matter what. She told Jane that Ed had had several affairs in the past and had always returned to her. She did not think he was serious this time either, although Marie acknowledges that he had asked for a divorce, had moved out of the home three months ago, and had begun legal proceedings. Nevertheless, she thinks that he will change his mind again and come back to her and their two children.

Marie also indicates that the only reason she had agreed to mediation was that she is unable to carry the expense of their home by herself. The couple had greatly disparate incomes, and although Marie had been the motivating force behind their buying their home, she is not able to figure out how to pay the expenses of the house by herself. Ed had told her that he could not afford to pay for his own apartment plus the mortgage on the house and child support.

Although Jane spent the first two sessions working with the parents, she is aware that there are important parties to this mediation who have not yet had a voice in discussions— the children. The children, ages 12 and 14, are old enough to have an opinion about how they want things to be. They are key stakeholders who should be involved in the decision-making process. However, Jane knows from many past mediations that it is advisable to establish the working agenda and at least reach some initial agreements prior to involving the children.

Ed and Marie have many pent up feelings— anger, frustration, hurt. It is sometimes difficult to keep them on track and avoid accusations and incriminations. When a meeting gets off track because the discussion wanders from one subject

to the next, it's time for Jane to help the parties refocus. Asking a question is a polite way of getting the parties back on track to deal with the agreed-upon goals. Another option is to make an observation about what is happening and the importance of keeping to the agenda. Jane finds that she must periodically reflect back and reiterate out loud the goals of the mediation and of the particular session. When she does not pull the parties back to the goal, valuable time is wasted.

Although Jane demonstrates empathy and uses her social work skills to enhance communication, her goal is to assist the couple to reach agreement. Here, Jane serves as a go-between in getting various members of the family to communicate better. Communication then forms the basis upon which mediation can take place. But unlike a therapeutic relationship, the mediator must keep the discussion focused on the agenda. A challenge in many mediations is to avoid or curtail disagreements that are not pertinent to the agreed-upon agenda (Newberry, 2002).

During the sessions, Jane helps the couple to converse directly. Jane does not seek a particular outcome, only that there be an agreement. As a mediator, Jane is concerned that any agreement reached be clearly understood by all parties and, further, that it be fair to each. Social workers offer an appropriate balance—offering direction to clients while letting them determine their own outcome ("Mediation Is a 'Natural'," 2001). Unlike the arbitrator (who may be called in, for example, to handle an employee grievance), the mediator does not have the power to impose a binding solution. If the parties cannot reach agreement, her work is done (Lemmon, 2002).

As a social work mediator with a legal background, Jane carries out a number of social work functions. However, mediation also has its own knowledge skill base, and social workers who want to do this type of work need to further their education in mediation-specific studies. Mediators are required to have formal training in the mediation process and beginning mediators work under a qualified supervisor. Formal training is available through professional seminars and workshops and university-based programs.

Social work mediators insert themselves into conflict resolution as a neutral party and enter into this role only when they can maintain a stance of impartiality and neutrality (Fishman-Green, 2002). Impartiality refers to the mediator's attitudes toward the issue and people involved. An impartial mediator acts without bias in word and action and is committed to helping all parties rather than advocating for any single person (NASW, 1991). A mediator should have no relationship with parties or vested interests in the substantive outcome that might interfere or appear to interfere with the ability to function in a fair, unbiased, and impartial manner.

Mediators do not make decisions for the couples and families with whom they work (Fishman-Green, 2002). Instead, they encourage dialogue, listen, and help to improve the communication to ensure that each party is cognizant of where the other is coming from. Mediation is not counseling, but clinical skills can be useful. The mediator tries to promote the couple's understanding of each other. The goal is not insight, per se, but to move the parties to the point where they are ready to negotiate how finances and property will be divided and how child visitation will be arranged. In addition, the social work mediator tries to help parties, as appropriate, to accept the reality of the situation. For example, as in the case of Ed and Marie, one party may not want a divorce, but the other party is insistent.

The social work mediator also provides information and referral services, which may range from needs identification (an accountant may be needed, for example) to specific referrals to financial planners, attorneys, psychologists, or other professionals. Jane studiously avoids one potential problem in mediation work—offering legal advice. For social workers, this would mean the unauthorized practice of law. Although Jane is also an attorney, her role here is mediation,

and adherence to the boundaries of the defined role is important. There is often a fine line, but a social work mediator must know when to refer the parties to mediation to an attorney.

As with other social work interventions, the success of mediation depends largely on the confidentiality of the process. The mediator should not reveal to other parties any information received during private sessions without the express permission of the parties from whom the mediator received the information. However, there are legal and ethical circumstances in which confidentiality cannot be maintained and the parties must be helped to understand and accept these limitations. For example, the mediator might be compelled to testify in court or in other ways reveal information gathered during the mediation process.

Mediation is not an appropriate intervention for all types of conflict. The social work mediator must assess whether each party has the capacity to engage in mediation and has the support necessary to be an effective participant. If the parties are not suitable candidates for mediation, the social worker should be able to inform them about alternative dispute resolution processes that are available (NASW, 1991).

Social workers have also used mediating skills to help opposing sides in landlord–tenant disputes and in union–employer labor negotiations. School social workers, too, have used the principles of mediation to teach students about conflict resolution.

In recognition of the growing role of social workers in mediation, *Standards of Practice for Social Work Mediators* were developed under the auspices of NASW (1991). The practice standards for social work mediators are guided by several principles, including

- mediation is a method of social work practice
- the mediator is responsible to the system of parties involved in the dispute or decision-making process rather than to

any single party or client

- mediators should be familiar with and trained in the theory and practice of mediation—in addition to social work education, the social work mediator needs specific training and practice experience in mediation and conflict resolution
- social work mediators should be accountable, both to the client and to colleagues, for the professional and ethical application of their skills and services delivery.

The standards were developed to promote the practice of social work mediation; provide direction and professional support to social work mediators; and inform consumers, employers, and referral sources by providing them with a set of expectations for social work mediators.

Standards for the Practice of Mediation by Social Workers

Standard 1. Social work mediators shall function within the ethics and stated standards and accountability procedures of the social work profession.

Standard 2. Social work mediators should remain impartial and neutral toward all parties and issues in a dispute.

Standard 3 The social work mediator shall not reveal to outside parties any information received during the mediation process.

Standard 4. Social work mediators shall assess each conflict and shall proceed only in those circumstances in which mediation is an appropriate procedure.

Standard 5. The social work mediator shall seek at all times to promote cooperation, to prevent the use of coercive tactics, to foster good-faith bargaining efforts, and to ensure that all agreements are arrived at on a voluntary and informed basis.

Standard 6. The social work mediator shall recommend termination of the process when it appears that it is no longer in the interest of the parties to continue it.

Standard 7. The social work mediator is responsible for helping the parties arrive at a clearly stated, mutually understood, and mutually acceptable agreement.

Standard 8. The social work mediator shall develop an unbiased written agreement that specifies the issues resolved during the course of mediation.

Standard 9. Social work mediators shall have training in both the procedural and substantive aspects of mediation.

Standard 10. A social work mediator shall have a clearly defined and equitable fee structure.

Standard 11. The mediator shall not use any information obtained during the mediation process for personal benefit or for the benefit of any group or organization with which the mediator is associated.

Standard 12. Social work mediators shall be prepared to work collaboratively as appropriate with other professionals and in conformance to the philosophy of social work and mediation.

FAITH-BASED SERVICES

On January 29, 2001, just a few days after assuming office, President George W. Bush announced the creation of the White House Office for Religious-Based and Community Groups, stating:

It is one of the great goals of my administration to invigorate the spirit of involvement and citizenship. We will encourage faith-based and community programs without changing their mission. We will help all in their work to change hearts while keeping a commitment to pluralism. ("Bush on the Creation," 2001, p. A18)

Social services agencies under religious auspices have had a well-established and distinguished role in the history of public–private relationships and have long been a major source of services delivered under purchase of service contracts (Gibelman & Demone, 1998). The Bush plan, however, seeks to open the doors wider to nontraditional providers, such as congregations whose primary mission is to serve the spiritual needs and interests of the community. At the time of this writing, legislative proposals to provide incentives and opportunities for faith-based providers face an uncertain outcome in Congress. Nevertheless, the administration has made clear its objective to enhance the service delivery role of faith-based groups, both traditional and nontraditional (Gibelman & Gelman, 2002).

According to Barker (1999), *sectarian services* are "social welfare programs that began their existence under the auspices or with the financial support of religious organizations or that are oriented to providing social services primarily to members of a specified religious group" (p. 429). Many of these sectarian agencies provide publicly funded services under government contracts. Examples include the network of Catholic Charities and Lutheran Social Service agencies.

Sectarian agencies seek contract funds for a variety of reasons, such as recognition of emerging needs in their catchment area, desire to initiate or expand services, and increased demand for current services (Levine, 1998). They know from past experience that the probable trade-off for entering into contracts is the reluctant embracement of an open door in regard to race, ethnicity, and religion, as the acceptance of public dollars entails an antidiscrimination obligation. Such sectarian agencies may also seek to fulfill their religious missions through programs that do not receive or use government funds, as in the case of camp scholarships.

Jewish Community Centers

Jewish community centers (JCCs) were founded, staffed, and maintained by social workers for much of their more than 100-year history (Altman, 1988; Rosen, 1985; Sweifach, 2002). The JCC, in its earliest days, was primarily concerned with socialization and acculturation of the

Jewish immigrant. Today, JCCs provide an array of social, recreational, and cultural services.

As the mission of the JCC has evolved, its labor force needs have also shifted. This shift has been described as a move toward an interdisciplinary structure, with social workers functioning as guests (Sweifach, 2002). Now, JCCs hire from the fields of education, recreation, and Jewish studies, among others, to meet the requirements of current programs and services (Sweifach, 2002). Social workers, however, maintain a strong presence and carry out diverse roles, ranging from planning and implementing programs for teenagers and older citizens to provision of child care to fundraising and management. Social workers also carry these role responsibilities in the Young Men's and the Young Women's Christian Associations throughout the country—the Christian equivalent to JCCs.

The following case vignette illustrates some of the multifaceted functions performed by a social worker in a JCC.

SCHOLARSHIPS FOR CAMP

Orli is one of 10 social workers employed by the JCC, which is located in a large, midwestern city. As part of its year-round program for teens, the JCC works in conjunction with a Jewish summer camp, referring youths and teens to it. In addition, the JCC sponsors a scholarship program to provide financial support for families who are not able to pay the cost of the camp. The program is funded through private donations and the JCC's executive director believes that all those in need should receive some aid. So far, the program has been able to provide some financial aid to all who qualify.

Families interested in enrolling their children in camp complete an application form. One of the questions on the form asks parents to indicate whether they wish to be considered for a scholarship. Social workers such as Orli then contact the parents who have indicated an interest in financial assistance.

One of the families assigned to Orli is new to the neighborhood and not currently a member of the JCC. The mother, Mrs. Greene, is a single parent with three children; the father deserted the family. She is employed as a secretary and has difficulty making ends meet. Mrs. Greene learned about the camp program from a local rabbi. She is worried about her children's adjustment to a new neighborhood, their lack of proximity to grandparents and aunts and uncles, and the short- and long-term impact of the father's desertion. She wants them to meet new friends and to have social outlets that will ease the transition for them.

Orli reviews Mrs. Greene's application and telephones her to set up an appointment. Because of Mrs. Greene's work schedule, the appointment is scheduled for evening time. Orli requests that Mrs. Greene bring with her a copy of her most recent tax return and make some preliminary notes about her monthly expenditures. Orli explains over the phone that the scholarship program is based on financial need.

Orli has never been very comfortable with this part of her job; she is concerned that she is ill-equipped to assess financial need and that prying into people's finances can be demeaning to them. In her mind, such need determination is reminiscent of her earlier employment in a public welfare setting. Nevertheless, she recognizes the origins of this program within the Jewish tradition of taking care of one's own. Such programs are also in keeping with the JCC's dual mission to promote Jewish continuity and to provide social services.

The JCC has encouraged social workers to take a holistic view of the applicants for camp scholarships. The person-in-environment perspective is actuated by assessing not only financial circumstances, but also family strengths and needs. Social workers are expected to provide information and, as appropriate, referral for social services to meet family needs. They inform clients such as Mrs. Greene about the network of Jewish services available in the community. Also explored are public and community programs under nonsectarian auspices for which the clients may be eligible.

Orli determines that Mrs. Greene meets the criteria for camp scholarships for her three children. This determination is made on the basis of calculating net expenses against net income. Orli also determines that Mrs. Greene and her family are eligible for a minimum membership rate in the JCC, which will allow the children to access the full array of JCC programs for youths and teens.

Orli informs Mrs. Greene that she cannot make any promises—the final decisions are made by a committee composed of JCC member volunteers. However, she is optimistic that camp scholarships will be available. She also provides Mrs. Greene with a timeline in which the decision will be made.

Orli then prepares a report summarizing the content of the interview and, with greater specificity, the financial review that took place. Relevant financial information is also appended to the report. Orli compiles similar reports for the other nine families she has interviewed. Some do not meet the criteria, but this is to be expected.

The next step is to meet with the other social workers to prepare a comprehensive report for the volunteer committee. The director of social services is present for this meeting. In total, 75 parents had been interviewed. Of these, 50 meet the criteria for a scholarship. The next task facing this task group is to prioritize the applicants on the basis of both financial need and the psychosocial assessment that was conducted. Although the JCC will try to provide scholarships for the 50 families (totaling 85 children), Orli and her colleagues are aware that the amount awarded may need to be adjusted, depending on the total funds available for scholarships. It takes a lot of time to divide the list into three categories: highest priority, middle priority, and lower priority.

It is the director of social services who meets with the volunteer committee two weeks after *the staff has made its recommendations. The applications for the 50 families had been sent to the six committee members in advance, but in summary form. Orli and her colleagues had prepared a summary narrative sheet and a one-page financial report, culled from the fuller documentation they had collected.*

The committee members compliment the staff on a job well done. They review the amount of funds available in this year's budget for scholarships and find that there is a shortfall of about $7,500. The members agree to either contribute themselves to meet this shortfall or to find donors who are able to make sizable contributions.

Orli and her colleagues demonstrate the multiple functions carried out by social workers in JCCs. First, there is a direct services function, screening applicants not only on the basis of financial need, but also on the basis of their individual circumstances. This entails conducting a preliminary psychosocial assessment—preliminary in the sense that the social worker evaluates and determines the extent to which the client wishes to discuss circumstances beyond the immediate purpose of the interview—determining eligibility for a camp scholarship. Orli is aware that she must respect the wishes of the client in terms of the breadth of the interview. However, as she listens to Mrs. Greene talk about her family, Orli remains "tuned" to other JCC services that may be useful to the family and makes referrals, as appropriate. This function falls under the realm of information and referral. These referrals may be to other community agencies, both sectarian and nonsectarian, or to programs within the JCC.

Even though the JCC is a sectarian agency, it provides services to people of all religions. However, for this particular scholarship program, almost all of the applicant families are Jewish. This is because the camp offers a uniquely Jewish experience—emphasizing culture, activities, and educational programs that are of most interest to people of the Jewish faith. Nevertheless, a non-Jewish family with interest in the camp scholarship program would be considered using the same criteria as for Jewish families.

The information Mrs. Greene provides is not confidential, in the sense that her application and a written report of the interview will be submitted to other social workers within the JCC and to a board committee for review and final decision making. Orli explains the limits of confidentiality, but assures Mrs. Greene that basic identifying information—name, address, phone number—is deleted from the reports and documents to be reviewed by others.

Orli's functions also include preparing a coherent, fact-filled report that will be reviewed and used by the senior administrators of the JCC and the committee of six volunteers. How well the information is presented, Orli knows, will affect the decision-making process.

It is not unusual for community agencies to establish financial criteria for scholarships or even eligibility for certain programs. Fee-for-service arrangements are typical in nonprofit agencies, but most have a sliding-fee scale that takes into account the client's ability to pay. Many social workers may not be as comfortable dealing with financial matters as they are within the psychosocial realm. However, agencies often operate with scarce resources, and priority may be given to clients who most need services. In this regard, financial information is required.

PUBLIC WELFARE

Public welfare is both a concept and a specific program. In conceptual form, public welfare refers to "the relative well-being of a society and its people as manifested by a nation's policy of providing for the protection and fulfillment of its citizens" (Barker, 1999, p. 391). In its more specific form, public welfare has been associated with programs of public assistance. Ginsberg (1983) defined public welfare as "welfare that is organized, directed, and financed by government, rather than by voluntary contributions or activities" (p. 3). It includes programs of financial assistance, such as Temporary Assistance to Needy Families, medical assistance (that is, Medicaid), food stamps, and social services, a large portion of which are now purchased from private and other public providers of services (Ginsburg, 1983).

Twenty-five years ago, a discussion of social workers in public welfare would have emphasized the professional function within the public agency setting. In the late 1960s and early 1970s a number of factors coalesced to deprofessionalize public welfare functions, in part stemming from the separation of income maintenance (cash assistance) and service provision mandated under the 1967 amendments to the Social Security Act and the declassification of some civil service positions. Declassification refers to the reduction in standards and work-related experience required for public sector jobs. Those positions still designated as professional (requiring a BSW or MSW) tend to be within the "soft" services areas, such as child protective services or adoption. The services delivery functions associated with child protection and child welfare are delegated to separate departments or units, such as a division of youth and family services or administration for children's services. Income maintenance positions previously occupied by social workers are relegated to a new category of income maintenance workers and clerks, for whom professional qualifications are minimal or not required. The net result is that public welfare agencies retain primarily those functions associated with the provision of cash assistance to those who qualify, using nonprofessionals to make determinations of eligibility (Hagen & Wang, 1993).

Although social work is the most common profession among personnel in public welfare, the majority of employees have not studied social work nor do they hold a degree in this field (Gibelman & Schervish, 1996). Nevertheless, social workers continue to work in public welfare settings, even if in decreased numbers. This set-

ting is often attractive to BSW level social workers who seek to gain valuable experience working with vulnerable populations.

In more recent years, there has been an increased emphasis on the function of case management in public welfare. Welfare reform efforts have embraced the concept of case management as a means to tighten accountability and move clients through the services system. The following vignette highlights the case management and advocacy functions carried out by social workers in public welfare.

DEALING WITH THE SYSTEM ON
BEHALF OF A CLIENT

Amy is a supervisor in the Lakeland County Department of Income Security. She first came to the department as an eligibility worker 10 years ago. Through a scholarship program made available by the agency, she obtained her MSW degree four years ago and was quickly promoted to the position of supervisor. In this position, she supervises 25 eligibility workers.

Lakeland County, like local welfare departments throughout the nation, now operates under the Temporary Aid to Needy Families (TANF) program, which replaced Aid to Families with Dependent Children in 1996. Under TANF, mothers of children over age three are required to enroll in work training, a component of which includes placement in a job once the training is completed. If the recipient is not employed by the end of two years, he or she becomes ineligible for TANF. Further, there is a five-year lifetime limit on benefits.

Jennifer, who holds a BSW, is one of the eligibility workers supervised by Amy. In a recent case conference, Jennifer tells Amy about one of her clients, Ms. Allen, whose TANF benefits are scheduled to be terminated next month. Ms. Allen is one of the successful graduates of the job-training program. She has learned word processing and has recently been offered a job. However, in her last visit with Ms. Allen, Jennifer learned of the mother's concerns about her financial status. Ms. Allen had figured out that her financial situation would actually worsen once she began employment. She would no longer be eligible for food stamps and Medicaid, and the subsidy she would receive for child care still required a copayment. As a new employee earning minimum wage, Ms. Allen will not be eligible for the company's health insurance benefits for six months. She would thus have to pay, out of pocket, for any medical expenses for her three children or purchase private health insurance. With rent, utilities, transportation, food, and clothing expenses, Ms. Allen simply did not know how she would survive.

Jennifer agreed with Ms. Allen's assessment of the pending financial situation. She asked Amy about the possibility of obtaining an exception for Ms. Allen, whereby her Medicaid and food stamp benefits would continue for the first six months of her employment. Amy knows that exceptions are not often granted, but she feels that Ms. Allen's case warrants intervention. Amy thus prepared, with the facts provided by Jennifer, a memo to the department's commissioner asking for the waiver. She indicated in the memo the merits of the situation and the need for a timely decision before benefits are terminated. Once Ms. Allen is terminated from benefits, it will take a lot of time and paperwork to restore her benefits should the exception be granted.

Three weeks have gone by and Amy has not heard from the commissioner. She prepares a follow-up memo, again urging that the exception be granted. A copy of the original memo is attached. Meanwhile, Ms. Allen's benefits will be terminated next week.

This vignette exemplifies some of the frustrations that have been associated with work in impersonal, large bureaucracies. TANF is intended to reduce welfare dependency, as well as control public welfare expenditures by getting people off the welfare rolls as quickly as

possible. Although the "welfare to work" component of the program has merit, it is still the case that recipients usually get jobs that initially pay only the minimum wage or a little above—often totaling less than public benefits when food stamps, Medicaid, and child care benefits are considered.

Jennifer, based on the information provided by Ms. Allen, determines that this client's longer term financial independence will be jeopardized if she loses the benefits that she now receives, an assessment with which Amy agrees. Both Amy and Jennifer engage in planning and advocacy to obtain an exception to the rules for this client. Advocacy is targeted to the specific situation of Ms. Allen but has policy implications for others who may be in similar circumstances now or in the future. Amy carries out the function of mediating between the interests of the client and the administrator of the department who is responsible for granting any exception. Her negotiating position, however, is stymied, at least for the moment, by the failure of the commissioner to respond in a timely way. Amy continues her advocacy role by preparing a follow-up communication to the commissioner. Meanwhile, Jennifer continues to work with Ms. Allen around budgeting and self-sufficiency issues, and together they explore community resources.

A social worker assisting a client on public assistance may devise empowerment strategies to help that client effectively negotiate the welfare bureaucracy. However, the focus is then on the client's specific circumstances and not the larger political and economic issues that underlie welfare dependency. It is helpful if the social worker is knowledgeable about relevant advocacy groups in the community, or how such groups might be organized if none exist (Lens & Gibelman, 2001).

Although relatively few professional social workers are employed within the public welfare system, the profession of social work has taken an active advocacy and policy development role in relation to economic need and societal response.

Some social workers have sought to use the media to articulate their concerns. For example, the NASW New York City Chapter Executive Director Robert Schachter, responding to an editorial in the New York Times concerning the transfer of people from welfare when their benefits run out, wrote a letter to the editor which was published. Schachter objected to the termination of welfare benefits for 50,000 New Yorkers and argued that even a smooth transition to a state-mandated safety-net program is insufficient since September 11. "Given the cooperation between the city, the state and the federal government in light of the disaster, it is reasonable to expect our elected leaders to find a way to put a moratorium on welfare time limits," Schachter wrote (cited in "Letter Urges Time-Limits Moratorium," 2002, p. 11). In his letter to the editor, Dr. Schachter reformulated and clarified the issue and offered an alternative. These and other aspects of macro practice in regard to financial security are discussed more fully in chapter 11.

DEVELOPMENTAL DISABILITIES

Developmental disability is "a condition that produces functional impairment as a result of disease, genetic disorder, or impaired growth pattern manifested before adulthood, likely to continue indefinitely, and requiring specific and lifelong or extended care" (Barker, 1999, p. 126). More specifically, developmental disabilities are defined by the 1984 amendments to the Developmental Disabilities Assistance and Bill of Rights Act of 1975 (P.L. 98-527) severe and chronic conditions that

- are attributable to mental or physical impairments or a combination of both
- are manifested before the person reaches age 22
- are likely to continue indefinitely
- result in substantial limitations in three or more major life activity areas

- require a combination and sequence of special, interdisciplinary, or generic care, treatment, or other services that are of an extended or lifelong duration and are individually planned and coordinated.

Conditions classified as developmental disabilities include cerebral palsy, Down syndrome, epilepsy, mental retardation, and autism. There may also be significant overlap of symptoms among these conditions (DeWeaver, 1995). It is estimated that there are approximately 4 million people in the United States with developmental disabilities (U.S. Department of Health and Human Services [HHS], 2003).

Although there are many different conditions that may qualify as developmental disabilities, there are some general characteristics and needs of this population:

- significant and continuous functional limitations in three or more major daily life activities: self-care, receptive and expressive language, learning, mobility, self-direction, and so forth
- functional limitations related to environmental contexts
- the need for individually planned services and supports on an extended or indefinite basis
- the need for multiple, interdisciplinary services in the areas of health care, social services, education, housing, and financial support. (HHS, 2003; Freedman, 1995)

As advances in medical care and biomedical technology continue, people with severe developmental disabilities are living longer. Social workers are needed to assist in planning and coordinating long-term services and support for both the affected individual and his or her family (Freedman, 1995).

Social work's ecological perspective is useful in working with people with developmental disabilities. Social workers can be involved at a micro or macro level—working with either individuals and families or groups and communities. On a micro level, social workers carry out the functions of assessment, diagnosis, advice and counseling, referral, and coordination. On a macro level, social workers use their knowledge and skills to identify and mobilize groups and communities to better access available resources. Finally, social workers also use their skills in planning, advocating, and empowering to press for changes in long-term social conditions such as poverty to prevent developmental disabilities or to minimize the negative consequences (Freedman, 1995; McDonald-Wikler, 1987). The mix of micro and macro functions is illustrated in the following vignette. Abbe Greenberg is an actual social worker practicing in New Jersey.

ENSURING THE LEAST RESTRICTIVE ENVIRONMENT

When Abbe Greenberg decided to be a stay-at-home mom, she looked for a part-time job opportunity that afforded significant scheduling flexibility. Abbe's brother, Steven, age 30, has developmental disabilities. Although earlier engaged in full-time social work practice as a youth group supervisor, Abbe had become involved with the state's Division of Developmental Disabilities. As a sister—and volunteer—Abbe had worked with the state agency to help Steven become eligible for an independent living program. Other parents heard about Abbe's work and contacted her to see if she could help them. The result was the initiation of a private case management practice.

Many young adults with mental or emotional disabilities may qualify for government-sponsored programs. But negotiating the system can be a daunting experience even for experienced professionals. Abbe, as an MSW student, had concentrated in community organization. She therefore had some of the requisite skills to assist families to identify and obtain the benefits that would allow adult children with disabilities to live in the least restrictive environment.

Many parents of adult children with disabilities grow fearful that, as they age, they will not be able to provide the care that their children may need. In addition, long-term planning is seen as critical in the event of serious illness and, of course, the likelihood that the adult child will outlive the parents. This situation is the context for many of the cases Abbe handles in her private case management work.

One day Abbe received a phone call from the Matthews family concerning their 26-year-old daughter Melanie. Abbe is on the Division of Development Disabilities' list of eligible "support brokers" and Mrs. Matthews had heard from an acquaintance that Abbe had helped another family in the area. The support broker list includes a brief biography, and the Matthews thought that Abbe was ideal to work with them. First, she has a brother in the program. Also, she is a social worker and lives in the same community.

Mr. and Mrs. Matthews are getting older and have been thinking for some time that they needed to make a long-term plan for their daughter. Melanie suffers from cerebral palsy, a condition she has had since birth, and is wheelchair bound. Although she does not have any diagnosed mental or psychological problems, living independently has, until recently, seemed an unlikely option. Melanie is not an appropriate candidate for a group home because of her high-level mental functioning and proven capabilities to obtain and hold a job. Melanie has an associate's degree and works part-time in a telemarketing job.

Last year, the Matthews learned about the housing program run by the Easter Seals Foundation under contract with the state. This program was established for young adults with physical, mental, or emotional disabilities who have chosen to live as independently as possible. The family signed Melanie up for the program, and she has been on the list for some time. They also attended community meetings. Just recently, the family was notified that Melanie's name is now at the top of the eligibility list and it is time to begin the assessment process. This entails a thorough psychosocial assessment of Melanie by a support broker and discussions with her family members, individually and together, about their involvement once Melanie is living on her own.

Although the Matthews and Abbe had spoken a few times, no formal brokering contract had been signed. It would have been premature to do so, as the waiting list was long and it might be months or even years before Melanie was ready to begin the assessment process. But now, the time had come. Abbe met with the family in their home to discuss the program and her approach to preparing Melanie for independent living. The Matthews were now ready to sign an initial six-month contract, which Abbe drew up. This contract laid out specific activities and outcomes that would occur during the six-month period. These included the following:

- getting to know Melanie, her needs, abilities, resources, and desires, which would involve meeting with Melanie twice a month
- developing a long-range living plan for Melanie, which would take into account her special needs (for example, Melanie requires an overnight staff attendant to stay with her and assist with bathing and dressing; Melanie also needs transportation arrangements as she works part time).

The outcome is a plan—a plan that is reviewed with Melanie and her parents. With the family's approval, a meeting is scheduled with the staff of the Division of Developmental Disabilities. Abbe submits the plan to the assigned staff person at the division in advance of the meeting. The meeting, at which all parties are present, involves some negotiating. The division staff is ever mindful of costs and challenges several of the items in the budget Abbe has prepared. Abbe has to convince the staff that, for example, the cost of a gym membership is appropriate, as Melanie requires special exercises. The membership must be at a club where there is a pool lift.

Although there is some bickering back and forth, the plan and budget are approved. Final plan approval is facilitated by a self-determination coordinator who also works for the division but is present as an advocate for Melanie. The task of finding a suitable apartment now begins. In the interim, Melanie's parents, who are elderly, have been approved for 25 hours per week of respite care while Melanie continues to live at home.

Once an apartment is located, Abbe will oversee the process of getting it equipped for a wheelchair-bound person. Then arrangements will need to be made for the in-home services that will make independent living possible. Once Melanie is in her own apartment, Abbe will continue to work with her to ensure that her needs are being met and to monitor her progress. Each month, Abbe will submit a report to the developmental disabilities office about Melanie's progress and any newly emerging needs she may have.

As highlighted in this vignette, Abbe carries out both direct and indirect services functions. At the direct services level, she interviews Melanie and her parents and conducts a psychosocial assessment as the basis for developing an initial case plan. Abbe and the family then contract about the components of the plan and the expected outcomes. In the macro realm, Abbe carries out the functions of budgeting, brokering, mediating, and advocating for the family with the Division of Developmental Disabilities. Abbe then works with and on behalf of Melanie to locate a suitable apartment, equip it, and aid Melanie in her transition to independent living through support, coaching, and case management. In addition, Abbe locates and facilitates the acquisition of the concrete services Melanie needs, including home care and transportation. Prior to

Melanie's move into the apartment, Abbe also arranged respite care for the parents.

Abbe is an approved support broker. To qualify as a contracted services provider for the Division of Developmental Disabilities, Abbe has taken a special training program offered by the state. One does not need a background in social work to qualify, but Abbe feels that her MSW and employment history as a social worker heighten her credibility with potential clients.

HOUSING

Social workers who enter the field of housing have the task of helping disadvantaged populations who need assistance to obtain quality and affordable housing in the housing market. The disadvantaged groups most often faced with housing issues are quite diverse. The homeless population is one group that needs assistance because shelters provide temporary housing without long-term solutions, as discussed in Chapter 5. In addition, people with mental illness, developmental disabilities, physical handicaps, and parolees, among others, need assistance in finding housing. Group homes are one solution, but many communities resist such homes due to fears of lowered property values and possible violence from the residents. As a result, a social worker may be involved in balancing the needs of clients to live in the least restrictive setting against the fears and concerns of community residents.

But it is not only people with disabilities or special needs who require assistance with housing. In some cities, such as San Francisco and New York, there is a serious housing shortage. Rental costs may be exorbitant, if rental units can be found at all.

Currently, 1.8 million housing vouchers are supplied to families, elderly people, and people with disabilities. Nevertheless, the system is strained. The demand for the voucher program has grown concurrent with an increase in rental prices. Rising rental costs mean that the vouchers

cover less of the monthly cost, the result of which is to price some low-income people out of the market altogether because they cannot make up the difference. Landlords, too, are dropping out of the program because they have less hassle and more rental income without voucher program participation (Kunkle, 2002). In 2001, in the District of Columbia, more than 40 percent of those with vouchers failed to find and lease a privately owned rental property before the vouchers expired 60 days after issuance (Kunkle, 2002).

The federal role in housing, to date, has included some recognition of the interplay between housing and other social problems, such as illegal drug trafficking, vandalism, violent crime, truancy among youths, and teen pregnancy. The question becomes one of addressing the totality of these issues, not just revamping the physical facilities. Here, the active participation of social workers is critical. Predicated on a neighborhood-based services model within the structural context of the community, "one-stop" service centers have been created to provide comprehensive programming, reflecting the understanding that the problems and potential of people, families, and neighborhoods are interdependent and interrelated parts of a whole. A core element of this approach is that of community partnerships and collaborations to achieve community-wide solutions. Residents of that community dominate the planning and governance of such services.

Social workers in the field of housing have an opportunity to engage in a variety of social work functions and are limited only by their own creativity. Social workers advocate for expanded and new public policies that improve the condition of low-income households and vulnerable populations. They also work to organize neighborhood residents; provide counseling and relocation assistance; coordinate tenant–landlord relations; plan for social services to assist neighborhood residents; and help neighborhoods, communities, and cities develop realistic housing assistance programs. In addition, social workers utilize their referral skills and provide linkage with other resources. The following case scenario highlights the organization and advocacy roles of a social worker in the field of housing.

REVITALIZATION OF A HOUSING PROJECT
Longwood Apartments is a deteriorating public housing project in a densely populated city that has been plagued by crime. A multifaceted strategy is needed to improve conditions at Longwood and it is just such an approach that is advocated by the Community Preservation Development Corporation (CPDC). CPDC is a private nonprofit organization, and in partnership with the U.S. Department of Housing and Urban Development, CPDC has purchased the Longwood Apartments with the goal of renovating the facility to improve the living environment for the residents. Janelle Baker, a social worker, is director of program development for CPDC. Her role is to evaluate and pursue the most effective and efficient ways to improve the project.

As Janelle begins to research the housing environment, she finds that according to U.S. Department of Housing standardized measures, public housing in this city is considered the worst in the nation. However, for the residents of the Longwood Apartments, like so many other public housing projects, housing represents only a piece of the problem.

Longwood was designed and built in late 1966. Two hundred and fifty of the units were scheduled to be purchased immediately by the city's housing authority and up to 50 percent of the remaining units could be leased by the housing authority as public or assisted housing. This plan was intended to ensure both racial and economic integration. In the early 1970s residents had begun to move in, and the complex was well maintained and safe. However, by 1978, economic stagnation and decline in the surrounding area became a real issue and a source of tension between residents of differing economic status. In

1981, two different attempts were made to bring in businesses to the area in an effort to revitalize the community. However, both attempts were met with great resistance from the community.

Janelle is now aware of the history of the development and past attempts to improve the facility. She decides that her first step should be a needs assessment. Janelle gathers a group of 22 key informants who are local services providers in areas such as schools, retention centers, health clinics, day care facilities, welfare offices, and drug rehabilitation facilities. Using a survey-type questionnaire, Janelle first gathers information from these key informants regarding needed services. The identified areas include education, such as tutoring and dropout prevention; substance abuse, such as drug education and prevention and alcohol treatment services; safety issues, such as dark hallways and vandalism; and need for recreational facilities and opportunities.

In addition to the key informant survey, Janelle also conducts a survey of residents of Longwood Apartments. Like the key informants, residents identify education services, safety measures, substance abuse services, and recreational facilities as needed in the community. In other meetings with the residents and service providers, Janelle concludes that the concept of one-stop services seems particularly salient in this environment. From her research, Janelle has learned that this structure for delivering services maximizes service effectiveness while minimizing the red tape of a disconnected bureaucracy. Because all of the services are coordinated in one physical setting or may even be under one organizational auspice, duplication of services is eliminated. Within this environment, individuals and families receive only those services they need and are not denied any services they seek.

Janelle then decides to develop a grant proposal to submit for funding to pursue the development of a neighborhood services center in the Longwood community. After obtaining input from the residents, Janelle develops goals and objectives and a rationale for the proposal using the information she has gathered. She then cites examples of similar successful projects piloted in other communities. Throughout the proposal, Janelle reiterates the need for resident participation in defining community needs and planning strategies to meet these needs. Janelle suggests that one-stop services should at least include the following elements: tutoring, employment training and placement, counseling, family planning, pre- and postnatal care, parent education, health services, day care, youth mentoring, drug and alcohol services, and recreation.

Janelle identifies the likelihood that a neighborhood services center in the Longwood community would meet with success since there are already a number of public and private agencies on the premises. These agencies include an income maintenance satellite office; the Mayor's Empowerment Program Office, which assists residents in obtaining services; Project Care, which provides health care to area residents; and Mason House, which provides various social services. However, the service providers are currently spread throughout the complex, and many residents are not aware of what is available to them on site. In the grant proposal Janelle details that an additional resource for Longwood Apartments is the unused space within the nearby central plaza area—the space would be ideal for locating a one-stop services center. After completing the grant proposal and discussing any last-minute issues with the resident leadership council, Janelle submits the proposal to the city and, with hope, awaits word of the outcome.

In this scenario, Janelle engages in many different social work functions spanning both the micro and macro arenas. First she engages in assessment and identification to determine problem areas confronting residents of the Longwood community. Janelle also engages in enabling and empowering as she assists residents to obtain the necessary services and engages them in planning and decision making. In helping residents access services, Janelle uses sound

referral practices. Furthermore, she organizes and mobilizes the residents to identify problem areas that need to be addressed. Janelle then engages in program development, coordination, and consultation as she surveys both residents and key informants in order to complete a needs assessment. Finally, in preparing the grant proposal, Janelle carries out the social work function of planning to determine methods of fulfilling the stated goals and objectives.

Social workers entering the field of housing services will be confronted with a range of needs and will use both direct services and program planning and advocacy skills. Regardless of the setting—urban, suburban, or rural environment—or in a public or private agency, the need for social workers is great.

INTERNATIONAL SOCIAL WORK PRACTICE

International social services are generally targeted at poor, displaced, and oppressed populations in the poorest countries of the world. Services range from relief efforts in life-threatening situations to program development focused on family support, increased income, proper nutrition, family planning, and basic education. The list is extensive and includes, as well, championing the protection of human rights (Allen, 1998).

International practice includes consultation and assistance to other nations in developing social welfare institutions and services. As the following examples illustrate, many social workers serve as volunteers, consultants, or both to social welfare institutions in other nations or to United States or other relief organizations:

Howard University School of Social Work Professor Fariyal Ross-Sheriff worked in Pakistan organizing the repatriation of Afghan refugees. (Slavin, 2002)

Social worker Beth Vann was part of a small team of social workers who were dispersed among a small proportion of the refugee camps in Guinea, on the west coast of Africa. There she provided casework and counseling services to women and families. The refugee camps were filled with people from neighboring Sierra Leone and Liberia, both wracked by civil war and' unrest. Female refugees brought with them tales about rape and abuse. In working with this population, generating trust and getting the women to talk about their experiences were the first steps in helping victims put their lives back together and look to a more positive future. To meet the needs of the women and children, Vann used organizing and advocacy skills. She applied for emergency funds for basic health care needs, legal protection for victims, and programs to meet emotional and social needs of the refugees. Vann works as a consultant with the United Nations High Commission on Refugees. ("Making a Difference in Guinea's Harsh Land," 2000)

Social workers Margaret Rubin of New Jersey and Nancy Phillips of Illinois lived and worked in India as part of Project India, run by the Colorado-based organization CrossCultural Solutions. Rubin worked in New Dehli for several weeks in an effort to convince parents to have their children immunized and attend school. Phillips researched and documented child labor abuses and helped educators to provide informal education services to the street children of New Dehli. ("Social Work in the Public Eye," 1998b)

Social worker Lynne Stevens has played a pivotal role in establishing programs to assess and treat women who are victims of violence in South America. Her work with the International Planned Parenthood Federation (IPPF) began when the organization recognized that many female victims of violence were not able to effectively use planning services because they were being battered and had lost control over their own lives. Stevens, an expert in domestic violence, was hired as a consultant to develop a gender violence program. The initial outcome was a pilot program at four family planning clinics in Caracas, Venzuela. Stevens assisted with the development of materials and the identification of potential referral sources. She also provided on-site a week of intensive training so that the clinic staff, numbering about 150, would be able to ask the right questions and provide appropriate responses. The longer term outcome in Venezuela was passage of a statute to criminalize violence against women. IPPF has received funding to expand the gender violence program to other countries, including the Dominican Republic and Peru. (O'Neill, 2000a)

Social work educators have also loaned their expertise to social welfare and educational institutions in other countries.

- Donald Maypole of the University of Minnesota–Duluth taught courses in addiction studies and administration at Attisba School of Social Development in Riga, Latvia. Hunter School of Social Work Professor Mimi Abramowitz lectured in Sweden on issues related to gender and on the U.S. welfare system at the University of Gothenburg. She also spoke on these issues to the Swedish press, American Embassy staff, the Swedish Confederation of Trade Unions, and the National Board of Health and Welfare. ("Social Work in the Public Eye," 1998a)
- Social worker Jon Steimel spent eight weeks in the Republic of Estonia where he conducted training and provided consultation to social welfare agencies. There, he worked with administrators, child care workers, and social workers

about the special needs of children who have experienced significant loss. The training component was oriented to staff of Estonian orphanages, where there are an estimated 1,000 children awaiting foster care or adoptive placements. ("Social Work in the Public Eye," 2000a)

- Norma Berkowitz, a retired social work educator, created an organization to provide assistance to centers dealing with people harmed by the nuclear accident at Chernobyl. In 1993, Ms. Berkowitz traveled to Russia and Belarus where she met mental health workers working to alleviate the psychosocial impact of the Chernobyl disaster. These workers lacked funds and basic tools to do their jobs. Upon her return to the United States, Berkowitz created FOCCUS (Friends of Cherynobyl Centers, U.S.), a volunteer group established to aid the health and mental health workers trying to help the tens of thousands of people dealing with the physical and emotional impact of the disaster. In the following years, FOCCUS has provided direct consultation, training, professional materials, and moral support to the staff of the centers and has linked the centers to other educational, medical, and humanitarian aid programs. In 2000, Ms. Berkowitz received a Millennium International Volunteer Award from the U.S. Department of State in recognition of her work. ("Social Work in the Public Eye," 2000b)

Former NASW President Terry Mizrahi believes that an increase in the influence and visibility of social workers in international affairs is needed. In the view of Terry Hokenstadt, professor at the Mandel School of Applied Social Sciences, Case Western Reserve University, globalization goes beyond economic matters to include a social dimension (Slavin, 2002).

The International Federation of Social Workers (IFSW), which represents half a million social workers in 77 countries, and the International Association of Schools of Social Work (IASSW) both have consultative status at the United Nations, which permits them to advocate on such matters as development, refugees, health care, human rights, discrimination, aging, children's rights, and peacekeeping. There are a number of U.S. social workers who hold leadership positions in and are active with these organizations. NASW is the largest member organization of the IFSW. In that role, NASW examines IFSW's efforts to define the social work response to the international crisis in Afghanistan and other countries with sensitivity to the national political priorities of the United States. At the same time NASW seeks to ensure that the response is consistent with social work values and the NASW *Code of Ethics* (2000) and takes into account the diverse views of NASW members.

International exchanges to promote social welfare development work two ways. Valdimir Fokine, president of IASSW, visited the United States in March 2002 seeking contacts and alliances to bolster professional social work in Russia. The profession of social work has a mere 11-year history in that country (O'Neill, 2002). Many of the issues facing Russia are similar to those encountered worldwide: ensuring standards of social work education, gaining recognition of and providing information about the profession of social work, developing and enforcing professional standards, and optimizing the use of computer technology to enhance education and practice.

With globalization comes heightened concern for the conditions of people throughout the world. Communications are of such a sophisticated nature that events occurring in the furthest corners of the world may be the subject of media headlines in the United States as the events unfold. The expansion of the boundaries of our awareness has brought heightened attention to human rights violations and ethnic and racial disharmony and the concurrent need for international action to eliminate violence, discrimination, poverty, and disease. More positively, the obligation to promote peace and social and economic well-being is the concern of every social worker (Allen, 1998).

NASW, in its Practice Update (2002), issued a statement on its *Role in the Promotion of Equitable International Development: Working to Give Social Workers a Voice*. Excerpts from that statement follow.

The U.S. Government spends less than half of 1 percent of the federal budget for international development. When aid is measured as a share of national income, the United States now ranks second from last among donors.

The needs of vulnerable populations all over the world are great. The disparity between rich and poor countries is so extreme that it undermines the basic premise of the world.

Health and education are essential elements in the growth of any society. Nutrition, population, and maternal and child health are subtexts in that equation: they are also basic to economic growth, sustainable development, building civil society, and defusing political unrest around the world. Social workers can make a difference by adding their voices to those already heard in the international development arena. The NASW, the largest social work organization in the world, seeks to engage in the international policy debate and provide a perspective gained in over one hundred years of serving human kind.

NASW continues to be a significant partner in networks such as the United Nations–United States Association (UNA–USA), the largest grassroots foreign policy organization in the United States. Here, the goal is to promote the interests and contributions of the social work profession in meeting the needs of the developing world, social and economic development, world peace, and a more equitable status for vulnerable populations.

NASW also participates in conferences and workshops sponsored by multilateral development agencies (for example, the International Monetary Fund and the World Bank), international development agencies (for example, the U.S. Agency for International Development and the U.S. Department of State). The purpose of these efforts is to promote the social work profession's readiness to be a viable partner in policy dialogue and program development and implementation.

These and other efforts by individual social workers, educational institutions, and agencies provide important linkages and practical assistance in developing social welfare services around the globe. These examples also shed light on some of the skill demands of social work in the international arena. The macro social work practice skills of planning, management, and community organization are important for international social work, as well as overseas experience. Interest and experience in organizing and managing projects have also been identified as important attributes for this field (Healy, 1987).

CAREER OPPORTUNITIES

This chapter has provided a broad overview of the areas of practice that are important to the social work profession, but do not employ a numerically large proportion of social workers. In many of these areas of practice, social workers are the minority profession in a host setting. Interdisciplinary collaboration is an essential component of work in these host settings. Social workers must be confident in their own skills, knowledge, and abilities to provide the necessary services to their clients. These skill requisites are highlighted in the following examples of career opportunities.

Licensed Clinical Social Worker

The Center for Justice and Accountability is a legal services organization that represents torture survivors in lawsuits filed in U.S. courts against human rights violators. The center seeks a full- or part-time licensed clinical social worker. Duties include: assess the clinical and social needs of survivors and their families; initiate or improve local services to them; support clients and witnesses during litigation and assist with any retraumatization; undertake outreach to refugee communities and organizations to inform them of available legal and social services; act as liaison with U.S. torture treatment centers. Must have experience working with trauma, driver's license, and clinical license. Fluency in Spanish and some trial experience are desirable. (*NASW News*, June 2001, p. 16)

Social Worker

The Committee for Public Counsel Services (CPCS), the Massachusetts public defender agency, seeks a full-time social worker for its Salem (Essex County) office. The committee provides legal representation and advocacy to its indigent clients who are charged with primarily serious felony offenses, including sexual offenses. The 11 attorneys in the Salem office serve people who are before the state's superior, district, and juvenile courts. Duties include psychosocial assessments; record gathering; advocacy in human services systems; treatment referrals; court appearances; and consultation with attorneys. Candidates must have an MSW and relevant graduate internship or postgraduate experience. Preferred experience includes an LICSW, with three to five years postgraduate work; work with or clinical assessment of persons presenting with a variety of clinical issues including major mental illness and substance abuse issues; and previous forensic or advocacy work experience. (*NASW News*, June 2001, p. 18)

Clinical Program Manager III

Director, Forensic Facility, Clinical Program Manager III–Forensics, in the State of Nevada, Lake's Crossing for the Mentally Disordered Offender. The clinical program manager reports to the administrator of the mental health division and the developmental services, and functions as the director of Lake's Crossing center, a maximum security facility serving the entire state. Current staffing of 80 serves a residential census of approximately 60 and also offers clinical services in urban jails throughout the state. The incumbent plans, organizes, implements, and directs the programs of the agency and manages the clinical, administrative, and security staff through subordinate supervisors. Minimum qualifications require a master's degree from an accredited school in clinical psychology; clinical social work, counseling, or a curriculum related to a forensics mental health program; and four years of postmaster's degree management experience in a complex human services delivery organization requiring integration of services with a variety of public and private sector agencies, all four years of which required managing multiple program units and supervision of professionals in a forensics mental health program; or a PhD from an accredited school in clinical psychology; clinical social work, counseling, or a curriculum related to a forensic mental health program; and two years of postmaster's degree management experience in a complex human services delivery organization requiring integration of services with a variety of public and private agencies, all of which included responsibility for the development and management of program budgets, and management of multiple program units and supervision of professionals in a forensics mental health program. The two years of forensics mental health program experience must have included one year in a locked, inpatient program for mentally disordered offenders. (*NASW News*, April 2000, pp. 15–16)

Social Worker, Intercountry Case Management

International Social Service seeks individual to broker agency case work services for people in vulnerable situations resulting from migration across national boundaries. Responsibilities include case management–interagency coordination. Qualifications include minimum BSW; five years experience in human services; excellent communication skills. Licensing and MSW preferred. Bilingual a big plus. (*NASW News*, June 2001, p. 18)

Juvenile Detention Therapist

Arizona's Children Association, Juvenile Detention Therapist. Master's degree in social work or related field required. Must have knowledge, background, and experience in juvenile justice. Responsibilities include assessing youths in juvenile detention facilities and conducting psychoeducational, coping skills, and problem solving groups with youths in detention. (*NASW News*, May 2001, p. 14)

Psychiatric Social Workers

Atascadero State Hospital, a nationally known accredited forensic mental health hospital, is accepting psychiatric social worker applications. Qualified individuals are encouraged to apply for several new positions resulting from the opening of a 258-bed hospital expansion. MSW required. If not California licensed, supervision available. Social workers are an integral part of interdisciplinary teams. Duties include assessments, social histories, groups, and working with community agencies. (*NASW News*, March 2002, p. 19)

Clinical Instructor, Clinical Assistant Professor

The Clinical Center for the Study of Development and Learning at the University of North Carolina at Chapel Hill invites applications for a clinical instructor–clinical assistant professor. Responsibilities include participating in interdisciplinary evaluations by conducting family assessments and interpreting evaluation results for children with developmental disabilities and their families. In addition, this individual will be expected to participate in teaching, clinical supervision, and research activities. Minimum requirements include a master's degree in social work with experience in the field of childhood developmental disabilities. Clinical social work degree or eligibility is required. Doctorate in social work or related field preferred, with experience in obtaining external funding and management of community-based projects. A minimum of two years of experience working with children and families in a health-related or clinical setting is required. (*NASW News*, June 2000, p. 17)

Senior Clinician

New York certification plus two years experience. Half time at county jail doing inmate mental health assessment, crisis intervention, discharge planning, court and probation consultation, and officer training; half-time psychotherapy at mental health clinic. (*NASW News*, March 2002, p. 24)

Clinicians

The School for International Training in Brattleboro, VT, announces a new Certificate in Psychosocial Peacebuilding and Conflict Transformation for experienced clinicians interested in working in war-torn regions of the world. The program includes a three-week institute at the school, online course work, and an international internship. (*NASW News*, April 2002, p. 14)

Social Worker

Louisiana State University Health Sciences Center, Department of Public Health, is seeking to fill several new correctional clinical social worker positions for its juvenile corrections program. A variety of clinical work experiences are available, including diagnosis, treatment, and case management. Work location is at Jetson Correctional Center for Youth in Baton Rouge, LA. Excellent opportunity to participate in this nationally innovative and cutting-edge program. Available positions are classified civil service. Required: MSW degree and two years of professional experience in social work. Desired: experience working with juvenile offenders. (*NASW News*, May 2001, p. 14)

Clinical Positions, Forensic Mental Health

National behavioral health care agency seeks well-rounded professionals to join the mental health service at the Correctional Treatment Facility in Washington, DC. Opportunities to be involved in creative program development, to provide assessment, treatment, and a variety of forensic mental health evaluations to a diverse population. Preferred candidate will have a background in testing, skills in rapid assessment and crisis intervention, experience in forensic mental health, and knowledge of brief intervention models. Culturally competent clinicians especially sought. Full- or part-time positions available at several levels: MSW (LCSW); doctorate in psychology or licensed professional counselor with background in forensic mental health. Must be licensed or eligible for licensure within the District of Columbia. Specialized forensic supervision available; competitive salary and benefits. (*NASW News*, June 2000, p. 15)

LCSW

Fun, nonprofit housing corporation seeks LCSW—preferred—with two years supervisory experience to work with low-income and homeless population. Flexible hours, great salary and benefits. (*NASW News*, September 2000, p. 22)

Christian Social Workers

North American Association of Christians in Social Work connects Christians in social work throughout North America with colleagues who share a similar identity, vocation, and faith commitment, supporting their efforts to actively integrate their faith and practice. The association also offers JobNet—finding jobs for Christians in social work has never been easier (see http://www.nacsw.org). (*NASW News*, April 2000, p. 18)

Social Workers

The New Jersey Juvenile Justice Commission has opportunities for individuals who have earned a master's degree in social work to become involved in researching, planning, and administering treatment programs to meet the rehabilitation needs of juvenile offenders housed in the Hayes Unit of the Johnstone Complex located in Bordentown and the Female Substance Abuse Program currently located in Trenton, to be relocated to the Camden County area. Interested candidates must possess an MSW and one year experience in social casework or a supervised field placement accredited by the Council on Social Work Education. We offer a competitive benefits package. (*NASW News*, May 2001, p. 18)

Executive Director

Impaired Lawyers and Judges Program, Executive Director—the Judges and Lawyers Assistance Program has an opening for an executive director. The program, recently established by the Indiana Supreme Court, will provide assistance to members of the Indiana legal community whose ability to practice is impaired by disease, chemical dependency, mental, or physical health problems. The executive director will administer the program, assist in identifying and intervening with impaired persons, participate in developing program guidelines, supervise staff and volunteers, and maintain the program's records. Applicants should have such education, training, and experience as will demonstrate the ability to assist impaired judges, lawyers, and law students. (*NASW News*, May 1998, p. 16)

Executive Director

Cleveland International Program, a nonprofit agency, serves approximately 45 participants from all over the world each year. These are midcareer professionals, mostly from the fields of social and human services—some from business and government—who are placed for internships with career-related host agencies and housed with host families. Most internships are for one year. Staff of five. Candidate must possess several years of management experience in human services administration; master's degree or equivalent preferred. (*NASW News*, February 1999, p. 22)

Family Service Coordinators

Employee-owned Science Applications International Corporation (SAIC) is the nation's largest high-technology and health services firm. With the recent acquisition of Bellcore, SAIC and its subsidiaries have estimated annual revenues of nearly $4 billion and more than 30,000 employees at offices in over 150 cities worldwide. Currently, we are seeking family service coordinators to work in Germany with American families and their children with developmental delays. Positions require master's degree in social work; LCSW; two or more years experience providing clinical case management or services coordination for children with disabilities and their families; experience and training providing family-centered care. (*NASW News*, March 1998, p. 17)

Director of Continuous Quality Improvement

Louisianan State University Health Sciences Center, needs a director of Continuous Quality Improvement, in the Juvenile Correction Program. Incumbent in this position will be administratively responsible for the quality improvement plan and reporting for the University Health Sciences Juvenile Corrections Program and will develop, implement, and evaluate the clinical services for the statewide juvenile corrections facilities; coordinate program evaluation activities; implement quality assurance mechanisms; oversee data collection. Develop reports and other communications. Faculty position in the Department of Public Health and Preventive Medicine at Louisiana State University's Health Sciences Center. Required qualifications: master's level or above in social or behavioral sciences (nurse, social worker, or psychologist); administrative experience working in health care systems; minimum five years experience; excellent verbal and written skills; ability to work with diverse staff; must be able to travel occasionally to statewide sites. (*NASW News*, May 2002, p. 16)

Social Workers

HealthConnections International, an international placement agency, has full-time positions available, minimum one-year commitment, for social workers in a variety of settings based on area of expertise throughout the Republic of Ireland. Full benefits, salary $30,000–$36,000 U.S. equivalent depending on years of experience. Travel assistance. Requires MSW or LCSW plus two years of experience. (*NASW News*, June 2002, p. 14)

Qualified Mental Retardation Professional

Duties: develop and implement a continuous active treatment program for each profoundly mentally and physically handicapped resident child to enable each individual to function as independently as possible and prevent skill regression; monitor and modify treatment programs as needed; share responsibility for several children with a mental age of six to nine months; establish and implement appropriate training goals; oversee patient safety and development. Bachelor degree in education or human services, one year working with persons with mental retardation or other developmental disabilities. (*NASW News*, March 1999, p. 19)

Program Director, Developmental Services

Rutland Mental Health Services, a private, non-profit company located in the heart of ski country in the Green Mountains of Vermont, is seeking qualified candidates for program director of developmental services. The person oversees a staff of 135 people serving individuals and families through Rutland County, manages an annual budget exceeding $8.7 million, and is responsible for providing leadership in planning, organizing, directing, implementing, and evaluating the activities of the developmental services program. We require a proven track record in a management position, preferably with five years of experience in staff supervision; a master's degree in special education, social work, psychology, or related program of study; certification as a qualified mental health professional; financial or budget management experience; and strong written and verbal communication skills. (*NASW News*, September 2000, p. 25)

Individuals Serving Developmentally Disabled Clients

Denver Options, Inc., Denver, CO, is a non-profit agency serving people who have developmental disabilities. We are looking for enthusiastic, supportive people to join our team. We offer professional growth, excellent benefits, and a great team environment. For information about our career opportunities, please visit our web site at www.denveroptions.org. (*NASW News*, June 2000, p. 14)

Staffing Consultant

Our company, a 39-year leader in staffing, is seeking a program-oriented individual to visit mentally retarded or developmentally disabled and other social services facilities and discuss our services. Lots of people contact and the opportunity to help NYC's best agencies improve their services through innovative supplemental staffing strategies. Excellent opportunity to advance your career from clinical to program management. (*NASW News*, May 2001, p. 18)

REFERENCES

Allen, J.A.V. (1998, September). From the president: Advocacy, from global to local. *NASW News*, p. 2.

Altman, M. (1988). Competencies required of Jewish community center professionals today and tomorrow. *Journal of Jewish Communal Service, 64*, 256–257.

Barker, R. L. (1999). *Social work dictionary* (4th ed.). Washington, DC: NASW Press.

Barton, W. H. (1995). Juvenile corrections. In R. L. Edwards (Ed.-in-Chief), *Encyclopedia of social work* (19th ed., Vol. 2, pp. 1563–1577). Washington, DC: NASW Press.

Bodaken, M. (2002). *We must preserve the nation's supply of affordable housing.* National Housing Institute. Retrieved December 6, 2002, from http://www.nhi.org/policy.affhsg.html

Bonczar, T., & Glaze, L. (2000, July 23). *Bureau of Justice press release.* U.S. Department of Justice, Office of Justice Programs. Rretrieved March 21, 2001, from http://www.ojp.usdoj.gov/bjs

Bureau of Justice Statistics. (2002). *Corrections: Probation and parole.* Washington, DC: U.S. Department of Justice, Office of Justice Programs. Retrieved December 6, 2002, from http://www.ojp.usdoj.gov/bjs.

Bush on the creation of a White House Office tied to religion. (2001, January 30). *New York Times.* Retrieved February 15, 2001, from http://www.nytimes.com/2001/01/30/politics/30BTEX.html.

Compton, B. R., & Galaway, B. (1999). *Social work processes* (6th ed.). Pacific Grove, CA: Brooks/Cole.

Corcoran, J., Stephenson, M., Perryman, D., & Allen, S. (2001). Perceptions and utilization of a police–social work crisis intervention approach to domestic violence. *Families in Society, 82*, 393–398.

Dane, B. O., & Simon, B. L. (1991). Resident guests: Social workers in host settings. *Social Work, 36*, 208–213.

Developmental Disabilities Assistance and Bill of Rights Act of 1975, P.L. 98-527, 98 Stat. 2662, 1984 Amendments.

DeWeaver, K. L. (1995). Developmental disabilities: Definitions and policies. In R. L. Edwards (Ed.-in-Chief), *Encyclopedia of social work* (19th ed., Vol. 1, pp. 712–720). Washington, DC: NASW Press.

DiNitto, D. M., & McNeece, C. A. (1990). *Social work: Issues and opportunities in a challenging profession.* Englewood Cliffs, NJ: Prentice Hall.

Fishman-Green, R. (2002). *Mediator neutrality: How is it possible?* Oakland, CA: John Ford & Associates. Retrieved February 8, 2003, from http://www.mediate.com.

Freedman, R. I. (1995). Developmental disabilities: Direct practice. In R. L. Edwards (Ed.-in-Chief), *Encyclopedia of social work* (19th ed., Vol. 1, pp. 721–729). Washington, DC: NASW Press.

Friend, C., & Mills, L. G. (2002). Domestic violence and child protective services. In A. R. Roberts & G. J. Greene (Eds.), *Social workers' desk reference* (pp. 679–683). New York: Oxford University Press.

Frontline. (2002). *Juvenile justice: Basic statistics.* Public Broadcasting System. Available from http://www.pbs.org/wgbh/pages/frontline/shows/juvenile/stats/basic.html

Gabel, K., & Johnston, D. (1995). Female criminal offenders. In R. L. Edwards (Ed.-in-Chief), *Encyclopedia of social work* (19th ed., Vol. 2, pp. 1013–1027). Washington, DC: NASW Press.

Garvin, C. D., & Tropman, J. E. (1998). *Social work in contemporary society* (2nd ed.). Needham Heights, MA: Allyn & Bacon.

Gibelman, M., & Demone, H. W., Jr. (Eds.). (1998). *The privatization of human services: Policy and practice issues.* New York: Springer.

Gibelman, M., & Gelman, S. R. (2002). Should we have faith in faith-based social services? Rhetoric versus realistic expectations. *Journal of Nonprofit Management & Leadership, 13,* 49–65.

Gibelman, M., & Schervish, P. (1996). Social work and public social service practice: A status report (1996). *Families in Society, 77,* 117–124.

Gibelman, M., & Schervish, P. (1997). *Who we are: A second look.* Washington, DC: NASW Press.

Ginsberg, L. H. (1983). *The practice of social work in public welfare.* New York: Free Press.

Goren, S. (1981). The wonderland of social work in the schools: Or how Alice learned to cope. *School Social Work, 6,* 19–26.

Gothard, S. (1987). Juvenile justice system. In A. Minahan (Ed.-in-Chief), *Encyclopedia of social work* (18th ed., Vol. 1, pp. 5–9). Silver Spring, MD: National Association of Social Workers.

Hagen, J. L., & Wang, L. (1993). Roles and functions of public welfare workers. *Administration in Social Work, 17,* 81–103.

Healy, L. M. (1987). International agencies as social work settings: Opportunity, capability, and commitment. *Social Work, 32,* 405–409.

Hiratsuka, J. (1993, September). Hard times alter views on "hard time." *NASW News,* p. 3.

Isenstadt, P. M. (1995). Adult courts. In R. L. Edwards (Ed.-in-Chief), *Encyclopedia of social work* (19th ed., Vol. 1, pp. 68–74). Washington, DC: NASW Press.

Kunkle, F. (2002, August 5). Housing vouchers no magic key. *Washington Post,* p. A1.

Legal Aid Society. (1998). *Annual report.* Retrieved September 22, 1999, from http://www.legalaid.org/ar99/crimd.htm.

Lemmon, J. A. (2002). Mediation and conflict resolution. In A. R. Roberts & G. J. Greene (Eds.), *Social workers' desk reference* (pp. 282–293). New York: Oxford University Press.

Lens, V., & Gibelman, M. (2001). Advocacy be not forsaken! Retrospective lessons from welfare reform. *Families in Society, 81,* 611–620.

Letter urges time-limits moratorium. (2002, February). *NASW News,* p. 11.

Levine, E. M. (1998). *Church, state, and social welfare: Purchase of service and the sectarian agency.* In M. Gibelman & H. W. Demone, Jr. (Eds.), The privatization of human services: Policy and practice issues (pp. 117–153). New York: Springer.

Loose, C., & Thomas, P. (1994, January 2). "Crisis of violence" becoming menace to childhood. *Washington Post,* pp. A1, A19.

Lynch, R. S., & Mitchell, J. (1995). Justice system advocacy: A must for NASW and the social work community. *Social Work, 40,* 9–12.

Making a difference in Guinea's harsh land. (2000, May). *NASW News,* p. 13.

McDonald-Wikler, L. (1987). Disabilities: Developmental. In A. Minahan (Ed.-in-Chief), *Encyclopedia of social work* (18th ed., Vol. 1, pp. 422–434). Silver Spring, MD: NASW.

McNeece, C. A. (1995). Adult corrections. In R. L. Edwards (Ed.-in-Chief), *Encyclopedia of social work* (19th ed., Vol. 1, pp. 60–68). Washington, DC: National Association of Social Workers.

Mediation is "a natural." (2001, November). *NASW News*, p. 6.

Miller, J. G. (1995). Criminal justice: Social work roles. In R. L. Edwards (Ed.-in-Chief), *Encyclopedia of social work* (19th ed., Vol. 1, pp. 653–659). Washington, DC: NASW Press.

National Association of Social Workers. (1991). *NASW standards of practice for social work mediators.* Silver Spring, MD: Author. Retrieved December 9, 2003, from http://www.familymediationcouncil.com/Standards%20of%20Practice%20for%20 Social%20Work%20Mediators.htm

National Association of Social Workers. (1996). *Code of ethics.* Washington, DC: NASW Press.

National Association of Social Workers. (2002). *The National Association of Social Workers' role in the promotion of equitable international development: Working to give social workers a voice* (Practice Update, 1). Washington, DC: Author.

Netherland, W. (1987). Corrections systems: Adult. In A. Minahan (Ed.-in-Chief), *Encyclopedia of social work* (18th ed., Vol. 1, pp. 351–360). Silver Spring, MD: National Association of Social Workers.

Newberry, S. (2002). *Three questions you can ask to make any meeting more effective.* Retrieved February 8, 2003, from http://www.mediate.com

Office of Juvenile Justice and Delinquency Prevention. (1999). *Juvenile justice: A century of change.* Washington, DC: Author.

Office of Juvenile Justice and Delinquency Prevention. (2002). *Causes and correlates of delinquency program.* Retrieved December 10, 2003, from http://ojjdp.ncjrs.org/ccd/oview.html

O'Neill, J. V. (2000a, February). Women victims of violence aided. *NASW News*, p. 14.

O'Neill, J. V. (2000b, February). Victim aid becoming full-fledged field. *NASW News*, p. 3.

O'Neill, J. V. (2002, May). Fokine visits NASW. *NASW News*, p. 6.

Parsons, R. J. (1991). The mediator role in social work practice. *Social Work, 36,* 483–487.

Roberts, A. R. (1995). Victim services and victim/witness assistance programs. In R. L. Edwards (Ed.-in-Chief), *Encyclopedia of social work* (19th ed., Vol. 3, pp. 2440–2444). Washington, DC: NASW Press.

Roberts, A. R., & Rock, M. (2002). An overview of forensic social work and risk assessments with the dually diagnosed. In A. R. Roberts & G. J. Greene (Eds.), *Social workers' desk reference* (pp. 661–668). New York: Oxford University Press.

Rosen, B. (1985). The role of the Jewish community center and Jewish continuity. *Journal of Jewish Communal Service, 62,* 119.

Slavin, P. (2000, April). Activist's training helps cheat death verdicts. *NASW News*, p. 9.

Slavin, P. (2002, March). Profession has global role. *NASW News*, pp. 1–2.

Social work in the public eye. (1998a, March). *NASW News*, p. 15.

Social work in the public eye. (1998b, May). *NASW News*, p. 13.

Social work in the public eye. (1999, May). *NASW News*, p. 13.

Social work in the public eye. (2000a, January). *NASW News*, p. 19.

Social work in the public eye. (2000b, April). *NASW News*, p. 13.

Suppes, M. A., & Wells, C. C. (2000). *The social work experience: An introduction to social work and social welfare.* New York: McGraw-Hill.

Sweifach, J. S. (2002). *The relationship of social work functions to job responsibilities within JCCs.* Unpublished doctoral dissertation, Yeshiva University, Wurzweiler School of Social Work, New York.

Treger, H. (1995). Police social work. In R. L. Edwards (Ed.-in-Chief), *Encyclopedia of social work* (19th ed., Vol. 3, pp. 1843–1848.) Washington, DC: NASW Press.

U.S. Department of Health and Human Services. Administration on Developmental Disabilities, (2003). *ADD fact sheet.* Retrieved November 18, 2003, from http://www.acf.dhhs.gov/programs /add/Factsheet.htm.

Validity of social workers' testimony upheld. (2000, November). *NASW News*, pp. 1, 6.

Vallianatos, C. (2000, November). Social workers intervene at police stations. *NASW News*, p. 37.

Victims of Crime Act of 1984, P.L. 98-473, 98 Stat. 2170.

Violent Crime Control and Law Enforcement Act of 1994, P.L. 103-322, 109 Stat. 2147.

Wilkerson, I. (1994, December 13). Crack's legacy lives on. *New York Times*, pp. A1, B12.

Yardley, J. (2002, February 19). *Trial in case of drowned child opens. New York Times*. Retrieved February 21, 2002, from http://www.nytimes.com/2002/02/19/national/19MOM.html

Young, D., & LoMonaco, S. W. (2001). Incorporating content on offenders and corrections into social work curricula. *Journal of Social Work Education, 37*, 475–493.

Chapter Eleven Social Planning, Community Organization, and Policy Practice

T
he social work functions of planning, community organization, and advocacy crosscut all areas of practice. The proportion of social workers engaged in macro social work—interventions with larger systems to affect change in communities, agencies designed to serve people, and society—is relatively small, but these activities constitute an important component of the profession's history and mission. Macro practice has also been referenced as "indirect" social work practice, which often does not involve immediate or personal contact with the clients served. This type of social work practice is "aimed at bringing about improvements and changes in the general society. Such activities include some types of political action, community organization, public education campaigning, and the administration of broad-based social service agencies or public welfare departments" (Barker, 1999, p. 285).

Netting, Kettne, and McMurtry (1998) similarly defined macro practice as "professionally guided intervention designed to bring about planned change in organizations and communities" (p. 3). These authors further articulated macro activities as going "beyond individual interventions," but the need, problem, issue, or concern may be identified in the course of working one-on-one with clients.

SOCIAL WORKERS IN MACRO PRACTICE

The *Code of Ethics* of the National Association of Social Workers (1996) identified policy or macro practice as a basic obligation of the profession and its members:

> Social workers should engage in social and political action that seeks to ensure that all people have equal access to the resources, employment, services, and opportunities that they require in order to meet their basic human needs and to develop fully. Social workers should be aware of the impact of the political arena on practice, and should advocate for changes in policy and legislation to improve social conditions in order to meet basic human needs and promote social justice. (p. 27)

The involvement of social workers in macro practice has waxed and waned throughout the profession's history. Policy practice, including legislative advocacy, social action, and social policy analysis, has been termed the "neglected side of social work intervention" (Figueira-McDonough, 1993, p. 179). Mobilization for macro interventions tends to occur in one of several situations, including (1) when government offers program and financial incentives to do so, such as during the War on Poverty; (2) when there is a perceived assault on social programs, such as during the Reagan administration and then the Clinton administration, when the Republican-controlled Congress promised substantial change in ways antithetical to the values and interests of the social welfare community; or (3) when a broad social movement is ignited to change oppressive social conditions, such as the civil rights movement. At such times, social workers seek to protect and promote their own status and programs as well as the services and benefits received by their clients.

Earlier in her political career, Senator Barbara Mikulski (D-MD), then U.S. Representative from the State of Maryland and a social worker, addressed the obligation of social workers to involve themselves in advocacy, activism, and politics. She urged social workers to become involved with "nitty-gritty" campaigns—going door to door, stuffing envelopes, working on fundraisers, taking people to the polls on election day, and working with people to register to vote. She also posed the challenge of social workers themselves running for office. "I am trying to change the political landscape, and I encourage you to do the same" ("Social Work Skills and Political Action," 1984, p. 8). Leon Ginsberg (1988), among others, also addressed the salience of political involvement:

It would be difficult to overstate the importance of political activity to large numbers of people, including the profession of social work and those it serves. Few arenas have more potential for benefiting or harming people. The distinctive culture of politics is the backdrop before which the major decisions about social welfare in the latter part of the twentieth century are made and implemented. (p. 247)

There is substantial agreement within the profession that the voice of social work needs to be heard, both to protect those policies that protect and enhance the lives of citizens, and to promote a new and more positive social agenda (Cohen, 1995).

ADVOCACY

Advocacy is a multifaceted concept. *It refers to* the act of directly representing or defending others and, within a social work professional context, incorporates the championing of the rights of individuals and communities through direct intervention or empowerment (Barker, 1999).

Advocacy has been a component of social work practice from the time of the charity societies and settlement house movements of the 1870s. The role of advocate is incorporated in the NASW (1996) *Code of Ethics,* and *advocacy* is defined as "a basic function of social workers, speaking out on behalf of the client to achieve changes in the conditions that contribute to the client's problems and securing and protecting a client's existing right or entitlement" (Barker, 1999, p. 12).

Advocacy at the macro level—the focus of this chapter—refers to those interventions to change the environment on behalf of many clients in similar circumstances (Mickelson, 1995). It encompasses a range of activities in the political sphere, among them educating and lobbying decision makers (the legislators) and opinion makers (the media) and building coalitions. The approach is typically pragmatic, emphasizing consensus building, data collection and research, and the use of mainstream administrative channels to effect change (Dluhy, 1990; Haynes & Mickelson, 2000; Richan, 1991; Smucker, 1991).

Advocacy for and on behalf of clients is a function that runs through most social work practice, no matter what setting or level of practice. A component of advocacy is client empowerment, although it may be more highly embraced in theory than practice (Hartman, 1993). Advocacy may also take the form of political lobbying or employing organized demonstrations, as the vignettes below illustrate. In addition, policy analysis can also be seen as a form of advocacy, as such analyses are used to influence the dialogue about social problems, the development of social policy responsive to the problems, and the impact or outcome for the people affected.

Advocating Takes Purpose, Motivation, and Energy

Advocacy is often undertaken by organizations or coalitions of organizations and individuals with a keen interest and stake in an issue or cause. A team of New York social workers, Lou Levitt, PhD, and Aaron Beckerman, PhD, epitomize what advocates can accomplish. Their work also show the components of advocacy, the steps involved in the process, and the importance of viewing the "big picture" and being persistent and highly motivated to promote change.

Levitt and Beckerman are both professor emeriti of Yeshiva University, Wurzweiler School of Social Work, in New York. Upon their retirement from a full-time academic role, they decided to turn their attention to social action. This was not a new career phase, as both men had long been involved in advocacy. At this time, however, advocacy became their primary activity. Their effort, still gaining momentum, is called "Rekindling Reform." This effort seeks to address the need to link social and health problems of the population and to combine both community social care and health services. Concern is with the overarching question of how any proposal for universal health care can be shaped to meet the needs of vulnerable populations, including elderly people, children, minorities of color, women, people who are chronically ill, people with a history of mental illness, people who are physically disabled, and immigrants.

Rekindling Reform involves an extensive array of activities under the broad rubric of organizing and advocacy, all directed to targeted outcomes. Desired outcomes include developing a consensus for comprehensive health care reform among the sponsoring organizations and strategies for influencing legislative action both in Congress and at the state level. Sponsoring organizations now number 40, and the list continues to grow. Gaining sponsors is one of the organizing tasks. Recent meetings to gain sponsors have included the New York Business Group on Health, the Council of Municipal Employee Retiree Organizations, and the New York City Central Labor Council.

Building a planning committee of knowledgeable organizationally-based health professionals was an essential first task. Consensus building and strategizing among the members of the planning committee are process oriented as well as content focused. The initial project was a lecture series on the universal health care systems of other countries with comparable economies. Outstanding health policy experts gave the lectures. The texts of these sponsored lectures, delivered by policy experts from the United Kingdom, Germany, Canada, and France, will be published in a special edition of the *American Journal of Public Health* (2003, Vol. 93(1)) and in other newsletters and journals. The next phase is a draft statement of principles, prepared by the seminar participants, that should be incorporated into any plan for universal health care, and an outline of the kinds of strategies needed to accomplish such reforms. The work on this draft, which began in June 2002, has been sent to participating groups for their comments.

Organizing and advocacy almost always involve some costs. Cognizant of this fundamental fact, Levitt and Beckerman took their proposal early on to potential backers. The result was a $25,000 grant from the Bronfman Philanthropies. This grant has been used primarily to underwrite the costs of the lecture series. The search for additional funds by the planning committee to support the effort is ongoing. The planning committee issues periodic progress reports to the sponsors, which may include an appeal for further assistance, particularly of a financial nature. Additional foundations are being contacted to inform them about Rekindling Reform and determine whether submission of a proposal for funding would be appropriate. Levitt, Beckerman, and others on the planning committee would then assume responsibility for writing the proposals. Since foundations typically support specific program efforts, proposals might include subsidization of publications, dissemination costs, establishment of a World Wide Web site, and employment of staff to carry out many of the functions initially undertaken on a volunteer basis.

In establishing and maintaining a social action movement, the issues involved are detailed by Levitt in the following interview:

AN INTERVIEW WITH A SOCIAL WORK ADVOCATE

Q: Tell me about your background and interest in advocacy.

A: *Having spent almost 50 years as a social worker before retirement from full-time teaching, I appreciated the fundamental importance of health care to the people my students and I were helping. Health care issues have been woven through every aspect of the practice experiences I had in the first half of my career as a practicing social worker. For example, during my employment with Mobilization for Youth in the heyday of the War on Poverty, I directed a project designed to help teenage drug abusers move away from addiction. It was the first group of teens to move through "detox" together. Much work with Beth Israel Hospital was involved. When I became executive assistant to the NYC Commissioner of Social Services, health protection and food provision were very serious problems. Lessening the bureaucratic hurdles of Medicaid was of deep concern to our staff. I worked to devise a means to get rid of the nonsensical surplus food distribution that required old and frail people to negotiate a monthly allotment of items, such as an 80-pound cheese package.*

In the second half of my career I focused on teaching social policy and administration of social services. During this time period, I served first as vice president and then as president of the NASW New York City chapter. In that capacity, I testified on behalf of the profession on the

first day of public hearings of the Moreland Act Commission to Investigate Nursing Homes. This kindled my interest in health care reform. I incorporated some of my own learning into my teaching career, involving my students in learning about the growing problem of Medicaid mills. Because Medicaid reimbursement was so low, and enforcement of standards for care was so lax, group practices in poor neighborhoods had taken to maximizing their income by examining and treating large numbers of people, spending very little time with each patient. A new administration at the New York City Department of Health had criticized this phenomenon publicly. They welcomed our concern. I took the entire class on one snowy morning to the department's offices where they received an orientation from a deputy commissioner who gave them the names of all the clinics in the lower east side health district. Armed with a letter of introduction from the health department, teams of two students each fanned out to visit these clinics and find out more about their practices. We compared notes in class when all of the teams had completed their work and confirmed the facts attendant to rushed treatment and examination. The class wrote a report to the department and received acknowledgment and appreciation for their contribution.

I also served as the university's community relations representative for three years. In that capacity, I became a member of the advisory board to the homeless shelter at the 168th St. Armory. What a sight: a massive gym floor with 800 beds, row on row with mattresses folded in half . . . waiting for nightfall and its daily influx of desperate men with no other place to escape the cold. AIDS, alcohol abuse, other drug abuse, TB—all were part of the statistics and discussion. I became president of the Northern Manhattan Improvement Corporation, a wonderful social agency providing badly needed housing services in Washington Heights. Charlie Auerbach (also on the Wurzweiler faculty), Aaron

Beckerman, and I collaborated on a study that identified small families on welfare as most at risk of becoming homeless. They fell farther and farther behind in their large rent payments, using their food money for rent payments to a great extent. One wondered about the effect on their health, especially the children. Thus, I was no stranger to considerations of health policy and the consequences of the absence of adequate health care for people of whom I had intimate knowledge.

Q: Why did you become involved in Rekindling Reform?

A: Two years ago, shortly after both Aaron Beckerman and I retired from full-time teaching and I had moved to Great Neck, we sat on a park bench to discuss what we might do together to act on the values that had prompted both of us to become social workers. Aaron had been even more intimately involved in health issues stemming in part from his work at the NYU medical school where he had pioneered the teaching of a seminar on the humanistic aspects of medicine. We decided that we would work together in helping to build the movement to achieve universal health care.

We sensed a quickening of the political pulse in the sharpening of the contradictions that had begun to characterize our country's health care system. We thought we could "catch the wave" of renewed interest in health care reform which would be generated by the reduction of benefits and increasing costs which were being experienced by many groups.

We felt that we had something to offer on the basis of our professional experience and the wide network of relationships we had in social work and other professions. We knew the problems of adding to the social movement were not only political, but also attitudinal. Many people believe real health care reform is an impossible dream. The extent of political power and resources that had been brought to bear in the defeat of the Clinton health policy proposals was

so overwhelming that many had reached the pessimistic conclusion that universal health care in the United States was impossible.

Aaron and I had been key figures in planning an interdisciplinary conference in 1997 on the cutbacks in health and social services funding which were then beginning. Many good papers were delivered by a range of professionals in the human services, all of whom focused on the consequences of these cuts. Three hundred people attended. The proceedings were widely disseminated and every member of the New York State legislature received a copy. We were truly witnesses to the emerging patterns of socially induced harm, a product of these fiscal retrenchments, which translated to a diminished commitment to health and social welfare.

The relationships we had developed in the planning and implementation of this conference were still extant. One of the key planners was Dr. Victor Sidel, a leader in the American Public Health Association and a key person in the movement for universal health care. Dr. Sidel introduced us to other health professionals in the Physicians for National Health Program and has maintained a helpful interest in our work since then. The rest is history.

Q: What is Rekindling Reform?

A: Rekindling Reform seeks to revive debate and discussion about how our country can provide quality health care to all people living here. We think that our present health care system is intrinsically unfair as it denies the assurance of health care to over 40 million people.

From its modest beginning, Rekindling Reform now has 40 sponsors. It will be expanding its sponsorship and will be attracting additional support from labor, business, and faith-based organizations. We have carried out a successful five-lecture series dealing with the universal health systems of other advanced industrial nations with universal health care. These presentations sought to explore and educate about how these systems work so that we can examine the elements that could usefully be adapted in the development of a United States system of universal care. We think that the present structure of the system wastes an enormous amount of money in the administration of health care with its proliferation of payers, all with their brand of excessive paperwork. We think the system is insane from a public health point of view in its inability to provide protection for so many members of an interdependent society. We are looking for informed alternatives.

We will be promulgating a statement of principles that should be incorporated into any system of national health insurance to be developed here. We are working on plans for a program involving an examination of how any system of universal health care needs to be shaped to meet the needs of vulnerable populations.

Q: What social work skills were used to get this effort off the ground?

A: *The most important contribution we made was one of perspective—the recognition that we needed to build a broad movement capable of attracting and involving people of different political persuasions and ideologies. What would unite us would be an agreement that comprehensive reform of health care was necessary rather than adherence to one particular view as to how this should be accomplished. We believed we should build from a base in the health professions since the general population viewed us as having particular expertise. That was a logical step because it was these professions and their clients that were being made to bear the brunt of the growing contradictions in health care.*

We believe we are both good listeners, tuning in on the concerns and perspectives of others and ready to modify both content and format of the work of the group to meet identified needs and styles. We were sensitive to the fluid states of readiness to accept and work with others. The group grew because the original participants reached out to involve others and then these people did the same. We worked hard to

evolve the program out of these interactions rather than suggesting formula-laden approaches out of our own experience.

Using our networking skills, we reached out to an older retired health policy professional who had been bypassed by the new centrist leadership in health policy because of his commitment to methodologically sound practices. He contributed his ideas freely and forcefully, helping to shape the decisions that led to the sponsorship of the lecture series. I believe he saw in Rekindling Reform something similar to what we saw—an opportunity to utilize oneself consciously in the advancement of a social movement in a way which called upon all the knowledge and skill one had accumulated over a lifetime of professional work. This is what motivates us.

We showed respect for the deep competence and knowledge of members of the planning group who had spent their entire careers in health care. We were very patient as we went over draft after draft of idea papers as each individual contributed his or her suggestions. We were conscious of the need to involve nurses as well as physicians and we were gratified when the New York State Nurses Association came on board. Their president elect was most helpful in the early days of conceptualizing purpose and drafting program.

Once the basic program thrust was agreed upon, we became the chief operating figures in developing the plans to carry them out. We had the time that the fully employed health professionals lacked and the skill and experience to translate group decisions into organizational reality. We welcomed the contributions of the physician who headed up Physicians for a National Health Care Program. A natural leader, his intelligence, insight, and patience helped to jell the group's ideas and establish a program.

We used e-mail consciously to keep everyone informed of both progress and problems, not hesitating to ask for advice and not reluctant to accept it. We did not have enough women mem-

bers of the planning committee at first and we raised the issue instead of waiting for it to become a destructive factor. More women were added and took hold in the leadership of the work. Our willingness to work hard became a kind of model for others as well—leadership by example, if you will. We welcomed the readiness of others to assume responsibility for phases of the organization's work rather than trying to hold all of the reins ourselves. That is a sensitive area and requires constant monitoring of the willingness of others to pitch in and use their initiative.

We did a lot of the reaching out to new groups based on the recommendations of others. That involved both public speaking and individual and small group interaction and development of rapport. We were constantly on the lookout for ways in which we could merge our work and interests with those of other likeminded individuals and groups. We heard about the development of a Web site by a group of veteran participants in health care reform. One of the members of our planning committee was also a member of that group. We worked with him to set up a meeting in which I participated. Voila . . . we identified common interests, agreed upon working methods, and the Web site collaboration is now a reality.

Aaron is busy developing a Listserv (or electronic mailing list) in which all of the names of interested individuals will be entered. We continue to identify bridge-linking figures who can serve as the basis for new contacts in expanding our work.

Q: What outcomes are sought?

A: *We want to contribute to the development of a broad social movement that can become an important force in the enactment of national health insurance. Health is the one aspect of the human condition that can unite all people. It is an aspect that affects all of the clients of members of this profession and the very work of this profession. It is eminently worth the effort that we, and many others, are investing*

to realize the urgently needed goal of universal health care coverage. (Levitt, personal communication, April 15, 2002)

Advocacy Takes Planning

A systematized advocacy effort is predicated upon an established plan detailing the "how, who, when, and what" for intervening in the political process around a specific issue (Lens & Gibelman, 2000). As the interview with Lou Levitt shows, planning is the basis upon which to build a social action movement. Beyond planning, advocacy involves perseverance, a focus on outcomes, and a significant amount of process.

As the Rekindling Reform movement illustrates, various skills are involved in the advocacy process. These include the following:

- **Data** *Collection and Research Skills.* In order to effect change, advocates must gather facts and information about the issue or situation they wish to change. This is accomplished through the use of policy analysis, advocacy, and planning skills.
- **Public Relations and Media Skills.** Working with the press is extremely important in advocacy and involves writing good press releases, organizing press conferences, and maintaining good relationships with specific journalists who write about the area of advocacy concern. The skill base includes public education, professional writing, research, networking, and coordination. Levitt and Beckerman have sought to educate the public about health reform issues by, among other activities, monitoring press accounts and writing "letters to the editor" to clarify specific points.
- **People Skills.** People skills are basic to social work practice. In Rekindling Reform the people skills of persuading, negotiating, mediating, accommodating, and educating are involved. These skills are needed, for example, to gain organizational

sponsors, convince funding sources that they should fund the project, keep alliances focused on the common agenda, and mediate disagreements.

- **Knowledge of the Legislative Process.** Advocates must know how political forums operate, which committees are important, and where decisions are made in a legislative body. Here, social workers use their analysis and networking skills.
- **Fundraising.** In order to run productive grassroots organizations, advocates must be skilled in writing grant proposals, approaching funding agents, and developing effective promotional campaigns. Also involved in this process is researching various funding sources to match their interests with those of specific elements of the proposed effort.
- **Networking and Alliance Building.** Skills in forming alliances and coalitions with other groups and agencies lead to much greater influence than any single agency or group could bring to bear. There is power in numbers.
- **Use of Technology.** Today, the tasks involved in advocacy are facilitated by the use of technology—telephone campaigns, direct mail, electronic mail, and World Wide Web pages (Fitzgerald & McNutt, 1999). The speed of communications and the numbers of people who can be reached have made advocacy more accessible and feasible for many social workers.
- **Organizing.** Social work advocacy also includes helping to organize and participate with community and professional groups who come together around a specific problem or issue, exemplified in the perceived need to jump start health care reform from a different perspective. This type of advocacy practice generally falls under the rubric of community practice and embodies the profession's empowerment tradition and social justice

values (Weil & Gamble, 2002). Enabling, brokering, mediating, and educating are among the advocacy skills that may be employed to achieve change in the socioeconomic and political conditions that affect the well-being of clients (Barker, 1999; Lens & Gibelman, 2000; Mickelson, 1995).

Advocacy takes time, knowledge, skill, and, often, some money.

ASSESSING IMPACT OF SOCIAL POLICY

A small proportion of social workers have a primary work function related to policy analysis, although a much larger number of social workers may conduct such analyses as a component of their job. Barker (1999) *defined policy analysis* as

> systematic evaluations of a policy and the process by which it was formulated. Those who conduct such analyses consider whether the process and result were rational, clear, explicit, equitable, legal, politically feasible, compatible with social values, cost-effective, and superior to all the alternatives, in the short term and in the long run. (p. 366)

Social workers are in a unique position to document human conditions and services needs of individuals and groups and the ways in which community social welfare systems can be improved to better meet human needs. Frontline social workers can count the numbers of people coming to soup kitchens and the numbers who are turned away from shelters because they are filled to capacity. This information can be provided to decision makers to document utilization and unmet need. Social workers can also vocalize the human impacts of fiscal cutbacks or the frustrations experienced by families who get the runaround from an agency to which they have turned for help.

As welfare reform has been reexamined during 2002 and 2003, efforts on the part of social workers to document the impact of social policy provide important data to support a professional position. One such effort, sponsored by the New York City chapter of NASW with funding from the United Way of New York City, was undertaken to document the impact of eligibility time limits on low-income people (O'Neill, 2002a).

Under the direction of Dr. Mimi Abramowitz, principal investigator of the study, researchers interviewed senior staff of 107 New York City nonprofit human services agencies. The findings revealed that clients and the agencies that service them have been significantly affected by welfare reform but not in a positive direction. For example, findings showed that changes in welfare policies have intensified the economic insecurity of low-income families, with the result that they are requesting more and different types of services from nonprofits. The combined impact of welfare reform, managed care, and new child welfare laws has interfered with the capacity of these agencies to provide the support, treatment, and advocacy clients need and request (Abramowitz, 2002). These findings point to policy recommendations on the part of the profession of social work and its labor force as welfare reform faces reauthorization. The social work position on welfare reform and the efforts being expended to influence the nature of the reauthorization are discussed later in this chapter.

Policy studies are carried out through university-affiliated research institutes, professional organizations, think tanks, such as the Urban Institute or Independent Sector, and individual researchers. A number of schools of social work, for example, have established research centers with government start-up funds. Social workers have also been pushing for the creation of a federal social work research center, but the proposed legislation stalled in the 107th Congress because of the nation's preoccupation with the War on Terrorism. Nevertheless, the legislation has picked up strong congressional support and a Senate sub-committee report included language directing federal agencies to explore ways to involve social work in research projects, with a progress report due back to Congress (O'Neill, 2002b).

The *Urban Institute*, which includes social work researchers among its personnel, has sponsored ongoing analyses of current social welfare issues that provide data sources for formulating professional positions. For example, as part of its Assessing the New Federalism project, the Urban Institute issued a report on "The Cost of Protecting Vulnerable Children II: What Has Changed Since 1996?" Among its findings, the study revealed that states target little funding to prevention services. Social workers can use such findings to advocate for channeling some of the over $15 billion spent annually on child welfare services to prevention programs ("Reform's Effect," 2002).

POLITICAL INVOLVEMENT OF SOCIAL WORKERS

Social workers engage in political activity largely by writing letters to public officials, discussing political issues with friends, attending political meetings, and joining politically active organizations (Ezell, 1993). A substantial proportion of social workers also make campaign contributions and campaign for candidates for political office. Others participate on an ad-hoc basis, depending on the issue and its salience to them. For example, a person may decide to volunteer to be a poll monitor on election day for one of the political parties, particularly if the outcome of the election is strongly felt. Or these same strong feelings may motivate a person to be a volunteer for a specific candidate throughout the campaign—calling voters, stuffing envelopes, answering phones, knocking on doors, and so on. A highly involved and motivated person may serve as a volunteer, as well, during the entire period in which the elected official is in office, engaging in tasks that are assigned on an as-needed basis.

Many social workers, however, believe that politics is not of personal or professional concern and that policies are made somewhere "out there"—removed from the day-to-day practice world. This view is remarkably persistent. Scholars and activists argue, however, that policy practice is a legitimate and essential component of social work that ranges from direct work with individuals where the emphasis is upon policy matters (such as empowerment and change) to interventions in larger scale systems (Flynn, 1992; Haynes & Mickelson, 2000). Policy practice, then, emphasizes the *environment* in the person-in-environment paradigm or the *situation* in the person-in-situation paradigm.

The NASW maintains an ongoing effort to involve social workers in politics. For example, NASW has established an advocacy Web site to provide resources and encourage its members to exercise continued political activity. The need for social work involvement is made clear in the words of Debbie Stabenow, MSW, U.S. Senator from Michigan:

It is easier to spend a few months and some money electing the right people than to spend years and a lot of money trying to get the wrong people to do the right things. (NASW, 2002e)

Other reasons include the following:

- shaping the policies that affect our clients by advocating for social justice
- adding the social work perspective to debates and issues—social workers under-stand how policies affect people representing the profession's interests
- working together for common goals. (NASW, 2002e)

Political Action

A small proportion of social workers have job responsibilities within the political action realm. Several social workers hold elective office, as dis-cussed below. Others may work on the staff of an elected official in the role of policy analyst. Or a social worker may be employed by a state or national organization in which advocacy is a core function. An example is the government affairs office and Political Action for Candidate Election (PACE) subsidiary of the National Association of Social Workers (see case vignette below). Since its inception, PACE staff and volunteers have worked to encourage, motivate, and facilitate social worker involvement in the electoral process. This effort is based on the conviction that social workers can influence elections (and therefore public policy) by voting, expressing their opinions to their elected officials, and remaining informed about the legislative agenda.

One way in which NASW promotes grass-roots advocacy involvement of its members is through its automated lobbying system, Congress Web, which allows members access to their senators and representatives. Between April and December 2001, 727 members used the automated lobbying system, for a total of 2,614 contacts with members of Congress. The largest number of contacts concerned the Clinical Social Work Medicare Equity Act of 1999, reintroduced in 2003 (S. 343/H.R. 707), which was not, however, acted upon before the 107th Congress adjourned. (You can visit Congress Web online at http://www.socialworkers.org /advocacy/default.asp.)

More frequently, political action is a component of community organization practice or an activity in which social workers engage as independent citizens based on their personal convictions and commitment to social change. Examples in this latter category include participation in demonstrations. For example, social workers joined hundreds of people who are poor and their allies in October 1999 for the March of the Americas, a demonstration organized by the Kensington Welfare Rights Union to bring visibility to the plight of the poor in America. This march took participants, including representatives of a network of more than 40 organizations united under the title of the Poor People's Economic Human Rights Campaign, through 32 cities over a one-month, 400-mile journey. The group also filed a petition with the United Nations charging the United States with violating the 50-year-old Universal Declaration of Human Rights by failing to provide accessible health care, quality public education, affordable housing, jobs, and a living wage (Beaucar, 2000).

In 2000, NASW Rhode Island chapter Executive Director Kate Coyne-McCoy demonstrated in front of the offices of Blue Cross Blue Shield Rhode Island to demand that the insurance company return its $29 million of surplus funds to consumers. She attempted to hand deliver a letter to the company's chief executive demanding that Blue Cross and Blue Shield lower its premiums and expand health care coverage ("Social Work in the Public Eye," 2000b). This kind of advocacy, even on the individual level, helps bring visibility to these issues and, in this case, the local press as well.

Also in 2000, social work students, along with students in law, medicine, nursing, and public health, joined with elected officials, experts on gun violence, and celebrities to participate in "First Monday 2000: Unite to End Gun Violence," a national campaign sponsored by the advocacy group Alliance for Social Justice. The goal was to bring attention to, educate, and stimulate discussion about reducing gun violence. The scheduling of the event was to coincide with the first day of the U.S. Supreme Court term. Social worker Monica Haines served as organizer for the Alliance for Justice (Vallianatos, 2000).

These kinds of activities fall within the category of political activism, in which individuals or groups engage in activities that seek to influence the decisions and viewpoints of elected or appointed officials and the electorate. According to Barker (1999), these activities are

> coordinated efforts to influence legislation, election of candidates, and social causes.

Social workers engage in political action by running for elective office, organizing campaigns in support of other candidates or issues, fundraising, and mobilizing voters and public opinion. Political action also includes lobbying, testifying before legislative committees, and monitoring the work of officeholders and government workers. (p. 366)

The involvement of social workers in the political process has given the profession greater recognition and influence and has resulted in tangible gains in public policy of benefit to our clients. The NASW and schools of social work have long encouraged social workers to be active in politics, either professionally or voluntarily. This emphasis appears to have had an impact. A survey of social workers in one state revealed that they are more politically active than the general public and engage in a variety of political activities ranging from the simple act of voting to organizing and facilitating election campaigns (Hamilton & Fauri, 2001).

Testifying

Testifying is a specific activity associated with the goal of influencing the direction of change and promoting change. The goal of providing testimony is to inform and educate and, in so doing, help policymakers see your views about the issue or problem and what action is needed.

Much has been written in newspapers and aired on television and radio news reports about the role of special interests in seeking to sway the opinions of policymakers in a manner beneficial to the group. C-Span and CNN, for example, often air congressional hearings on issues that are controversial and for which special interest groups have organized to influence legislators' views on their behalf. Examples include efforts on the part of oil companies to gain access to Alaska's oil fields through changes in environmental protection laws. But it is not only big business that seeks to persuade through testimony. Health and human services groups, too, seek to influence the opinions of policymakers in a manner consistent with their missions and the client groups they represent.

There are many examples of activism among social workers in the form of testifying before local, state, and national legislative committees and commissions. Michael Sherraden, for example, Director of the Center for Social Development, Washington University at St. Louis, provided testimony in October 2001 to the President's Commission on Social Security on asset building for low-income Americans. He expressed the concern that "the pronounced shift toward asset-based domestic policy in the United States has excluded the poor." Sheridan was quoted as saying that "asset-based policies have the potential to exacerbate inequality and, indeed, are doing so because the poor are being left behind" (as cited in "Social Work in the Public Eye," 2002, p. 15). Among several recommendations, Sherraden suggested that the poor should be brought into 401(k) plans, individual retirement accounts, state college savings plans, and all of the other tax-advantaged asset-building strategies that benefit those who are not poor.

The opportunity to provide testimony is available to many social workers at the federal, state, and local levels. To do so involves active monitoring of the key legislative issues of interest to the individual social worker or groups of social workers. Sometimes "experts" may be invited to testify. At other times, individuals or groups with a bona fide interest in and knowledge of the subject may sign up to testify. Those with a bona fide interest may include citizen groups and their representatives, such as health and advocacy organizations (for example, American Cancer Society and the Lupus Foundation of America). Such testimony may be highly personal and emotional, such as when the actor Michael J. Fox testified about his personal experiences with Parkinson's disease.

Testimony is oriented to a specific audience. The goal of testifying is to present facts in a manner that will influence and persuade deci-

sion makers to take a particular course of action. In this sense, testimony is not neutral. Although testimony includes elements of policy analysis, it is more goal directed, forceful, and clearly expressive of opinion than most forms of policy analysis, as illustrated in the following vignette.

CORPORAL PUNISHMENT IN THE SCHOOLS
Susan, a school social worker and chair of the state's pupil personnel services group, learns that the state legislature's education committee will be scheduling hearings on corporal punishment in the schools. These hearings are, in part, motivated by a recent case in which a junior high school teacher engaged in a physical altercation with a student whose arm was broken in the struggle. The press has picked up on this incident, and there has been a public outcry both in defense of and in opposition to the teacher's actions. Although it is known that the student was fighting with another student and that the teacher intervened to break up the situation, the principal of the school suspended the teacher. The teacher's union has come to his defense.

Many parents are also sympathetic. But the rules are clear—physical contact with students for any reason is strictly forbidden. The fact that the student sustained serious physical injuries complicates an already complicated situation. Corporal punishment is thus again on the legislative committee's agenda. State law already prohibits corporal punishment in the schools. The question before the committee is whether this stance should be reconsidered.

The pupil personnel services group, composed of school psychologists, counselors, and social workers, concludes that their collective voice needs to be heard on this issue. However, it is not so simple to come up with a position on which there is consensus. This group supports the maintenance of the existing legislation prohibiting corporal punishment in the schools. But they feel that they can bring attention to issues that may not have been considered, such as unusual circumstances in which the use of physical constraints can actually save lives or protect other students. The group also has another agenda: Testifying is an opportunity to bring attention to the small but growing organization, to educate political leaders about pupil personnel services, and to create positive opinion and action orientation among the group itself.

The preparation of the written testimony was the responsibility of a small subset of the group. One member took primary responsibility for the initial draft, which was then circulated for comment. This process entailed clarifying the position of the group in regard to corporal punishment; the testimony must reflect the group's preferences and priorities. The several draft versions of the testimony were also sent, via e-mail, to the subgroup members for comments and clearance. Susan and her colleagues continued to work on developing and refining the testimony in the weeks before the hearing. They found it a challenge to limit the facts and arguments to only 10 pages—the maximum length for written testimony, as specified by the education committee.

On behalf of the pupil personnel services group, the written testimony is being submitted to the legislative committee two weeks in advance of the hearing; this provides time for the committee members to read it and other written testimony submitted. Susan then spends a lot of time preparing for the verbal presentation. She knows that she will have only five minutes to speak. She knows she must quickly gain the attention of the committee members and that the arguments must be succinct, logical, and backed by facts. Susan knows that she will not have time to present all arguments in the five minutes she is allocated and that she will need to bring attention to a few key arguments that may not have been considered or discussed by others providing testimony.

Based on the reading she has done on the subject of testifying and her discussions with colleagues who have testified before legislative committees on other topics, Susan is mindful of the

need to demonstrate competence, trust, and enthusiasm. She must also adhere to the established protocols for presenting and do so in a manner respectful of the process.

Susan arrives at the appointment room half an hour early. She uses this time to place handout materials on a table set aside for that purpose. She also familiarizes herself with the layout of the room. She does not plan to read her statement verbatim. Rather, she has an outline in front of her that consists of the major points she wishes to make. She has practiced the oral presentation several times, in front of a mirror, her family, and her colleagues.

Susan begins by thanking the committee for the opportunity to provide testimony and identifies herself and her organizational affiliation on whose behalf she speaks. She then provides a brief statement about the group's position on the issue of corporal punishment, followed by recommendations for action. These recommendations are "reasonable," as they are based on the specific circumstances and past debates and actions on the issue of corporal punishment in the schools. She then provides relevant background to support these recommendations.

Although Susan initially thought that she should provide the background before introducing the recommendations, she had learned in her preparation that maintaining attention, in this case of the congressional subcommittee, is difficult and that one has to hit the key points early and forcefully.

A few of the points Susan intended to make during this testimony were abandoned. This is because the points were covered in testimony presented earlier in the day. Because Susan had sat through all of the testimony she was able to modify the content of her presentation based on what other speakers had already provided. Thus, she had a bit of extra time to emphasize some issues not addressed by others. She was also able to reference earlier testimony and build upon it.

Nowhere in her testimony does she use the first person. This is not the time for personal *opinions, and although the testimony clearly states a point of view, that viewpoint is based on analysis of facts. The goal is to provide facts in such a way as to persuade, inform, and motivate.*

Susan concludes her testimony by indicating her willingness to entertain questions. She is aware that some of the questions may not be "friendly," in that some representatives on the subcommittee may have already thought about the issue in a way counter to the recommendations Susan has presented. Several questions are, in fact, asked of her. Susan did not know the answer to one of the questions and said so. "Fudging" is not appropriate in these circumstances. In fact, the questions allowed Susan extra time (not "on the clock") to elaborate upon some of her earlier points. Following the questions and answers, Susan thanks the committee for the opportunity to speak.

In this vignette, Susan, representing a coalition of school mental health professionals, sought to present information to legislators to influence their opinion and potential actions about corporal punishment in the schools. In general, testimony is given on behalf of an organization; the person providing the testimony speaks on behalf of a group, not for him-or herself. (The exception may be when an acknowledged expert is called to testify—perhaps a social scientist who has conducted empirical research on the subject, or an older child who has been subjected to corporal punishment and wants to inform others about the deleterious impact of the experience.)

Susan had learned as much as possible in a short period of time about testifying and, in this process, researched the literature and consulted with colleagues who had more experience than she in this forum. Susan had learned the basics about parliamentary procedure guiding the hearings and about each of the members of the committee.

With assistance, she had reviewed the arguments for and against changing the law about cor-

poral punishment and was prepared to counter any questions from those of an opposing viewpoint. The homework served the group well. The written testimony is concise and well documented, and the recommendations are clear and based upon substantive evidence. The written statement was completed in advance, and copies had been distributed to all members of the committee and to their staff. In addition, extra copies of the written testimony were available on site. The group is aware that the written testimony will be entered into the *Congressional Record* or other formal proceedings and that it may be referenced in the future. For that reason, extra care was taken to ensure that the final document was letter perfect.

The volunteer in charge of public relations for the group prepared, in advance, a press release about the testimony and the position of the pupil personnel services group, as well as background about the group itself. This step is intended to influence the debate of others outside the committee members who hear the testimony.

Susan is aware that her role does not end immediately following the oral testimony. Within a day of the hearing, Susan writes a letter to members of the committee who were present, in which she expresses her appreciation for the opportunity to testify and restates the salient points of her testimony. In addition, she circulates copies of the testimony to the leadership of the state's pupil services group, on whose behalf the testimony was provided. Finally, a copy of the testimony is included in the group's quarterly newsletter. Here, the purpose is to promote a sense of group accomplishment; it is a good form of internal public relations.

It is difficult to assess the impact of individual and group testimony. Testimony is given on both sides of an issue, and legislators may have strong positions and not be open to new perspectives. But testifying provides an important opportunity for social workers to be heard and a written record of the testimony to be recorded. Group members, as well, are typically pleased about the visibility they receive.

SEEKING AND HOLDING POLITICAL OFFICE

Social workers have held and do hold elective office, although admittedly in small numbers. In 1916, Jeannette Rankin, at 36 years of age, became the first woman and the first social worker to be elected to the U.S. House of Representatives. As a suffragist, pacifist, and Republican, her early experiences in working in agencies concerned with children led her to wonder if she was doing enough. During her political career, Rankin supported legislation to benefit underrepresented and vulnerable populations. She supported national women's suffrage, the extension of child welfare reform, legislation to provide loans to farmers, and tariff legislation that benefited workers (Harris, 1986).

In more recent years, there has been a slow but identifiable trend toward more social workers attaining and serving in elected public office (Nieves, 2000b). At the beginning of 2002, there were two professional social workers in the U.S. Senate and four social workers in the House of Representatives (NASW, 2002d). Barbara Mikulski (D) is the senior senator from Maryland. A graduate of the University of Maryland School of Social Work, Senator Mikulski began her career as a social worker with the Baltimore Department of Social Welfare. She was first elected to the U.S. House

of Representatives (1976–1986) before her successful run for the Senate in 1986. Senator Mikulski is the senior female Democratic senator, the first Democratic woman to hold a senate seat not previously held by a husband, the first Democratic woman to have served in both houses of Congress, and the first woman to win a statewide office in Maryland (NASW, 2002d).

Also in the Senate is Deborah Ann Stabenow (D-MI), who is serving her first term after a long career in Michigan social services and politics. With an MSW from Michigan State University, Senator Stabenow served as Ingham County, Michigan, commissioner from 1975 to 1978, and served as the commission's youngest and first woman chair from 1977–1978. She won election to the Michigan House of Representatives in 1978 and served in the state house until 1990, when she was elected to the Michigan State Senate (NASW, 2002d).

As of November 2003, the four elected social workers in the House of Representatives are Susan Davis (D-CA), Barbara Lee (D-CA), Ciro D. Rodriguez (D-TX), and Edolphus ("Ed") Towns (D-NY). All hold MSW degrees. In addition to these national elected posts, social workers across the country serve in a range of political positions, from school boards to city and county offices and state legislatures. (A synopsis of social workers in elected office is provided in Table 11-1.)

TABLE 11.1

Social Workers in Elected Office, 2003

POLITICAL BODY	BSW	MSW	DSW/PHD	UNKNOWN
U.S. Congress		6		
State Legislature	12	46	3	3
County/Borough	2	13		2
City/Municipal	5	35	2	
School Board	2	25	4	4
Other	9	8		
Total	**30**	**133**	**9**	**9**

Source: "Social Workers in Congress," *NASW News*, p. 15.

NASW encourages social workers to run for office because they are trained communicators with concrete ideas about how to empower communities. Social workers understand social problems and are knowledgeable about human relations, and their commitment to improving the quality of life brings a vital perspective to public decision making. They make good political candidates because they are well educated, articulate, and experienced in public speaking, comfortable at persuasion, and knowledgeable about their communities; they understand how policies affect individuals and communities, understand social problems, and are committed to social justice (NASW, 2003a). Running for office (and winning!) provides social workers with the opportunity to contribute to the policy-making process on a direct and continuous basis.

Over the years, social workers have also held important appointed positions. Social worker Charles Curie was selected by President George W. Bush in July 2001 and confirmed by the Senate to be administrator of the Substance Abuse and Mental Health Services Administration (SAMSHA). This federal agency, under the umbrella of the U.S. Department of Health and Human Services, is charged with improving the quality and availability of substance abuse prevention, addiction treatment, and mental health services throughout the United States ("Member Named to Head SAMSHA," 2001). With its budget of $3 billion per year and 550 staff members, SAMSHA houses the Center for Mental Health Services, the Center for Substance Abuse Prevention, and the Center for Substance Abuse Treatment.

In 2000, Kansas social worker Cassie Burdine Lauver was appointed director of the Division of State and Community Health at the U.S. Health Resources and Services Administration's Maternal and Child Health Bureau ("Social Work in the Public Eye," 2000b).

Josie Torralba Romero, professor of social policy and clinical practice at San Jose State University School of Social Work, was named in 2000 to be one of the new members of the national team that advises SAMHSA's mental health center on mental-health-related activities and policies ("Social Work in the Public Eye," 2000a). Also in 2000, Shirley Buttrick was appointed by District of Columbia Mayor Anthony Williams to a three-year term on the Mayor's Advisory Committee on Child Abuse and Neglect ("Social Work in the Public Eye," 2000a).

These examples of social workers who have held or currently hold elected or appointed political positions suggest that the body politic is an important, albeit nontraditional, arena of practice.

Endorsing and Supporting Political Candidates

Throughout the years, NASW has also endorsed and campaigned for political candidates who are considered to favor sound social policies. In 1984, NASW took a high-risk course of action by declaring its endorsement, before the primaries, of Walter Mondale to be the Democratic Party nominee for the presidency of the United States (Stewart, 1984). In the following years, NASW, through its Political Action for Candidate Election (PACE), endorsed and actively campaigned for presidential candidates Michael Dukakis in 1988, Bill Clinton in 1992 and 1996, and Al Gore in 2000.

PACE, first formed in 1976, takes an active stand in electoral politics at the national level, including financial contributions to candidates who receive endorsements. Endorsements are based on the priority-issue preferences of members (as determined by periodic surveys conducted by PACE) and the consistency of candidates' views with member preferences.

Endorsements of political candidates are made on the basis of their support for NASW policy positions, not by political party affiliation. PACE considers the following:

- issues that candidates support or oppose
- viability of campaign (money raised, name recognition of candidate)

- whether the current officeholder is seeking reelection
- relationship to the social work community
- building an electoral presence for future campaigns
- leadership position of the incumbent, such as committee assignments
- affirmative action goals for candidates from underrepresented groups. (NASW, 2002a)

Lobbying

Either as individual citizens committed to social justice and social change or as part of their assigned job responsibilities, many social workers engage in lobbying at the local, state, or federal level. The purpose of lobbying is to influence the opinion of decision makers. It can take many forms, including petitions, telegrams, telephone calls, and face-to-face meetings. Social workers are effective lobbyists because they can talk about issues from personal experiences. And social workers' expertise in fact-finding, communicating, negotiating, and mediating can help decision makers make the "right" decisions.

Lobbyist is the term used to described "interest groups and individuals who seek direct access to lawmakers to influence legislation and public policy" (Barker, 1999, p. 280). The term originated from the practice of some of these people to wait in the lobbies outside the legislative chambers to influence legislators in respect to some current issue. The role of the lobbyist includes mobilizing constituent pressure, monitoring all legislation of relevance, providing technical assistance, offering research results of relevance, and developing relationships with aides and other lobbyists.

As the professional association representing social workers, the National Association of Social Workers, which is incorporated as a professional association and not limited in lobbying in the same way as charitable organizations, has always included the exercise of influence in social policy making to be among its priorities. In this respect, NASW speaks for and represents its full membership although, of course, not all members always agree with the positions taken. Efforts include advocating for legislation to improve health, welfare, and other human services programs. Advocating for civil rights and for appropriate recognition of the social work profession is also a focus (NASW, 2002b). At the start of 2002, for example, NASW reiterated its general arena of concerns and commitments:

As Congress continues to fight terrorism at home and abroad, NASW will work to continue the vital role of government in providing needed supports for individuals, families, and communities. NASW will work to ensure that the role of professional social workers is acknowledged, protected, and supported in federal legislation.

NASW nationally and internationally is concerned about a range of issues that affect the quality of life for people in the United States and the ability of social workers to provide quality services. This year, we will focus our legislative advocacy in the arenas of health and mental health, child welfare, economic equity, civil rights, and education. (NASW, 2002a)

Lobbying efforts are usually oriented to achieve a specific end, such as passage of legislation, increased appropriations, and language of regulations, to name a few. In some cases, the effort may be to prevent passage of a law or to stop budget reductions. Along this line, NASW designates specific areas of concern that are then detailed in the association's statement of legislative priorities ("Legislative Agenda Adopted," 2001).

Over the years, the NASW leadership has placed increasing emphasis on government relations as a priority activity. The dual agenda of NASW in government relations is to influence the social policy agenda in a manner consistent with the profession's commitment to vulnerable populations and to protect and improve the status of the social work profession and its membership.

Welfare reform, in some incarnation, is typically on the political agenda of each presidential, congressional, or gubernatorial campaign. Advocacy groups representing social work and social welfare were active in the welfare reform movement of the 1990s. However, opposition to the Temporary Assistance for Needy Families (TANF) program expressed by many organizations representing social work interests, including NASW and the Child Welfare League of America, was infrequently heard or heeded (Lens & Gibelman, 2000). Advocates themselves decried their lack of influence, claiming they had been locked out of the debate (Vobejda & Havemann, 1995). One newspaper headline decried, "social workers could undermine welfare reform," and noted that NASW had "opposed all efforts to trim welfare benefits and to require work" (Payne, 1996, p. A16).

The social welfare community was portrayed as a negative force against positive change. The outcome of the 1995–1996 social welfare community's lobbying effort to influence the shape and form of welfare reform was disappointing to much of the social welfare community. The NASW legislative staff, however, used the experience to organize a more effective effort the next time around. Capacity building has been part of this longer term effort.

In many ways, the stakes involved in the reauthorization are now higher for the social welfare community and the clients it represents than was the case in 1996. The immediate goal of TANF—to get people off welfare—has been realized. Maryland, for example, has reduced its welfare rolls by 66 percent. But this does not mean that the people who are no longer receiving benefits are gainfully employed and economically self-sufficient. It simply means that they have reached their lifetime limit for federal assistance. It is unclear as to whether and how well states may opt to continue benefits with their own funds. State budgets are seriously strained. A complicating factor is that each state has its own set of rules and requirements, leaving the fate of welfare recipients dependent on geography and the savvy of their caseworkers (Vallianatos, 2002). The possibility that racial and ethnic discrimination will affect who gets what also looms, given the level of discretion that states may exercise.

The following vignette illustrates the ongoing work of the government relations staff of NASW to influence the 2002–2003 debate about welfare reform. The case takes us to an arbitrary point in the process; NASW's work continues until both houses of Congress approve the reauthorization. Information about NASW's work on this initiative is drawn from an interview with Dave Dempsey, manager of NASW's Government Relations and Political Action Office, and augmented by articles in the *NASW News* in 2001 and 2002. As appropriate, citations to the literature are provided as they shed light on the nature of the social work functions carried out in this government relations and political action work.

GOVERNMENT RELATIONS AT NASW
Reauthorization of the Personal Responsibility and Work Opportunity Act (PRWOA) of 1996 has been at the top of the agenda for NASW's government relations staff. The decision to focus on the reauthorization of welfare reform was made in conjunction with the volunteer committees of the association and key volunteer leaders. The first task was to delegate responsibility to both staff and volunteers. Dave Dempsey, manager of the Government Relations and Political Action Office at the NASW national headquarters in Washington, DC, oversees and monitors the effort.

Cynthia Woodside, a lobbyist in NASW's government relations office, was assigned to work exclusively on the issue of welfare reform. Sherri Morgan, MSW, JD, and a member of NASW's legal counsel staff, was assigned to work on welfare reform one day per week. In addition, Will Dickey, a second-year MSW stu-

dent at the University of Houston who was fulfilling his second-year field placement at NASW, worked with Ms. Woodside on research. Mr. Dempsey has a law degree and 24 years of experience as a trial attorney.

Terri Mizahri, former president of NASW, appointed a Blue Ribbon Panel on Economic Security comprised of seven NASW members with expertise in the subject area. The panel's composition includes a mix of educators–researchers and practitioners–administrators and one TANF former client who is now an MSW student. The panel is expected to amplify social work's voice on the issue of poverty in America and to contribute to the debate over reauthorization of the PRWOA ("Economic Security Panel Named," 2002). Panel members assist in identifying relevant research by social workers and others; are available to reinforce the national office's media message by serving as social work experts in their issue areas; serve as resources in the legislative arena; and provide resources for member education programs at the chapter level.

On April 7, 2002, panel members had the opportunity to meet with Senator Hillary Clinton (D-NY) to discuss the impact of welfare policy on social services agencies (Stoesen, 2002). Ms. Mizahri sees this panel—and the overall effort to influence the debate about reauthorization of PRWOA—as an essential component of the profession's advocacy role. The success of the effort is seen as predicated on thorough planning. This planning process involves (1) establishing goals; (2) developing internal capability; (3) forging interorganizational alliances; (4) determining volunteer and staff needs for the effort; (5) hiring and deploying staff and providing training for them; and (6) establishing, maintaining, and strengthening internal and external communication systems. A high level of coordination and the use of multiple strategies are required to actuate this initiative.

The following goals were formulated within the context of the overarching goal of influenc-

ing the debate and ultimate content of the welfare reform reauthorization:

- to raise recipients out of poverty, not just lower caseloads (from caseload reduction to poverty reduction)
- to provide programs to remove specific barriers to employment, such as mental health and substance abuse problems, domestic violence situations, and racial and ethnic discrimination
- to revitalize the welfare administration infrastructure, including training case workers, collaborating with qualified professionals, instituting appropriate case load size, and streamlining the service provision process. (O'Neill, 2002c)

These goals, however, are seen as stopgap measures while working toward universal systems of support, including health care, food, housing, child care, and education. In November 2001, this list of recommendations for shaping reauthorization legislation was submitted to the U.S. Department of Health and Human Services (NASW, 2001).

The strategy developed by NASW to achieve these goals is multifaceted. One strategy involves the use of lobbying techniques, with a focus on the committees involved in debating and reaching consensus on welfare reform. Early in this process, Ms. Woodside began to meet with individual members of the House Committee on Education and the Workforce. During these meetings, which most often involve committee staff rather than elected representatives, Ms. Woodside described the NASW goals and responded to questions about where NASW stands on alternate proposals. A skillful response involved significant knowledge about other proposals on the table and an assessment of the degree of comparability between these other proposals and those offered by NASW.

Ms. Woodside monitors developments on a daily basis. New developments constantly emerge. The Bush administration provides new or clarifying insights into its position. The president's proposals include requiring more adults to work, requiring them to work more hours, encouraging "healthy" marriages, and discouraging out-of-wedlock births ("Next on Welfare," 2002). However, these proposals do not include additional funds for grants to states for assistance or child care. States are thus being asked to do more with less, at the same time in which unemployment rates are up and the economy is in a slump—thus diminishing employment prospects for those with few marketable skills. The government relations staff seeks to analyze the meaning of these emerging proposals and to get information out to its allied organizations and its members about the interpretation and implications of the administration's statements and positions.

Part of the NASW strategy is to be visible and, through the use of the media, to make its voice heard. Ms. Woodside has already been interviewed by Robert Pear of the New York Times. Other media contacts are being cultivated. These steps are taken in recognition that the media is an essential link in the advocacy chain, especially with such a volatile and emotional issue as welfare reform. The government relations staff is cultivating its own media contacts but is concurrently working with organizational allies to bring added visibility to its viewpoint.

Creating Alliances

Former NASW President Terry Mizrahi (2002) articulated the importance of a unified intra- and interorganizational approach to influence the shape of welfare reform:

In order to be effective in the campaign now under way to shape the reauthorization of the Personal Responsibility and Work Opportunity Act of 1996, including Temporary Assistance to Needy Families, we need our legislative, policy, practice, and research arms to work in concert. And we need to help refocus the debate from ending

dependency to creating opportunities and from one based on moral imperatives to one guided by practical solutions. (p. 2)

It is axiomatic that there is strength in numbers. Coalition building is an essential component of any advocacy campaign whether at the local, state, or national level (Dluhy, 1990; Haynes & Mickelson, 2000). Forging alliances and working in concert with other national organizations are major components of this effort to influence the direction of social welfare policy. Toward this end, NASW is an active member of the Coalition on Human Needs, comprised of over 100 groups. It is also a member of the National Coalition for Jobs and Income, a large, umbrella advocacy group. In addition to enhancing the influence of each individual member group, alliances also tap the resources and skills that each organization possesses.

NASW initiated one additional group, called the Training Work Group, the purpose of which is to address labor force needs attendant to any changes in welfare reform legislation. Members of this group include the Children's Defense Fund; Child Welfare League of America; American Federation of State, County, and Municipal Employees; Service Employees International Union; American Public Human Services Association; National Urban League; Center for Law and Social Policy; Center on Budget and Policy Priorities; and the National Partnership for Women and Families.

Joan Zlotnick, executive director of the Institute for the Advancement of Social Work Research (IASWR), completed a report of all research conducted by social workers about the impact of welfare reform since its passage in 1996. This NASW–IASWR collaboration was based on a shared commitment to promote the use of social work research in practice. The preparation of the research compilation is consistent with the IASWR goals of developing research, bridging research and practice, and informing policy making with research

(Vallianatos, 2001), while providing valuable information that may be used by NASW and others in furthering their legislative agenda.

Interorganizational Relations

As the issues take shape, groups enter the lobbying effort with new or modified positions. Alliances built by NASW need to be newly crafted based on common areas of concern defined in the here and now. For example, prior to enactment of the 1996 welfare reform law, the National Governors' Association (NGA) lobbied for stringent work requirements. In 2002, the NGA urged Congress to relax those requirements for some people on welfare, concluding that the sluggish economy and rising unemployment make the work requirements for some families appear unrealistic. Further, the governors believe that some welfare recipients need more education and training to secure jobs (Pear, 2002). These views, modifying the NGA position prior to the 1996 reform effort, are more consistent with those of NASW, making a closer alliance possible.

The government relations staff has, since the new 107th Congress was elected, worked diligently to form relationships with newly elected officials and congressional staff of both parties as well as to strengthen relationships with returning members who have new roles. This effort continues into the 108th Congress. In fact, this relationship building for networking purposes is a major component of NASW's lobbying effort. The network of contacts is utilized each and every day to gather information and to monitor developments in regard to welfare reform and other issues of concern to social work and to effect changes in legislation. Information gathering from congressional and other sources, particularly other national organizations, is an ongoing activity. Utilizing modern technology (e-mail and fax), Ms. Woodside and her colleagues share new information from Congress and discuss whether new developments warrant any adjustments in strategy. For example, a

2002 White House proposal sought to encourage communities to conduct campaigns to promote marriage on moral grounds as well as one means to prevent or ameliorate economic dependency. One component of this proposal was tied to welfare reform, in which $300 million a year would be allocated to state and local governments to experiment with programs to foster strong marriages. The funds would be granted as a "waiver," in which states could use part of their welfare allocation in ways not originally intended (Goldstein, 2002).

Based on informal discussions with government relations staffs of other organizations in the alliance, Ms. Woodside concludes that this proposal does not warrant isolated action, such as a grassroots letter writing campaign. Even among the Republican leadership, the idea has raised serious questions of feasibility. The staff concluded that it is better to look at the broader picture than to spend time on a subissue that is not likely to go anywhere. NASW staff feel that the combined impact that can result from interorganizational collaboration is extremely important. When it is time to mobilize NASW constituencies, Ms. Woodside and her colleagues will prepare materials for use in contacting legislators.

The NASW relies on its members, chapters, and national staff to carry out its legislative program. The membership has already been activated in several ways, an effort which has spanned several years. The NASW maintains an advocacy link on its Web site (http://www.social work ers.org) to provide members with up-to-date information about legislation and the legislative process. The NASW Government Relations and Political Action Office established an alliance with NASW chapters in seven states to strengthen social workers' clout at the legislative level. An action plan was developed to use a number of grassroots strategies to make NASW's presence felt in Washington with the new Bush administration. A field organizer position was added to the national staff ("Legislative Network Assembled," 2001) to activate membership through the advocacy LISTSERV and "Congress Web" software, which allows members to locate their own congressional representatives.

Each of the participating chapters has recruited a federal legislative liaison to be the contact person between the chapter and the national office on legislative issues. In turn, each liaison is responsible for recruiting from 15 to 20 members from the chapter's legislative network or general membership to serve as a rapid-response team on legislative developments. These teams will use the communication methods set up and maintained by NASW, including the Congress Web link. Op ed pieces and visits with legislators in their home districts are also facilitated ("Legislative Network Assembled," 2001).

The government relations staff works concurrently on a number of strategies to influence the decision-making process. Staff frequently meet to discuss strategy in light of new information gathered. Internally, Ms. Woodside coordinates efforts with the staff of PACE in regard to supporting decision makers who might be amenable to influencing their colleagues about the "right" decisions on the subject of welfare reform or who have stood up for an NASW position. Ms. Woodside and other staff frequently attend political fundraising events to meet politicians and gain their ear. Member contacts are also used. For example, if a social worker in Kansas is known to have been active in the campaign of a senator from this state or is in a key position related to experience with a legislative issue and that member comes to Washington, a visit might be arranged with the senator, NASW staff, and the member. Face-to-face contact between constituents and members of Congress and lobbyists is considered an effective tool of influence (Richan, 1991).

Money and Influence

PACE, a subsidiary of NASW, raises funds on a voluntary basis from social work contributors. These funds are used to influence the achievement of NASW's political agenda. PACE has a discretionary budget of $7,500 per quarter to use in a manner that may benefit achievement of the NASW legislative agenda. In this welfare reform effort, a decision has been made to target available funds to Republicans who may be "on the fence" and amenable to listen and act in ways consistent with NASW's legislative platform. (Donations are made to the reelection committee, for example, of targeted representatives or senators.)

Staff are aware that the NASW platform, in general, resonates more with Democrats than with Republicans. But precisely because this is the case, outreach efforts to Republicans who may be swayed are seen as more important than providing funds to those already committed to a position in line with that of NASW.

Although there is recognition that the funds available through PACE are meager compared with those of big business lobbies, staff is nevertheless cognizant that a good-faith contribution to a political war chest may win allies among those elected officials who are open to reconsideration of their party's position.

A Juggling Act

The functions performed by Dave Dempsey, Cynthia Woodside, and other government relations staff on any given day may vary, but all relate to the goal of influencing the course of social policy development. Communication is a vital component of the advocacy effort. A lot of time is spent in meetings, on the telephone, and writing letters and action alerts. Much time is also spent on Capitol Hill meeting with members of Congress or their staff and then in NASW's offices to follow up on these visits by telephone.

Multiple strategies are implemented concurrently. This implies a kind of juggling act— keeping all of the balls in the air at the same time. There is a constant need to establish daily and weekly priorities as the reauthorization effort gains momentum. On any given day, staffs follow legislative developments on Capitol

Hill, communicate with coalitions of which NASW is a member, and keep members up to date through the Web site, fax, and e-mail about developments and the implications for action at the local level. These efforts will continue to the finish—when PRWORA is reauthorized. The reauthorization timetable was 2002, but due to lack of agreement, the deadline has been extended quarter by quarter. The latest extension of the current law runs through March 2004 (NASW, 2003c).

The social work functions involved in the above processes include monitoring the legislative process, information gathering and information disseminating, mobilizing the membership, working collaboratively with other national organizations on a shared agenda, preparing policy analysis and position statements, drafting legislative language, dealing with the media, visiting with congressional staffs and others for face-to-face contacts, participating in coalition meetings, devising and redevising strategies in light of emerging developments, and preparing written materials that may be used by members and other groups to influence decision making. For Mr. Dempsey and his staff, these tasks have taken on increased urgency in light of the anti-social-welfare sentiments associated with many of the reauthorization proposals.

Although welfare reform is a high priority for NASW's government relations program, other areas receive attention by staff. For example, in 2002 NASW assumed lobbying responsibilities for the Action Network for Social Work Education and Research, a coalition of seven social work organizations that have come together to promote passage of the National Center for Social Work Research Act ("NASW to Lead Lobbying Effort," 2002). If enacted, this bill would establish a center to collect, develop, and promote research that can be used to demonstrate the effectiveness of delivery systems and specific interventions, as well as development of new services and improvement in existing services.

COMMUNITY ORGANIZING

Community organization has been defined as "an intervention process used by social workers and other professionals to help individuals, groups, and collectives of people with common interests or from the same geographic areas to deal with social problems and to enhance social well-being through planned collective action" (Barker, 1999, pp. 90–91). A social worker in community organization may assist a community group by acting as a facilitator to help the group recruit members, define problems, and develop advocacy strategies (Weil & Gamble, 2002). In addition, increasingly social workers are mobilizing community resources in an effort to meet local needs during times of scarcity (Martinez-Brawley, 1995).

During the 1960s community organization was a more visible form of social work practice than it is today. Although community organization may have faded from the center spotlight, its methods have become more sophisticated in the ensuing years, new issues are being addressed, and more diversified range of tactics are being employed (Hiratsuka, 1990).

Many social work activities incorporate the principles and methods of community organization, including planning and implementing community-based services, networking, outreach, and coalition building. Community organizing is evident in the efforts of social workers to bring people together to solve problems or improve services. They may occupy positions as social planners, grassroots program developers, or social activists.

In the wake of the 1992 Los Angeles riots, social workers mobilized to help heal affected communities. Although this event occurred over a decade ago, the severity of the racial and ethnic unrest manifested during the riots remains a comparative reference point when incidents of other community unrest arise. In the Los Angeles case, the violence exploded after a jury acquitted four white police officers of nearly all charges in the beating of Rodney King, an African American motorist (Hiratsuka, 1992a).

Virtually all Americans had watched, countless times, the videotape of that beating and held strong opinions about it.

Many social workers responded in the aftermath of the Los Angeles riots, going into schools, disaster centers, and communities to provide crisis counseling, deliver food and clothing, and mediate ethnic tensions, racism, and bigotry. The Korean American Social Workers' Association sent bilingual social workers into those areas hardest hit in the riots in an attempt to sooth racial tensions and to minimize the violence as the Asian American population attempted to come to terms with the violence and destruction largely aimed at them and their property. The following vignette highlights the range of social work interventions carried out by social workers in the hours, days, weeks, and months following the riots.

Helping to Heal a Community

Leslie Dang, a 34-year-old Korean American social worker, works as a community outreach worker for the Los Amigos Multi-Cultural Service Center in Los Angeles. In the aftermath of the Los Angeles riots, Leslie and her colleagues visit the stricken area of the city and find themselves knee-deep in rubble and the ruins of businesses and lives. The primary questions she hears from members of the Asian American community are "Why me?", "Why us?", and "Why do they [African Americans] hate us so much?" Her job, over the long run, is to work with community residents to answer and resolve these questions. For the short run, the immediate agenda is to assess individual and family needs and link residents of the community with assistance in the form of housing, food, and clothing. Soon, there will be the need to help residents apply for business loans to rebuild their businesses and to work with local banks and nonaffected businesses to do their share in revitalizing the community.

Leslie spends the first day on the streets, talking with residents and assessing the types of serv-

ices they will need. She then returns to the office and begins the networking process of contacting community agencies to arrange for necessary services provision and to coordinate the efforts of neighborhood agencies. Within the heart of the Asian community, Leslie organizes a "town meeting," inviting everyone in the community to attend, not just the affected merchants. Three police officers, functioning as a crisis-response team, also attend in an attempt to reassure residents that the police will step up efforts to protect Asian American businesses should anymore violence occur. The residents are angry; they want to know why the police did not do more. With Leslie's help in facilitating the discussion, police are able to answer the residents' questions and address their concerns, at least to a point where a dialogue has been opened.

Following the town meeting, Leslie invites social workers from the Association of Black Social Workers of Greater Los Angeles to attend a separate meeting. Out of this combined effort, a task force takes shape, which includes Asian American business owners, the three police officers, and leaders of the African American community, as well as African American, Asian American, and white social workers. The job of this task force is to open channels of communication among all the various ethnic communities in Los Angeles to facilitate a better understanding among people who need to live and work together. Regular meetings are scheduled with the location of the meeting shifting from one ethnic community to another, allowing everyone equal access. Various city officials attend in an attempt to show concern and involvement in efforts to stem the rising tide of violence among divergent ethnic communities. Leslie acts as the facilitator during the entire formation process of this task force while dealing on a daily basis with helping those eligible for federal assistance to obtain it as quickly and efficiently as possible.

Leslie also holds special group meetings for adolescents within the Asian American commu-

nity in an attempt to minimize any kind of organized, violent response to what many in the Asian American community consider targeted looting and destruction. Leslie particularly reaches out to the Asian American gangs through her community connections and is successful in opening channels of contact with this volatile segment of her target population. Having established one task force, Leslie works with other social workers to address the adolescent population, including gang members. Although she helps initiate several programs, other social workers and identified civic leaders perform the necessary follow-up tasks.

Through Leslie's efforts, an ongoing coalition of ethnic leaders carries on the work of healing wounds and building networks for problem solving within the stricken communities. When she began her work in Los Angeles following the riots, Leslie carried out the functions of assessment and needs identification to determine what problems had to be addressed immediately and in the longer term. She then used her information and referral skills to help needy residents access necessary services. Organization and coordination functions also were important in Leslie's efforts to facilitate communication among community groups.

Organizing Demonstrations

One method of achieving social change is to organize group action to call public or political attention to a problem or issue of interest and concern to the group. Examples include organizing marches or sit-ins in highly visible settings or picketing the entrances of buildings. The media, for example, periodically call attention to organized demonstrations against the companies that employ child laborers in American-owned or American-operated factories overseas. Social workers, too, have long used confrontational methods to call attention to issues of social justice and social welfare. An example of such strategies follows.

USING CONFRONTATIONAL TECHNIQUES
Kettlebrook is a low-income housing project in Chicago, IL. The complex has 25 separate housing units, but only 10 of them are still occupied. After the other 15 units were vacated, the landlord simply refused to rent them. The 10 remaining units are in complete disrepair. Neither the heat nor the electricity work regularly, paint is peeling from the ceilings and walls, and termites have begun to eat away the floors.

Kelsey Green is a social worker with the department of social services and she has a client who lives at Kettlebrook. Kelsey is disgusted with the deterioration of Kettlebrook and she begins to talk to and work with the tenants. They first attempt to meet with the landlord, but this fails to produce results. Kelsey then helps the tenants to organize themselves. The following week, all of the tenants gather to picket on the street in front of the landlord's home. The landlord never leaves his house, and the tenants come back every day for a week. Kelsey arranges for the media to be present, and the press coverage brings the support of the surrounding community. Finally, the landlord concludes that the adverse publicity is harmful and that it will cost him less in the long run to make the necessary repairs than to face possible rent strikes and perhaps even a government investigation of conditions.

As noted earlier, a motivating force for social workers to engage in macro level interventions is their perception of a threat to themselves and those they represent or, in the case of Kettlebrook, the failure of discussions and negotiations have failed and the necessity for new strategies be explored. One tactic that has been employed to achieve desired ends is the job action, which includes workplace organizing, lobbying, educating, protesting, and sometimes strikes.

There are no hard and fast rules concerning when to initiate a job action, but the time has come, in general, when a group of social workers identify conditions that endanger the lives of clients and employees or when it becomes impossible to provide quality services (Hiratsuka, 1992b). Most job actions are held during the process of contract negotiations. Issues may concern salaries, caseload size, supervisory issues, and worker safety. Sometimes services may be disrupted in the short run. But the intended outcome is long-term improvements, which are often the result of calling public attention to problems. In turn, pressure is brought on administrators and legislators to act. Job actions are typically associated with unionism.

SOCIAL WORK AND UNIONS

Some social workers belong to unions, such as the American Federation of State, County, and Municipal Employees. Unionization of social workers has a long history. In the 1930s, New York social workers formed the Association of Federated Social Workers and conducted the first social work strike, which took the form of a two-hour work stoppage. Local 19 of the United Office and Professional Workers of America also organized social workers employed by Jewish welfare organizations. During the 20th century, social work participation in unions addressed working conditions, with particular attention to caseload size and salaries. However, at various times, such as during the 1930s and 1960s, union activity also focused on client-related issues. Through unions, social workers sought policy development or change to address poverty, hunger, unemployment, racial discrimination, and the spread of fascism in Europe (Nieves, 2000a).

Executive Vice President Linda Chavez-Thompson of the AFL-CIO articulated some of the commonalities of purpose between unions and the social work profession. Like social work, the labor movement emphasizes partnership building with natural allies located in communities. In Chavez-Thompson's view, "organizing and coalition-building are especially important when workers' productivity has increased but

their earnings have not" (as cited in "Leaders Put Partnership into Practice," 1998, p. 5).

It is estimated that there are about 125,000 social workers in the United States who belong to unions, representing about 25 percent of the professionally trained social work labor force (Tambor, 1995). Barth (2001), extrapolating from the U.S. Bureau of the *Census Current Population Survey*, similarly found that 24 percent or about 204,000 social workers reported being a member of a union. Barth also found that nearly 89 percent of social work union members are in the public sector, with about half of these employed at the local government level.

Social workers' participation in job actions or strikes, whether on behalf of their profession or the clients they represent, is supported by the profession's ethical code. However, ethical considerations must be weighed. According to the NASW *Code of Ethics* (1996):

> Social workers may engage in organized action, including the formation of and participation in labor unions, to improve the services to clients and working conditions. The actions of social workers who are involved in labor–management disputes, jobs actions, or labor strikes should be guided by the profession's values, ethical principles, and ethical standards. Reasonable differences of opinion exist among social workers concerning their primary obligation as professionals during an actual or threatened labor strike or job action. Social workers should carefully examine relevant issues and their possible impact on clients before deciding on a course of action. (p. 22)

Market forces, particularly managed care, have in recent years influenced a higher level of social work participation in unions. For example, the Clinical Social Work Federation has affiliated with the Office and Professional Employees Union of the AFL-CIO. The unit is called the National Guild of Health Care Professionals (Nieves, 2000a). In New York City,

Health Care Workers Union 1199–SEIU Health and Human Service Union worked collaboratively with several professional organizations, including the city's NASW chapter, to defeat legislation that would have deregulated hospital social work. This same union has also worked proactively with social work coalitions to seek passage of a social work licensing law (Rosenberg, 2002). The alliance between the New York City chapter and 1199–SEIU is considered by NASW to be a pilot project that may help to establish union–social work association relationships in other localities (Nieves, 2000b). The NASW–union relationship was furthered in late 2000 when the New York City and New York State chapters of NASW signed an agreement with 1199, the Hospital and Human Service Employees Union–SEIU, AFL-CIO, to form an alliance. The purpose of the alliance is to enhance the political and legislative work of each organization (Carten & Schachter, 2000).

Sometimes, social work activism in unions is totally client centered. Social worker Arturo Rodriquez is a long-time employee of the United Farm Workers (UFW). He signed with the UFW in 1973 upon his graduation from the University of Michigan School of Social Work. In May 1993, he was named president of the union, a position he still holds, succeeding Cesar Chavez, who died earlier that year (UFW, 2002a). He had first become active with the UFW's grape boycott in 1969 as a college student. Upon receiving his MSW, Mr. Rodriquez expanded his union organizing activities by organizing boycott campaigns in Detroit.

In a 1987 interview, Mr. Rodriguez described for NASW his earlier activities as Mid-Atlantic director of the table-grape boycott and a member of the union's national board. There he utilized a variety of means to achieve the union's goals, including the application of social marketing techniques for social causes. Mr. Rodriquez said that his social work skills, including organizational skills, research, and ability to assess a community and target efforts, have served him well in his job ("Social Worker Helps Chavez with Boycott," 1987).

The Grapes of Wrath campaign and table-grape boycott began in July 1984 and received more than 1,000 endorsements from politicians, labor leaders, and organizations. The campaign focused on free and fair organizing elections, banning the use of specific pesticides that can cause cancer and birth defects, and instituting tests to determine pesticide residue on fruits and vegetables. Although union members engaged in picketing, this was only one of many strategies employed. The importance of augmenting direct confrontation techniques, such as picketing, with other strategies was accentuated by the conservative national mood.

In planning public education campaigns, Rodriguez targeted audiences that were likely to be sympathetic to the cause, such as labor, Chicanos, other minorities, and religious and academic communities. The campaign focused on the hazards to consumers as well as farm workers, thus broadening its appeal to and participation in consumer and environmental groups. To raise funds and, at the same time, engage in public education strategies, Rodriguez oversaw the implementation of direct mail, films, sales, and other fundraising solicitation techniques. Mr. Rodriguez has utilized these strategies throughout his career with the UFW.

Mr. Rodriquez exemplifies how communication skills can be used effectively to convey information about social issues and the means of addressing them. The following op ed column, written by Mr. Rodriguez (2001), argued eloquently against pending legislation (reprinted here in its entirety).

UTILIZING THE PRESS TO EDUCATE AND ADVOCATE HISTORIC PROPOSAL FOR FARM WORKER LEGALIZATION
Arturo S. Rodriguez
"*Congress can help thousands of America's undocumented farm workers emerge from the*

shadows of fear and abuse. It can do that by passing breakthrough legislation negotiated last fall between the Cesar Chavez-founded United Farm Workers and the nation's agricultural employers—even though the industry has since broken its word to back the compromise agreement.

"Undocumented farm workers would use this historic proposal to earn temporary legal status for themselves and their families, and eventually permanent status. With the measure, the often skilled men and women whose labor produces this country's rich bounty of food could win the protections other American workers enjoy—and some day fully participate in the society they feed.

"Under the compromise UFW–grower farm worker legalization bill, undocumented farm workers and their families would legalize—or adjust—their status.

"They would have the freedom to choose for whom they work and to join a union of fellow workers to collectively protect their interests. These workers would still need to labor in agriculture for a minimum period of time over six years to be eligible for legalization.

"The compromise would also make it easier for growers to obtain foreign workers in cases of legitimate labor shortages—with less paperwork and government oversight.

"This compromise enjoyed broad bipartisan support in both houses of Congress last year. It would have been enacted during the lame-duck session in December but for fierce opposition from Texas Republican Sen. Phil Gramm.

"Now growers have abandoned key parts of the negotiated measure by backing a new bill by other far-right Republican lawmakers, including Sen. Larry E. Craig (R-Idaho). Craig's bill would preclude many if not most undocumented farm workers from becoming legal residents.

"In a classic 'Catch 22' scenario, the Craig plan says undocumented workers seeking to legalize would be barred from non-farm jobs until they worked 150 days a year in agricul-

ture. Many would not be able to do that given the industry's short harvest seasons, oversupplies of labor and chronic unemployment. Yet the Craig bill also says these workers couldn't stay in the country for more than 60 days without seeking employment.

"Craig's legislation would lower the pay for temporary foreign farm workers imported to the United States under an existing federal program. And it would continue the discriminatory exclusion of these imported foreign laborers from the basic federal law protecting the on-the-job rights of domestic farm workers.

"Late last year, the growers agreed with farm worker advocates to jointly support this historic compromise. We hope they will change their minds and honor their word."

Mr. Rodriquez is a community organizer. Through a variety of activities, his role is to facilitate planned efforts to achieve specified goals (Barker, 1999). These goals relate to social justice, economic and social development, and other improvements for a specific constituency—farm workers.

Influencing policy making is an important component of the job. In the op ed article, Mr. Rodriguez sought to influence public opinion in support of congressional action to legalize 500,000 undocumented immigrants and give them the right to join a union (Garcia, 2001). He did this through presentation of facts, persuasive analysis of the facts, and an appeal for reconsideration and further dialogue. The issue of legalized status for immigrants has become all the more pressing since September 11, 2001, in light of congressional sentiment, backed by substantial public support, to restrict immigration to the United States and to enforce illegal immigrant laws.

Part of community organizing is to help communities help themselves through collective action. Here, the focus is on involving volunteers and other citizens in a community in decision making, human services planning, and coordinating with agencies and professionals. According to Barker (1999), the process includes

> identifying problem areas, analyzing causes, formulating plans, developing strategies, mobilizing necessary resources, identifying and recruiting community leaders, and encouraging interrelationships between them to facilitate their efforts. (p. 91)

Mr. Rodriquez epitomizes a community organizer—a very successful one. The successes are evident in the attention the UFW commands. For example, candidates running for political office in Texas have courted the UFW endorsement (Bisbee, 2002).

Testifying is yet another forum in which Mr. Rodriguez forcefully brings attention to social issues and details action plans designed to influence the course of policy making. Such activities highlight the extent to which the UWF is both a union and a civil rights movement (UFW, 2002b).

Rothman, Erlich, and Tropman (1995) detailed three basic models of community intervention—locality development, social planning, and social action. Locality development attempts to correct a problematic situation or achieve social progress with the participation of the entire community. For effective locality development, social workers must exhibit skill in performing needs assessments and conducting research to determine realistic development goals (Weil & Gamble, 2002). Social planning usually addresses long-term goals of the community and emphasizes a technical process of problem solving for substantive social issues. At this level of community intervention, social workers must be able to identify necessary community resources and plan, manage, and negotiate to best achieve the desired social changes (Weil & Gamble, 2002). Finally, social action presupposes the existence of a disadvantaged segment of the population that must be organized in order to make demands on the larger community for

fair and equal treatment. Social action practitioners frequently focus on challenging the existing power structures in society and carry out the functions of advocacy, education, and organizing (Martinez-Brawley, 1995; Rothman et al., 1995; Weil & Gamble, 2002).

Due to the individuality of each and every community, there is no one correct method of community organizing. Community organizing emphasizes the creation of an egalitarian environment in which community services are as much a result of attitude as they are a collection of techniques. In working to organize formal and informal resources to achieve social justice aims, social workers must be able to effectively carry out the functions of advocacy and enabling as well as referral, planning, organizing, and coordination (Martinez-Brawley, 1995). As formal resources continue to diminish, a social worker's ability to organize and mobilize community and informal resources will become increasingly important.

Social workers involved in community organization must be able to help people discover their own strengths so that they may become self-sufficient. Si Kahn (1995), one of the most well-known and respected community organizers, explained the challenge facing social workers in this field: "to reach, teach, and organize people in ways that transform their understanding of power and their relationship to power—not just individually, but collectively" (pp. 575–576).

SOCIAL WORKERS PROVIDING CONSULTATION

Social work consultation refers to a problem-solving process in which advice and other helping activities provided by the consultant is offered to an individual, group, organization, or community that is faced with some type of problem. Consultation can be distinguished from supervision. Supervision is a relatively continuous process that encompasses many areas of concern. Consultation, on the other hand, typically occurs on an ad hoc or temporary basis and has a specific purpose and focus (Barker, 1999).

A *consultant* is one "with a special expertise or access to those with the needed expertise whose skills are sought by professionals or organizations" (Barker, 1999, p. 101). The social work consultant often does not work for the organization that is experiencing the problem or that seeks advice but rather is retained because of his or her special expertise to solve a specific problem. "Consultants advise or educate about the nature of the problem or possible solutions or find better ways to achieve the organization's goals" (Barker, 1999, p. 101). However, the consultant does not have any authority over those to whom advice is given and the advice may be accepted in total, accepted partially, or ignored.

The role of consultants in human services organizations is broad and is limited only by the resources and constraints of those who hire them. Consultants are hired to contribute their knowledge and experience on topics which range from interior decorating to crisis programs, fundraising, and staff training (Walsh & Moynihan, 1990). The process by which the need for a consultant is recognized and acted upon deserves attention, as the support of the board of directors, advisory board, or other authorizing entity, and staff in this decision can make all the difference in how well the consultant is received and the recommendations followed. The following vignette highlights a situation in which an agency decides to use a consultant and the range of roles upon which a consultant may be called upon to carry out.

AN AGENCY IN TROUBLE:
LOOKING FOR DIRECTIONS
The Children's Center, a not-for-profit residential treatment center serving emotionally disturbed youth, has fallen on difficult times. For the past 10 years, the largest portion of the center's funding (70 percent) was derived from a

contract with the state's department of human resources. The state, in turn, was the main source of referrals to the program. But in 2000, a new governor was elected with a twofold agenda: (1) to pare down the size of government and (2) to cut taxes. The governor immediately announced that he would be reviewing all existing contracts and that none should be considered "safe."

The executive director, Nancy, who recently received a doctorate in social welfare, realizes that the very existence of the agency is in jeopardy. Despite discussions at board meetings over the years about the need to diversify sources of center funding, the day-to-day management of the agency and the false security of the 10-year history of state funding meant that a long-range funding plan had never evolved. In addition, in the aftermath of the September 11, 2001, terrorist attack, the outpouring of charitable giving has been targeted to charitable organizations providing immediate and direct assistance to victims, such as the American Red Cross. Smaller agencies providing local services to specific populations have been hard hit because monies have been allocated elsewhere.

In consultation with the board president, an ad hoc committee on fiscal development is immediately convened. At the first meeting of the committee, Nancy is charged with the responsibility of locating a consultant who can assist in devising a fund development plan. The committee also realizes the importance of coordinating with other services providers facing the same threat of contract termination and to activate the agency's constituency (parents of the children served, other public and voluntary community agencies, government officials "friendly" to the agency, and influential community residents who have donated funds in the past). Within a few days, Nancy is able to obtain information about existing and newly forming coalitions in the state and in the community that are mobilizing to fight the cutbacks in contract funds. Several of these groups include the families of the clients served by family and children's agencies. A number of committee members volunteer to serve as agency liaisons to these coalitions.

Nancy has also been on the phone to her colleagues at other agencies to obtain a list of potential consultants with expertise in fund development. Based on the recommendations she receives, Nancy develops a "short list" of three names and calls them. Nancy explains the situation to each and arranges appointments to meet with them individually. As preparation for these meetings, Nancy asks the potential consultants to prepare a brief proposal outlining their initial thoughts on possible directions and cost estimates for consultant time.

Within a week, Nancy meets with the three consultants. The selection is relatively easy. One person, Monica Smith, stands out as a person with experience helping agencies in similar circumstances. Monica has an MSW degree, but her career path has been nontraditional. She also obtained an MBA and developed expertise in fundraising and fiscal development. In recent years, she has worked as a consultant to not-for-profit organizations, mostly those concerned with health and human services.

Nancy is comfortable with Monica's style and approach and thinks that she will work well with the committee. Monica, however, makes clear that she cannot "solve" the agency's problem. Rather, her job, as she explains it, is to guide the agency's decision makers to identify alternatives and make decisions. Nancy's proposal also emphasizes the decision-making responsibility of the committee and, ultimately, the board of directors. The proposal, in fact, details the process—a highly interactive one—in which Nancy will engage with the agency and its elected and staff leadership.

Monica begins her consultation assignment by spending two days in the office reviewing financial records, past proposals—both those funded and those rejected—fundraising and public relations materials, and interviewing staff responsible for income-generating activities. A meeting with the ad hoc resource development committee is set for the following week.

As Monica reviews the agency's financial history and current status, she realizes that the current financial crisis should have been anticipated and that the agency had made a common mistake—it had grown dependent on government contracts and had not considered that this funding stream might someday "dry up." Creating a more diversified and secure funding base is, of course, the long-range goal. However, a crisis plan needs to be developed in the short run to deal with cash flow problems.

Monica develops a series of options for presentation to the ad hoc committee. She knows that some of the options will not be popular, particularly those that concern laying off some of the staff. Other cost-saving strategies will be proposed, including curtailment of some non-revenue-producing programs and cancellation of recently ordered computer equipment. Cost savings is only part of the picture, though. Monica will also propose that the entire board, many of whom are well connected in the business community, engage in face-to-face fundraising with their associates to seek contributions. Perhaps a "challenge" program could be set up, with each board member responsible for soliciting contributions of $25,000.

Monica discusses each of these ideas with Nancy in terms of their implications for the agency and the likely reaction from the ad hoc committee and board members. This type of strategizing is important to assess the potential climate of the meeting and to anticipate the issues that will be raised. She hopes to elicit additional ideas from the ad hoc committee before meeting with the full board. The following weeks and months will involve the active participation of the board and staff; although it will be a tough road, it is possible to turn the financial situation around.

In this vignette, there are two social workers. Nancy, as executive director, uses her administrative skills, including those of fiscal management, to identify the agency's troubles. She then engages in information sharing with her board of directors, communicating to them the nature and scope of the problem in a timely way, and identifying the initial steps that will be taken to address the problem. Nancy then mobilizes her personal and agency resources to identify and select an appropriate consultant and negotiates the terms of the agreement. Collaboration between Nancy and the consultant, Monica, by design occurs on an ongoing basis.

Resource mobilization and development is a concern to all social welfare agencies. In this case, Nancy identifies the problem and seeks to institute a process that will result in mobilization of resources. Resource mobilization is

the process of bringing together and making available the organization's assets including existing funds, funds to be raised from the constituency and other sources, information base, personnel and volunteers, and the knowledge and talents of board members and others who can be called on for assistance. This process depends on the organization's making clear its needs and mission, identifying the population to be served, and communicating this information to the public. (Barker, 1999, p. 412)

Nancy and her board, however, are also aware that they need outside assistance in developing short- and long-term fiscal development plans. This issue has been on the "back burner" for so long that a crisis has been allowed to happen. Outside assistance is seen as an important way to get the agency moving in the right direction. Consulting is oriented to helping a person, group, organization, or larger system to mobilize internal and external resources to deal with problems and change efforts. Nancy is confident that an outside perspective can help overcome

past obstacles to strategy development and can establish an accountability system to keep up the momentum. She also recognizes her own limitations in regard to fund development expertise and looks forward to help in learning new skills.

Monica conducts a form of needs assessment by reviewing past records and proposals and interviewing staff. She then engages in planning, organizing, and program development to identify several strategic options to meet the agency's crisis. Finally, Monica carries out the function of coordination and review to discuss all issues with Nancy in preliminary strategy sessions. Ultimately, the board of directors, with facilitation from Nancy and Monica, will develop a plan of action, for which Nancy will have implementation responsibility.

Tight budgets are a problem faced by many human services agencies. Addressing financial development needs is an ongoing concern of social work managers. A recent study conducted by Mimi Abramovitz, PhD, sponsored by NASW's New York City chapter and funded by the United Way of America, revealed that many nonprofit agencies that serve low-income communities are strapped to capacity to meet the demand for additional services brought by welfare reform (NASW, 2002c). Charitable giving patterns also influence the financial status of nonprofit organizations. For example, in the aftermath of the September 11, 2001, terrorist attacks, there was an outpouring of charitable giving, but targeted to agencies specifically providing services to victims and their families. Charitable contributions to other agencies were significantly down. Thus, the situation of the children's center, highlighted in the preceding vignette, may, to varying degrees, typify the plight of many agencies.

Consulting is frequently carried out primarily as an **independent** function, much like social workers who maintain private practices. The nature of the consultation will depend on the expertise of the social worker and the niche he or she wishes to occupy. A look at classified ads in any issue of the *NASW News*, under "miscellaneous," will show ads by social workers offering assistance with thesis writing, help with attracting clients, software for private billing, seminars and training, among other services.

Consultation can include an advocacy component, of which the activities of social worker Sonya Chadwell of Laurel, MS, offer one example. Ms. Chadwell established her own business to represent people in social security and supplemental security income cases. Unlike lawyers who typically present only medical facts in hearings with an administrative law judge, Ms. Chadwell adds psychosocial evaluation to her representation of clients ("Entrepreneur's Niche," 2002).

Ms. Chadwell used her resource development and community skills to develop the information she needed to establish a practice. This included consulting with the regional social security administrator to find out about protocols for representing clients and how to represent clients as a nonattorney. She also invested in brochures outlining her services and distributed them to churches, hospitals, and social services agencies, among other sources.

Once there is a contract with a client, Ms. Chadwell begins by getting releases and obtaining clients' medical records. These records are forwarded to the appropriate parties. Sometimes, it is helpful to have a physician write a letter on behalf of the client, and Ms. Chadwell is the one to assess whether this step is needed and then to follow through with the physician ("Entrepreneur's Niche," 2002).

Payment does not come from the client. The compensation rate is set by the government and the amount is up to 25 percent of the initial payment to the client, to a maximum of $4,000. The Social Security Administration calculates the amount due and sends her payment directly. Not all clients requesting services are accepted by Ms. Chadwell. She needs to believe that they have a reasonable chance of winning the appeal based on the facts of the case. In addition to the

satisfaction that comes from successful advocacy for clients, Ms. Chadwell also enjoys the flexibility in hours and working from home.

CAREER OPPORTUNITIES

Although social work is often thought of as a predominantly clinical profession, the macro functions of social work are equally important. Administration, program planning and development, supervision, policy analysis, research and evaluation, community organization, and consultation are all means by which social workers can use their knowledge and skills to be active players in shaping the programs and policies that guide our nation's actions toward the most vulnerable in our society. Terry Mizrahi (2001), former NASW president, described the challenge to the profession:

> The commitment and competence of our vast social work profession must be communicated more powerfully to policymakers, politicians, the press and the public. Like the mosaic of glass in a kaleidoscope, the many facets of our profession form an intricate pattern reflecting our diversity and a unified whole at the same time. That colorful and vibrant image needs to be projected onto the landscape in ways that shape the debate and direction of social policy for years to come. (p. 2)

A brief sampling of career opportunities in macro social work are listed below. However, these selections only begin to scratch the surface of the rich array of opportunities for creative, professional growth in this field of practice.

Grants Manager

United Jewish Communities, Washington, DC, office, seeks grants manager with graduate degree and minimum five years of grant writing experience to secure grants from foundations, government agencies, corporations, and individuals. Must have excellent writing and research skills, ability to work at fast pace, and meet deadlines. Knowledge of the Jewish community helpful. (*NASW News*, March 2002, p. 19)

Research Specialist

The Casey Family Program, a nonprofit child welfare agency headquartered in Seattle, has reopened its search for a full-time research specialist. Principal responsibilities include design, plan, and coordinate evaluation research studies; design data collection forms and code books; code data; supervise the data entry and coding process; manage research databases; conduct statistical analyses; write and edit research documents, articles, chapters, and reports; coauthor articles for conferences and professional journals; and consult with research and nonresearch staff and consultants regarding study design, analysis, and implications. Research services is committed to involving children, parents, and Casey staff whenever possible in research design, implementation, and interpretation. Minimum qualifications are MSW or MA degree (psychology or other closely related field); PhD preferred. Research project leadership and program evaluation experience (including research methods and analysis techniques), and knowledge of child welfare and family social services required. Intermediate knowledge of statistics and experience conducting statistical analysis. Ability to prepare work plans, delegate tasks, and keep supervisor informed of progress. Ability to communicate diplomatically and work effectively in a team both as a leader and as a member. Experience writing technical reports and articles, and presenting research findings to professional and lay audiences required. Some travel required. Casey offers a competitive salary and an excellent benefits package. (*NASW News*, February 1999, p. 23)

Social Work Consultant

Opportunity for leadership in interdisciplinary holistic care program of national long-term care organization of 240 facilities. Background should include current successful experience as consultant or social worker in long-term care Medicare facility. Must have written and verbal communication skills necessary for consultation, training, and development of manuals to support quality care. Need to combine geriatric social services knowledge with sensitivity and tact relating to administration, staff, and regulatory agencies. This position requires relocation to our central office in Sioux Falls, SD. Travel involved. MSW required. Salary is commensurate with qualifications. (*NASW News*, November 2001, p. 16)

Associate Director, Human Services
Social Policy Pillar

United Jewish Communities, Washington, DC, seeks senior professional with 10 plus years experience in human services planning or government administration to manage our national human services and social policy initiatives. Work with national leadership, local communities, organizations, and colleagues to develop and implement program priorities. Fast paced, challenging, and creative environment. Excellent management, budget, administration, planning, and communication skills essential. Knowledge of human services and Jewish communal system preferred. (*NASW News*, April 2002, p. 15)

Director of Social Work Research Center

The newly established University of Arkansas School of Social Work is searching for a tenure track faculty member to be the director of its Social Work Research Center. Salary is competitive. Rank is open based on qualifications and experience. The center has received a three-year congressional appropriation of $921,000. Its focus is social work research and instruction to assess, analyze, and develop policy recommendations and practice interventions to reduce poverty. Opportunities and responsibilities include direct the Social Work Research Center; participate in developing a nationally competitive

MSW program; teach in a PhD program in public policy; participate in designing a state of the art social work technology laboratory; merge the roots of social work with 21st century approaches to address poverty and social injustice; develop a successful career in social work education and research while enjoying a high quality of personal life. Requirements are DSW or PhD in social work or related field or MSW degree accredited by the Council on Social Work Education; and agreement to attain Arkansas licensure within two years; world view consistent with social work values and ethics; substantial record of research productivity; record of success in acquiring external funds, especially federal research funds; record of success in practice and teaching; student centered; skills in the integration of technology in social work education and research; skills in teamwork and maintenance of a collegial work environment; skills in graduate curriculum development. (*NASW News*, July 2001, p. 16)

Executive Director

NASW's Michigan chapter seeks applications for executive director of the 8,000-plus member Lansing-based state chapter; staff of 6; $650,000 budget. The successful candidate must contribute to unity of the profession and association through effective leadership; facilitate inclusion of diverse perspectives consistent with the NASW Code of Ethics; build association capacity through fundraising and resource development; oversee administration of the association, including fiscal, personnel, and program management; effectively build team relationships with the governance structure; establish, maintain, and strengthen effective relationships with external organizations; advance NASW social policy position to strengthen the image and influence of the profession. Minimum requirements are graduate degree in social work; 10 years postgraduate social work experience, including five years in administration and management; experience in a leadership position in a large complex organization; demonstrated commitment to diversity and affirmative action; experience in fundraising and resource development. (*NASW News*, May 2001, p. 17)

Bilingual Social Worker

Provide a wide range of services to Cantonese-speaking individuals and families. Serve as neighborhood development counselor. Assist in racial harmony projects, parental training, and voter registration. Bachelor degree in social work plus one year of experience in similar job or as a school social worker required. Must speak, read, and write Cantonese. Applicants must show proof of legal authority to work in the United States. (*NASW News*, April 2002, p. 15)

Executive Director

Search reopened: Advocacy Unlimited, a statewide consumer run advocacy organization for people in recovery with psychiatric disabilities, is seeking an executive director. We are looking for an individual with proven leadership skills, who can direct internal operations as well as interface with community groups, and state and federal agencies. Candidates with personal experience with psychiatric disabilities are strongly preferred. (*NASW News*, May 2002, p. 14)

REFERENCES

Abramowitz, M. (2002). *Jeopardy: The impact of welfare reform on nonprofit human service agencies in New York City.* New York: National Association of Social Workers New York Chapter.

Barker, R. L. (1999). *The social work dictionary* (4th ed.). Washington, DC: NASW Press.

Barth, M. C. (2001). *The labor market for social workers: A first look.* New York: John A. Hartford Foundation.

Beaucar, K. O. (2000, January). March seeks to give poor a voice. *NASW News*, p. 16.

Bisbee, J. (2002, February 10). Candidates fight for highly-prized UFW endorsement. *Monitor.* Retrieved November 18, 2003, from http://www.ufw.org/mon21002.htm.

Carten, A. J., & Schachter, R. S. (2000, September). *Currents* (NASW New York City Chapter), pp. 1, 7.

Cohen, R. H. (1995, October). Looking ahead: Time of singular peril is time to act. *NASW News*, p. 2.

Dluhy, M. K. (1990). *Building coalitions in the human services.* Newbury Park, CA: Sage Publications.

Economic security panel named. (2002, April). *NASW News* pp. 1, 12.

Entrepreneur's niche: Social security claims. (2002, May). *NASW News*, p. 12.

Ezell, M. (1993). The political activity of social workers: A post-Reagan update. *Journal of Sociology & Social Welfare, 20*, 81–97.

Figueira-McDonough, J. (1993). Policy practice: The neglected side of social work intervention. *Social Work, 38*, 179–188.

Fitzgerald, E., & McNutt, J. (1999). Electronic advocacy in policy practice: A framework for teaching technologically based practice. *Journal of Social Work Education, 35*, 331–341.

Flynn, J. (1992). *Social agency policy.* Chicago: Nelson-Hall.

Garcia, O. R. (2001, August 8). UFW chief rallies support for proposals. *Bakersfield Californian.* Retrieved November 18, 2003, from http://www.bakersfield.com/local/v-print/story/647729 p-690896c.html.

Ginsberg, L. (1988). Social workers and politics: Lessons from practice. *Social Work, 33*, 245–247.

Goldstein, A. (2002, March 23). Marriage promotion link to child support eyed. *Washington Post*, p. A8.

Hamilton, D., & Fauri, D. (2001). Social workers' political participation: Strengthening the political confidence of social work students. *Journal of Social Work Education, 37*, 321–332.

Harris, D. V. (1986, October). Social workers urged to follow profession's activist tradition. *NASW News*, p. 2.

Hartman, A. (1993). The professional is political. *Social Work, 38*, 365–366.

Haynes, K. S., & Mickelson, J. S. (2000). *Affecting change: Social workers in the political arena* (4th ed.). Boston: Allyn & Bacon.

Hiratsuka, J. (1990, September). Community organization: Assembling power. *NASW News*, p. 3.

Hiratsuka, J. (1992a, July). L.A. burning: Social workers respond. *NASW News*, p. 3.

Hiratsuka, J. (1992b, May). Social work puts it on the picket line. *NASW News*, p. 3.

Kahn, S. (1995). Community organization. In R. L. Edwards (Ed.-in-Chief), *Encyclopedia of social work* (19th ed., Vol. 1, pp. 569–576). Washington, DC: NASW Press.

Leaders put partnership into practice: Union support sought. (1998, March). *NASW News*, p. 5.

Legislative agenda adopted. (2001, March). *NASW News*, pp. 1, 8.

Legislative network assembled. (2001, June). *NASW News*, pp. 1, 8.

Lens, V., & Gibelman, M. (2000). Advocacy be not forsaken! Retrospective lessons from welfare reform. *Families in Society:* Journal of Contemporary Human Services, *81*, 611–620.

Martinez-Brawley, E. E. (1995). Community. In R. L. Edwards (Ed.-in-Chief), *Encyclopedia of social work* (19th ed., Vol. 1, pp. 539–548). Washington, DC: NASW Press.

Member named to head SAMSHA. (2001, October). *NASW News*, pp. 1, 10.

Mickelson, J. S. (1995). Advocacy. In R. L. Edwards (Ed.-in-Chief), *Encyclopedia of social work* (19th ed., Vol. 1, pp. 95–100). Washington, DC: NASW Press.

Mizrahi, T. (2001, July). Social work: A kaleidoscopic view. *NASW News*, p. 2.

Mizrahi, T. (2002, April). Aiming for economic security. *NASW News*, p. 2.

NASW to lead lobbying effort for research center. (2002, April). *NASW News*, p. 13.

National Association of Social Workers. (1996). *NASW code of ethics.* Washington, DC: Author.

National Association of Social Workers. (2001, November 30). *Recommendations for the reauthorization of the Personality Responsibility and Work Opportunity Reconciliation Act.* Author. Retrieved January 4, 2003, from http://www.social workers.org/advocacy/welfare/legislative/ recommend.pdf

National Association of Social Workers. (2002a). *Advocacy agenda: Second session: January–December 2002*. Retrieved January 4, 2003, from http://www.naswdc.org/ advocacy/agenda2.htm

National Association of Social Workers. (2002b). *Facts about the National Association of Social Workers*. Retrieved November 18, 2003, from http://www. socialworkers.org/nasw/default.asp

National Association of Social Workers. (2002c, February 22). *Non-profits struggling in world of welfare reform* (Press release). Washington, DC: Author. Retrieved November 18, 2003, from http://www.socialworkers.org/pressroom/2002/ 022202.awsp.

National Association of Social Workers. (2002d). *Social workers in Congress*. Retrieved November 18, 2003, from http://www.socialworkers.org/pace/ congress_ swers.asp.

National Association of Social Workers. (2002e) *Why social workers should be involved*. Retrieved November 23, 2003, from http://www.naswdc. org/advocacy/why_ involved.asp.

National Association of Social Workers. (2003a). *Why social workers should run for office*. Retrieved November 23, 2003, from http://www.socialwork-ers.org/pace/ why_run.asp.

National Association of Social Workers. (2003b). *Demographics of social workers in elected office, 2003*. Retrieved November 24, 2003, from http://www. socialworkers.org/pace/ characteristics.asp.

National Association of Social Workers. (2003c). *Once again, TANF reauthorization pushed off until next year*. Retrieved November 24, 2003, from http://www.socialworkers.org/advocacy/updates/ 110703.asp.

Netting, F. E., Kettner, P. M., & McMurtry, S. L. (1998). *Social work macro practice* (2nd ed.). New York: Longman.

Next on welfare. (2002, March 1–7). *Washington Post National Weekly Edition*, p. 24.

Nieves, J. (2000a, January). Social work collective bargaining? *NASW News*, p. 2.

Nieves, J. (2000b, October). Project shows NASW's progress. *NASW News*, p. 2.

O'Neill, J.V. (2002a, January). Welfare reform found to stress agencies. *NASW News*, p. 4.

O'Neill, J.V. (2002b, January). Research bill delayed. *NASW News*, p. 8.

O'Neill, J. V. (2002c, February). Welfare overhaul advised. *NASW News*, pp. 1, 10.

O'Neill, J. V. (2002d, March). Web-based advocacy on the rise. *NASW News*, pp. 1, 16.

Payne, J. L. (1996, December 9). Social workers could undermine welfare reform. *Bergen Record*, p. A16.

Pear, R. (2002, February 24). Governors want Congress to ease welfare's work rule. *New York Times*. Retrieved February 25, 2002, from http://www.nytimes.com/2002/02/24/politics/ 24GOVS.html

Personal Responsibility and Work Opportunity Reconciliation Act of 1996, P.L.104-193, 110 stat. 2105.

Reform's effect on families studied. (2002, January). *NASW News*, p. 5.

Richan, W. C. (1991). *Lobbying for social change*. New York: Haworth Press.

Rodriguez, A. S. (2001, July). *Historic proposal for farm workers legalization*. Knight Ridder Publications. Retrieved November 18, 2003, from http://www.ufw.org/knoped701.htm

Rosenberg, J. (2002). *Social workers in unions*. Unpublished doctoral dissertation, Yeshiva University, Wurzweiler School of Social Work, New York.

Rothman, J., Erlich, J. L., & Tropman, J. E. (1995). *Strategies of community intervention: Macro practice* (5th ed.). Itasca, IL: F.E. Peacock.

Smucker, B. (1991). *The nonprofit lobbying guide: Advocating your cause—and getting results*. San Francisco: Jossey-Bass.

Social work in the public eye. (2000a, September). *NASW News*, p. 17.

Social work in the public eye. (2000b, October). *NASW News*, p. 15.

Social work in the public eye. (2002, January). *NASW News*, p. 15.

Social work skills and political action make a potent mix, Mikulski asserts. (1984, January). *NASW News* p. 8.

Social worker helps Chavez with boycott. (1987, March). *NASW News*, p.12.

Stewart, R. (1984, October). From the president. *NASW News*, p. 2.

Stoesen, L. (2002, June). Clinton given group's welfare views. *NASW News*, pp. 1, 10.

Tambor, M. (1995). Unions. In R. L. Edwards (Ed.-in-Chief), *Encyclopedia of social work* (19th ed., Vol. 3, pp. 2418–2426). Washington, DC: NASW Press.

United Farm Workers. (2002a). *Biography of Arturo S. Rodriguez.* Retrieved November 18, 2003, from http://www.ufw.org/asrbio.htm

United Farm Workers. (2002b). *UFW history.* Retrieved November 18, 2003, from http:// www.ufw.org/ufw.htm

Vallianatos, C. (2000, June). Students take action on gun violence. *NASW News*, p. 3.

Vallianatos, C. (2001, November). Stronger partnership on research emerges. *NASW News*, p. 5.

Vallianatos, C. (2002, February). Welfare limits: Disaster in the making. *NASW News*, p. 3.

Vobejda, B., & Havemann, J. (1995, May 21). Traditional welfare constituencies put out by lack of input in reform. *Washington Post,* p. A4.

Walsh, J. A., & Moynihan, F. M. (1990). Using external consultants in social service agencies. *Families in Society, 71,* 291–295.

Weil, M. O., & Gamble, D. N. (2002). *Community practice models for the 21st century.* In A. R. Roberts & G. J. Greene (Eds.), *Social workers' desk reference* (pp. 525–534). New York: Oxford University Press.

Chapter Twelve A Look to the Future

Many of the functions carried out by social workers across the wide range of practice areas and settings have been identified in earlier chapters. However, the profession is closely intertwined with the society of which it is a part. Thus, what social workers do very much depends on the context of the times—the prevailing economic, political, and social climate. It is this larger context that defines the circumstances in which social workers practice—with whom, where, for how long, and concerning what types of problems.

CHANGING CONTEXT OF PRACTICE

As in the past, the sociopolitical environment serves to constrain or, alternately, expand the boundaries of social work practice. Examining the problems that are emerging now or that are taking on different dimensions helps to clarify professional mandates for the future. These problems include, among others: AIDS; societal violence, particularly violence among youths; economic stagnation; inner-city decay; continued feminization of poverty; industrial downsizing and worker displacement; and the growth in the proportion of elderly people in our society.

President George W. Bush began his presidency with a declaration of the "compassionate conservative," translated to mean compassion from a distance, with little government involvement in social matters. The least government is

the best government. But after September 11, 2001, there was an immediate turnaround, with new and burgeoning roles for government—basically in the area of "homeland" safety. Quickly, for example, airport security was "federalized," with the result that the civil service labor force is growing rather than shrinking—a reflection of the enlarged role of government. At the same time, the aftermath of the terrorist attacks and the engagement in a War on Terrorism and War with Iraq have led to a congressional preoccupation with two priorities: disaster and defense.

Prognosticating about the context of social work practice in even the immediate future has grown more difficult by the events of September 11, 2001. We are still in a reactive mode and the longer-term effect of war in the Middle East in regard to our social and political culture cannot yet be assessed. Prior to September 11, American society was plagued by a variety of social problems and unmet human needs that continue to warrant societal attention and action. For example, the achievement of full civil rights remains illusive for many people in the United States and, of course, throughout the world. Affirmative action, one of the landmark achievements of the civil rights era, continues to be challenged in the courts. Racial tensions continue to simmer and sometimes erupt. The black–white racial dichotomy in regard to power and resources has translated, in this new millennium, to struggles among Latinos, Native American Indians, Asian

Americans, and immigrants who seek to embrace their fair share of the American dream.

Economic tides have turned from their strong point in the 1990s, reverberating in plunging stock market tallies, growing unemployment, and increasing claims for public benefits. Americans have begun to identify government, Wall Street, and private industry greed as unacceptable phenomena within society. Newspapers report daily on the many examples of corporate greed. The intolerance of excesses attributed earlier to government has now shifted to the private sector. In the early years of the 21st century, Enron has come to epitomize all that is wrong with private industry. It is within this context that social work carries out its societal role.

The elimination of poverty remains illusive in this nation of riches; despite the economic gains during the 1990s, people who are poor remain entrenched in that status (Kilborn & Clemetson, 2002). The boundaries between the haves and the have-nots have grown, rather than diminished, with a shrinking middle class. Economic and social disparities challenge the quality of life for many Americans, including access to the education, health care, and cultural resources that have heretofore provided the route out of poverty.

The concept of inclusion is eagerly embraced in the abstract but more illusive in the concrete. Demographic trends and conditions that show the ingrained patterns of discrimination based on race, age, gender, sexual orientation, and physical and mental ability continue to challenge our social institutions (Allen, 1999). Globalization has made political, economic, and social conditions throughout the world an unavoidable concern in the United States—for example, witness the escalation of disharmony between Arab and Jewish Americans. Political, social, and economic conditions at home and, increasingly, abroad shape the agenda for the social work profession.

The terrorist attack on the United States on September 11, 2001, also heralded a new con-sciousness of individual and collective crisis and the long-term impact of trauma. Public understanding of the health and mental health consequences for those directly and indirectly affected grew experientially, with public service announcements urging Americans to seek and receive help. However, what has not changed, according to NASW Executive Director Elizabeth Clark,

> are tensions about funding priorities; problems with mental health service capacity; limited research on interventions; risk and protective factors; the numbers of people with mental illness in the criminal justice system or who are homeless; limited coordination between mental health service providers; and an increase in the sale of street drugs. ("Perspective Is Urged on September 11 Reactions," 2002, p. 5)

Rising Costs, Diminishing Access, and Accountability Demands

Closely intertwined with the political scene is the health care reform movement and its potential impact on what social workers do. The failure to enact health care reform legislation during the Clinton administration allowed, by default, the private market (such as insurance and managed care companies) to impose their own restrictions, which may well extend far beyond any limitations the federal government might impose. The impetus for some type of reform has never been off the political agenda. A key question is whether and to what extent social workers will be included as care providers in any legislation that finally is passed. In the interim, health costs continue to escalate. Medicaid spending, for example, rose 13.4 percent between 2001 and 2002—threatening government budgets (Broder, 2002). The pressure to curtail services exists side by side with demands to address the health care needs of the 37 million Americans who lack any form of health insurance.

The practice of social work will increasingly emphasize accountability to funding sources and to the general taxpaying public. The demand by funding bodies, consumers, and accrediting agencies that helping professionals be able to document the outcomes of their interventions is both consistent and strengthening. In the current climate of managed care and cost consciousness, social workers are aware there is a growing need to demonstrate that treatment leads to the desired results in a cost-effective manner. However, the state of the art of assessing the outcomes of social work services has lagged (Vallianatos, 2000).

University- and agency-based researchers have been devoting more attention to developing evidenced-based practice guidelines. To date, the successes of social work interventions have been largely anecdotal. The challenge is to empirically assess outcomes without trivializing the complexities of treatment (Vallianatos, 2000).

Demands for measurable outcomes have also meant new career paths within social work. For example, positions carrying the title Director of Quality Improvement have added to the expanse of job titles covering the totality of the profession. Here, requirements might include knowledge of quality improvement standards, program evaluation methods and procedures, and experience with the use of computerized information systems for clinical care records. Similar demands for accountability are occurring in regard to the private practice of social work. These demands go beyond demonstrating the outcomes of interventions. Managed care companies may impose their own requirements on their providers, such as access to case information that may be considered a violation of clients' confidentiality.

There is justifiable concern about the evolution of managed care systems and the impact on health and mental health services. The risks in managed care concern both potential limitations on the role of social workers within this system

and the quality and quantity of services that will be available to clients in need of social work services. The issues of quality of services and of assuring the adequacy and appropriateness of services continue to occupy the profession. The need to document the effectiveness of social work services has never been more important; social workers must continue and expand research efforts about the outcomes of different types of interventions. Past NASW President Josephine Allen (1999) articulated the research mandate:

> We must demonstrate that social work is effective. We must continually prove the efficacy of our methods of intervention, of predicted social work outcomes and of social work theories with their articulated variables. Empirical research that generates data which respond to these and other efficacy issues is essential. We must demonstrate our productivity and be accountable. The call for individual and collaborative research efforts by social workers in academia and social workers in agency and community practice must be answered—and answered in greater volume. It is in this way that we increase our credibility as well as our influence. (p. 2)

Social work is concerned with improving the quality of life for individuals, groups, and communities and addressing the social maladies of society. This professional mandate involves a critical link between research, practice, and policy. Practice-based research and evidence-based practice are two of the terms that have been used to describe the imperative for social workers to understand, use, and contribute to research and policy (Mizrahi, 2002; O'Neill, 2000a). Historically, there has been a pronounced lack of rigorous research to shed light on the most effective means to prevent or resolve human problems (Inouye, Ell, & Ewalt, 1994). The centrality of research in informing public policy is aptly stated by Inouye et al. (1994):

Policy formulation and debate in the areas of health care reform, crime, welfare reform, and child and family welfare have drawn on relevant research when it was available, but all too often these discussions have revealed critical gaps in convincing research-based knowledge. Advocacy for an enhanced mental health benefits package in health care reform, for example, was hampered, according to Clinton administration officials and their opponents, by limited knowledge about the use of these services by varied socioeconomic and ethnic groups. (p. 629)

Visions of the Future

Modern society has grown increasingly sophisticated in its ability to project the world of the future. Although there may be some surprises in the social scene brought about by forces that cannot be predicted with great accuracy (for example, natural disasters, global conflict), we have some fairly accurate knowledge about what the future holds for our society and for our profession. We know, for example, that the absolute and proportionate number of older people in our society is increasing; many will require services ranging from those associated with the creative use of leisure time to those concerning the provision of home health care. The number of people who are poor will also continue to grow, especially children, as the middle class continues to shrink (Hopps & Collins, 1995) and as the impact of welfare reform manifests itself fully. Violence as a means of conflict resolution—on the streets in the case of drug wars and in the home in the case of domestic violence—will continue to threaten our safety and humanity, until such time as alternative means of resolving conflicts are taught and accepted. Creating an ethnically and culturally diverse society able to live harmoniously becomes increasingly more important as demographic trends reveal an even more heterogeneous population.

Biotechnology has solved some of the mysteries of disease, elongated life, and led to the abil-

ity to genetically engineer life itself. These advancements have not only created new practice arenas for social workers, such as genetic counseling, but also created new ethical dilemmas about the nature and quality of life. Such advances would have been unimaginable two decades ago. New methods of practicing social work and of learning how to practice, through social work education and training, have resulted. It is clear that technology will have an even more profound influence in the future on the nature of society and how social work responds to newly created societal conditions.

We can anticipate that social workers will play a continuing and growing role in working with people with AIDs as the affected population increases numerically and across gender, racial, and socioeconomic lines, and reaches pandemic proportions globally. New and expanding social work roles are reflected in curricula changes within schools of social work. In recent years, we have seen an increasing array of courses offered in specialty areas such as homelessness, AIDS, pharmacology, gerontology, and managed care.

For the profession of social work, the mandate is strong for capacity building to influence decision making, both domestically and internationally. The involvement of social workers in the political sphere, including running for elective office and supporting candidates who can promote a social agenda which emphasizes inclusion, civil rights, and a more equal playing field for many in our society, remains a consistent need (Allen, 1999). Social workers continue to gain sophistication about successful functioning in the political world. Positive developments in regard to professional involvement in politics are evident, as discussed in cjhapter 11, in the growing number of social workers who are elected and appointed to official positions at the national, state, and local levels and the increasingly active participation of social workers in political campaigns.

Is social work able to adapt to changing times and to the expanding boundaries of the profession's purview? Some say no. Kreuger (1997), for example, forecasted the end of social work. In his view, new cyber technologies will render traditional interventions obsolete. The knowledge explosion, too, will threaten the profession's knowledge base. Finally, changes in political and economic structures, manifest in corporate domination, will eliminate the role of social work in this society. Other commentators see a dynamic and changing profession (Allen, 1999; Gibelman, 1999; Mizahi, 2001; Stewart, 1984). Social work now holds a dominant position among the mental health professions; there are more clinically trained social workers than members of other core mental health professions combined (O'Neill, 1999). In this era of managed care, social workers are often considered to be the less costly, more outcomes-oriented of the mental health professions. Such views suggest a promising future for social work.

Environmental factors are an important determinant of the parameters of social work concerns and the nature and focus of social work practice at any given time. The nature of social work in the future will be affected by the influence of both intraprofessional developments and external, environmental conditions and demands.

THE CHANGING PROFESSION

Forty years ago, the government employed the largest proportion of social workers. Mental health was far behind child welfare and family services as the major arena of social work practice. The for-profit sector as a setting of social work practice was virtually nonexistent, and the private practice of social work was limited by the then ineligibility of most social work services for third-party payments. Social workers held leading managerial roles in public welfare, and the executives of most nonprofit social services agencies held MSW degrees (Gibelman & Schervish, 1997). Interventions focused on relationship and process.

In the beginning of the 21st century, we also see a very different profession (Gibelman, 1999):

- Mental health is the fastest growing area of social work practice.
- Private practice has become an increasingly important alternative for the provision of social work services.
- Technology is an important force driving how services are managed and delivered.
- The for-profit sector has become an increasingly significant alternative for delivering social work services.
- Competition with allied professionals, such as psychologists, counselors, marriage and family therapists, public administrators, and even business administrators for direct services, supervisory, and administrative positions, has increased.
- Managed care has altered and holds the potential of limiting the role of social workers, as well as the quality and quantity of services available to the clients in need of social work services.
- Social workers are held accountable for the outcomes of their services, not just for the process.
- Scientific advances have implications for human well-being.
- Ethical challenges continue to expand with scientific advances.

With the identification of new social concerns or the compounding of existing social problems, the boundaries of the social work profession continue to broaden and change. In some instances, social workers are at the forefront of identifying new arenas of practice; at other times, social workers respond to the social welfare agenda defined by others. The labor market also limits or, conversely, opens opportunities for social workers, the dynamics of which relate to the state of the economy and the constraints or expansions of public social policy. Examples of these boundary-changing and boundary-spanning areas are discussed in the following sections.

Scientific Advancements

The frontiers of science continue to expand. First, we were introduced to Mollie, the cloned sheep. Human cloning was no longer a futurist fantasy. President Bush is opposed to any type of human cloning, in part because of the possibility that a market for human eggs and egg donors would lead to "designer babies," making life a commodity rather than a creation (A. Goldstein, 2002). Others argue that although cloning would not be acceptable for reproductive purposes, it should be permitted in research to pursue treatments derived from cloned embryo.

A similar ongoing ethical and political battle concerns embryonic stem cell research, the cells of which are derived from the human fetus. Evidence is strong that the microscopic cells could lead to treatments for spinal cord injuries, Alzheimer's and Parkinson's diseases, and other chronic, debilitating, or fatal diseases (Connolly, 2002). But ethical and religious arguments are also compelling. People on both sides of the issue battle in the political arena.

These scientific advancements bring with them enormous new opportunities to enhance life. But they also bring the prospect of misuse or abuse. Some see these interventions as tinkering with human life in unacceptable ways. These advances are relevant to the profession because social workers, as discussed in chapter 5, work with individuals and families who face health crises in which the products of scientific research—transplantation, cell replacement, or in vitro manipulation—can mean the difference between life and death. Social workers are among those counseling people in these situations and helping them cope with the choices that become possible in a high-tech age. With these advances, however, come arrays of moral, ethical, and legal questions about which social workers need to be knowledgeable to aid their clients. For example, when eggs or sperm are donated, who are considered the "real parents"? Do payments to surrogate mothers unfairly take advantage of low-income women? What about

custody disputes over embryos, which have already taken place in the courts? When human organs for transplant are scarce, who should get priority? These and other questions continue to emerge as we grapple with the long-term implications of the scientific revolution.

Changing Services Delivery Systems

The preference for Americans and their elected leaders to "privatize" as many public functions as possible has been evident for the past 15 years, and political and societal support for this movement is increasing rather than abating. An important impetus to privatization has been the reduction in government funding for social welfare programs and the preference of government to purchase services rather than provide them directly (Gibelman, 1995). This movement suggests that social services will increasingly be delivered by not-for-profit and for-profit agencies.

In recent years, for-profit organizations, also known as proprietary organizations, have increasingly entered the human services market, particularly in such settings as nursing homes, home health care, residential treatment centers, and adult and child day care. Although these organizations employ social workers and other mental health professionals, for-profit organizations are owned and operated as any other business (Gibelman & Demone, 2002). Their purpose is to sell a set of services, and their operations reflect the goal of yielding a profit for investors and stockholders (Horejsi & Garthwait, 1999). Given that for-profit groups have as their "bottom line" the goal of making a profit, services may be modified to ensure that the criterion of success is achieved. To what extent clients may receive different, less effective, or perhaps even better services is as yet unclear. For over two decades, the health and mental health professions have been arguing the various benefits and liabilities of for-profit services. Concerns have been expressed about the money-making motivation and its impact on the quality of care, cost of services, accountability, and ability of nonprofits to compete (Barbakow, 1997; Bloche, 1998; Estes & Swan, 1994; Gibelman & Demone, 2002; H. Goldstein, 1998; Hilzenrath, 1997; Ottaway, 2001). The opportunities for social workers to practice in for-profit settings are growing and issues of access, quality, and accountability of services are rising exponentially.

Social Workers and Technology

Technological change deserves special mention, as its speed and range of influence are pervasive in our society and in our profession. The development of an "information superhighway" has had a profound affect on this society, including the frequency, speed, and nature of communications between people. Technological change has led to improvements in products and services, growth of new industries, and the need to retool and re-educate people for a changing work environment (Macarov, 1991). Technology has also, directly and indirectly, impacted on what social workers do and how they do it. These impacts range from enhanced research capability to new and emerging forms of case management.

Social work agencies and social work practitioners have embraced technology as a means to facilitate professional work. Computerized information services have become indispensable to many social services organizations as a necessity to efficiently record, store, analyze, evaluate, and consolidate useful information. In addition, computer technology has vastly expanded the ability of social workers to deliver services (Butterfield & Schoech, 1997).

Initially, computer technology was used within social services agencies to provide information to administrators, through management information systems and data processing, and by researchers to evaluate programs. Agencies have increasingly adopted standardized data collection formats to meet the demands of funding sources for accurate and detailed information about service provision.

The application of computer technology in direct services to clients is also evolving. Examples include self-administered psychiatric diagnostic interviews; self-administered programs dealing with assertiveness, self-esteem, and stress; and clinical mental health assessments. Computer-conducted interviews are also being used to collect case history data and to screen clients at risk of suicide. Counseling via computer is another example of the clinical application of this technology. A July 2001 ad in the *NASW News* invited applications for licensed–certified, insured, practicing therapists to conduct therapy over the telephone in a national intrastate network.

Satellite communications have made the world smaller; we get instant news, and social workers are among those who have extended the boundaries of their concerns to events happening in other countries. With the democratization of Eastern European countries, these nations are forced to grapple with a range of social problems. Increasingly, countries such as Hungary, Poland, and Romania are turning to social workers in the United States to assist in establishing social work education and training programs and to establish formal social welfare systems.

Future technological advances are on the horizon. Conceivably, virtually all the activities carried out by social workers face to face could be accomplished online, including counseling, visits, consultations, research, supervision, and social work education (McCarty & Clancy, 2002). Web cameras are expected to revolutionize the way therapy carried out over the Internet is conducted, making interactions between the social worker and client face to face in virtual time (O'Neill, 2001).

Although technology has made many services more accessible, and communication between social worker and client is easier and faster, liability concerns also arise, particularly in regard to client confidentiality and privacy of records. Information technology is being used for transmission, storage, or data management, making imperative the removal of individual identifying information to ensure privacy protection. Providing online treatment poses particular confidentiality and record-keeping concerns ("Mental Health Bill of Rights," 2002).

Concerns about potential misuses of technology led NASW to issue a practice update about its use in the practice of clinical social work (Coleman, 2002). The NASW practice guidelines urge social workers to follow federal and state statutes regarding the use of technology (for example, cellular phones, answering machines, facsimile machines, and computers) in their practice. For example, wireless and cordless phones have radio transmitters that make it easy for calls to be intercepted, intentionally or inadvertently. To protect patient confidentiality, clinical social workers should not use cell phones to communicate with their clients or in matters concerning their clients. Similarly, answering machines should be situated in a secure location with the volume turned off so that others are unable to hear incoming messages. Voicemail is a good alternative, as long as the system is not shared with others. The practice update also offers the suggestion that social workers exercise caution when leaving messages for clients on answering machines.

A volunteer committee of the Association of Social Work Boards (ASWB) has been looking into the practice of online therapy, including ways to deal with this phenomenon ethically and responsibly. Online therapy is not appropriate for everyone. People who have problems with reality testing, depression, eating disorders, and disorders which require medication, such as schizophrenia, would not, be good candidates for online treatment. Legal regulation of practice is also a thorny issue, since a clinician residing in Iowa may be treating someone in California. The California licensing board would not have jurisdiction over the practitioner in Iowa ("Licensing Group Looking Toward Standards," 2001). Practitioners of all disciplines may find

information related to Web-based therapy from a new professional association for mental health counseling on the Internet, the International Society of Mental Health (http://www.ismho.org). The ASWB is considering the development of a model law and standards governing the use of online therapy.

Technology is also being harnessed to reach distance learners. Computer-assisted instructional programs, for example, can be quite useful for practitioners to learn skills such as making a diagnosis, keeping an interview focused, and crisis counseling (Hopps & Collins, 1995). Electronic conferences and training sessions are being used by schools of social work and training institutes to reach students on branch campuses or those who live at substantial distances from training locations.

Computer bulletin boards are being used to exchange information, post notices and advertisements, access and copy files and software, and send cost-effective and speedy messages. These bulletin boards have also been initiated for the wider social services community, such as the National CUSSnet (Computer Users in the Social Services) (Hiratsuka, 1995). The Internet provides a means for ongoing dialogue among colleagues on issues that may range from stress management to advocacy strategies to forestall pending budget cuts. The Internet has also been put to use to facilitate communication about social work jobs. For example, the Web site http://www.mentalweb.com offers to post jobs, post resumes, and help users find a job. The Web site, according to its advertising, specializes in creating links between employers and employees in the mental health field. A comparable Web site has also been made available for professionals serving older Americans: http://www.Aginghelp.com. This site includes job opportunities in the aging field, resources for goods and services, and information-sharing opportunities.

These boundary-changing influences are merely suggestive of the wide range of economic, political, and social forces that affect the definition of social work and the nature of social work practice now and into the future. These influences also impact upon the profession in terms of the degree to which social workers are passive recipients of societal changes or active players in defining how science, technology, and infrastructures to meet people's needs are designed and used.

Unifying Themes

The profession of social work is committed to and incorporates within it a strong and consistent value base that has been remarkably consistent over time. Social workers operate from a purpose and perspective that is rooted in a set of core values that include "service, social justice, dignity and worth of the person, importance of human relationships, integrity, and competence" (NASW, 1996, p. 5). These values are adaptable to changing circumstances involved in the human condition and how society sees fit to address such human needs.

Other unifying themes have been offered. NASW Executive Director Elisabeth Clark, PhD, ACSW, defined power as a key descriptor of what social work is about:

> I am not thinking only in terms of the power of our numbers (over half a million strong), but of the power for good—to bring about positive social change and to help right the wrongs of society. Power is the ability to do, to act and to influence. . . . Social workers also have the power of knowledge, skills and values.
>
> The power of social work spans the "micro" to the "macro." The power of social work is evident in the clinical setting and in private practice. The power of social work can be seen in the cutting-edge research that not only identifies social problems, but also substantiates interventions that work. The power of social work is found in the classroom where a new generation of social workers is

being trained and nurtured. And the power of social work is noted in the leadership of community, state, and federal agencies and in elected offices. (Clark, 2002, p. 2)

Social workers have an important role to play in defining the profession of the future. The profession of social work is affected not only by the environment in which it functions but also by the directions it sets for itself. As Macarov (1991) noted in this regard:

> Without forecasting there is no freedom of decision. Only insofar as we try to influence the direction that the future will take are we exercising choice, rather than resigning ourselves to the inevitable or—to be more precise—to capriciousness. (p. 3)

Social work can initiate its own transformation, based on the preferences of its labor force and in response to the identification of conditions in need of change—both societal and professional. Former NASW President Terry Mizrahi (2001) referenced the current times as "challenging and contradictory" for the profession:

> Exploding technology and national wealth create incredible possibilities for progress. But the influences of corporations and conservative government policies increasingly polarize the haves and have-nots, denigrate professional competence and values and ignore or oversimplify social problems and solutions. (p. 2)

THE NEW PROFESSIONALS

The shape of the social work profession of the future can also be discerned from data on the primary fields of practice and social problem concentrations selected by master's students currently enrolled in social work education programs. For the 1999–2000 academic year, 32,582 students were enrolled in MSW programs. The overwhelming proportion of students were preparing for practice at the direct services level, followed by "other," and third, a combination of community organization and planning and administration and management (Lennon, 2001). This phenomenon is consistent with past trends.

One index of the social work profession of the future also can be discerned from data on the primary fields of practice and social problem concentrations selected by these same master's students and trends in postdegree employment of practicing social workers. The fields of practice and social problem concentrations of master's students were identified on the basis of reports provided by social work education programs (Lennon, 2001).

Although "not yet determined," "none," or "other" were listed for more than half of the enrolled students, of those for whom a concentration was designated, the largest proportion were in mental health followed by family services. However, family services and child welfare, when combined, ranked first among primary fields of practice, followed closely by mental health, and lagging behind but still a major area, health. The dearth of social work students concentrating in aging, substance abuse, community planning, occupational social work, public welfare, and developmental disabilities shows a consistent pattern with the proportion of practicing social workers represented in these areas among the NASW membership (Gibelman & Schervish, 1997).

Of course, concentration of studies does not always translate to the field of practice in which graduates find employment. Here, employer needs, reflected in available job openings, have a major impact on employment decision making. It is also difficult to determine whether student concentration preferences reflect labor market needs or personal choices independent of the job market. Doelling, Matz, and Kuehne (1999) examined the job market experience of 1998 MSW graduates based on data submitted by 1,788 graduates from 19 social work educa-

tion programs. Consistent with earlier analyses (Gibelman & Schervish, 1993, 1997), Doelling et al. found that mental health, child welfare, and school social work were the most frequently cited fields of practice, whereas rehabilitation and public assistance–public welfare were the least frequently cited. Only 6 percent of the 1,788 graduates worked in the field of aging.

A later national survey of 1,534 MSW graduates from 20 schools of social work across the country found the fields attracting the largest number of graduates were, in proportionate order, mental health (23 percent), child welfare (18 percent), school social work (10 percent), family services (9 percent), and aging (8 percent) (O'Neill, 2000d). A follow-up survey was conducted of year 2000 MSW graduates, with consistent findings—23 percent found work in mental health, 20 percent in child welfare, 11 percent in school social work, and 10 percent in health (O'Neill, 2002c). These findings are also consistent with the field of practice preferences long held by social workers.

An ongoing issue of concern is whether changes in social trends are accurately reflected in what social workers do and how they do it. For example, in light of the growth in the proportion of elderly people in the U.S. population, one might reasonably expect gerontology to be a growth area of professional practice. However, as discussed in Chapter 8, social work labor force patterns indicate otherwise (Gibelman & Schervish, 1997; Lennon, 2001). Other data (O'Neill, 2000d) suggest a slight upward trend in the proportion of MSWs employed in the field of aging, but a gap is still apparent between social need and social worker job preferences. In this situation, in which demographic trends are irrefutable, it is the profession that will need to modify its course if it is to maintain an appropriate "fit" with its external environment. The job market reflects sociopolitical and economic trends, limiting some areas of social work practice and broadening other areas.

THE JOB MARKET

For those considering a career in social work or those already in social work but contemplating a change in what they do, an inevitable concern is about the status of the job market. How "open" is the market and in what areas? Government labor force statistics suggest an optimistic future. In 2001 the U.S. Department of Labor, Bureau of Labor Statistics (BLS) projected that the U.S. labor force will increase by 17 million between 1998 and 2008, reaching over 155 million by 2008. This translates to a growth rate of about 1.2 percent per year. For the same time period, it is projected that the number of social workers will rise from 604,000 to 822,000, an increase of 36.1 percent or 3.1 percent per year (Barth, 2001). These data suggest that the social work labor force will expand significantly within the next decade.[1]

Expanding Areas of Practice

The job market continues to reflect arenas in which sizable public dollars are allocated. For example, in September 2000, a front page article in the *NASW News* proclaimed that there were about 1,000 child welfare vacancies in Los Angeles alone (O'Neill, 2000b). In that state, there are fewer social work graduates per capita than in any other state with more than 10 million population ("Social Work Jobs Going Unfilled," 2000).

At the same time, selective cutbacks in state and local governments across the country often translate to job cuts. Some of these cuts are in the areas in which research has consistently demonstrated the need for more and better qualified social workers. For example, Massachusetts' social workers have protested the layoff of 12 percent of the state's child welfare caseworkers, a step taken by the state legislature in response to the diminution of state revenues and a projected shortfall of $2 billion. Layoffs of child welfare workers were part of an overall strategy to reduce the public payroll across all government agencies (O'Neill, 2002a). To focus public attention on the potential consequences of these cutbacks, the NASW Massachusetts chapter sponsored a "Remembrance Vigil" in Boston in memory of the 115 children who died of child abuse and neglect. Other social work efforts include media campaigns, lobbying, and coalition building (O'Neill, 2002a).

Many openings also exist in the field of aging because of the increasing proportion of older people among the U.S. population. Competition is keenest for sought-after mental health clinical jobs, particularly in urban areas. At the same time, positions in rural areas often go unfilled. Flexibility in location may be an important factor in seeking and securing a social work position. Shortages also exist in fields of practice that have not traditionally been favored by professional social workers, such as corrections, disability, home health, and welfare.

The identified need for more social workers to fill vacant jobs now and into the future, particularly in certain fields of practice such as child welfare and aging, is influenced by the overall status of employment in the United States. However, unlike many sectors of the economy, the job market for social workers tends to improve at those times when other sectors of the economy falter.

Following a sustained period of economic growth during the 1990s, the U.S. economy hit a substantial slump late in the year 2000, continuing and worsening in 2002. In April 2002, the unemployment rate, which had been at an all-time low, surged to 6 percent, the highest level in almost eight years (Leonhardt, 2002).

---

[1] Government calculations of the number of social workers presently in the labor force vary. For example, according to estimates by the BLS Occupational Employment Statistics, the number of social workers is significantly lower than the figure derived from the *Current Population Survey*. In part, the difference has to do with who is counted—whether, for example, human services assistants are included—and whether it is degree or title of position that is considered. Despite differences in the actual count, the important point is the projected growth in social work.

This contrasts sharply with early figures for 2000, when the unemployment rate stood at 3.9 percent and wages were rising in all sectors of the economy.

Economists have suggested that the easing of recession and economic recovery may not necessarily be accompanied by job recovery. Although companies have added jobs to their payrolls, these jobs have almost exclusively been of a part-time or temporary nature. Employers seem to be cautious about the state of the economy and do not wish to make long-term commitments in the form of regular hiring (Leonhardt, 2002).

Unemployment and recession often result in financial, health, and mental health stress for sizable portions of the citizenry. In addition to the social and emotional ramifications of difficult economic times are the attendant practical needs, such as job retraining, financial management (debt consolidation, for example), and temporary financial assistance. The psychosocial and concrete needs that are the byproduct of a changing economy create new services needs that are within the purview of social work.

The samples of classified notices that appear throughout this volume also point to another trend: the desirability of having or obtaining a variety of skills. For example, those who know how to use computers, who can read and understand financial statements, or who speak a second language have "bonus" skills that are attractive to agencies that hire social workers. NASW Executive Director Elizabeth Clark put it this way: "If you're a bilingual, culturally competent social worker, you can virtually write your own ticket" (as cited in O'Neill, 2002c).

Classifying jobs by field of practice has also become more difficult. An ad for a supervisor in a child welfare agency may call for applicants to have a strong background in mental health. The ad may further include descriptors related to skills in evaluating the outcomes of service. Thus, classification of the position as child welfare becomes somewhat arbitrary. The position might

also be listed in this volume under mental health or macro practice, the latter a reflection of the evaluation component of the job description.

Reports of an open job market are particularly bright for those with a doctoral degree in social work. There is a substantial market for doctoral graduates who are skilled researchers; job opportunities in this arena reflect the growing demand that human services organizations document that social work interventions work. There are also a large number of vacancies within social work education each year, in part due to the growth in the number of social work education programs across the country and also attributable to the significant number of retirements of academics who were hired during the expansion period of the 1960s (O'Neill, 2000c, 2000e). Doctoral graduates are also filling top managerial positions in human services organizations.

The open job market for social workers has led to some gains in salaries, a phenomenon that often occurs when there are more open jobs than people to fill them. Nevertheless, social work salaries remain relatively low compared to those of other professions. In general, government jobs (at the federal, state, and local levels) pay better than jobs in the nonprofit sector.

The changing national political climate and ongoing promises (or threats) of deep budget cuts cause understandable worry among social work students and those currently employed who have begun to witness selective retrenchments. The job market for social workers is also affected by what is known as "supply and demand." Jobs—numerically and in specific fields of practice—may contract or expand. The issue of supply, however, relates to how many qualified people are available to fill existing job slots (demand). In the later part of the 20th century, with a booming economy and near full employment, the number of students applying for and enrolling in social work education programs dropped considerably (Lennon, 2001). When this happens, the pool of eligible social workers available to fill job vacancies also decreases. In such circumstances, the time is ripe for adjustments upward in the salaries offered. Supply and demand is a potent force affecting the conditions of work.

Other options were available to college graduates that offered, perhaps, greater monetary incentives and career opportunities. It was common to defer graduate education because the labor market was in need of more people, and employers were willing to pay for them. The social consciousness that is more prevalent in times of scarcity was, true to form, less apparent within this socioeconomic context. The pursuit of careers in public service, including human services, tends to be greater when societal attention on social issues is more pronounced and social programs to meet human needs are in a growth spurt. This constriction in the number of newly entering social workers may, in fact, be an important self-regulation of labor force size. But, as we have experienced before, the job market bounces back, although perhaps in a somewhat modified form.

In this new millennium, we see a very different labor market. Private industry is no longer on a hiring binge. Bonuses to new recruits straight out of college are a thing of the past. Many of the "dot-com" industries have collapsed. Layoffs in the financial, consulting, manufacturing, travel, and technology fields are an everyday occurrence. The job market for new college graduates has been termed the worst in nearly a decade (Browning, 2002). College graduates are considering different directions, notably in the public services, and careers that involve postgraduate education. Data are not yet available on the potential increase in applications to and enrollment in social work education. But the Law School Admission Council reported that applications for Fall 2002 are up by over 25 percent (Browning, 2002). Similar upward trends have been noted in applications for professional education in business, nursing, engineering, and pharmacy (Mangan, 2002). If trends hold to past patterns, there will be a rise in the number of students enrolling in social work education programs.

Social work has consistently been featured by *U.S. News & World Report* in its annual tally of "best jobs for the future," including the specialty areas of employee assistance counseling, private practice psychotherapy, home health care, family counseling, and gerontology ("Home Health Social Work," 1995; "More Growth in Social Work," 1997; "Social Work Again Top," 1999). In the early years of the 21st century, it is fairly common for a classified ad to promise a sign-on bonus, payable after six months of satisfactory job performance. Other incentives include employer-covered relocation expenses. These add-on benefits would not be offered if there were an abundance of locally qualified social workers to fill the vacancies.

Although many beginning social workers intend to enter independent practice once they have a clinical license and at least two years of clinically supervised experience, the realities of the health care industry suggest a less lucrative field for social workers than might have once been the case. A recurring advertisement in the *NASW News* raises the question: "Is managed care threatening the survival of your practice?" Offered is a manual entitled "How to Partner with Managed Care: A 'Do It Yourself Kit' for Building Working Relationships and Getting Steady Referrals," which includes strategies for coping and thriving in a managed care environment. Even if social workers are able to master these techniques for relationship building with managed care organizations, the fact remains that these companies set reimbursement rates and impose their own reporting and accountability requirements on the practitioner.

Forecasts of gloom for social work careers are offset by some positive predictions. The best prognosis, however, comes from the proven resilience of the profession in unfavorable political times. Social work, as noted throughout this volume, continues to expand and adapt its boundaries to fit societal context.

Labor Market Trends

A review of classified advertisements from 1998 to 2002 reveals some interesting insights about the job market. First, numerically, the classified ads follow social work employment preferences. A preponderance of ads in the *NASW News* (excluding academic positions), for example, are for jobs in the field of mental health and family and children's services. Although aging has been singled out as a field of practice in which the social work labor force is woefully inadequate in size and specialization (Barth, 2001), the reality is that few job ads appear in this practice area. One can hypothesize that employers have sought to advertise elsewhere to recruit social workers or people in related disciplines because past experience in recruiting through the *NASW News* has not produced the desired results.

Similarly, there is only an occasional ad for jobs that would fall under the categories of macro and "other" practice areas. In regard to macro practice, the exceptions are executive director or other management positions for which opportunities remain substantial. However, jobs for social work researchers, policy analysts, and program planners are scarce, at least under the rubric of social work positions and as advertised in the professional association's newsletter. The classified ads also highlight a number of significant trends.

Growth in For-Profit-Sector Opportunities.

Ten years ago, a classified advertisement for a social work position within a for-profit corporation would have been a rarity. In the new millennium, such ads have become commonplace, as highlighted in many of the career opportunities listed at the end of each chapter.

Proprietary social services refers to the delivery of social services for profit. The most frequent form of for-profit practice in social work is independent or private clinical practice. But proprietary practice also extends to macro areas, such as consultation. For-profit agencies provide services such as home care combined with social services for the elderly. And, as noted above, the privatization of human services has led to the creation of a new and growing network of proprietary agencies ready and willing to compete for contract dollars.

Specialization.

Given the enormous breadth of the profession of social work, it is both logical and necessary that a system of specialization develops within it. Although beginning social workers may seek and hold more generalist-type positions, in which they work with diverse demographic populations with a range of problems (such as in a public welfare or child welfare agency), typically social workers begin to focus their growing knowledge and skills on a specific type of problem area, such as homelessness, chronic mental illness, or juvenile delinquency; target populations, such as children and youth; infants, senior citizens, and marital couples; or goal-oriented services, such as providing housing for runaway youth, preventing child abuse, or rehabilitating substance abusers.

A social work specialist is one whose orientation and knowledge is focused and whose technical expertise and skill in specific activities are highly developed and refined (Barker, 1999). Specialization is both efficient and expedient for the individual social worker and for employers, as it reduces the amount of on-the-job training and learning that is necessary and provides for a higher level of expertise. Social workers develop their specialist expertise through on-the-job experience and through participation in continuing education. Continuing education is now frequently required by state licensing boards as a condition of maintaining one's license; a specific number of continuing education units must be taken within specified time periods (Barker, 1999; Maidenberg, 2001).

Part-Time Employment.

Another emerging trend in the social work labor market is the increasing use of part-time employees. Many classified ads highlight this trend. The motive seems clear in this era of cutback management: to keep employer costs down. Hiring two part-time employees is substantially less expensive than hiring one full-time worker. This is because part-time employees are not entitled to the same level of fringe benefits as full-time employees, which, including pension plan and health and disability benefits, can come to 27 percent or more of total salary. This trend in social work employment mirrors that of the overall employment market. In addition to cost-savings, another advantage, from the employer's perspective, is that the agency can recruit and retain a more specialized labor force.

Another variation in the labor market is the use of per diem or contracted job employment. For example, social workers may be hired by an adoption agency to do home studies; they are paid on the basis of each completed home study. Or a social worker may be retained to provide in-home services on a case-by-case basis. A recent classified advertisement concerned an opening for a psychotherapist, who would do private outpatient work. Qualifications sought were experience with inner child, adult children of alcoholics, and sexual abuse as well as experience with Gestalt, psychodrama, and action therapies. The ad specified that applicants must be willing to work flexible hours, days, and evenings. Pay was on a fee-for-service basis (*NASW News*, November 2001, p. 21). Translating this ad into the labor market of today, the agency sought a part-time worker who is flexible in terms of work time, has a high level of specialization, and is willing to accept pay on the basis of the number of contact hours with clients.

Still another variation in conditions of work concerns temporary positions. Such employment has been associated with the corporate sector, particularly in regard to clerical and technological positions. Some people have favored this type of arrangement in that it affords them maximum flexibility without long-term commitments and the chance to "test the waters" in a number of different work environments. Sometimes "temping" leads to a full-time job offer.

The concept of a temporary workforce has been relatively unknown within the helping professions. This may be because professionals interested in part-time or flexible employment have long had the option of establishing a private practice. The situation is changing. Now, some hospitals and other types of health care agencies (for example, home care agencies or nursing homes) use temporary workers whose services are procured through an intermediary—a staffing agency. One example is "Social Worker, PRN," which was established by social worker Joan King Upshaw in 1978; this staffing agency originated in Overland Park, KS, but has since expanded to several large cities throughout the country (Blank, 1997). Other agency examples are Social Work Associates, Inc., in Baltimore, MD, started by social worker Arlene Saks, and Delta-T Group, a consulting, management, and temporary staffing agency; both companies service the mid-Atlantic states (Maryland, Virginia, and Washington, DC). Social workers are placed in social services or social work host agencies (for example, hospitals and schools) to fill in when staff are on maternity or family leave or during peak vacation season or high utilization periods. Temporary workers may also be used to cover evening and weekend hours. Social workers are assigned specific responsibilities, such as discharge planning, psychosocial assessments, and home visits. These positions may last anywhere from three months to two years (Blank, 1997).

As social services agencies are forced, in the current environment, to seek cost-saving measures, the use of part-time employees is likely to increase. However, several concerns have been raised about part-time, contractual, and temporary positions for social workers. Concerns center on the long-term implications of replacing regular employees with those who cost less because they receive no benefits. A second concern lies in the practice implications, specifically in regard to how clients might be affected by this trend in services delivery.

Flexibility. Flexibility is an asset—it is required in this job market in terms of hours of work (some weekends, some evenings, and perhaps also willingness to travel. But more important is the demand by employers for social workers who evidence flexibility in terms of handling a diverse workload requiring a large range of skills.

A July 2001 ad in the *NASW News* read as follows:

JUVENILE ASSESSMENT CLINICIAN
Master's degree in human services field: LCSW, LPC, LPA, or CD certification preferred. One year of experience conducting bio-psycho-social assessments for school-age children, including written summary, referrals, follow-up, and limited case management services; also crisis intervention services. Successful applicant completes assessments on-site at various locations including Mat-Su Youth Facility. Must be willing to work evenings, weekends, and rotating on-call hours. Computer literate. Requires five years clean and sober; background check; TB testing. (p. 15)

First, this job requires time and travel flexibility. The successful candidate may be a social worker but could also have professional credentials in a related field (see discussion below on this subject). Credentials are desired in the form of certification or licensure. Experience is needed—a minimum of one year of specific work with school-age children and in conducting assessments. In addition to education, experience, and credentials, the successful applicant also needs to have computer skills. Apparently, it is expected that some applicants will have personal experience with substance abuse; perhaps such experience is even considered desirable. The clean and sober requirement, TB testing, and background check further suggest that the applicant may have a personal history related to substance abuse and even the criminal justice system.

Flexibility is not only required of social workers, but also may be offered to them. An ad in

the June 2002 *NASW News* sought applicants for an advice hotline. Here, social workers would have the opportunity to work from home on a national call-in service. The employing agency described itself as "an exciting new company that provides advice about a variety of personal problems troubling our diverse American public" (p. 17). Among the requirements for the position are strong interpersonal skills, including warmth and the ability to engage others, good listening skills, a pleasant telephone voice, and comfort working with client populations on the telephone. This type of job may portend of things to come in the future.

In summary, positions require a particular set of skills. Often, the successful applicant must be a specialist with solid generalist skills and a "jack of all trades," willing to assume a complex job assignment that requires task, time, and travel flexibility.

Selective social work labor force shortages translate to expanded opportunities for social workers, but flexibility is key in regard to location, practice setting, and field of practice. The shortage of qualified social workers to fill vacancies creates a paradoxical situation. Selectively, social welfare organizations are molding jobs so that vacancies can be filled by paraprofessionals. The agency then takes on the task of training the paraprofessional to take on specific tasks, often in concert with and under the supervision of social work professionals (O'Neill, 2002b). To the extent, however, that paraprofessionals are able to provide quality services under supervision, the end result may mean fewer jobs for professionally trained workers.

Degree and Experience Requirements. Classified advertisements often specify the requirement that eligible applicants be licensed or license eligible. Frequently cited "buzz" words appearing in classifieds include experiential requirements in total quality management, case management, clinical and administrative supervision, grant writing, and contract management. Many jobs now require a combination of clinical and administrative skills and designated job functions reflect this multidimensional emphasis. Requirements are emphasized and often form the major portion of classified ads.

Social workers are often in competition with other human services professions, such as psychologists, counselors, marriage and family therapists, public administrators, and even business administrators, for direct services, supervisory, and administrative positions. In earlier years, the classified ads under such categories as "social work," "mental health," and "counseling" generally specified the MSW degree as a requirement. By the mid-1990s, a discernible trend was evident—social work was becoming one of several eligible professions for jobs that heretofore required a social work degree. By 2002, a sizable proportion of classified ads, including those in the *NASW News* as well as local and national newspapers, included several disciplines eligible to apply for jobs that earlier would have been within the exclusive province of social work. For example, an advertisement for a clinical director in the *NASW News* (2002, March) listed as educational requirements either a master's level psychologist or a licensed social worker with a minimum of two years of supervisory experience.

Degrees in counseling, psychology, psychiatric nursing, and marriage and family therapy are sometimes listed as acceptable. Similarly, there is a growing tendency for a degree in business or public administration to be listed as a qualification for management positions, combined with clinical or supervisory experience. The terminology used in the classifieds shows this trend: "human services or related degree"; "social worker or psychologist."

In a similar vein, many of the jobs list the bachelor degree as the baseline requirement, with a master's degree cited as "desirable" or "preferred." Or, in other cases, no degree requirement is specified. This trend may relate to several phenomena:

- by not listing a degree as a requirement, employers have greater flexibility in their hiring decisions
- hiring of less experienced or less educated personnel may be a means of controlling personnel costs
- declassification has downplayed degree requirements within certain agencies, particularly public sector agencies.

The current fiscal constraints felt by most human services agencies may lead to pressure to hire social workers who cost less—those holding the BSW as opposed to the MSW, the less experienced versus the more experienced practitioner. Public agencies in particular have been prone to deprofessionalize social work services ("State Criteria Downgrading," 1999).

Although there may be increased competition between social workers and other helping professionals for jobs, this phenomenon may work both ways. Social workers are also expanding into nontraditional areas of practice. The skills possessed by social workers can be transferred to and used in related occupations. These may include counseling roles in public schools or human resources work in businesses (Barth, 2001). National health agencies are expanding their range of services to include professional assistance as well as self-help and patient education, providing a growing arena for social work practice. Higher educational achievement (that is, an MSW versus a BSW or a PhD versus an MSW) is also equated with greater career choices. For example, management, research, and policy positions are rarely open to those with a BSW but are frequently open to those with MSWs or above.

Social workers newly entering or relocating within the job market need to look beyond the social work section of classified advertisements and search for related opportunities that draw upon and require the skills social workers possess. These include positions under such headings as mental health, mental retardation, health, administration, coordinator, advocacy, management, and education.

Choices and Constraints. As noted above, the labor market for social workers is influenced by a large number of inter- and intraprofessional factors. The supply of social workers available at any given time is contingent upon the education and career choices of a large number of individuals (Barth, 2001). It is not only a matter of choices to enter social work but also the availability of other professional options when choices are being made. If professional schools of psychology, for example, are cutting back on admissions, then the pool of candidates interested in social work education might increase. On the other hand, if educational options are open and the chances of earning a higher salary in psychology are better, social work will be the likely loser.

The labor market itself is an important variable in the future of the profession. Throughout this book, the inextricable link between social work and the larger sociopolitical environment has been emphasized. The profession is a product of and intertwined with this society. Its authority comes largely from federal, state, and local laws that serve to expand or contract the nature and breadth of human services available to those who need or desire them.

BEING A SOCIAL WORKER

Individuals elect to become social workers for any number of reasons: a personal experience in which a social worker played a significant role, the "calling" to help, the prerequisites of a job, or the availability of a scholarship to study social work. The motivations likely cover a broad spectrum.

Chances are that people motivated to become social workers do not do so because of the prospect of becoming rich or famous. Social work is hard work, and sometimes it can be frustrating. But frustration is probably an emotion everyone who works, regardless of the occupation, feels at some time. Toby Weismiller, who at the time was interim Executive Director of NASW, celebrated the work of the profession in a column entitled "Honoring the Everyday Heroes" (Weismiller, 2001). Her words capture the complexity of what social workers do within the context of our society, our institutions, and our profession.

> Despite gains in professional recognition, social workers still struggle with working environments, both in agencies and in private practice, that run contrary to our purposes. We must contend with the squeeze for resources, unreasonable caseloads and workloads, bureaucratic snarls, unsafe working conditions, interprofessional turf battles and frequent challenges to the effectiveness of our practice. . . . These dynamics continue to be part of the reality most members must cope with every day.
>
> So, what is the response of the typical social worker? You always seem to find a way to reframe the problem, partner with another agency, challenge the rules for accessing services, streamline the process, reach out to others for support and keep on working for the client.
>
> I believe this approach is fundamental to both who we are as individuals and how we are trained as professionals. I have found that many who are drawn to social work as a vocation tend to be optimists; they see the possibilities in people and in life situations. This inclination is cultivated and refined in our professional education, which teaches us to identify the strengths in individuals, families and communities and begin the helping process there. . . . I have also encountered many people who tell stories about how social workers changed their lives at times when they felt desperate and alone. You are there for others at each of life's fragile and difficult junctures. Everyday heroes. (p. 2)

REFERENCES

Allen, J.A.V. (1999, February). From the president: New millennium, ongoing challenges. *NASW News*, p. 2.

Barbakow, J. C. (1997). Point-counterpoint. Not-for-profits vs. for-profits: Is one better patient care? *Health Systems Leadership, 4*, 16–17.

Barker, R. L. (1999). *Social work dictionary* (4th ed.). Washington, DC: NASW Press.

Barth, M. C. (2001). *The labor market for social workers: A first look.* New York: John A. Hartford Foundation.

Blank, B. T. (1997, Fall). Temp positions an option in social work. *New Social Worker, 4*, pp. 11–13.

Bloche, M. G. (1998). Should government intervene to protect nonprofits? *Health Affairs, 17*, 7–25.

Broder, D. S. (2002, May 27–June 2). States in fiscal crisis. *Washington Post National Weekly*, p. 4.

Browning, L. (2002, February 22). Not wanted: '02 graduates seeking jobs. *New York Times.* Retrieved February 23, 2002, from http://nytimes.com/2002/02/22/business/2GRAD.html

Butterfield, W. H., & Schoech, D. (1997). The Internet: Accessing the world of information. In R. L. Edwards (Ed.-in-Chief), *Encyclopedia of social work* (19th ed., 1997 Suppl. pp. 151–168). Washington, DC: NASW Press.

Clark, E. J. (2002, March). Power in numbers, power for good. *NASW News*, p. 2.

Coleman, M. (2002, January). *Using technology in the practice of clinical social work* (Clinical Social Work Practice Update 2). Retrieved September 6, 2002, from http://www.socialworkers.org/practice/updatecsw0201.htm

Connolly, C. (2002, June 9). Waging the battle for stem cell research. *Washington Post*, p. A6.

Doelling, C., Matz, B., & Kuehne, J. (1999). *Job market of 1998 MSW graduates* (Mimeo). St. Louis, MO: Washington University.

Estes, C. L., & Swan, J. H. (1994). Privatization, system membership, and access to home health care for the elderly. *Milbank Quarterly, 72*, 277–298.

Gibelman, M. (1995). Purchasing social services. In R. L. Edwards (Ed.-in-Chief), *Encyclopedia of social work* (19th ed., Vol. 3, pp. 1998–2007). Washington, DC: NASW Press.

Gibelman, M. (1999). The search for identity: Defining social work—past, present, future. *Social Work, 44*, 298–310.

Gibelman, M., & Demone, H. W., Jr. (2002). The commercialization of health and human services: Neutral phenomenon or cause for concern? *Families in Society, 83*, 387–397.

Gibelman, M., & Schervish, P. (1993). *Who we are: The social work labor force as reflected in the NASW membership.* Washington, DC: NASW Press.

Gibelman, M., & Schervish, P. (1997). *Who we are: A second look.* Washington, DC: NASW Press.

Goldstein, A. (2002, April 10). Bush presses for human cloning ban. *Washington Post*, p. A2.

Goldstein, H. (1998, April 9). Making charities' for-profit arms more accountable. *Chronicle of Philanthropy*, pp. 45–46.

Hilzenrath, D. S. (1997, December 3). Doctors lash out against profit motive in health care. *Washington Post*, pp. B11, B14.

Hiratsuka, J. (1995, February). Computerizing: A calculated approach. *NASW News*, p. 3.

Home health social work called "hot track." (1995, January). *NASW News*, p. 10.

Hopps, J. G., & Collins, P. M. (1995). Social work profession overview. In R. L. Edwards (Ed.-in-Chief), *Encyclopedia of social work* (19th ed., Vol. 3, pp. 2266–2282). Washington, DC: NASW Press.

Horejsi, C. R., & Garthwait, C. L. (1999). *The social work practicum: A guide and workbook for students.* Boston: Allyn & Bacon.

Inouye, D. K., Ell, K., & Ewalt, P. L. (1994). Social work research and social policy. *Social Work, 39*, 629–631.

Kilborn, P. T., & Clemetson, L. (2002, June 5). Gains of 90's did not lift all, census shows. *New York Times.* Retrieved June 5, 2002, from http://www.nytimes.com/2002/06/05/national/05CENS.html

Kreuger, L. W. (1997). The end of social work. *Journal of Social Work Education, 33*, 19–27.

Lennon, T. M. (2001). *Statistics on social work education in the United States: 1999.* Alexandria, VA: Council on Social Work Education.

Leonhardt, D. (2002, May 4). U.S. jobless rate increases to 6%; highest in 8 years. *New York Times.* Retrieved May 4, 2002, from http://www.nytimes.com/2002/05/04/business/04ECON.html.

Licensing group looking toward standards. (2001, July). *NASW News,* p. 4.

Macarov, D. (1991). *Certain change: Social work practice in the future.* Silver Spring, MD: NASW Press.

Maidenberg, M. (2001). *Factors which influence social workers' participation in continuing education.* Unpublished doctoral dissertation, Yeshiva University, Wurzweiler School of Social Work, New York.

Mangan, K. S. (2002, February 15). Professional-school enrollments boom as many parts of the economy tank. *Chronicle of Higher Education,* pp. A45–A46.

McCarty, D., & Clancy, C. (2002). Telehealth: Implications for social work practice. *Social Work, 47,* 153–161.

Mental Health Bill of Rights Project. (2002). *Joint initiative of mental health professional organizations: Principles in the provision of mental health and substance abuse treatment services—A bill of rights.* Retrieved November 19, 2002, from http://www.socialworkers.org/practice/mental.htm

Mizrahi, T. (2001, July). From the president: Social work—A kaleidoscopic view. *NASW News,* p. 2.

Mizrahi, T. (2002, June). From the president: The research–practice connection. *NASW News,* p. 2.

More growth in social work jobs foreseen. (1997, January). *NASW News,* p. 8.

National Association of Social Workers. (1996). *Code of ethics.* Washington, DC: NASW Press.

O'Neill, J. V. (1999, June). Profession now dominates in mental health. *NASW News,* pp. 1, 8.

O'Neill, J. V. (2000a, February). Solution-focused therapy gains adherents. *NASW News,* p. 6.

O'Neill, J. V. (2000b, September). Social work jobs abound. *NASW News,* pp. 1, 4.

O'Neill, J. V. (2000c, October). Profession needs work force data. *NASW News,* pp. 1, 6.

O'Neill, J. V. (2000d, October). Survey profiles MSW graduates. *NASW News,* pp. 1, 6.

O'Neill, J. V. (2000e, November). Few social workers follow path to Ph.D. *NASW News,* pp. 1, 6.

O'Neill, J. V. (2001, July). Webcams may transform online therapy. *NASW News,* p. 4.

O'Neill, J. V. (2002a, May). Chapter fights state caseworkers' layoffs. *NASW News,* p. 1.

O'Neill, J. V. (2002b, June). Paraprofessionals: Answer to shortage? *NASW News* p. 3.

O'Neill, J. V. (2002c, June). Survey eyes job market for grads. *NASW News,* p. 12.

Ottaway, D. B. (2001). Private social welfare initiative draws scrutiny. *Washington Post,* p. A1.

Perspective is urged on September 11 reactions. (2002, June). *NASW News* p. 5.

Social work again top career pick. (1999, February). *NASW News,* p. 1

Social work jobs going unfilled in California. (2000, September). *NASW News,* p. 4.

State criteria downgrading beaten back. (1999, April). *NASW News* p. 4.

Stewart, R. (1984, November). From the president. *NASW News,* p. 2.

U.S. Department of Labor, Bureau of Labor Statistics. (2001). *Tabulations from the Current Population Survey, 2000 annual averages.* Washington, DC: Author. Retrieved October 8, 2002, from http://www.bls.gov.

Vallianatos, C. (2000, September). Social work steps onto proving ground. *NASW News* p. 3.

Weismiller, T. (2001, March). From the director: Honoring the everyday heroes. *NASW News,* p. 2.

Index

About the Author

Margaret Gibelman, DSW, is professor and director of the doctoral program in social welfare at the Wurzweiler School of Social Work, Yeshiva University, in New York City. She teaches courses in management/administration, child welfare, social policy, and social work education. Previously, she was on the faculty of Rutgers University School of Social Work and the Catholic University of America, National Catholic School of Social Service.

Dr. Gibelman's social work experience includes clinical, supervisory, educational, and managerial roles. In the latter category, she served as executive director of the Lupus Foundation of America and the National Association of School Psychologists. She was also associate executive director of the Council on Social Work Education, the accrediting body for social work education programs in the United States. She has served as a consultant to the Asthma and Allergy Foundation, the National Association of Social Workers, and the Council for Accreditation for Services to Families and Children.

Her scholarly work has focused on human service delivery systems, including privatization, management and financing of social service agencies, the social work profession, and the social work labor force. Related areas of scholarly work include ethical conduct in research, managed care and its impact, and professional women's issues, including pay equity and the glass ceiling. She is senior author of *Who We Are: The Social Work Labor Force as Reflected in the NASW Membership* (1993) and *Who We Are: A Second Look* (1997), both published by NASW Press. The first edition of *What Social Workers Do* was published by NASW Press in 1995.

MORE RESOURCES ON THE SOCIAL WORK PROFESSION FROM NASW PRESS

What Social Workers Do, *2nd Edition, by Margaret Gibelman.* A much-awaited sequel to Gibelman's best-selling book, this second edition provides a panoramic look at social work and offers practical information about the current status of various service areas. It makes extensive use of case studies and demonstrates the connection between what appear to be diverse specializations by highlighting the intersection between practice functions, practice settings, and practice areas.

ISBN: 0-87101-364-9. 2005. Item #3649. $49.99.

Social Work Career Development: *A Handbook for Job Hunting and Career Planning, 2nd Edition, by Carol Nesslein Doelling.* Updated to respond to changes in the job market and the profession since the best-selling first edition, this unique handbook addresses in detail the career management and job search needs of social workers across job functions, fields, or degree levels, including self-assessment exercises, strategies for researching the job market and networking, details on resumes, curriculum vitae, and portfolios; tips on selecting master's and doctoral programs, and much more.

ISBN: 0-87101-363-0. 2005. Item #3630. $49.99.

Lessons from Abroad: *Adapting International Social Welfare Innovations, by M.C. Hokenstad and James Midgley, Editors.* Regarded as among the world's leaders in formulating social work policy and practice, U.S. social workers have much to learn from colleagues in other nations. The third in an NASW Press series on international social work edited by Hokenstad and Midgley, this book examines how domestic policies and practice can be enhanced by documenting, analyzing and judiciously adapting innovative approaches emanating from other countries.

ISBN: 0-87101-360-6. 2004. Item #3606. $44.99.

Changing Hats while Managing Change: *From Social Work Practice to Administration, 2nd Edition, by Felice Davidson Perlmutter and Wendy P. Crook.* A unique and useful guide for practitioners who want to broaden their repertoire of professional choices and are either moving up the administrative ladder or considering making a career move in that direction. In user-friendly language, *Changing Hats* addresses the major challenges that face social workers in these complex times and presents a picture of the various roles and responsibilities of administration, illustrating them with lively case studies.

ISBN: 0-87101-361-4. 2004. Item #3614. $44.99.

A Dream and a Plan: *A Woman's Path to Leadership in Human Services, by Lorrie Greenhouse Gardella and Karen S. Haynes.* The helping professions are rich with women who have the imagination and aspiration to be successful leaders, but lack confidence or opportunity. Written from an inclusive, multicultural perspective, this empowering book offers practical guidance on pursuing career advancement, overcoming barriers, and cultivating mentorship. A pragmatic and motivating text for social workers, students, and human services providers, as well as for experienced managers.

ISBN: 0-87101-359-2. 2004. Item #3592. $34.99.

Prudent Practice: *A Guide for Managing Malpractice Risk, by Mary Kay Houston-Vega and Elane M. Nuehring with Elisabeth R. Daguio.* Today, practice is more specialized and licensing regulations, professional standards, and statutes are more complex. The best defense in our increasingly litigious society remains competent, ethically conscientious practice. *Prudent Practice* offers practitioners a complete practice guide to increasing competence and managing the risk of malpractice. Included in the book and on CD-ROM are 25 sample forms and five sample fact sheets to distribute to clients.

ISBN: 0-87101-267-7. 1996. Item #2677. $45.99.

(Order form and information on reverse side)

ORDER FORM

Qty.	Title	Item #	Price	Total
__	What Social Workers Do, 2nd Edition	3649	$49.99	_____
__	Social Work Career Development, 2nd Edition	3630	$49.99	_____
__	Lessons from Abroad	3606	$44.99	_____
__	Changing Hats while Managing Change, 2nd Edition	3614	$44.99	_____
__	A Dream and a Plan	3592	$34.99	_____
__	Prudent Practice	2677	$45.99	_____

	Total
Subtotal	_____
Postage and Handling	_____
DC residents add 6% sales tax	_____
MD residents add 5% sales tax	_____
NC residents add 4.5% sales tax	_____
NJ residents add 6% sales tax	_____
Total	_____

POSTAGE AND HANDLING
Minimum postage and handling fee is $4.95. Orders that do not include appropriate postage and handling will be returned.

DOMESTIC: Please add 12% to orders under $100 for postage and handling. For orders over $100 add 7% of order.

CANADA: Please add 17% postage and handling.

OTHER INTERNATIONAL: Please add 22% postage and handling.

❒ **Check** or **money order** (payable to NASW Press) for $ _____.

❒ **Credit card**
   ❒ Visa   ❒ MasterCard   ❒ American Express

_____   _____
Credit Card Number   Expiration Date

Signature _____

Name _____

Address _____

City _____ State/Province _____

Country _____ Zip _____

Phone _____ E-mail _____

NASW Member # (if applicable) _____

(Please make checks payable to NASW Press. Prices are subject to change.)

NASW PRESS
P. O. Box 431
Annapolis JCT, MD 20701
USA

Credit card orders call
1-800-227-3590
(In the Metro Wash., DC, area, call 301-317-8688)
Or fax your order to 301-206-7989
Or order online at www.naswpress.org

CPWD05